KV-420-049

Henry Fralick.

PIONEER COLLECTIONS

COLLECTIONS AND RESEARCHES

MADE BY THE

PIONEER SOCIETY

OF THE

STATE OF MICHIGAN

SECOND EDITION

VOL. X.

LANSING
WYNKOOP HALLENBECK CRAWFORD COMPANY, STATE PRINTERS
1908

PREFACE TO SECOND EDITION—VOLUME X

In comparing this volume with the first edition, not many changes will be found, as the object of the revision was to correct obvious errors and to make brief explanatory comments rather that to substitute the editor's opinions and style for those of the contributors to the archives of the Society. But even this has called for a great amount of research to verify dates and statements of fact. Only errors obviously due to the carelessness of copyists or printers have been corrected without explanation; where there is a probable mistake, a brief comment, or another spelling of the name or word, has been inserted in brackets.

The usual plan of using foot notes, was not available, because, by so doing, the paging of the first edition would not have been preserved and the Index to the first fifteen volumes would have been of use only for the first edition; therefore the notes have been gathered into an appendix, each numbered with the page to which it refers.

The work of revision has been done as directed by the Board of Trustees under authority given by Act No. 62 of the legislature, approved April 25th, 1907.

HENRY S. BARTHOLOMEW,
Editor of Second Edition

STATE LIBRARY, June, 1907.

PREFACE TO FIRST EDITION

It is with pleasure that the Pioneer Society of the State of Michigan presents to the public the tenth volume of its historical collections. The infancy of this society is past, and henceforward its work promises to be not of an experimental or miscellaneous nature but of an assured historical character. This fact is attested by the abundance of valuable historical material already in the hands of the Committee of Historians, and which continues to accumulate. So abundant has this material become that not infrequently papers of no little interest must unavoidably be laid aside for future reference and use. Attention is called to the fact that the present volume, the first of its kind, is made up entirely out of this accumulated material, the first two hundred nine pages comprising articles of exceptional interest from several of the most enthusiastic contributors to the society's collections.

The balance of the volume is occupied by the "Haldimand Papers," a small number of which were published in Vol. 9. Since the publication of the first installment a strictly chronological arrangement of these papers has been thought to be most advantageous, as presenting a consecutive and connected history, and those herewith presented have been arranged in that manner, all documents pertaining to a given year being grouped together. The great interest of these papers increases with prolonged acquaintance, and the committee earnestly bespeaks for them a careful perusal by all in any way interested in historical research. Installments of these papers will appear in several succeeding volumes.

The long delay in the publication of the present volume is greatly regretted, but it is also hoped that it will receive no less warm a welcome from its expectant friends. To all who have in any measure contributed to its interest and value the committee returns its most sincere acknowledgments.

MICHAEL SHOEMAKER, *Chairman.*
HARRIET A. TENNY, *Secretary.*
WITTER J. BAXTER,
OLIVER C. COMSTOCK,
RILEY C. CRAWFORD,
WYLLYS C. RANSOM.
Committee of Historians

LANSING, January 27, 1888.

CONTENTS

OFFICERS OF THE PIONEER AND HISTORICAL SOCIETY OF MICHIGAN, 1874-1887

PRESIDENTS

Judge Albert Miller, Bay City	April 22, 1874—Feb. 3, 1875
Oliver C. Comstock, Marshall	Feb. 3, 1875—Feb. 2, 1876
*Jonathan Shearer, Plymouth	Feb. 2, 1876—Feb. 7, 1877
Witter J. Baxter, Jonesville	Feb. 7, 1877—Feb. 6, 1878
John J. Adam, Tecumseh	Feb. 6, 1878—Feb. 5, 1879
Michael Shoemaker, Jackson	Feb. 5, 1879—Feb. 5, 1880
†Hezekiah G. Wells, Kalamazoo	Feb. 5, 1880—Feb. 3, 1881
‡John C. Holmes, Detroit	Feb. 3, 1881—June 7, 1882
Charles I. Walker, Detroit	June 7, 1882—June 5, 1884
Francis A. Dewey, Cambridge	June 5, 1884—June 18, 1885
Henry Fralick, Grand Rapids	June 18, 1885—June 9, 1886
M. H. Goodrich, Ann Arbor	June 9, 1886—June 2, 1887

RECORDING SECRETARY

Mrs. Harriet A. Tenney, Lansing	April 22, 1874——————

CORRESPONDING SECRETARIES

Ephraim Longyear, Lansing	April 22, 1874—Feb. 6, 1878
§John J. Bush, Lansing	Feb. 6, 1878—Feb. 5, 1879
George H. Greene, Lansing	Feb. 5, 1879——————

TREASURERS

‖Alvin N. Hart, Lansing	April 22, 1874—Feb. 3, 1875
O. M. Barnes, Lansing	Feb. 3, 1875—Feb. 6, 1878
Ephraim Longyear, Lansing	Feb. 6, 1878——————

*Jonathan Shearer died Sept. 26, 1881.
†Hezekiah G. Wells died April 4, 1885.
‡John C. Holmes died Dec. 16, 1887.
§John J. Bush died Oct. 11, 1886.
‖Alvin N. Hart died August 21, 1874.

MICHIGAN

PIONEER AND HISTORICAL SOCIETY

BIOGRAPHY OF HENRY FRALICK

TWELFTH [ELEVENTH] PRESIDENT OF THE MICHIGAN STATE PIONEER SOCIETY

Hon. Henry Fralick, Grand Rapids, is a native of New York, and was born at Minden, Montgomery county, on the 9th of Feb., 1812. His father, Abraham Fralick, originally from Columbia county, N. Y., was a captain in the war of 1812. His grandfather was one of a family of 15 boys, 11 of whom were engaged in the revolutionary war, in which four of them were killed; of the seven who returned, all were wounded. His mother was Mary E., daughter of Henry Keller, of Minden, N. Y., who was quite prominent in the community, having been a member of the assembly and the senate of the State. Mr. Fralick received his education in the district schools of his native county and in Wayne county, where his father removed in 1824. The next three years were spent in assisting with the work on the farm, at the end of which time the family removed to Plymouth, Mich. In 1829 he left home to seek his fortune; going to New York, he worked on a passenger boat of the Erie canal for two years, becoming captain of the boat the second year. In 1832, at New Bedford, Mass., he shipped as a hand before the mast, on a whaling vessel bound for the South Atlantic and Indian oceans. On this voyage he was gone two years, touching at a great many different points, and bringing home a full cargo of whale oil and bone. In 1834 Mr. Fralick shipped as third mate in a merchant vessel bound for Rio Janeiro and other parts of South America. He was gone on this voyage about seven months, after which he was engaged for another year on several coasting vessels, when he returned to Michigan. In 1836 he went to Detroit and became clerk at the Michigan Exchange, the principal hotel in the city. Here he remained nine months, when he returned to Plymouth, and became clerk in the store of Henry B. Holbrook. In 1838 he bought out Mr. Holbrook's stock of dry goods, and engaged in business for himself. In a few months he took in as partners Messrs. Austin and Penniman, the firm name being Austin, Fralick & Co.; and, after carrying on this business for three years, sold his interest, bought a lumber mill, and built a flour mill. After two years he sold his mills to Mr. Austin and again engaged in the sale of dry goods. In 1860 Mr. Fralick sold his store and goods. About a year and a half afterwards he came to Grand Rapids, where he bought out the interest of Mr. Aldrich in the bank of Ledyard & Aldrich; the firm then became Ledyard & Fralick, and as such carried on a very successful banking business for about five years, when it was dissolved, and the City National Bank, of Grand Rapids, was organized, since which time Mr. Fralick has been a stockholder and director of this bank.

Upon the firing on Fort Sumter, in 1861, he, with his brother and Mr. Penniman, raised, equipped and filled the muster-roll of the first company in the State, which enlisted for three years; and throughout the rebellion he gave his energy and means to aid the government in its vigorous prosecution of the war. In 1867 he again bought a stock of goods, and engaged in the mercantile trade for about two years, when he sold out to Mr. Remington and began the real estate business, in which he still continues. In 1872 he, with others, formed the Grand Rapids Chair Company, with a capital of $300,000. Of this company he was director for three years and president two years, when, on account of press of business, he resigned. Mr. Fralick has been justice of the peace, supervisor and county auditor. He has served for thirty years as a school officer, and for four years as president of the board of education of the city of Grand Rapids. He is and has been a trustee and the treasurer of Olivet College for the last six years, and has been a member of the legislature for three different terms. In 1850 he was a member of the constitutional convention, which formed the present constitution of the state; and in 1853 he was elected state senator and was appointed chairman of the select committee on the Maine law question. He presented to the senate a petition, with 100,000 names annexed, in favor of the passage of the Maine law in Michigan, and in pursuance thereof he presented a bill which, after amendment, became a law. In 1871 he was appointed by the governor of the state a member of the relief committee for the distribution of the funds sent to help those who were sufferers by the fire which had devastated the western part of Michigan. To the duties of this committee he devoted, gratuitously, seven months of his time; and the self-sacrificing labors that he put forth in behalf of these sufferers can never be forgotten. In 1875 he was again appointed by the governor one of the state board of managers to represent Michigan at the national centennial exposition, to the discharge of which duty he devoted about ten months; and it was largely to his continued and successful efforts that the state of Michigan owes the prominence which she held at the exposition. He has been for many years a member of the executive committee of the State Agricultural Society, and its president for two years; also a member of the State Pioneer society for a number of years, a member of its executive committee four years and its president one year.

In 1837, on the 23d of May, he was married to Corinna A., daughter of Henry Lyon, who was one of the first settlers of the town of Plymouth, Mich. Mrs. Fralick died on the 16th of October, 1840. On the 22d of April, 1842, he married Jeannette Woodruff, of Plymouth, Mich. They have four children, one son and three daughters. Being highly regarded for the soundness of his judgment, and ever ready to help by his influence and counsel, he has held for eight years the position of president of the board of trustees in the First Congregational church of Grand Rapids. In the public career of Mr. Fralick, every step is marked by conscientious effort, based on principle. Emphatically, he is a man of energy, sterling integrity, and unselfish generosity. A portrait [frontispiece] of Mr. Fralick may be found in this work.

FIFTEENTH ANNUAL REUNION OF THE PIONEERS OF KALAMAZOO COUNTY AT AUGUSTA, AUGUST 9, 1886

ADDRESS OF WELCOME AND RESPONSE—SECRETARY'S REPORT

The 15th annual reunion of the Pioneer Association met at Augusta to-day at 11 o'clock. Eight well filled cars left this city at 10:30 this morning.

The day was very fine and all went merry as could be asked for. The train stopped at Comstock and Galesburg and arrived at Augusta at 11 o'clock. Here a cordial welcome was given the visitors. The streets were spanned with an arch of welcome, the stores and houses were decorated, flags were displayed, the band played and the people turned out to greet the visitors.

In a little while a large company gathered at the grove on the hill where a platform was prepared for the speakers, seats for the audience, tables for the dinner and other conveniences for the guests. After a short season of visiting the oral exercises began, opened by music. Then followed the invocation. Then Hon. E. W. Hewitt delivered the following address of welcome:

"*Ladies and Gentlemen, and the Pioneers of Kalamazoo County:*

Upon me has fallen the pleasure of welcoming you, and of thanking you for your presence upon this appointed day.

We will try hard to prove our appreciation of your kindness by doing our best to make the day an agreeable and happy one; a day to which you may look back without a feeling of regret, and with bright hopes of a future reunion.

We came here young, now we are old with not many years before us.

We have had our joys and our sorrows in the years that have passed, but let us banish from our hearts all sad and sorrowful memories and enjoy the pleasures of to-day with all the spirit of 50 years ago. Again, let me bid you a hearty welcome in the name of our townsmen.

To which President Williams gave this response:

In behalf of this audience and the Pioneer Association I take great pleasure in tendering our earnest and hearty thanks to the friends and good people of Augusta for their courteous reception and untiring efforts to make this occasion everything desirable and long to be cherished in our memories; we are placed under many obligations for the privileges of this meeting in this social capacity in this beautiful grove, arranged for the enjoyment of all present. And who among us is not alive to the sweet associations that give tone and vigor to life? for that is the object of this meeting in part, to mingle our voices together in the common bond of brotherhood. I see around me here to-day familiar faces of 50 years ago, of those who have been side by side with us from youth's manhood to old age. May it not be pertinent for us to ask, where on the dial plate of time are we to-day? Far over the ridge and noon-time of human existence; our history made up, and departure at hand. Thus it is through all ages, ranks and conditions. This great culmination of human life is being constantly repeated and again replenished by troops of succeeding pilgrims, and when we are all gathered home to our fathers the world in its routine will move on until the fiat vibrates from shore to shore that time will be no more."

The secretary then read his annual report:

Again we are met in annual reunion, once more to greet each other—once more to say "hail and farewell!" perchance again and again to meet—just as likely to meet no more upon this shore of time—one of us to fall, it may be, in the pathway homeward, another to live beyond the period when all his companions shall have passed the portals into the land beyond. * * * * The way of this our world-pilgrimage is full of uncertainties and mystery. Not only the incoming and outgoing of life are hidden with a manifold veil, but even the short path itself. As around the Egyptian temples, so around the greatest of all temples Sphinxes lie; and reversing the Sphinxes, he only solves the riddle who dies.

Since our last meeting with the farmers' harvest festival at Vicksburg, so pleasantly remembered—one of the most delightful meetings of the many that have been held since the first reunion at Kalamazoo in 1871—quite a number of the pioneers have bowed their heads, closing their eyes to earthly scenes, and joined the countless host that no man can number in that mysterious realm beyond man's ken, seen only with the eye of faith. Among these are many whose existence has been very useful and honorable—men and women, the aged and the youthful, the good, the true and the beautiful, who have contributed their share to the substantial benefits, as well as the sweet amenities of life, whose place can never be filled to those most intimate with them—lives precious to the presence and the well-being of kindred and friends and to the world. There have been fewer, it is true, in the twelve months, of great names and of persons of the higher ranks and spheres of political and social matters than in the year before; yet not less useful or beloved in their own circle of acquaintances and in their familiar places in the home and neighborhood that have known and esteemed them. Among these are John I. Hogeboom, aged 75 years; Dr. Melancton Freeman, 86 years; Preston I. McCreary, 80 years; George N. Goodrich, 61 years; Joseph Skinner, 84 years; Horace Sawyer, 79 years; Eli Johnson, 88 years; Harriet Watts, 85 years; Benjamin F. Smith, 82 years; Peter Kniss, 98 years; Philo D. Clark, 71 years; J. B. Ide Clamax, 70 years; Mrs. Alonzo Thompson, Charles Culler, 74 years; Rev. Samuel Boyles; Richard S. Gagee, in Missouri, Oct. 20; Dan Frank, Kansas City, 53 years; Hamilton Wyman, 79 years; Dr. Chapin (though not a pioneer exactly) was a well-known and long time citizen; Bushrod Spaulding; John Coleman at Wayland; Elizabeth Carroll, Kalamazoo, 100 years.

At this time it is well to recall the views of Hon. Stephen F. Brown at the last reunion to continue the annual meetings of the pioneers of this county, and at each and all of them to tell again and again the story of the early settlement of this county and to recount the bravery and endurance, the privations, the patient and unremitting labors of the pioneers, men and women, and the noble, unselfish, honest and sterling character, who all were helpful to each other, making common cause of difficulties, sharing each other's trials, disappointments, and sorrows, and rejoicing, too, with those who were successful as if they were members of one family. In the meetings which have been held heretofore very much of the history of those early days and very many of the names of the hardy pioneers, founders of our present prosperity, have been rescued, and placed upon the printed page for those who came after them to read and to admire.

By an amendment to the constitution of our society the election of officers is to be held at the annual reunion. That election will therefore take place at the close of the meeting, and I would suggest that a committee be appointed by the meeting or by the chair, as you may deem proper, to recommend officers for the ensuing year. It might be well to appoint that committee now, to give them time to confer and report at the close of the meeting. The officers are: president, vice-president, secretary, treasurer, historical committee and executive committee. With these suggestions I will close the report.

Thereon F. Giddings gave in a clear voice his recollections of early Ross. We give below an outline of this interesting paper.

In opening, Mr. Giddings made some amusing remarks touching his debut as a public speaker, as this was his first endeavor, "but in making such an attempt," he said, "I had rather trust myself near the spot where I learned my A B C's, feeling that you who knew me in boyhood days, and you who have been my friends in manhood as well, would excuse any shortcomings in my oratory while giving you a man's recollection of boyhood days spent in Augusta and vicinity 35 years ago." He claimed to be a pioneer, though the county had a good start, and these old fellows had been here before him; "but I came just as soon as I could, and that was just as soon as any pioneer got here. I was even worse off than the pioneer who boasted that when he came here he had but one shirt to his back. I did not have even that article of wearing apparel." He began his career here on Christmas day, 1843, in a family then "living on the territorial road over across the river there in Charleston; I concluded to stay and be one of the family." * * * "My father and mother moved from their farm in Charleston to Augusta in the spring of 1847. Augusta was not much of a town in those days. People were few and the houses decidedly scattered, but like some larger cities of this day rents were scarce. My father found a habitation then located about where T. C. Wood's store now stands. It was not large but the rooms were as good as a palace. My memory for two or three years succeeding that date is rather imperfect for reasons of infirmities of age (at that time), but I know that the leading and only mercantile establishment was kept in the exchange building by Caleb Kirby. I think the Augusta mills were being built and 'Clipnockee' had great expectations during those halcyon days. About 1850 my intellect began to clear and I became a man about town." Mr. Giddings then devoted considerable space to a description of the centers of trade and business firms. Augusta in those days was not even a flag station on the railroad, for there was no flag. If any one had ambition or money enough to get away from town and take a ride on the strap rail, they stopped the train by getting on the track and swinging hat or bonnet as a signal for a halt. There was no passenger house needed, and the freight house was anywhere along the track between the bridge and the west switch. Sprague's store was the headquarters for all the news and gossip, and Fullerton's shoe shop served as a temple of justice. The people seemed to exist without churches, and education was imparted by Seth Pratt and L. L. McCloud in the old school-house. The speaker alluded in serio-comic sentences to the old quaking and at times submerged bridge, a band of Indians, to Jed Thompson (afterwards a valued locomotive engineer on the Central), the track walker, to spike down the snake-heads on the railroad. Mr. Giddings mentioned a number of the farmers and the improvements on the east and south side of the river, the Burdicks, Bushes, Cockes, Crosby, Whitford, Bloss and others. In turn the speaker gave a pretty full description of the sections all about Augusta and the names of the farmers, even to Ross Center, at that time and for years the voting place of the town. He concluded his paper as follows:

"The boys of those days were all good boys. They had to be, because good-sized hazel bushes grew close to town. The most of them grew up to manhood and took up the journey of life far from these scenes. A few yet remain, substantial men in this their childhoods home. Of those that were men when we were boys, few remain; the majority have passed away to their final home and those that are left are living on borrowed time. Soon those original pioneers will be all gone, and then we boys must take up the burden and be the old men and the pioneers for the boys that come after us. May our record be as clear, and their veneration for us be as deep, as ours towards those that preceded us."

Godfrey Knight, who with other pioneers was on the platform, was introduced to the audience. Mr. Knight it is claimed is 100 years old, and is certainly a very active man for such an age. Rev. J. T. Robe, the first Methodist minister in the county, was also present on the stage, as well as a score of others. Mr. Allen Smith, one of them, was introduced and sang a song, "In this hour of earnest labor," in a clear voice, though more than 80 years of age.

THE POLITICAL CAMPAIGN OF 1840, WITH INCIDENTS, ANECDOTES, AND RECOLLECTIONS OF ITS DISTINGUISHED EDITORS AND ORATORS, NORTH AND SOUTH

BY A. D. P. VAN BUREN

The following is the admirable paper read at the pioneer reunion at Augusta by A. D. P. Van Buren, August 9, 1886. It was prepared at the request of the State Historical Society. All who remember that campaign will recognize how faithful is the presentation Mr. Van Buren has given:

Mr. President, Pioneers and Fellow Citizens:

The early settlers in this State fought their great battle in the wilderness, during the first pioneer decade. At the close of that decade was fought one of the greatest political battles known in the history of American politics. This battle resulted in the great whig victory of 1840.

This campaign was distinguished by a masterly *coup d'etat* of the whigs, that enabled them to get into power once more. The controlling thought of the whig leaders at the outset was to secure an available candidate for the presidency. Availability in a presidential leader was the inspiring motive of the party. Here a great difficulty met them. Henry Clay—the "gallant Harry of the west"—the undisputed head of the whig party, must be disposed of. If nominated he could not be elected. The time had come with him, as it had in previous years with William H. Crawford, "his very eminence had become fatal to him: He was formidable to all candidates, and all combined against him." Hence the gallant old whig leader, by some strange mixture of whig "algebra and alchemy," was disposed of. For, in the nominating convention, Gen. Scott got 16 votes, Henry Clay 90 and Gen. Harrison 148.

From the beginning of this campaign a bitter political contest was expected—the severest known in our country. The previous success of Gen. Jackson had taught the whig leaders that the military element not only gave *eclat* to his cause, but gave it an impetus that nothing else could. Consequently in selecting "General" William Henry Harrison an "odor of gunpowder" would constitute an attraction to rally the masses; and, in the smoke of the coming battle, the enemy would not be able to discover that their nominee did not have the civil qualifications, nor the brilliant military fame, that Gen. Jackson possessed. But, should they be able to discern this weakness, the statesmanship of John Tyler, the nominee for vice-president, would, by association and reflection, cast its glamour over their leader, and they would work up and reproduce his war record so as to dazzle the American people with the military fame of their presidential nominee. On the other side, Mr. Van Buren's late administration had been very acceptable to his party, and he was renominated with the full assurance of a re-election by the people. The old whig and democratic parties at that time were in the zenith of their political power and prestige. Noble old foes, they had met to decide on this chosen battlefield whether a whig or a democratic president should be at the head of our national affairs for the next four years. Never was a name chosen for a political battle cry with such a magnetic power to electrify and arouse the masses, as the whig shibboleth of "Tippecanoe and Tyler too." It had the rallying power of "Old Fritz," on the Prussian soldiers, or *"Vive l'Empereur,"* in Napoleon's day on the French people. This battle cry was first happily introduced in song by Gen. Louis Grinier, who wrote most of the whig songs for this campaign. It was, you remember, in the famous song beginning:

> "Oh what has caused this great commotion—motion, motion, our country through?
> It is the ball that's rolling on
> For Tippecanoe and Tyler too, for Tippecanoe and Tyler too;
> And with them we'll beat little Van
> Van, Van—Van. Oh, he's a used up man,
> And with them we'll beat little Van."

This song was sung throughout the land. Its liquid notes rolled off the tongues of the singers into the hearts of the people. A very learned and a very wise man has said, "Let me make my country's ballads and I care not who makes her laws." Here the making and the singing of whig ballads made a president of the United States and the law-makers of the land. If the whig orators were inspired for the occasion, and carried the multitude by the irresistible power of their eloquence, Apollo himself seemed to have given the whig poets and singers the captivating power of song that carried every-

2

thing before it. Never before had the people been so influenced by the songs of a political campaign. Ossian E. Dodge of Boston, the celebrated singer, was hired to make a tour of the country and sing at the whig meetings. He came into Michigan with Frank Granger of New York, and sang at a mass meeting in Marshall. In addition to this, Mr. Van Buren and the democratic party had two powerful influences against them, each strong in itself, but truly powerful when united. One was the entire whig party acting as a determined body, the other was "the large league of suspended banks, headed by the bank of the United States," which was desperately in earnest to beat back the democrats and get a national charter. The surest way to do this was to elect a whig president. Money, in political campaigns as well as in war, must furnish the sinews of strength. By mutual support the banks were able to pass their notes as money, and not being subject to redemption it could be furnished without constraint. Consequently the whole interest of this great moneyed power was directed against the democratic party. The press was bought, the debtors were intimidated, and the business pursuits coerced, while the poor man was flattered and cajoled by promises of better times, of speedy reaction in labor which would give him $2 a day and plenty of work. This constituted the soul of whig stock—promises of higher wages and better times.

Then they began a system of fault-finding with, and charging of political crimes against, the democratic party. The spirit of grumbling and fault-finding inspired both whig orator and poet. And they always ended their complaint against the democrats with glowing promises that were addressed to all business pursuits and personal interests of the community. They shouted and sung higher wages to the laboring man. "Two dollars a day and roast beef," and a hundred other like phrases, calculated to catch the ear, move the heart, and fire the passions of the masses. They harangued the people and made them believe that Mr. Van Buren's re-election would be the downfall of all prices, the stagnation of all trade, the destruction of all labor, and the ruin of all industries. The phrases given out by whig speakers in congress were caught up and re-echoed by the editor and stump-speaker, and made the inspiring theme of song for the hustings. The newspapers in all the trading districts kept the people stirred up with such advertisements as these: "The subscriber will pay *six* dollars a barrel for flour if Harrison is elected, and *three* dollars if Van Buren is. The subscriber will pay five dollars a hundred for pork if Harrison is elected, and two dollars and a half if Van Buren is." And so on through the whole catalogue of marketable articles, and through the different kinds of labor. And these advertisements were signed by responsible men, large dealers in the articles mentioned, who were able to fix the market for them. Thus the business, the prosperity, the pecuniary interests, and the hopes of the laboring man were all to bud and blossom and yield abundant fruit in the political El Dorado that was to be inaugurated if Harrison was elected. No inducements were spared to influence the passions and the imaginations of men. The democrats taunted the whigs with their nominees's having lived in a "log cabin" and drinking hard cider as a beverage. The whigs seizing the words, adroitly put them to their own use, and gave them a talismanic power in the campaign that the "little magician" was not able to withstand. Immediately the terms "log cabin," "hard cider," and "coon skins" were taken as symbols of the party, and to express its identification with the poorest and humblest of the people. Then began the monster processions and parades. An old campaigner of that time exclaims, "Oh, it were worth five years of peaceful life to have witnessed the scenes that were then enacted!" Log cabins, as if by the power of magic, sprung up in the crowded marts of the great cities, in the large towns, and in all the small hamlets and cross-roads throughout the country. Each rough cabin was ornamented with coon-skins like the frontier hut, while the cider barrel, with the gourd dipper in it, was free to all who wished to drink. These rude cabins, thus furnished, were the tabernacles to which all the people were invited to come. They were the headquarters of "whiggery;" each cabin being a recuiting office where the young and old were treated to hard cider, sworn into service and joined the crusade against the democracy. It was by these public gatherings that the ranks of the whigs were increased, and their doctrines spread over the land. The whig orators and their singers went from place to place like modern revivalists, in Moody and Sankey style, trying to convert democratic sinners from the errors of their ways over to the pure doctrines of whiggery. Log cabins on wheels drawn by ten or fifteen yokes of oxen, that were tricked off with ribbons, whig banners and gewgaws, and canoes on wheels ornamented in a similar manner, were a picturesque part of the processions. The great orators, the Websters, Clays, Prentisses, McDuffies, the Corwins and Ewings addressed the great mass meetings, while the lesser ones harangued the people in the small towns and at the gatherings in the rural districts. The power was practically in the hands of the politicians, and it can truthfully be said that the campaign of 1840 produced more politics to the acre than any ten years before or since in the history of this country. For this campaign was the greatest thing that American politics ever did. At Dayton, Ohio, a whig gathering covered ten acres by actual measurement, and the people, like Xerxes's army, were too numerous to be counted. A whig flag floated over almost every house in the city, and every flag denoted free access to the building over which it waved. A rough estimate of the gathering put it at from 90,000 to 100,000 people. Gen. William

Henry Harrison, the whig candidate, was there and addressed this mass of enthusiastic whigs. The south, chagrined because Clay was not nominated for president, entered slowly into the campaign, but eventually threw her whole power into it.

The political oratory of that day accomplished ten-fold more than does the stump speaking of to-day. There were but few newspapers then, and the influence of the orators was supreme when compared with what it is in these times.

This famous political campaign, like those of other presidential elections, had its comic side. And should some of our ambitious authors study the newspapers of those times a mass of genuine wit and humor could be collected. The elequent and brilliant speeches, the songs that accompanied them, the jokes, the travesties, anecdotes and satire, would fill volumes.

At the head of the whig journalism of that day was Thurlow Weed, the Warwick of American politics. As editor of the Albany Journal he exerted a powerful influence in this campaign, and the great whig victory was largely due to him. He had, in Edwin Croswell, democratic editor of the Albany Argus, a foeman worthy of his steel. Albany at that time was the center of New York journalism.

Gen. James Watson Webb was the Roland of the whig press in New York city, and did good work for the whig cause as editor of the Courier and Enquirer. But he found his *Oliver* in Moses Y. Beach, democratic editor of the New York Sun. And the General also found, that, after his duel with Beach, he was lamed in one leg for life.

William Cullen Bryant was at this time an able, reliable democratic editor of the New York Evening Post; while James Gordon Bennett, editor of the New York Herald, was then as ever after, a trimmer and espoused any party's cause out of which he could make the most money. But to Horace Greeley must be assigned the post of honor in making the whig songs the most effectual weapon in the presidential campaign of 1840. In that year he started, in Albany, the *Log Cabin* (fit suggestion to starting them all over the land), to aid in the election of Harrison and Tyler, and threw such force and variety into it that it ran into an immense circulation, and became the basis of the Tribune, established in 1841. A file of the old *Log Cabin*, with its whig editorials, speeches and songs, would be choice reading now as giving a good political history of that period. Greeley's followers sung themselves hoarse for—

"Tippecanoe and Tyler too."

And the Van Burenites shouted for their favorite in the famous ditty beginning—

"When this old hat was new
Van Buren was the man, &c."

"Living men," says a writer of that time, "who saw those days," will not forget the monster parades of the whigs after the Maine election, when they chorused the popular refrain opening and ending—

"Oh! have you heard the news from Maine, Maine, Maine."

But, as we have stated, it was by political oratory and song that this campaign was made successful. Newspapers being few, the people relied on the stump speaker as their oracle and leader. He was the Moses to conduct them to the promised political inheritance. And they gathered at the hustings about the speaker's stand to hear him deliver the political law and commandments, as the children of Israel did in the tabernacle to hear the law read to them. There were then no short hand reporters to write down the speech as fast as it was delivered, no telegraph wires to send it to the press two thousand miles away to be put in type the next two hours, and no lightning express trains to scatter one hundred thousand copies of it, in the next twenty-four hours, from Maine to California. That wonderful feat was reserved for these days in which the editor has usurped the place of the public speaker.

But the orator of forty-six years ago had almost unlimited sway over the masses; that was the golden period of political oratory in our country. Politics absorbed all other interests. All work seemed to be laid aside, and every man's business, especially every whig's, was to attend the political meetings; and not only the men but their wives and children flocked to the hustings. It was the year of jubilee for the young folks, who were everywhere delighted with the grand processions and parades, the witty speeches, the singing, the bands of music playing amid all the attractions and display of whig pageantry. The whole whig party had turned into political gypsies, and, with traveling orators went camping out over the country, holding whig revivals, and preaching and singing their political gospel everywhere they went. Steamboats and all public conveyances were crowded with parties singing whig songs, or doggerel ballads made for the occasion, accompanied with the music of drums, fifes and fiddles. Political rivalry had assumed most destructive features. The stump speaker, like the border chieftain summoned his adherents about his standard, and by the potent spell of oratory awakened among them an enthusiasm for his cause, a loyalty to his party, a fidelity to its leader that was worthy of the days of chivalry. The democratic party led by its Roderick Dhu, the whig party by its Fitz James, and the abolition party by its bold McGregor, waged a war of conquest against each other.

But that power of the political orator has departed. The press of to-day, as we have said, has taken it from him, for it has not only usurped the power of the stump speaker, but of the politician as well. The press has so instructed and educated the people that they not only do their own reading and thinking, but they have so far solved the political problems and mastered the science of government that they have not so much need of instruction from the public speaker as in the old days.

It was another master stroke when the whigs called a general convention of all their adherents in New England on Bunker Hill, September 10, 1840. Fifty thousand New England whigs assembled on that occasion, and a great number of whigs from every other state in the Union met with them. Daniel Webster addressed this vast multitude, and gave a declaration of their principles and purposes. The report of this great mustering of whigs on Bunker Hill, of Webster's great speech and declaration of purposes, gave *eclat* to the whig cause. It was really the grand bugle blast that aroused the whigs to arms all over the Union. It is said that Webster planned the whig campaign of 1840, and advised them to begin at once holding mass meetings all over the country. That they must raise the whig standard and address the people in all the rural districts of the land. This was a kind of tactics worthy of a Napoleon. To it undoubtedly the whig party owed their great victory. It was, at any rate, a great hit, and started a movement that swept like wild-fire over the country, for, as soon as the open-air meetings were started, the "great commotion," like the Irish rebellion, "broke out forty thousand strong" simultaneously all over the Union.

Says Hugh S. Legare: "The subject of popular eloquence, always an attractive one in a free country, has been invested for us with a more than ordinary interest in the memorable campaign of 1840."

In this campaign greater multitudes assembled than were ever addressed by those great masters of eloquence, Pericles, Demosthenes or Cicero. The great orator is born of a great occasion. This political campaign inaugurated in America the out-door mass meeting, which gave birth to that most popular orator known as the "stump speaker."

A history of this great political movement would be very incomplete without giving a full mention of the conspicuous part that the south took in it. The south, disappointed that Clay was not made the whig standard bearer of the campaign, Achilles like, for a while at least, "sulked in her tent." But—

> "The war that for a space did fail,
> Now trebly thundering swelled the gale,"

with the battle cry of "Tippecanoe and Tyler too," throughout the entire southern border.

The great southern orators, Clay, Prentiss, McDuffee, Crittenden and others, led the campaign against the democracy in the south. But to S. S. Prentiss, "America's most brilliant orator," as he is called, must be awarded the highest honors, and the most effectual work of any orator north or south, in the campaign of 1840. Probably no public speaker of modern times was ever so great a favorite with the nation at large, or ever had such a splendid field for the display of his oratorical powers, or, by them, ever accomplished so much for the cause of a political party. He was continually besieged with invitations to address whig associations, Tippecanoe clubs, mass meetings, grand conventions, log cabin raisings, mustering at barbecues and whatever other strange names designated the political gatherings of that *annus mirabilis.* Hundreds of these invitations, of course, he could not accept. By the most urgent solicitations from northern whigs, he made during the summer of this year, a tour of the northern states, in which he may be said to have been the hero of successive oratorical triumphs. In writing to his sister at this time he says: "I have made speeches at St. Louis, Chicago, Detroit, Cleveland, Buffalo, Syracuse, Albany, New York, Newark, Portland," and many other places. He said in his Portland speech: "Rarely has the history of the world presented such a scene as that now passing before our eyes. We behold this whole nation, from the shores of the Atlantic to the Mississippi, rising up as one man and flocking together in every state, city and village to discuss and hold counsel upon the administration of public affairs."

As illustrative of the people's estimation of Prentiss as an orator, and of the power of his eloquence, I give the following from a distinguished southern gentleman: "I heard the great speech of William Pinckney upon the Missouri question in the United States Senate in 1820. I sat near by and listened to that of Mr. Clay upon the same subject in the House of Representatives. They were, perhaps, the greatest speeches of their lives, and were most powerful in their influence upon the action of Congress. The speech of Mr. Pinckney was perhaps the most finished and masterly piece of oratory ever listened to on this continent. That of Mr. Clay was grandly eloquent; Mr. Pinckney's though admitted to be the most convincing, stirred no feeling as did the burning words of Mr. Clay. A few weeks after I was in the courtroom in Columbia, South Carolina, and heard George McDuffee in a celebrated criminal trial, and this was the only speech I ever listened to that I thought approached the eloquence that I have often heard from Prentiss." As an evidence of Prentiss's great eloquence I give the following: It was at a dinner-table in Newark, New Jersey, in 1844, a distinguished gentleman, in company with William C. Dawson and Chief Justice Lumpkin, of Georgia, and John Bell, of Tennessee, was talking about orators. During the dinner a lady present said: "I was tempted once (it was in 1840) to go and hear S. S. Prentiss make a political speech in this city, and he held me spell-bound for three hours. I consider it an era in my life." "Did you ever hear him, Judge Lumpkin?" asked the distinguished gentleman above alluded to. "I never did," was the reply. "Then, sir," continued this gentleman, "you should seek an opportunity to do so, for certainly he is the greatest master of modern eloquence. I had heard and read much in the current news of the day in relation to his ability and could scarcely believe that heaven had vouchsafed such powers to any man as were ascribed to him. I was discourteous enough to laugh at my lady friend there, who asserted that he had held her spell-bound for three hours. I was incredulous as to the existence of any human power being such as to enchain my attention for so long a time, and I was tempted to go for once to a political meeting to hear this man from the woods of the west. I found an immense concourse present. There were at least one thousand ladies seated all around the rostrum in the open air just where you have been speaking to-day. I wished to be near the speaker and pushed my way, with the privilege of age, through the throng, until, reaching a convenient distance, I found standing room. It was just as Mr. Prentiss rose to speak. I took out my watch to time him. The cheering was vociferous and I failed to hear his commencement and started to replace my watch in my pocket. I was arrested by a most startling thrill of words and stopped to listen. And I did listen with an attention and interest I had never given to an orator before. So intense was my interest that every faculty, every feeling was concentrated upon the man and the wonderful flow of burning words. It seemed the incarnation of eloquence. There was a witchery in his words clothed in tones so mellifluous that they not only enraptured but stabbed the heart, and I lost the consciousness of passing time, and when he closed I found my hands holding my watch at the pocket's mouth waiting the power to replace it. I looked at it and found I had been listening for more than three hours, and though over seventy years of age, I felt no fatigue. A friend, a clergyman, who had followed me into the crowd, stood pale and agitated, looking at the man after he was seated. As I approached him he explained: 'Will you ever again doubt that God inspires man?'"

A similar instance was given to the writer by E. W. Hewitt, of Augusta, Michigan, who knew Prentiss, and had often heard him speak. Mr. Hewitt says he was once relating to John Van Arman, the distinguished criminal lawyer of Chicago, some instances of the wonderful power of Prentiss as an orator, and Van Arman laughed at him, and ridiculed the idea of a man's having such power. When Van Arman came back from the Mexican war with the Michigan soldiers, he heard Prentiss at New Orleans deliver that eloquent address to the returned volunteers from Mexico. Hewitt, aware of this, when he next met his old friend Van Arman, asked him what he thought now of S. S. Prentiss' oratory. The reply was: "I can say, like the Queen of Sheba, that you did not tell me one-half about this wonderful orator. I never heard before, and I never expect to hear again, such eloquence from mortal lips."

But the prince of all writers in fierce invective, brilliant paragraph, keen wit and pungent satire, was George Dennison Prentice. Beginning as editor of the Louisville Journal in 1831, he soon became a host in the opposition to Jackson, Van Buren and Polk; and his epigrams, bright and sharp, often bordering on the severest personalities, were far more effective than the heavy columns of his editorial foes, Duff, Green, Francis P. Blair, Shad Penn, Thomas Ritchie and others. And yet while Prentice could sting like a hornet, he could sing like a nightingale. It is not often that one who could throw such venom into his paragraphs, could produce such sweet music from his rare poems. As editor of the Louisville Journal, he exerted a powerful influence towards securing the great whig victory of 1840.

The northern and southern democrats, as well as northern and southern whigs, seemed to vie with each other in their efforts to defeat their respective foes. Although the democrats did not expect a defeat, yet it was apparent in the early part of the campaign that whigs began to abound in the land. Thus "the great commotion" surged on, sweeping like a mighty wave over the entire country. The result of this monster political revival was, hundreds of thousands of the American people "experienced" whiggery, and "Tippecanoe and Tyler too" were respectively elected president and vice president of the United States. THEN, the exultant whigs shouted and sang:

"In Lindenwald the 'Fox' is holed,
The coons all laugh to hear it told."
Ha—ha—ha, etc., etc.

Among the prominent democratic orators in Michigan at this time were G. V. N. Lothrop, of Detroit, Edward Bradley, Gen. Isaac E. Crary, Abner Pratt, Thomas B. Church and John VanArman, of Marshall, Charles E. Stuart, N. A. Balch, of Kalamazoo, Flavius J. Littlejohn, of Allegan, and John S. Chipman, or "Black Chip," as he was called, of Centerville. Who that heard them, can ever forget those eloquent democratic stump speakers.

Among the well known whig orators were George Dawson, editor of the Detroit Advertiser, and whom Daniel Webster introduced to the great whig convention of '40 in Fanueil hall, Boston, as "the eloquent Geo. Dawson of

Michigan." Besides him there were James Wright Gordon, and Henry W. Taylor, of Marshall, Horace Mower and Marsh Giddings, of Kalamazoo, and others, all able and eloquent whig orators.

Many of the old citizens here present will remember the whig mass meeting in 1840 at Kalamazoo, when a log cabin was erected and made the headquarters of whiggery for the occasion. But who can ever tell how many locofocos' heads and politics were turned by hard cider that day. The editors of the Free Press and Advertiser were bitter opponents throughout this campaign. The former said in his paper that, at the whig dinner in Kalamazoo, "Dawson and McGraw and their friends ate fried skunk and fricasseed coon."

Dawson made, on this occasion, a ringing, eloquent speech that carried the people to the highest pitch of enthusiasm. Sometime before this meeting a malignant libel had been published against him. It came out in hand bill form, and was circulated about the streets of Kalamazoo the day before the speech was made. While Dawson was speaking this libel was handed him with the request that he read it. He took the paper and, looking over the vast crowd before him, said, "I'll read it, and (referring to the low tone in which a democratic speaker had read a similar paper against himself) I'll read it loud, too." Then, holding up the paper, he began to read, giving running comments on each sentence. I wish I could give you every word of that libel and Dawson's withering comments, but I cannot. I recall the closing sentence: "The whigs wanting an editor for the Advertiser, could not find one on earth, so they went to the depths of hell and there found Dawson." Then, twisting his mouth into comical shape, he replied, "That is the best of evidence that there are few whigs in hell. Any of the scum of hell would do for a locofoco editor."

The two most distinguished and brilliant men of the south, S. S. Prentiss, statesman and orator of Mississippi, and Geo. D. Prentice, journalist of Louisville, Kentucky, were each unsurpassed in their own field, by any person north or south, in the power each exerted towards the election of Harrison and Tyler. They were both born and educated in New England, and having attained their majority settled in and became adopted sons of the south. And though both so distinguished, they never met each other.

Justice A. R. Brown, of Galesburg, Michigan, rode forty miles to hear Webster speak at Stanhope and Morristown, in New Jersey, during the campaign of 1840. Webster at Morristown spoke from the steps of the hotel and an umbrella was held over him to shield him from the rain, while his ten thousand hearers stood in the rain for some an hour and a half listening to him. At this time Justice Brown heard Ogden Hoffman and Commodore

Stockton, eloquent whig orators, speak. The old whig party at this time with its Webster, Clay, Prentiss, Choate, McDuffee, Corwin, Ewing, Hoffman and other eloquent speakers overshadowed the democratic party in statesmanship and brilliant oratory.

The democrats were sanguine of victory and surpassed themselves in their efforts to defeat "Old Tip and Tyler." Dr. J. A. B. Stone, of Kalamazoo, remembers hearing George Bancroft and Peter Parley (Samuel G. Goodrich) make eloquent speeches in Boston on Saturday night before the election on Monday. Bancroft's peroration was full of hope and democratic fervor. "Fellow citizens," said he, "I have but one word to say to you in closing—it is—*advance!* We must win in this contest. The whig party has great and eminent men in it; it has Webster, Clay and Choate, but we must defeat it. And I repeat, we must advance, it is now but a short time till the election on Monday next, and, democrats, I say again we must advance to victory on that day."

But that Monday brought an overwhelming defeat to the democratic party. I was a young democrat then, not old enough to vote, but I felt the tremendous whipping that the whigs gave us at that time, just as much as if I had been a voter. The old democratic party, probably, never got over the effects of that defeat. But the American people will never forget the splendid fight that this redoubtable old party made in this campaign against its time-honored whig foe. And we shall never forget the gallant fight that its own orators made in this State. In fact it has ever seemed to us that the masterly and eloquent defense of the democratic cause that was made by Edward Bradley, Charles E. Stuart, Flavius J. Littlejohn, General Isaac E. Crary, Thomas B. Church and other democratic orators of central Michigan, won for them, as did the bravery and gallant conduct of Francis I. at the battle of Pavia, all the honors of a personal victory. In truth the democrats had the better cause, and although the whigs gained the day in 1840, the case was appealed to the people four years later and the democrats won the election.

But the reform, the better times, the "two dollars a day and roast beef," promised by the whigs were not realized by the laboring man. This was pithily put in an able speech made by Thomas H. Benton in the United States Senate some years after the election. There was a cry of hard times and distress throughout the land. Mr. Benton exclaimed: "Distress! What, sir, are not the the whigs in power, and was not all distress to cease when the democracy was turned out? Did not they carry the elections? Has Mr. Van Buren not gone to Kinderhook? Is General Jackson not in the Hermitage? Are democrats not in the minority in Congress, and expelled from office everywhere? Were not "Tippecanoe and Tyler too" both elected? Is not whiggery in entire possession of the government? Have they not had their extra session called to relieve the country, and passed all the relief measures? Yet the cry is distress! and the remedy is—a national poultice of lamp-black and rags!"

There were two important planks in the whig platform of 1840, one was "a national bank," and the other "protection." S. S. Prentiss, while speaking in favor of American industry, in his great speech at Newark, was interrupted, either by an honest inquirer or possibly a hostile politician, who loudly cried out to him, "Will not that system make the rich richer, and the poor poorer?" The orator instantly, but courteously, turned to the interrogator and thanked him for putting the question, and then, slowly turning his gaze, with an appropriate and corresponding motion of his arms, as if surveying the stately edifices surrounding the park in which he was speaking, he said: "My friend, I am informed that, much to the honor of your city, those elegant dwellings that adorn this park, and the glittering equipages standing before some of their doors, or now rolling through your streets, belong, almost exclusively, to mechanics, or to the sons of mechanics. It is a splendid testimony to the enterprise, skill and industry of Newark, and enough to gladden the heart of every patriot. But, let me tell you, that but for the blessed influence of that protection which the government has hitherto afforded our manufacturers, you who have worked in your shops would be doing so now, and you whose sires—to their honor be it spoken—were blacksmiths and shoemakers, would be mending the old axes and shoes that they made, instead of occupying the palace-like dwellings that surround us."

One of the great events of this campaign was Henry Clay's memorable speech at Nashville, Tennessee, in the autumn of that year. Some four hundred of Tennessee's fair daughters had invited him to speak in Nashville at that time. Over thirty thousand people listened to this eminent whig statesman and orator on this occasion. This speech was one of the most eloquent of the campaign.

Was ever personal influence used with such effect before as by the whigs in this election? Who will ever be able to tell how many thousands were induced to vote for "old Tip" by a glass of hard cider or a whig dinner? The latch string to every log cabin was out, and, as it was said, every democrat who entered and partook of the hospitality within, by some strange infatuation, came out a whig voter.

Nicknames and invective were used as legitimate weapons in this contest. Gen. Jackson was called "old Hickory," hence the hickory tree was an emblem of democracy. General Harrison was called "Tippecanoe" or "old

Tip" from the victory he won over "the Prophet," Tecumseh's brother at the battle of Tippecanoe. The canoe, filled with singing girls, that formed such a picturesque part in the whig processions, with the miniature log cabin and other pageantry, was a symbol for Tippecanoe. The whigs built their log cabins entirely of oak. They were very careful not to have any hickory in them, as that was a locofoco emblem. Webster was called "the dark browed and sunken eyed;" Van Buren, the "Fox," or "Little Magician;" Thomas Ewing, "the crafty and cruel;" Frank Granger, "the pitiless and remorseless." A whig couplet touched off Thomas H. Benton and Amos Kendall—

"There's Benton, the braggart, full of humbug and salt,
And heaven-born Amos, unspotted with fault."

When Mr. Gouge's work on banking came out, Amos Kendall said, "I have heard a great deal about banks on gouging, but this is the first I ever heard of Gouge on banking."

Every device was resorted to to further on the whig cause. Medals about the size of a silver dollar, with a log cabin on one side and a bust of "old Tip" on the other, were made and sold for a trifle to the children, who wore them, and what pleased the child did also the man, for everybody wore these baubles.

Thomas Corwin, the statesman, orator and prince of stump speakers, was at this time in the full vigor and freshness of his unmatched faculties. Wit, humor, poetry, logic, anecdote, graphic power of illustration, an inimitable mimic and *raconteur,* a classical scholar and profound reasoner, he lacked nothing as a popular orator to captivate, convince and carry the crowd with him.

A friend of the writer's went some forty miles during this campaign to hear Corwin speak. It was at a mass meeting in Ohio. As Corwin came upon the stand he bowed, and, without saying one word, he took a large wooden knife, and with it cut a huge johnnycake that was on the table before him, into small pieces. Then laying the knife down he took a piece of the johnnycake and threw it out among the crowd. Thus he continued till every piece of the cake had been thrown among the vest audience before him. Then looking intently a moment at the wondering crowd he exclaimed, "Thus, fellow-citizens, the government at Washington is squandering the public moneys among its favorites all over the union." Then, after this most forcible and impressive illustration of how the democratic administration was squandering the public funds, he began his speech, or rather continued it, for no one in that vast multitude before him ever forgot that most happy illustration at the beginning of one of the greatest speeches they ever listened to. Somebody has said "it was worth going twenty miles to hear John Randolph say 'Mr. President.'" When it was announced that Tom Corwin was to speak in any part of the country distance seemed to be out of the question—it never was too far to go and hear him. Who shall attempt to estimate the influence Tom Corwin's speeches had in the election of Gen. Harrison? That influence was powerful in securing the great whig victory.

The barbecue, although known in some parts of the north, belongs exclusively to the south, and one must have seen it and engaged in it in this southern clime, to have known what it really was.

While sojourning in Mississippi some years after this campaign and while its memories were yet fresh and vivid in the minds of the people, the writer heard frequent mention made of the "barbecues of 1840." And among them was one that awakened memories of distinguished southern orators who had made the occasion one never to be forgotten by their brilliant speeches. This barbecue was on Colonel Heborn's plantation, which was about half way between Vicksburg and Jackson. Col. Heborn, one of Mississippi's chivalrous sons, had invited the people generally, whigs and democrats alike, to this barbecue. A large company of young men mounted on horses in true cavalier style, and came from Jackson. Among them was E. W. Hewitt, referred to above, who has given the writer additional particulars concerning this gathering. It was held in a beautiful grove on the plantation. Seats were arranged about the stand in a half circle, while ladies in their carriages formed a picturesque group in the rear.

After a bounteous feast had been enjoyed, Col. Heborn, master of ceremonies, took his seat on the speaker's stand with the distinguished guests seated on either side of him. Each of the speakers selected was to consider himself a "free lance" in the discussion of whatever subject he might choose. Governor Jones, of Tennessee, a staunch whig, was first called out. He, taking the occasion as a golden opportunity, made a telling whig speech that brought rounds of applause from the enthusiastic crowd. He was followed by Robert J. Walker, democrat of the manor born. It is needless for me to say that he could make a good after-dinner or platform speech. The man who could capture a national democratic convention as he did that of Baltimore in 1844, when he was the dextrous Saladin who met B. F. Butler, the champion of the Van Buren cause in that convention, and after defeating him by a masterly speech, carried James K. Polk against all opposition into a triumphant nomination by that body. Such an orator was ready for any occasion, and he now made a speech whose potency and convincing logic seemed to sweep the first speaker's argument away like cobwebs. But before closing he referred to the distinguished orator S. S. Prentiss who was to follow him. "I know, fellow citizens, that he will captivate you by the charm of his oratory and win you and convince you by the wierd power of his argument. Yes, and I shall be sitting there on the seat beside you, and shall also be won over and convinced with you." And Mr. Walker took his seat. Col. Heborn then introduced S. S. Prentiss, "the eloquent Bayard of the south." The occasion, graced and honored by the refined audience composed of the beauty and chivalry of Mississippi, the distinguished speakers present, (he had been Robert J. Walker's law student), and above all the cause of the grand old whig party, all these now fully inspired him. And, as he stepped forward to begin his speech you could see not only the glory of the occasion, but the *gaudia certaminis,* beam from his countenance. He made one of the most brilliant and memorable speeches of his life and took his seat amid deafening applause. Gen. Anderson, a democrat of the genuine Bourbon type, followed Prentiss. He was a superb platform speaker. He was equipped with every requisite for the orator; with the wit and ridicule of an O'Connell, the fund of anecdote, play of fancy and droll humor of a Corwin, all of which he could admirably use to give edge to the most trenchant logic, or point to the most vigorous argument. He seemed master of the situation, now turning argument, now ridicule, against the strong points of the whig speakers, till there appeared to be nothing left of them. Then again he would turn the tide of wit and humor against his opponents, keeping the audience convulsed with laughter, till everything they had heard from the whig orators was laughed away or forgotten. The plaudits of the crowd were showered upon him as he retired. This barbecue was a remarkable event in the campaign of '40 in Mississippi.

I questioned Mr. Hewitt as to his recollections of these speeches. He replied: "They were all excellent; each one unequalled of its kind and just such a speech as only such an orator could make. But that speech of Prentiss', nobody could equal. It is as distinctly impressed on my mind to-day as excelling all the other speeches of that occasion, as Prentiss excelled all other orators of his time."

A QUARTER OF A CENTURY OF TEACHING

HISTORICAL ADDRESS DELIVERED BY A. D. P. VAN BUREN, AT THE REUNION OF DR. AND MRS. J. A. B. STONE'S PUPILS, AT KALAMAZOO, SEPT. 23, 1885.

Mr. Chairman, Honored Teachers, Old Schoolmates and Fellow Citizens:

It is said that the true function of the historian is to keep the past alive for us. But how much of the past do we find thus secured? Or rather how little does that reverend chronicler of the deeds of men tell us of the years that are gone. We get but a meager outline, a mere synopsis of the public acts of rulers, leading men, and remarkable events. All else, and often the best part, is unrecorded. And as we recede from this unwritten past, time robes it in the mellow light of romance, or throws the glamour of enchantment over its achievements, which then pass into the age of chivalry, and are regarded as more beautiful and attractive than true. The novelist and day-dreamer find it delightful to enter this realm of the by-gone, "this lazy land where it seemeth always afternoon." There is much of our school-day life of which we can say, as we do of the singing of Sontag or Lind, or of the acting of Booth or Garrick: "Well, this delightful thing has been, and all that is now left of it is the feeble print upon my brain, the thrill which memory will send along my nerves; and as we live longer the print and thrill must be feebler, and when we pass away the impression will have passed from the world." Consequently the most delightful part of our school-days, like the song of the bird, a strain of music, or the orator's eloquence, cannot be written, it is only retained by the memory and the feelings. You will remember, fellow students, the beautiful line of Virgil that we used to quote so often and which to-night I can again quote as applying most fittingly to the things that we did in our school days, forty years ago. *"Forsan et haec olim meminisse juvabit,"* perhaps it will delight thee to have remembered these things hereafter. True there is the old quotation.

Our past, then, the history of the school we would give to-night, lies mostly in this unrecorded by-gone; for although the history of the Kalamazoo branch of the Michigan university, and of the schools of Dr. and Mrs. Stone succeeding it, have been written, yet how little of the real history of this quarter of a century of teaching, so invaluable, has been given. How little can be given. We can give but a mere outline of it this evening. Had I the wand of Prospero to wave over our past, and reproduce, or bring to light but one session of our school, in the golden days of the "old Branch," what a delightful retrospect it would be to the teachers and students of that school here to-night. Memory is now busy with those past scenes.

"My eyes make pictures when they are shut."

I see the old Branch standing half hid among the trees on the corner of the park. I hear—

"The old school bell's familiar sound
Peal out among the oaks once more;
Though I had heard it many a time,
It never rang so sweet before."

We are all going to school again. We are once more sitting in our seats at early morning prayer. Again the class bell rings; our teacher sits in his arm chair on the platform, with text-book in hand; we are reciting our lessons. The varied school day routine goes on; students, who study in their rooms, drop in to recitation. It is a fine day in June, the windows are up, "the air is balm and rosemary." I hear the hum of the busy hive all at work.

"Methinks I've cast full forty years aside,
And am at school again. The gentle breeze
That trembles through the windows bears"

the fragrance of the clover blossoms, the song of birds from the trees, and the tinkle of "old crumple horn's" bell from the park lot. Class after class come and go. I hear the light tripping of feet down the stairs, the door opens, a bevy of girls with text-books in hand come in to recite. Others having recited trip up stairs to their seats again. I see their bright eyes and smiling faces. I hear passing words with each other as they go in and out. Thus fancy restores the whole scene till we are all once more at school. Fellow students, in thought the picture is real, and

"Life is but thought, so think I will,
That you and I are schoolmates still."

The Branch building was a two-story frame structure. Dr. Stone had charge of the young men in the room on the first floor; Mrs. Stone of the young ladies in the room above. There was but one government. All the difficult or appeal cases in Mrs. Stone's room were referred for settlement to the principal. The curriculum was ample, including all those studies that would fit a student for the university at Ann Arbor, or he could go through a part or the whole university course here if he chose. Most of the classes below were made up largely of young ladies who came down to recite, and young men sometimes formed part of the classes in Mrs. Stone's room. There was also a small room on the second floor called "No. 3," designed for the tutor's department, which was usually rented by some of the advanced students, one of whom acted as tutor in hearing certain classes recite. Two or more students usually occupied "No. 3," there being room for a bed in it. This was the room where the students held all their meetings and attended to all their club affairs, and at the close of the term, here is where they held their once famous jubilees, sung songs, responded to toasts, made speeches, and gave the parting hand.

The Kalamazoo Branch had attracted and drawn together within its walls a large number of students from various parts of this state and from other states. The young men and young ladies whose names were enrolled as its students in the spring of 1843 would have done honor by their intellectual endowments to any academy in the land. The school itself was popular, the branch universities established in different parts of the state were near enough together to awaken in the minds of the people of the new state a desire for a higher education, and they were far enough apart to afford each other a patronage sufficient to secure a large membership. It was not long before this branch, under the superior organizing power and able management of Dr. Stone, became one of the best known and most popular in the state.

These branches were really young universities equipped with the curriculum that was to be used in the main school at Ann Arbor when that should be opened. In the meanwhile they pioneered and led the way up from the log school-house to the State University. They had, as the times demanded, played the pedagogue by instructing the young through the rudimentary branches, then played the professor through the preparatory degrees, and often through the full college course. So that when the university was finally declared ready to begin her work there were hosts of students all over the state ready to form and fill up her classes from freshman to senior. Thus the university was fitted for her work and set going. And as the branches closed their doors, and retired from their field of labor, they could truthfully have said to the State University, "Your success is now more than half assured, go to work and secure the rest yourself."

It was in May, 1843, when Dr. J. A. B. Stone and his wife, Mrs. L. H. Stone, appeared on this scene of educational labor, where they continued to work uninterruptedly one quarter of a century. Both of them had had experience in teaching, he in academies, in Middlebury College and in Newton Theological Seminary, while Mrs. Stone, besides her teaching in Vermont, had extended her experience to teaching in the south. After pecuniary aid in 1850 had been withdrawn from the Branch the building was used for the ladies' college, which was then in process of erection. Dr. Stone, who had been so instrumental in building the upper college, was made its president, while Mrs. Stone, equally efficient in building the ladies' college, became principal of that, which was dedicated in 1859.

Dr. and Mrs. Stone were the first and successful advocates of a full collegiate course for young women in our state. Being both unequalled as organizers and educators, nothing short of a complete education for both sexes would have satisfied them. In a historical sketch of Kalamazoo College, prepared at the request of the trustees by the Rev. S. Haskell, the secretary of the board, we find the following description of the work done by them in their connection with the college:

"To Professor J. A. B. Stone fell the lot of following Dutton, and the short course of one is in contrast with the long course of the other. Dr. and Mrs. Stone commenced their labors in 1843, and they twain have been one flesh and one spirit in these labors uninterruptedly until the present time. Their work has been multiform and multiplex. There is nothing which they have not touched, from the gravel beneath all material foundation stones to the finale of each pupil's edification in learning and character, their means the while spreading as diffusely through the work as their labors have done. With the entrance of the institution upon its full college career Dr. Stone was appointed its president, and has so continued through these nearly nine years, Mrs. Stone thoroughly occupying the position of principal of the female department."

It may be said of Dr. and Mrs. Stone as regards their long career as teachers in the schools of Kalamazoo, that in their labor for their pupils both as to education and character, "they builded better then they knew." The teacher who imparts a love of study to the pupil, has conferred an invaluable bequest; it is like giving him the "philosopher's stone" that will enable him to turn his time and talent to the acquisition of the golden treasures of knowledge. This is worth all else that books and schools can give, for it leads to the making of the full scholar and the full man. We got this love of study from our teachers, and MORE, there was a power of character that did so underlie and enforce the work of the intellect—that did so arouse and energize their pupils, so call forth their strength and the pleasure of its exercise—as to make the hardest work agreeable.

The course of study pursued at the Branch, under the personal direction of Dr. and Mrs. Stone, was used as the means to develop the moral as well as the intellectual powers of the student. They were in fact, as well as in law, our teachers *in loco parentis*, for they not only taught but trained the students in their course day by day, ever impressing on their minds, till it became ingrained in their natures, that it was morals that gave the highest value to scholarship. The Kalamazoo Branch was our Rugby, and its principal was our Dr. Arnold, whose words seemed half deeds, and their presence in our thoughts was a potent moral force ever with us.

"Our teacher absent was our teacher still."

Wherever we went his instruction went with us as an inspirer to high thoughts and high deeds. Education, he would say, was valuable, culture was above education, character was above culture, and the christian sentiment gave the highest value to character. "The figure is in the stone and the sculptor only finds it." The figure here was character, and it was the educational work of our teachers to develop that in its fullest perfection. The pupil saw that by following the instruction of the teacher it would not only make the most of his time and studies, but the most of him.

By such training the general habits of the student were made to conform to those rules of educational and moral life that are essential to the development of the highest type of the scholar and the man. Moral and religious instruction was made valuable to us, not so much by direct teaching, or what we were brought to know, as from what we were brought to feel by the unconscious influence of the life and character of our teachers, and by the illustrious examples that were daily brought to our attention as models and guides for us in life.

Who shall attempt to estimate the good effects of such teaching on the pupil, and through the pupil on the society in which he moves? What shall we say, then, of the hundreds of pupils who, from 1843 to 1868, have gone forth from the halls of learning presided over by Dr. and Mrs. Stone, to mingle in the affairs of the world wherever their lot may have been cast? Who shall estimate the corrective influence of such lives upon society, or the benefit they have conferred upon mankind?

INCIDENTS

If anything could "beguile the old Gray Beard of his pinions," or cause him to forget to turn his glass this evening, perhaps it would be the reproduction of some of the incidents of the "old Branch days." But alas, how many of them have

"Gone glimmering through the dream of things that were,
A school boy's tale, the pride and wonder of an hour."

Wednesday afternoon was declamation and composition day for the young men below, and composition day for the young ladies above. If they got through with their exercises first, which they often did, they came below to hear us declaim. At one time a knot of young ladies had conspired to flurry or disconcert the declaimer, and cause him to break down if they could. This was not general. They selected certain students whom they wished to victimize on such occasions. Consequently when one of these students was on the stage and heard the patter of feet hastening down stairs he knew that trouble was brewing for him. One day William Eames had just taken the stage when the accustomed footfalls were heard on the stairs. Dr. Stone told him to wait till the young ladies were seated. I can see him now standing at ease, calmly waiting for the wave of Dr. Stone's hand to begin. He was the Cicero of our declamation set. Graceful, humorous, eloquent or pathetic, there was a charm in his manner and delivery that always made it a pleasure to listen to him. Although there was something mischievous in the young ladies' glances at Eames when they came in, yet it was doubtful whether they meant to attack him at that time. We sat anxiously waiting to hear what he had in store for us. And what do we hear:

"Old Grimes is dead, that good old soul
Whom we shall see no more," &c., &c.

That was enough. Instantly a masked battery of eye-shots, grimaces and jeers was let loose on him for daring to declaim that old, antiquated ballad, that the very urchins in the streets had repeated till it was worn to tatters. Of course this attack was made on the sly, when the teacher did not see them. But it was all useless, for Eames had struck the pathetic in the famous old ballad, and, despite all their efforts to confuse him, he turned upon his tormentors and rehearsed the plaintive story of old Grimes with such pathos and tenderness that the young ladies' opposition was hushed and subdued into admiration of the declaimer. Eames left the stage triumphant. William Eames, one of the noblest of our school-mates, died in early manhood.

At another time Charles Beckwith, now judge of the supreme court of Buffalo, had just begun to declaim, when the door opened and the young ladies entered. He stopped till they were seated. They immediately, by look and gesture, attempted to disconcert him. But he was not to be flurried. Watching the opportunity when Dr. Stone was not looking at him, he turned towards them, and, putting his finger to his nose, deliberately made the John Tyler manipulation (then in full vogue) which said to them more defiantly than words could—"you can't come it!" Then going on with his declamation, acquitted himself so handsomely that he even won praise from these young ladies.

There is another incident connected with our declamation days that is yet clearly impressd upon my memory. It is the case of Darius J. Davidson of Union City. He being now a Detroit lawyer it won't hurt him if I tell it here. Davidson had failed every time he had attempted to declaim. He finally concluded that if the rule to declaim was imperative he would have to leave the school. I advised him to try once more. He replied that it was simply impossible for him to get on that stage and "speak a piece" before the school. But after a long talk, he agreed to try again. He selected the first part of the Declaration of Independence. He thought he wouldn't fail on that, for he knew it by heart already. He had two weeks to practice on it, in the meanwhile, he declaimed it to me six or eight times without missing a word. His Wednesday came. I was his prompter, and took seat midway between the door and stage. Davidson's name was called; he took the rostrum, made his bow and begun: "When, in the course of human events"—a pause; I prompt —"it becomes necessary"—he repeats and pauses, I prompt—"for one people" —a pause; I repeat, and look up—Davidson was striding down the aisle past me, and as I looked back he shot out of the door, and disappeared from sight. One of the students said to him that "he stalked out of the school room, like a perfect 'Colossus of Rhodes.'" Davidson afterwards said that when he had uttered the first ten words it began to grow dark before him and he knew nothing till he found himself out on the lawn standing bareheaded under a burr oak tree.

It is said that the critical period in the student's school days is found in his Latin course. That the little god holds his court in the verbal realm *"amo"* (love), and that it is in this realm that the student first meets his destiny. Consequently we have the adage—"Love and Latin do not work well together." Charles Kingsley has thus described this period:

"When all the world is young, my lad,
  And every tree is green,
And every goose a swan, my lad,
  And every lass a queen,
Then hie to boot and horse, my lad,
  And round the world away,
Young blood must have its course, my lad,
  And every dog his day."

As said, the young student usually meets his fate in the word *amo*. If he can conjugate that verb correctly through all its moods and tenses, and pass unscathed the arrows of the little god, he is safe. Now I mention no names, and I refer to no student of the old Branch when I simply say that if the walls of some of their rooms could repeat the verb *amo* as they had heard it conjugated, it would be something like this:

"Amo, amas,
I love a lass
As cedar tall and slender;
Sweet cowslip's grace
Is her nominative case,
And she's of the feminine gender."

We would know then, I say, in what student's room the little god had held sway.

The students sustained a debating society. This was in fact a continuation of the old "Burr Oak Club" which had been the arena where the older citizens had discussed the mooted questions of their day. Many of the students received great benefit from this club. Sometimes the citizens would come and discuss a question with us.

A paper called the Mirror was edited by two of the students, who were elected as its editors. The Mirror was very popular, and among its numerous contributors were some able writers. It was "published" every Wednesday afternoon when the elocutionary exercises were over. Charles Beckwith and the writer of this address were the editors for 1845. I remember that, at the close of our editorial year, we divided the manuscript articles of the correspondents, he taking a portion, I the rest. Among my collection of these papers I lately found a package written in the years 1843, '44 and '45. The handwriting of many of them was familiar to me, and through the mask of a fictitious name signed at the bottom, I could read the name of some old classmate of forty years ago. As I looked over these contributions to the old Mirror, they seemed to "shed the light of other days around me." What thoughts and emotions crowded upon me as I recognized in these *"noms de plume"* the names of Edwin C. Hinsdill, Wyllis C. Ransom, Charles Beckwith; of James A. Duncan and Wells R. Marsh, both of whom died in full manhood, when there was the promise of a brighter future before them. And here was the name of Dwight May, distinguished as student, lawyer and for the high positions of trust he has held in this state, and whose death a few years ago we all mourned. Here were the names of Elias Cooley, Myron Hinsdill, Gibson Brown, and here I find "Justitia"—George A. Hinsdill, the Byron of our school—splendid fellow, with an intellect that a prince might envy, the fine things in whose conversation were always worth noting down. After having risen to prominence in the profession of law in the west, he died when his usefulness was most needed in the upbuilding of a new state. The names of George Trask, John Goodrich and George Fitch bring vividly to mind three old school mates who have "gone to the other side." They made their mark, the first two as business men, the latter as editor and newspaper manager. And here, under the *noms de plume* of some of the fair correspondents of the Mirror, I read the names of Minerva Cornell, Caroline M. Swayzee, Eliza A. Hays, Genevieve Hinsdill, Cornelia A. Clark, Refella Brown, Zilpha Foote, and others of our old schoolmates. We hope during this reunion to read you some of these contributions to the Mirror.

And now I must close. This is a remarkable gathering—one never to be forgotten. When we older students, now gray-headed men and women, entered the Branch, the younger class at this reunion were not born. Some of the younger students here are children of the older ones, and some are pupils of the older students; thus Dr. and Mrs. Stone have taught several generations of pupils here in Kalamazoo. And here in this assemblage of their pupils we find the three periods of life, youth, manhood and age, represented. Holmes has said: "Youth longs, manhood strives, and age remembers." The oldest students here to-night have passed through the ardent, ambitious period of youth when the great desire was to get an education; and they have entered the arena where "manhood strives," and there they have found whatever of success they have achieved in life has been mostly due to the valuable instruction and thorough training they have received as pupils of these honored teachers. And now they have reached the period where "age remembers." We remember that we were taught to aim high in life—"to shoot an arrow at the sun every morning." That the habit of getting good lessons, of always trying to do our best, once established, would lead on to fortune. Yes, old schoolmates, memory is busy to-night with our school days. We can read on its tablets the history of that happy period. "History," says Shelley, "is the cyclic poem written by time on the memories of men." Would that I could gather from the memory of each student here at this reunion the brightest and best recollections of his or her own school days; I would transcribe them all into one beautiful poem and present it, in their behalf, as a souvenir to our dear teachers on this happy occasion.

HISTORY OF THE FREEWILL BAPTIST CHURCH OF COOK'S PRAIRIE

BY HON. JOHN C. PATTERSON

[Read at the Semi-Centennial Anniversary of the Church, March 12, 1886.]

It is fitting for us to-day, on the fiftieth anniversary of the organization of this church, to recall in memory those pioneers who planted this vine in the wilderness, to take account of the fruit it has borne and of its present fruitfulness, and to estimate the possible fruitage of the future. This church and society to-night possess the accumulations of the half century, and are enjoying privileges which were secured long before the present generation was born. As we convene in this cozy chapel and occupy these cushioned pews, surrounded by these broad, cultivated fields and beautiful homes of luxury, we cannot properly appreciate the comforts and privileges we enjoy without looking back, through the clouds and sunshine of fifty years, to the rude place of worship, the narrow fields and the plain homes of the fathers and mothers who gave this church existence.

Let us go back in imagination to March 12, 1836, and glance at Cook's Prairie as the founders of this church saw it when they convened to take upon themselves that solemn covenant with all its obligations. We find ourselves in the territory of Michigan, with a population of about one hundred thousand. Our commonwealth has not yet been admitted into the national union as a state. We are in the township of Homer, which at that time comprised all the territory now contained in the townships of Homer, Clarendon, Eckford and Albion, and the greater part of the territory of the city of Albion. The equalized valuation of the township of Homer as thus constituted in 1836, was $146,250.00, equal to about one-half of the property now owned by the members of this church and society. The equalized valuation of this same territory, in 1885, was $4,961,687.00. In the fall of 1836, the sum of $336.94 taxes was apportioned to the township of

Eckford. In 1885 the sum of $4,117.43 of the state and county taxes was assigned to Eckford. In 1836, $740.57 of taxes were apportioned to the townships of Homer, Clarendon and Albion, and in 1885, $17,967.39 were assigned to the same territory. Fifty years ago the combined wealth of all the members of this church and society did not exceed $6,000.00; to-day it exceeds $300,000.00.

This church organized on the twelfth day of March, 1836. The township of Eckford was set off from the township of Homer and organized as a separate township by an act of the territorial legislature on the twenty-third day of March, 1836; the township of Albion, by an act of the state legislature on the eleventh day of March, 1837, and the township of Clarendon on the sixth day of March, 1838. In March, 1836, there were not three hundred acres of land improved within miles of this spot, and to-day there is scarcely an acre of unimproved land, unless reserved for timber, for miles away. There were only three small frame houses on the prairie at that time. The pioneer log cabin, with parlor, sitting-room, dining-room, kitchen and bed-room all combined, was the prevailing style. The village of Homer, or "Barneyville," and the city of Albion, or "The Forks," were only prospective municipalities, and not actually populated. But few public highways were laid out and opened. The marshes, creeks and rivers were crossed on old beaver dams, or forded. The cross-ways and bridges were yet unbuilt. The clearings and fences were few and the trails and pathways ran in various directions across the broad commons, as suited the convenience or pleasure of the traveler. The primitive burr oak trees were standing here and there like the remnants of an old orchard. There was no undergrowth of timber, save here and there a thrifty clump of hazel bushes. The ground was sodded with the strong roots of the prairie grass, which in summer grew two or three feet in height and waved in the winds like a heavy growth of golden grain. Wild deer were as common on these plains then as sheep are now. Wild turkeys and prairie chickens were more numerous than the domestic fowls are now. No locomotive's shrill whistle was heard at night and no rumbling cars by day. The silence of the night and the peaceful slumbers of the hopeful pioneer were often disturbed by the hideous howl of the prowling wolf, but each dawn of day was heralded by a grand chorus of wild bird song. It was before the age of railroads, telegraphs and telephones.

In March, 1836, there was but one religious organization in this vicinity. On the fourteenth day of December, 1835 (less than three months before) the First Congregational church of Homer was organized by the Rev. Calvin Clark at the residence of Deacon Henry Cook. Henry Cook and Medad Bordwell were among the trustees then elected. This organization seems to have been soon after abandoned. The same persons were among the number who organized the Presbyterian church of Homer on the thirteenth day of September, 1837. The Methodist Episcopal church of Homer was organized on the fifteenth day of April, 1839. It will be seen from these dates that the Prairie church is the oldest religious organization in this part of the county. The first Freewill Baptist church planted in the territory of Michigan was formed near Ypsilanti, March 14, 1831, five years before this church was formed. Other Freewill Baptist churches have been established in the territory before this, but so far as I have been able to learn all of these older churches have ceased to exist, and to-day Cook's Prairie church is the oldest Freewill Baptist church in the state.

THE FOUNDERS

The pioneers of Cook's Prairie and vicinity came from New York and New England. In their new homes they missed the church privileges and the religious teachings of the east, and with Puritanic zeal set about building new altars of worship. Among the first settlers on the prairie were Elder Samuel Whitcomb, a native of New Hampshire, and Elijah Cook, Jr. a native of New York. They came into the territory together from western New York in 1834, and purchased adjoining farms. Elder Whitcomb purchased the farm now occupied by Erastus Stead, and Mr. Cook the farm where he afterwards lived and died, and which is now owned by Francis Andrews. They made their purchases and returning to New York, made preparations for moving their families to their new homes. Mr. Cook determined to purchase more land, and on the twenty first day of January, 1835, accompanied by his son-in-law and daughter, Daniel Dunakin and Eliza Ann Dunakin and Eli T. Chase, he started from Clarkston, Monroe county, New York, for Cook's Prairie, by private wagon conveyance, of the prairie schooner type, and after a journey of twenty-two days in mid-winter, arrived at their destination on the twelfth day of February, 1835. Messrs. Dunakin and Chase were young men, just past their majority, and came to make a home in the west. Mr. Dunakin purchased the farm where he so long lived and where he died, now owned by his son-in-law, Edwin L. Owen. Mr. Chase bought eighty acres of the farm where he now resides. After paying one hundred dollars, the government price for the land, he had three dollars left, a surplus capital with which to make improvements. His means in hands is a fair sample of the accumulated wealth at that time of many of the early members of this church and society. But improvements and a home were in due time made. In 1837 Mr. Chase married Margaret, the only daughter of Elder Samuel Whitcomb. Mr. Cook, after transacting his business, went back to New York, returning in the spring with his family, and accompanied by Lionell Udell and family. In August, 1835, Elder Whitcomb moved his family from Alabama, Genesee county, New York, and settled on his farm. Jacob Rosecrantz, a native of Pennsylvania, came from Orleans county, New York, and settled on the farm now owned by the estate of Perry Herrington, in January, 1836. The same year John Blake, a native of Maine, came from Clarendon, New York, and settled on the farm, where he afterwards lived and died, which is now owned by B. F. Witherbee.

Elder Whitcomb had been a minister in the Freewill Baptist denomination some years. Soon after his arrival he began preaching in the red school-house then standing about five-eights of a mile south of this chapel and nearly opposite the present residence of Albert Andrus. The school-house was small, but with its two rows of seats behind the two rows of high desks around three sides of the room it accommodated all the worshipers. A number of Christian men and women were among the hearers, and a small congregation was gathered. It was determined to organize a Freewill Baptist church, and on that March afternoon, just fifty years ago to-day, a meeting was called at the school-house for that purpose. Let the record of that meeting as recorded at the time in the bold hand-writing of Elijah Cook, Jr., relate its own history:

RECORD OF THE FIRST FREEWILL BAPTIST CHURCH IN HOMER, CALHOUN COUNTY, MICHIGAN TERRITORY.

Homer, March 12, 1836.

A meeting of brethren and sisters assembled to associate and confer on the subject of entering into church covenant with God and with each other. The meeting was opened with singing and prayer by Elder Samuel Whitcomb.

1st. Appointed Elder Samuel Whitcomb to the chair.

2d. Appointed Bro. Elijah Cook, Jr., secretary *pro tem.*

3d. Voice of the assembly was in favor of forming a church.

4th. Read the Freewill Baptist treatise on their faith.

5th. Moved and carried by twelve brethren and sisters that it is their duty and privilege to enter into church covenant together.

6th. Read a covenant from Colby's Journal and unanimously agreed to receive the same as theirs.

7th. Received and read the letters of command from the different churches for embodying.

The church covenant read and which was taken by this little band of christians in the wilderness was as follows:

"We are agreed in repairing to the Scriptures of truth as our only and all-sufficient rule of faith and practice, believing that there is no man wise enough to revise the laws of Christ or to alter them for the better. Neither do we consider ourselves or any other society perfect in a strict sense so but that we are liable to errors and imperfection, and of course if any man or men fix a book of discipline to govern the church by, it must be an imperfect one. The Lord Jesus

Christ has given us a perfect law of liberty and we are not willing to exchange a perfect law for an imperfect one. We therefore consider that the Scriptures are sufficient for the church to make their appeal to on any and every occasion, for saith Paul to Timothy, 'All Scripture is given by inspiration of God and is profitable for doctrine, for reproof, for correction, for instruction in righteousness; that the man of God may be perfect, thoroughly furnished unto all good works.' If, therefore, we are thoroughly furnished, we need nothing more than to consider the Scriptures of truth as our only and all-sufficient rule of faith and practice, hoping and praying that we shall all be led by the same spirit by which they were written. Therefore, under these considerations, we not only consider it our duty but esteem it our privilege to be embodied together as a church, and having first given ourselves to God, we now give ourselves to one another by the will of God to watch over each other for good, and to build each other up in the most holy faith, to bear one another's burdens, and so fulfill the law of Christ. And now, as brethren and sisters in Christ, as children of one family, and heirs of the grace of God, we covenant, unite and agree to stand by each other and do all we can to strengthen and encourage each other on our heavenly journey; and also to preserve a union and harmony in the church by attending to the worship of God and all the ordinances of His house. And may the Lord grant us grace and wisdom that we may shine as a light in the world and that this church be as a city set on a hill that cannot be hid. Therefore, as an evidence of our thus uniting as above mentioned, we give orders to the clerk to enroll our names together."

Daniel Dunakin, Eliza Ann Dunakin, Eli T. Chase and Catharine Cook were received upon letters from the Freewill Baptist church of Clarkston, N. Y.; Solomon Russell, by letter from the Freewill Baptist church of Elba, N. Y.; Jonas Cutler and Janet Cutler, upon letter from the Freewill Baptist church of Alabama, N. Y., and Samuel Whitcomb, Jacob Rosecrantz, Clarissa Rosecrantz, Melissa Haskell, John Blake and Elijah Cook, Jr., were received upon verbal expression. The right hand of fellowship was given by Elder Whitcomb. It was determined by vote that their covenant meetings should be held once in four weeks, and that the name of the church should be The First Freewill Baptist Church of Homer, Michigan Territory. The name was changed April 24, 1841, and The First Freewill Baptist Church of Cook's Prairie was adopted as the name of the ecclesiastical organization.

Of the thirteen persons who became charter members of this church fifty years ago, only one, Eli T. Chase, the chairman of your committee on this anniversary, survives.

Soon after the organization Simeon Cowles, Sarah Cowles and Lucinda Blake united with the church. July 23d the names of Harriet Watkins and Harriet Townsend were added; September 9th Stephen H. Wilson united and October 9th Mandanna Udell became a member; November 15th the names of Henry R. Cook and Lewis Whitcomb were added to the church roll and on the 3d of December, 1836, Chester Smith and Abigail Smith became members of the church family. No others united during the first year. Eleven persons besides the charter members took upon themselves this church covenant during that year. Of this number Martha Blake and Henry R. Cook are with us to-night; Lewis Whitcomb resides in Washington territory; the rest have passed over to their final reward.

It is not the purpose of this paper to name the members, but simply to mention those who organized the church and those who united during the first year of its existence. The latter can justly be classed among the founders of the enterprise.

Solomon Russell took a letter from the church January 9, 1838, and Jonas Cutler, Janet Cutler, Harriet Watkins and Harriet Townsend took letters in November, 1838, to join the Concord church. At the same time Stephen H. Wilson and wife were dismissed by letter. Melissa Haskell, the wife of Timothy Haskell, of South Albion, took a letter in 1841, to unite with the Bellevue church. Sarah Cowles took a letter in March, 1841, to unite with the Battle Creek church. Four of the charter members and four of the early members thus withdrew from the church in its infancy. Simeon Cowles died in 1839, and Mandanna Udell died in April, 1842.

BRANCHES

The church worshiped in the old red school-house, where it was organized, until the brick school-house opposite the present church edifice was built. The services were held in the new school-house until this church was completed in 1860. Under the leadership of Elders Whitcomb and Cook, this church was instrumental in organizing Freewill Baptist interests in other localities. In 1841 Elder Whitcomb organized a church in Burlington, and a dozen or more churches were organized within a radius of forty miles by Elders Whitcomb and Cook, prior to 1846. A branch of this church was formed at the house of David Cummings, in Clarendon, on the 18th of July, 1842, with power to transact local business. David Powers, Horace B. Hayes, Rufus Sarz, Lovina Sarz, Abram Vreeland, Thomas Clark, Issac Vreeland, Fanny Vreeland and T. Deming were received as members of this auxiliary society. This branch remained visible but a short time. Some of the members afterwards became identified with the mother church.

On the 23d day of March, 1846, the Freewill Baptist Church of Eckford was organized at the Olive school-house by Elders Samuel Whitcomb and H. S. Limbocker. Twelve members, viz., Daniel Dunakin, Eliza Ann Dunakin, Eli T. Chase, Charles Olin, Cynthia Olin, John Whitcomb, Nancy Whitcomb, Sarah Cowles, Augustus Lusk, Ann Lusk, William Markham and Louisa J. Hawkins united as the charter members. Eight of the number were members of this church and seem never to have severed their connection. The Eckford church had a visible existence until October, 1851, and enrolled thirty-seven members. The same pastors divided their labors between the two churches. When the Eckford church ceased to exist, by common consent of the members of that, and by the votes of this church in 1853, the records of the two churches were consolidated and the active members were transferred to this organization. Although the Eckford church had an independent organization for a time, it seems to have performed the functions and in fact to have been a branch of this church.

INCORPORATION

The society, in the pioneer days, possessed no church, no communion set, and no church property. The deacons took care of the baptismal robes, and the librarian of the Sunday school carried his library in a basket. A legal board of trustees to manage the temporalities of the church was unnecessary. In May, 1858, it was determined to build a place of worship, and the plan of this chapel was substantially adopted. To acquire the authority to hold property under the laws of the state, a religious corporation then became a necessity. Articles of association for that purpose were signed on the 9th day of May, 1859, by Franklin Mead, E. H. Cook, Elijah Cook, H. R. Cook, J. L. Cook, E. T. Chase, Alfred Stiles, Wm. Beedon, Cyrus Heath, F. P. Auger, Caleb McComber, T. O. Dunton, L. Richey, E. Andrus, Green Wells, H. B. Richey, A. Mumbrne, David Patterson, John Blake, H. B. Hayes, A. C. Hopkins, Luther Rogers, Bela F. Putnam, Wm. McNitt, Joseph E. Daniels, Wm. Rosecrantz, S. Underwood, Lafayette Andrus, Wm. Putnam, Joshua Henshaw and Mark Humphrey. The first meeting to elect trustees was held April 26th, 1859. The pastor of the church, Rev. F. P. Auger, was elected chairman and Henry R. Cook clerk. E. H. Cook, who was elected trustee for three years, Franklin Mead for two years and Eli T. Chase for one year, constituted the first board of trustees. Deacons John Blake and Joseph E. Daniels were the inspectors of this election and executed the certificate required by the statutes, which was filed and recorded in the county clerk's office on the 30th day of April, 1859. The incorporation of the society was thereby completed under the corporate name of "The Freewill Baptist Society of Cook's Prairie." Henry R. Cook has held the office of clerk of the society for twenty-seven years continuously—from the incorporation to the present time. Eli T. Chase was reelected trustee for five successive terms and has held the office for sixteen consecutive years—the longest continuous service of any one. E. H. Cook was trustee for twelve years in succession. Franklin Mead was trustee for eight years, was out of office two years and then served on the board for nine years. He has served the society seventeen years in that capacity; the longest service of any trustee. Joseph E. Daniels and A. C. Hopkins have each served three years; L. J. Andrus, nine years; Horace B. Hayes, eight years; Albert Andrus, six years; William Ashley, three years and Theodore Cook five years. Few moneyed corporations have exercised their franchises as strictly and kept their records as accurately as this religious corporation. The proceedings and records of this society can be safely followed as precedents. They reflect great credit upon the clerk and trustees who have transacted the business. Elder Elijah Cook donated this church site to the society by an absolute conveyance, executed by himself and wife, on the 27th day of April, 1859.

CHURCH, BUILDINGS

The plan of the church as proposed by Mark Humphrey, architect and builder, in 1858, was adopted. The frame was raised on the first day of July, 1859. The ladies of the society served dinner on the grounds. The building was completed at a cost of about $2,200 and was dedicated in August, 1860. President Edmund B. Fairfield, D. D., of Hillsdale College, preached the sermon on the occasion. The chapel has been slightly remodeled since it was first erected, and in 1877 the sheds were built.

PASTORS

Elder Samuel Whitcomb was pastor of the church from its organization until 1841, but was absent for some months on different occasions during the time. Elder H. S. Limbocker labored with the church as an evangelist and as supply on one or more of these occasions. Sometimes services were held once in four weeks and sometimes once in two weeks. The ministers received from twenty-five to one hundred and seventy-five dollars a year as salary, and were compelled to work on their farms during the week to support their families and to prepare their sermons while following the plow. Elder E. Hall was pastor from 1840 to 1841. Elder Limbocker became pastor in 1842. I am unable to ascertain how long he remained. It is probable that there was no regular pastor of the church a portion of the time until 1847. Elder Cyrus Coltren preached in 1847 and 1848. Professor Horace Wellington was pastor in 1849 and 1850. Rev. Edmund B. Fairfield, D. D., ministered to the church for a time in 1851 and 1852. Elder Schuyler Aldrich was pastor from 1852 to 1855. Elder Elijah Cook supplied the pulpit in 1856 and at various other times. Rev. Ranson Dunn, D. D., preached as a supply on various occasions. In 1857 Elder F. P. Auger became pastor and remained three years. He was an able preacher and a good business manager. Under his leadership a new departure was taken and the Sunday school, church and society were conducted upon business principles. The means were raised and this church edifice was erected under his ministrations. Elder O. D. Auger, a brother of Elder F. P. Auger, was pastor from 1860 to April 7, 1861. Elder John Ashley was pastor from 1861 to 1867, Elder Geo. R. Holt was pastor from 1867 to 1870, Elder A. W. Ensign was pastor from 1870 to 1872, Elder A. J. Marshall was pastor from 1872 to 1873, Prof. J. S. Copp was pastor from 1873 to 1876, Elder G. S. Chappel was pastor from 1876 to 1877, Elder John Ashley was pastor from 1877 to 1881 and Elder F R. Randall was pastor from 1881 to the present time. In those early days when from poverty or other causes the church had no regular pastor, the members met regularly in their covenant and social meetings and kept the organization together. President E. B. Fairfield, Prof. D. M. Graham and Prof. H. E. Whipple have occupied the pulpit for short periods. Elder Wm. H. Osborn was pastor of the Eckford church for some time. Elders Whitcomb and Limbocker and Professors Wellington and Graham also ministered to the Eckford church at various times as pastor or supply.

The first twenty years of the church history may be classified as the pioneer period. The people were pioneers, they had pioneer preaching and pioneer singing. The jaded farm horses before a lumber wagon constituted the most stylish turnout seen going to church. I have seen whole families drive up to the old schoolhouse in lumber wagons, drawn by oxen. Calico dresses and coarse shoes had not been deprived of church privileges and excluded from the house of God. The fathers and mothers did not ride so fast on the road to church as do their children and grand-children today, but they started early and were quite as prompt. They put in a full day's worship each Sunday. No twenty minute sermons were delivered. The morning sermon (as near as I can now time its length) was about two hours long, after which was an intermission of about half an hour, when the lunch basket was passed around; then came Sunday school and after Sunday school another short sermon, then all returned to their homes, conscious of having given good time, at least, in their worship. They had no organ, no church choir, but the congregation, when led by the enthusiastic voice of Elder Elijah Cook, never failed to sing "with the spirit and understanding." Many of us can recall the thrilling eloquence and the impressive power of Elder Whitcomb as he gave expression to his agonizing petitions, to his overflowing gratitude and sublime adoration, in prayer. We can also recall the inspiring power and religious fervor of Elder Cook in social meetings in the exercise of his rare gift of song.

6

DEACONS

Cornelius Putnam, Charles Smith, Charles Olin, Ira J. Wilkins, Horace B. Hayes, John Blake, Joseph C. Daniels, Elisha H. Cook, Lafayette J. Andrus, Theodore Cook and H. H. Sheers have held the office of deacons in this church, and Daniel Dunakin was chosen in the Eckford church.

MINISTERS LICENSED AND ORDAINED

Twelve members of this church and its branches have been licensed to preach, and ordained to the christian ministry on the recommendation of this church, during its existence, whose names are as follows: Stephen H. Wilson, E. Hall, David Powers, Elijah Cook, Jr., Lewis J. Whitcomb, Walter H. Watkins, Stephen Mead, William H. Osborn, George R. Holt, Henry B. Richey, Ennis Maynard, and J. D. McColl, D. M. Graham, and Horace Wellington, were ordained on the recommendation of this church. Walter H. Watkins and Wm. H. Osborn were members of the Eckford church or branch.

MEMBERSHIP

This church has been the spiritual home of nearly five hundred members; during the half century nearly five hundred persons have taken that solemn covenant just read. This flock has had its sunshine and its shadow, its prosperity and its adversity. It has had its joys, its revival and times of spiritual growth, and its sorrows, its indifference and times of spiritual decline. Yet in the light of the years, it seems to have had more of sunshine than of shadow, more of prosperity than of adversity. It has been a power for good in this community, in the denomination and state. Whether this church has been "as a city set on a hill that cannot be hid," as was devoutly prayed by its founders in that christian covenant taken by them fifty years ago, can only be judged by its works. Has this organization, through its members, done anything for the cause of religion, christian education, human freedom, and for gospel missions? Has it fulfilled its mission? By its fruits shall it be judged.

CAUSE OF RELIGION

Who can outline the religious influence of this church? Who can describe the spiritual influence of any active christian church, of the impulses of morality and piety, of the assurances of faith and of the hopes of immortality and of heaven, there inspired? We can only gather a few leaves from the wayside and breathe the incense as it arises from the altar. We may note the good deeds of charity and feel the general influence of brotherly love; but we cannot on earth reach the choicest fruits of a christian church; the golden fruitage can only be gathered in heaven. The pastors of this church have been earnest and devoted men. They have preached the gospel from the Book itself. They have quoted poetry, not from Shakespeare and the modern poets, but from the Psalms and Isaiah. They have quoted authority, not so much from Tyndall, Huxley and Darwin as from the sermon on the Mount; from John and St. Paul. A number of powerful revivals have been had and lasting religious impressions have here been made. No one can question but what this church has exerted a great influence upon the morality of this community. An enthusiastic Sabbath school has been continually maintained for nearly two score years, in which the old and the young have been interested students of the Bible. This Sabbath school has been in fact, the nursery of the church. A majority of the members of the church, at the present time, were first members of the Sabbath school.

EDUCATIONAL CAUSE

To appreciate the important part performed by the members of this church in the educational movement, we must go back fifty years in the history of our state and of the Freewill Baptist denomination and consider the standard of public sentiment upon the question as it then existed. The commonwealth of Michigan was then in its infancy. The people had not then had the influence of a graded school in every village and city. They had not lived beneath the light of our great university, nor had the benefits of our numerous denominational colleges. Neither pastor nor people had enjoyed the educational advantages which they now possess. There was no college in the Freewill Baptist denomination and its oldest seminary had then been in existence only four years. The first Freewill Baptist church was organized by Benjamin Randall on the 30th day of June, 1780, and the denomination thus founded was not fifty-six years old when this church was organized. The ministers were mostly uneducated men. Says a denominational historian: "Prejudice against an educated ministry and education for the ministry predominated during the first sixty years of the denominational existence, and for a long time previous to 1840 the denomination had been losing from its ranks many ministers of piety and promise on account of its position on the question of education." Elder David Marks tells us that when he determined to acquire an education he was accustomed to hide his grammar from his ministerial brethren to avoid their expressions of disapproval. It is but just to say that this sentiment was not confined to the Freewill Baptist denomination, but that it was common with many other religious sects and was a result of the limited educational advantages of the day. Our present public school system has since revolutionized this condition of affairs in the state and our numerous denominational schools have worked a change in the church. Prior to 1840 the subject of education had been discussed in denominational circles in New England, and on the 15th day of January, 1840, the Freewill Baptist Educational Society was organized at Acton, Maine, "to provide means for the intellectual and moral improvement of young ministers." This indicates the educational status in the east. The denomination, comparatively speaking, had no schools for higher education and but very few educated members and ministers. Strange as it may seem to us, the question of an educated ministry and the educational movement were subjects of excited discussion and were opposed with the greatest earnestness in denominational circles.

Elder Samuel Whitcomb, the organizer and first pastor of this church, was the earliest advocate and the leading champion of an educated ministry and of the educational movement as a part of the denominational polity in Michigan. He had the sagacity to foresee that the church of the future would require an educated ministry. As a means to that end, we find him, soon after this church was established, advocating with his accustomed zeal, the establishment of a denominational school in the state. Elijah Cook, Jr., who began preaching soon after, heartily endorsed this policy and pushed the measure with all his stalwart power. During these early years Elders Whitcomb and Cook preached and organized churches in Calhoun, Branch, Jackson, Eaton and Barry counties. They advocated the necessity of an educated ministry in their pulpits and agitated the question of a denominational school in the state. Wherever these evangelists labored the educational movement, so called, in the denomination, was brought before the people, and their churches were pushed to the front, far in advance of the other churches in the state. Among the prominent laymen in the denomination who took a leading position at that early day in the educational movement, I am able to mention Daniel Dunakin and Eli T. Chase, of this church, Heman Cowles and Thomas Dunton of Battle Creek, Joseph S. Blaisdell of Assyria, Joseph C. Bailey and Jonathan Videto of Spring Arbor, and Rosevelt Davis of Blackman. Elder H. S. Limbocker, one of the early pastors of this church, was also one of the pioneer leaders in this movement. At that time the members of the denomination were few in numbers, widely scattered and poor in purse. The yearly meeting, first organized in the state at Leoni in 1839, contained only four hundred and sixty communicants. The agitation of the educational cause prior to 1844 had been principally carried on, as it had been begun, by Elders Whitcomb, Cook and Limbocker, and it had been mostly confined to communicants in Calhoun and in adjoining counties where they had preached. These old fathers, though uneducated themselves and identified with an uneducated denomination and living in an uneducated age, recognized education as the handmaid of religion and preached this truth to their congregations. The ways and means, the plans and possibilities for a denominational school were for years the subject of conversation between Elders Whitcomb and Cook as they met in neighborly intercourse. While Isaac E. Crary and John D. Pierce at Marshall, in the province of statesmanship were discussing and perfecting the plan of our state public school system, laying its foundation broad and deep to be crowned by our great university, Samuel Whitcomb and Elijah Cook, Jr., here on Cook's prairie, in the domain of church polity, were discussing and perfecting the plan and laying its foundations broad and deep for a denominational school in the state, to be crowned by Hillsdale college.

ORGANIZED ACTION

The denominational yearly meeting was to convene for its fourth annual conference at Franklin, Lenawee county, in June, 1844. The Calhoun quarterly meeting at that time contained the churches situated in Calhoun and adjoining counties. The delegates from this quarterly meeting to the yearly meeting were appointed some weeks before the yearly meeting was to convene. Samuel Whitcomb and Elijah Cook, Jr., from this church, Heman Cowles and Thomas Dunton, from Battle Creek, and Joseph S. Blaisdell, of Assyria, were the delegates appointed. They all favored the educational movement, and after their appointment conferred together and determined to bring the subject of a denominational school before the yearly meeting for action. Elder David Marks was at that time the most prominent leader in the educational movement and was high authority in the denomination. After preaching for twenty years with zeal, power and success he was then pursuing a regular course of study at Oberlin College. Elder Cook wrote a letter to Elder Marks informing him of the measure proposed to be brought before this yearly meeting and urged him to be present to advocate the cause. Elder Marks was prevented from being present by sickness, but he wrote Elder Cook a letter, which was read to the conference, approving the proposed action.

The yearly meeting convened at Franklin in June, 1844. Lewis J. Thompson delivered an address before the conference on christian education. Elder Whitcomb, early in the business session of the conference, made a motion to raise ten thousand dollars to establish a denominational school within the limits of the yearly meeting. Rosevelt Davis seconded the motion and it was discussed at length and at different sessions of the conference. It was a new measure to the great majority of the delegates and they were not prepared to grapple with the question and assume the financial burden. The motion was advocated by Elders Whitcomb, Cook and others. The approval of the measure by Elder David Marks, with the magic power of his name, was marshaled in its support. The motion trembled in the balance and seemed doomed to be lost. Laurens B. Potter (now Elder Potter of Lansing), believing that the measure would be lost, unless modified in some way, drafted a resolution to establish a denominational school in the state and to call a convention of the churches at Jackson to perfect the plan and to carry the resolution into effect, and offered it as a substitute. The vote was taken on this resolution, Samuel Whitcomb, Elijah Cook, Jr., Heman Cowles, Thomas Dunton, and Joseph S. Blaisdell, the five delegates from the Calhoun quarterly meeting, voted in favor of the measure; the rest of the conference were silent and did not vote. Do we fully realize the importance of this vote? The vote of these five men on this measure, originally introduced by Samuel Whitcomb, gave to the denomination, to the state and to the world, Hillsdale college.

The convention provided for in this resolution convened at Jackson in July or August, 1844, and appointed Cyrus Coltren (who was afterwards pastor of this church two years) agent to procure subscriptions, and determined to locate the school where the most contributions for the enterprise should be raised, having due regard for the healthfulness of the locality. Cook's Prairie competed with Leoni, Jackson, and Spring Arbor for the school. Elder Cook tried to procure from Deacon Henry Cook the high grounds in the center of the prairie, now occupied by the buildings of Theodore Cook for a site. Spring Arbor raised the largest subscription and secured the prize. This community, headed by the generous subscriptions of Elijah Cook, Jr., Daniel Dunakin, Eli T. Chase and others contributed liberally to the enterprise. We must remember that a hundred dollars then was more of a sacrifice for the majority than a thousand dollars would be now. It would be less burdensome for this church and society to raise fifteen thousand dollars to endow a Whitcomb professorship of theology, or a Cook's Prairie professorship of natural sciences in Hillsdale college now, than it was to raise the few hundred dollars donated to establish Michigan Central college at Spring Arbor then. The school opened on the 4th day of December, 1844. Henry R. Cook, Stella Mead and Laura Hayes from this church were among the first students. During the first term of the school the treasury and the wood pile of the institution were exhausted at the same time. Henry R. Cook volunteered to divide his time between his books and the woods. He shouldered his ax, and felled the trees in the woods, and prepared the timbers for the sleigh, a neighbor volunteered to haul the wood to the school room and Stephen Mead and others prepared it for the stove, and thus the members of this church, in that emergency, saved the infant college from freezing out and kept the school open.

The legislature of 1845 granted a charter to the school, but refused to give the authority to confer degrees. Elijah Cook, Jr., was the first trustee named in that charter. The first building was commenced in 1845. Daniel Dunakin laid the stone foundation with his own hands as a part of his contribution to the enterprise. The charter of the college was amended in 1850 and the power to confer degrees was bestowed. This was the first denominational college chartered in the state of Michigan and the first ever chartered in the Freewill Baptist denomination. Elijah Cook, Daniel Dunakin, Eli T. Chase and E. H. Cook were among its most influential trustees. When the question of moving the college from Spring Arbor arose, the trustees from this church held the balance of power and turned the scale in favor of removal and thereby multiplied the usefulness and greatness of the college tenfold. These men staked their fortunes for this college enterprise. The old charter at Spring Arbor made the trustees jointly and severally liable for all judgments that should be obtained against the corporation. A suit was commenced against Elijah Cook, Daniel Dunakin and Eli T. Chase, impleaded with the Michigan Central college and other trustees, but a favorable decision of the court saved them from loss. Daniel Dunakin and Eli T. Chase were members of a committee of five selected by the board of trustees to determine the new location of the institution, and they joined in the report locating the college at Hillsdale. Eli T. Chase for some time held the title of the property at Hillsdale in trust for the college. After the grounds were obtained and the buildings were nearly completed at Hillsdale, the courts decided that the special charter granted to the school at Spring Arbor could not be used at Hillsdale without legislative consent. The new constitution of the state, which went into effect in 1851, prohibited all special college charters. It had been the established policy of our state up to that time to reserve the power of conferring collegiate degrees exclusively for the university. At that time the power to confer degrees had never been granted to any institution aside from the university, except to the Michigan Central college at Spring Arbor. In this case the legislature fixed the standard of scholarship so high that it deemed it impossible for the institution to reach it, or the power would not then have been given.

Daniel Dunakin was elected from this district to the house of representatives, in the state legislature, in 1854. He was on the prudential or building committee of the new college at Hillsdale without a charter and had a deep interest in the enterprise. Undoubtedly he did more work than any other member of the legislature of 1855 to change the policy of the state and to secure the passage of the general college law. Largely through his influence the law was passed and Hillsdale college was the first institution to incorporate under its provisions. The policy of the state was changed and, as the result, we now have a number of flourishing and useful denominational colleges in the state. Daniel Dunakin and Elijah Cook were elected members of the first board of trustees at Hillsdale, and Mr. Dunakin served on the board until his death in 1875. Franklin Mead has also served on the board of trustees several terms. This church and society have contributed thousands of dollars to build and endow Hillsdale college, and have sent scores of students to its classic halls. Has this church, through its members, done anything for the educational cause? Samuel Whitcomb, the organizer and first pastor of this church, was the pioneer leader in the educational movement of the denomination in the state of Michigan, and he can properly be called the father of Hillsdale college. He was the great leader in this march of progress in the peninsular state. And by his side, as he marshaled his forces to battle with prejudice and ignorance, as his wise counselors, efficient supporters and trusted lieutenants, under the banner of progress, we always found Elijah Cook, Daniel Dunakin and Eli T. Chase. Had it not been for the far seeing sagacity and the early labors and brave leadership of these men action would not have been taken at Franklin, and the school would not have been opened at Spring Arbor in 1844. Had it not been for the influence and votes of the trustees from this church, in 1852 and 1853, the school would not have been removed to Hillsdale and to a broader field of usefulness. In fact, had it not been for the lives and labors of these men, the Freewill Baptist denomination to-day would not have had its grandest possession, Hillsdale college, with its fifteen thousand men and women, disciplined by its hand, scattered all over the world. Truly these fathers builded better than they knew, but they had the "hearts to conceive, the understandings to direct and the hands to execute."

ANTI-SLAVERY CAUSE

It is now an easy matter to be opposed to human slavery; in fact it is almost impossible to find a pro-slavery man or woman, north or south. It was not so forty years ago. The democratic party then in power favored slavery, the free-soil or Wilmot proviso wing of the party, was in the minority. The whig party at that time had a strong anti-slavery element, yet it was compromising with the devil on the slavery question. These two parties then moulded public sentiment and controlled legislative measures. In those days to be an abolitionist was to be an object of derision and contempt. It required earnest convictions and moral courage for a church to espouse the cause of the slave, and stamina of character and strong individuality for a man to defy the prevailing sentiments and become an outspoken abolitionist. Early in the anti-slavery agitation this church took a decided stand, and on the 19th day of May, 1838, in its monthly covenant meeting, passed a resolution to do all that its members could consistently do to advance the cause of the abolition of slavery. This church was in advance of the denomination on this question, for the Freewill Baptist denomination did not make the question of slave ownership a test of church fellowship and refuse to admit slaveholders to its communion until its general conference in 1839. Soon the individual members of this church began to sever their relations with the old political parties on account of their positions on the institution of slavery. In 1844 Eli T. Chase voted with the abolition party, when it cast only eleven votes in the township of Eckford. Soon after Samuel Whitcomb, John Whitcomb, Elijah Cook, E. H. Cook, Horace B. Hayes and others whose names I cannot now give, became champions for the African slave and voted the abolition ticket. I can recall some of the sneers that were directed against these advance guards of universal freedom. When we remember that it is often easier to be shot at than to be laughed at, we can form some idea of the strong convictions and moral courage of these men in those early days. In 1854 Eli T. Chase, E. H. Cook and Daniel Dunakin were members of that immortal convention "under the oaks at Jackson," and helped organize the republican party; that instrument, in the hands of God, which destroyed the hideous institution of slavery in our land and gave back to the African race the God given right of liberty.

PATRIOTISM

This church and society has not been wanting in patriotic efforts. They contributed liberally of their means and sent scores of men to vindicate the America flag, and to serve the union on the bloody field of battle. Among these patriots who gave their lives for their country I find the names of Smith Rhodes, Orlando Crocker, Harrison Richey and Cicero Kennedy on your church roll, and from your society I recall the names of Sewall A. Jennison, Hoyt Henshaw, Sylvester Mumbrue, Lester Mumbrue and Bert. Spaulding. Some died in the dismal camp, some on the field of battle, and some starved in the loathsome prison pen.

"Dust may return to dust, but deep
Within the hearts of freedom's sons,
Embalmed forever, love shall keep

The memory of these faithful ones;
And coming years shall swell our lays
And weave new laurels for each head,
While grateful freemen sing the praise
Forever due our noble dead."

MISSIONARY CAUSE

This church has contributed something, at least, to the cause of missions. The ladies have not only maintained their church society here, but have extended their labors over broader fields. The Freewill Baptist Woman's Missionary Society of the Calhoun and North Branch quarterly meeting and the Woman's Missionary Society of the St. Joseph Valley yearly meeting were organized, and, to a great extent, have been conducted by the ladies of this church. This church, this quarterly meeting and this yearly meeting all owe their flourishing missionary organizations to the ladies of the Cook's Prairie church. The labors of Mrs. Electa Potterson French, Mrs. Julia Hofer Cook and Mrs. Alma Dunakin Owens and their co-workers from this church will not soon be forgotten. The seed that they have sown will bring forth fruit throughout the world wherever Freewill Baptist missionaries are spreading the gospel of Christ.

CONCLUSION

This church has lived and labored fifty years. Has it fulfilled its high mission? Will it live and labor another fifty years? Who of us will be present at the centennial anniversary of this church fifty years from now? Will this church be visible then? These questions come crowding upon us at this hour. This church to-day has one hundred and fifty members bound together by the strongest ties of harmony and brotherly love. It owns this neat and valuable church property and is free from debt. Its wealth has increased since the fathers commenced to worship here fifty fold. I can see no reason why this church vine should not grow, be thrifty and bring forth rich fruit at the end of the century. The fact that one of the original thirteen members is with us to-night, though past three score years and ten, yet young and joyous in spirit, gives us hope that many of the church and society of to-day will live to celebrate the next semi-centennial anniversary and carry the traditions of the present time to that generation, as Mr. Chase to-night brings the traditions of the fathers and spreads them before us. What a rare combination of privileges Mr. Eli T. Chase has enjoyed. How appropriate it is that he, as chairman of the executive committee, should have charge of this anniversary celebration. He is not only the sole survivor of the church as organized fifty years ago, but is the only man now residing in the township who voted at the first township meeting held in Eckford in 1836, and is the only man surviving who voted at that election except Andrew Herrick, now of Homer. As a man of deeds, not of words, he has taken an active part in the religious and social questions of this church and community, and has participated in the educational and political affairs in his township, county and state. He has lived to see the educational movement triumph in his denomination, and the sentiment of his church completely revolutionized on the subject. He has lived not only to see the institution of slavery wiped out, but to see the slave made a citizen and enfranchised. What a blessing to see these fond hopes all realized. He has helped to make this history, and now it must be a source of great satisfaction to him, and it will be a support to him in his declining years to feel conscious that the world is freer, wiser and better for his having lived in it.

We have consecrated grounds in our midst. Just across the way in your beautiful prairie cemetery are the graves of Samuel Whitcomb, Elijah Cook, Catherine Cook, Daniel Dunakin, Eliza Ann Dunakin, Jacob Rosecratz, Clarissa Rosecrantz and John Blake, eight of the first members of this church—eight of the founders of this church fifty years ago. In the wilderness they planted it for me and you. With grateful hearts let us ever cherish their memories, and as spring time shall come in each fleeting year, cover their graves with sweetest flowers of love.

Let every Spring Arbor and Hillsdale student remember that to Samuel Whitcomb, Elijah Cook, Daniel Dunakin, Eli T. Chase, E. H. Cook and Franklin Mead he owes a personal debt of gratitude. Let every Freewill Baptist who appreciates the progress of his denomination and its educational institutions remember that here the seed was sown and here the plan was conceived and here the influences were started, out of which has grown Hillsdale college. Let the christian and the patriot remember that this church has been on the right side of all great, moral and religious questions, has been in the front ranks of many of the reform movements of the day, and has done much for right living, for right ruling, for man and for God. From the achievements of these humble men, under God's blessing, may we not learn a lesson and take courage, remembering that

"We live in deeds, not years, in thoughts, not breaths,
In feelings, not in figures on a dial.
We should count time by heart throbs. He most lives
Who thinks most, feels the noblest, acts the best."

HISTORY OF THE METHODIST EPISCOPAL CHURCH AT GALESBURG

CONTRIBUTED BY A. D. P. VAN BUREN

[John S. Martin, in Galesburg Enterprise, June 12, 1885.]

The Methodist Episcopal society, in connection with Galesburg and vicinity, was organized in July, 1838, by Rev. James T. Robe, now living in Kalamazoo. Its membership at that date were Jabez Rogers, wife and daughter, Mrs. Warden, Moses McClellan and wife, Mrs. Hannah Austin, Mrs. Luke Rugg, Mrs. J. Burnette and son—nine persons. Their place of worship from the date of organization to 1837 was Mr. Rogers' residence, a double log house that stood on the west side of the present David Vosburg farm; from 1837 to 1840 in a log school-house built on Henry Rogers' farm, now owned by Luther Eldred; from 1840 to 1845 in a frame school-house 15 rods north from the southwest corner of Ralph Tuttle's farm, now owned by Mr. Carr; from 1845 to 1848 in the Baptist church in this village; from 1848 to 1852 in the Presbyterian church; then one year in the "Variety Store," now a part of Mr. Knapp's present residence; then for a time in the Baptist church again. In January, 1855, their first house of worship was dedicated; built where the Adventist church now stands. They occupied this church until June, 1871, when it was burned to the ground, without insurance. They met then for a short time in the Baptist church again until the basement of their present edifice was ready for occupancy. On December 23, 1875, the church was finished and dedicated and the society has worshiped in it to the present date. The following ministers have served the society from its organization, figures below being date of appointment:

Year.	Pastor.	Presiding Elder.
1832......	J. T. Robe......	James Armstrong.
1833......	R. C. Meek......	"
1834......	J. T. Robe......	Richard Hargraves.
1835......	S. S. Williams......	"
1836......	E. L. Kellogg, H. B. Beers......	"
1837......	E. L. Kellogg, Jacob Colclazer......	Aaron Wood.
1838......	William Tod, H. Worthington......	J. Ercanbrack.
1839......	H. Van Order, O. S. Mills......	"
1840......	R. R. Richards, R. H. Cook......	"
1841......	R. R. Richards, Edward S. Kellogg......	J. F. Davidson.
1842......	J. W. Birer, R. R. Richards......	"
1843......	J. T. Parker, J. T. Hudson......	"
1844......	S. C. Stringham......	"
1845......	Daniel Bush......	William Sprague.
1846......	R. R. Young......	"
1847......	V. G. Boynton......	"
1848......	R. L. Farnsworth......	"
1849–50...	V. Mosher......	Francis B. Bangs.
1851......	A. Wakefield......	"
1852......	A. Dunton......	Resin Sapp.
1853......	I. C. Abbott......	"
1854......	"	George Bradley.
1855......	F. Gage......	J. Jennings.
1856......	R. Sapp......	"
1857–8....	S. Steel......	"
1859......	I. C. Abbott......	E. Holstock.
1860......	V. G. Boynton......	F. B. Bangs.
1861......	A. Billings......	"
1862–3....	H. M. Joy......	"
1864......	W. W. Johnson......	R. Sapp.
1865–6....	A. J. Van Wyck......	"
1867......	G. W. Sherman......	"
1868......	"	T. Lyon.
1869......	"	I. Coggshall.
1870......	J. W. Miller......	"
1871–2....	D. Engle......	"
1873–4....	C. L. Barnhart......	H. C. Peck.
1875–6....	L. W. Earl......	"
1877–8....	H. P. Henderson......	J. W. Miller.
1879–80...	J. A. Sprague......	"
1881–2....	J. P. Force......	W. J. Aldrich.
1883–4....	E. S. Mechesney......	"

EARLY MICHIGAN

BY WILLIAM H. CROSS

[Read before the Branch County Pioneer Society, December 28, 1885.]

Michigan territory in 1820 had a population of 8,765; in 1830, 31,639. It then comprised all the territory north and west of Ohio, Indiana and Illinois, and east of the Mississippi. In 1834 was added to it all the country west of the Mississippi river and north of Missouri, with a delegate in Congress to ask for what he wished, but with no vote to give to obtain it.*

How is it to-day? We have Michigan, Wisconsin, Iowa, Minnesota, Nebraska, Colorado, with twelve United States senators, nearly one seventh of the senate, forty one members of the house of representatives, over one eighth of that house, and much more than one eighth of the brains and business of either house, with over 9,000,000 of the best educated, intelligent, active and independent inhabitants of the globe; and this is what Michigan of 1834 has become in 1885, within fifty one years. The world does move in the northwest.

My first fall and winter in Michigan and my first night, fifty nine years ago, were spent in the woods alone. On the last day of September, 1826, I came to Tecumseh, on the river Raisin, the then western farming settlement of the territory, consisting of about twenty five families. The next day but one (the first being Sunday) I went to work for Peter Low, digging potatoes. I worked ten days and was taken with a severe attack of bilious dysentery and was unable to do any work for four weeks. I then went with my brother Robert J., who had been preparing a place and cutting logs for a house on our lands, four miles above the village and two from any settler, to assist him what I could and be company for him. Through the month of December we got our house up, a building of 16x18 feet inside, with a shingle roof, two floors, a glass window, and board doors; a decidedly aristocratic mansion for those days, for it had a stick chimney above the edge of the roof. About the middle of January our stock of corn, on which we depended for our corn meal for bread and for feeding a team of oxen, had got so low that it became necessary for one of us to go to Monroe, thirty five miles, for that and other needed supplies for winter and spring. I was not strong enough to chop but thought I could go, and left with my oxen and sled, the snow being nearly a foot deep. The first day I went about twenty miles to the mouth of the Saline river, the next day to Monroe, and traded some deer skins and peltries we had got of the Indians, and with a little money bought a barrel of Ohio flour, a barrel of salt, a few groceries, nails and other needed indispensable things for cabin use, and, with what corn I could haul, got back seven miles toward home. Next day I got to what was known as the Big Prairie, where were some stacks of hay, put up by Mr. Evans, of Tecumseh. As I neared the prairie, I cut a number of logs of beech and maple wood, loaded them on my sled to make a fire with when I got to the hay stacks, and just at dusk I got there, when I took the cattle from the sled, turned them in their yoke to the side of the stacks and let them help themselves, and I made a fire with my wood, then thawed out some bread and pork I had with me, which was hard frozen, made my supper, and creeping into the hay stack as far as I could, with my blankets, made myself as comfortable as I could for that severely cold night, being eight miles from a settler's cabin, that being my first night in the woods alone. The next day I got home, some seventeen miles, about sundown, with my load of about 1,200 pounds of much needed things for future use.

FIRST WINTER IN COLDWATER, 1830–31.

After the winter of 1826-7 we spent three more winters in Tecumseh, making improvements on our farms, but in June, 1830, we sold out our farms there, and in October, 1830, bought that part of your city lying on the east three-fourths of section 21. The four winters spent on the Raisin made us conclude that the winters of Michigan were much less severe than they were in Ontario county, N. Y., for they had proved so; but those of 1830-31 and 1831-2, the first we spent in Coldwater, forced us to the conclusion that either a change from the eastern watershed to the western made harder winters, or that the Indians were correct in their declaration that the white men brought more snow and colder weather with them to kill off their ponies and the game upon which they depended for their living, for these first two winters, 1830-1 and 1831-2, were much more severe than any we had before met in Michigan. And these winters we had to bring our provisions for ourselves, and most of our corn and grain and part of our hay for our stock from Tecumseh, nearly sixty miles, and on such roads as the frontiersmen had opened on the line of the Indian trail, with not a stream bridged but all to be forded, and it was cheerfully done, for our hearts were strong, our minds determined. Our anticipations of good farms, freedom from rents, independence from landlords and from being required to change places at another man's command,

and all the future bright and blooming with promise of future fortune, we were willing to work and win, only asking life and health for us and ours, and the results were fully accomplished in all southwestern Michigan.

The Grand Haven Herald recently sent out a request for all persons settling before May 14, 1826, to communicate with it. We condense from nearly two columns of interesting letters the year of settlement, name and present location of all who responded. In 1815, A. L. and B. O. Williams, who reside at Owosso, E. S. Williams, Flint, and their sister, Mrs. M. A. Hodges, Pontiac, came to Michigan; S. C. Manson, East Saginaw, aged 85, came to Detroit in 1817. C. C. and H. A. Rood, Grand Rapids, J. E. Voorheis, Frankfort, Mrs. J. E. Gillett, Lansing, Mrs. N. Frost, Cheboygan, David Knox, Sr., St. Joseph, and J. M. Dewey, Owosso, came in 1823. Mrs. Hope Leman, North Newberg, Shiawassee county, Simeon French, Detroit, Ezekiel French, Dubuque, Iowa, Mrs. W. Green, aged 83, and Mrs. George Collins, Farmington, aged 89, John Geddes, aged 84, and J. J. Parshall, aged 61, moved into the territory in 1824. Edward Hawley, Kalamazoo, Philo Parsons, Ypsilanti, aged 79, J. D. Ackerman, Union City, Mrs. A. Beardslee, Flint, Allen Tibbits, Coldwater, aged 81, Mrs. J. E. Hawkins, Fenton, 81, Herman N. Hicks, Ann Arbor, 68, Orange K. VanAmberg, Brighton, Rufus Thayer, Plymouth, 85, William Power, Farmington, 70, Ira Hough, Plymouth, 83, Leland Green, Farmington, 83, Allen Durfree, 83, and A. Kingsley, Livonia, came in 1825. Dexter Briggs, Livonia, 81, Earl D. Hamblin, Imlay City, Roswell Burt, Davisburg, Sullivan Armstrong, Tremont, Alfred J. Armstrong, Ashland Center, and Horace Carpenter, Ann Arbor, 80, come in 1826.

I add the following persons in St. Joseph county; also the names of persons now residing in St. Joseph county who came to Michigan before and in 1826:

	To Mich.	To St. Jo.
Alvin Calhoun	1817	1827
John W. Fletcher	1824	1829
George W. Thurston	1824	1827
David Knox, Sr	1823	1823
William Connor	1825	1827
John Sturgis, 2d	1824	1827
William H. Cross	1826	1830
Hamden A. Hickox, born in Michigan	1809	....
Miss Althea Lawrence, "	1817	1827
Miss Mahala Hampson, "	1824	1829
Mrs. Sarah Fletcher, "	1823	1830

No doubt there are others, but I am not sure, and I hope may be added those from your own county besides our old friend Allen Tibbits as above.

What a host of memories must William B. Sprague have in store, who has lived in every president's time from Washington to Cleveland.

EARLY DAYS IN MICHIGAN

BY ALFRED L. DRIGGS, OF CONSTANTINE

[From the St. Joseph County Advertiser, July 9, 1885.]

There are few persons now living, who, from personal experience, have any idea of the trials, adventures and hardships of those who, over 50 years ago, went into the wilderness of Michigan to carve out homes for themselves. It must be hard for the present inhabitants of this densely populated, highly cultivated and prosperous state to realize that but little more than 50 years ago it was really and truly a howling wilderness—the home of wild animals, and Indians, more savage and more dreaded than the wild animals. It seems almost like a dream that all this growth and improvement had so recent a beginning. While enjoying the bountiful present, a knowledge of the past and of the early days in Michigan will not be unprofitable, and I trust not uninteresting. By request of some of my friends, I will give a partial sketch of events, and my experience the first five years in Michigan.

At the age of 21 I left my parents' home in Middleburgh, Schoharie county, N. Y., on the first day of May, 1831, for Michigan. I arrived in Detroit, I think, on the 13th, and three days later at Jackson. The county seat had just been located there. I soon rented the only saw mill in the county, near the village, which I ran until the middle of July, when I was taken with the ague, and had it on and off until the first of October. I then left Jackson for White Pigeon in company with Daniel Hogan, then a merchant at Jackson, who had a horse and buggy. At that time there was not a bridge over any river, creek, or marsh between Jackson and White Pigeon.

There were only two rough board houses at Marshall; only two buildings at Kalamazoo, a log house by Bronson, the first settler in the town, and a board shanty by an Indian trader, named Austin. I left Kalamazoo for White Pigeon, at that time the only place of trade, except Niles, in southwest Michigan. At White Pigeon there were three stores, by Barry & Willard, E. S. Swan, and Kellogg Brothers; a fine hotel kept by A. Savery, the only land office in the west part of the state. I boarded at the hotel, having the ague part of the time. I left White Pigeon the fore part of January, 1832, for Detroit, with the intention of returning to New York in the spring, in case I did not get rid of the ague. I had a ride to Hog Creek, 30 miles east of White Pigeon. I stopped over night at a log house kept by Judson. My bed was on the bare floor, with no clothing except what I had on. At that place two men from the east, Wales Adams and William A. Kent, had just built a cheap saw mill on Hog Creek, and neither had any knowledge about a mill. They induced me to stop over a few days and instruct them.

While I was at White Pigeon I formed the acquaintance of a young man by the name of King, from Connecticut. He was at the hotel with the ague while I was there; he had heard I was stopping at Hog Creek; he came to see me and ask me if I knew of any speculation. I told him I had examined a good mill site two miles north on Swan creek, in first-rate heavy timber land. I told him I had no means to improve the site (I had the previous fall entered the land on Broad street, where O. C. M. Bates now resides). He convinced me he had sufficient means to improve the site. We at once entered into partnership, he to furnish the means and I the experience. Without delay we commenced,—about the middle of February,—cutting roads, building a log house, and getting out timber for a saw mill frame; we had hardly commenced getting the timber out when he received word from his friends east that he had better locate further west; he left me with a lot of hands and not fifteen dollars at my command; he assigned over to me what he had advanced, and I was to pay him in two years. I went on with the improvement. I could obtain anything I wished on time, my credit was unlimited, better than it is at this time. My mill was framed and raised. I found a millwright. I previously bought a yoke of oxen and a wagon on time. I sent one of my hands with the ox team to Detroit for the irons and castings, as they could not be obtained nearer. I had previously engaged them. I was endorsed by Oliver Raymond, who was at that time a resident of Sturgis, and was well acquainted with the furnace man, A. M. Hurd. My man was obliged to stay at Detroit until the mill irons were completed. I sent my note payable one year from date for $150, by previous agreement. I started the mill about the middle of October. I settled with the millwright by giving him my note for $125, payable one year from date. After I started the mill I had only cut a few logs when the dam broke and came near upsetting the mill. I soon repaired both mill and dam, and started the mill again. For more than four months I was not out of sight of the mill, and ran it alone that time eighteen hours out of every twenty four. I soon had piles of lumber about the mill, after supplying the demand in Branch and St. Joseph counties, but I was heavily in debt and must raise money and was at a loss how. The roads through the heavy timber lands were impassable to haul half a load. There was no snow that winter, and I was obliged to haul logs on trucks. I conceived the idea of clearing out the creek about five miles to the openings for the purpose of conveying my lumber to some market. I hired the only man who was willing to assist me in the tedious job of working in ice water in the month of March. The creek was cleared. I then employed men rafting the lumber in cribs, some 1,500 feet in a crib. One man on a crib with a pole would run down the creek some five miles to a bank in the openings, haul it out, and that was his day's labor. That was repeated, rafting and running till I had about 100,000 feet on the bank. Then I hired teams to haul the lumber to Colon lake and St. Joseph river. Then it was rafted and run down said river to the mouth and Lake Michigan. There was but little or no demand for lumber there.

I was told they had started a town across the lake at the mouth of Chicago river, where it was thought I might make sale of my lumber. There was a vessel lying there—I think the only one on Lake Michigan—with part of a load of flour bound for that town across the lake. I bargained with the captain to put a deck load of lumber on his vessel. I also chartered the vessel to return and take a cargo. I was to pay $200. We came in sight of the town; the vessel was anchored over half a mile from shore, the lumber put on a scow and rowed in the river and put on the bank. There was no harbor there. I soon ascertained I had come to a poor market to sell my lumber, about 20,000 feet of clear whitewood. I at last made sale to a man by the name of Williams who was then keeping a 7 x 9 grocery. He was the only man there who was able to purchase the lumber. There were at that time about a dozen cheap houses or shanties, and one respectable one, called a hotel, the only one that had any paint on it, was located where the Tremont house now stands. There was a fort, and soldiers stationed there, which was commanded by Col. Whistler. I was in the place two days, intending to leave for home the next morning and not return to St. Jo. for the cargo I had bargained for. I was aware I could not sell it. Late in the afternoon my friend Williams was hunting for me to inform me the captain of the vessel had taken out a warrant to arrest me for a breach of contract for not returning for the cargo, as he had heard from some source I would not. I was not long paying my bill at the hotel, and struck out for the beach of the lake. I traveled some time after dark, I think about 15 miles. Was out of the state and safe. That was the first and only time I ever ran away from an officer. I stopped over night at a log hut near the beach. The man had a squaw for his wife. I took to the beach next morning, by way of Michigan City and Laporte, home. I also ran another raft the next year, 1834, down the river to the lake. In the month of June, 1836, I sold my mill and 400 acres of heavy timber land adjoining, for $4,500, and other lands, etc., for $1,500. Chicago was then heard of. Some thought it might make a smart town. I thought I might speculate. I went there on horseback with $6,000 on my person. I could then have bought hundreds of acres now covered with buildings. I did not invest. I thought it only a mushroom town located on a wet marsh. There had been considerable improvement made since I saw it three years previous, in very cheap houses, even a small brick one. I returned with my money. I bought that summer twenty two hundred acres of land in Branch and St. Joseph counties and the following fall bought and built on Broad street.

THE EARLY SURVEYS OF MICHIGAN

WASHINGTON, MICH., *June 12, 1886.*

Harriet A. Tenney, Recording Sec., State Pioneer Society, Lansing:

MADAM—I enclose to your address a paper in reference to the public land surveys of Michigan, which may be of interest and worthy of preservation. Having been an active participant in these surveys since 1849, and knowing many of the deputy surveyors, am pleased to note a desire on the part of those who would preserve historical data and reminiscences of the past to deal justly and secure accuracy. In vol. 5, page 115, of the "State Pioneer Collections," the paper entitled "The life and times of William A. Burt, of Mt. Vernon, Michigan," should be credited to Geo. H. Cannon, of Washington, Macomb county, Michigan, and *not,* as it erroneously is, to Scott Cannon, as no such person is known to exist.

With great respect, etc.,

GEORGE H. CANNON.

To the Editor of the Post and Tribune:

In a recent number of your paper Mr. George S. Frost, in his historical address, is represented as saying that "Mr. Trowbridge copied a list of the names of the white inhabitants of the territory for the census of 1820." And after recounting the places of settlement which were then over that vast country, says: "The public surveys had not yet extended even into this peninsula." This is an error, as the linear surveys of that date had occupied a large area of the southern portion of the territory; parts of Oakland and Macomb counties having been surveyed as early as 1817 and 1818.

GEORGE H. CANNON,
Dept. Surveyor U. S. Lands.

Washington, Mich., December 25, 1882.

To the Editor of the Post and Tribune:

In your issue of December 27 I find the following from the pen of Mr. George H. Cannon, the well known surveyor and "land-looker" of Macomb county:

In a recent number of your paper Mr. George S. Frost, in his historical address, is represented as saying that "Mr. Trowbridge copied a list of the names of the white inhabitants of the territory for the census of 1820." And after recounting the places of settlement which were then over that vast country, says: "The public surveys had not yet extended even into this peninsula." This is an error, as the linear surveys of that date had occupied a large area of the southern portion of the territory; parts of Oakland and Macomb counties having been surveyed as early as 1817 and 1818.

I think that the following will show that an attempt, at least, was made to survey a portion of our state as early as 1815, although Mr. Cannon places the earliest date at 1817. The document which I copy below is on file at the general land office at Washington, and through the courtesy of the Hon. E. M. Marble, United States commissioner of patents, several months ago, a copy was secured for me from the Hon. A. C. McFarland, commissioner of the general land office. In addition to establishing a date I think it will prove of interest to your many readers as illustrating in what opinion the lands of our beautiful peninsula were held in 1815. It is proper to add that, acting upon the suggestion of the surveyor general, the congress repealed the act making appropriation of Michigan lands for the soldiers and I think appropriated other lands in lieu thereof located in Florida. The document referred to I have never seen in print, and I copy it verbatim as follows:

SURVEYOR GENERAL'S OFFICE,
Chillicothe, November 30, 1815.

SIR:—

The surveyors who went to survey the military land in Michigan Territory have been obliged to suspend their operations until the country shall be sufficiently frozen so as to bear man and beast. Knowing the desire of the government to have the lands surveyed as soon as practicable, and my earnest importunities to urge the work forward, they continued at work suffering incredible hardships until both men and beasts were literally worn down with extreme suffering and fatigue—the frost set in early, and the ice covered nearly the whole country, but broke through at every step, and the pack horses could not be got along with them, they were therefore obliged to submit to the climate and its attendant rigors, and desist for awhile, intending to attack them again as soon as they think it possible to proceed.

I annex a description of the country which has been sent to me and which I am informed all the surveyors concur in, it was only yesterday I received it and heard of their return—so soon as their health and strength is recruited I expect to see them all, only one of them having been here yet—in the mean time I think it my duty to give you the information, believing that it is the wish of the government that the soldiers should have (as the act of congress expresses) lands fit for cultivation, and that the whole of the two millions of acres appropriated in the territory of Michigan will not contain anything like one hundredth part of that quantity, or is worth the expenses of surveying it, perhaps you may think with me, that it will be proper to make this representation to the president of the United States and he may avert all further proceedings—by directing me to pay off what has been done and abandon the country—congress being in session other lands could be appropriated in lieu of them and might be surveyed as soon as those in Michigan—for when the ice is sufficiently strong to bear man and beast, a deep snow would still embarrass the surveyors. I shall therefore wait to hear your answer to this communication before I proceed any further thinking I should be unfaithful to my trust if I had lost any time in communicating the information received.

The country in the Indian boundary line from the mouth of the great Auglaize river and running thence for about 50 miles is (with some few exceptions) low wet land with a very thick growth of underbrush, intermixed with beech, cottonwoods, oak, etc., from thence continuing and extending from the Indian boundary line eastward, the number and extent of the swamps increases, with the addition of numbers of lakes from 20 chains to two and three miles across. Many of the lakes have extensive marshes adjoining their margins, sometimes thickly covered with a species of pine called "Tamirak," and other places covered with a coarse high grass, and uniformly covered from six inches to three feet (and more at times) with water. The margin of these lakes are not the only places where swamps are found, for they are interspersed throughout the whole country and filled with water as above stated, and varying in extent. The immediate space between these swamps and lakes, which is probably near one-half of the country, is, with a very few exceptions, a poor, barren, sandy loam land, on which scarcely any vegetation grows, except very small scrubby oaks. In many places that part which may be called dry land is composed of little short sand hills, forming a kind of deep basins, the bottoms of many of which are composed of a marsh similar to those above described—the streams are generally narrow and very deep compared with their width; the shores and bottoms of which are (with a very few exceptions) swamp beyond description; and it is with the utmost difficulty that a place can be found over which horses can be conveyed. A circumstance peculiar to that country is exhibited in many of the marshes; by their being thinly covered with a sward of grass, by walking on which evinced the existence of water or a very thin mud immediately under that thin covering, which sinks from 6 to 18 inches from the pressure of the foot at every step, and at the same time rising before and behind the person passing over. The margins of many of the lakes and streams are in a similar situation, and in many places are literally afloat. On approaching the eastern part of the military lands towards the private claims on the strait and lake the country does not contain so many swamps and lakes, but the extreme sterility and barrenness of the soil continues the same—taking the country altogether so far as has been explored and to all appearances together with the information received concerning the balance, is as bad—there would not be more than one acre out of a hundred, if there would be one out of a thousand that would in any case admit of cultivation.

With great respect I am your obedient servant,

EDWARD TIFFIN.

The Hon. Josiah Meigs, Commissioner G. L. office, Washington.

The above is an accurate copy, including peculiarities of orthography, punctuation, grammer, etc.

Imagine the shade of our former surveyor general visiting again the scenes of his early life at Chillicothe, at Tiffin, Ohio, and then making a rapid journey across the territory of Michigan in any direction. Possibly, however, he was misled by willful misrepresentation on the part of his surveyors. An example of that kind can be cited in relation to the alleged "survey" of some of our northern counties. Take, for example, Gladwin county: there is probably nowhere in the west a county that is so inaccurately surveyed as it is; indeed, it is generally believed that the party of surveyors who were to lay out that county, and upon whose skill generations of people must depend for accurate descriptions of their farms and homes, got on a big drunk of ten days' duration at the old "Webster House," in Saginaw City, and actually in order to make up time "surveyed" Gladwin county in one of the bed rooms of that erstwhile famous hostelry. The late "Curt." Emerson used to say this was a fact, and any man who has ever tried to establish a corner in that county will need few arguments to convince him of the truthfulness of the story.

May it not be presumed that much of the odium which for many years attached to Michigan, and which materially retarded its settlement, may be directly traceable to the influence which the promulgation of the above report in congress had upon the minds of those people who were seeking new homes in the then far west?

W. R. BATES

Philadelphia, December 29, 1882.

THE TOWN OF GREEN

ADDRESS OF C. D. RANDALL AT THE ANNUAL MEETING OF THE BRANCH COUNTY PIONEER SOCIETY IN COLDWATER, DEC. 23, 1885

[Revised and enlarged for the State Pioneer Society.]

Mr. President, Ladies and Gentlemen:

The following interesting and touching correspondence I present here, after mature deliberation, for my preface and apology:

COLDWATER, Dec. 17, 1885.

Hon. C. D. Randall, Coldwater:

DEAR SIR—Will you have the kindness to give our pioneers about a three minutes talk on "The Town of Green," at our pioneer meeting the 23rd inst.

Yours truly,
J. G. PARKHURST, *President.*

REPLY.

Gen. John G. Parkhurst, President:

MY DEAR SIR—Yours of the 17th inst., requesting me to tell in three minutes all I know of "The Town of Green," is at hand. The time suits me exactly. I am sure I can tell all I know about it in that time, and will try to do so, relying upon you to help me out on the last minute, as I may not have material enough for the allotted time.

Yours truly,
C. D. RANDALL.

And now fate or the president of the society has placed me on the program with this dry subject, right after the delightful music, right after the address of Dr. Alger, the "Old Man Eloquent," and the interesting and touching tribute by Hon. Harvey Haynes to the memory of Hon. Roland Root and others of our fellow pioneers who have left us during the past year. I had a vague idea that the town of Green was lying about here somewhere or had been here sometime, but just where and when I did not know. Consulting encyclopœdias brought no consolation. There was nothing in the American, Johnson's, Chambers' or Britannica about this ancient town. Almost as a last resort I consulted the president's message, but although it contained everything else, he had, alas, forgotten to speak of the town of Green. Then I consulted the statutes of the Michigan Territorial Council and talked with the oldest pioneers, who were in Michigan before I was born. We came here in 1835, but when we arrived the town of Green had had its brief career and had passed into history. We came to the place where this old town was, but it was here no more forever. Yes, Branch county was once the town of Green. Not this county alone but Eaton and Calhoun and "all the country north of Eaton" composed this town. The section of this act organizing this town was approved Nov. 5, 1829, and reads as follows:

SEC. 5. That the counties of Branch, Calhoun and Eaton and all the country lying north of the county of Eaton, which are attached to and compose a part of the county of St. Joseph, shall form a township by the name of Green, and the first township meeting shall be held at the house of Jabez Bronson in said township.

The house where the meeting to elect township officers was held was in that part of the town of Green which was some years afterwards named Bronson, after Jabez Bronson. It was a long, low, log house, but however low, such houses always had a chamber above for sleeping room. It was a little way back from the street, near where the flouring-mill now stands.

This building, notable as the birthplace of the olden town, was at the same time a private residence, a hotel, a town house and the seat of justice. By law the courts could not be held in a bar room. In this house it was the only room large enough for that purpose. But the sturdy pioneer, Bronson, was equal to emergency. He had the liquors removed to a rear room just before the court convened. Then the justice, who was Mr. Bronson, with due solemnity, correctly proclaimed, "Gentlemen, this is not a bar room, but a court room," and thereupon he would proceed with the trial, no one questioning the correctness of his statement. When the town of Green was organized there were justices of the peace to be provided, and Governor Cass appointed Mr. Bronson, who was the first judicial officer in Branch county. He removed from Connecticut in 1828 to Bronson's Prairie, which was named for him. He was about 50 years of age, a ship builder by occupation. In his travels to the west he married a Canada widow and they came on to

Branch county. In trying cases he depended more upon his judgment than on the territorial statutes. He was not educated. He was also the early postmaster. Bronson held courts for about one year before they were held in any other place in the county. For many years Bronson's Prairie was the favorite resort of lawyers, the litigation being extensive. The itinerant peddler was often a victim in this court. Passing through, he was arrested and required to show his license. If he had none he was fined to the extreme penalty of the law. It he was authorized, in some way he still had to pay the costs of court.

It was in the house of the pioneer Jabez Bronson where the first election of the great town of Green was held—a town that embraced several counties and somewhat over. These large towns existed in the days when Michigan territory reached to the Mississippi and shortly after to the Missouri—as Michigan has always been a growing state.* Counties sometimes were very large. Brown and Michilimackinac counties once reached across the lake into what is now Wisconsin. The people were few and could not fill the land, and so the land reached out and took in the people.

Wayne was the first great county. In 1796 it was all of lower Michigan, part of upper Michigan, part of Indiana and Ohio, and extended over into Wisconsin.* It had subsequently reductions and enlargements by proclamations or statutes until it took its present form in 1826. Brown, Crawford and Michilimackinac counties were striking examples of this reaching out to take in all the people. By the proclamation of Gov. Cass in October, 1818, they comprised the entire Michigan territory, to which the Indian title had been extinguished, reaching to the Mississippi, excepting the counties of Wayne, Monroe and Macomb, which were then about their present dimensions.

The changes in the geography of this state, from its French occupation over two hundred and fifty years ago, would form an interesting study. And the maps showing the English settlements and control, the extinguishment of the Indian titles by treaty after our government ascendancy, would be very valuable. That Massachusetts and Connecticut once projected through southern Michigan is an interesting fact, and like many others relative to our early history, is little known.

But for a town our hero Green was greater than any county was for a county. I do not know of any town that ever had so much true greatness. I find no records of the first town meeting held in the log house of Jabez Bronson. I can see who are there, certainly Bronson, Richardson, and some, if not all, of the other officers who were elected. Probably there were not over twenty or thirty voters present. There is said to be no record of the second meeting of the town of Green. But the reports of the officers elected and

* See appendix, page 54

their other official acts show there was such an election. The Hon. William H. Cross, now living in Centerville, and who was present at the second town meeting in 1831, writes me: "The town meeting was held at the old Trading House on the west bank of Coldwater river in 1831, the first Monday in April. Col. A. F. Bolton was occupying the old building, making preparations for the erection of a hotel on the east side of the stream, then being put up for him by Harvey Warner. After selecting Col. Bolton for chairman, and John Morse and Columbia Lancaster, then of Bronson, as clerks, we elected John Morse town clerk, Seth Dunham, of Bronson, supervisor, John G. Richardson, collector and Willard Pierce, Edward S. Hanchett and myself as commissioners of highways, besides three assessors. There were about thirty persons present. Of these there are only two besides myself now living. One is Willard Pierce, who returned east and a short time since was living in Connecticut. The other is Columbia Lancaster, now of Vancouver, Washington territory. He was the second lawyer in St. Joseph county and has for forty years been a prominent citizen of Oregon and Washington territories, and at one time a delegate in Congress."

But the third meeting is recorded. It was at Pocahontas Mills, near Branch, April 2, 1832—over 53 years ago. An interesting feature of this meeting was the auditing of the account of John G. Richardson, the town collector for 1831 and 1832. The amount presented showed he had collected taxes to the amount of $56.82 and had actually paid out $59.32, leaving his due $2.50. What a contrast between 1831-2 and 1885! I think the present assessed valuation of Branch county alone, which is not one tenth of the old town of Green, is $17,000,000. This year our taxes are higher than usual, and if they are one per cent on the valuation—and they approximate that probably—then the amount of taxes we pay in 1885 will be about $170,000. Don't we poor tax ridden modern citizens, when thinking of those halcyon days of low taxes and little property, wish we were back again enjoying the thirties? There is, however, nothing so interesting to me as the consideration of the names and characteristics of the town officials of Green.

I know more about them than I do of the town which they survived. I well remember the ancient collector of taxes, John G. Richardson. My father bought his farm near Bronson village, and he then moved farther east into the woods. He was a strong, healthy hunter, never had the ague, killed many a deer, never did much farm work, spent years in devising a perpetual motion, which never moved. But the greater dream of his life, in that long ago, was to go far away to the Pacific, to Oregon. But he died many years since on his farm on the west line of Bethel, near Bronson, and never saw his dreams of Oregon or a perpetual motion realized. His widow remarried and I, as solicitor, procured a divorce for her second husband on the ground of desertion. She was, I think, the first white woman who settled in Branch county and the mother of the first white child born in this county, and in that part that it would seem was then about the most prominent in the county. At that town meeting others were elected to office whose names are very familiar to us, who still survive, beloved and honored: William H. Cross, treasurer; Allen Tibbits, commissioner of schools and assessor; and Harvey Warner, overseer of highways for Coldwater Prairie. It was voted at this meeting that the next town meeting should be held at the house of John Morse, which is the present old Phœnix House in Coldwater.

The life of the town of Green was as brief as brilliant. Measured by the importance of historicial facts connected with it, some might compute its life as lengthy, but its years, as measured by the sun struggling through our then miasmatic atmosphere, was only about three. In 1832, on the re-organization of townships, the name of Green was dropped; the west half of Branch county being named Prairie River, from a stream in the southwestern part now called Hog Creek, while the east part of the county was called Coldwater. But though the legislative council, in 1832, crowded the name of Green off the atlas, yet some one still clung to the ancient name. Here is a ringing section that is given with an emphasis by an act of the legislative council, April 23, 1833:

"Sec. 1. Be it enacted by the legislative council of the territory of Michigan, that the township of Prairie River, in the county of Branch, *shall* be called Green, and by this name of Green *shall* hereafter be known and distinguished, any law to the contrary notwithstanding."

The italics are mine, and seem necessary to give the spirit of the one who drafted the section. It is written as though it closed a dispute and settles the fact that Green *was* to be remembered. This brought Green to the front again. It was not so large as it once was, but it comprised several of the present townships. It was big enough to feel pretty well, but alas, its glory was transient. It flashed up a moment only to go out in darkness forever. This town of Green, the grandchild of the greater Green, was born April 23, 1833, and the legislative council gave it life; but March 11, 1837, there was an act by a new power. Michigan had become a state, and then the legislature, by an act to organize townships, enacted this section:

"Sec. 60. All that portion of the county of Branch known as the township of Prairie River and the village in said town known as York shall, on and after the first Monday of April next, be known and designated by the name of Bronson."

Please note that this act makes no reference to the act of 1833, which changed the name of Prairie River to Green. It ignores it—boycotts it entirely. Whether the legislature considered the act of 1833 unconstitutional, or desired to show a lack of respect to the memory of Green, history does not relate. Hence the second existence of Green was longer than the first, being three years, ten months and eighteen days, and then passed off from our county atlas forever. It became

> "One of the simple great ones gone,
> Forever by and by."

Why the name of Green had become unpopular I cannot tell. No aged pioneer can tell me why it came or why it went. The name of Prairie River was soon lost for both town and stream, though the Hon. Wales Adams, who owned a saw mill on the creek where it ran slow and up hill by the marsh to turn the wheels, strove to have the name retained, but it soon degenerated into "Hog Creek." I think the town was named for General Green, but I do not know. No pioneer I have asked can tell me. They were probably not consulted, nor the town either, the territorial council, in their wisdom and discretion, fixing upon this name. In size the town must have had something over 1,800 square miles, to say nothing of "all the country lying north of Eaton," which, unless explained by statute, reached to the north pole, and certainly to Mackinac. But the statute of Nov. 4, 1829, in establishing St. Joseph and Cass counties, included Kalamazoo, Branch, Barry and Eaton counties for judicial purposes, as a part of St. Joseph county, explains the expression "all the country lying north of Eaton." In the statute of Nov. 4, 1829, the expression is used, "all the country lying north of township number four north (being the north line of Eaton) of the base line, west of the principal meridian and south of the county of Michilimackinac and east of the line between ranges twelve and thirteen." This tract is attached to St. Joseph for judicial purposes and by the act organizing the town of Green is made a part of it. This is a triangular tract boundary commencing at the intersection of the principal meridian with the north line of Ingham, thence west about fifty miles to a point about four miles west of the southeast corner of Kent, thence northeast to the headwaters of Thunder Bay river or the southwest corner of Montmorency county, thence south on the principal meridian, about 150 miles to the place of beginning, making a tract containing about 3,750 square miles. Add to this the about 1,800 square miles of Branch, Calhoun and Eaton and the town of Green contained about 5,550 square miles, being in extreme length about 225 miles, and greatest width fifty, and in shape somewhat like an Indian arrow.

"All the country lying north of Eaton," etc., is the western part of the territory to which the Indian title was extinguished in 1819. As this title was not extinguished when Brown and Michilimackinac counties were organized, this diagonal line formed the south and east line in that part of the state, of the county last named. It is necessary to determine the early boundaries of towns and counties to consider these Indian treaties.

I have tried to find some good moral hid away under the ruins and name of this great old town, but save the lesson relative to the brevity of all sublunary things, I find nothing fruitful for that purpose.

But after all, I think I do see a good lesson for the young in the names and lives of some of the old town officials of Green, who for over fifty years have survived their arduous labors. When we see to-day Mr. Cross, the treasurer, Mr. Tibbits, the assessor and school commissioner, and Judge Warner, the commissioner of highways, hale and hearty in body and mind, enjoying their eighties, it does seem as though there was after all something of advantage in good, honest, temperate lives, that makes men respected and gives them fullness and ripeness of years. So to-night for myself, and I think I may also in your behalf, I extend to these survivors of the township officials of Green most hearty congratulations and best wishes for yet many years.

And to the memory of the town of Green, I say:

"Hail and Farewell!"

(Although a short address by Mr. Randall on the same subject was published in vol. 9, the one here given being much more extended, it was deemed advisable by the committee to insert it in vol. 10.—Ed.)

THE EARLY HISTORY OF HORTICULTURE IN MICHIGAN

BY J. C. HOLMES, OF DETROIT

[Read before the Michigan State Pomological Society at Battle Creek, February 25, 1873.]

The many very large, rough, hardy pear trees, the many ancient apple orchards and old Morello cherry trees that we find scattered along on the old farms, on each side of the Detroit river, testify to us that the early settlers in that vicinity were not unmindful of the value to themselves and their posterity of the plantations of fruit trees.

The heavy clay soil along the banks of the Detroit river seems admirably adapted to the growth, health and longevity of pear trees, if we may judge from the present condition of many of these old trees that rise to a height of sixty or seventy feet and bear large annual crops of very good pears, known only by the general cognomen of "Old French Pears," their origin running back beyond the knowledge of the oldest Frenchman of our time.

Tradition says that some of the early French missionaries brought pear seeds, scions and trees from Normandy and planted a few around each little habitation along each side of the river from Monroe to Mt. Clemens. I have seen it stated that several pear trees were brought from France in 1749 and planted along the river side from the Brush to the Witherell farm in Detroit, a distance of nearly one mile. How correct this statement is I do not know, but it seems to be a well ascertained fact that in no other locality in this country can such trees be found as the ancient pear trees that are now standing on the banks of the Detroit river. It is not unusual for them to bear a crop of thirty or forty bushels each. A short time since Mr. William L. Woodbridge, of Detroit, told me that he had many times taken a crop of fifty bushels from one of these old pear trees that stood on his father's farm.

These old pear trees seem to be as hardy as the oaks of the forests; no disease has ever attacked them; they flourish under neglect about as well as does the Canada thistle. Very few of them receive much care, yet they bear their full annual crops as regularly as a well kept apple orchard.

In many of the old apple orchards in the vicinity of Detroit we find the Snow apple, the red and white Calville, the Detroit red, the Pomme Gris or grey apple, and the Rosseau.

The late Gov. William Woodbridge owned a farm adjoining Detroit on the west; it is now annexed to and is a part of the city of Detroit. About the year 1825 Gov. Woodbridge bought of Grant Thorburn, of New York, two thousand apple trees and some pear trees and planted them on his farm, making two good orchards. He had the leading varieties of apples of that day, viz.: the Rhode Island Greening, the Baldwin, Yellow Bellefleur, White Bellefleur, Gloria Mundi, Spitzenburg, Roxbury Russet, Twenty Ounce apple, Fall Pippin, Early Harvest, Black Gilliflower, and many others. He also had the Snow apple, white and red Calville, Detroit red or black apple and Pomme Gris or grey apple. The scions of the six varieties last named he procured from some of the old orchards in Windsor and Sandwich, Canada, opposite Detroit, and engrafted them into some of the trees that he bought of Mr. Thornburn. In other orchards in the vicinity of Detroit, where these varieties of apples are grown, I find that for the most part scions were taken from Canadian orchards near Detroit and engrafted into the old trees. The farthest back that I have been able to trace these apples toward their origin is to the year 1796.

Some years since, as I was passing through the orchard of Mr. Francis Baby, of Windsor, Canada, for the purpose of getting specimens of apples for exhibition, I noticed a very handsome, bright red apple, at that date, September, not ripe. Its name Mr. Baby did not know. Mr. James Dougall, son-in-law of Mr. Baby, and a near neighbor, who was well acquainted with the orchard, had never noticed this tree or its fruit, so we concluded to wait until it was ripe, then take another look. A short time afterward I received from Mr. Dougall specimens of this fruit, accompanied by a note in which he says: "Mr. Baby informs me that he received the original trees, which are yet standing, and from which I took the specimens I send you, from Montreal, in 1796, along with other kinds, and he thinks it had no particular name, but says it is one of the Calvilles. Captain Cowan, who commanded a small vessel on the lakes, and who had formerly been a gardener to Gen. Washington previous to his being president, brought up the trees in his vessel for Mr. Baby from Fort Erie, and as he was an excellent grafter, he took scions from each variety received by Mr. Baby for the purpose of engrafting them into trees in Detroit. I find some of the specimens of fruit are very good, while others from the same tree are very inferior. Some of the fruit is stained red to the core, and some specimens are white throughout. The specimens with stained flesh are always the best. This remark holds good as against the red Calville and the Rosseau, which apples belong to the same class."

In the Baby orchard, among the trees brought from Montreal in 1796, were the Snow, Calville, Pomme Gris and other apples that were leading varieties in the orchards in Canada. I afterwards found this handsome but nameless apple in some of the orchards on Grosse Isle, under the name of Bourassa. The only work in which I find the Bourassa apple mentioned is J. J. Thomas' Fruit Culturist. The apple of which I am speaking does not correspond with his description.

In an English fruit book, by William Forsyth, published in 1802, in his list of apples introduced into England from France, I find mentioned Le Calville d'Automne, which, judging from Forsyth's description, I think must be the nameless apple that I have alluded to. Besides this variety, he mentions the Pomme Gris, from Canada, and the red and the white Calville as being highly esteemed in England. The Snow apple, or Pomme de Neige, or Fameuse, known by all these names, is also mentioned by Forsyth. All the fruit books speak of it as a native of Canada, with one exception, viz.,

Chauncey Goodrich, in his "Northern Fruit Culturist," published in Burlington, Vermont, says: "This fruit is said to be a native of Montreal; we believe it was brought from France by the first settlers of Canada. Wherever they went, either in Canada or the United States, they planted this apple."

In Hovey's Magazine of Horticulture for 1851, under the head of "Descriptions and Engravings of Select Varieties of Apples," he says: "The Fameuse, though an apple of American origin, and known to most European writers on fruit, from the time of Forsyth, does not appear to have been generally known to American pomological authors. Neither Thatcher or Cox, the earliest authorities, notice it; Mr. Kenrick was the first to give a full account of it in his American Orchardist. That a variety of so much merit should not have been long since more extensively cultivated, is somewhat surprising; for as an autumn apple, both on the score of beauty and excellence, it has few superiors."

Mr. William L. Woodbridge, son of Gov. Woodbridge, started a small nursery, mostly of pear trees, on his father's farm in 1833, when he was a school boy; with the help of one man, and with the attention he could give it himself, he was quite successful in raising trees. He raised many apples and pears from seed, some of them were very superior in flavor and beauty. He raised some trees from seeds of the Snow apple, the grain was finer and the skin lighter colored than the true Snow apple, but the flesh had the peculiar flavor and snowy whiteness of the parent.

In 1836 Mr. Woodbridge sold between three and four hundred pear trees from his nursery, to be taken to Chicago. Among them were the Seckel, Summer Bon Chretian, French and English Jargonelle, Pound, Bartlett and White Doyenne. Mr. Woodbridge thinks this was the first lot of pear trees sold from a Detroit nursery, and that his was the only nursery in Detroit at that time, and it was not a very extensive one.

In the utumn of 1830, or thereabouts, Gov. Woodbridge bought in New York twenty thousand small trees and plants and had them shipped from Buffalo on a schooner for Detroit. On the way up the vessel stopped at Huron and was obliged to remain there till the next spring, being frozen in. When she arrived at Detroit the trees and plants were found to be dead; the whole lot being a total loss.

One of the first nurseries established in Michigan was that of E. D. and Z. K. Lay, near Ypsilanti. A short time since, I addressed a note to Mr. E. D. Lay, who still resides on his farm at Ypsilanti, asking some questions with regard to his nursery, in answer to which I received the following:

YPSILANTI, *February 10, 1873.*

"SIR—At your request I send you an account of the nursery started and carried on in the town of Ypsilanti, on the plains east of the now city of Ypsilanti.

In the spring of 1833 I came to Michigan, then a territory, to select a place for establishing a nursery, and selected the above location. In the fall of 1833 my brother, Z. K. Lay, and myself came to Ypsilanti and brought with us about twenty five thousand cultivated trees, mostly of one season's growth, from the nursery of Asa Rowe, near Rochester, New York. They consisted of one hundred and thirty varieties of apples, seventy five varieties of pears, forty of peaches, three of apricots, three of nectarines, twenty of cherries, twenty of plums, three of quinces, fifteen of strawberries, forty of grapes, native and foreign, together with currants, gooseberries, raspberries, &c., also a large assortment of ornamental shrubs, evergreens, roses, peonies, herbaceous, perennial flowering plants, &c.

In the autumn of 1834 we erected a small greenhouse and filled it with plants. I think this was the first greenhouse built in Michigan. In the autumn of 1836 we erected a larger greenhouse and filled it with a choice collection of tropical plants. I do not know that there was any nursery of fruit trees in Michigan at the time we started ours on the plains, near Ypsilanti.

The leading varieties of apples cultivated at that time were the Baldwin, Bellefleur, Tart Bough, Canada Red, Snow, Rhode Island Greening, Fall Pippin, Summer Pippin, Green Newton Pippin, Porter, Rambo, Golden Russet, Talman's Sweet, Green Sweet, Esopus Spitzenburg, Swaar and Twenty Ounce Apple.

The leading varieties of pears were the Bartlett, Buffum, White Doyenne, Flemish Beauty, Seckel and Stevens' Genesee.

Of peaches, the Early Anne, Sweetwater, Royal Kensington, Prince's Red Rareripe, Orange, Pound, Barnard, Early York, Malta and Red Cheek Melocoton.

Apricots and nectarines we found were too tender for cultivation in this climate.

The principal varieties of cherries cultivated at that time were the Amber Heart, American Heart, Black Heart, Black Tartarian, May Duke, Ox Heart, Carnation, and White Tartarian. The plums were Coe's Golden Drop, Duane's Purple, Green Gage, Bleeker's Gage, Huling's Superb, Smith's Orleans, Washington, Yellow Gage.

The persons making the first and largest purchases of trees from the nursery, except in our immediate vicinity, were John Bertram, J. Henry, J. D. Pierce, Sidney Ketchum, George Ketchum, C. D. Smith, Isaac E. Crary, and others of Marshall and vicinity. In the course of the first five years of our nursery we sold trees that went to Lenawee, Hillsdale, Branch, St. Joseph, Kalamazoo, Jackson, Kent, Shiawassee, Genesee, Oakland, Livingston, Wayne and other counties in the state.

There has been a decided improvement in the varieties of fruit since we started the Ypsilanti nursery, particularly in pears. A large number of the varieties we brought to Michigan proved to be worthless; so also with our collection of apples, a large number of the varieties proved to be unworthy of cultivation in this state. Of the persons who started nurseries in Michigan between 1837 and 1840, I remember the names of Willis of Battle Creek, Dunham near Kalamazoo, and White near Monroe. Most of them closed their nurseries within a few years."

In 1841 George Foster started a small nursery in Detroit, on Michigan avenue, near Cass street, and in connection therewith a seed store on Jefferson avenue, between Woodward avenue and Bates street. The nursery was called the Detroit Nursery. This arrangement continued but a year or two.

In the autumn of 1842 William Adair and George Foster entered into copartnership, and the firm held forth at what was known as the Michigan garden, located on Randolph street, between Lafayette and Croghan streets, on the Brush farm, Detroit. They dealt in fruit and ornamental trees and greenhouse plants. Mr. Foster soon retired from the firm and Mr. Adair has continued the business alone from that time to the present, not having a partner either in business or household affairs. His garden is now located where it has been for many years, on Jefferson avenue, corner of Adair street, near Bloody run.

At an early day, about 1836, Mr. Charles Hastings started a nursery on his farm in Troy, Oakland county. After a time Mr. A. C. Hubbard became interested in this nursery and the firm was then Hastings and Hubbard. Subsequently Mr. B. M. Davis was admitted a member of the firm; then, for a short time, the firm was Hastings, Hubbard and Davis. After a few years, the health of Mr. Hastings having failed, he withdrew from the firm. Messrs. Hubbard and Davis purchased some land on the Porter farm, on what was then known as the Porter road in Springwells. That road is now known as 24th street, Detroit. They moved their nursery from Troy to this location, where it has remained ever since. Mr. Hubbard died in the autumn of 1871, leaving Mr. B. M. Davis the sole owner of the nursery.

The extensive greenhouses connected with this nursery are owned by Davis, Taplin & Co. Mr. Taplin was an employé of the late firm of Hubbard and Davis, but is now a partner with Mr. Davis. Mr. Davis has charge of the nursery and Mr. Taplin of the greenhouse.

Mr. T. W. Dunham had a nursry four and a half miles south of Kalamazoo, as early as 1840. He called it the Kalamazoo nursery.

In 1844, Gibson and Russell, at Jackson, had for sale fruit trees and shrubbery from the Ypsilanti nursery.

In 1844, Mr. S. B. Noble had a nursery in Ann Arbor, where he sold fruit trees and ornamental shrubbery.

At about 1840, Mr. Willis started a nursery at Battle Creek.

In the autumn of 1835 I passed through Battle Creek. About the only business going on at that place then was the building of a canal to lead the water from one river to the other so as to utilize it in the running of machinery.

In 1840 Mr. White, familiarly known as Variety White, had a nursery at Monroe.

The first horticultural society in Michigan of which I have any knowledge was partially organized at the Northern hotel, in Detroit, on the evening of March 5, 1846. At that meeting there were present, William Adair, John Ford, J. C. Holmes, Thomas Hall, M. Howard Webster, John Lumsden, John B. Piquette, Robert Radford, Robert Stead and Henry D. Hastings. J. C. Holmes was called to the chair and Henry D. Hastings appointed secretary. Having adopted a preamble and constitution and appointed a committee to draft by-laws, the meeting adjourned to meet at Mechanics' Hall on the evening of March 16th.

On Monday evening, March 16th, the society met according to adjournment. Permanent officers were elected and by-laws adopted.

The officers elected were:

President—John Winder.

Vice-Presidents—John C. Holmes and Benjamin G. Stimson.

Corresponding Secretary—M. Howard Webster.

Recording Secretary—John Lumsden.

Treasurer—Thomas Hall.

The committees appointed were as follows:

On Fruits—Adrian R. Terry, Wm. Adair, Samuel Barstow, George Duffield.

On Trees and Shrubs—George V. N. Lothrop, Lewis Hall, Bela Hubbard, John E. Schwarz.

On Greenhouse Plants and Florist's Flowers—John Ford, M. Howard Webster, John C. Holmes, Wm. B. Wesson.

On Indigenous Plants—Bela Hubbard, John B. Piquette, F. F. Merceron.

On Vegetables—Thomas Hall, Robert Stead, Henry D. Hastings, Thomas W. Lockwood.

The membership consisted of

William Adair, Samuel Barstow, George G. Bull, George Duffield, John Ford, Thomas Hall, Henry D. Hastings, John C. Holmes, Lewis Hall, Bela Hubbard, Thomas W. Lockwood, George V. N. Lothrop, John Lumsden, F. F. Merceron, J. H. Morris, William R. Noyes, John B. Piquette, Francis Raymond, Robert Stead, John E. Schwarz, Benjamin G. Stimson, Adrian R. Terry, John Winder, M. Howard Webster, William B. Wesson.

In 1846 the society held several exhibitions of horticultural products, as well as meetings for conversations, lectures and discussions.

For the purpose of showing what were the leading varieties of fruit under cultivation, and who were some of the fruit growers in and near Detroit at that time, I will give the names of some of the exhibitors and fruits exhibited in 1847. Among the varieties named you will probably recognize some that were long ago discarded and stricken from the list as unworthy of general cultivation in Michigan.

At the society's exhibition on August 24, 1847, Mr. Marvin Hannah, of Albion, exhibited Red Magnum Bonum, Blue Gage, Green Gage, Yellow Gage and Damson plums. Bela Hubbard of Springwells; French Jargonelle and Seedling pears, Imperial Gage and Blue Gage plums. A. C. Hubbard, of Troy; Orange Pippin and Seedling apples of 1846 and Bleeker's Scarlet plums. J. C. Holmes, of Detroit; a collection of apples and pears. James Dougall, Amherstburg; C. W. Prince's Yellow Gage, Purple Seedling, Pond's Seedling, Imperial Gage, Blue Seedling, Mediterranean and Washington plums, American Summer Pearmain, Summer Queen, Hawthornden, Sweet Bough, Keswick Codlin, Alexander and Lyman's large summer apples, English Jargonelle pears. Zeri Phelps, Plymouth; Cheeseborough Russet, Golden Pippin and Sweet Bough apples, Prince's Imperial Gage plum. Roswell Root, Plymouth; Early Harvest, Spice Sweet and Golden Pippin apples. H. Weeks, Plymouth; One dish and three large clusters of Washington plums. Jonathan Shearer, Plymouth; Prince's Imperial Gage plums and Red Rareripe peaches. John G. Welch, Plymouth; Sweet Bough, Golden Pippin and Spice Sweet apples. John G. Bennet, John Tibbits, M. Shutts, E. J. Penniman, D. Averill, Henry Fralick, John Westfall, Wm. Blackmore, H. B. Holbrook, Andrew Bradner, David Warner, John Kellogg, "Grafter" Warner, E. Starkweather, John Barker, John Miller, Moses Lyon and Henry Lyon, of Plymouth, each exhibited early apples—mostly Sweet Bough, Spice Sweet and Golden Pippin. James V. Campbell, Detroit; A large cluster of Blue plums, Mediterranean plums and Black Cluster grapes. All these fruits exhibited in August were, of course, early fruits. You will notice that plums were very plenty then, the curculio not being so destructive in Michigan as it has been since.

Here are some of the names of exhibitors and fruits at the exhibition held in Detroit, on the 28th and 29th of September, 1847:

Doct. Cobb, of Detroit, exhibited Albert Gallatin, Teton de Venus, Orange Cling, Red Cheek Melocoton and Seedling peaches; also Isabella grapes.

James Dougall, of Amherstburg, now of Windsor, C. W., where he has a nursery, exhibited Isabella, Catawba, Black Cluster, Fox, White Muscadine, Golden Chasselas, Esperione, Black Frontignan, Green Swiss and Sweet Water grapes; Purple Gage, Coe's Golden Drop and Damson plums; Red Rareripe, President and Monstrous Pompone peaches; Passe Colmar, White Doyenne and Easter Beurre pears; Ribston Pippin, Alexander, Hawthornden, Pennock's Red Winter, Small Pomme Gris, Dominie, Keswick Codlin, Flushing Spitzenburg, Large Pomme Gris, Labute, White Calville, Royal Russet, Monstrous Pippin, Bourassa, American Summer Pearmain, Pomme d' Neige, Baldwin, King of the Pippin, Esopus Spitzenburg, Male Carle or Charles Apple, Bullock's Pippin, Scarlet Pearmain and Rosseau apples. Charles Hastings, of Troy, Oakland county, exhibited Viegalien, Bleeker's Meadow, Marie Louise, Summer Bon Chretien, Autumn Bergamot and Steven's Genesee pears; Pound Royal, Summer Queen, Summer Pippin, Talman's Sweet, Wine, Yellow Bellefleur, Holland Pippin, Detroit Red, Monstrous Pippin, Baldwin, R. I. Greening, Yellow Newtown Pippin, Swaar, Westfield, Seek-no-further, Twenty Ounce Pippin, Doctor, Court Pendu Plat, Roxbury Russet, Pomme d' Neige, Pound Sweeting, Romanite, Golden Sweet, French Pippin, Hubbardston's Nonesuch and Esopus Spitzenburg apples; Orange, Portugal and Common quince; Alexander grapes and Pine Apple peaches. Joseph R. William, Constantine: Buffum pears; Maiden Blush, Holland Pippin, Pomme d' Neige, Rhode Island Greening, Fall Pippin and several varieties of apples not named.

Hubbard & Davis, Troy; Pine Apple Cling, Incomparable, Orange Cling, Albert Gallatin, Red Cheek Melocoton, Columbia and Mellish's Favorite peaches; also a large collection of apples, a few pears and grapes.

James Allen, Pontiac; Twenty Ounce Pippin, Fall Pippin, Detroit Red, Spitzenburg, Rhode Island Greening, Cheeseboro Russet, Golden Pippin and several other varieties of apples; French Jargonelle, Stevens Genesee and English Jargonelle pears.

Jabez Warner, Plymouth, from the orchard of a neighbor; Twenty Ounce Pippin and several other varieties of apples.

Rev. Mr. Ruggles, of Pontiac; Apples and quinces.

James M. Edmunds, Ypsilanti; Catawaba and Isabella grapes.

Bela Hubbard, Detroit; Apples, pears, plums, quinces and grapes.

Linus Cone, Troy; Collection of apples.

There were many other exhibitors, but the names of exhibitors and the kinds and varieties of fruits exhibited, already mentioned, will suffice to show us what fruits were grown in the several localities and by whom they were raised.

Many excellent varieties of fruit have been added to our list since that day.

In addition to the names of exhibitors already given, there were at subsequent exhibitions in other years, several persons who exhibited large collections of apples, pears, peaches, plums and grapes. Among them I may mention E. D. Lay of Ypsilanti; O. M. Bronson, Waterford; B. G. Stimson, Detroit; Wm. B. Wesson, Detroit; A. Whitehead, Pontiac. Judge Barkery, Plymouth, made collections from the orchards in that town and entered them for exhibition in the names of the proprietors of the orchards. He took great interest in the welfare of the society, and was generally present at the exhibitions, bringing large collections of fruits from Plymouth gardens and orchards.

At the annual meeting in March, 1848, the following officers were elected:

President—J. C. Holmes.

First Vice President—M. Howard Webster.

Second Vice President—Wm. R. Noyes.

Corresponding Secretary—Thos. W. Lockwood.

Recording Secretary—Francis Raymond.

Treasurer—Wm. B. Wesson.

At the annual meeting held in March, 1849, the officers elected were:

President—Rev. George Duffield.

First Vice President—Bela Hubbard.

Second Vice President—B. M. Davis.

Corresponding Secretary—E. R. Kearsley.

Recording Secretary—Warren Isham.

Treasurer—Wm. R. Noyes.

At the annual meeting held in March, 1850, the following officers were elected:

President—Rev. George Duffield.

First Vice President—E. R. Kearsley.

Second Vice President—B. M. Davis.

Treasurer—Francis Raymond.

Coresponding Secretary—H. Howard Webster.

Recording Secretary—B. G. Stimson.

The officers elected for 1851 were:

President—B. G. Stimson.

First Vice President—John Ford.

Second Vice President—T. H. Hinchman.

Treasurer—Francis Raymond.

Recording Secretary—Bela Hubbard.

Corresponding Secretary—Wm. Adair.

Librarian—Bela Hubbard.

The officers elected for 1852 were:

President—A. C. Hubbard.

First Vice President—Thos. W. Lockwood.

Second Vice President—Francis Raymond.

Treasurer—Stephen Smith.

Recording Secretary—Chas. Betts.

Corresponding Secretary—Bela Hubbard.

The interest in the society was well kept up until 1852. In that year there was a great falling off. There were four exhibitions in 1852, but they were very small compared with former years.

At the annual meeting held in March, 1853, there were but few present, and the society then died out.

As the society now here in session is a Pomological Society I have spoken only of the fruits exhibited by the Detroit Horticultural Society, thinking you would be more interested in the history of the fruit department than in the departments of flowers and vegetables, and it would make my paper too lengthy to speak of all the departments of horticulture in detail; but our tables were always graced with an abundance of beautiful flowers and excellent vegetables. Indigenous flowers from our own fields and forests always held a conspicuous place in the shows.

I think I do not like the name of Pomological Society as well as I do that of Horticultural Society, for the former designates only one department of horticulture, while the latter embraces every kind of horticultural product. I am found of delicious fruits; I am equally fond of beautiful flowers; I love to see a well kept orchard, so also a well kept flower and vegetable garden. I love to see the choicest products of each on exhibition by the same society, and an endeavor on the part of the society to foster the cultivation and exhibition of the riches of Flora, as well as the riches of Pomona. I am glad to know that although this society makes the advancement of the pomological interests of the state its leading object, it does not ignore flowers, but has a place for them in its premium lists.

On the 9th day of September, 1853, a convention of nurserymen from the southern part of Michigan was held at Jonesville, Hillsdale county. The object of the meeting was to establish, as nearly as possible, uniform prices for fruit trees; also for the purpose of discussing such subjects connected with horticulture as might be deemed interesting and beneficial, not only to nurserymen, but to all the citizens of our State. A schedule of prices was reported to the convention, and, after some discussion, it was adopted. This meeting adjourned to meet at such time and place as the chairman and secretary might deem fit to appoint.

In pursuance of this adjournment a convention of nurserymen and fruit growers was called and met at Adrian, Michigan, on the 24th of February, 1854. At this meeting the following gentlemen were present: B. W. Steere, Isaac Chase, A. G. Eastman, D. K. Underwood, and B. F. Strong, of Adrian; Charles E. Perigo, Toledo; John Merritt, Tecumseh; C. H. Hageman, Blissfield; C. C. Cooley, Hudson; Haynes Johnson, Jr., Hillsdale; Jesse Maxson, Pittsford; John T. Blois, Jonesville; J. C. Holmes, Detroit; A. R. Bentley, Monroe.

The meeting having been called to order, J. C. Holmes, of Detroit, was called to the chair, and J. T. Blois, of Jonesville, elected secretary. After the transaction of some business the following list of prices was reported, discussed and adopted:

Resolved, That our price for apple trees of medium size, or from 5 to 7 feet high, shall be not less than 18¾ cents each, nor less than $16.00 per hundred. Extra sized trees at proportionate prices. Dwarf apple trees from 25 cents to 37½ cents each. Plum trees shall not be sold less than 50 cents each; our price for peach trees shall not be less than 20 cents each, or $15.00 per hundred. Apricot and Nectarine trees, on peach stocks, shall be from 37½ to 50 cents each. Quince trees of medium size shall be from 25 to 50 cents each. Our price for hardy grapes, from two to three years old, shall not be less than 25 cents each.

The following constitution was then adopted:

ARTICLE 1. This association shall be called The Michigan Nurserymen and Fruit Growers' Association.

ARTICLE 2. Any practical nurseryman, fruit grower or friend of horticulture may, by a vote of the society, become a member.

ARTICLE 3. The objects of the association shall be to extend the acquaintance of the members and to advance generally the horticultural interests of this and neighboring States.

ARTICLE 4. The officers shall consist of a president, vice president, and a secretary, who shall also act as treasurer. They shall be elected by ballot, and hold their offices for one year, or until their successors shall be elected. They shall perform the duties usually devolving upon such officers, and form an executive board.

ARTICLE 5. The society shall hold annual meetings on the first Tuesday in December, at which time the annual election of officers shall be held.

ARTICLE 6. By-laws not inconsistent with this constitution may be adopted, and from time to time altered and amended by a majority of the members present.

ARTICLE 7. This constitution may be altered and amended at any annual meeting by a vote of two-thirds of the members present.

The society adjourned to meet in Adrian the next June, but for some cause, it did not meet again until the 9th of January, 1855, when it held its annual meeting in Adrian. No permanent officers having been elected, J. C. Holmes, of Detroit, was called to the chair, and J. T. Blois appointed secretary.

On motion of Mr. Perigo, of Toledo, Ohio:

Resolved, That the afternoon session be devoted to the regular business of the association and, at the request of several citizens of Adrian, that the evening be devoted to a general conversation and discussion of subjects connected with horticulture.

The following gentlemen were elected members of the association: Sterling Perkins, of White Pigeon, Rev. E. H. Pilcher, B. J. Harvey, Ira J. Thurston, J. Mandeville, Chas. M. McKenzie, J. N. Chandler, Adrian; S. O. Knapp, Jackson; Harvey Smith, Pine Lake; Warren Gilbert, Rome; Henry P. Hanford, Bristol, Indiana; Wm. H. Loomis, South Bend, Indiana; Doct. E. M. Hale, Jonesville, Mich.; Lewis Miller, Lockport, St. Joseph county, Mich.; Mr. Wilcox, Flint; William Bort, Niles; and M. L. Dunlap, Leyden, Cook county, Ill.

The subject of cleaning seeds of fruit trees, and raising seedlings was introduced. Mr. Bentley, of Monroe, Mr. Thurston, of Adrian, Mr. Holmes, of Detroit, Mr. Steere, of Adrian, Mr. Blois, of Jonesville, and Mr. Bort, of Niles, participated in the discussion.

The subject of grape culture was discussed by Messrs. Pilcher, Holmes, Steere and Perigo.

In the evening the society met in the office of T. M. Cooley, now Judge Cooley.

Specimens of several varieties of apples were presented for consideration by Messrs. Scott, Strong, Cooley, Eastman and others.

The subject of apples being introduced, the discussion was participated in by Messrs. Underwood, Scott, Perigo, Blois, Perkins, Bort and Holmes. The subject of strawberries was discussed by Messrs. Underwood, Perigo, Bort, Scott, Strong, Steere and Cooley.

The constitution of the society was amended by striking out in article 5, the words, "The first Tuesday of December," and inserting "The second Tuesday in January."

The following officers were elected for the ensuing year:

President—J. C. Holmes, Detroit.

Vice President—J. E. Perigo, Toledo.

Secretary and Treasurer—J. T. Blois, Jonesville.

The third annual meeting was held at Jackson on the 8th of January, 1856. The following gentlemen were elected members: J. E. Beebe, W. R. Gibson, J. T. Wilson, D. Cook, W. T. Howell, R. Dunning, Doct. D. Foote, J. M. Harwood, M. McNaughton, Wm. Hayden, of Jackson; E. Moody, Wright

Corners, N. Y.; Ira C. and A. A. Olds, of Hartford, Van Buren Co., Mich. The schedule of prices of fruit trees was discussed, but no changes were made. Many specimens of apples were placed upon the tables by the members.

On motion the question of separating seeds from the fruit, also the treatment of stock seedlings was discussed by Messrs. Blois, Steere, Moody, Willson, Beebe, Dunning, Foote and Holmes. The question of pruning in the nursery was then discussed.

At the evening session of the 9th of January, the examination of fruits on exhibition and the discussion of their respective merits, occupied the evening.

Messrs. Cook, Moody, Holmes, Gibson and Blois were the principal speakers.

At the morning session on the 10th of January, the pear and grape questions were discussed by Messrs. Moody, Knapp, Beebe and Holmes.

The association then proceeded to the election of officers for the following year, with the following result:

President—A. C. Hubbard, Detroit.

Vice President—J. T. Blois, Jonesville.

Secretary—W. R. Gibson, Jackson.

The society then adjourned to meet at Jackson, on the 2d of September.

On the 2d of September, 1856, the association met at Jackson. The president, Mr. Hubbard, being absent the chair was occupied by Mr. J. T. Blois, the vice president. The following gentlemen were elected members:

S. B. Noble, James De Puy, T. E. Gidley, H. T. Buck, P. B. Loomis and S. Gidley.

A large collection of fruit was exhibited at this meeting The principal questions discussed during the session were the quality and the cultivation of several varieties of apple, pear, peach, strawberry and grape. The discussions were participated in by Messrs. Foote, T. E. Gidley, Willson, Knapp, Bort, Noble, Blois and Steere. Another subject discussed was the frauds that had been practiced upon western nurserymen and amateurs by eastern venders of trees. The society then adjourned, and this was the last meeting it ever held.

The Nurserymen and Fruit Growers' Association having been winter killed, or from some other cause died out, there was a call from Clinton county, Kalamazoo county and other places for a meeting to be held at Jackson for the purpose of organizing a state horticultural society.

In September, 1857, pursuant to this call, a meeting was held at Jackson to form a state horticultural society. The meeting was called to order by Mr. C. K. Gibson of Jackson. On motion, T. T. Lyons of Plymouth was elected chairman and V. B. Merwin, of Moscow, secretary.

A constitution and by-laws were adopted and the association organized as "The Michigan State Horticultural Society."

The following officers were elected:

President—Hezekiah G. Wells, of Kalamazoo.

Secretary—R. F. Johnston, of Detroit.

Treasurer—P. B. Loomis of Jackson.

Directors—Hiram Walker, Detroit; D. W. Underwood, of Adrian; John T. Blois, Jonesville; Linus Cone, Troy; J. W. Nelson, Grand Rapids; Wm. Bort, Niles. After the reading of letters from persons who were unable to be present, the society adjourned.

The first annual meeting of this society was held at Kalamazoo on the 7th of January, 1858, under very favorable circumstances. There was a large attendance, and a good display of fruit. An extract from a Kalamazoo paper says: The display of fruit was large and most beautiful, one of the finest ever made in this State. Indeed we are assured that, for excellence, beauty and variety, this collection surpassed the exhibit of the New York State Horticultural Society, made at Rochester last winter. Over one hundred different varieties of winter apples, raised in this State, were here exhibited, arranged tastefully on plates, and spread upon a double row of tables.

At 3 o'clock P. M. the meeting was called to order by the president. The secretary being absent, Mr. T. T. Lyon, of Plymouth, was elected secretary *pro tem.*

The following officers were elected for the ensuing year:

President—H. G. Wells, of Kalamazoo.

Vice Presidents—E. T. Graves, of Battle Creek, and B. W. Steere, of Adrian.

Secretary—T. T. Lyon, of Plymouth.

Treasurer—Stephen S. Cobb, of Kalamazoo.

The society continued in session three days, during which time considerable business was transacted. The President delivered an address upon the subject of horticulture. Several committees were appointed to report upon various subjects connected with horticulture; reports that were made by these committees were discussed; a list of apples was recommended for general cultivation, and a list was made of apples that promise well; and a list that was, in the opinion of the society, unworthy of cultivation.

Contributors of fruit were A. C. Hubbard, Detroit; Jeremiah Stanard, Ionia; Samuel Johnson, Kalamazoo; J. T. Willson, Jackson; D. McKee, W. Taylor, E. Merrill, George D. Rice, S. S. Cobb and A. Buel, of Kalamazoo; Joshua Clemens, Leoni; B. Hathaway, Little Prairie Ronde; and T. T. Lyon, Plymouth.

This society held an exhibition in Detroit on the 30th of June and 1st of July, 1858. The specimens of horticultural products exhibited were excellent, but not so abundant as the officers of the society had reason to expect, consequently there were but few visitors. The exhibition seems to have been almost an entire failure with regard to the number of articles exhibited and the number of visitors in attendance. I think this was the last effort the society made to hold an exhibition of horticultural products, or a meeting of any kind. It went the way of all the rest; it died out.

In those early days of which I have spoken we had no trouble in ripening peaches and plums in Detroit, but the subsequent cold winters and the curculio have wrought somewhat of a change in that regard.

Peach trees grow stronger, and I think they are more healthy and longer lived grown in a heavy, strong soil like that of Detroit than in light soils. I have never seen a case of the yellows there; sometimes, in a cold, wet, backward spring, the leaves curl and fall off, but the trees soon recover from this. The borer is not so fond of working in peach trees grown in a heavy soil as it is in trees grown on a light soil.

I have now spoken of some of the fruit trees of olden times and of horticultural societies that have had their day and retired from the field.

This new Pomological Society seems to be doing a good work; it is not only new, but it is strong, active, energetic. You and I are part and parcel of it. I hope it will be well sustained so that it may be able to accomplish the good it seeks to do.

DETROIT THREE SCORE YEARS AGO

LEADING MEN OF THE EMBRYONIC METROPOLIS OF MICHIGAN. LOCAL REMINISCENCES OF A REMOTE PERIOD AND OF INTEREST TO MOST RESIDENTS

PRESENTED BY EPHRAIM S. WILLIAMS, OF FLINT

Sixty years ago Detroit contained a population of 1,200; Buffalo, 2,095; Cleveland, 500; Chicago and Milwaukee were nowhere.

The home of Congressman Hurd was only heard of in song as the place "where potatoes, they grew small on Maumee," and there was no dispute about the second and third cities in Michigan. With the exception of the settlements on the Clinton river, river Raisin and along the straits, the territory was a wilderness in possession of Indians and wild animals. The following items and incidents are copied from the Detroit Gazette, progenitor of the Free Press, the only newspaper then in Michigan, published by John P. Sheldon and Ebenezer Reed:

September 26, 1820, obituary of Col. Daniel Boone.

The names of those holding official position in 1821 were: Lewis Cass, governor; Robert A. Forsyth, governor's private secretary (Mr. Forsyth was a brother of Mrs. B. B. Kercheval, who recently celebrated her 85th birthday, surrounded by her daughters and grandchildren, at the home of her son-in-law, Hon. Moses W. Field); William Woodbridge, secretary of the territory; Augustus B. Woodward, James Witherel and John Griffin, judges of the United States court. The governor and judges constituted the legislature. Austin E. Wing, sheriff; Paul D. Anderson, John R. Williams and Abram Edwards, county commissioners; David C. McKinstry, county treasurer; Thomas Palmer, clerk; Charles Larned, prosecuting attorney; Conrad Ten Eyck, city treasurer; Solomon Sibley, delegate to congress; Jonathan Kearsley, United States receiver; James Abbott, postmaster; Lemuel Shattuck, secretary of the lyceum; C. C. Trowbridge, secretary of the first Protestant society of Detroit; John J. Deming, clerk of the United States court.

Gov. Cass and Solomon Sibley return from their Chicago treaty August 21, 1821.

The Scinaps exploring company depart on their first exploration, October 9, 1821. This company was organized to explore the wild country which now constitutes the northern counties of the lower peninsula of Michigan, and the results of their explorations were of so favorable and important a character that they were published in the National Intelligencer and other papers of the day.

Col. Stephen Mack finishes six miles of the road towards Pontiac.

The first public sale of lots at Pontiac took place July 18, 1821. Sixty village lots were sold at prices ranging from $20 to $70.

Independence was celebrated for the first time in Macomb county, July 4, 1821; Thomas Ashley, president; John Stockton, vice president.

There were four flouring mills in Michigan, aside from wind mills, viz.: that of Col. Mack, at Pontiac; of Capt. Ben Woodworth, at Paint Creek, Rochester; of Marsh & Co., at Monroe, and A. Edwards' horse or team mill,

Detroit. The latter was known as the Ox mill, and was situated on the river front of the Cass farm.

Wheat sells at $2.01 per bushel. Flour at this time was put and sold in sacks. The first export of flour from Michigan took place in 1827, when 200 barrels were shipped to the east by Miller & Jermain, of Monroe.

Three hauls of 1,660 whitefish are taken at Grosse Isle, 1826.

Charles Jackson, Jeremiah Moore and Levi Cook were a committee of arrangements for the installation of Detroit Lodge of Free Masons, December 21, 1821.

The Indians, Ke-taw-kah and Ke-wa-bis-haw, were executed for the murder of W. S. Madison and Charles Ulrich, after having first a Protestant and then a Catholic sermon preached to them.

Rev. Eleazer Williams,* missionary to the Oneida Indians, arrived July 12, 1821, with a deputation of the Six Nations, on a visit to their brethren at Green Bay.

Capt. Benj. Woodworth, a carpenter by trade, who came to Detroit in 1807 to build the Gov. Hull house, the first brick building in Michigan, figures at the time as a sort of Caleb Quotem. He keeps a hotel (the old Steamboat hotel), runs a ferry to Windsor, is captain of an artillery company, carries on a grist mill at Rochester and runs the only line of stages in Michigan between Detroit and Mt. Clemens, the route being on the river bank and across the Grand Marais. Capt. Woodworth died two or three years ago at St. Clair, 92 years of age.

Rev. Platt B. Morey, of the Methodist Episcopal church, died at Mt. Clemens, December 20, 1821.

Dr. R. B. Rice and Israel Lee are appointed commissioners of insolvent estates in Macomb county.

Benjamin Stead, an old citizen, died at his residence in Hamtramck, now Detroit, September 25, 1821.

Thomas Palmer and Mary Witherell are married, August 20, 1821.

De Garmo Jones advertises goods; A. C. Canniff, boots and shoes; I. O. & I. E. Schwars, fur and peltries; Oliver Newberry, general dealer, under the printing office; John Hale, general stock; William Brewster, large stock; F. F. & J. Palmer, general stock, brick store, where the Board of Trade building now is, and John I. Williams, general stock, corner Jefferson avenue and Bates street. George A. O'Keefe, long to be remembered for his wit and oddities, advertises a law partnership with Samuel T. Davenport. I. L. & H. S. Cole, the latter a talented and popular lawyer and an eloquent and pleasing speaker, advertise their office in the Steamboat hotel. Robert Stewart is made commissioner on the estate of John Gleason. Peter Van

Every and Oliver Williams each paid $10 for tavern license. Melvin Dorr was licensed a retailer.

The following names are appended to a call for a public meeting, August 10, 1821, to send Hon. Sol. Sibley as delegate to Congress: Daniel LeRoy, John Farrar, Jeremiah Moore, Melvin Dorr, Henry Sanderson, Charles Jackson, Levi Cook, J. L. Whitney, William Brewster, B. Woodworth, Chauncey S. Payne, Julius Eldred, Samuel Sherwood, Robert Smart, Samuel Ward, John Palmer, B. F. H. Witherell.

The following names of prominent citizens were appended to a call for a public meeting: A. G. Whitney, George McDougall, John Hunt, J. Visger, J. Bartlett, O. W. Miller, William Durell, W. W. Petit, Joseph Campau, John Palmer, B. Stead, John McDonell, John Hale, George Leib, John J. Leib, Thomas Palmer, H. J. Hunt, James May, James Connor, Oliver Williams, James McCloskey, A. L. Williams.

The loss of the steamer Walk-in-the-Water is briefly announced. She went ashore November 1, 1821, near Buffalo Light, and a long account, signed by the passengers, was copied from a Buffalo paper, to which the names of Thomas Palmer and his wife, Mary A. W. Palmer, of Detroit, who were returning from their bridal tour, were attached. Their son, Senator Thomas W. Palmer, has now in his possession two paintings by an artist who was a passenger, and who presented them to Mrs. Palmer. The Walk-in-the-Water was 330 tons burden,

The new steamer Superior, the second on the lakes, Capt. J. Rogers, arrived at Detroit on her trial trip from Black Rock, May 25, 1822. She was 410 feet keel, 29 feet beam, 50 horse power engine and 346 tons burden.

Jerry V. R. Ten Eyck, city clerk, calls a public meeting to take into consideration the plan for water works.

A meeting was held in the council hall to reform the judiciary, and separate the judicial from the legislative functions of the government.

March 11, 1822, the Bank of Michigan elected the following officers:

President—John R. Williams.

Directors—Stephen Mack, Henry J. Hunt, Abram Edwards, Phillip Lecuyer, Peter J. Desnoyers and Barnabas Campau.

A. Edwards, J. P. Sheldon and P. J. Desnoyers were elected county commissioners.

Shubael Conant advertises a house occupied by Dr. Henry for sale.

Of all the above mentioned officials and business men but one survives at the present time, Col. John Roberts.

"Alas, what is there in human state,
Or who can shun inevitable fate?
The doom was written, the decree was past
E'er the foundations of the world were cast."

HISTORICAL DETROIT

HENRY A. FORD

I.

An old town like Detroit seldom fails to present many historic sites and other points of special interest to the antiquary, or to any citizen or stranger of average intelligence. This city, from its age, its occupation by several nationalities at the different periods of its earlier history, and its character from the beginning as a military post, is peculiarly fortunate in the number and interest of its historical associations. The central lower part of the city, for several blocks along and near the river, is replete with them. The plan has been mooted of marking, by inscription on metal plates or otherwise, after the fashion of old European cities, the more interesting of these locali ties; and the praiseworthy suggestion will doubtless materialize soon or late in the hands of a society formed for the purpose, or by private beneficence. Meanwhile, in a brief series of papers devoted to our historic localities, we will do what we can to deepen the interest and heighten the pleasure of citizen or visitor, in his casual walks about the ancient burgh.

Let us take position at the postoffice, and proceed thence. The observer here, or at the intersection of Congress and Woodward, is apt to notice with some surprise a phenomenon not common in river towns—that he is at the bottom of a long and gentle slope from the northward, corresponding to a similar rise of ground between him and the river. Obviously, he is in the bed of an old-time stream—in this case the Savoyard river (more anciently the Rigolet des Hurons), named from a native of Savoy, who had a pottery upon its banks in the early days. This brook—for it should hardly be dignified as a river—took its rise several blocks east of Woodward avenue in a willow swamp on the Guoin farm, near the present meeting of Riopelle and East Congress streets. It flowed in an irregular course near the line of Fort street east, crossed Woodward avenue at Congress, where it was spanned by a rude wooden bridge, and thence ran in general parallelism to the Detroit, which it entered at about Fourth and Woodbridge, in a bay which then stretched along the fronts of several of the old farms. It was bordered by rather narrow belts of low, marshy ground, upon one of which, the southern, the postoffice now stands. Within a little distance to the west and south, on the higher bank back of the pickets of the old fort, stood a lofty oak whose hollow trunk held an image of the Virgin, and which was said to mark the spot where Father Constantin del Halle, founder of the church of Ste. Anne perished during an Indian attack in 1705. So the legend goes at least.

Setting our faces toward the river, and walking down to the corner of Griswold and Jefferson, we are directly upon the primitive French settlement about Fort Pontchartrain. In a little cove at the foot of Griswold, Cadillac landed with his queerly costumed band of soldiers and colonists, July 24, 1701. The hamlet he commenced was built upon the contracted plan of old world towns, so that within the 120 feet that measure the breadth of Jefferson avenue were comprised two French streets and the little blocks of dwellings between them. The fire of 1805 swept them all away, and the last of their immediate successors, the famous Campau house, disappeared a few years ago from the site, No. 140 Jefferson avenue, now occupied by the stately Palms building. Mr. Campau is said to have built upon or very near the ground occupied by Cadilac's headquarters. Between this and the southwest corner of Griswold, upon the north side of the old Ste. Anne's street, of 15 feet width, and within 20 feet of the present south line of Jefferson, stood the later Ste. Anne's church, built in 1723 of logs, with two modest spires and two bells. It followed its predecessors in a fiery ordeal; and its successor upon the same site, built in 1755, was burned in the fire of 1805, but men are still alive who can remember the ruins that long marked the spot. The first Catholic cemetery in Detroit adjoined the church directly in the modern avenue. All burials previous to 1723 were probably in the military cemetery, just back of the First National Bank.

Still standing upon Jefferson avenue and looking westward to the intersection of Second, one could formerly have seen the sparkling waters of the Detroit, as they here came up to the high bank that formed the front of the Cass farm. In those days the river margins of the Cass, Jones, Forsyth, Labrosse, Baker and Woodbridge farms abutted on a beautiful though not deep bay, long since destroyed by the filling and "made ground" which began with the improvement of the Cass farm for residence and business. The banks were high with a good road near the brink, and furnished a favorite promenade and driveway to the Detroiters of bygone generations.

The solid little building used by the First National Bank has an interest of its own, having been erected in 1836, the "wildcat" days, for the bank of Michigan. It was bought by the United States in December, 1842, for

$32,000, and long used for the postoffice and federal court house. It stands as is well known, upon the site of the east gate of the stockade about Fort Pontchartrain, which acquired special renown as the "Pontiac gate" after the failure of the treacherous Indian attempt in 1763. From this gateway, on the 31st of July in that year, marched the red coats under Capt. Dalzell to the massacre at Bloody Brook, and through it fled back the remnants of that ill starred band after their terrible repulse. The stockade of 1807, built by Gen. Hull, extended far beyond this, reaching from the Cass to the Brush farm near the Biddle house, and from the fort on the second terrace, whose site is now crossed by Fort street, to the river. It had gates and block houses on each side on the line of Jefferson avenue.

Walking down Griswold street from the bank corner, we have on our right the site of the "King's palace" and garden, names which mark the later English regime, when the palace or official residence was built for Gov. Hamilton, the "Hair-buyer General," as George Rogers Clarke designated him in the Vincennes campaign of 1778, from his offer of premiums for scalps of American patriots. The site is now partly covered by the fine buildings on the south side of Jefferson avenue.

Turning westward on Woodbridge, we are at once upon the historic ground where the beginnings of Detroit were made. Somewhere here, upon a site that can not now be precisely identified, was the first Ste. Anne's church, piously commenced only two days after the landing. Nor are the exact limits of Fort Pontchartrain probably now to be defined. Mr. Farmer, in his "History of Detroit," says that this first of the Detroit military works stood between Jefferson and Woodbridge, on the west half of the block between Griswold and Shelby, probably crossing Shelby and occupying a part of the ground now covered by the Michigan Exchange. In 1760-61 the tract contained within the stockade reached from the present line of Griswold to 50 feet west of Shelby, and from the alley between Larned and Jefferson to Woodbridge. Twenty eight years later, in Revolutionary times, when the citadel was at the corner of Jefferson and Wayne, and just before the Fort Lernoult (afterwards Shelby) was built, all the ground between Griswold and Cass, Larned and the river, was included. The original fort—a rude log affair, but strong enough for its purpose—was about 200 feet square. About 1858 the stumps of some of the cedar pickets enclosing it were found by workmen making excavations in the rear of the Michigan Exchange. The council house stood near the river, between Griswold and Shelby.

II.

The close of the first article of this series left our pedestrian upon the site of old Fort Pontchartrain and the original French settlement, about the intersection of West Woodbridge and Shelby streets. Near this spot stood the first building occupied (1838) by a public free school in this city. It was a plain two story frame, 40 by 80 feet, not built for the purpose, and having a convenient grocery in the first story, with outside stairs leading to the school room in the second. The house was erected on piles, upon the primitive river bank, a site now just east of the old Board of Trade building, on Woodbridge street. Passing along that street to the corner of Wayne, we are upon ground where once were the waters spanned by the narrow plank road or causeway leading out to the first dock pushed from the adjacent shore into the Detroit—a small and very simple affair, on light piles, and composed of timber, logs, and loose stones. With the increase of commerce and the advent of steamers, new and more substantial wharves were constructed, and this was suffered to fall into decay. The space it occupied, and more in the vicinity, was transformed into "made ground" many years ago by the enormous filling of 25,000 cubic yards of earth.

In the new volume of Mr. Parkman, "Montcalm and Wolfe," an extract is made from the narrative of Father Bonnecamp, chaplain to the expedition of Celoron to the valley of the Ohio in 1751. He was here for a day, on his return from the expedition, and records that "the situation is charming. A fine river flows at the foot of the fortifications," which, as we have seen, extended but little below Woodbridge. From this point, or a few rods beyond, the river trenched rapidly upon the present shore, forming the beautiful bay mentioned in our first number, which was skirted by a high bank. At First and Second streets the waters encroached upon the line of Jefferson avenue; and north of it, in a superb site upon the bank, stood the old Cadillac or Cass house, destroyed in 1882, which had to be moved but a short distance to reach its final resting place on Larned street.

The name given to Jefferson avenue, like so many others—would there were more—in the city, is itself historic. It is one of five Presidential names given to our principal avenues by the governor and judges of Michigan territory, in their replatting of the town after the sweeping fire of 1805—Washington, Jefferson, Adams, Madison and Monroe. It begins with the entrance of Woodbridge at First street. Starting from the ancient shore of the Detroit at this point, and now facing eastward, we pass presently the location of the citadel or arsenal at the northwest corner of Jefferson and Wayne, connected with Fort Shelby by a covered way. The house of the military storekeeper, for a long time Capt. Perkins, was a small frame a little below, on the avenue, where Mrs. Perkins became as noted for the floral beauty of her front yard, as her husband for the neatness of his buildings and grounds, with their piles of ordnance, shot, and shell. Between Wayne and Cass stood one of the old time block houses, on the line of the Hull stockade, the last one built; and, after the fire of 1805 this was used as the public jail. At the northwest corner of Jefferson and Cass stood the dwelling of Judge May, built of stone from the chimneys left by the fire. This succeeded the block house in use as a jail, but by 1815 it was abandoned for an old wooden building on the same side of the avenue a little beyond Shelby. The May residence was enlarged and became the excellent and widely reputed hostelry known for many years as the Mansion house. A small frame part of it, removed to another part of the city, was in existence only seven or eight years ago. On the opposite, the northwest corner, in the old Newberry building, afterwards the Garrison house, was the first telegraph office opened in the city, for the Speed line, some time in the 40's.

At Jefferson and Wayne the bluffy bank was finely utilized by Lieutenant Anderson for the placing of his 24-pounders, August 16, 1812, to resist the advance of Brock's force from Springwells; but the cowardice of Hull prevented the effective resistance he had planned.

Passing now rapidly the former site of Ste. Anne's church in the avenue, between Shelby and Griswold; of the Campau house of 1805, at No. 140, with Cadillac's headquarter's site thereon not far away, and of the guard-house and east or "Pontiac" gate of the old fort, where the First National Bank now stands, we come in a block further to the crossing of Woodward avenue, just below which, in Woodward, long stood the primitive market-house of the city. One of the old Godfroy homesteads stood opposite to the eastward, on Woodward and Woodbridge. The police station on the latter street stands upon the exact site of the Godfroy barn.

At Jefferson and Randolph, where Fireman's hall now stands, was the government council house of the later dominations, opposite the notable two story brick residence—the only one in town when built—of Gov. Hull, on the Biddle house corner. Looking down to the northwest corner of Woodbridge and Randolph, we see another of the old time hotel sites, where Woodworth kept an inn as far back as 1812, and where his famous Steamboat hotel long flourished. At the foot of Randolph were the original city water works, on the Berthelet wharf, with the reservoir in rear of the Fireman's hall. The last relics of the latter water works, with the well remembered round tower, have but lately disappeared from the foot of Orleans.

At or near Brush street ran the east front of Hull's stockade, with a gate and block house here. The old church at the corner of Beaubien, occupied as a carriage factory and warehouse, was the First Congregational, built in 1845. Next beyond St. Antoine, on the south side, is a noticeable row of old dwellings, dating back to the 30's and 40's. A number of venerable mansions remain on the avenue, though most of them are much changed by modern reconstructions. The oldest are probably the Trowbridge house, at No. 494, built about 1826, and the Brush homestead at 462, put up in '28, and reconstructed in '70. Part of the Van Dyke house, at No. 308, was built in 1836; and the Moran residence, 393, is also an old one. But would you see the older Moran home, the most venerable building in Michigan? Drop down from Jefferson on Hastings one short square, turn to the right a few steps, and there, at No. 182 and 184 Woodbridge east, half hidden behind a wilderness of weeds and with one or two of the ancient pear trees still towering above it, is the ruinous old building of 1734, wherein the late Judge Charles Moran was born.

Returning to Jefferson avenue, little of historic interest, save an old mansion here and there, presents itself until the Pontiac tree is reached, in the valley of Bloody brook, the last visible memorial of the Indian massacre here wreaked by the great Ottawa chief and his painted braves upon the English troops, July 31, 1763. Alas! that is no longer a surviving memorial. Its partial decay was observed last year, and this spring it totally refused to put forth buds and leaves. Its wood is already beginning to be worked up into souvenirs. A few rods below, upon ground now deeply covered, stood one of the early mills, whose ruins, Judge Campbell says, could still be seen forty to fifty years ago.

In Mount Elliott cemetery, a little off the avenue, the grave of Major Hamtramck may be visited, and a mile or so beyond, near the river, at the southeast corner of the Wesson place, with a grand old elm still dominating it, may be seen the quaint little dwelling built for him by one of the Chapotons in 1802, and where "The Frog on Horseback," as Hamtramck was called from his small size and singular appearance when riding, died the next year.

Upon the site of the present water works until lately stood one of the last of the old French dwellings, known as the Van Avery or Chauvin house. It was built by Thomas Stewart and Jean Limarre, in 1769, with a solidity and honesty that never failed to command the admiration of visitors. The great pear trees near it, planted in 1790, were known as the "Twelve Apostles."

The traveler thence to Grosse Pointe will pass the scene of the terrible battle in which an Indian tribe was almost annihilated in 1712, at Presque Isle, now Windmill Point, and will find some old habitations at Grosse Pointe and about L'Anse Creuse, the little bay beyond.

III.

The saunter along Jefferson avenue brought us to one or two points of antiquarian interest at the crossing of Woodward. Only a square below this, at the southwest corner of Woodbridge and Woodward, opposite the Mariner's church, is the first known site of the Detroit postoffice, where Judge Abbott, who held the postmastership from 1806 to 1831, dispensed for many years the hatfuls of letters and papers that made up the mail for the settlement. The office afterwards occupied the first floor of a building on the Mariner's church corner. A few rods below this and seventy seven feet above Atwater street, was the margin of the river in the days preceding the improvements along a few blocks of the city front.

Walk now two squares up Woodward, turn to the right on Larnard one block, and view with reverent regard the oldest church building, by far, left standing in the city, and still occupied for religious purposes.* The present Ste. Anne's church, at least the fourth or fifth of the name in Detroit, is lineal descendant of the little log-and-bark building whose erection was begun by Cadillac's people within the stockade about Fort Pontchartrain the second day after landing. The venerable stone pile at Larnard and Bates was commenced in 1817, but not finished till 1832, though occupied long before. The devoted Father Richard, whose statue appears on the east front of the city hall, contributed his entire pay as delegate in Congress towards its building. A Catholic cemetery of an acre's size was located here in 1797, and in it the remains of Colonel Hamtramck first reposed. Along here, between Bates and Randolph, Larned and Michigan Grand (now Cadillac Square), the ground was perhaps fifty feet above the general level, forming the original "Piety Hill," a name since appropriated for a locality far up town, near Cass park.

A little north of Ste. Anne's, on the west side of Bates, near Congress, was the first building, a very plain affair of twenty four by fifty feet, occupied by the University of Michigan in 1817, and for a few years thereafter. Passing on to the southwest corner of Randolph we are upon the site of the original Ste. Marie's hospital, opened by the Sisters of Charity, June 9, 1845, in a much older log cabin; and, looking down to the northwest corner of Jefferson and Randolph, we may see in our mind's eye the little one story brick building which held the Detroit bank as long ago as 1806.

Facing now westward on Larned, our pedestrian may go on to Wayne, where, at the northeast corner, flourished the Washington market from 1835 to 1852. At Nos. 164 and 166, between First and Second streets, stood, until

* Ste. Anne's was demolished in the early summer of 1886.

August, 1882, the strongly built frame dwelling which tradition affirmed to have been erected on the banks of the Detroit, then but a little way to the southward, by Cadillac, for the chief of the Hurons, one hundred and seventy nine years before. The whole ancient part of it, with its massive oak and pine beams and sills, was in admirable condition when torn down to make way for the present brick buildings.

Returning to Woodward and pausing on the west side of the aveune, we face the first church row, and the only one ever erected in Detroit. On the northeast corner stood the original Presbyterian church edifice, a rather stately one for its time, as may be seen by the picture of its burning, now hanging on the east wall of the public library. Next and north of it was a little building of brick, occupied for a session room; beyond that the first St. Paul's Episcopal church; and finally, on the other side of Congress, the Methodist meeting-house of a generation ago. At an earlier day the Protestant cemetery of the petty hamlet here included a part of the avenue in this locality, between Larned and Congress. Above this, to the city limit, Woodward avenue presents little of historic interest. It is worthy of notice, however, how closely the First Methodist church has clung to this avenue. Its next building, torn down but a year or two since, stood on the southwest corner of State and Woodward, and the superb edifice now occupied is just beyond the Grand Circus at Woodward and Adams. The original building occupied by this society, but never dedicated, I believe, was put up in 1834, only two squares west of Woodward, and was abandoned because it was so far out "on the commons," and difficult to reach in bad weather. It is now occupied as a dwelling, at the southwest corner of Gratiot and Farrar. On the flat-iron lot close by, upon which is the public library, long stood the county jail, which was succeeded by the Clinton street prison. Opposite it, on the site of the First Presbyterian church, was erected the gallows for the execution of the Indian, Kishkaukon, who defeated its purpose by suicide in his cell. At Farmer and Gratiot stood the old Pontiac depot, removed in 1842 from the site of the first railway station in the city, at Dequindre and Jefferson where it was established in 1838. About 1850 the cars coming down Gratiot avenue stopped upon the opera house site, on the Campus Martius, which was finally abandoned for the Brush street depot. The Central depot, for the ten years 1838-48, was on the site of the city hall, the trains moving in and out on Michigan avenue.

Fort street, historically, is one of the most interesting of Detroit thoroughfares, as its very name suggests. Near its western terminus, on the river bank, may be visited a well preserved, though small, enclosure or fortification of the mound-builders. Upon and near the ground now covered by Fort Wayne were the copious natural fountains or springs that gave the name to Springwells; and, in the vicinity, several interesting burial mounds could be seen forty or fifty years ago. Hereabout were pitched the wigwams of the Pottawatomie village, whose site was granted by the tribe to Robert Navarre, "son of the scrivener," one of the most notable of the early French residents. The Huron village was on the Jones farm, now a long way within the city limits. Not far from Twenty fourth street ran Knagg's creek, at the mouth of which, on the Detroit, stood his old red windmill, erected in or before 1795, and remaining until this century was well advanced. The late Mrs. Hamlin made it the scene of one of her entertaining "Legends of Le Detroit." From this shore it is worth while to cast a glance across to the spire of the Sandwich church, marking the site of the Huron mission removed thither by Father Potier in 1747, upon the enforced abandonment of the mission on Bois Blanc island.

At Fort and Fourteenth streets, on the northwest corner, may be observed with some interest the venerable Piquette house, occupied in 1874 as the Little Sisters' Home for aged poor. Three squares beyond, at the railway crossings, some traces are left of the banks of Campau's Mill river, later Cabacier's and finally May's creek, which entered the Detroit not far from the Central depot. The mill—a *maulin banal,* or public mill, in the earliest times, for grinding grain—stood at this crossing. Precisely at Cass street we strike the west line of the military cantonment attached to Fort Shelby in 1815, and at Wayne the boundary of the fort itself. This was built in 1778 by the British troops under their commandant here from whom it was originally named Fort Lernoult, and extended from Wayne to a line about half way between Shelby and Griswold, and from Lafayette nearly to Congress street, the glacis running well down to the bank of the Savoyard river. During the war of 1812-15 its name was changed to Fort Shelby, in honor of the gallant governor of Kentucky, who personally led his troops at the battle of the Thames. Fort and Shelby streets, of course, derive their names from it. The stump of the flagstaff, a well kept fragment of Norway pine, now in the public library, was dug up a few years ago, during excavations for the cellar at the residence of the Hon. John Owen, No. 61 Fort street west. The military cemetery was a little to the northwest, between Lafayette and Michigan avenues.

Another fortification, but a petty circular affair of about forty feet diameter, with a parapet ten feet high, was thrown up in 1806, in consequence of an Indian scare, far out in the woods, near the northeast corner of Park and High streets, and was called Fort Croghan, sometimes Fort Nonsense.

At the crossing of Fort and Griswold, on the northwest corner, one may recognize the old First Baptist church, now occupied for business purposes, Looking up Griswold we see the old Territorial and first State Capitol of Michigan on State street, reconstructed to its present shape as the high school building in 1875, three years after the city hall was finished. Not far to the northwest of this, at No. 43 West Park, near Grand River, stood the first building erected by the Detroit school board—a small wooden affair costing $540.

Pushing several blocks out on Fort street east, between Rivard and Russell, on the south side at No. 253, is the plain frame dwelling in which the young Lieut. Ulysses S. Grant resided when stationed in Detroit, away back in the 40's. Returning by Congress street, the house No. 185, between Hastings and St. Antoine, may attract attention as the place of meeting between John Brown of Osawatomie and some of his Detroit sympathizers, Dec. 12, 1859, before he made his ill starred attempt at Harper's Ferry. At the corner of Beaubien is one of the old Beaubien homesteads, to the rear of which was removed, from the site of Charles Busch's hardware store, the Dr. Brown house, one of those built next after the fire of 1805. If the wanderer cares now to walk far enough up St. Antoine to reach Elizabeth, he will find on the northwest corner another of the ancient Beaubien houses, now occupied by the House of Providence.

Farmer's "History of Detroit" has been the chief source of information for these papers, although free use has been made of Roberts' "sketches," Mrs. Hamlin's "Legends" and many other publications.—*The Detroit News.*

DETROIT IN 1838

BY HENRY A. FORD

Materials for the study of Detroit fifty years ago do not abound, except in the memories of a few living men. The directory system had yet reached scarcely any of the infant cities west of the Alleghanies; and the paucity and brevity of local sketches in the newspapers of those days afford but narrow fields for investigation. Happily about the time when the first tentative efforts were made to transform Michigan from a territory to a full fledged state, it entered the intelligent brain of Mr. John T. Blois, teacher of the Detroit Latin and English school, to compile a gazetteer of the incoming commonwealth, as a source of accurate information at home and a guide to immigrants from abroad. The result appeared early in 1839, in a neat 16 mo. volume of 418 pages, apparently printed in New York, and published there by Robinson, Pratt & Co., in Detroit by Messrs. Sydney L. Rood & Co. A few copies of this, in the original covers of figured blue cloth, still exist, and are unique and invaluable relics of the early days of Michigan as a separate state.

Mr. Blois brings his statistics and other data, so nearly as he can, down to October, 1838. The state had then provided for thirty nine counties, of which Arenac (but recently organized), Barry, Sanilac, Gratiot, Montcalm, Isabella, Clinton, Gladwin, Oceana and Midland were as yet unorganized. It was making rapid progress, however, and the legislature, which was then charged with such business, had provided at its last session for the erection of seventy two townships. The population, at the close of 1837, numbered 175,000 (besides 7,914 Indians), against 87,278 in 1834 and 32,538 in 1830. There were but two chartered cities—Detroit and Monroe—and twenty three incorporated villages. Of the 56,451 square miles of territory only 25,636 had been surveyed, and the Indian title to at least two thirds of the upper peninsula had not yet been extinguished. The northern part of that region was still sometimes called "the Siberia of Michigan." But in that and other portions of the state a geological survey under the lamented Dr. Douglass Houghton was progressing with excellent results, under an appropriation for three years of $12,000 per annum. The public lands were being sold at government offices in Detroit, Monroe, Kalamazoo, Flint and Ionia. The era of wild speculation was not yet over, and under the new banking law of the state forty five wildcat banks had been started between Aug. 15, 1837, and April 3, 1838, when an alarmed legislature put a stop to inflation of this kind. Fifteen banks were already existing under older laws, and altogether had a nominal capital of more than $10,000,000. Twenty four railroads, with a total length of 1,011 miles, had received special charters, and three or four others, aggregating 591 miles, were provided for under the internal improvement system of the state, which likewise contemplated several canals and sundry river improvements. Five state roads or turnpikes had been made, all pushing out from Detroit, and one of them, the Chicago road, being 254 miles long. The whole state had but sixty eight mail routes, only three of these directly reaching Detroit. The larger lake steamers, of 250 to 472 tons, numbered but nineteen, and the largest yet launched upon these inland seas was the "Illinois," of 755 tons, built here. The entire tonnage owned in the Detroit district in 1837 was but 6,994, against 995 in 1830.

The industries of the State were as yet light and comparatively unimportant. The estimated value of the agricultural product of 1837, based in part upon the census of that year, gave $2,114,366 for 1,691,499 bushels of wheat; $1,163,446 for oats; $1,319,045 for corn and $36,573 for rye; making a total of $4,633,430. Neat stock was estimated at $4,480,500; horses, $1,405,-800; hogs, $1,636,425; sheep, $95,515; total, $7,617,240. Mining had hardly yet begun. The Clinton salt works were going; Mt. Clemens had a glass factory and was doing a little ship building. Incomplete census returns in November, 1837, exhibited 433 saw mills, 114 grist mills, 23 carding machines, 12 cloth dressing establishments and 16 distilleries. The vast industrial development of Michigan was yet mainly in the future.

Wayne county at this time had 23,400 people, being little more populous than Washtenaw with 21,817 and Oakland with 20,163; but apart from Lenawee, which had 14,540, it had more than twice as many as any other in the state. Its only villages were "Dearbornville," which had about sixty families and the United States arsenal, just completed; Plymouth (or "Plymouth Corners"), about 300 population; Northville and Flat Rock, about 250 each; Redford "small," and Gibraltar, fifteen to twenty families. Detroit had yet no suburb of Springwells, except as a farming settlement, and Hamtramck is set down as "three miles" from the city. The Central railroad was running across the country as far as Ypsilanti; the "Pontiac road" was in operation to Royal Oak, and the "railroad to Shelby" was in course of construction. The depot was upon the Campus Martius, where the opera house now stands. The county sent two senators and seven representatives to the state legislature.

Detroit was in 1838 not only "port of entry" and "seat of justice for Wayne county," but also "capital of the state of Michigan." The state house, otherwise the county court house, now built around by the high school building, is named as a "commodious edifice of brick, constructed in the Ionic order 90 feet by 60. The portico in front is supported by six columns and the entablature at the sides by pilasters. The steeple, crowned with a dome, is 140 feet high." The view from this was thought to be exceeded by but two others in the country, those from the state house in Boston and from St. Michael's church in Charleston. On the 1st of January of that year the place had a population of 9,278 against 4,968 in 1834, 2,222 in 1830, 1,517 in 1828, 1,442 in 1826, 1,110 in 1820, and 770 in 1810. Thus within a decade the population had once increased by 50 per cent, had once more than doubled, and again nearly doubled. With very few exceptions all lived below the Grand Circus, and along not more than a mile's front upon the river, "more or less densely settled." Most of the business was done on Jefferson avenue, but Woodward avenue was "becoming of increased importance." Atwater, "upon the river," and Woodbridge, "running parallel with it upon the declivity," were "mostly occupied by stores and dealers in the heavier articles of merchandise." There were 4 banks with $2,250,000 capital, 27 dry goods, 25 grocery and provision, 14 hardware, 10 forwarding and commission, 8 drug, 7 clothing and 3 book stores, 8 silversmiths and jewelers, 27 lawyers, 22 physicians, 3 markets, 4 printing offices, issuing 4 weeklies (1 religious), 3 dailies, 1 tri-weekly and 1 educational monthly. The little city had also a Mechanics' hall, a theater, museum, circus, public garden, and a number of federal and state offices. In manufacturing there were 3 iron foundries, 1 brass foundry, 2 breweries, an edge-stool and a sash factory, and "a large steam saw mill." Much wholesale trade was already done, one half to three fifths of all merchandise sold going to the interior. No great amount of any product was exported, except fish. The fur trade had declined, although the American Fur company still kept its agency here. Forty seven lake vessels of all kinds were owned in this city, with an aggregate tonnage of 5,164. For their accommodation 5,900 feet of wharf had been made. About three steamers and as many sail vessels arrived and departed daily. The steam ferry to the Canada shore was running. Western emigration passing through afforded a large source of profit, especially in the season of navigation.

The town was quite well and modernly built, nearly all the huts and cottages of the French period having disappeared. Wooden buildings were much the more numerous; and as many of them occupied leased grounds, the sight of houses in process of removal was more common than now. The business quarter had several fine brick blocks and the city had "altogether a cheerful and comely appearance," with "not a few outward indications of high cultivated taste and refinement." The principal public buildings, besides the state house or capitol, included the city hall on the Campus, a $20,000 brick structure, 100 feet by 50, with two stories and a basement, the lower story occupied for a market; St. Paul's church, brick, with a 115 foot tower; the Baptist church, a plain affair at the corner of Fort and Griswold; St. Anne's, still standing on Larned street, but then its two spires were "in front," and were backed by an octagonal dome 30 feet high; and the old Bank of Michigan building, costing $40,000. There were eight church societies, two Catholic, one colored, and one each of Episcopalians, Presbyterians, Methodists, Baptists, and German Lutherans. The Catholics had one and the Protestants another orphan asylum, the latter in "a handsome two story brick edifice," on the familiar site then "a mile and a half above the city." The public schools of the place were grouped in seven districts which together had 4,355 children of school age. A branch of the state university was located here. Three free schools were maintained by the ladies' free school society (Protestant), specially for indigent children, who were furnished books and all needed supplies; and others were the St. Clare English and German (Catholic) and the French female charity schools. The chief private schools were the Detroit female seminary, in care of Prof. and Mrs. Wilson; the young ladies' institute, conducted by Mrs. Hector Scott and her daughters; St. Clare's seminary and several schools for boys, taught by Profs. Blois, Mitchell and Bacon. The state library, kept at the capitol, already numbered 1,900 volumes; the Detroit young men's society had made a good beginning with 1,200; and there was also a circulating library of about 1,000. The society named had been in existence for six years, the historical society for about ten, the state literary institute was organized the same year, and several other organizations of the kind had been made here.

The system of water supply demands a passing notice in closing. Steam power, forcing water from the river, was giving but partial service, and a plan had been mooted to utilize the current of the stream in generating a power for further use. This had been superseded, however, by the works which stood until a quite recent day at the foot of Orleans street, where the tall chimney may still be seen. This was then "the upper part of the city," and a brick tower was here being erected, sixty four feet in diameter and going to a height of fifty feet above the river, supporting a cast iron reservoir twenty feet deep, with a capacity of 425,000 gallons. Water was to be taken 450 feet from the shore and 6 feet below the surface of the river, through a 12 inch pipe. A 25 horse power engine would do all the work. One hundred fire hydrants were to be connected, each capable of throwing a stream into the third story of any building in the city. The cost of this modest system was estimated at $100,000 and it was to be finished in 1839.

The sewerage of the city was already pretty good; but the streets were mostly in primitive condition, and bad in the spring and after hard rains. Paving with wood, however, had hopefully begun.—*Detroit Post and Tribune.*

DETROIT NEARLY FIVE DECADES AGO.

There is possibly no greater pleasure reserved for old age than to take a retrospective view of a life well spent, to mark the stepping stones to success in the past, and to be able to enjoy the fruition of well directed effort. The every day occurrence of a business man receiving a telegram from Buffalo or Chicago, telephoning to his wife that he will not be at home that night, and in a few hours arriving in one or the other of these cities, would appear even more wonderful than the wildest story in the Arabian Nights to an inhabitant of Detroit fifty years ago, if it were possible that he could be resurrected and made witness of the uses of our modern improvements and discoveries. Strange as it would undoubtedly seem to him of a half a century ago, yet the people of the present time have become so accustomed to the new modes of living that there are already many young business men who do not possess the faintest idea of what the lives, manners and customs of their grandfathers and great-grandfathers were two generations ago.

Postmaster Codd has in his possession a work that reflects a great deal of the life of this city when its population was less than 10,000. It is a "Directory of the City of Detroit with its environs and register of Michigan for the year 1837." It is a book of about 200 pages, and professes to contain "a classification of the professions and principal trades in the city, every information relative to officers of the municipal government, to public offices and officers, to churches, associations and institutions, to shipping, steamboats, stages, &c. Also, a list of the State and County Officers, &c., &c., by Julius P. Bolivar MacCabe." It is printed by William Harsha, father of Walter Harsha, present clerk of the United States circuit court.

The first thirty six pages are given up to advertising, thus showing that there were many shrewd business men here at that time. Among these advertisements may be found much to amuse. One page announces that: "The Detroit Evening Spectator and Literary Gazette is published on an imperial sheet, on Wednesday and Saturday evenings at $4 per annum. Its first page is devoted to belles lettres and science; its second, to the current news of the day, and editorial matter, comprising comments on passing events, full reports on important public meetings, remarks on literary and moral subjects, etc., etc. The two remaining pages are devoted to advertisements." At that early date the city possessed a Detroit museum. It was situated on the corner of Jefferson avenue and Griswold street. By its advertisement "the public are respectfully informed that this establishment has lately been fitted up in a neat and elegant style, with many additions and improvements. An entire new cosmorama has been erected with new and splendid views. * * Phantasmagoria, and phantascopal illusions will be exhibited every evening at 8 o'clock."

"Capt. Charles Walsh would present his unfeigned thanks to the citizens of Detroit, and the public, who have so kindly extended to him the very liberal patronage he has been favored with at his establishment. He takes pleasure in stating that 'The Shades' has become a resort for gentlemen such as he is exceedingly happy to wait upon, and flatters himself that in time his unwearied endeavors to please will give his place the character he intends it shall bear." The "Capt." does not state where his place of resort was located.

H. Vaughan, keeper of the "Franklin retreat," begs leave to inform the public that he is now receiving his winter supply of oysters, together with other delicacies of the season." James G. Crane & Co., hatters, announce the receipt of goods, "all of which will be sold low for cash, and no growling."

At the time this directory was published there were three banks here: The Bank of Michigan, the oldest institution of the kind in the city, having a branch in Kalamazoo, capital $100,000, with the privilege of increasing it to $250,000, in the bank and branch; the Farmers and Mechanics' bank of Michigan, capital $100,000, and the Michigan State bank, capital $100,000. In 1834 Detroit possessed only four wards and a population of 4,973 persons. Three years later there were 9,763 persons in Detroit. There were seven churches, two of which were Catholic, one Episcopalian, one Presbyterian, one Methodist, one Baptist, and one German Lutheran.

Under the heading of charitable institutions appears the following: "Wayne county hospital and poorhouse—Fort Gratiot road, established in 1832, under the direction of the Rev. Mr. Kundig. This establishment is supported by a county cess. The average number of its inmates ranges from 25 to 40. Three ladies of the order of St. Clair superintend the institution." Of the orphan asylum it says: "This benevolent institution is situate on the Fort Gratiot turnpike road, at a distance of two miles from the city. The number of children left destitute by the ravages of cholera in 1832, suggested to the Rev. Mr. Kundig, R. C. Clergyman, (who in the exercise of his ministry braved the dangers of this pestilence as he walked through its 'valley of death') the necessity of then establishing this asylum."

There were three markets. The city market, on the first floor of the city hall; the Berthelet, at the corner of Randolph and Woodbridge streets, and the Washington, corner of Wayne and Larned streets. In 1837 seven railroads had been chartered to run into the city, and two of them were at that time in the course of construction. They were the Detroit & St. Joseph road, whose whole length was 196 miles, and the Pontiac and Detroit road.

The directory proper, containing the names of the residents of the city, is comprised in 38 pages, each page averaging 30 names. An appendix shows that Levi Cook was then mayor, George Byrd city clerk, James A. Vandyke city attorney. Israel Noble is quoted as sexton, and the city got along with three constables. H. V. Disbrow was chief engineer of the fire department and there were five fire wardens for each of the five wards. A mayor's court held by the mayor, recorder and aldermen, or any three of them, was held on the second Monday in every month. Sheldon M'Knight was postmaster and Andrew Mack collector. T. E. Tallman was county clerk, and the sheriff, John M. Wilson, was content with two deputies.—*Detroit News.*

THE GLADWYN AND PONTIAC FABLE

BY HENRY A. FORD

"Edmund Kirke" (Mr. J. R. Gilmore) apparently accepts without question the old story of Gladwyn and the Indian girl, and even furnishes it with a new picture, one truer to the probabilities of such a scene than the elaborate painting of the late Mr. Stanley. The story itself is familiar enough to all readers of western or aboriginal history, and need not be repeated. But, after passing almost unchallenged for nearly a century and a quarter, it is time to inquire whether the incident belongs to veritable history or to romance —whether it has sufficient warrant in contemporary accounts, or took its origin in the legends and traditions of the wild woods. This inquiry will justify the brief space we care to give to it.

The hero of this tale is Major Gladwyn, English commandant of Detroit and its dependencies in the year of grace 1763, and for some time before and after. The attempt of Pontiac and his warriors to seize the fort and massacre the garrison by an act of treachery succeeding the present to Gladwyn in a particular manner of a belt of wampum at the end of the great Ottawa's address, occurred May 7th of that year. The commander's full official reports have never been reached in the search for authentic accounts of the transaction; but, in a brief statement to his superior, Gen. Amherst, dated one week after the attempt, he simply says: "On the 7th he (Pontiac) came, but I was luckily informed the night before that he was coming to surprise us." Not a word of Gladwyn's has ever been discovered giving color to the tale that Pontiac's plan was disclosed to him by an Ojibwa (Chippewa) mistress, or any other Indian girl.

Two months later, in early July, a private letter was written from Detroit which was presently given publicity in the Newport (R. I.) Mercury for August 22, 1763. The writer thus tersely tells the story: "The Ottawas and some of the Chippewas to the number of 300 came to the fort and held a treaty with Major Gladwyn, who had information the evening before that the Indians were determined to fall upon and murder the officers and soldiers in council, while they were to have parties at the different merchants' houses, to treat them in the same manner," etc.

Had there been valid ground for the tradition, it could hardly have failed to be noticed in the famous "Pontiac Manuscript," discovered in this city many years ago, the supposed work of a French priest here at the time, and describing events with great particularity and minuteness. If any Indian woman had visited Gladwyn with information of the attempt, and the incident was known among the garrison, he too must have known it, and in his garrulous way would have recorded it. But he writes nothing of the kind—on the contrary says "the plot was disclosed to Gladwyn by a man of the Ottaway tribe." But he does say further that the next day Pontiac sent four of his warriors from the Ottawa village (just above the present site of Walkerville) to the Pottawatomie town (at Springwells, now the west end of Detroit, near the fort) to seize an Ojibwa girl whom he suspected; that they took her before Gladwyn but learned nothing from him to criminate her, and she was then taken to Pontiac, who beat her severely with a kind of racket or Indian ball club. A similar story was told long afterward by an old Indian to Henry Conner, the interpreter and trader, son of the Moravian pioneer near Mt. Clemens, and very likely has some foundation in fact, though it proves nothing for the historic truth of the woman's guilt.

No other contemporary letter, narrative, or official report has yet been found attributing the betrayal of the plot to an Indian girl. The story has been given reputable currency, chiefly by Mr. Parkman, the historian, who inserts it in much detail in his noble work on "The Conspiracy of Pontiac."

His immediate authority was a letter from the late Henry R. Schoolcraft, who rested his statement not upon documentary evidence, but upon the tradition related to him by Conner, including the death of the woman by falling into a kettle of boiling maple sap. It had long before, however, been related and had got into literature. Jonathan Carver heard it on his visit to the northwest six years after the conspiracy, and embodied it in his book of travels. Other accounts are much later, but are in their origin altogether traditional, though in several cases made by persons living at the time of the treacherous attempt and subsequent siege under Pontiac. Pelletier, or Peltier, a descendant of one of the two *coureurs des bois* found here by Cadillac in 1701 was then 17 years old; and he told it to Gen. Cass in 1824, sixty one years afterwards. Maj. Thompson Maxwell, at Gen. Cass's request, dictated his reminiscences of the siege to the late C. C. Trowbridge in 1821, fifty eight years after. He was an illiterate man, and his relation is full of blunders. Other narratives given late in life by St. Aubin, Guoin, Mr. Meloche, and others are evidently affected by the romance with which old age will clothe the simplest occurrence of early days. In the total absence of any documentary evidence or contemporary statement it must be held that the story grew to its present proportions and brilliancy from the mere suspicions of Pontiac and his brutal punishment of the Indian girl which subsequently in the legends of the prisoners and the savages received its variegated embellishments, that have lost nothing at the hands of successive historians. Mrs. Sheldon in her history of Michigan says that a soldier at the fort named William Tucker, who during captivity among the Indians had been adopted into a tribe, learned the designs of Pontiac from his savage sister and disclosed them to Gladwyn. This is very likely the correct version of the affair and the soldier's "sister" may plausibly enough have been the woman scourged by the haughty Pontiac.—*Detroit Tribune.*

THE OLD MORAVIAN MISSION AT MT. CLEMENS

BY HENRY A. FORD

One of the most obscure episodes in the annals of the northwest, so little noted that Judge Cooley's recent history of Michigan (in the "American Commonwealth," series) has not the least reference to it, is yet fraught with the highest interest to the reader of heroic and daring deeds, undertaken for civilization and christianity. It illustrates grandly the devotion, courage, endurance, and missionary enterprise of the Moravian brethren, who, next to the indefatigable "black robes" were the first emissaries for Christ among the savages of the new world.

The *Unitas Fratrum,* otherwise called the Moravian or Bohemian brethren, trace their origin back of the Reformation to the time of John Huss. Early in the last century his disciples were expelled from Bohemia and Moravia by their fierce persecutors. Among their sympathizers in the neighboring state of Saxony was the noble Nicholaus Ludwig, Count von Zinzendorf, the youthful son of a Saxon minister of state, and already eminent for his piety. He admitted a small party of the Hussites to reside upon his estate, organized them and the refugees and converts who joined them in considerable numbers into a church, and so became the founder of the Moravian brotherhood. Beginning to preach the gospel he presently devoted his entire property and energies to the propagation of the faith. In 1736 he was banished from Saxony, and five years later came to America and established the Moravian church at Bethlehem, Pa., where its chief seat in this country still remains. After nearly twenty years' service among the savages and the people of his native land, to which he was allowed to return, he died upon his ancestral estate, May 9, 1760. He left more than 100 works of his authorship in prose and verse, some of which, used as hymn books by the pious Moravians, are said to be characterized remarkably by indecent figures and allusions.

No christian church, not even the Roman Catholic, has been more distinguished for zealous missionary spirit in the face of tremendous difficulties than the Moravian. From the Cape of Good Hope to Labrador and Greenland, and from the steppes of Asiatic Russia to the deep forests of the new world, their mission stations have been planted with astonishing success. From Bethlehem the missions, principally among the Delaware Indians, were pushed rapidly westward into the tangled wilderness, during the latter half of the eighteenth century, until in 1771 they paused for a time in the fertile valleys of the Tuscarawas and the Muskingum. Here were founded stations of some permanence, bearing the beautiful names of Schonbrunn, "The Shining Spring;" Lichtenau, "The Pasture of Light;" Salem, "Peace," and Gnadenhutten, "The Tents of Grace." The last was a favorite designation among the Moravians, no fewer than five of their American stations bearing it, including that founded in Michigan.

In the Ohio country the founder and continuing head of the mission was the Rev. David Zeisberger, for sixty two years a most devoted and energetic servant of the church among the aborigines. He was born at the hamlet of Zauchtenthal, Moravia, April 11, 1721, and ended a career of great usefulness in his 88th year, at Goshen, in the Tuscarawas valley. He was the founder of New Gnadenhutten, near Mt. Clemens, Mich., and thus has place among the heroes of our state history. His biographer, Bishop de Schweinitz, describes him as of small figure, but well proportioned; his face pleasing and cheerful, but seamed by endless care and the exposures of his long life among the savages; his dress neat and plain. He had become taciturn as an Indian, and often spoke in terms rather befitting the council house than a christian church. This quality proved of eminent service to the patriot cause at a critical period of the revolution, and there was one eventful moment when the single voice of Zeisberger, pleading successfully before the council of Delaware braves against alliance with the British, possibly saved American independence. He had been adopted into the tribe of the Onondagas by a name signifying "On the Pumpkin," and had great influence with most of the tribes which he encountered.

Upon the low bluff on the south side of the Clinton river (a century ago called the Huron), a little outside the southwest corner of the corporation of Mt. Clemens, and only twenty miles from Detroit, a slight depression in the open field a few rods from the residence of Mr. Henry E. Steevens, and perhaps a few aged fruit trees, are the only visible memorials of the Moravian occupation in Michigan. The history of the events precedent to the settlement, of the settlement itself in July, 1782, and its abandonment four years after, has many points of interest, but must be briefly told in these columns. Fortunately for our narrative, however, as well as for the future historian, new and important light is now thrown upon the record by the recent translation and publication in two goodly octavo volumes, of the diary of Zeisberger, which has lain in the original German and in manuscript for nearly a hundred years. With the invaluable aid of this the story is newly compiled.

During the revolutionary struggle the Delaware nation had suffered terribly from both sides for their persistent neutrality. The christian Indians in the river valleys of Ohio lived directly upon the war path traversed by the Wyandottes and other tribes in alliance with the British, and the hardy borderers of Pennsylvania and Virginia; and so were between two fires. In the fall of 1781, under orders from Detroit, the British headquarters in the northwest, they were forcibly deported from their peaceful and prosperous villages and left utterly destitute upon the Sandusky plains, from which they were forbidden to return. A winter of awful cold and hunger had been passed in a wretched cluster of huts a few miles below the present Upper Sandusky, and when, in March following, a hundred of the miserable exiles had been allowed to go back to their towns to gather the standing corn, they were seized, brutally murdered and scalped by a party of frontiersmen, who wrongly held them responsible for some of the fresh atrocities in the settlements. The feeble remainder had been peeled and plundered, persecuted and threatened, scattered like partridges upon the mountains. Zeisberger and his pious associates were stripped of even the clothes they wore; and several months after, when summoned to Detroit, they were still in a state of abject raggedness and destitution.

It was in October, 1781, that the British commandant at Detroit, Major De Peyster, of generally happy memory, sent for the missionaries in Ohio to answer before him the charges made against them of sympathy and complicity with the American cause. The summons was answered by Zeisberger, Heckewelder, Sensemann, and Edwards, with five of the christian Delawares. The second of these, although not so long in the service as Zeisberger, became the most famous of the Moravians in America, partly by his writings on the Indians, which are still highly esteemed, and partly from his superior qualities. The historian Hildreth says: "In disposition he was like the Apostle John, while his companion, Zeisberger, partook of the spirit of St. Paul." He was English born, but son of a German refugee, and died at Bethlehem Jan. 31, 1823, aged 80 years. Although much associated with Zeisberger in Ohio and elsewhere, he was not a founder of the mission on the Clinton, but several times visited and labored there, and should have honorable mention in the story of its brief career.

The little party was but poorly equipped for the journey to Detroit, and had a painful time struggling on horseback through "the deep swamps and troublesome waters" of northwestern Ohio. Somewhere near the present site of Toledo Zeisberger records: "We met to-day, as indeed every day as far as Detroit, a multitude of Indians of various nations, who were all bringing from Detroit horse loads of wares and gifts, and in such number that one would think they must have emptied all Detroit." Arriving at the River Rouge, which he calls the "Rush," they could not get over for want of a boat, and "had to pass the night three miles from the city, under the open heaven, but had nothing more to eat. We could see very plainly," he adds, "the city and the whole country round about, on both sides the river, which is about a mile wide." The next day they crossed in a canoe, and "came at once to Detroit, after we had first passed through the settlement this side of the city, which is thinly settled, and is built like a village along the river." They were at first rather cavalierly received by De Peyster, but after considerable detention and much questioning, were fairly vindicated, when his demeanor changed, they were kindly treated and allowed to return to their Indians on the Sandusky. Zeisberger's diary, however, does not quite bear out the tale usually told of absolutely cruel and oppressive treatment accorded them there. He speaks always well of De Peyster, to whom the mission on the Clinton was afterwards much indebted. His notes of the visit and of a brief residence here the next year, awaiting the arrival of the christian Indians, include many interesting memoranda of the Detroit of more than a century ago. A minor problem of local history is solved by his mention of "Yankee hall," a building near the fort, so called from the occupation by the American prisoners brought in by the Indians. This has heretofore been known in our local literature only by the corrupted name of "Jakey hall." Mention is made of "the palisades in the shipyard," which lay near the foot of Woodward avenue. Long afterwards, upon a Lake Erie island, Zeisberger observed "much red cedar timber," quantities of which were taken to Detroit for ship building. The "upper end of Germantown," a locality in or near Detroit, not yet identified, was the scene of the baptism of four children by the missionary,

The missionaries received a fraternal call from the French priest (Father Peter Simple), "quite an old man, with whom, however, we could not speak, for he knew no English." In various parts of the diary, Detroit morals receive but doubtful compliments, as the following: "It is wonderful here, and pleasant, if any one is found who shows a desire for God's word, for the place here is like Sodom, where all sins are committed." The merchants reported of the christian Indians "that they have paid their debts to the last penny, saying it could well enough be seen that they were an honorable people, and better than all the inhabitants around Detroit, who do not like to pay their debts, and add thereto." Many well known or totally unknown citizens of Detroit at that time come into the narrative, as Elias Schmidt (baptized by Zeisberger, June 23, 1782), Isaac Williams, the Indian trader, and his companion, Cassedy "Homes" and his wife, "some gentle people," who went in sleighs over the ice on the lake to visit the mission, McKee and Elliot, the famous (or infamous) British agents and traders, a "merchant from Detroit," who had his two children baptized respectively John and Mary, and others. "A man by the name of Halse" was found living near the mouth of the Detroit river, whose child Heckewelder baptized. Baptisms had been conducted here, it seems, with considerable looseness: "As there is no ordained preacher of the Protestant church in Detroit, the justice baptizes the children also, or the commandant, if it be asked of him; but to many this is not satisfactory, and they are scrupulous about it." Hence the Moravians are often resorted to for this ordinance, and occasionally for marriage.

A period of great scarcity of food in Detroit is noticed July 18, 1784. One of the Indians had just returned to the mission and reported "nothing to be had for cash. With his own eyes he saw a Spanish dollar offered a baker for a pound of bread and refused. A hundred weight of flour costs £7 13s, and is not to be had." At another time, the same summer, two Frenchmen from Detroit brought word that "in the settlement there is a very bad outlook. They said that most people there had no bread and lived from the weeds they cooked and eat."

March 1, 1782, another summons was received by Zeisberger and his companions on the Sandusky, this time that "the teachers and their families" should be brought to Detroit. It was now the intention of De Peyster, whose mind had again been poisoned by the Wyandottes, to keep the missionaries here or send them away to Bethlehem; but after a time he consented that they should found a new mission station in the vicinity of Detroit, and send for their christian Indians. Under the depressing influences of another removal, but particularly of the horrible massacre of their brethren and sisters on the 7th and 8th of March, in the Tuscarawas valley, the Delawares slowly arrived, and on the 20th of July Zeisberger and John G. Jungmann, with their wives, Wm. Edwards and Michael Young, who were unmarried, and four Indian families, in all but twenty five persons, set out in a sail boat for the Clinton river, on whose banks, at the site already indicated, a small tract for a mission had been procured from the Chippewas. "Three miles from the city we came to an island where we took aboard our two pilots, who were to conduct us to the appointed place." It was evening of the next day before the devious windings of the little river had been traversed for a few miles, and the destined point reached. Here, among much excellent forest, the diarist noted "wild cherry trees, which had a fine red wood, of which in

Detroit the most beautiful cabinet work is made." The place was evidently the site of an old Indian town, of which many "corn holes" and other indications were observed.

Religious services were held the same evening around the bivouac fire, for which the Moravian text of the day seemed specially fitting: "For ye shall go out with joy and be led forth with peace." Tents were pitched, but in a few days huts were erected, which in due time became substantial cabins. Only two rows were built, one on each side of a street, "full four rods wide," each lot having a front of three rods or fifty feet, very nearly. Accounts vary as to the number ultimately erected, from twenty to thirty. A rude chapel, not much larger than the other buildings, was first occupied on the 5th of November. There was no blockhouse or stockade, but the little church was slightly fortified.

This Moravian station appears to have existed during several months of its short life, without a name. It is not mentioned by Zeisberger by the favorite name of Gnadenhutten until Sept. 4, 1783, and it was not until Loskiel wrote his history of the Moravian missions that it received the designation by which it has since been known as New Gnadenhutten. The settlement was founded under auspices that well entitled it to be called "Tents of Grace." Everybody at first was kind. Major De Peyster had supplied the infant colony with unusual liberality. "He said," Zeisberger wrote, "we must not think he had put us where we must suffer want; he wished to supply both us and our Indians with food until we ourselves had a harvest and could supply ourselves." In a single issue from the government stores he provisioned the colony for six months. Shortly after this De Peyster was superseded by "the Lord George Hay," as Zeisberger in his simplicity calls him, who was also favorable to the mission, and showed it many kindnesses. The diary enables us to fix almost to a day the time of Governor Hay's death, which occurerd here, since by these memoranda he was buried Aug. 2, 1785.

The merchants of Detroit were similiarly hospitable. "When we came into the city we were welcomed everywhere, people were glad to see us, gave us good wishes and showed themselves serviceable to us. There were some people who offered us on credit or upon payment to provide our Indians for fishing, with flour, corn and all materials in the winter when the lakes were frozen—an important matter for us, and one that always interested us." Hunting and fishing in the vicinity of the village were excellent, and the second summer their humble crops began to be available. The characteristic feebleness of Indian agriculture, however, had not greatly improved under the influence of the missionaries, and but twenty five to thirty acres had been improved when the station was broken up.

Besides their modest husbandry, the hunting and fishing, sugar making in the season, and frequent religious service at all times of the year, the Indians made canoes, baskets, brooms, bowls, ladles and other simple articles, for which ready market was found in Detroit. A salt lick was found somewhere in the back country, from which the Indians returned, "having boiled a good lot of excellent salt, which is just the thing for them, salt being here a scarce thing." In the spring of 1783 "some Indian brethren went to the mouth of the river to help block out his house for a white man, who wishes to settle there and invited them "the first note, we believe, of civilized settlement in Macomb county, elsewhere than at New Gnadenhutten. As before hinted, visits of Detroiters to the mission were frequent.

December 19, 1785, some of the Indian brethren went "to lay out and make a new and straight road to Detroit." This, when finished, became the famous "Moravian road," the first wagonway made in the interior of Michigan. It was "twenty three and one half miles from our town to Detroit, straight through the bush."

The annals of the four years at New Gnadenhutten are comparatively uneventful. The winter of 1783-4 was terribly severe. The "gentle people" from Detroit who visited the station January 10th, "simply to see our town," reported "that by the thermometer it has not been so cold for twenty eight years as it is now, it being seven degrees lower than in the whole time." On the 24th, Zeisberger makes entry: "This week it snowed several days in succession, and the snow was now three feet deep, so that it was hard to get firewood." And a few days later: "It has snowed nearly every day, and the snow gets ever deeper. Our Indian brethren, about whom we are most anxious and distressed, have many of them, nothing more to eat. * * * No one had thought there would be such a winter. Old settlers in Detroit say that as long as they have lived there the snow has never been so deep." Within three days, however, by the help of snow shoes, more than a hundred deer were shot, which removed all the present fear of famine. But the streams were frozen hard, and out upon the lake, a mile from the shore, the ice was three feet two inches thick, and did not go out till May. The snow was finally five feet deep, and remained till late in the spring. Most of the season was spent in a struggle for comfort, if not for life.

The mission grew only by natural increase and the immigration of christian Delawares formerly in Zeisberger's flock. It was started, we have seen, with but nineteen Indian souls, including children. On Christmas, 1782, he writes: "There were together fifty three of us, white and brown." Many of the converts came from the Shawanese towns in Ohio the next May, and in his last entry for the year he says: "Twenty six brethern have this year been absolved and sixteen reädmitted to the holy communion." Natural increase in 1783 did not quite keep pace with death—five against six. Among the births was Susanna, daughter of Richard Conner, born Dec. 16th, and baptized the Sunday following.

But one new communicant was received in 1784, one woman baptized, eight children born, three couples married, two adults died. At the end of 1785, the last entire year spent at New Gnadenhutten, Zeisberger was able to record only the baptism of two adult women and two girls, as many persons admitted to the communion, one child dead during the year. "The inhabitants here on the Huron [Clinton] river are 117 Indian souls." There were probably no more when the removal occurred, less than four months afterwards.

No impression whatever had been made upon the heathen Chippewas, none of whose villages were in their vicinity. Friendly relations were maintained, and there is no account of Indian alarm at the settlement, a remarkable thing for a pioneer town. But when the Chippewas heard that the war of the revolution had closed, and the chief claiming the land on the river had died, they began to suggest the removal of the mission whose heads were formally warned by a deputation of the heathen in the middle of January, 1786. A few weeks afterwards they were advised by the governor of Detroit to comply with the wishes of those whose hospitality they had so far peacefully enjoyed, and on Thursday, the 20th of April, the congregation betook itself to the chapel for the last time, and, after solemn service of thanksgiving, loaded their canoes, and in the afternoon paddled sorrowfully down the river. At Detroit they took two sailing vessels for the Cuyahoga, upon whose banks they settled in poor shape for a time, and, after some further wanderings, a remnant of them finally located at Fairfield, a few miles beyond Chatham, Canada, and near the battle field of the Thames, where Tecumseh was killed. Their improvements on the Clinton were purchased by Maj. Ancrum, the British commandant at Detroit, and John Askin, the trader, for a total sum of $450. Some of the cabins were occupied by tenants for a number of years, but all long since disappeared, leaving no trace except the cellar of Richard Conner, indicated near the beginning of this narrative.

"None of us all remained behind," says Zeisberger, "save Conner's family, who himself knew not whether to go nor what to do." He was the sole Moravian layman who had been allowed to settle there. Richard Conner (originally O'Conner) was a native of Ireland, but had migrated from Maryland to the wilderness west and married a white girl who had been a captive among the Shawanese. After Lord Dunmore's campaign against the Ohio Indians (1764), they settled in Pittsburg, but went to the Moravian town of Schonbrunn to seek their son, who was now himself a captive. Here they so commended themselves that, against Moravian usage, they were permitted to remain. June 14, 1782, they followed the missionaries to Detroit in a ship from Sandusky "on account of the unrest caused by war," but did not go to the mission till the last of March, 1783. The rest of Conner's life was spent at the Moravian site, where he died April 17, 1808. He left four sons, James, John, William, and Henry, who became somewhat notable in the pioneer days of eastern Michigan, and are well remembered by a few of the old citizens of Detroit. The last named, called Wah-be-sken-dip by the Indians, was renowned for his great strength, and was a superior interpreter and trader among the savages. He fought with Harrison in the battle of the Thames, and was present at the death of Tecumseh. Richard Conner's only daughter, Susanna, was born at the mission Dec. 16, 1837, the first child of white parents born within the limits of the present Macomb county. She married the late Judge Elisha Harrington, whose farm covered the site of the old mission. A part of the tract was subdivided in 1837, during the internal improvement mania, to form the village at the beginning of the Clinton & Kalamazoo canal, at first called Casino, but later known as Frederick. A few ruinous houses are all that now remain of it.—*Detroit Tribune.*

WATERTOWN THIRTY YEARS AGO

[TUSCOLA COUNTY]

The following paper was read by the Hon. Enos Goodrich of Watertown, at the pioneer picnic at Mayville, August 21, 1884:

The year 1854 was one long to be remembered in the early history of northern Michigan, for it was in that year that the passage of what was known as the "Graduation Law" gave an impetus to settlement such as the state had not known since the speculating days of 1836. Steadily but very slowly had been the march of improvement for the intervening eighteen years. Many of the wild lands of Michigan had been in market from twenty to forty years without a purchaser. This state of facts, not only in Michigan, but in other frontier states, prompted Congress, in the year 1854 to reduce the price of all lands having been in the market twenty years or over, down to prices from one dollar to twelve and one half cents an acre, according to a graduated scale, governed by the time they had been in market. This act was intended for the benefit of actual settlers, but like most other benevolent acts it was in many cases perverted to purposes of speculating. Nevertheless there is no doubt but it resulted in actual benefit to the country.

At the time of the passage of the "Graduation Law" about three quarters of the lands of Watertown were still the property of the government, and the portions that had been located were almost exclusively taken for the timber.

The speculating epoch of "wildcat days," which ran wild over the southern counties, had just dipped over the border and taken three small tracts in Watertown near North lake. On the 19th day of December, 1836, Calvin C. Waller, had made a small entry of land on sections 32 and 33, and the 23d day of January, 1837, Alva Bishop invaded the township by making a location on 33. But who Calvin C. Waller and Alva Bishop may have been are facts not known to the writer. Whether they have gone to join the majority of the pioneers of that early period in the better land, or still live in other climes must remain for others to tell. And now the wilds of Watertown enjoy a long season of unbroken repose, until John McCartney invades the very heart of the township by a location on section 21 under the date of October 18, 1851. During the next succeeding three years quite extensive tracts of land were located for their timber. Principal among the locators are the names of Chester Baxter, who, I think, was a Vermonter, and Royal C. Remmick and Enoch J. White, both citizens of Michigan, both widely and favorably known to our early pioneers, and both of whom, after a long and successful career, have years ago passed from the scenes of earth. Of those who purchased lands in Watertown, not far from thirty years ago, I present an imperfect list of such as are known to be living and such as are known to have passed away.

Among the living are Nathaniel M. Berry, Charles Dickinson, Joseph Colling, Thomas Duncan, James Docherty, Samuel P. McNeil, Franklin Wright, James McCartney, Jacob W. Brown, Patrick O'Neil, Nathan Potter, Nathan N. Wilson, Thetford; Edward H. Thompson, Flint; John H. Markell, James H. C. Blades, Fenton; Jasper Johnson, Curtiss Coffeen, Samuel Salein, Oakland Co.; James L. Cain, Enos Goodrich. Among those known to have passed away we have to record the names of George Turner, Ira S. Begel, Alphant J. Glynn, Charles Merrill, Benjamine Decker, Samuel McNeil, Amos L. Hinney, Ira Davenport, Merrill Henry.

In looking back over the past thirty years it is almost wonderful to note the very large percentage of early pioneers who have been spared through the vicissitudes of life, to assist in pushing on the grand work of improvement, and who, like the old guard of Napoleon. can still stand side by side and answer to the roll call of Watertown's early founders. But who can say how long the list I have presented to-day will remain unbroken. As the Hon. Andrew Parsons said to us when he dismissed the senate of 1835, "It is not probable that we shall all meet again in time." Were it within the province of my subject I might here waft away your thoughts to the untrodden regions of the future, in imagination contemplative of what Watertown is destined yet to be, but my theme leads me to linger with the past. But before passing from this stage of the subject it is meet that we should pay a passing tribute to the memory of two of Watertown's old settlers, who within the past few weeks have been suddenly called away from the scene of their earthly labors. Benjamin Sperry and Henry E. Chaplain, though not among Watertown's very earliest settlers, may justly be classed among its pioneers. It must be at least a quarter of a century since these two men sat down among us and united their labors with ours in pushing forward the work of improvement. And nobly and manfully did they do their work, closing their labors only with the closing hour of their lives. One day early in July just passed, I was driving from Fostoria to this village, and met Mr. Sperry, also driving his team; he seemed hale and vigorous, cheerful and active as I had known him in the years of the past. It was the last time I ever saw his honest face; perhaps in less than an hour from that moment, in returning homeward, near the spot where I met him, his team took fright and dashed him to death. Scarcely had the startling news died away, when it was heralded that old Mr. Chaplain, while in the act of carrying a pail of water had dropped down dead; "Heart disease" was the verdict, though why should we wonder that after 84 years of active service the wheels of life should at last stand still. Thus ended the earthly career of two of Watertown's most respected pioneers.

How often do we see the world run wild over some military chieftain, whose only merit is that he has steeped the earth in the blood of his fellow beings. In this connection let us call to mind the language of the poet:

> "A wit's a feather and a chief's a rod,
> An honest man's the noblest work of God."

But I must return to linger a little while with our primeval forests. Thirty years ago to-day there was not a white settler in Watertown. From one extremity to the other it was clad in a garb of almost the heaviest timber that I ever saw. Here grew the beech in the greatest perfection I ever saw it in any country. Here too were found the different varieties of maple in perfection. Oak was not abundant, but the rock elm and the linden or bass-wood were abundant, and of the finest quality. On interval lands the black ash and the American elm towered side by side in nature's grandest form.

Here, too, the poet Burns might have embraced his "Highland Mary" beneath the "Gay Green Burk" (or birch), but the "Hawthorn Blossom" was rarely if ever found. A few swamps of cedar of the most impenetrable character made a safe home for the owl, the wolf, and the wildcat. Along the gentle hillsides the dark green hemlock cast its sombre shadow—while towering high over all waved and murmured the green branches of the magnificent pine. I will not stop to weary you with details of height, diameter, and circumference, but will say that during a lifetime spent largely in the midst of pine timber I have seldom if ever seen the pine of Watertown equaled, and certainly never surpassed.

Why is it that the denizen of the forest loves his toil? Why is it that he shrinks from no hardships and murmurs at no privation? It is that he is brought in daily and hourly contact with the scenery of nature where he imbibes

> "Health in the gale and freshness on the stream."

He takes the blessings of nature from the fountain head. The late William S. Patrick, of Flint, widely and well known as an adroit and accomplished woodsman, once assured me that "he never in his life spent a long day in the woods." Beguiled by the presence of the ever varying works of God the forest dweller drinks in inspiration from the works of nature by which he is surrounded. The poet Armstrong in speaking of the atmosphere of the crowded city says:

> "It is not air
> That from a thousand lungs wreaks back to thine."

The blind poet Ossian, when reclining on the mossy banks of his native highland, drank in inspiration from "the sounding woods of Garmallar," which gave to his wild, weird songs a freshness that will go with them while poetry shall be read and time shall endure.

But to, return. It was thirty years ago the 20th of last April when Marcus Tetesouth, Alfred Fox and myself left our camps in Millington, and with our packs and equipage climbed the rugged hills and threaded the ravines along the section line west of Watertown center. That night we slept in an Indian wigwam on section 21, and near the line now dividing the farms of Mr. Hoyle and Didymer Johnson. Our next night we slept on the north bank of Elm creek, a little below the Fostoria brick yard, on land now owned by Linus Hart. But why pursue our journey further, now that my comrades are gone. For the past twenty seven years Alfred Fox has slept in the Goodrich cemetery, and Marcus Tetesouth has reposed in the Millington cemetery for a dozen years at least. My own wanderings have been long and weary to bring me here in your presence to-day.

It was late in September 1854, when in company with Nathaniel M. Berry, the first settler of Watertown, and nearly a dozen other adventurers I came clambering and blundering through windfalls and cedar swamps, from the old Farrell saw mill in Marathon to the quarter post between sections 26 and 25, and one half mile west from the present village of Fostoria. Several of the company after making choice selections of land left them never more to return, with a solemn conviction that town 10 north, range 9 east, was too far from paradise; and of the whole company Squire Berry was the only one that ever perfected his claim and made a home of it, myself excepted. Between that late September evening and the close of the year, so far as the best date can be gathered, there was but one more actual settlement perfected in Watertown and that by a genius known as "Trait Crosby," who staked his claim where Henry Kincaid now lives, on the southeast corner of section 25, one mile east of Fostoria. He remained but a short time and like the wind that "bloweth where it listeth," no one knew when e'er he came or whither he went.

Several cabins were erected in October. Franklin Wright and Alphant Glynn who came together from Ohio, and Samuel McNeil and his son "Perry" from Genesee county in this state, were among the very first beginners, but their cabins remained empty until the following spring. The advent of 1855 brought with it a swarm of settlers and from that period onward Watertown has been getting out of the woods. If her citizens are worthy of their opportunity, health and prosperity, wealth and happiness lie along their future pathway. As to myself, I feel that my earthly journey is drawing to its close. One week ago last Monday I passed my seventy first mile stone. My life was begun and my youth spent in the wilds of western New York. Emigrating to Michigan in 1836, when it was a territory, the years of my mature manhood were spent in the county of Genesee, and for the last quarter of a century I have looked upon Watertown as my home. And as I look back over my past life my greatest satisfaction is derived from the thought that I have helped to cause the wilderness of three new counties "to bud and blossom as the rose," and my greatest regrets for the future arise from the fact that it is not for me to settle and improve a few more counties.

THE SCHOONER MINK, AND OTHER ITEMS

BY EPHRAIM S. WILLIAMS, OF FLINT

In a former article, where I spoke of our family (the family of Oliver Williams) coming to Detroit in the autumn of 1815 on board of the schooner Mink, I overlooked an incident relating to the Mink that I think should not be passed by.

The schooner Mink (report said) was built upon Lake Superior, by the Hudson Bay company, for the transportation of their goods and furs up and down that lake. The Mink, by accident or otherwise, ran the rapids of the Sault Ste. Marie safely, and for many years ran on the lower lakes. I remember hearing it said that she was driven down the Sault river in a gale of wind. It seems impossible, when one stands and sees the Indians run those rapids, with their canoes, requiring the greatest skill to clear the rocks in safety, yet the schooner Mink made the trip without touching a rock. Perhaps no other animal but a "Mink" could have succeeded as well, being a water animal. I must say we thought very poorly of her as a passenger vessel in 1815, for her accommodations were very poor indeed; the cabin was only four or five feet high and we could not stand upright in it, and the bilge water scented the cabin awfully, so bad that the family camped on the deck under a tent made with sails that the captain was kind enough to furnish us.

In the days when the Pontiac railroad was run (or walked) by a single horse, there was an old couple who took passage from Pontiac for Detroit. Mr. Alfred Williams, called Salt Williams, was on board the train. The old lady became fatigued and, addressing Mr. Williams, not knowing he was one of the proprietors of the road, she remarked that they went very slowly and she would like to know when they would get to Detroit. Mr. Williams (Salt) stuttered badly, and he replied to the old lady as follows, "I don't k-k-now if we e-v-e-r shall g-e-t there; a sh-o-r-t time ago a cou-p-le about m-m-i-dd-le age tried it and they d-d-i-e-d of old age before they got to D-d-e-troit, and I g-g-u-ess we sha-ll." The old lady said she thought it was about so.

Mr. Williams had a splendid white horse that all delighted to drive, especially the ladies. When Mr. Schuyler Hodges died, in 1845, Mr. (Salt) Williams proposed that his white horse be put before the hearse at the funeral as he was not only handsome but a great favorite of all the family and friends. This was done, and when the funeral procession was about twenty rods from the house the horse stopped and refused to move another step. Mr. Williams tried every way to have him proceed, but no, he would not stir. A man was sent to the livery stable to get another horse to take the place of the white one, and the procession had to wait for the change.

I have heard it said that some horses will not go in front of a hearse, and old Charley was one of that kind. Mr. Williams coaxed and patted him, but it was no go; he would look around, shake his head, and refuse to move; when he was unhitched he walked out and was all right. Mr. Hodges was a particular friend of the horse, he drove him frequently, and the old fellow did not propose to do that kind of duty.

FLINT TWENTY YEARS AGO

PRESENTED BY EPHRAIM S. WILLIAMS OF FLINT

"How wondrous are the changes,
Since twenty years ago."

Editor Citizen:—A little after the hour of noon, in one of the faultless autumnal days of which the denizens of Michigan are so proud, twenty years ago, I descended from a seat beside that loquacious Jehu, John Stevens, on one of the three great stages of Boss's line, on that day running between Fentonville and East Saginaw, at the door of the "Carlton house" in Flint, where I was met by the stately proprietor of the "line" with unlighted cigar between his lips and the genial presence of the landlord, John B. Hamilton.

Recalling vividly, after the lapse of two decades, my conflicting emotions as I stood among strangers in the little place which I had chosen for my future home and with whose interests, mercantile and social, I was destined to become identified for so long a period, and of my impressions of the place then, and of the place and people as my acquaintance with both increased, it seemed a fitting time—and perhaps not entirely without interest—to revive some of the old recollections, and conjure into our presence some of the faces and forms which long ago were familiar in various situations in life and helped to make up the society of this newly dubbed city.

Entering the city on my elevated seat, my first impressions of Saginaw street were more favorable than had my advent occurred two or three years earlier, for the devastation caused by the fires on either side had been in part overcome by the erection of the block north of Kearsley street, including the Citizens' bank buildings and the Dewey block. The Williams' block on the northeast corner of Kearsley street was completed and the postoffice, with E. S. Williams as postmaster, located in the rear, was proud of its new and first display of letter drawers and boxes; W. I. Beardsley occupying a corner with the first "news depot." The Presbyterian and old Episcopal churches were well up town and Dr. Willett felt little apprehension of being elbowed out of home by business encroachments. Since that day the vacancy south of the Dewey block has been filled, the entire block below Union street built and the block of fine shops between the railroad track and river, the entire block south of First street to the Presbyterian church, the row below Union street on the east, except the old Thurber block, the entire row of fine buildings between Kearsley and First streets on the east, except the City hotel and the two stores of James Decker and Charles Harrison, the Bishop block above the old Hazelton building, the Gazley block, Bishop's, Judd's and Pratt's fine stores and the Charles block, between First and Second streets and covering the ground of the old Gazley rookery, the Rev. D. E. Brown's residence and the old Episcopal church; and since the fire, which wiped out the "Irving," the splendid blocks which include the four story Masonic Temple and the adjoining new hotel, besides several brick stores between Second and Third streets, the city hall, court house, etc. So much for Saginaw street.

The Williams block spoken of above was built by E. S. Williams and was the first block of brick stores of three stories built in Flint in 1853-4. All business except in the mills was confined to Saginaw street. And how changed the business personæ of the city! Before the advent of Smith or Judd or Stone; of Spencer, or Davidson, or McIntyre!

Then James Henderson was the oldest and best known merchant, and Dewey & Crosman had but recently issued their "New Store" ad, while "Cotharin's" was still the place to find whatever could not be found elsewhere. The farmer, driving into the city with his load of produce, could seek his own market unmolested, for the present custom of buying on the street was not seen, and Henderson's or Dewey's, Grant Decker's, O'Donoughue's, Fox's, or the mill, comprised nearly the limit of the market facilities. Old residents will easily recall the trains of Indian ponies laden with maple sugar, or baskets, or blackberries, the entire stock of which it was confidently expected Charley Dewey or Cotharin would buy. These were all general stores and sold anything from nails to a lace shawl. H. C. Walker and Morrison were also engaged in the dry goods trade; Jas. C. Decker, W. R. Hubbard (son of Diodate Hubbard, one of Oakland's pioneers) and J. H. Townsend dealt more exclusively in groceries; and Forsyth, Higgins and Paul Stewart confined their trade to hardware and stoves. The Clarks, Frank Frary, Wesson, Witherbee and Dr. Moon furnished the drugs, while Drs. Lamond, Drake, Clark, and the new fledged M. D.'s, Axford and Wilson, helped to dispense them, Dr. Eldridge being the only homœopathic practitioner at that time, and Drs. Smith and Rea pulled teeth. W. L. Sholes, Dewstoe, Ford, Sutton and Lee were knights of the shears and tape measure; and Joe Cauffman and Lieberman sold clothing ready made. Barker & Ripley, John Quigley, A. L. Stewart and John Delbridge cared for the shoeless, while Skidmore crowned the head and Uncle Dave Mather the hands. True, and Beecher and Lounsbury supplied the necessary articles of jewelry and kept old Time's implements in order, while Stevenson added to these useful employments the pleasant duty of supplying the mental food for old and young to be found in books. Holmes, Charles, Miller and Sullivan supplied the houses with furniture, while George Hill furnished in addition the last narrow tenement the citizen required and Johnson placed at the head the marble slab which told their virtues. Gazley, Pursell, Knickerbocker and Vassault harnessed the horses and Pruman and Wicks shod them. E. H. Hazelton and A. W. Brockway discounted the western money for you, and Fenton, Newton, Davis, Thomson Howard, Carr, Chauncey Wisner, O. Adams, C. K. Williams, George K. Cummings *et al.* read the law for a consideration; Charles Hascall dispensed justice and Charley Griswold and Jake Farley served the papers. Very many incidents of those days, though not very remote to many of the older citizens remaining, come to one's mind, of which space forbids the mention; and one recalls the familiar faces of many then daily seen on the streets who have forever passed from our view (and whose absence which twenty years may effect) each with his peculiar characteristics, and with whose name is associated some reminiscence of early days of the little city; the dignified Fenton and the courteous Avery, the brusque Benj. Pierson, the facetious George Cumings, the genial Roosevelt, the shrewd Gregory, the Hendersons, the Walkers, C. S. Payne, Witherbee, Crapo, Robert Page, R. W. Jenny and

George Crocker. Then the "Pinery" (now 4th ward) had just been cleared of its trees, and a few scattering houses stood in that now populous ward. The site of the Thayer house was then the abode of Ross's stage horses. All west of the Baptist church, save two or three little dwellings, was a broad cow pasture, the entire suburbs much less extended, and the population but about one third its present number.

I trust I have not occupied too much space in these imperfect recollections of twenty years ago.

I do not claim for them absolute accuracy, and mention only such names as readily came to my mind."

This "Twenty Years Ago" must have been written twenty or thirty years ago, and more have been the changes and improvements since that time. The Carleton House he mentions was, afterwards, the Irvin, and was burned with all the buildings on that side of the street from the Williams corner (which still stands), to the river. These have been since rebuilt, with fine brick buildings for business, to the river, and the beautiful new iron bridge over the river on Saginaw street.

In the spring of 1855 the first charter election was held and Grant Decker was elected the first mayor. That spring we had unusually high water. There was a very handsome enclosed bridge (painted white), a noble structure, but the water raised it from its foundation, and it swung around, end to the stream, and floated down stream majestically, more like a large noble steamer than a bridge. The entire population of the city was on hand to witness the departure of our noble bridge. The water at this time was up to and over Union street to the Masonic temple and Brant house, and where now the F. & P. M. R. R. depot stands and the Thayer house is the water was up to the middle of the windows of several residences. All had to move out of their dwellings. The river was crossed for a long time by a boat ferry. The west side of Saginaw street from Walker's corner was burned to the river. It was soon rebuilt with very fine two story wooden buildings, mostly all painted white and making a good appearance when finished and occupied for business. Fire again burned it all out nearly to the river, then it was rebuilt with brick as at present, and thus we have progressed.

Notwithstanding all these disasters we had lots of fun and many laughable incidents—which cannot well be laid before the public—yet the few left now have many a good hearty laugh over those times, and enjoy talking them over frequently.

RETROSPECTION

BY EPHRAIM S. WILLIAMS, OF FLINT

[Incidents connected with the building of the old court house now (March 3, 1886), being torn down at Saginaw City; the contract for the erection of the building signed nearly half a century ago; the bids for doing the work, the name of the contractor, etc.]

Forty eight years ago to-morrow (March 3, 1886) marked the day that a contract was signed for the erection in Saginaw county of a building suitable to the needs and requirements of the county officials of that time. The day upon which this forty eighth anniversity may be recorded will also witness the destruction of the building. Workmen for the three weeks past have been engaged in tearing it down, and its forty eighth birthday may only be written on a pile of debris. This old structure to-day, as compared with the new building, which has been termed a "palace" and other synonymous names, dwindles into mere nothing; yet forty eight years ago, when the initial steps towards its construction were taken, it was regarded by those who were about to build it as a structure of which they could feel proud, and they undoubtedly did. Accustomed to meeting in private houses, in small, incommodious halls, it was no more than natural that they should regard the bundle of specifications, and not long after the building which grew out of them, with a smile of satisfaction.

From the dim and dusty records of the proceedings of the township board of nearly fifty years ago was learned a brief history of the preparations for the construction of the building. At a meeting of the board held on the 2d day of March, 1838, a resolution that a building for the use of county officials be constructed was introduced. There were present at this meeting, Jeremiah Riggs, a supervisor; A. Ure and A. Miller, two justices of the peace; and E. S. Williams, the township clerk. Those five persons laid the plans for the building that has served the county for so many years. Many old residents will remember the forms and faces of those five persons. References are not at hand at present to say much of these early incidents. E. S. Williams, brother of Gardner D. Williams, now deceased, is still living. In the early days he was a prominent resident of Saginaw City and county. He has been spoken of in connection with Harvey Williams, the pioneer, whose popularity is well remembered. Mr. Harvey Williams came to Saginaw many years after G. D. and E. S. Williams. Mr. E. S. Williams is now a resident of Flint, and recently passed his 84th birthday. He has accumulated enough of this world's goods to be able to live comfortably in his old age. He occasionally makes this city a visit and his cordial greeting always makes him welcome.

A. Miller refers to Judge Albert Miller, of Bay City, brother of Mrs. Jewett, of this city. Mr. Miller is too well known in this city to require much mention here. He was prominent in every movement of importance in the early days. Mr. Miller still visits his friends and acquaintances in this city. He has been spending some time of late in looking up documents pertaining to the early history of this State, which to him is always interesting.

Andrew Ure, a member of the township board, and who was active in building the old court house, was the father of Robert and John Ure, and was by occupation a farmer. He long since went "to that bourne from whence no traveler returns," but his name will always be remembered in connection with early events.

Of Jeremiah Riggs, whose name is also attached to the proceedings of the township board, but little is known. Suffice it to say, that his name is recorded with others whose deeds were honorable and advantageous to the early settlers. (Mr. Riggs was an early pioneer of Saginaw and Genesee counties, known as Judge Riggs.)

At the meeting spoken of above the bids for the construction of the county building were opened. There were four in all, as follows:

Asa Hill and Benjamin Stevenson	$11,500
W. L. P. Little	12,000
R. H. Burrdick	11,000
Bunker & Tuthill	11,950

It seems from the record that the bids in some manner were unsatisfactory to the board, for, on motion of Albert Miller, "the board proceeded to sell the contract for the erection of the building at auction, reserving all rights, etc." The record further shows, upon the yellow tinged pages, that Mr. W. L. P. Little was made the auctioneer, and was instructed not to receive any bid less than $2,500. On March 3d, forty eight years ago on Wednesday of this week, the auction took place, and the contract was "knocked down" to Asa Hill at $9,925. The work was commenced immediately, and the building completed in about a year.

During this time, in the month of October, occurred the death of the contractor, Mr. Hill. This necessitated some changes, the result of which was an agreement between his bondsmen and the township board to go on and finish the building.

This is a synopsis of how, when and by whom the old court house was erected. Since that time many varied scenes have been enacted beneath its roof. Its walls have looked down upon a court of law and justice, upon the disturbed atmosphere of a democratic or republican convention, upon public meetings called for the discussion of events of public importance, and lastly upon a scene of happiness and sociability such as the Kermis, held two or three months ago afforded. A more fitting scene for a building that for half a century had served the public, could not have been selected. Its outlines will always occupy a place in the minds of the citizens of this city.

The subject of building a new court house was agitated for years before any movement of prominence was taken. The subject was brought to the notice of the board of supervisors by the members from East Saginaw, who, representing their city, liberally offered to build a $100,000 court house for the county if the people of the county would consent to the removal of the county seat to the other side of the river. The removal of the county seat, the people of this city, it is quite superfluous to say, would not hear to, but the citizens not willing to be outdone, immediately took action and through the council, made a similar offer to the board, that they would erect for the county a $100,000 court house. The proposition was considered by the board, and caused at the time some warm arguments from both sides. A vote decided, however, that Saginaw should have it. On March 14, 1882, the legislature passed an act enabling this city to issue bonds for a sum not exceeding $100,000 for the purpose above mentioned.

On April 6, 1882, a special election was held to give the citizens of this city an opportunity to express their free opinion regarding the step about to be taken. The election resulted in 860 yeas and 52 nays. A contract was made between the city and the board of supervisors and the way seemed clear.

But an entirely unlooked for obstacle soon arose. East Saginaw individuals seeing that Saginaw City was rapidly getting the best of the bargain, sued out an injunction restraining the further progress of the work. The litigation that followed brought to light some irregularities which rendered void everything that had been transacted. On March 13, 1883, the legislature passed another act in the matter. On May 10, 1883, another election was held, which resulted in a vote of 350 to 37. The work was again taken up, the bonds were issued, the bids advertised for and a contract let to Dawson & Anderson at $92,713, upon plans drawn by architect F. W. Hollister. Mr.

Hollister was also appointed by the committee as supervising architect. Ground was broken in September, 1883. The corner stone was laid with imposing ceremonies on the 28th of May, 1884. The stone occupies a conspicuous position on the east corner of the court house. It is a fine sandstone block 37 inches square and 24 inches thick. It bears the inscription in old English letters, "Saginaw County Court House, A. D. 1884," on one side, and on the other, "F. W. Hollister, architect; Dawson & Anderson, builders."

The plans and specifications as prepared by Mr. Hollister were carried out to the end, with but very few changes, and those of minor importance, and right here we wish to congratulate this genial and whole souled gentleman, upon the success he scored in drawing these plans. His plans have been perfect and the representation of them that now occupies the most prominent block in the city is, we think, all that the citizens of this city could wish them to be. Since planning this official palace, Mr. Hollister has achieved many triumphs throughout the state of Michigan, among which may be mentioned the capturing of the $1,000 prize for presenting the best prepared plans for the new "Soldiers' Home." Mr. Hollister also prepared the plans for the new Presbyterian church, recently dedicated, and also for the M. E. church. Several private residences finished and in progress also mark the popularity that ingenuity and sound ideas are bringing to this gentleman in his chosen profession. Mr. Hollister also drew the specifications for the furniture, of which mention shall be made further on. A full description of the building is too lengthy for the society's records; yet it's a very fine and beautiful building, costing $112,000.

Mr. Asa Hill, spoken of as the contractor of the old court house of forty eight years ago, who died October, 1838, was brother-in-law of E. S. Williams, they marrying sisters. Mrs. Hill, in after years, married Mr. Royal W. Jenny, of Flint, who died February 12, 1876, leaving a widow and two children, a son and daughter. Mrs. Jenny resides in Flint, and with her, the unmarried daughter. Her son is married, has two children, and resides in Walkerville, Ont. Mr. Jenny was born January 13, 1812. Mr. Jenny was proprietor and editor of the "Genesee Democrat," which is still published in Flint.

Mrs. Jenny is the only survivor of a large family that came to Michigan the spring of 1822 in the steamer Superior, her grandfather and wife, Mr. Janess Harrington, her father and mother and four sisters and three brothers, herself making a family of eight children. Mr. Harrington purchased a farm of 160 acres near Auburn, Oakland Co., a beautiful place, where he lived and died. He also purchased a tract of land of the government, in the township of Farmington, for the purpose of giving each grandchild 160 acres as a marriage gift, which he did while he lived. Grandfather Harrington was born January 27, 1763, and died Oct 13, 1825. He was a soldier of the Revolution seven years, most of the time with Gen. Washington's army. He married Martha Gould, in Vermont, March 13, 1785; who was born July 8, 1766, and died Oct., 1829, near the old homestead in Oakland county, at one of her granddaughter's, Mrs. Horace Johnson.

INDIAN DEEDS OF REAL ESTATE

[From the Detroit Evening News, May 5, 1885.]

Miss Ouellette, of Windsor, is at work in the Wayne county register of deeds' office making a transcript of the original deeds of land, dating from the Indian grants in 1770-76 to later dates. The old records are remarkably well preserved and the penmanship forms excellent specimens of chirography. The documents are in French, and the names appearing speak the antiquity of many of the families now prominent in Detroit. A number of the land grants made out by the aboriginal occupants of the soil are signed by the Indian chiefs, hieroglyphics taking the place of signature, the settler or official writing the name underneath. One chief deeds a strip of land, and scratches what is supposed to represent the sum. Another chief, known as "Kegon," makes some wandering European happy by affixing the figure of a fish to the conveyance of a strip of land. "McKaugh" scrawls the figure of a bear, while "Wawaskeisch" appends a flying deer, suggestive of the fleeting nature of the land claimed for centuries as his inheritance.

"The curious often ask why the land in this vicinity was laid out in such narrow strips, running from one to three miles back from the river," remarked James A. Visger, deputy register of deeds. "The fact is the early settlers were afraid to separate themselves for fear of attack from their many foes. As a consequence they would negotiate with the chiefs for from 600 to 1,200 or 1,500 feet frontage on the river, running for miles back. This gave them sufficient territory, besides an equitable division of the river front, and secured them the advantage of mutual protection. The purchase price of this valuable property would astonish you. A horse, a rifle, a half dozen blankets, even a drink of whisky, would purchase miles of land. Frequently the transfers were the results of friendship without compensation."

"How do the records of Michigan lands interest the Canadian authorities?"

"The deeds now being copied cover both sides of the river. The records were captured by the British in the war of 1812, and by a subsequent understanding between the Canadian parliament and congress they were returned to Detroit, it being understood that our friends across the water should have access at any time to the documents."

EARLY HISTORY OF ELISHA W. RUMSEY, ONE OF THE FOUNDERS OF ANN ARBOR

BY A. D. P. VAN BUREN

It may be well to state here the historic fact that Elisha Rumsey and John Allen, with their wives, both of whose first names were Ann, were the founders of Ann Arbor. The Elisha Rumsey of Ann Arbor fame was only known in his early life in New York as Walker Rumsey, having assumed the name Elisha after he came to Michigan. Why he changed his name the following letter from G. M. Peck to T. B. Lord, from whom I received most of this reminiscence, will explain. It is said now that Rumsey's full name was Elisha Walker Rumsey:

East Bethany, N. Y., *February 14, 1881.*

Friend Lord: Yours of the 26th of December was duly received. I was so busy that I did not get posted in your matter for some time. Walker Rumsey was a resident of Bethany in 1817 (or before), and lived in a log house on the Joel Miner farm, near the "poppe tree" on the ridge south of the road. This poplar tree is thus accounted for: An old Indian stuck a cane, cut from a limb of a poplar tree, into the ground at this place, and it grew into this tree. The house was afterwards burnt. Rumsey then went from there to the "Corners," and you know his wife died there. In 1818 he bought wheat at 31 cents a bushel, had it floured at the Tomlinson Mills, and shipped to Albany by a six horse team. The next winter, 1818, he bought pork at Canadea and packed it. Rodney Taylor helped him cut and pack it, and send it to Albany. In this way he became acquainted with Trotter & Co., the firm in Albany who bought his pork, and who sent him $3,000 to buy cattle with. He advertised for the farmers to bring in their cattle on specified days at the center of Bethany and Stafford, but *he* failed to appear. Some time before this his wife and he had become acquainted with Ann Sprague, a grass widow of prepossessing attractions. Now, Rumsey, after receiving the $3,000, went with Ann Sprague to Canada with his pockets full of money. After getting there he found, if caught in that country, it would be worse for him than if caught in the states; hence, *he now starts for Michigan.* A young lawyer in Batavia got wind of his movements, and went to Albany. Trotter came back with him, and they pursued and found Rumsey, and took him to Albany, leaving Ann in old Gen. Isaiah Churchill's home. On reaching Albany the matter was personally arranged, and Rumsey came back to Bethany. Soon after this he was reärrested, taken to Albany, and locked up again. Esquire Churchill went to Albany, and Rumsey, who owned the Taylor farm at the time, turned that out, which, with Churchill's security, released him. After this he lived with Ann Sprague as his wife.

Public opinion was so strong against both him and his wife that *they pulled up and went to Michigan.*

Capt. Taylor, an old man now in his eightieth year, and from whom Mr. Peck got most of this sketch of Walker Rumsey's early life, says that Ann Sprague was a smart, fine looking woman, had lived in his home and was kind in caring for Mrs. Taylor while she was sick with the dropsy. Thus it turns out that Elisha Rumsey, one of the founders of Ann Arbor, was *Walker* Rumsey, of Bethany, Genesee county, N. Y., whose escapade with Ann Sprague we have given. Mr. T. B. Lord, now of Comstock, Kalamazoo county, had previously given the writer of this paper the same account of Walker Rumsey as Mr. Peck and Mr. Taylor have given in this letter, which they afterwards sent, by his request, to him. Mr. Lord also says that Walker Rumsey's brother Henry came to Michigan, and became surveyor general of the new territory. The writer of this sketch has not written it for any other purpose than to subserve the purposes of history in giving a faithful portrait of E. W. Rumsey, although we were compelled, as Cromwell compelled the artist, to "paint him, warts and all." By Rumsey's dropping the name *Walker,* which was in bad repute in New York, and assuming the name Elisha, he got out from under a cloud and had a clear sky in Michigan.

ALL ABOUT A MARRIAGE LICENSE

BY COL. HENRY RAYMOND

The Tribune of Jan. 21, 1885, contains an interesting narrative of events by "Pioneer" that brings to mind a certain event of nearly the same period, somewhat in the same line, and the writer only regrets he does not possess the happy faculty of narration of "Pioneer."

It was in 1832, the writer was resident in a very sparsely settled town in Wayne county, and at a township meeting had the honor of being elected town clerk. Not long subsequently he was called upon by a young, green looking fellow who demanded a marriage license, and was told that he did not require such a document. He, however, insisted that he did, for a minister had refused to marry him without and the license he must have. The official being green in office, was not in his own mind positive that the fellow was not right. But what sort of a paper to make him next puzzled his brain. He had no idea what the law required in the way of examination of the applicant, but proceeded thus:

"What is your name?"

"Joseph Streight."

"Your age?"

"Seventeen."

"The woman's name?"

"Betsey Bates."

"Age?"

"Thirty seven."

"When is the wedding to take place?"

"Next Sunday."

"Well, I will make out the paper and leave it at the postoffice for you Saturday. I must look at the law."

"All right," he says, "only be sure to do it."

The writer had a neighbor friend, who had been a justice of the peace; a comical fellow, who pretended to know more than he really did, but I went to him for counsel. Said I, "Is a man required to have a license from the town clerk to get married?" He believed there was such a law but did not think people paid much attention to it. "Well," I said, "a party has applied and insisted on having one and I don't know the first word of a form or what the law requires."

"O," said he, "never mind that. You know that, here in the woods, if we want a thing and haven't got it we make it, and I'll help you make the thing."

After a good deal of racking of brains and waste of ink and paper the following comical document came forth, written in bold hand, covering a whole page of foolscap. (It was arranged that I should write what my friend dictated):

"In the name of the sovereign people of the territory of Michigan, and in accordance with the laws enacted by the government and council, and approved by the president of the United States of America; and

"Whereas, one Joseph Streight proposes to marry one Betsey Bates, and the said people have sworn by the holy St. John and the big horn spoon there is no legal impediment to the contrary;

"Now, therefore, this is to permit the said Joseph to be joined in holy wedlock to the said Betsey, and may the Lord have mercy on his soul.

"Given under my hand at M———, this — day of ———, 1832. R———, Clerk."

About twenty five years after the foregoing the writer was introduced in the corridor of the state house at Lansing, to Rev. Mr. B., of Albion. The reverend gentleman scanning the writer closely for a moment, said: "Are you Mr. R., who a long time since lived in the town of M., Wayne county?" "I am." "Was you town clerk?" "Yes, why?" "I was then just commencing to preach; was filling an appointment in a little log school house in what was known as the Mud street settlement. After the service I was approached by a rustic lad with an application to perform the marriage ceremony. 'Yes;' I said, 'if it is close by.' 'O,' he replied, 'my gal is here and we'll have the job done right now, and here is my license.' Well, by the time I had read that unique document (which I still keep and laugh over with my clerical brethren as a relic of pioneer days and its many crudities) and partially recovered from the convulsive laughter it occasioned, the parties came in and were duly spliced."

"Now, Mr. B.," said I, "did you not preach your first public sermon one warm summer day in the shade of some trees near the residence of a family by the name of Bird, in that same settlement?" "I think that is so."

"Yes, and I was present; thought you rather green but would improve by practice. Good day, elder!"

LEGENDS OF INDIAN HISTORY IN SAGINAW VALLEY

BY EPHRAIM S. WILLIAMS, OF FLINT

I notice with pleasure an article upon the defeat and extermination of the Socks from the Saginaw country by the Chippewas and other tribes, which I have always understood to be the fact, and Saginaw derives its names from the fact of its having been the Socks' country, the Indian name being Saw-gee-nong, meaning the Socks' country, also as regards their superstitions and notions that the country they had captured from the Socks was haunted by the *Mun-e-soos* or bad spirits of the Socks, or in their phrase, the bad Indians. I will give a little of my experience of twelve years' residence among them.

The fact is, they carried their fears and superstitions to a very great length and at many times to their very great loss of property. Many of their frights I have witnessed and have tried to persuade them otherwise, but to no purpose, they having so long been deluded.

There was a time, every spring, when the Indians from Saginaw and the interior, would congregate in large parties upon the Saginaw bay for the purpose of putting up large quantities of dried sturgeon, which made a very delicate dish when properly cooked and was much used in those days, by the first families in Detroit. At the Point Au Gres, so called in those days, being a shallow point making out into the bay, with a smooth limestone bottom, the sturgeon would run up the smooth point in large numbers, working up until quite up shore, and lie like floating cord wood. The Indians camped here on the point and would select the best at their leisure, flay them, hang them across poles in rows about four feet from the ground and the rows about two or three feet apart. Then a gentle smoke was kept under them until perfectly dry. A common sized sturgeon, when flayed, would be about the size of an ordinary deer skin. When dry they were folded and packed in nice packages for keeping for their summer use and for market. About the time this is accomplished the *Mun-e-soos,* more properly poor, lazy, worthless Indians, would come from a distance, having an eye to supplying themselves with provisions they never labored to obtain, except by theft. They (the Socks) would now commence, in different ways, to excite their own fears that the *Mun-e-soos* were about their camps, by firing guns at night in the woods in the rear of their camps, and also dropping a certain painted kind of quills near their camps so the children and women would find them. These were certain indications their enemies were near at hand. After a few nights, they became so frightened, they would take to their canoes and flee, leaving many times almost everything they possessed, fleeing for the Saginaw river. The *Mun-e-soos* or robbers would then rob their camps of what they wanted and escape to their homes, with perhaps their summer supplies of fish and often sugar and dried venison. They rarely if ever took any articles of property, as it might lead to discovery and detection.

Being the time of year I usually made my annual trips along the bay and lake shore, looking after our spring trade and collection of furs, going as far as Thunder bay and looking after our trading post at the Sable river, where we kept three men during the winter, at these times I have often met them fleeing as above mentioned, sometimes twenty or more canoes. I have stopped them and tried to induce them to return, and we would go with them; but no, it was the *Mun-e-soos*, and nothing would convince them differently, and away they would go frightened almost to death.

I have visited their deserted camps at such times, gathered up their effects that were left, and secured them in some one camp or lodge from the destruction of wild animals. After a time they would return and save what was left. During these times they were perfectly miserable, actually afraid of their own shadow. At other times, having a little bad luck in trapping or hunting, they would become excited, and often say game has been over and in their traps and they don't catch anything—have known them to go so far as to insist that a beaver or an otter has been in their traps and has gotten out, or was let out by the *Mun-e-soos*, or that their traps are bewitched or spell bound by the "bad Indians," that their rifles have been charmed by the *Mun-e-soos* and they can't kill anything. Then they must give a great feast and have the medicine man or conjurer, and through his wise and dark performances the charm is removed, and all is well again; traps and rifles do their duty, and the poor beaver, otter, deer, bear, etc., again suffer, much to the profit of the traders and pleasure of the Indians. These things have been handed down for generations.

I have had them come frequently miles, bringing their rifles to me, asking me to examine and re-sight them, declaring the sights had been moved, and in most instances they had (but by themselves in their fright). I always did, when applied to, re-sight and try them until they would shoot correctly, and they would go away cheerful and thankful. I would tell them they must keep their rifles and traps where the *Mun-e-soos* could not find them. They never forgot these little favors, but would bring me some choice present, such as beaver's tails, which are a most delicate dish, and often a nice fat ham of venison. The reason for their coming to me was that I always kept a splendid rifle and was considered a good marksman. The young hunters would come and practice shooting at a mark with me. I have spent hours in shooting with them. They thought it very strange I would beat them shooting off hand, and they always resting their rifles. I have practiced with hundreds of them and never found an Indian I could not beat at any distance. This fact made me quite popular with them. I have often attended their feasts by invitation. These are always conducted with much solemnity, and the invited guest or guests are always seated at the head of the feast, and the head of the animal cooked for the feast is always placed in a dish before the guest. Sometimes it is a bear, deer, coon, or dog, a dog, being esteemed the greatest delicacy of them all. They usually at these feasts, after the table is cleared away, close with what is called a pouch dance, which is a very solemn affair, but very amusing to the invited guests, the guests never being allowed any part therein.

I meant to have mentioned an incident, which was very amusing. When the sturgeon run up on Point Au Gres as spoken of, some of them are very large and lie quite stupid. A young Indian, a little fellow, would wade in, straddle one of these, strike his tomahawk into its nose, and away the sturgeon goes full speed through the water, the young Indian guiding him by the handle of the tomahawk until fatigued, then runs him ashore, to the amusement of lookers on, the young fellow receiving many cheers.

Some of these fish are very large, often weighing one hundred pounds or more. The Indian name for sturgeon is *mon-e-meg.*

In Mr. Williams' "Personal Reminiscences," in vol. VIII of Pioneer Collections, he calls the evil spirits "manesous" and instead the Sock Indians, he calls them Sauks.

In Long's Chippewa vocabulary sturgeon is translated *onnemay* instead of *mon-e-meg.*

REMEMBRANCES OF EARLY DAYS

INDIANS AND AN INDIAN TRAIL—A TRIP FROM PONTIAC TO GRAND BLANC AND THE SAGINAWS

BY EPHRAIM S. WILLIAMS, OF FLINT

In the days past and gone, as we traveled from Pontiac to Grand Blanc and Saginaw, following the only road, the long traveled Indian trail, over the beautiful oak openings being burned over by the Indians, perfectly clean, and in June covered with beautiful flowers of almost all colors, it was like traveling through flower gardens—there could scarcely be anything more pleasant and beautiful. The openings were in gentle rolling swells, and from those you could look for miles in many places over the country, like looking through extensive orchards, and see deer, often in herds from ten to fifteen or twenty, feeding upon the acorns—nothing more beautiful.

Now the deer are killed or driven back, the beautiful openings cultivated, converted into splendid farms, and more sad, the old pioneers of those days, who toiled and suffered many privations of pioneer life, are almost all gone to their rest, but such is life.

Perhaps about half way, going towards the north, a few feet from the trail, were some very singular tracks, or what resembled tracks. The Indian legend was that an Indian warrior being shot on the brow of one of these ridges, ran down the slope, near the trail, making very long steps, or perhaps jumps, leaving deep impressions in the ground, the steps being from six to eight feet apart. Taking from seven to nine steps, then falling, his shoulder and hip made an impression in the ground. This was said to have been in some of the Indian wars, years and years before. These prints of feet and body were kept sacred by the Indians up to our day. They kept them free from leaves and clean for so many years they were worn down several inches. All Indians passing stopped and had certain ceremonies over them, and the young men would try and make the jumps from step to step. We almost always stopped and examined them. These steps and marks in the ground were preserved and kept as perfect as possible until the country became settled and made into beautiful farms.

A Mr. Brainerd, an early settler in the town of Grand Blanc, wrote a sketch of some of his pioneer life. He speaks of these steps (I quote his words): "When about half way to Pontiac from Grand Blanc a party of Indians were on their way to Detroit to engage in war. One Indian would not consent to fight on either side; of course he was shot. He reeled, and ran down the side of the trail, making nine tracks and falling upon his hip and shoulder. These were always called the 'Indian nine tracks.' I have been on the spot several times, and tried to go through the performance for the novelty of the thing. The trail and steps were quite deep, and the 'nine tracks' were all very plain to be seen in 1834."

I will mention another incident of an Indian legend which Mr. Brainerd mentions. He says: "There was a hole dug and stoned up, about four feet deep, and two feet or more across, one mile from my place, on the bank of Thread river. Report has it that in 1812 the Indians took a white man prisoner at Detroit, and brought him out here, dug and stoned up this hole, then placed the man in it and burned him. The stones show the effect of fire. I have been at the place often; it could not have been dug for a well, for the Indians never take the trouble to dig for water."

Mr. Brainerd more than probably formed a wrong opinion of the stone well being made to burn a prisoner in. I think I can solve the problem more satisfactorily about the use of the well. I have seen many such places. The Indians dig them, stone them up, or throw stones in loose, then build heavy fires in the pit, heating the stones as hot as possible. They then fill the pit, over the heated stones, with a certain kind of roots, cover them over tight; the hot stones cook the roots, for several days, which prepares them for food. Some of these roots are very poisonous in their natural state, but after this cooking they make a safe and good food. This, I am satisfied from experience, was the use made of the well, instead of burning white men, as Mr. Brainerd says. I have eaten the roots spoken of, in the Indian camps, and they were very palatable.

Many of our early settlers formed very strange ideas of the Indian character, and their doings, which has caused so many strange notions about the Indians by the early pioneers, and many of them have been handed down to the present time. I quote again from Mr. Brainerd:

"In the spring of 1833, on the first Monday in April, we held the first township meeting, at the center of the town of Grand Blanc, at the house of Rufus Stevens. J. R. Smith offered a resolution: Resolved, that we call this township 'Grand Blanc' (carried). Norman Davison was now elected supervisor; Jeremiah R. Smith, township clerk; Lyman Stow, Rufus Stevens and Charles Butler, assessors." (I wish to say here this Lyman Stow spoken of was the first postmaster in Flint. The mails were so small that Postmaster Stow carried the letters around in his hat and delivered them as he met his neighbors, and was looked upon as a great convenience.) "John Todd, Jonathan Dayton and Edmund Perry, commissioners of highways. The overseers of highways, district No. 1, George Oliver; No. 2, Jonathan Davison; No. 3, Norman Davison; No. 4, Ira Dayton; four districts extending to Saginaw, Fentonville, Lapeer and Pontiac. At this town meeting an amusing incident occurred. After the election was over one of the citizens being fired by the results of the day and a portion of whisky, mounted his horse and rode upon the stoop of the house to bid us good bye. The floor of the stoop gave way and precipitated horse and rider into the cellar; the cellar extended under the stoop. All these adventures helped to cheer the path of the pioneer."

July 8, 1833, we held another election for delegate to Congress for the county of Oakland. Austin E. Wing received 42 votes, William Trowbridge one vote, Lucius Lyon, 12 votes. For member of the legislature, Thomas I. Drake received 51 votes. Grand Blanc bears off the palm of all towns in the county for her first town meeting and county officers of the day. Mr. Brainerd continues: "This year, 1834, has been one of pain and sorrow for the pioneer in this part of Michigan. The spring seemed very backward. Emigration had become so great among us it settled our part of the town fast; a good many log houses had to be built and I think it caused sickness. The houses were made of green logs, and in the summer the sap in the logs soured and smelled offensively in hot days. Living and sleeping in them I think caused much sickness, such as fever and ague and chill fever; a number died of fever this fall."

There were hardly well ones enough to take care of the sick; those days were truly discouraging.

Mr. Brainerd says: "We had to send to Pontiac for all our groceries except a few articles. Soda for cake we made of cob ashes; our coffee is made out of burned bread; tea, sometimes out of sage leaves, and sometimes from sassafras root bark. Our sugar some of us made from our maple trees. Ginger we sent to Pontiac for, and often found it mixed with corn meal."

I will now continue my course towards Saginaw. Between Grand Blanc and Flint the Indian trail passed over a beautiful rise of ground, which the

Indians had cleared and surrounded with plum trees, which bore any amount of wild plums, red and yellow, the finest I ever saw. This spot was, perhaps, forty or fifty feet in diameter, the trail passing through nearly in the center of this beautiful, green grass spot, where all travelers, both white and Indian, stopped. The Indian always stopped, as it was a place of Indian worship. Beside the trail, nearly in the center of this spot, stood a very peculiarly shaped stone, perhaps four feet high, erected by the Indians as one of their idols or gods. They called it Bab-o-quah. They never allowed themselves to pass this stone without stopping and talking a lingo with their god and having a good smoke from the red pipe of peace and friendship. This was always a matter of worship, and conducted with much solemnity on their part.

As we journeyed to and from Saginaw we always arranged our time so as to stop, bait our ponies to the fine grass and refresh ourselves from our lunch baskets, which we always carried well supplied, we having a regular old fashioned pioneer sit down lunch party talk over, by telling some funny incident some of us had experienced. Talk of pioneer society meetings now a days! They are nothing to the enjoyment we took in those days, as I see it.

In the early days of 1823-4 Capt. Jacob Stevens located and built a log house in Grand Blanc, one of the first in the town, his son Rufus building the first. Looking about for stone for the back of his fire place (stone were very few and far between in those days), he came across the Indians' Bab-o-quah, or their god of worship, loaded it on his stone boat, drew it home and placed it in the back of his fire place. All went well for a time, but at last the Indians missed their idol, Bab-o-quah, and were quite excited about the loss. Searching about, they discovered where it was. They at once appointed a delegation to wait upon the captain and insisted upon his returning Bab-o-quah to its original position, saying to him that he had committed almost an unpardonable offense, and nothing would answer but returning the stone. The captain and family were a little uneasy, fearing some ugly fellow might do some harm. He offered to pay them to let him keep it, but no, never would they sell their fancied god, and he was obliged to take the stone from his fireplace and replace it where he found it, placing it in the same position, and at once. They named the captain from this transaction after the stone, Bab-o-quah, and he was known and went by that name as long as he lived and was known by that name throughout the land. The stone stood there afterwards until the land was purchased and made into farms. What became of it or who got Bab-o-quah I never knew, but presume some of the settlers got it and may have it still. If I ever knew the English of the word Bab-o-quah I have forgotten it.

I will mention another incident in this connection, which has just come to my mind. Sometime in the years 1836-37 or '39, I don't remember which, Col. David Stanard located on a farm on the Tittabawassee river. Mrs. Stanard and her daughter were in Pontiac on a visit, anxious to get home. Brother G. D. and myself were going to Pontiac with a double team on business. The Colonel wished we could bring his wife and daughter home with us. Mrs. Stanard applied to us at Pontiac, being anxious to get home, the winter being near its close. We said to Mrs. Stanard we feared we could not make it very comfortable for them, as we had about a load; she replied that she was anxious to get home, as it might be the last opportunity, as winter was about at an end. They would give us as little trouble as possible and could and would put up with all the inconveniences of the journey, having had some experience in settling in an early day on a farm near Pontiac, and keeping hotel in Pontiac in its earliest days. The Colonel's family being old friends and neighbors, we were willing to make an effort to comply with their wishes. Mrs. Stanard and daughter were perfect ladies and some of the noblest women of those pioneer days, or any other days. We therefore decided to take them and do the best we could to make them comfortable. The first night we stayed with my sister, Mrs. Rufus Stevens, at Grand Blanc. We started early the next morning, in hopes to get to Saginaw that day, but the sleighing not being good, we had to go slowly, night coming on when we were at what was then called Bird Run; now called County Line, a railroad station and quite a village with fine farms surrounding. We drove up on to a little rise of ground that was covered with a young growth of pines; we cleared away the snow under the pines and laid down plenty of pine boughs for a bed fountain. We had plenty of bedding, Mrs. Stanard having provided for an emergency of this kind, and with our own blankets we were well provided. Making a good fire and keeping it through the night, we made the ladies very comfortable. They were jolly and enjoyed the trip very much. Mrs. Stanard got out the lunch baskets, which were well supplied, and prepared a fine supper, which we all enjoyed after a hard day's travel. After the evening's chat, all retired, brother and myself keeping fire. The ladies said they rested very well. Next morning after taking breakfast we went on our way rejoicing and arrived at Saginaw before night. Col. Stanard had but the one daughter, a splendid young lady, who in after years became the wife of Morgan Drake, a lawyer in Pontiac, where they lived and died.

I often think how would the ladies of the present day like such traveling as our wives and daughters went through with and were obliged to, summer and winter, camping out at all times. There was some pioneer life about this I think, yet they all enjoyed it, and had any amount of fun.

The Colonel died, I think, on his farm on the Tittabawassee river; Mrs.

Stanard and daughter returned to Pontiac, lived and, in after years, passed away.

This Tittabawassee river in early days was called Tiffin river, named by the surveyors after Surveyor General Tiffin, of Ohio. The early settlers, not pleased with the name, changed it to the Indian name, Ta-tu-ba-war-say, the meaning of which is the river running around the shore—as it does make off around the Saginaw bay and Lake Huron.

REMEMBRANCES OF EARLY DAYS IN SAGINAW IN 1833

BY EPHRAIM S. WILLIAMS, OF FLINT

In those days there lived in Saginaw City an old Indian trader (then retired) by the name of John Baptiste Desnoyers. He became very much excited over stories the Indians had told him over and over again, that there were copper mines, very rich ones, far up Pine river in Gratiot county. He had several pieces of native copper, which the Indians had given him, which they said they obtained from the rocks, and they said the place was a secret and they dare not inform the white man where it was, for the Great Spirit had enjoined upon them secrecy, under penalty of some severe punishment. But Desnoyers worked upon one who professed to know all the secret by promise of presents, and paying him well if it proved a success. Under a solemn promise that he, Desnoyers, would never tell who gave him the information, the Indian agreed to pilot and go with Desnoyers to a spot near where the copper was. He could not go to the place, for he would be struck down by the Good Spirit, yet he would go so near as to point out or tell where to find the copper rock. After all this having been accomplished by Desnoyers in great secrecy, he came to me and gave me the secret as a confidential friend, and proposed that I should join him in the enterprise, and we would make an exploration privately.

I must say that I had very little faith in the story, knowing the Indian character and their strange ideas, but I could make the trip a business one, as we were going through a good country for trade with the Indians, therefore I went prepared to trade. We made our arrangements and in a few days started in a canoe, with our wise Indian for a guide up the Ta-ta-ba-wassay to Forks, thence to Pine river, far above the present St. Louis, in Gratiot county. It was tedious, for the stream was quite rapid, but at last we came to high bluff banks and some little indications of rocks and gravelly shore. The banks were perhaps from twenty to thirty or forty feet high, the shore was about twenty to thirty feet wide and in about the centre of it there was a large boulder. As we drew near this place our Indian became very nervous and uneasy, manifesting some fear. As we landed here our Indian said that in the high bank was the copper mine, but he could not and would not go any farther. He lay in the canoe a little farther down the stream from where we landed. We then went up and examined the surroundings, but could not find any indications or signs of mineral. We then examined the boulder and found it worn quite smooth by the Indians. It was a sacred Indian god, which they all stopped and worshiped by a speech and friendly smoke. They made speeches and left pieces of tobacco for the spirits to have a smoke. They also left other articles, and among them were pieces of copper, which we afterwards learned were cut from the copper boulder on the Ontonagon river, Lake Superior, by Indians. They looked upon them as sacred, and by leaving the pieces they dedicated them to their god, Boulder, and this was one cause of our informant's being so fearful of his being known, for probably he was one who robbed their god. The Indians are very peculiar in such matters, standing in great fear of offending the Good Spirit. This was the foundation of his story and trick upon Desnoyers.

We explored the high land back from the river, but did not find any rocks or indications of copper, but we found splendid farming land, which has since been converted into fine farms. Thus ended our early exploration for copper on Pine river, yet I made it a profitable trip, as I gathered many valuable furs, going prepared for trade. These rivers, in those days, abounded with Indians and game, and the Indians were good hunters and trappers. So ended one of many silly Indian humbugs.

Speaking of the copper boulder that was taken from Lake Superior and dedicated to the Washington monument by the State of Michigan, my father visited that boulder in very early days, even before the war of 1812, and he cut quite a piece of the pure native copper from it, and took it to his family in Concord, Massachusetts, before we moved west. I remember it very well; it was looked upon as a great curiosity and wonder, hardly credible in those days, especially in that old Yankee land. I think that when the family came west it was donated to some of my father's and mother's friends.

I give a description of a trip I made to Lake Superior in the year 1846:

The party consisted of Mr. Sherman Stevens, Mr. Hinsdale, who was a brother-in-law of Mr. Stevens, my brothers, A. F. Williams, late of California, and James M. Williams, now living in California, and myself. On our arrival at the Sault Ste. Marie we purchased a good boat, well equipped with oars, sails, etc., with a good tent and plenty of supplies, and started to coast it up Lake Superior, a jolly crew. The Sault canal was being excavated, and a steamer was being hauled across the portage from the head of the rapids into Lake Superior. She was then near to being launched into Lake Superior, but she was having some trouble, and was delayed several days. This steamboat was built at Black Rock or Buffalo by a Mr. Palmer. She was built and rigged as a full rigged brig, a beautiful vessel and the only brig on the lake at the time. Not proving a success as a brig she was made into a steamboat and named the Julia Palmer. I think she was named in honor of Mrs. Palmer, wife of the owner. We left and coasted as far as the Ontonagon river, stopping at all the points of interest, such as Eagle River, Eagle Harbor, and all the then mining points of interest. We encountered several heavy winds that we could not stand, always making for land, endeavoring to make some outlet of a small stream down the mountains, where we found splendid trout fishing, and we enjoyed catching the beautiful little fellows. They would take the bait about as fast as we could take care of them. The mouths of these little runs down the mountains would be dammed up with sand that was washed up by the winds, forming little ponds that were full of trout; our bait was a small piece of white pork, and we often took a hundred trout in a very short time. While two fished, two cooked and kept camp, taking turnabout. As we left the Ontonagon river on our way down, after a while we saw down the lake in the distance what we supposed was the steamer Julia Palmer, steaming for the first time up the lake for Copper Harbor. We were rejoiced to see her, for we were about tired of coasting. Giving three cheers for the Julia Palmer, we put in our best energies to get to Eagle Harbor before night, supposing the Julia Palmer would leave the next morning for the Sault, which she did, and we sold our boat and took passage down on our way home on board the first steamboat that was ever on Lake Superior.

There were several passengers on board and we requested the captain to run down by the Pictured Rocks, which he did, it being a beautiful, bright afternoon. The view of the rocks was beautiful beyond description. On our passage down the lake we passed near to and the spot was pointed out to us where Dr. Douglass Houghton was drowned. I felt sad, very, for I was intimately acquainted with him; he was with us much of the time at Saginaw when he was locating the salt well for the state at Salt Spring on the Ta-ta-ba-was-say. Messrs. G. D. & E. S. Williams took the contract and made the brick for the well. The doctor often urged us to use our mill steam power for boring a salt well near the mill at the foot of Mackinac street, city of Saginaw, he pointing to the spot to bore, saying we were in just the best place to strike the salt basin, which in after years proved so, and was and is now worked by the Williams Brothers, sons of Gardner D. Williams. They manufacture from one hundred to one hundred and fifty barrels per day, using the surplus steam from their saw mill.

In the years 1836, '37 and '38 we had living with us in Saginaw a gentleman and his family, consisting of his wife and two beautiful daughters, by the name of Joseph J. Malden, formerly a sea captain. The captain and his family were very much esteemed and respected. Mrs. Malden was a good, motherly, lovely woman; the daughters were married in Saginaw; the eldest was married to James Busby, one to a Mr. Beach, and the other to a Mr. Palmer. Mr. Palmer established a tannery, the first in Saginaw. In a few years he died, and at about the same time Mrs. Malden died. Both were much missed in our little settlement. The captain remained with us a few years; he received the appointment of light house keeper at the Island of Mackinac.

Mrs. Palmer went with her father to Mackinac and kept house for him, and the last I knew of the captain he was at the Mackinac light house. He subsequently became blind and died about 1880 at Alpena. In 1861 I visited the captain and his daughter while we were stopping at the Mission house on the island for a few days.

In after years the city procured and located a fine cemetery ground above the city and the citizens purchased lots; all who had been buried in past years were removed to the cemetery; Mr. Palmer and Mrs. Malden were removed. On attempting to raise the casket of Mrs. Malden, it was found that it could not be raised by the ordinary means; a power was provided to raise the casket, and upon examination it was found that the body had become petrefied to solid stone and was just as natural in looks as it was on the day she died, not a particle of change. This was a very singular incident, as no other body in the same ground, even near Mrs. Malden's, was so changed. Mrs. Malden in life was a fleshy woman, weighing probably, 175 or 200 pounds.

In 1836 Mr. Palmer went to New York on business, and while there he bought a very fine gold, English lever capped watch, paying for it one hundred and twenty dollars. After his return and while erecting his tannery buildings and putting down his tan vats, he found it was costing more than he had expected. He then proposed to me to trade watches, saying he rather have more lumber and not quite so much watch. I had an English lever watch with the works similar to his, but in silver cases; it cost me forty five or fifty dollars; we traded and I paid the difference in lumber. My reason for speaking of this is that I have the same watch now and I have carried it since the year 1836 (fifty years) and it has always been and still is a faithful old friend, but it will not run on railroad time, or wrongly called I think, standard time. I concluded to let my clock run on old solar time, and as I was around among our town's people, and the city had adopted railroad time, I would start my old companion watch of fifty years on standard time. To my surprise after a day or two my old friend stopped; I thought nothing, but started it again. The next day it stopped again, struck, perhaps, for better time. I tried it again, but at twelve o'clock in the day or night it would stop. I thought it strange, so I said, now my dear old friend, I will not ask you to do that I dislike to do myself and I cannot approve of, so I set the old fellow on the good old solar time, God's time, and I have had no trouble since, except that it runs a little slow, like its master. Perhaps you may think this is a little mixed, but it is true, and I assure you that the old watch and myself are pretty good friends and much attached to each other. The cases of this watch of fifty years are as bright and perfect as most of the new ones of the present day.

[The following lines were composed by my old esteemed friend, Capt. Jos. I. Malden, Saginaw City, 1838, while suffering under the horrors of fever and ague, and addressed to the malignant spirit supposed by the writer to preside over it.]

Avaunt, gaunt fiend, why, wicked demon, why
Comest thou again on me thy art to try?
Sure, I've not challenged thee, in dews, mist or rain,
Then why here now to torture me again?
What, twice in one season, why, thou worse than devil,
Bane of my health, and source of every evil,
Will you not stay your hand until you cause my death?
Say, would it not give thee pleasure to stop my breath?
May not perdition catch thy shivering form?
To fiery regions may'st thou quick be borne,
Thence drowned in sulphur, if thou need must shake,
Nor here again to come my health to break.
Or, if cold thou lov'st, may'st thou to Greenland go,
There buried in some everlasting snow,
Or in some iceberg's icy heart be bound,
And ne'er again by mortal man be found.
Or bound on some snow cap'd height on sterile Labrador,

And never have permit to haunt my family more,
Nor ere again in triumph thus to roam
O'er this fair land which I have made my home.
Oh, for the tonic mixture's efficacious power!
With what good will a bottle or two I'd shower
On thy curs'd form, thou wicked elf,
But that I could not get to save myself.
Ah, did friend E. S. Williams know of these, thy tricks,
I think a remedy he could quickly fix
Would drive thee hence—sulphur or quinine,
Salts or Peruvian bark mixed with generous wine.
Or did our Bunnel know of this, my case,
With nostrums certain he would hither pace;
But, oh! I'm left alone the war to wage
With thee, accursed imp, thou hast the (withering gaze.)

INDIAN REMINISCENCES OF CALHOUN AND KALAMAZOO COUNTIES

COLLECTED AND CONTRIBUTED BY A. D. P. VAN BUREN

CALHOUN COUNTY

The Indians that formerly occupied Michigan were of the Algonquin family. The larger branch called Ojibways or Chippewas inhabited the northern part of the peninsula; the Ottawas, the region south of them. The Pottawattomies occupied the lower part of the peninsula and spoke one of the rudest dialects of the Algonquin language. In 1822 there were five thousand six hundred and sixty nine Ojibways at Saginaw. Since 1800 the Pottawattomies have inhabited the lower part of the Michigan territory, living in scattered bands independent of each other. And as they are the only Indians connected with the early history of central Michigan our narrative bides with them.

There are but meager traces of antiquity, and no trace of government among them. The Chippewas and the Ottawas were under British influence during the war of 1812. The Pottawattomies were friendly to the American cause. These three tribes ceded all their lands about Lake Superior to the United States, and removed south of the Missouri river.

In 1870 there were four thousand nine hundred and twenty six Indians in Michigan. In 1874 there were only sixty Pottawattomies of the Huron band in this state. They lived in a rude hamlet situated on a patrimony of one hundred and sixty acres of original timbered land in the southern part of Calhoun county near Nottawa Sepe Prairie on which was formerly located the Nottawa Mission. The Methodist Episcopal church established this mission here in 1840, when they built a large log structure for a mission house, and a smaller one for a school house. The dwellings were of poles laid up like a log house, and covered with shakes. Rev. Manassah Hickey, now of Detroit, assisted by his sister and a young man by the name of Crane, had control of this mission and school.

After Sau-au-quet's death John Ma-gau-go* aspired to the chieftancy of the Pottawattomie nation. He was a man of noble bearing, and was succeeded in 1833 by his son John, whom most of the early settlers in this part of the state well remember. He became chief of the Michigan band, and was in the full sense a most noble specimen of his own race. In 1838 or '39 the grand council of the Indians was held in the Indian Reserve school house, and Muck-moot was present. There were then assembled five hundred of this tribe.

John Ma-gua-go had three sons, Man-do-ka, Mo-qua and Me-mie. That they were agile and muscular in all physical sports, and good wrestlers, many of the early settlers' sons can testify. Mar-chee was the chief's sister; or Mar-chee-o-no-qua was her full Indian name. She was said to have been a beautiful woman in her younger days and preserved traces of it long in her old age. Her second husband was Capt. Hatch, the Indian trader. They parted, and she married Buel Holcomb, known as "Bue" Holcomb, with whom she lived many years, and they separated. Mar-chee the writer knew well. She was the medicine woman among her people, and the doctoress in many families in the white settlement on Dry Prairie and the region about the mission. I have often met her at Isham Simond's hospitable home on Dry Prairie, where she was usually called in case of sickness of any of the inmates, and where she was esteemed highly, not only for her skill as

*The chiefs of this band, beginning with the settlement of the whites here have been *Pierre Morreau*, an accomplished Frenchman, who married an Indian woman and spent his after life with the Pottawattomies as their chief; *Cush-ee-wus* and *Pee-quoit-ah-kiss-ee* were legitimate chiefs, but were supplanted by *Morreau* and his son, *Sau-au-quette*, who virtually governed the band; the former till he died a poor drunken wretch, the latter till he was assassinated at Colon, St. Joseph county. At *Sau-au-quette's* death "old" *John Ma-gua-go* became chief, he was succeeded by his son *John Ma-gua-go*, and he by *Phineas Bamp-ta-na-by*, the present chief.

doctoress, but for many virtues of a good Indian woman. And I remember Pont-sig-na, Mar-chee's daughter, by her Indian husband. Pont-sig-na was a beautiful young girl—the dusky belle of the forest. As I saw her one Sabbath morning walking in the open wood near the rude village gathering wild flowers, she recalled these lines of Scott:

"And ne'er did Grecian chisel trace
A nymph, a naiad, or a grace
Of finer form and lovelier face.
* * * * * * * * *
A foot more light, a step more true,
Ne'er from the heath flower dashed the dew."

Pont-sig-na was educated at Albion and died before she was twenty years old.

MARY

Rev. Manassah Hickey, as we have said, was the pastor of this little flock, had his home with them, as did Miss Hickey and Mr. Crane. Mary, the wife of Man-do-ka, was the interpretess. She had been educated at Albion. She was an intelligent, comely Indian woman of some thirty years of age. One Sabbath morning, in the spring of 1847, I had gone with a party of young men and ladies from the school district north of the mission, where I was teaching to attend church with the Indians. We had got there early, and going into the log chapel seated ourselves and waited the gathering of the dusky congregation. Soon a young Indian came in, and taking down a long tin horn that hung behind the door, he stepped out in front of the chapel and wound it so loudly and musically that we could hear the twanging notes peal out, whisk off and die away in the distant arcades of the forest. Repeating this two or three times he stepped back into the chapel and hung up his horn again. Soon these children of the forest began to assemble in the rude log church. Quietly, with the careful Indian tread, old and young came in and took seats. Some half hour later the Indian who had given the first summons to church on the horn took the instrument, and, stepping in front of the door, wound it as he had done before. The flock all assembled, Hickey took his stand by a small table, and Mary took seat in a chair by his side, ready for her work. They had hymn books and the New Testament, I believe, in the Indian language. To hear these quiet worshipers sing—

"Oh, for a thousand tongues to sing
My great Redeemer's praise,"

in the Pottawattomie language, with its liquid accent and beautiful monosyllabic distinctness, when uttered by Indian lips, was a great pleasure to us.

An Indian once said to Hickey, "White man don't sing that hymn right. Indian would sing:

> 'Oh, for *ten* thousand tongues to sing
> My great Redeemer's praise.' "

After the hymns and the prayer, Mr. Hickey began his sermon. He would deliver a sentence in English and then pause till Mary repeated it to the Indians in their own tongue. It was very interesting to us to sit in that room whose quiet seemed like the stillness of the forest about us. Very interesting, I say, to listen to Hickey's sonorous voice, as he pronounced his sermon, paragraph at a time in distinct English, and then listen to the same sermon given forth again paragraph after paragraph by Mary's musical voice, in the beautiful Indian language. As Hickey became animated, or emotional, his interpretess would also, until, at times her feelings would so overpower her, that her head would fall back against the wall, her voice grow weaker and weaker, till her lips would move with no audible sound. Hickey would then stop till Mary revived, when he would go on as before.

Of the two sermons, his to the whites in English, and Mary's to the Pottowattomies in Indian, I think Mary's was the most effective. She had the best listeners, and then her Indian words as they left her lips went more effectually to the hearts of her audience than Hickey's did to his, because the Indians are more gifted as listeners. From the old patriarch of eighty years, to the little Indian boy or girl, they seemed to feel that they were in the house of God. The very moment that they entered the door of the chapel, worship began. They were in the presence of their Creator. They are worshipers to "the manor born."

"MO-SHA"

There was, at this time, living at the mission, an Indian from the far west called the "Mississippi Indian." This was Mo-sha. By those who admired his speaking he was called the "Mississippi orator." "He that only hears Demosthenes loses the better part of the oration." We could not understand what he said, but we saw and heard Mo-sha, and in his manner and action we thought he evinced much of the orator. Surely the Demosthenic test of making action the principal thing in oratory would have made Mo-sha an orator. We, at least, found Indian delivery admirable. No public speaker was more distinct in elocution than Mo-sha. He spoke the pure Indian with an articulation and modulation that was faultless, and his gesture was just what the word naturally required. He followed the instruction of a great master—"suit the action to the word, the word to the action." Although we understood scarcely a word of what he said, yet we were so interested in him while he was speaking that we were sorry when he took his seat. What was it that held us as with a spell?

> "'Twas the charm of delivery—the magical art
> That thrills like a kiss from the lip to the heart."

Here, thought I, is a model for some of these "Boanerges" in the pulpit, who, not only "tear a passion to tatters," but tear their words into fragments and drive their meaning out of the minds of their hearers. Mary left her husband, Man-do-ka, and went with another Indian to Canada. Mo-sha died a few years later at the mission.

SARAH, THE SISTER OF MARY

Mary had a sister named Sarah, who was also educated at Albion, I am informed. Sarah belonged to the "Slater Mission," which was located near Gull Prairie, in Barry county. She was, I believe, interpretess, for Rev. Leonard Slater at the above named mission. Sarah was much more accomplished in education and the graces of our schools and society than Mary was. She was younger, and like Mary, was comely, but a more attractive Indian woman.

Mung-woo-dans was chief of a western tribe of Indians far towards the Rocky mountains. Sarah was one of the Indian party with which Mung-woo-dans had made the tour of Europe. On their return to this country I met these tourists at Battle Creek. This was in the summer of 1853 or '54. I think I never saw a nobler specimen of mankind than this Indian chief. He was tricked off in true Indian warrior style. His head gear was of eagle's feathers; around his neck and hanging over his shoulders was a broad necklace of grizzly bear's claws. As he walked the streets of Battle Creek all eyes were upon him. What a splendid highland chief he would have been. Scott could have said of him—

> "And if thou said'st I am not peer
> To any lord in Scotland here,
> Lowland or highland, far or near,
> Lord Angus thou hast lied."

He lectured in the evening to the citizens of Battle Creek, in the old Universalist church. He said there was such a throng crowded about them, in some of the cities on the continent, that they dared not go into the streets. They visited Louis Phillipe in Paris, and other kings in Europe; also Queen Victoria in London. He lost two of his children while in Europe. He was not an orator, though a forcible and pleasant speaker, and exhibited some characteristics of Indian oratory in his distinct elocution, fine modulation of voice and impressive delivery. The party stopped at the old Battle Creek house. Prof. Copeland of Detroit, at that time, had one of the square rooms on the second floor for an art gallery, whose walls were hung with his beautiful monochromatic paintings. He was the first to introduce crayon paintings in Battle Creek. A lady from Boston, stopping at the Battle Creek house, was delighted with Sarah, the Pottawattomie tourist. As they passed by the art gallery I invited them in. They were both much pleased with the paintings. I asked the Boston lady which of them she considered the finest. She pointed to Diodate, Byron's home in Geneva. This was a beautiful work of art. I then asked Sarah the same question. She immediately pointed to a wild winter scene in the woods called "The Bear on the Ice." This was characteristic of the race to which she belonged; nature had more charms for Sarah; while on the other hand a fine work of art had won the lady from Boston, as art had more charms for her and her race.

REV. HENRY JACKSON, OR "STORM CLOUD"

Bam-me-no-de-no-kaid, signifying storm cloud, came here from Canada, where he was born, brought up and educated as a Wesleyan Methodist. He was government interpreter and business agent for the Pottawattomies. He was highly esteemed by the Indians at the Nottawa mission. He did not live here, only came when business required. His home was with the Ottawas at Wayland, Allegan county. Jackson was a Chippewa and has lectured at Battle Creek on the "Manners and Customs of the Chippewas." He was better acquainted with the history and traditions of the Indians in Michigan than any other person in the State. And it is greatly to be regretted that these histories and traditions were not secured by the State Pioneer Society before his death. He became dissipated some time before he died. He died at Holland a number of years ago. He was a forcible speaker, earnest and pathetic in his appeals to his red brethren. While he was with this mission he was a very useful man, and had he lived and remained in the work he began he would have been of great use to his race.

KALAMAZOO COUNTY

[Read at the Annual Pioneer Reunion of Kalamazoo county, held at Vicksburg, August 5, 1885.]

Mr. George Torrey, secretary of the association, then presented his annual

SECRETARY'S REPORT

Pioneers, Ladies and Gentlemen:

Once again we meet in this part of the county and for the third time, to hold our annual reunion and picnic, and to hear the voices of pioneers in song or story of the olden time, to meet long separated friends and acquaintances of former times, to look each other in the face, to grasp hands that have grown harder and more wrinkled since they used to meet more often in friendly clasp, to talk over the days that are no more, the scenes that are vanished except in memory, and to recall the form, and the face, and the character of friends who have gone before—a happy privilege, indeed, vouchsafed us.

Owing to the fact that so many other meetings were in progress last season, and a heated political canvass being at its height, the usual annual reunion was postponed, much to the disappointment of many. It is the only year since 1871, when the society was organized in Kalamazoo, that a meeting has not been held, and every gathering has grown larger and larger and seemed to be more and more enjoyed. But the circumstances were such last season as fully warranted the postponement.

This year while the officers of the society were discussing where to hold the meeting, a very kind and cordial invitation was received from the officers of the harvest home festival to meet with them at this place, conveying with their kind message the assurance that the pioneers would be well cared for. We knew that, for we were acquainted with the great hearted officers of that association and those who were members thereof; we did not parley a moment, but accepted, very happy to be with them. This gathering, therefore, will have less the features of a distinctive pioneer reunion than those heretofore held, though on a former occasion here the meeting was of a union character and a very delightful one, except its termination was a drenching rain storm.

Since we last met, two years ago, at Galesburg, in that pleasant grove by the river, death has been very busy with members of this society and pioneers of the county, prominent for good work, and leading citizens of the county, among these the noblest and best the county has ever known. As I call the names of many of these it will be unnecessary to pass a eulogy upon them or to tell you who they were. Personally they were known to nearly all of you; you have many a time grasped them by the hand in cordial fellowship. You have met them in business circles, on social and friendly occasions, in patriotic, philanthropic, benevolent and christian enterprises for years past. You have often heard the voices of some of them, at our pioneer reunions, and you have listened with pleasure to their utterances. Their names are associated with leading events in our history, both county and state, and among them are those who have sat down with princes, statesmen, judges, and the great men of the nation and of the world. I need not recall the tall and majestic form of Judge Wells, who never failed to be at a pioneer picnic and contribute to its chief interest by his inimitable and always attractive powers as a historian and story teller. Where could be found his equal in depicting the characteristics of noted pioneers; yea, the very form and color of those times? I know of no one that could match him. How greatly we miss his presence to-day. There was Wm. G. Dewing, the great hearted philanthropist, one of the fathers of the pioneer society, of whose virtues and work I might speak for an hour without exhausting the theme. Allen Potter, whose name is a synonym for all that is worthy and good; John Millham, the sturdy farmer and honest man, whose word was as good as his note, and his experience and skill as a farmer was worth a mint to others as well as himself; Martin Turner, the ingenious and ever ready mechanic and millwright, generous friend and neighbor, who as a farmer and artisan has from the first contributed so much to the development and prosperity of the county; Horace Phelps, another builder up, and in every fibre a noble man; Alexander Buell, Elon G. Huntington, Henry S. Parker, Lucius L. Clark, for nearly fifty years a leading merchant and man of many friends; Capt. R. C. Dennison, the genial and generous hearted citizen, soldier in the war and provost marshal at the time of the draft; Robert S. Babcock, merchant and banker; William Skinner, the well known farmer of Cooper; Chas. S. d'Arcambal, for over 30 years druggist in Kalamazoo; Mr. Gage of Texas; Willard Dodge, Caleb Sweetland, David Sergeant, and many others. They have passed from the stage of action to the sphere of rest and reward. But they have a place in our memory that can never be effaced.

The secretary would feel that the many pioneer women who have lived and have done so much in the work of making this county what it is, who have so often met with us and have contributed so greatly to the pleasure and interest of these meetings were worthy of honorable mention, but unfortunately I have but an incomplete list of these mothers in Israel. We hope at a future meeting to speak of them and place their names upon our pioneer record.

At the annual meeting of the society held in Kalamazoo, March 8th, a quorum being present, it was voted to amend the constitution so that the election of officers should take place at the annual reunion instead of at the winter meeting as heretofore. I would suggest, therefore, that it would be in order to appoint a committee from those here assembled, without any formalities, to submit the names of proper persons to act as officers of this society for the ensuing year.

Hon. Stephen F. Brown was then called upon, and though surprised and unprepared he made the most of his opportunity, and for fifteen minutes he held the closest attention of his audience.

Five little girls then sang "Bye Bye Baby, Bye Bye," and were loudly applauded.

A committee consisting of Mr. J. Lemon, Mr. J. M. Neasmith, Mr. A. D. P. VanBuren, Mr. Hackett, Mr. G. F. Brown, was appointed to nominate officers of the society for re-election. Mr. A. D. P. VanBuren then delivered the following carefully prepared and valuable papers:

THE "INDIAN" JOHNSON, AND SOME OF THE POTTAWATTOMIE BANDS TO WHICH HE BELONGED

The following sketch of the life of "Indian" Johnson I got from the old pioneer, William Harrison, of Climax, who not only knew Johnson, but was well acquainted with, and had lived for years a neighbor to his father, John Johnson, in Shelbyville, Shelby county, Kentucky. When William Harrison, or "Uncle Billy," as he was familiarly called, came to Climax in 1830, he found among the Indians here this white man called Indian Johnson. He had four wives, and was a man of importance among the Pottawattomies in this region. Uncle Billy's log cabin, on Climax, was a kind of a rude Mecca, to which his early friends here, the Indians, were accustomed to resort with offerings of berries, maple sugar, venison, and so forth. He was always on good terms with them, and says that he and his family would have starved in those early days when they could find nothing to "browse on," had it not been for the kindness of their Pottawattomie neighbors. He was always a favorite with them, so much so that they named him Sam-okay-ma-co, which means the good man. Among his particular Indian acquaintances were four brothers, Sam-o-ka, who had been a petty chief in his tribe, Not-a-wa, Pe-ash-y and Pe-ne-moo. These names and many others of the old Pottawattomie band were as familiar as household words to the early settlers in Climax and the region about it. Uucle Billy soon found that Johnson was a white man, and strongly suspected that he was of the Kentucky family above mentioned. He wrote to his old neighbor, John Johnson, at Shelbyville, who sent two of his other sons to Climax, where they found their long lost brother—a complete Indian in all but his having been born a white child. The facts in his life are as follows: Two of Johnson's children had been stolen many years before from his home in Shelbyville, Kentucky, and no trace of them had ever been found. One was quite a lad, the other an infant in the cradle, whom his Indian captors must have killed, as he was never seen or heard of afterwards. The lad was kept and had thus been reared by the Indians.

Johnson, having been identified by his brothers, went back with them to his "old Kentucky home." But he was now more Indian than white man, and, after staying some years or so, he came back to his forest home in Michigan, where he died some years afterwards. Pe-ne-moo's squaw was Johnson's daughter. Johnson would never join the Indians in their pow-wows, but on such occasions he would come to his friend's, Uncle Billy's, home. Mrs. Dr. L. W. Lovell informed the writer that Johnson at times in his talk with the settlers seemed to feel the full sense of his lost manhood, that he was now, as compared with the whites, an inferior person—an underling. And a feeling of sadness would come over him as he would say: "Me not Indian. Me born white. Me white man."

Sam-o-ka, and Johnson as interpreter, came to Stephen Eldred, Climax, with the bitter complaint that "Che-mo-ka-man had killed their dog." The Indian dogs would kill the settlers' pigs, and then the settler shot the Indian dog, whereupon the owner of the dogs would come to the white man claiming from twenty to thirty dollars for every dog killed. Mr. Eldred, on the occasion referred to, told Sam-o-ka and Johnson that unless they kept their dogs from killing his pigs he would report them to the Indian agent at Detroit, and they would get no more presents from the government. There was no more annoyance, says Mr. E., of this kind. But the Indians were generally what might be called good, accommodating neighbors. Says Mrs. L. W. Lovell: "We could not have done without the Indians. They were our marketmen and women. They brought us venison, huckleberries, maple sugar and many other things that we in a new settlement needed." Pe-ne-moo had a patch of land on Major Lovell's farm that he for many seasons cultivated. Here he raised corn, beans, pumpkins, and other vegetables; his wife, Johnson's daughter, being half white, seemed to have more energy and thrift than the other squaws. She was a member of the M. E. church, and a few years ago communed with its members at Climax. At the time of the removal of the Indians westward by the Government, Sam-o-ka and most of the Pottawattomie band known here went to Canada. Says Judge Eldred: "While I was at the 'corners' a few years ago, a squaw came up to me, apparently much pleased, as she held out her hand and exclaimed, 'How do you do, Judge Eldred, don't you know me? Me Pe-ne-moo's squaw!" The Judge was very happy, he said, to meet this good Indian woman. She and her husband had returned from Canada. About this time Not-a-wa, who also had returned from Canada, met an old settler on Climax. The old Indian seemed to be sad and melancholy as he said: "Me remember when it was all woods about this place. Plenty of deer, plenty of hunting, plenty of Indian here then. All gone now. Me go, too, soon!" Pam-pla-pee, another of this old band of Pottawattomies, remembered he said, when the dry marsh, or rather clayey land, north of McNary's, in LeRoy, was a large lake abounding in fish. He had caught fish there many times. Sam-o-ka never came back from Canada. Some few years ago one of his tribe informed the writer that the old chief, or, as he was accustomed to say when a little squiby, "Me, Sam-o-ko-ma-co, cheep," was yet alive in Canada, and he was a good Indian, and he had a very fine squaw. But now they are gone—all gone—those old familiar acquaintances and helpful friends of the early settlers of this region.

The Indians were friends and very kind neighbors to the early settlers. They treated us so much like kith and kin, that we called them our "country cousins." And although extremely backwoodish in habit and mode of living, yet we could not wish for kinder and more accommodating neighbors. To use an Indian simile, "the smoke from the wigwam ascending upward united with the smoke ascending from the white man's cabin, into one volume. So white man and Indian became one in friendship." The Indians were often of great help at raisings; a log house or barn could not, at times, have been raised without their aid.

One day Sam-o-ka came to a logging bee at our neighbor Jonathan Austin's clearing in Battle Creek township. "Uncle Billy" Harrison, as the old Indian came to the clearing, remarked, "an Indian will drink all the whiskey you give him. I will prove it." So pouring into a pint basin, the only drinking cup the settler had, over a gill of whiskey, the old chief drank it off without breathing. Billy then filled the basin nearly half full, which the old fellow swallowed and smacking his lips said, "Me like'm squibee." He soon began to reel and was taken and laid under an oak tree, where he slept all the afternoon. Towards nightfall he got up and took the trail for his wigwam.

Uncle Billy's son Jerry, like his father, had the strength and muscle of an athlete in wrestling, jumping or "pulling sticks." While the young Indian boys were as lithe and agile as panthers at all athletic sports, Jerry could generally "down them" at a "back hold," but at a "rough and tumble," the Indian's "foot was on his native heath," and there he usually came off victor.

Among the Indian playmates of Jerry were Pe-ne-moo's sons, whose friendship for him continued till his death a few years ago. After Jerry was married these friends of his boyhood would each summer spend a week or two with him.

The following incident is so illustrative of an Indian trait that we give it here: A son of Pe-ne-moo had informed Uncle Billy that he was about to get married. "Then you come here with your wife," says Billy, "and I kill dog; make big feast for you." This was agreed to. During the "bridal tour" to their friend's home on Climax, young Pe-ne-moo and his wife camped in the woods over night near a settler's clearing. In the morning the young Indian's fine broadcloth coat was missing, and could not be found. On reaching Billy's hospitable home the story of losing the coat was told, and that "a che-moke-a-man had stolen it," for Pe-ne-moo had traced out the thief, who was the settler living near where they had slept over night. The latter denied taking the coat; and drove the Indian off. This excited a spirit of revenge in the Indian, and nothing but revenge could now satisfy him. Says he to his friend, "Me kill him for stealing Indian's coat." Uncle Billy was alarmed, for he knew Indian revenge would find satisfaction, and that young Pe-ne-moo would kill this settler. Consequently he replied, "You must not kill che-mo-ko-man. Me tell you what to do. He got fat hog. Steal 'em hog; that is better. Hog worth more than coat." Billy found this the dernier resort. The Indian followed his advice, stole the hog, and thus the settler's life was saved.

NOONDAY, THE OTTAWA CHIEF. HE WAS IN THE BATTLE OF THE THAMES, AND SEES COL. R. M. JOHNSON SHOOT TECUMSEH, WHOM HE CARRIES OFF THE BATTLE FIELD

Rev. Leonard Slater established a mission among the Indians at Grand Rapids sometime in 1826. Here he first met the Ottawa chief, Noonday. And it was here that the old chief was converted to christianity some time in 1830 or '31, with a number of other Indians of his tribe. Deacon Edwin Mason, of Richland, from whom I received most of the facts in this sketch, first saw the chief Noonday, in 1832, on Gull prairie, as he, with his Indians, was on his way to Malden to get their annual presents. The early settlers of Gull prairie were then just in the midst of the excitement over the rumors that Black Hawk and his Indians were coming into Michigan to murder them all. Deacon Mason had a talk with Noonday and among other things asked him which side he would take in case Black Hawk did come into the territory. He replied: "Me and my Indians will help the white folks if they need us."

Mr. Slater established his mission in Prairieville, Barry county, some one and one half miles from Richland, in 1836. He bought several hundred acres of land of Luther Hill for the use of the Indians. Deacon M——— remembers that in November of 1832 Elder Merrill came on horseback to his log cabin inquiring the way to Grand Rapids, whither he was going to organize a Baptist church, and to baptize Noonday and the converted Indians. The elder on his return told Deacon M——— that he had to sleep in the woods one night both going to and coming from Grand Rapids. Noonday was an old man long before he came to Gull. He occasionally visited the settlement on the prairie, but was always the same taciturn, dignified, commanding person. Though the settlers now and then talked with him, through an interpreter, few of them knew that he had ever done an act that had caught the ear of fame. Yet the redman's Clio, the penless scribe tradition, whose function was to keep alive the memory of famous deeds, had often told the braves around the council fire, and they had told their children that Noonday had fought bravely on the British side in one of the memorable battles of our second war with England. It is well known that both the Chippewa and Ottawa tribes fought with the English in the war of 1812. Noonday had a wife and family. After his conversion he lived a true christian life, never failing to hold family worship, gathering all the inmates of his household about the family altar morning and evening. I do not know whether he had children of his own, but he had several adopted children. He took great interest in the mission work, and especially in the school in which, through his influence, all the children of his tribe were gathered. He was looked upon by all his people not only as their counsellor, but as the wise patriarch who was to look after their temporal and spiritual wants. Miss Susan Parker, Amasa Parker's sister, was the first teacher in this school which was organized in 1838. She afterwards married Rev. Mr. Davis, and died at Ann Arbor, a number of years ago. The next teacher was Rev. Leonard Slater's daughter, Frances, who became the wife of Cornelius Mason. She, too, is dead. Noonday, when visiting the school, would never let a wrong or improper act go unrebuked or unpunished, often chastising a refractory pupil for the teacher.

Mr. Slater always preached to the Indians in their language, with which he had made himself familiar. He had early sought instruction from Noonday in the Ottawa dialect. He would first deliver his sermon to the old chief, in order to get his criticism as to its correct Indian, before he preached it to the rude worshipers in the chapel. The mission lasted some ten years. Noonday died when some one hundred years old in 1845 or '46, and is buried near the spot where the old mission house stood. A plain slab marks the grave where the old patriarch of the Slater mission sleeps. His wife at her death was laid beside him.

Noonday never learned to talk English, but always spoke to his white friends through an interpreter, who usually was Mr. Slater. From an article by D. B. Cook, editor of the Niles Mirror, published in the Century Magazine of June, 1885, I get the following historical facts concerning Noonday: Mr. Cook's father, Phineas Cook, was an early settler in the region near Gull prairie. He says: "I had in 1838 an interview with Noonday, chief of the Ottawa tribe. The chief was six feet high, broad shouldered, well proportioned, with broad, high cheek bones, piercing black eyes, and coarse black hair which hung down on his shoulders. He possessed wonderful muscular power. He was converted to christianity by Rev. Leonard Slater, Missionary at the Slater mission at Grand Rapids, and afterwards came with his friend and pastor to the new mission near Gull prairie. Noonday was at the battle of the Thames." Mr. Cook's diary runs thus: "After rehearsing the speech which Tecumseh made to his warriors previous to the engagement, and how all felt that they fought to defend Tecumseh more than for the British, he was asked:

"Were you near Tecumseh when he fell?"

"Yes, directly on his right."

"Who killed him?"

"Richard M. Johnson."

"Give us the circumstances."

"He was on a horse and the horse fell over a log, and Tecumseh with uplifted tomahawk, was about to dispatch him, when he drew a pistol from his holster and shot him in the breast and he fell dead on his face. I seized him at once and with the assistance of Saginaw, bore him from the field. When he fell the Indians stopped fighting and the battle ended. We laid him down on a blanket in a wigwam, and we all wept, we loved him so much. I took his hat and tomahawk."

"Where are they now?"

"I have his tomahawk and Saginaw his hat."

"Could I get them?"

"No; Indian keep them."

"How do you know it was Johnson who killed him?"

"General Cass took me to see the Great Father, Van Buren, at Washington. I went to the great wigwam, and when I went in I saw the same man I see in battle, the same man I see kill Tecumseh. I had never seen him since, but I knew it was him. I look him in the face and said: 'Kene kin-a-poo Tecumseh,'" that is, you kill Tecumseh. Johnson replied that he never knew who it was, but a powerful Indian approached him and he shot him with his pistol. "That was Tecumseh; I see you do it."

Noonday finished his story of Tecumseh by telling of his noble traits, the tears meanwhile trickling down his cheeks. There is no doubt of the truth of his unvarnished tale.

It was believed by some people that Noonday was at the burning of Buffalo. But Rev. Leonard Slater's son George, now living in Richland, assures us that Noonday told him just before his death that he was not at the burning of Buffalo.

Wash-ta succeeded Noonday as chief of the tribe; but in a short time after the chief's death he went north with the few Indians at the old mission. Lewis Gen-ro* was an Indian well known on Gull prairie at this time. He, when living at Grand Rapids, had been sent to state's prison for "holding his wife's father in the fire till he burned to death." This was done when Gen-ro was drunk. After serving his time in prison he came to Gull prairie. He had learned the shoemaker's trade in prison. Rev. L. Slater built him a shop, and furnished him with an outfit for his trade. But, Indian like, he worked by fits and starts, and finally went north with the rest of his band.

NOONDAY, THE OTTAWA CHIEF, WAS AT THE BURNING OF BUFFALO

In a previous article on this subject published in vol. 9 of these collections, it was claimed that Noonday was not at the burning of Buffalo; that the old chief had persistently asserted this to be a fact. Since then the writer has got fresh information from Mr. Joseph Merriman, now of Yorkville, this county, who settled on Gull prairie in 1836, and lived for many years near neighbor to both Rev. Leonard Slater and Noonday. He was intimately acquainted with both. And he assured the writer that Mr. Slater had told him that Noonday had given him the correct story of his life, and that he was at the burning of Buffalo. But he had enjoined the utmost secrecy in regard to it upon Mr. Slater, as he feared that those who were injured by the burning of Buffalo might yet seek revenge on him. And furthermore it was a deed that he had repented of, and were it known among the people here it would create a *babble* about him and would prejudice many against him. Mr. Slater kept his word, and not till after Noonday's death did he divulge this fact. Mr. Merriman is positive that the above statement is true. And he is too well known for sterling integrity of character by his old friends here for any one to doubt the truth of what he says in this matter.

In a public "talk" that Noonday had, in an early day, with the people of Gull, he was asked what side he would take if there should be war with the

*Gen-ro was said to have been half French; he talked English about as well as the settlers. He was a powerful man, fully six feet in height and well proportioned. He had "offered to bet that he could whip or throw any man in Kalamazoo county." No one accepted his challenge. H. B. Brownell, now of Galesburg, then living on Gull prairie, had wrestled with Gen-ro at "side hold" many times. And when Brownell had his choice of hold, he threw Gen-ro; but if the Indian had his choice, he threw Brownell. Hence between them, at "side hold," it was a "Roland and an Oliver." Gen-ro was not a bad man, but was always feared when he had been drinking.

English or Indians again. He replied, "With you. You need not fear me or my tribe." He said the English had promised them if they would join them in battle they would always aid them when they needed help—furnish them support through life. "But," said the old chief, "they have not kept their word. They never did anything for us after we had done so much for them. We know you to be our true friends, and we shall always be yours."

Noonday was very much affected by the fact that the landlord at Prairieville was selling liquor to the Indians. The Indian agent, who then lived at Detroit, hearing of this, urged the people on Gull prairie to prosecute all such violations of the law. Mr. Merriman soon afterwards had this landlord arrested for the offense. But he pleaded so stoutly for mercy that Mr. Merriman and Mr. Slater, who assisted him in the prosecution, settled with him on his pledging himself under oath that he would not sell any more liquor to the Indians. Immediately after the landlord was set at liberty he arrested both Mr. Slater and Merriman with a criminal warrant and had them put in the jail at Hastings on the ground that they had no legal right to settle with him—that the court before which he was arraigned was the only authority to have decided his case. The arrested parties remained in jail over night. Mr. Slater the next day got himself bailed out. He then went home and in a few days got his friend out on bail. But the trial was yet to come. When the circuit court met at Hastings Mr. Merriman received a note from Judge Ransom requesting him to call on his boarding place in Hastings. Mr. Merriman did so, and was told by the judge, who had got the facts in the case, that he could go home as soon as he pleased, for, says he, "I shall not allow your case to be called, and that will put a quietus on the whole matter."

OLD "SHE-MOKE"

An old Indian who belonged to a band who lived south of Gull prairie had become well known to the settlers and had won their friendship by many a kind act. Some of his white friends had given him a new suit of clothes. It was a very amusing sight to see the old fellow, when completely dressed, in a full white man's costume. After scanning himself all over from head to foot he extended his arm, felt of the sleeve, stuck out his foot, felt of his pantaloons, took off his hat, surveyed it, placed in on his head, and, suddenly giving a jump some three feet from the ground, uttered a wild whoop and exclaimed—"She-mo-ko-man!" "Me, She-mo-ko-man!" After that he went by the name of "Old She-moke."

Mrs. Elihu Mills, being in feeble health, had expressed a desire for some fish. She-moke having heard it took his spear and started for the "Three

Lakes," in the south part of Richland. In less than two hours he was at Mr. Elihu Mills' door and presented Mrs. Mills with a large pickerel. He speared it in the day time, no one could tell how, but an Indian could do many things wonderful to a white man.

THE OLD INDIAN DOCTOR

There was an old Indian doctor well known by the first settlers in the east part of this county. His name we could not get. His home was originally near Schoolcraft. He died in the spring of 1833 and was buried in what was later known as the Catholic burying ground in Kalamazoo. His two sons were Cop-mo-sa and Chip-e-wa. He had a daughter who was deaf and dumb. She married a Frenchman by the name of Joseph Mouseau, who lived with the Indians as a trader. They had a son who was a bright boy. Hugh M. Shafter, who gave this bit of history to the writer, visited the Indian camp, which was located on the lands now owned by A. L. Rowland, in Charleston. Mr. Shafter asked Mouseau if his boy could speak French. He straightened up proudly as he replied—"He speak'em ma-jash English, he speak'em Indian, he speak'em French." Then turning to his deaf and dumb squaw wife, he said—"She no speak'em, but she good." Of the old doctor's family two died with the consumption; one called the "little one-eyed squaw," says Esquire Shafter, "was a smart little thing."

INDIANS IN KALAMAZOO COUNTY

The following letter from A. H. Scott, dated St. Joseph, Mich., Jan. 9, is to Mr. Henry Bishop, and is in answer to questions touching the Indians in this county at an early day. It will be found of great interest to many of our readers to whom the aborigines of this section were unknown:

"Your letter, dated Dec. 25, came to hand and I have felt it a duty to give the information desired in regard to the Indians of Kalamazoo county during the years of its first settlement by the whites as far as my memory will serve me. I came to Kalamazoo county early in June, 1833, as a member of the family of James Smith, in company with his brother Addison; Hosea B. Huston and E. Lakin Brown, carried on the merchandising business under the name of Smith, Huston & Co., and had two stores, one at Schoolcraft, and the other at Kalamazoo (or rather Bronson, as it was then called). I soon picked up enough of the Indian language to enable me to trade with them. They then owned a reservation of land ten miles square, which took in the eastern part of Gourdneck prairie, and had a small village or collection of wigwams in the grove just east of the prairie on the farm now owned by James N. Neasmith, Esq. The wigwams were all built with a frame of poles, covered with elm bark, with the exception of the wigwam of the chief (Sag-a-maw), which was built for him by his friends, the early white settlers, of logs and covered with oak shakes. You wish me to inform you how they received the first settlers, how they lived and how they mingled with and how they traded with the white man.

1st. I think as a class they received the early settlers very kindly and were inclined to live peaceably with them.

2d. How they lived? Deer were plenty in those early days and as they were good hunters they had no difficulty the greater part of the year in supplying themselves with meat. They also used the flesh of raccoons, muskrats, etc., for food. Fish were plenty in the rivers and lakes. They understood how to catch them both with spear and hook. They raised some corn on land that some of the early settlers plowed and fenced for them. In their season wild fruits, such as blueberries, blackberries, etc., were obtained by them for food, and also to swap with the white man for flour, salt, sugar, etc.

3d. How much they mingled with the white man? In our stores and in the dwellings and cabins of their acquaintances they made themselves very much at home. The squaws and pappooses would come in in crowds and sit down on the floor (never taking a chair) till they were so thick that you could hardly find a place to put your foot. They turned out *en masse* on all public days and at horse races and shows. They were greatly delighted with circuses. Shooting matches and foot races they took a great interest in.

4th. How they traded with the white man? The trade with the Indian at that early day was mainly an exchange (or, as they called it "swap") of their furs, venison, dressed deer skins, moccasins, blueberries, blackberries, cranberries, etc., for flour, salt, tobacco, powder, lead, sugar and all the articles that the Indians use to clothe themselves. I never knew an Indian to offer to sell to white people any part of the carcass of a deer except the ham. The price for a ham of venison was always two shillings; no more, no less, no matter how small or large it was. Whenever we sold a squaw any goods that had to be made up into any of their garments a needle and thread for each garment must be given; only the goods for one garment would be bought or swapped for at a time. It required a good knowledge of their ways and much patience to be a successful dealer with the Indians. We frequently sold them goods on credit and found them about the same kind of paymasters as the ordinary white man; some paid promptly, some after a long time, and some never paid. They would have been splendid customers if they had been blessed with plenty of money; but they were poor and thriftless, and I may with truth say a "vagabond race" and consequently their trade was of no great value. They received an annual payment from government, which was mainly in necessary goods for their use and comfort, and a small amount of silver money. The money was very soon gone and in most cases did them no good, but the goods furnished them by government were just what they needed, and added greatly to their comfort.

In regard to personal characteristics of any noted Indian, etc., I would say that the best specimen of an Indian that I ever saw in those early days was Sag-a-maw, the chief of all the Pottawattomies in and about Kalamazoo county. He was a man of great good sense, of noble bearing, of great integrity, and in every way a dignified gentleman. He was called a great orator among his people. He was a true friend to the whites. I have heard him make speeches to his people, and although I could not understand him, his manner and voice were very interesting, and the effect of his speech on his people was very great. He was the only Indian I ever saw who was polite and attentive to his squaw. When they came to the store at Schoolcraft to do their trading he would help her off her pony, and when they were ready to return he would place his hand on the ground by the side of her pony and she would place one foot in it and he would lift her with apparently great ease into her saddle, and no white man could have shown more respect and politeness. If he wished for any credit at the store he had it and paid promptly. Any Indian that he told us it was safe to trust was sure to pay us. He always told us never to trust his son Cha-na-ba, who was a very worthless fellow. * * In regard to the number of the Indians that lived in Kalamazoo county and vicinity in that early day, I can make no estimate that would be of any value. They were continually coming and going and scattered about in little squads. In regard to the effect it had on the character of the Indian in his contact with the white race I have no doubt but it was bad.

He seems (as many writers have said) to take in all the vices of the white man and reject all his virtues. Whiskey (the great demoralizer of the white man) was and is the principal factor in the destruction of all that is good in the Indian character when he comes in contact with the white race. The longer the Indians remained here among the whites the more worthless they became. Game became scarce, they were too indolent to work, and they became drunkards and beggars. The great end and aim of the most of them was to get whiskey to get drunk with, and as its cost was only about twenty five cents per gallon they generally got all that they wanted. When they purchased whiskey they usually announced that they were going to get squibby (drunk). The quality of the whiskey sold to the Indians was very bad, having been first watered and drugged for their especial use. I recollect in 1833 that some Indians came to Schoolcraft from Kalamazoo and made bitter complaint to Addison Smith about H. B. Huston. They said that he put so much bish (water) in his whiskey that it made them sick before they could get squibby (drunk). As to myself I sold no whiskey to Indians except during the first two or three years after my arrival in Schoolcraft. What I have said about the Indians has been mainly about those whose headquarters were near Schoolcraft. If you can glean any item out of this disjointed and lengthy letter that will aid in making up a true history of the early settlement of Kalamazoo county I shall feel well paid for what little trouble I have had in writing it. But I very much doubt if you can, as there are other persons still living in Kalamazoo county who were familiar with all the facts that I have attempted to set forth.

E. Lakin Brown came to Schoolcraft two years before I came, and is very well posted in all the ways of the Indians of those early days. Mrs. Thaddeus Smith came to Schoolcraft in 1830 I believe, and could speak the Indian language better than any white person that I knew when I came there. She was a great favorite with the Indians, and any day that they were in town you would usually find her sitting room filled with squaws and pappooses. Thanking you for your kind Christmas greeting, I must close by subscribing myself your old friend."—*A. H. Scott, in Kalamazoo Telegraph.*

DAILY LIFE, MANNERS, AND CUSTOMS OF THE INDIANS IN KALAMAZOO COUNTY

Below we give another interesting and valuable paper from the pen of Mrs. St. John* regarding the Indians of this portion of Michigan the tribes who owned and for hundreds of years inhabited and dominated over these happy hunting grounds:

1. Pokagon was the principal Pottawattomie chief in 1827. I remember one Pottawattomie chief who was called Blackskin and my brother (George) says he remembers of a chief or under chief called Whiteface being probably of a mixture of French blood. I am unable to say just what form of government the Pottawattomies had among themselves, but I suppose it was much like that of the Ottawas. When any important matter concerned the tribe

*Daughter of Rev. L. Slater.

or any differences too heavy to settle between persons, the chief called a council of head men who sat round in a circle, smoked tobacco and talked one at a time, while others occasionally gave short exclamations of assent or surprise or dissent or grunts of attention till the matter was discussed, and generally ended by agreeing with the chief.

It has been said by many that Indians are slow and stolid; that they were quick tempered, and when partially intoxicated would often stab each other (men and women). They all carried knives in sheaths hung to the belt. The knife blade was about seven inches long and turned back a little at the point and sharp. The United States government took notice of crimes committed among the Indians whenever such were perpetrated within the jurisdiction of the mission. Louis Geneau, an Indian, when drunk, pushed his wife† into the fire; he was tried and sent to Jackson prison for life. While there he was asked how long he would have to stay. He replied, "All time, spose." He was afterwards pardoned out. There were a number of chiefs at the same time. Father writes of three coming together once to the mission house to confer on some subject.

2. I think the Ottawas were superior to the Pottawattomies; first, in their dialect. It was a relief to hear the musical completeness of the Ottawa's speech after the labored pantomime of the Pottawattomie. Their darker skins and wilder Indian ways, I know, prove nothing; but we count that man the wisest who makes choice of the best things. The Pottawattomie tribe was probably superior in numbers and bodily vigor.

3. The Ottawas and other Indians lived in small communities or villages of wigwams of ten or a dozen or more, of poles sharpened and driven in the ground and fastened at the top by withes or strips of bark. They fastened strips of bark from pole to pole around the sides which made a sort of frame to hold the covering of bark, skins or matting, with an oblong mat hung over a doorway, and an Indian would dart through head first as quick and noiselessly as a fox might. A fire built in the middle would fill the wigwam with smoke until the blaze would drive it out at the open top. I often wondered why the concern did not take fire at the top, but the inmates would fearlessly build a brisk fire of sticks without seeming to care for the smoke and when the wood had burned down to bright, clean coals and the women had made some dough of meal or flour and put it in the hot ashes, and the kettle of sturgeon, or partridge, or coon simmered, then was the time to begin a big talk of the adventures of the day. And if it was winter or wet weather the deer skin moccasins were taken off and stretched out and dried and the wide

†Deacon Edwin Mason, of Richland, says it was his wife's father. H. B. Brownell, who also was in Richland when Gen-ro lived here, that was burned to death. They also say his name was Gen-ro, but this may have been a corruption of *Geneau*.

woolen bandages gathered around the foot for stockings, were hung round to dry for the next day, when the shoe must be again kneaded or rubbed to make it soft. The other parts of their dress have been truly pictured in Indian books. They soon found that our kind of dress was the best and adopted it; not caring to go back to their old costume, even though they would not "civilize."

The routine of life among the women was by necessity very simple. In early times the garments were made with few stitches, but fitted and fastened to the body by strings of deer skin. A pappoose cradle was a board with a sort of binding of soft, fine bark around the edge, with open work sufficient to pass a wide swaddling band round the knees and over the whole for the chest, and then a hoop or bow over the face, so that a blanket might hang loose to protect the little face from rain and wind. The mother carried it from place to place by a strong band across the forehead backward. Some times, when they came to the chapel, they would stand them up along the wall, like so many umbrellas.

There was no lack of affectionate care for the little ones. When they worried or cried the mother quickly went and loosened their harness, or took them and stood the board up beside them. The women were accustomed to be very valuable servants to their husbands, and on this account, if for nothing more, were esteemed and loved very much, the same as among the light skinned lords of creation. As to the courtships of the young people, it seems to me there was not much. In the absence of the elaborate customs of civil life, those suspicions and doubts which haunt the minds of young civilians were set aside, and the young Indian told his desires to the party of the second part, and if she was agreeable they both agreed. The children were taught those things which their parents thought were indispensable to success as an Indian. First of all, perhaps, to ride a pony and shoot with a bow, and it was a great practice among the boys to run and jump at a mark. The children were under law to venerate parents and superiors, to obey and wait upon them. They were punished in no systematized manner. Parents would shake, or push, or cuff the ears, but it was a right jealously held by the parents, and if the father thought his child had in any wise been insulted or punished at school he was quickly on hand to see about it. I think that wives were fully up to the standard of these times in domestic truth. When there were evidences of improprieties they were paler faces, and such were always held under a kind of scorn.

I never heard of any polygamy among the tribes, but my personal knowledge of practices were mostly confined to our own mission. The tendencies were all the other way. Each husband had a pride in providing for his squaw and pappoose, ponies and trappings, and he readily saw that the easiest way was the best. Some of the christian Indians told father that years before there were some of the tribe who were so heathenish as to take more than one wife.

4. They loved deeds of kindness done towards themselves, and would remember them and return the favor if they ever had an opportunity, and so it was counted no shame to beg, and when they came into any house hungry, they would say: "Howe-shum-bo-shin, quas-quis chebuckatah," give me bread, very hungry. One Sabbath morning, chief Noonday brought his adopted son to the mission school saying: "This is the morning that the Savior rose from the dead, and I wish to do something in memory of Him." They seemed to be chary of speaking much of their traditions and superstitions in the presence of the white teachers whom they acknowledged to be superior in knowledge, and were shy of criticism. Their minds seemed sharpened only to those things which were good in their daily life. They could take fish with a wooden spear split at the end, and would boil fish in a tray. They imagined when they died the (great) "Gitchie-Manitou" would give them what they most desired while in life, but they must love him while here to be blest hereafter. Once, in the hard, cold winter of 1827, when the snow lay deep on all the land, the hunters could find but little game, and the hungry tribe came begging round the mission. Some of them killed a bear; upon the good news the people assembled and roasted him for a feast; but, before eating, one of the chiefs made an address, which some one said was to the Manitou, thanking him for sending them that food just at that time. I think the Indians, in their native state, had no profanity. That was reserved for the white man to teach them.

Their moral code partook of the crude simplicity of their minds; to love and do good to their friends and kill their enemies. Sometimes, when drunk, they would come to kill father. One was sick and sent for father to come and cure him, but gave him to understand that if the medicine did not cure him he would kill him. Their idea seemed to be to get even with every one, good for good, evil for evil; nothing was harder for them than to forgive their own injuries.

I cannot say what festivals they had in early days, other than war-dances and medicine-dances. These last consisted in making as much and as horrible a noise as they could with dry gourd shells with a few pebbles in them, and a kind of drum made of deer skin shrunk over a hoop or bow. When these two were struck together and the medicine musicians grunted and chanted and yelled in chorus, imagine the noise if you can. A year they called a sun, a month was a moon. They knew no weeks, and when the missionaries began to make Sabbath regulations they took a stick and cut a notch in it for each day and a deeper one for the seventh.

5. Their wigwams were made as has been described, of such materials as could be found on or near the ground—poles and bark and mats. The light luggage was bundled on to the ponies, with the women and children. Their household goods were few and easily moved. A blanket or two was coat by day and bed at night; an iron pot was all the cook stove; and their wash-bowl was a marsh, a brook or a lake, and soap, alas, was not in fashion. But in their long hair was one of the ten plagues in force, and I saw them often take the same between thumb nails in as orthodox fashion as any New England mother ever did, and there were no fine-tooth combs to aid in the catch, and yet their glossy black heads were more comely than many a banged frizzle-top of civilization.—*S. E. ST. J., in Kalamazoo Telegraph.*

INDIAN COUNCIL

[From the White Pigeon Republican, Aug. 28, 1839.]

At a council held at Notawassippi, St. Joseph county, Michigan, on the 20th inst., between Isaac S. Ketchum, agent, on behalf of the United States and the remaining Indians in the states of Michigan and Indiana, of the Pottawattomie tribe, Red Bird, a chief, addressed the agent as follows:

Father:

You have waited with patience for us to come to the council and most of us are now here. We are happy to meet you all well; ourselves and our children are all well. To day we have dry ground, a bright sun and a clear sky, and the Great Spirit be with us. We are now ready to hear you, and to-morrow by 10 o'clock we will be ready to answer you.

Mr. Ketchum then addressed them as follows:

Chiefs and Warriors:

It is true that we have waited some time for the purpose of meeting you in council, and I am gratified to see you assembled. The object of this council originates from a treaty concluded between ourselves and the government of the United States, at Chicago, known by the name of the Chicago treaty, in which it was stipulated that you should give up peaceable possession of the lands ceded to the government of the United States, within three years from the ratification of that treaty, and remove west of the Mississippi river, upon lands that were ceded to you in that treaty by the government. Your Great Father has had several councils with you to carry this into effect, at no small expense, and you have deferred carrying that part of the treaty into effect. He now wants these lands for his white children. Your Great Father, the President of the United States, has sent me here fully authorized (here Mr. Ketchum produced his authority) to convene you in council and to ascertain whether you are now ready, or when you will be ready to carry that part of the treaty into effect. It is specified that the expenses of moving you to your new homes should be paid by the government of the United States, and not out of your annuities, as you were informed by some bad birds, and further, the government is bound to furnish you provisions for one year after your arrival at your new homes. The government is now ready to perform its part. I am also instructed to give you a history of your lands west of the Mississippi. The description I shall give you must be of a second hand nature, as I have never seen that part of the country, but it is from such sources that it can be relied on with the utmost confidence. The face of the country, as reported, is prairie openings and heavy timber, well watered with fine, rapid streams, filled with plenty of fish. The timbered lands are generally the same as here and the prairie also, and an abundance of game, such as deer, otter, muskrat, mink, etc., etc., and wild fowl of all kinds, such as turkeys, geese, ducks, prairie hens, etc., etc. The soil produces corn, potatoes, melons, etc., and in fact it is generally acknowledged by all white men who have seen it that it is better than this country and is very healthy. Now if you go there you can enjoy all these things and you will be on your own lands and not be trespassers. Here you are not on your own lands and are committing trespasses daily, and you will not be troubled with the whites. You will also get the annuities due and coming due to you. If you remain here you cannot expect one dollar to be paid to you, for it is particularly specified in that treaty that no annuities should be paid you east of the Mississippi. Your Great Father is determined to carry out his part of that treaty. It is therefore hoped you will be as willing on your part and to come to such conclusion that he will be satisfied, for he is your well wisher and knows that you would be much better off on your own lands than you are here.

After consultation among them, Muckmote, another chief, addressed Mr. Ketchum as follows:

Father:

We have held our consultation with the three nations, and what you said to us yesterday does not please us at all. You told us that we must go west of the Mississippi. In our former councils we always said we would not go, and our minds have not changed yet. At the council at Niles the same question was put to us and we said we would not go. You also wished to know when we would be ready to go. We say again, we will not go. We wish to die where our forefathers died. We have also been informed that the government would protect us. Yes, it will protect us while on our way west, but when we get there we are left to our own destruction, and there is not one of us that is so daring as to go. We are very poor, and one of our nation came back from there and told us that there was no bark to build lodges with, and our women and children would be obliged to live in tents, and it is well known that we are not able to build houses like your white children. Now, there are a great many whites that want us to stay here. They hunt with us and we divide the game, and when we hunt together and get tired we can go to the white men's houses and stay. We wish to stay among the whites, and we wish to be connected with them, and therefore we will not go.

Here Mr. Ketchum addressed them as follows:

You say the whites want you to remain here. Now, to show you that you are wrong in your impression, I will put the question to them and they shall signify the same by the uplifted hand. (So the question was put to a large assembly of whites, when every one lifted up their hands.) Now, sirs, you see that the white men want you to go. I still think that you had better reconsider the answer you gave to me, and carry that article of the treaty into effect, for your Great Father thinks you will be better off there than you are here. You say that you are poor, and I have no doubt of it, and the longer you stay here the poorer you will get. If you go west, you will, as I before stated, participate in the annuities, and that will afford you some relief, and I have no doubt but that you will prosper.

Then Red Bird said:

Father, you have heard our decision: we shall never go. The reason the whites lifted their hands is they are afraid of you. We will never meet in council again.

This concluded the council.

WHITE PIGEON'S GRAVE

[From the White Pigeon Republican, May 29, 1839.]

[It is well known that this village and prairie, as also the beautiful stream that flows along its southern border, take their name from an Indian chief whose grave may still be seen on a small eminence about one mile west of the village. The Indians were accustomed to regard this spot with much veneration. And it is said that in the first settlement of the prairie, on account of its elevated situation, it was chosen by one of the hardy and enterprising pioneers as the most eligible location for his future home; but scarcely was the toil raised shelter from the storm completed ere the forest children, avenging the desecration of their chieftain's dust, laid it in ashes.]

'Tis a chieftain rests beneath the sod
The red man dug for the brave;
Be sacred the spot where his warriors trod,
Where the Indian knelt to the Indian's God,
And wailed by his leader's grave.

And every year as the early spring
Crown'd the grove with its foliage wreath,
His people came, their wild flowers to bring,
And strew o'er the grave of their chieftain king,
And chaunt the wild dirge of death.

Yet time passed on—and but once again
The warrior belt and plume,
The worn with age, and the youthful came—
For strangers stood where their chief was lain,
And their dwelling was over his tomb.

Then the Indian mutter'd a vengeful curse,
And was lost in the forest shade,
But flames on the midnight darkness burst,
'Twas a fun'ral pyre to the chieftain's dust
Which that white man's cabin made.

As fades the frost from the morning sun,
Or the flower in *its* chill embrace;
So brief a race hath the Indian run,
So swift are the forest hunters gone
From before the pale-faced race.

But though forced from their homes have the red men been,
Or sunk to their forest grave,
Yet fix'd they have left upon wood and plain,
On the silvery lake, and the winding stream,
The titles their fathers gave.

And chieftain, tho' years may thy glory hide,
Nor thy warriors shall speak it again;
Yet while men shall inhabit the plain of thy pride,
Or thy beautiful river still flows at its side,
Shall thy name, White Pigeon, remain.

ALFRED.

WHITE PIGEON, May 18, 1839.

LINES WRITTEN ON THE BANK OF PIGEON CREEK

[From the White Pigeon Republican.]

A charm is on thee, winding stream,
    Whose waters glide so gently by,
And thy sweet murmuring accents seem
    The plaintive and the soft reply
To spirits wandering by thy side,
Where once they dwelt, the forest's pride.

Their graves were dug with fragrant bowers
    Of nature's planting o'er them waved,
Upon thy banks adorned with flowers,
    And by thy dimpling waters laved,
While mellow songsters tuned above
Their wildest notes of joy and love.

But ruthless hands thy course have stayed
    And turned thee from thy winding way;
Disrobed thee of thy forest shade,
    Thy forest songsters scared away,
Restrained thy lightly dancing wave,
And made thee, gentle stream, a slave.

Though mirrored on thy bosom now
    Are forms more bright, more fair than they!
Thy murmuring ripples as they flow,
    In whispering accents seem to say,
"More free our dimpling waters played
While forest children near us strayed."

DELIA

WHITE PIGEON, May, 1839.

EDWARD HUGHES THOMSON

[From the Wolverine Citizen, Flint, Feb. 6, 1886.]

It is difficult to realize and very sad to contemplate the fact that the stalwart form of Colonel Edward H. Thomson will never again be seen upon the streets of Flint; that his ever cordial greeting will never again be heard; that the inexhaustible fountain of his wit and anecdote will sparkle here no more; that the social circles where he was always the life and light, will never again be charmed by his conversation; that the listening crowd will no more be inspired from the rostrum by his dramatic lore; that the youthful aspirant for histrionic bays has lost forever the accustomed benefit of his kindly encouragement, criticism, aid, and instruction. It is sad, but alas too true, that the warm heart, the generous hand, the liberal soul, the cultured brain, the accomplished tongue, are cold and silent; and all that remains of Col. Edward H. Thomson has been laid to rest in Glenwood cemetery—baptized by him "God's Acre."

A newspaper is not the place for a biography, and none will be attempted here. Colonel Thomson's life has been active, distinguished, adventurous, and influential. It would afford material for an interesting volume, and it is to be hoped that some one competent to the task will assume the undertaking of writing his biography in an ample form. Meanwhile, the Citizen must confine this death announcement to a mere allusion to the more salient points in the checkered life of the deceased.

Edward H. Thomson was born at Kendal, in Westmoreland county, England, on June 15, 1810. He died from the effects of paralysis, at his residence in this city, very early on the morning of Tuesday, February 2, 1886.

When young Thomson was about three years old his family came to America and settled in the city of Boston, where he spent a few years. They afterwards removed to Westchester county, N. Y., where Edward H. entered and graduated from White Plains Academy. He studied law in the office of Millard Fillmore, afterwards president of the United States. After being admitted to the bar he practiced law in Buffalo, and in Cleveland, Ohio.

He enlarged his mind by several years' travel—two years being spent at sea, as a sailor before the mast. Soon after Michigan was admitted to the union, he adopted this state as his home and settled first in Atlas, then a part of

Lapeer county, and was appointed prosecuting attorney of that county by Stevens T. Mason, Michigan's first governor. In 1838 he settled permanently in Flint, and became a partner in the law firm of Bartow & Thomson. John Bartow was then and until his death regarded as one of the ablest jurists of his day; and to be associated with him was in itself a letter of recommendation.

In 1844-5 Mr. Thomson accompanied Dr. Douglas Houghton in his explorations of the Lake Superior mining regions, and in 1847 he was elected to the state senate, Hon. William M. Fenton being elected lieutenant governor at the same time. Thomson at once took a leading position in the legislature, and was the author of some important and successful measures, among them being the establishment of the institution at Flint, and the insane asylum at Kalamazoo.

He was subsequently appointed by Governor Ransom, commissioner of emigration, in which capacity he served for three years, part of the time in New York, and part at Stuttgart, in Germany; and he was largely instrumental in directing a stream of valuable immigrants to this state. In 1851, at the first World's Fair in London, he represented Michigan, as one of the commissioners of the United States, and, as usual, became distinguished for his social and business qualities. In 1858 he was again elected to the legislature; this time as member of the house of representatives.

Upon the breaking out of the civil war, he took a prominent and active position among the loyal union democrats, and was appointed by Governor Blair, a member of the state military board, with the rank of colonel. He afterwards became president of the board. His connection with "Camp Thomson," and the raising of the Tenth Michigan infantry volunteers in Flint, is too well known to need dwelling upon here.

He was for several years a member of the board of trustees of Union school district and in 1877 was elected mayor of this city. As predicated by his character and capabilities, in every official position he filled, Colonel Thomson was found occupying a front rank. Notwithstanding his busy life as a man of affairs, he never remitted the culture of his inborn taste for literature, the fine arts and the drama. He was a connoisseur in all, and has left behind him visible and durable memorials of his cultivated taste. They will be found in some features of St. Paul's church, in the best aspects of the city hall and in the interior ornamentation of the high school building. Glenwood cemetery, made roughly beautiful by nature, has been converted by art and taste into one of the loveliest "cities of the silent" to be found in this country. There also can Colonel Thomson's ideas be traced on every hand. He took much pride in it, and his artist's eye was never at fault. Only a few weeks since, during a ride through the cemetery with the colonel, he pointed out to the writer a number of additional improvements which he had in contemplation and intended to urge upon the directors as soon as the season was suitable. Little either of us then thought that his last work in that direction had been already accomplished.

It is supererogatory to speak of Col. Thomson's Shakespearean scholarship, or of his rare and splendid Shakespearean library—the collection of a long life time—now fortunately, one of the treasures of the state university. His Shakesperian lectures and readings had a state reputation.

Yesterday afternoon, after short religious services at the house, the casket was brought to St. Paul's church, escorted by Gardner's band and the Union Blues in uniform, and followed by the members of the bar of Genesee county in a body, and by the common council of the city. The bearers were the vestrymen of St. Paul's church. The regular services were conducted by Rev. A. W. Seabrease, the rector. A large congregation was present and a long funeral procession followed the remains to the cemetery.

A meeting of the bar was held on Tuesday afternoon, at the office of Messrs. Durand & Carton, when G. H. Durand, J. H. Hicok, C. D. Long, C. H. Wisner, and E. L. Bangs were appointed a committee to draft resolutions in relation to the death of Colonel Thomson, to be presented at the opening of the next term of the circuit court.

On the same day a special meeting of the common council was held, when resolutions were adopted which will be found embodied in the following proclamation by the mayor:

MAYOR'S PROCLAMATION

It is my painful duty to announce to the citizens of Flint the death of the Hon. Edward H. Thomson, which took place at his late residence in this city, at twenty minutes to one o'clock on Tuesday morning, February 2, 1886.

At a meeting of the common council on Tuesday morning the following resolutions were adopted:

Resolved, That the common council have heard with deep regret of the death of the Hon Edward H. Thomson, of this city.

Resolved, That as a body we desire to express the sorrow that we as a council and as citizens, feel in the death of a former mayor of our city, and one who has for so many years done so much for the social and material advancement of the city.

Resolved, That as a token of respect for the deceased, the city building be draped in mourning, and that the mayor and common council attend the funeral in a body.

Resolved, That the mayor be requested to issue a proclamation embodying these resolutions, and requesting the citizens generally to close their places of business during the hours of the funeral of the deceased.

Now, therefore, I, Mathew Davison, mayor of the city of Flint, would request the citizens, so far as possible, to close their places of business on Friday, the fifth day of February, 1886, at 2 o'clock P. M., and laying aside all ordinary business, attend the funeral of our distinguished citizen, as a mark of respect, and in some sense to show the esteem in which he was held by us.

D. D. Aitken, *Clerk* MATHEW DAVISON, *Mayor*

Dated Flint, Feb. 3, 1886

At a special meeting of the Glenwood Cemetery Association the following resolutions were unanimously adopted:

Whereas, Hon. E. H. Thomson, who for many years has been actively identified with, and for several years has been the president of this association, has been removed from earth, and

Whereas, We, the surviving officers and members of this association, unite in a common sorrow at his demise, therefore

Resolved, That as an association, and as individual members thereof, we, thus publicly, give expression to our regret.

Resolved, That in the death of Col. Thomson we recognize the loss of a public spirited, honorable man, a painstaking, conscientious official, and a patriotic citizen.

Resolved, That a copy of these resolutions be presented to Mrs. Thomson and to the newspapers of the city for publication.

COL. EDWARD HUGHES THOMSON

CONTRIBUTED BY E. S. WILLIAMS

On the morning of February 2, 1886, the spirit of Edward H. Thomson left its earthly tenement of clay, and the struggle between the angel of death and a wonderfully powerful constitution had ended. On New Year's day he was out on the street, a little feeble it is true, but he greeted everyone with a smile and one of those pleasant jests for which he was famous. On the Sunday following he was taken seriously ill, his lower limbs became partially paralyzed, and his physicians became alarmed. He rallied somewhat, but it was found that his whole system was badly shattered and must gradually decay. The paralysis finally affected his brain, and his condition was then recognized as almost hopeless. He was unconscious for several days, but again his constitution asserted itself, and he became quite rational. When conscious he greeted every visitor at his bedside with a pleasant remark and seemed to be almost himself again. But this was of short duration, paralysis again seized upon him, and it was known the end was near. Yesterday it was realized that that was the last day of his life, and family and friends anxiously watched each fleeting breath. At 12:40 A. M., with a little sigh, the soul flitted from the body, and family and friends were in the presence of the dead.

* * *

The parents of Edward Hughes Thomson lived for some time in the picturesque town of Kendal, Westmoreland, England, a beautiful little city of about 12,000 inhabitants, lying on the west bank of a pleasant stream which, but a few miles below, emptied its limpid contents into Morechambe bay, where rose and fell the tides of the ever changing and treacherous Irish sea. In this lovely spot, but a few miles from the Scottish borders and almost within sight of the Isle of Man, the man whom now we mourn was born on the 15th day of June, 1810. In the summer of 1813 his parents moved to this country, and settled in the city of Boston, Mass., where the father was in business for several years. In classic Boston the youth of young Thomson was spent, and there he received his early schooling. Afterwards he entered the White Plains academy in Westchester county, N. Y., and during a four years' course in that institution achieved a reputation of being a hard student and a lover of the muse and stage. After graduating from this academy he spent several years in wandering and sightseeing, doing very little work in that time, but acquiring much valuable information, and storing it away in his wonderful memory. Two of these years he spent on the ocean as a sailor before the mast, and these two years proved of great benefit to him, as he visited many lands which otherwise he would not have seen. Finally he settled down in Buffalo, N. Y., and began the study of law in the office of Sherwood & Fillmore, the firm being composed of Thomas T. Sherwood and Millard Fillmore, afterward President of the United States. In 1832 he was admitted to the Erie county bar, and practiced in Buffalo with some success, afterwards moving to Cleveland, O., where he continued in the law business. He went back to Buffalo and embarked in journalism for a time and gained the reputation of being a remarkably versatile and able writer. He assisted in the organization of the Buffalo Transcript and was on its staff for some time. The friendship between young Thomson and Millard Fillmore continued, and, up to his death, the President took a great deal of interest in him, and aided him in every way in his power.

At the time when Michigan was admitted to the Union and emigration from New York to this state was at its height, young Thomson decided to cast his lot in the Peninsular state, and accordingly in 1837 we find him located in the township of Atlas, which then formed a part of the newly organized county of Lapeer.

In 1847 he was elected to the state senate for the district embracing the counties of Genesee, Oakland, Lapeer, Shiawassee, Saginaw, Tuscola, and all of the counties north, including the upper peninsula. During the term of 1848 and 1849 he was chairman of the judiciary committee, of the committee on mines and minerals, and a member of the committee on state affairs. While he was in the senate he introduced the bills which resulted in the establishment of the institution of the deaf, dumb, and blind in this city; of the asylum for the insane at Kalamazoo; and also for the incorporation of the first copper and iron mining companies in the upper peninsula. He had accompanied Dr. Douglas Houghton in his exploration of the Lake Superior region in 1844-45, and had in this way become acquainted with its wonderful mineral resources.

Another important bill introduced by him was one for the promotion of foreign emigration direct into Michigan. His great interest in this measure was recognized by Governor Ransom, who appointed him as commissioner of emigration under the new law; an office which he filled for three years, first having his office in New York city, and afterwards establishing it in Stuttgart, in the kingdom of Wurtemberg, Germany. Here in a personal interview with the king he laid before him the details of his emigration plan, and afterward gave a full explanation of the vast resources of Michigan by the publication and distribution of a pamphlet of some sixty pages, giving in detail an account of Michigan's advantages as a place for new comers. This same information was also given to the public through the medium of the German press, and with such success that, during the first year, 2,800 persons emigrated from that country to Michigan. The total result of his energetic efforts was an accession of nearly twenty five thousand to the population of the state; and these were principally of a hardy and enterprising class of mechanics and farmers, many of them possessing considerable pecuniary means.

In 1851, while in London, he was appointed United States deputy commissioner of the first world's exhibition. In this position his assiduous attentions to American visitors, and his timely advice to American exhibitors gained for him great praise, while his brilliant social qualities made him an honored and welcome visitor in the homes of the nobility and gentry of the foremost city of the world. Upon returning to the United States he remained in Washington for several years, connected with the United States Senate, and afterward a prominent member of the "third house." His friendships in Washington numbered among them the greatest lights of the age, and his wonderful social talents and brilliant literary attainments made him very popular in the leading circles of the Capital. In 1856 he returned to Flint and resumed his law practice. In 1858 and 1859 he represented this district in the state legislature.

At the breaking out of the war, although he had always been politically opposed to Gov. Blair, the latter, recognizing his executive ability, appointed him a member of the state military board with the rank of colonel, and upon the resignation of Gen. A. S. Williams, he became president of the board. He was untiring in his efforts to raise, organize and equip troops, and his efforts were recognized as being invaluable at the time. The 10th infantry was organized at Flint and received the particular attention of Col. Thomson, who had complete charge of their camps here, which was named Camp Thomson, in his honor.

Since the war he has lived very quietly in our midst, contented to live with the laurels he had already earned. He has, however, served one term of three years as a member of the school board, and in April, 1877, was elected mayor of the city by a majority of 427, one of the largest majorities ever given to any officer of the city. He filled the office with great honor to himself and credit to the city, and at the expiration of his term retired permanently from politics.

Always a man of great literary tastes, during the years following the war he devoted his time very extensively to the study of English literature, and especially of Shakespeare and Shakespeareana, and was recognized the world over as an authority upon the thoughts and acts of the immortal bard of Avon. His Shakespearean library was one of the best of the kind in the world, and when he parted with it about three years ago, he did so with genuine sorrow. It is now the property of Michigan university and is valued at $10,000. Many of the volumes contained in it cannot be duplicated in the world at the present time.

Col. Thomson was a leader in everything he undertook, and at one period of his life studied for the stage. The result was that although he did not adopt the stage as a profession, he became a reader and elocutionist of rare ability; his keen literary perception enabling him to correctly interpret the exact meaning of an author at a glance. During the seventies his Shakespearean lectures and readings were greatly in demand throughout the state and were invariably spoken of in the highest terms.

Col. Thomson was one of the best dramatic critics. He was wonderfully quick to recognize merit and he encouraged it in every way in his power. Many a person of literary ability, fine conversational powers, or intelligence in reading, owes such ability, power and intelligence to the seed sown by

Mr. Thomson, who delighted to be surrounded by those whom he pleased to call his protegés, and these during the latter twenty years of his life may be numbered by the score.

Col. Thomson commanded a leading position wherever he was by his great mental endowment, and his influence was always exerted for good. He was always among friends, for to meet him was but to be his friend. Courtly, genial, the soul of honor, he was recognized as a prince among men.

Col. Thomson was a member of several secret societies and had attained to high honors among the Knights Templar, Odd Fellows, Masons and other organizations.

Col. Thomson leaves behind him a large number of relatives in the United States and England. He was twice married, the first time in Buffalo, when about 20 years of age. In 1841, he was married in this city to Miss Sarah T. Bush, daughter of David Bush of this city. His beloved wife still survives him with whom she journeyed for five and forty years. One son only is living, Edward H. Thomson, Jr. A daughter by his first wife is living, now Mrs. A. B. Wetherbee of Washington. A half brother of Col. Thomson, Charles Hughes, is a prominent attorney residing at Sandy Hill, N. Y.

As a citizen, Flint was always proud of Col. Thomson, as well might be. He had done much for it, and was public spirited beyond his means. His books, his travels, his wonderful brain, had given him a polish and courtesy to all, that put every one at their ease, and filled each one who greeted him with wonder at his great tact and conversational powers.

As a friend, he was the soul of honor, quick to forgive, slow to take offense and a gentleman in the highest sense in which the word can be used.

And so as citizen, man, friend, we follow him to his last resting place, tears must come, and as he is placed forever from our sight, we turn from the new made grave with hearts filled with emotions that our tongues are powerless to express and realize.

"He was a man which, take him all in all,
We shall not look upon his like again."

Edward H. Thomson will rest peacefully in Glenwood cemetery; the birds will sing their sweetest songs above his tomb, for he loved them; the flowers will don their brightest tints and shed their sweetest perfumes over his grave, for he loved them; and we will keep his memory green in our hearts, for he loved his fellow men. Blessed must be the man who loves his God, his fellow man, nature and books. His must be a soul indeed.

Peace to his ashes.

ANOTHER PIONEER GONE—BENJAMIN M. KING

BY JAMES W. KING

Benjamin M. King, one of the early pioneers of St. Joseph county, died at the old home, two miles southwest of Three Rivers, on Wednesday morning, Sept. 15, 1886, aged 79 years. He was born near Middletown, N. Y., and was christened after his grandfather, Benjamin Montonye, a Baptist minister, and soldier of the revolutionary war, the man whom General Washington chose to carry the false dispatch into the British lines, which gave to the enemy the idea that an attack on New York was contemplated by the combined American and French forces, and which finally resulted in the capture of Cornwallis and his army at Yorktown.

Mr. King remained in Orange county until manhood, and then went to Wayne county, where he lived for several years. Here he learned the shoemaker's trade, and when relieved from his apprenticeship married Martha Wetherbee. Soon after this event the young couple started for the then considered "out of the world" territory of Michigan. They reached White Pigeon in the month of May, 1832, and concluded to make their home in the prospective village of Eschol, the landmarks of which can be found two miles south of Three Rivers, on the east bank of the St. Joseph, where the new bridge crosses that stream. In the same year he and Samuel Fitch were drafted as soldiers in the Black Hawk war. They served their country just one month at White Pigeon, when the capture of Black Hawk was announced, and the command to which they belonged disbanded. In 1833, the subject of this sketch removed to Constantine, and, together with Daniel Arnold, of Hull and Arnold's famous band, rented a room and worked at shoemaking for some time. In 1834 he removed to Three Rivers, and lived in the Jacob McIntaffer house, the first habitation erected by a white man in this now prosperous city. About 1835 he built one of the first frame houses in Three Rivers. It occupied the site of the old Frye homestead. In 1836 he purchased 120 acres of land, two miles southwest of this city, built him a house thereon, and commenced in earnest the work of preparing a permanent home for himself and family. For many years he worked at clearing his farm in the day time, and at his trade evenings. In 1846 the mother of his family died, leaving him with five children, the eldest of whom was sixteen, the youngest two years of age. Two years later he married Miss Elza Van Buren, who died just six months ago. She was the daughter of Ephraim Van Buren, one of the earliest pioneers to Battle Creek. Mr. King, for many years, took a deep interest in public affairs. He was an active participant in the anti-slavery struggle, and during the war of the rebellion the Union had no firmer friend than he. He fought the battle of life like a true soldier, and well performed his part as a husband, father, and citizen. He leaves to mourn his loss four children, namely, John, of Waukegan, Ill.; James W., of Fabius township; Mrs. C. H. Howe, of Raymond, Dakota; and Mrs. M. R. Dickinson, of Rockford, Ill. Henry, the eldest son, died at his home, five miles northwest of this city, fourteen years ago.

The funeral services, conducted by Rev. George Frost, took place at the residence of the son, James W., and the remains were interred in Riverside cemetery.

BIOGRAPHICAL SKETCHES

REV. E. H. HAMLIN—AN EVENTFUL CAREER OF A MOST EXCELLENT AND USEFUL MAN

BY A. D. P. VAN BUREN

Elisha H. Hamlin was born August 1, 1808, in Berkshire county, Massachusetts. His father's family removed when he was a child to East Bloomfield, Ontario county, N. Y., where he received the common school education of that day. He was clerk in his brother's store in Murray, Ontario county, N. Y., from the time he was fifteen years of age till he was twenty seven.

He was married to Miss Maria Steadman, at Holly, New York, in 1829. His wife died some few years later. Soon after her death he entered Madison seminary, that Baptist seat of learning that became famous from the eminence its graduates afterwards achieved in the field of foreign missions. He remained in this seminary under the instruction of President Kendricks one year.

His ministerial record is as follows: He was ordained at Holly, N. Y., June 18, 1836. Soon after he came as a pioneer minister to Manchester, Michigan. Preached at Rome, Ohio, one year; at Jackson, Michigan, three years; to the first Baptist church in Chicago from 1843 to 1846; at Laporte, Indiana, three years. Was agent for the American Bible Society two years, with his home at Jackson, Mich. He preached three years at Piqua, Ohio; and in 1855 went to Clinton, Louisiana, where he preached thirteen years, returning to the north in 1868. He preached five years at Ceresco, Michigan. He came to Galesburg in 1873, where he lived till he died December 20, 1885.

One of the memorable events of his life was on the occasion of the fiftieth anniversary of the first Baptist church in Chicago, in October, 1883. Mr. Hamlin was fourth pastor of this church, and the oldest living pastor. The early record was:

Rev. A. B. Freeman..................................1833 to 1835
Rev. I. T. Hinton.....................................1835 to 1841
Rev. C. B. Smith......................................1842 to 1843
Rev. E. H. Hamlin....................................1843 to 1845

Mr. Hamlin's reminiscences given on that memorable occasion, and published in the Chicago papers, were very interesting. The above figures indicate that he was pastor of this church but two years. This was a mistake. He was there three years, as his own record proves it.

He leaves a wife and three children; seven of his children having died. The three surviving are Mrs. C. A. Dye, Miss Ella Hamlin, of Chicago, and Mrs. Robert S. Percy, of Clinton, Louisiana. Mrs. Hamlin will now make her home with her daughter, Mrs. William A. Foote, of Clinton, Missouri. She has a son, Charles D. Wood, living in Denver, Colorado.

Rev. L. B. Fish, of Paw Paw, says of Mr. Hamlin: "The first time I ever saw dear brother Hamlin was in the fall of 1836, when this state was a territory. He preached the second sermon I heard after coming west, in a log school house on the plain a few miles west of Manchester, Hillsdale county. From that time till now I have respected him, loved him, and honored him. He was always a gentleman of great refinement and purity; a most devout and consistent christian. He was more than an average preacher, and one of the best pioneer pastors. The impression he made on me when I was a boy as I used to see him, with my pastor, Rev. J. J. Fulton, and Dr. Piper, in protracted meetings, visiting, preaching, praying, singing, exhorting, and encouraging sinners to change their lives, lingers sweetly in my memory yet. He has gone to join a host of christian pioneers of this state, many of whom he has outlived, but has 'come down as a shock of corn fully ripe.' "

Mr. Hamlin's sterling christian character has been a living sermon for the good of every church to which he has preached, and for every community in which he has resided. A character that ever gave additional effectiveness to his pulpit discourse and to his ministerial labors.

Better than all sermons or printed creed,
Is christian living in word and deed;
Better than all precepts both old and new,
Is christian example from pulpit and pew.

His sermons were always able, clear, concise and instructive. His discourse was animated with the fervor and boldness of one who feels himself "thrice armed" in a righteous cause. Whether it were in church, Sabbath school, educational, temperance or mission work, in every good cause, his life has been devoted from first to last, to the service of his Master.

We have never known a minister who had so many sincere friends among the clergy of other denominations, or among the members of different churches wherever he has resided. This has been especially true of his life in Galesburg. Although he had retired from the pulpit when he came here, yet the Baptist church of this place has had in him its best counsellor and most zealous supporter. When in need of preaching, he has ever been ready to supply its pulpit, and help it in all its work. And when a pastor of any of our churches has been absent, he has kindly consented to preach to his flock; and on funeral occasions he has been a kind and sympathetic pastor to administer spiritual aid and consolation to the grief stricken and sorrowing. In so many ways has this good man endeared himself to this entire community, that all feel that they have lost a most valuable and dear friend. Says a brother clergyman, "no minister was ever more respected or honored by the Baptist church of this state, than Rev. E. H. Hamlin. Amid all the labors and trials of his long and useful services in the Baptist church, no cloud ever hung over his name, not the slightest imputation or stain ever attached to his character."

The funeral services were held in the Congregational church on Wednesday at 10:30 A. M., Rev. J. S. Boyden of Kalamazoo, assisted by Rev. Dr. Mather of Battle Creek, officiating. The remains were taken to Jackson for burial.

DEACON ISAAC MASON—AN OLD PIONEER DEPARTED

Deacon Isaac Mason was born in Cheshire, Berkshire county, Mass., Nov. 23, 1798; came to the Genesee valley, N. Y. in 1802; lived three years at Farmington, then removed to Pennfield, Monroe county, where he lived many years. He afterwards lived in Orleans and Cattaraugus counties. He came to Michigan in 1827 on a land hunting tour, and spent a large part of the year prospecting in Washtenaw and adjoining counties, and without locating any lands, returned to his home in New York.

Reminiscences of this visit to Michigan will be found in the fifth volume of the Michigan Pioneer Collections. Deacon Mason removed with his family to this state in May, 1839, settled on the Dr. John Beach farm in South Battle Creek, where he remained a number of years. In February, 1843, he took charge of the Hiram Moore farm on Climax prairie, living there five years, and afterwards spent three years on his farm in Charleston. While living on Climax, his home was a station on the underground railroad to aid escaped slaves on their way to Canada.

In 1858 he was appointed superintendent of the Kalamazoo county farm, which position he held until 1870, when he removed to Galesburg, where he lived till his death, which occurred on the 29th of December, 1885.

Deacon Mason had been married four times. His last wife, Mrs. Charlotte Thiers, died some four years ago. He leaves five children: Henry, who lives in Cattaraugus, N. Y.; Lee A., at Comstock, this county; Russell B., at Holton, Mich., and Mrs. Abel Hoag and Miss Mary Ann Mason, of Galesburg.

Deacon Mason united with the Baptist church in Pennfield, N. Y., in 1826, was made deacon in 1834. Was justice of the peace five years in Orleans county, N. Y. Was supervisor three years in the same county. Was supervisor one year in Charleston, this county, and one year in Comstock.

In his recollections of life in western New York, that he has given me I recall this item: "My old school teacher was hoeing in his garden one Saturday when a carriage drove up to his gate containing the 'Morgan abductors;' he dropped his hoe, went into the house, changed his coat, and getting into the carriage, rode off with them."

Deacon Mason was one of the memorable "nine" who voted for Jabez S. Fitz for governor, on the "free soil ticket," in Battle Creek, in 1841. He was originally a democrat, but early joined the abolitionists, and went with them into the republican party.

The military record of his sons is excellent. His eldest, James B., was colonel of the 11th Michigan cavalry and was killed at the battle of Clinch Mountain, Va., on the 4th of October, 1864.

Edwin D., after serving through the Mexican war, died on his return home at Jefferson barracks, just below St. Louis, July 7, 1848.

Henry C., now a minister of the M. E. church at Dayton, Cattaraugus county, N. Y., served in the 44th N. Y. infantry during the war for the Union.

Lee A. served in the Michigan 2nd infantry through the war for the Union.

George P., captain of Company A, Michigan 11th cavalry, was killed at Marion, Va., December 18, 1864.

Russell B., served through the war in the 7th Michigan infantry, and lives now at Holton, Mich.

How many men have caught the ear of public fame whose lives have been unworthy of the honorable record that Deacon Isaac Mason leaves.

His life, lengthened beyond three score years and ten, has been full of usefulness and good deeds to his fellow men. He has been a prominent and valuable member of the Baptist church for more than fifty years. And now, at the close of such an extended period of life, he has been gathered to his rest, like a full shock of corn. Few men have been so long and so well known in Calhoun and Kalamazoo counties as this worthy old pioneer. And, like many of those who have gone before him, he leaves the rich heritage of a good name to his family and friends, the best legacy to the history of those early days in Michigan in which he has taken so active a part.

LANKFORD BURDICK

ONE MORE OF THE OLD SETTLERS GONE

Lankford Burdick was born in Pittsfield, Massachussetts, on the 29th of May, 1797. When he was young his parents moved to New Lisbon, Otsego county, N. Y. His subsequent life in the state of New York was spent on the farm. On January 1, 1826, at Lewisville, Otsego county, he was united in marriage to Miss Caroline Toby, by the grandfather of the bride, Rev. Zacheus Toby, a Baptist clergyman there, ninety one years old.

Robert Burdick, with his family, emigrated from Otsego county, N. Y., in 1833, and settled in Charleston, Kalamazoo county, Michigan. With him came his sons Lankford, Alvan and Charles with their young families. The father and sons each locating separate lands formed the nucleus of a colony in this new region, and that part of Charleston was long and widely known as the "Burdick settlement."

Lankford and his family stayed the first week here in the hospitable cabin of the old pioneer, Asa Gunn.

Mr. Burdick's oldest daughter, now Mrs. H. W. Bush, of Chicago, informs the writer that in coming to Michigan they were one week in crossing Lake Erie, and when they began their journey from Detroit, inland with their ox team, they were two days going ten miles. There being no bridges over the streams, they forded them all till they reached Marshall, where they found the first bridge. She was then but four years old, and her graphic, childlike description of the new country, which was sent back to the friends east, was as follows: "There was a great deal of water and no bridges, a great farm with no fences, and one hundred and two mud holes."

When Lankford Burdick built his rude cabin in Charleston in 1833 the settlement on Prairie Ronde was but five years old, the one on Toland prairie was four years old, the one at Kalamazoo was scarcely four years old, and the one on Gull prairie was just three years old.

Mr. Burdick converted his wild burr oak lands into a valuable farm, which he, in 1853, sold to A. R. Holcomb, and removed to Galesburg, where he lived till the time of his death. He leaves four children: Mrs. Harvey W. Bush, of Chicago; Mrs. George A. Signor, of Arthur, Dak.; Mrs. W. A. Blake, of Galesburg, and Mrs. O. H. McConnel, of Jackson.

Mr. Burdick's life in Michigan embraces nearly the entire period of this country's history. He has well and faithfully performed his part in placing Kalamazoo county among the first in the state in point of good farming, thrift, and enterprise.

The traits that characterize the old days of half a century ago, presever-ance, industry, frugality, self reliance, and the knack that goes with it, were exemplified in this thrifty old pioneer's after life.

Mr. Burdick was a republican in politics, a most worthy citizen, and a prominent and valuable member of the Baptist church of Galesburg. In fact this church, which is the oldest in that denomination in western Michigan, has great cause to cherish the memory of Lankford Burdick, for the wise counsel and financial aid he has given it in times of its greatest need.

This church has been called, within the short space of sixteen days, to mourn the loss of its three most honored members—Rev. E. H. Hamlin, Deacon Isaac Mason, and Lankford Burdick.

The funeral services were held in the Baptist church, at 1 P. M., on Friday, the 8th inst., Rev. J. S. Boyden officiating.

BENJAMIN TOBY

Benjamin Toby was born on the 19th of November, 1796, in Massachusetts. He came from Otsego county, N. Y., to Charleston, Mich., in 1844, where he has lived till his death on the 9th inst. He leaves three children, Mrs. J. A. Ranny, of Augusta; Hiram and Geo. Toby, of Charleston. He was a member of the Baptist church of Galesburg. That church has within three weeks lost four of its oldest members. The funeral services were held at the late home of deceased in Charleston, Sunday, the 10th inst, at 1 P. M., Rev. J. S. Boyden officiating.

L. S. HOWELL

DEATH OF A WELL KNOWN FORMER BATTLE CREEK RESIDENT

L. S. Howell died of inflammation of the bowels at his late residence in Kalamazoo, October 28, 1885. He came with his father's family to Battle Creek in 1835. His father, Capt. David W. Howell, located 320 acres of land southeast of Battle Creek, including the farm of the late Jeremiah Brown, to whom he sold the portion known as the Brown farm. Capt. Howell taught school in Marshall in 1835 and '36, and he also followed Warren B. Shepard as teacher in the log school house in Battle Creek in 1837. After selling to Jeremiah Brown, Capt. Howell removed to New York state, where he died many years ago. He is well remembered by the oldest settlers in Battle Creek.

L. S. Howell was young when he came to Battle Creek and spent his school days and until he attained his majority in that place.

He learned the wagonmaker's trade, working for Elijah Clapp a number of years, and afterwards going into business for himself. He married Miss Frank Lockhart, of Galesburg, to which place he removed a number of years ago. He afterwards visited the south, took a trip to California, lived several years in Lincoln, Nebraska, and finally returned to Galesburg some few years ago. During the first of this month he removed to Kalamazoo, where he died, as stated.

Mr. Howell was a great lover of music, early mastering the accordion, out of which, it used to be said, he could get all the music it could produce. He next took the violin, with which he not only won his way to the best musical circles in this part of the state, but also in Rochester, N. Y., and other parts of the country he had visited. He was considered one of the best violinists in the state. For a few years past he had given his attention to piano tuning, in which business he had worked up a large practice in this part of the state.

He leaves a wife to mourn his loss. Mr. Howell was a quiet, unassuming man, not quick to form new acquaintances, rather holding to his old friends, to whom he was ever true, and in whose society he preferred to spend his leisure hours. So well known and appreciated was he by the lovers of music in western Michigan, that for a number of years past he was continually receiving invitations to aid with his violin in some musical concert or other public gathering.

Mr. Howell was of a social, reserved nature. The best part of life to him was in its quieter walks, far "from the maddening crowd." His death calls to mind recollections of the once favorite boarding place on Main street, Battle Creek, presided over by that landlady of the manor born, Mrs. Percy Smith. The set at table consisted of Marsh Giddings, Dwight May, M. H. Joy, Moses Sutton, Mr. Putman and wife, George Thomas and wife, and L. S. Howell, the writer, and a few others. Howell, with his accordion and violin, was ever a favorite with the inmates of "Aunt Percy's" home. But he has gone to the other side, and it is only a matter of time as regards his old friends following him.

LEVI DUNNING

Levi Dunning, one of our old townsmen, died at his late residence in Galesburg, of Bright's disease, on Tuesday, August 18, 1885, in his 77th year. Mr. Dunning was married in Genesee county, N. Y., 1832, to Miss Harriet Mills, the daughter of Asa Mills. Mr. Mills was a pioneer to western New York, and came with his family to Ann Arbor in 1826, where his son Loren yet lives. This was a noted pioneer family. Simeon, Willard and Augustus settled at Gull prairie in 1831, some of the other sons settling in Galesburg at an early period.

Mr. Dunning lived some years at Verona, Calhoun county, from there in 1852 he went to California and in 1854 came to Galesburg, where he lived till his death, as stated above. On his coming to this place he united with the Methodist Episcopal church at Galesburg. He was an industrious, hard working man, and as the fruits of his labor, leaves his family a fair property. In politics he was a republican, but whatever views he had, he held to them unswervingly. He was what we call a positive, angular man and he went through life unchanged, ready to give his opinions without stint or favor to friend or foe, a man of strong convictions, sincere purposes, who lived his religion. He was withal a man of strict integrity, a good citizen, a strong supporter of every good measure or enterprise that would benefit the community in which he lived. His son Edward went to the war and died in Andersonville prison. He leaves a wife and five daughters.

ISAAC CORY

Isaac Cory died at Cedar Springs, on the 21st inst. of consumption. Mr. Isaac Cory came to Galesburg with his brother Joseph, in 1835. He worked at his trade here, carpenter, for many years. Some ten years ago he removed to Cedar Springs where he died. Mr. Cory was one of our worthy citizens, while here filling various offices in the village and township and in all sustaining the reputation of a first class man and citizen. His wife died before he did. He leaves two sons and two daughters.

A. W. COOLEY

A. W. Cooley, who died at the home of his niece in Bedford, several days ago, came to this place in 1836, and worked a year or more for the old pioneer inn keeper, Ralph Tuttle; he also worked a year or more for Mr. Dunham, the pioneer nurseryman of Portage. Mr. Cooley first located in Ross where he purchased a farm. Of late years he has been well known here, at Augusta and Battle Creek. Though in poor health for a long time, yet naturally industrious and thrifty, he has proved the truth of the old adage, "better wear out than rust out;" for he always found some kind of work that he could do, and thus kept adding to his stores, besides being of benefit to the community where he lived. He never married. He had a clear memory of the early days in the eastern part of this county. The writer has obtained many important items in the early history of this region from this worthy old pioneer. He was a member of the Baptist church at Augusta and was a republican in politics. He had accumulated considerable property. His work is done, he has departed, leaving a good name among those who knew him.

GILBERT HIGGINS

Gilbert Higgins died at his home in Augusta on the 5th of September, 1885. Mr. Higgins came to Otsego in 1834. He was a millwright. He came to Augusta in 1835; built the first mill and the first frame house in that place. As a millwright he was a very useful man for this new country. He died in the house he erected in his robust manhood leaving a good name among his fellow men for the usefulness of his life and for his excellent character. He leaves a wife, a son and a daughter.

MAJOR OLIVER WILLIAMS

BY EPHRAIM S. WILLIAMS, OF FLINT

Major Oliver Williams was born at Roxbury, Mass., May 6, 1774, and died on his farm at Silver lake, Oakland county, Michigan, October 11, 1834. In the spring of 1819, Major Williams moved to Silver lake, from Detroit, where he had resided since 1815, and with three men cut their own road through the woods and drove the first horse team ever driven from Detroit to Pontiac. He settled on the south bank of Silver lake, in the town of Waterford, which was then on the frontier of civilization.

Major Williams had visited Detroit in 1808, and was at that place most of the time during the war of 1812; being present there at Hull's surrender.

MRS. MARY WILLIAMS (WIFE OF OLIVER WILLIAMS).

A paper, speaking of the death of Mrs. Williams, says: "Died at Pontiac, April 1, 1860. She was born January 11, 1777, in Concord, Mass. The last year of Mrs. Williams' life was one of intense suffering, which she bore with christian fortitude, in the full hope of a blessed immortality. Mrs. Williams leaves a large circle of relatives and friends to mourn her loss. For forty years she had been a resident of the county. From her position, Mrs. Williams became acquainted with many of the first emigrants and settlers of the county. Her kindness and courtesy to the early settlers won their esteem and none made her acquaintance who did not become her friends, and the attachment formed in the early settlement of the county remained unbroken during her life. For several years Mrs. Williams has resided with her daughter, Mrs. Schuyler Hodges, from whose residence the remains were yesterday removed and deposited in the Oak Hill cemetery beside her husband. Mrs. Williams was the mother of fourteen children, ten sons and four daughters, seven of whom only survive their parents: E. S. Williams of Flint; A. L. and B. O. Williams of Owosso; Mrs. Mary A. Hodges, of Pontiac, and Mrs. Harriet L. Rogers, A. F. and James M. Williams, of California. Mrs. Mary William had forty two grandchildren and sixteen great grandchildren."

The Boston Telegram says: "An old landmark gone. The Lee house, Concord, Massachusetts, built in 1688, was burned to the ground a short time since. It was a large, roomy, two story mansion, seventy five feet in length, and was repaired and fully fitted up at great expense three years since by

S. G. Wheeler, Esq. Its owner, when it was destroyed was Capt. Ellery. The Lee house was occupied during the revolution by Doctor Joseph Lee, a relative of Samuel Lee. Many years afterwards it passed into the hands of the old millionaire, Billy Gray, who sold it in 1820 to the late Joseph Bassett, Esq."

Mrs. Williams was born in this house and lived in it many years after her marriage, it being the property of her father, Samuel Lee. Many of her children were born while she resided in this home. The house remained her mother's after her father's death, until her family left for Detroit in 1815.

Mrs. Williams requested that $600 of her estate be appropriated for the erection of a family monument. Her children added to this amount sufficient to erect a handsome plain marble family monument, which stands on one of the most beautiful spots in Oak Hill cemetery, in Pontiac, surrounded by most or many of the members of her family. The monument bears the masonic emblems of the Master Mason, Mr. Williams having been a member of the order. It also bears the family coat of arms, which is the Williams family coat of arms in Wales.

HON. GARDNER D. WILLIAMS

In the State Republican, Lansing, we find the following obituary notice:

Hon. Gardner D. Williams died at his residence in Saginaw City, on Saturday morning, Dec. 11, 1858, aged 56 years. Mr. Williams was born in Concord, Mass., Sept. 9, 1804. He was the son of Oliver and Mary Williams, and brother of Ephraim, Alfred, Benjamin, Alpheus, and James; his sisters were Caroline, wife of Rufus W. Stevens, of Flint (both deceased), and Mary, widow of the late Schuyler Hodges, of Pontiac, and Harriet, wife of Geo. W. Rogers, of Pontiac (both deceased).

Mr. Williams went early into the Indian trade with his brother, E. S., for many years as agent of the American Fur company, speaking Indian fluently. His power over them was complete, owing to his dignity, his strength of will, and his taciturn, self-collected manner. In personal character, Gardner D. Williams was honorable, upright, liberal, and like the entire family, temperate. He was hospitable, as thousands now living can testify, who have sat at his table and have refreshed themselves after their long wood and river journeys to reach his home. As a husband and father he was kind and careful, a kindness and care which he extended to all relations and kindred who sought his aid. The deceased exercised a wide personal influence through the nature and extent of his business, and from the number looking to him.

The political influence of Mr. Williams was considerable, and was exercised with judgment, in such a manner as coincided with his views of right. He was a useful man in community, and held very many local offices, which he faithfully discharged, without benefit to himself, but because they were needful. He also held many other public offices at different times during his life, both under the federal government and the state government, in all of which, as well as those of a more local character above named, he acquitted himself with honor. He had at different times held the office of Indian farmer and of Indian interpreter, for the duties of which he was unusually well fitted, and if we are not mistaken, filled one of these up to the day of his death.

Mr. Williams was a commissioner of the first board of internal improvements, appointed March 21, 1837; was county judge of Saginaw county for several years, was elected senator from the Sixth district in November, 1844, and received the office of circuit court commissioner of Saginaw county during the same year. His brother, E. S., held the office of postmaster under President Jackson, for several years, and on leaving Saginaw in 1840, he resigned the office, and recommended to the department the appointment of his brother, G. D., to take his place as postmaster, which he received and held for many years.

Judge Williams leaves in his own immediate family a devoted wife, who mourns his loss deeply and sincerely, three sons and the remaining relatives to whom we have before alluded. Mr. Williams was a life long democrat and his three sons, also his four brothers, were all democrats of the old Jacksonian school.

Mrs. Eliza Beach Williams, widow of G. D. Williams, died Sept. 27, 1862.

CAROLINE LEE WILLIAMS

Caroline Lee Williams, daughter of Oliver and Mary Williams, was born at Concord, Mass., February 10, 1806, and died at Flint, Mich., January 5, 1847. She married Rufus W. Stevens, who died September 19, 1850. Mr. and Mrs. Stevens raised a family of one daughter and five sons and were the first family who settled in the township of Grand Blanc, Genesee county, the daughter and one son only now living.

ALFRED L. WILLIAMS

Alfred Leonzo Williams, son of Oliver and Mary Williams, was born July

18, 1808, in Concord, Mass., and died January 6, 1886, at his residence in Owosso, Michigan. Mr. Williams and his brother, B. O. Williams, purchased the land of the government, laid out the city of Owosso, settled there and commenced business under the firm name of A. L. & B. O. Williams. In 1831, accompanied by his brother Benjamin O., he threaded the forests between Pontiac and Shiawassee county and established a trading post on an eighty acre lot, previously entered by him. From 1832 to 1836 the two brothers were acting as agents for the American Fur company. In 1837 the post was abandoned. At his suggestion, land had been purchased from the government at what was termed "the Big Rapids." A little later some improvements were made on it. Mr. Williams saw in that locality, with its fine water power and good soil, well drained by the river, a possible future city, and with a strong determination to make it such, in 1837 he came to Owosso and began the city of Owosso, with whose interests in heart and struggles from that day to his last days he was fully though quietly identified. With his brother, the contract was taken to "grub and clear" forty miles of land from the center of the county to Lyons, westward, for the Northern railroad. One half of this was completed by them. In 1846 Mr. Williams was appointed county treasurer, after the embarrassments caused by the mismanagement of his predecessor. In 1850 he went to California and did active and lasting service in the construction of a water race, from Nevada City to what is known as "Rough and Ready," returning to Owosso in 1851. In 1852 he again went to California, having fitted out an expedition to go thence overland. In 1857 he was absorbed in the Amboy, Lansing & Traverse Bay railroad, now the Saginaw division of the Michigan Central. Of this road Mr. Williams was president. By securing land grants he did an important work, without which the development of the vicinity of Owosso could not have taken place. Considerable of his time during this enterprise was spent in New York, in the interests of the road. After the sale of the road, various enterprises, mainly mining in California and Honduras, South America, occupied his mind. In 1871 he went to London to enlist English capitalists in American mining interests.

Four years were thus spent. The gigantic scheme of his life—it may be said—was that of building a railroad from Richmond, Va., to Clifton Forge, and the development of vast coal fields and iron mines. The project was so far successful that the road was built, and the work in part developed. Financially the attempt was not a success. While not the chief object, it may be said that all other enterprises proved successful financially. Such in brief are some of those dry transcripts of events which crowded this life. Those who knew him could not fail to be impressed with the idea that he was set to be an executor of great designs, a leader, one made in constitution and capacity to direct men. In transactions with his brother, in whom he had, and with reason, the utmost confidence, there was much which he treated as in a careless manner, because of the consciousness that its care would burden his mind while he aimed at entering broader fields. From early life Mr. Williams was through all of it, very closely associated with his surviving brother in Owosso—a man who, in some essentials of his character, is the opposite of what Alfred was—who has so demeaned himself in all their business relations as to retain ever that confidence which grows up between boys in a well ordered home. Besides that the success which had crowned all other undertakings, and that large element of confidence in the worth of man, in his correct intentions, led him to have an undue confidence in mankind. Matters which others could execute and ought to execute, he confided to them for execution, no doubt often to his own detriment. Some would say, "Well, any man ought to know better, and he especially." True as meant, but what is meant by it? Simply this, that the intent of self care ought to be strong enough to keep man from an over confidence in men which works one's own harm.

ALPHEUS F. WILLIAMS

Alpheus F. Williams, son of Oliver and Mary Williams, was born in Concord, Mass, Nov. 12, 1812; married Miss Ann Simpson at Saginaw City and was a resident of that city several years. He went to California at an early day. A California paper contained the following.

Death of Col. Williams. The peaceful termination of an adventurous career.—Shortly after 4 o'clock yesterday afternoon Col. Alpheus Fuller Williams, of Oakland, breathed his last. Col. Williams was a remarkable man. He was essentially a pioneer. The thirst for adventure which dominated his character in youth clung to him to the last. He was born in Massachusetts in 1812 and reared in Michigan. His parents moved to the latter state, the then far west, when he was an infant in arms, and his boyhood days were passed amid those stirring scenes of early frontier life that live in history and tradition.

In 1849 Col. Williams caught the gold fever and left his Michigan home for California. He was then, at the age of thirty seven, a man of large stature and herculean strength, a fine shot, excellent horseman, and thoroughly versed in wood craft.

The long and dangerous journey across the plains was one round of pleasure for him and he took kindly to the rough life of the early Californians. He was one of the first men to build mining ditches in this state, and was also an original owner in the Blue Gravel company. He acquired a fortune in mining and returned to Michigan to lead a life of ease.

He soon tired of the older civilization and taking his family moved back to California. He engaged in mining in Nevada, Sierra and other northern counties, but made his home in Oakland. He was one of the earliest residents of the latter city and contributed materially to its development. Two years ago, at the age of seventy, Col. Williams formed a party to prospect Alaska for the precious metals—not only formed a party but assumed its leadership. A more striking illustration of the restlessness of the typical American pioneer could not be cited than this incident in the career of Col. Williams—a man seventy years old leaving a pleasant and attractive home in the garden spot of California to prospect the sterile and rugged mountains of the frozen north, not as a matter of necessity, but from choice.

His surroundings were so delightful that any man might have envied him. A loving and devoted wife and affectionate children and grandchildren were ever ready to anticipate his desires. And yet he wanted to get into a new country and rough it. So he went to Alaska with his party in a small schooner, was wrecked, suffered greatly from exposure, and never fairly recovered from the effects of the journey. Last year he wanted to visit Alaska again, but was deterred by ill health. His company sent up a schooner, however, and as yet nothing has been heard of her. Six months ago Col. Williams was taken ill and began to fail. His death yesterday was due to a complication of diseases, the heart and lungs being mostly affected. He leaves a wife, two sons and two daughters, all of whom are well known in San Francisco and Oakland. The sons are Gardner F. and Robert N. Williams, and the daughters are Mrs. E. B. Clement and Mrs. T. C. Van Ness. Col. Williams was a man of rugged integrity and leaves behind him a stainless name. Col. Williams was a Mason—a thirty second degree member of the Ancient and Accepted Scottish Rite of Free Masonry for the state of California.

HARRIET LOCADA WILLIAMS

Harriet Locada Williams, daughter of Oliver and Mary Williams, was born Feb. 10, 1814, in Concord, Mass., and died in San Francisco, on Sunday, August 31, 1884. Harriet married Geo. W. Rogers, who died April 9, 1859, at his residence, Pontiac, after a long and painful illness, which he bore with christian fortitude and resignation. "Mr. Rogers was born in New Haven, Vermont. He resided for some years at Vergennes, Vt. He took up his residence in Detroit, in 1840, and in the subsequent year removed to Pontiac, where he afterward resided. During his residence among us he has been identified with the best interests of the village, and has ever maintained a true and spotless character in all the relations of life. He was a faithful friend and brother, a kind and affectionate husband and father, and a good man whom a large circle of friends and acquaintances will mourn with sincere sorrow.

"Thus has been broken a link connecting the present with the age of the revolution; Mr. Rogers having been born on the very same day and hour which witnessed the last early breath of George Washington. Thus in the mellow evening of a well spent life a good man meets the common fate of all. When such men pass away we all may truly mourn.

"Mr. Rogers was a member of the Masonic fraternity, and was one of the founders of the lodge in Pontiac. He leaves a wife, two sons and two daughters to mourn his loss. One of his sons, Mr. Forde Rogers, resides in Detroit. His two daughters are married and reside in California."

The above remarks are taken from a Pontiac paper at the time of his death. The four children above were by his first wife, who was an Emmons, sister of the late Halmer H. Emmons, Esq., of Detroit.

MRS. MARY A. WALKER

Mrs. Mary A. Walker, wife of Hiram Walker, Esq., and eldest daughter of E. S. Williams, was born Sept. 25, 1826, and died Sept. 14, 1872. "None knew her but to love her, none named her but to praise." Her aunt, Mrs. R. W. Jenney, of Flint, was not able to attend the funeral of Mrs. Walker, but her daughter, Miss Belle Jenney, attended the funeral of her cousin. Upon Miss Belle's leaving for her home the friends made up a beautiful bouquet for her mother, Mrs. Jenney, and upon receiving the bouquet Mrs. Jenney composed the following lines:

IN MEMORIAM—MRS. M. A. WALKER

MY BOUQUET

My child, is this all you bring
  From the dear one we loved so well,
A bunch of flowers, so white and sheen,
  What is the story they tell?

Never a word, as you came or went,
From those beautiful lips you say!
My child, you forget the message sent.
Do tell me the sweet words, pray.

"A veil and a bridal wreath,
On her marble brow she wore!"
You cannot mean she's the bride of death,
'Mid friends who have gone before?

"You have guessed too well," oh yes,
'Tis the old, old story o'er;
Our lov'd one is with the blest
In the land of the evermore.

Mrs. Walker left a family of one daughter and four sons: Julia Elizabeth, Willis Ephraim, Edward Chandler, Franklin Hiram, James Harrington.

JENNIE MELISSA WALKER

Jennie Melissa Walker, daughter of Hiram and Mary A. Walker, was born February 13, 1857, and died May 1, 1870, at Aiken, S. C., in the 14th year of her age—a dear and lovely child—whither she had gone accompanied by her parents for the restoration of her health.

"Calm on the bosom of thy God,
Young spirit! rest thee now;
Even while with us thy footstep trod,
His seal was on thy brow.

"Dust to its narrow house beneath!
Soul, to its place on high!
They that have seen thy look in death,
No more may fear to die.

"Lone are the paths, and sad the bowers,
When thy meek smile is gone;
But oh! a brighter home than ours,
In heaven is now thine own."

MARY CAROLINE WILLIAMS

Mary Caroline Williams was born September 22, 1839, and died October 7, 1869, at the residence of her parents in the city of Owosso. She was the wife of Wm. W. Kilpatrick, Esq., and only daughter of B. O. and S. A. Williams.

The sudden death of Mrs. Kilpatrick fell like a pall upon our community. Being the daughter of one of the founders of Owosso, and at the time of her death, with one exception, the oldest born resident of the place, she may truly be said to have grown up with it. Actively coöperating in all enterprises for its moral and intellectual advancement, she has been from her childhood conspicuously identified with the social development of Owosso; while her excellent qualities of character and amiable disposition have always won the love and esteem of the community with which her life has been so intimately associated.

At the age of eighteen years she was confirmed by Bishop Doane, while a member of his school at St. Mary's hall, Burlington, N. J., and from that time she has ever been a zealous worker in the Episcopal church, and an humble, consistent christian. She was one of the earliest members of Christ church in Owosso, being the second communicant in the parish, and her labors have been unceasing in its welfare. From the organization of the Sunday school she occupied a position of teacher and labored indefatigably.

On the 30th of December she was married to Mr. William M. Kilpatrick, a prominent lawyer of Owosso. Surrounded by all that could make life desirable, with unclouded prospects for the future—a beautiful home, the gift of her parents, awaiting her occupancy—we all, so far as human foresight could anticipate, felt warranted in looking forward to a long life of continued usefulness in our midst; but mysterious are the ways of Providence. She now reposes, with her infant by her side, in Oakwood cemetery. The bereaved husband, parents and brothers have the heartfelt sympathy of the entire community. She was buried from her father's residence, on Saturday, Rev. H. Banwell, of Lansing, officiating. Although the weather was very inclement, the crowd of sympathising friends was so great that many could not gain admittance. The burial service of the church was read, and on Sunday morning next, Rev. Mr. Banwell will deliver the funeral sermon at Christ Church.

SCHUYLER HODGES WILLIAMS

Schuyler Hodges Williams was born July 3, 1845, and died January 25, 1866. The funeral of Schuyler H. Williams, son of A. L. Williams, Esq., of Owosso, took place on Sunday, the 28th of January, in the Congregational church.

Mr. Williams was one of the most talented and honored members of the junior class of the university. He died at Ann Arbor, on the 25th, after a very brief illness, which was not considered dangerous till the day before his death. The funeral was attended by a large concourse of sympathising friends, and the remains were followed to the grave by a deputation from his class, and by a number of the members of the Alpha Delta Phi fraternity, to which he belonged while in college, and who acted as pall bearers on the occasion.

He was a young man of fine promise, and beloved and esteemed by the professors as well as by his fellow students, for the uprightness of his character and genial disposition. Endeared to the hearts of those who knew him his loss will not soon be forgotten.

JAMES N. GOTEE

James N. Gotee, brother of Mrs. E. S. Williams, died at his residence in Saginaw City, on the morning of December 8, 1867, aged 53 years. Mr. Gotee was born in Cayuga county, New York, August 29, 1814. More than thirty years since he came to this state, making Pontiac his temporary resting place. Thence he removed to Saginaw in 1836, so that for thirty one years he has been a resident among us. The estimation in which he was held by his fellow citizens is evinced by the fact that he was elected to the office of justice of the peace and afterwards to that of county register, an office which he held for two terms. He was also placed in the responsible position of postmaster for eight years, in Saginaw City. He retired from the discharge of his official duties without the imputation of a stain upon his character. From earliest years he was a religious man, performing every duty, social, domestic and religious, with the utmost fidelity. His end was peace. At 5 o'clock Sunday morning he gently fell asleep.

At that self same hour, of the self same week day, on which the Lord of Glory burst the bonds of death, the emancipated spirit of James N. Gotee, we humbly trust and believe, was with the Lord. "Let me die the death of the righteous, and let my last end be like his."—From the funeral sermon of Rev. I. Leach.

JEROME N. GOTEE

Jerome N. Gotee, brother of Mrs. E S. Williams of Saginaw City, died at his residence on the 3d day of May, 1865, after a long and severe illness. Though in middle life, he was one of the pioneers of Saginaw county, and has shared largely in the confidence and esteem of his fellow citizens. Mr. Gotee held several public offices; was elected sheriff of Saginaw county, serving one or two terms with much credit, faithfully conducting the same, to the benefit of all concerned and with honor to himself.

ELIAS GOTEE WILLIAMS (SON OF E. S. AND U. M. WILLIAMS).

Last week we briefly announced the death of Mr. Elias G. Williams, son of our respected fellow townsman, E. S. Williams, Esq. To-day we give a more extended notice, for Mr. Williams' death was so sudden and, we may say, unexpected, that many of his friends and relations failed to hear of it until the last sad tribute had been paid to their departed friend, and can only express themselves in words of deep regret and sorrow at the loss of one that all who had the pleasure of being acquainted with knew but to love him and respect him. Mr. Williams was born in Saginaw City, April 11, 1838, and died April 23, 1884, being in the forty seventh year of his age. He fully realized how serious his illness was, and requested to be buried beside his little son in Glenwood cemetery, in Flint, and his remains were, therefore, brought to his father's residence here, from which the funeral took place on Saturday, the 26th of April. Mr. Williams, at the opening of the late civil war, enlisted in Colonel Fenton's Eighth Michigan infantry, and was appointed commissary sergeant, being afterwards promoted to the rank of quartermaster, and holding that position during his service with the regiment, which was about two years. Previous to joining the "Eighth" he was clerk and assistant postmaster under his father, in this city, for seven years and was greatly esteemed for his courtesy and obliging manners to the public. He left Flint for Windsor, Ont., about five years ago, where he was in business until a short time previous to his death.—*Flint city paper, April, 1884.*

MRS. AMOS LEE WILLIAMS

From the Owosso Weekly Press, Wednesday, March 31, 1886

Very suddenly has one of the most estimable ladies of Owosso, wife of Mr. Amos Lee Williams, been taken by death from a useful and comparatively active life. An exceedingly happy and beautiful home is left desolate. Her death occurred last Friday morning, March 26.

Mrs. Williams returned on Saturday previous to her illness from Southfield, Oakland county, where she was called about three weeks ago to attend the funeral of a brother. On Monday she performed some duties around her house incident to having been absent from home, which probably involved exposure to a delicate constitution, and at evening experienced a chill, followed by another the next morning, when Dr. McCormick was called in. He found slight congestion of the lungs, administered remedies, and Wednesday morning she appeared better; but at night drowsiness set in, which deepened into stupor the next day, indicating pressure upon the brain, presumably from the rupture of a small blood vessel. Dr. McCormick called in consultation Drs. Perkins and Hume, and Dr. Parkill, but nothing could be done to avert death, and she expired at 7 o'clock Friday morning. The case was necessarily rapid in its fatal termination. A notable feature was the remarkable elevation of temperature, the thermometer registering 109¾ degrees. We have been thus definite concerning the case because many erroneous statements have been made. Mrs. Williams' maiden name was Mattie Beardsley. She was married about twelve years ago, at her home in Oakland county, to our prominent and highly esteemed citizen, Mr. Amos Lee Williams, son of the late A. L. Williams, Esq., of Owosso, and on coming to Owosso identified herself with the cultivated and literary society of this city, bringing much grace and culture to the circles in which she moved. She was a devoted member of the Baptist church, exerting an active and beneficial influence, especially upon the young people of the church. She is a loss to society and to her church, but the heavy blow rests upon the desolate husband between whom and the departed wife there was a remarkable bond of companionship and enjoyment of their beautiful home. She was in the 51st year of her age.

Funeral services were held at the residence Sunday afternoon, at which there was a very large assembly of friends and citizens. Rev. Mr. Donnelly, pastor of the Baptist church, conducted the services.

There were present, relatives, Mr. and Mrs. Dewey and Mrs. Gunning, of Detroit, Miss Lottie Beardsley, Mrs. and Miss Irwin, Mr. Ira Beardsley and Misses Beardsley, of Southfield, Mr. Irwin and daughter, of Walled Lake, Mrs. Phelps and son, of Flint; also relatives from Bennington and Saginaw City.

MRS. E. S. WILLIAMS

[Remarks of a Flint paper upon her death.]

Died in this city, on the 12th of February inst., (1874) in peaceful hope of a blessed resurrection, Mrs. Hannah M. Williams, wife of Hon. Ephraim S. Williams, of this city.

Mrs. Williams was born at Aurelius, N. Y., June 5, 1809, and came to Michigan on the first trip of the steamer Superior, in May, 1822. She resided with her grandfather, James Harrington, near Auburn, Oakland county, until her marriage, March 13, 1825. In the fall of 1824 Mrs. Williams was one of a party of young friends, among whom was Mr. E. S. Williams, to whom she was afterwards married, who rode on horseback to Grand Blanc on a visit to Mrs. Rufus W. Stevens, a sister of Mr. Williams, thence from Grand Blanc to the present city of Flint. The company followed an Indian trail, then the only road of travel; crossed the river on the then rapids and where now is the mill dam, and standing upon the north bank viewed the beautiful spot for the future city of Flint, where she, after an eventful life, lived many years and died.

After her marriage Mrs. Williams and family resided in Saginaw City from the fall of 1829 to the spring of 1840; then after a few years passed in Detroit and Pontiac, made their home in Flint.

At an early age she made a profession of faith in Christ, and for over thirty five years has been a worthy and honored member of the Methodist Episcopal church.

Her life, passed for the most part in continued bodily suffering, has furnished the highest testimony of the power of divine grace to impart steadfast patience, cheerful submission, and continued joy of spirit in the midst of the sorest trials and affliction.

On the day before her death, with her mental faculties unimpaired, and with that wonderful self forgetfulness and care for others which characterized her whole life, she talked with her husband, with Mrs. R. W. Jenny, her only sister, and now the only surviving member of a large family, held a long conversation with the physician who had attended her for eighteen or twenty years, thanking him for his kind attention and expressed her perfect satisfaction with his treatment, gathered her children at her bedside and then directed messages for each of the absent ones. Of seven children given her five yet live; these with her husband, eighteen grandchildren and three great grandchildren mourn the loss of a most devoted and affectionate wife and mother.

Their loss is her eternal gain. Fully matured by discipline and grace, she was eminently ripe for heaven, and on Thursday morning at 5 o'clock with a sweet and peaceful smile as if angels whispered rest, blessed rest, she laid one hand across her breast, the other held by her husband, and with her eyes fixed upon her husband and a beautiful smile, yielded her spirit to God and passed from earth to heaven. "Blessed are the dead who die in the Lord!"

Speaking upon the death of Mrs. Williams, the Saginaw Enterprise says: "Death of Mrs. E. S. Williams. We are pained to hear of the death of this excellent lady at Flint, who expired on Thursday morning the 12th inst.

"The early settlers of the valley of the Saginaw will ever remember her with feelings of the highest respect and tender regard. She was the estimable wife of E. S. Williams, brother of the late Gardner D. Williams, of Saginaw City, and of B. O. & A. L. Williams, of Owosso.

"For a period of nearly a quarter of a century she has been an almost helpless invalid, and during the whole time she has suffered far beyond that of any person within our remembrance, and with a christian resignation that challenges admiration.

"We very much doubt whether the decease of any lady in this section of the state will recall more pleasant and happy recollections than the subject of this hasty notice.

"The hospitality of the whole family of the Williams' at an early day is well known to all who found a home, at that time, in what was familiarly known 'The Saganau.' We offer our sincere sympathy to her worthy husband and children, in the sacred hour of their sorrow."

The Saginaw Courier says: "A short sketch of a noble life and an illustrious death."

"Something more is necessary to constitute true heroism than the absence of fear in the hour and article of death. The untutored savage can calmly contemplate the preparations for his death by torture, and approach the stake chanting his death song, and die defying his enemies. This may be bravery of a stoical character, but fails in the true moral courage which patiently sustains a sufferer, and that sufferer a poor feeble woman, through a long series of years of cruel torture, in which a life lesson is taught us that true heroism is alone found in an implicit reliance upon the justice and mercy of God, by a faith which soars above earth, and, laughing at impossibilities, declares it shall be done. In view of such an instance as this, how pales into insignificance the glory of the dying gladiator, or the soldier on the battlefield. The sublime spirit of the martyrs of old is still found in the case of those who, with hand clasped in that of God, can say, under all circumstances, 'It is well!'"

These reflections are suggested by the death of the late Mrs. Hannah M. Williams, wife of the Hon. Ephraim S. Williams, of Flint, Mich., who died on Thursday, the 12th inst., or rather, passed away, for such do not die; for though putting off the mortal, still the immortal lives, not only in the law of rest and peace, but in the undying memory of good deeds and a blameless life of patient resignation to the will of God.

The services at the house were very impressive; Rev. J. McEldowney and Rev. Marcus Lane, Episcopal, were in attendance on Saturday, and made remarks suitable to the occasion.

Previous to the death of the lady she strove to sing the verse of a hymn she had selected some years before to be sung at her funeral, but her trembling voice could but tremulously articulate two lines of the hymn. At the services the choir sang the hymn, as follows:

SEEKING RELEASE.

"Let me go, my soul is weary
  Of the chains that bind it here;
Let my spirit bend its pinions
  To a brighter, holier sphere.
Earth, 'tis true, has friends that bless me,
  With a fond and faithful love,
But the arms of angels beckon
  Me to brighter worlds above.

"Let me go, for songs seraphic
  Now seem calling from the skies;
'Tis the welcome of the angels,
  Which to me seem hovering nigh.
Let me go, they wait to bear me
  To the mansions of the blest,
When the spirit, worn and weary,
  Finds at last its long sought rest."

[From another Flint paper.]

Mrs. H. M. Williams, wife of Hon. E. S. Williams, of Flint, died at her residence, corner of Kearsley and Beach streets, Thursday morning, at the ripe age of sixty five years. Mrs. Williams had been a terrible sufferer for thirty years from the effects of mercurial poison, administered in her early life as a cure for fever and ague. For a number of years, twenty or more, the poor sufferer has been unable to comb her hair, or to move her body in any direction to help herself, but never lacking assistance, she having a large circle of friends and relatives around her.

Her physician, Dr. I. N. Eldridge, of this city, has been attending her for nearly eighteen years, and had kept her in as comfortable circumstances as his ability would permit. She was indeed kind, industrious, and always patient through her long sufferings, and never known to complain, but always received her friends and neighbors with kind and friendly smiles, always enjoying their company.

On Thursday, the 10th instant, the Rev. E. McEldowney administered the sacrament to her, which she partook of as only a christian would, then on the 12th passed peacefully away. She always attended her church, when able, by her husband taking her in his arms, seating her in the buggy, and then taking her from the buggy and seating her in her seat in the church, having for many years to be carried from place to place, and drawn about her house in a chair made for the purpose.

The family and friends were accompanied by an escort of Knights Templar from Genesee Valley Commandery, of which Mr. Williams is an officer; arriving at Pontiac, were met by Pontiac Commandery of Knights Templar and band, and pall bearers of the old citizens of Pontiac, and escorted to the Hodges house, the home of Mr. W.'s sister, Mrs. Hodges, and on Sunday, after appropriate services by the Rev. Mr. Joslin, M. E., the remains were deposited in Oak Hill Cemetery in the family grounds.

THE HALDIMAND PAPERS

[Continued from Vol. 9.]

COPIES OF PAPERS ON FILE IN THE DOMINION ARCHIVES AT OTTAWA, CANADA, PERTAINING TO THE RELATIONS OF THE BRITISH GOVERNMENT WITH THE INDIAN TRIBES OF NORTH AMERICA AND TO MILITARY POSTS AND MARINE INTERESTS OF THE GREAT LAKES.

1762—1799

Note.—Care has been taken in publishing the following papers to follow the original copies as closely as possible, including orthography, punctuation, capitalization, etc. The references in brackets at the close of each paper, are to the filings in the Dominion archives at Ottawa.

CORRESPONDENCE, INDIAN COUNCILS, PROCEEDINGS OF COURTS, ETC.

FROM GENERAL GAGE. UNADDRESSED

Montreal the 13th July 1762.

Sir—I have twice visited the old Government books to satisfy your demand with respect to the titles of the Jesuits in the Government of Three Rivers & I send you all those which I have been able to find.

I am very sensible of the disasters that have been caused by your unhappy fire & I will be very happy to be able to furnish you with the necessary utensils to stop the progress of similar accidents in the future.

The magazines of this city have never been sufficiently supplied with such utensils & most of those which were stolen in last winter's fire were of the sort that I am better without.

We have no news here, either from Europe or the Isles. It seems to me that the provisions are a long time delayed, it is time that they arrived so as to send them to the Upper Country before the winter; I fear very much being left in the same predicament as last year when after all my trouble, the most of the provisions remained all winter at Fort William Augustus, without power to send them farther.

The Batteaux on Lake Superior are not sufficient.

Major Wilkins saw the Commander at Niagara & Gladwin at Detroit, the former major of the 80th regiment & the latter major of the 1st Battalion in place of Walters. Gladwin can send the same parties into Lake Superior as into all the other lakes.

Your Quarter Master left this morning for York to distribute the uniforms to your Battalion.

My wife and all the Gentlemen send you their compliments; have the goodness to present my respects to Madam Marguerite Bruyére &c.

I am with much consideration sir your very humble and very obedient servant.

(Signed) THOS. GAGE.

Do you know the road by Casco Bay. You can doubtless find the Indians who will give you the description of this route before you attempt it.

Endorsed:—General Gage M. R. the 13th July 62 received the 16th answered the 18th

[B 2. 1 p 68]

COURT OF INQUIRY

FORT PITT September 1st 1763.

A Court of enquiry held by order of Colonel Bouquet to examine into the reasons why an Indian named Andrew,* did not proceed with a Packet to Presqu' Isle.

The Court being assembled are informed by the Indian that on the Evening of the 29th of August he met four Indians of his own nation viz—Hurons near Venago [Venango], who told him that there were assembled at Presqu' Isle One Hundred and fifty Ottawas & Cheapwas determined to wait the arrival of any party of our Troops which might be sent to the relief of D'Troit. That they were in Possession of a Breast work Erected by our own Troops and had mounted two Swivells which had been buried by the Savages when they took the Block house, and that his informers said, they then had been

*See appendix

there twelve days, and had intended soon to march back and take the Swivels to their Grand Camp at D'Troit, consisting of 4000 men Composed of six different nations.

That they had another party of 15 men in a Canoe to Reconnoitre the other side of the Lake as far as Niagara.

That while they were at Presque' Isle they had seen one of the vessels going to D'Troit, but at a great distance, and that she did not attempt to come near.

This express informs likewise the Court that about Eight days after he had left D'Troit with Major Gladwin's dispatches for this Post, he had been told at Sandusky by some of his own nation That 400 men having sallied from D'Troit to attack an Ottawa village a League and a half from the Fort, had been obliged to retire after an action of six Hours with a loss of 150 Killed and Wounded. That the Officer who Commanded that Detachment & five other officers had been killed and Captn Rogers wounded in the Thigh, and that the four Indians he met near Venago Conformed this account which they had heard from the French.

John Stewart Captn.
42. Regt
David Haye
Capt. of Artillery.
Simeon Ecuyer
Capt. 60th Regt.

[B 22 p 88]

LIST OF THE UPPER POSTS UNDER THE FRENCH GOVERNMENT, OF THE GARRISONS THEREAT POSTED, AND OF THE NUMBER OF CANOES USUALLY SENT UP EVERY YEAR

Southern Posts

Fort of Niagara	Officers	5.	one detached.
	Serjeants	2.	No of Canoes
	Drummers	1.	to little Niagara
	Soldiers	24.	
	Chaplain	1.	
	Storekeeper	1.	
	Surgeon	1.	
		—	10

x Toronto	Officers	1.	
	Serjeants	2.	
	Soldiers	4.	
	Storekeeper	1.	
		—	5
x Fort Frontenac	Officers	3.	
	Serjeants	2.	
	Soldiers	12.	
	Chaplain	1.	
	Storekeeper	1.	
	Surgeon	1.	2
		—	—
		Carried over	17
Detroit & Depcies	Officers	4.	—
	Serjeants	2.	
	Soldiers	24.	
	Chaplain	1.	
	Surgeon	1.	
		—	17
Michilimackinac & Dcs	Officers	2.	
	Serjeants	2.	
	Soldiers	10.	
	Chaplains	2.	
	Interps	1.	25

[Q 5 part 1. page 387]

MONEY VALUES IN BRITISH STANDARD

	dwt.	grs.		£	s.	d
The Johannes of Portugal, weighing	18.	6	at	4.	16.	0
The Moydore	6.	8	at	1.	16.	0
The Carolin of Germany	5.	17	at	1.	10.	0
The Guinea	5.	4	at	1.	8.	0
The Louis D'or	5.	3	at	1.	8.	0
The Spanish or French Pistole	4.	4	at	1.	1.	0
The Seville. Mexico and Pillar Dollar	17.	2.	at	0.	6.	0
A French Crown or Six Livre Piece	19.	4.	at	0.	6.	8
The French Piece passing at present for £0. 4. 6 Halifax	15.	6	at	0.	5.	6
The British Shilling			at	0.	1.	4
The Pistereen			at	0.	1.	2
The French Nine Penny Piece			at	0.	1.	0
Twenty British Coppers			at	0.	1.	0

And all the higher or lower denominations of the said Gold and Silver Coins to pass current likewise in their due proportions.

[Q 2 p 294]

ORDINANCE FOR REGULATING AND ESTABLISHING THE CURRENCY OF THE PROVINCE OF QUEBEC.

Be it therefore Ordained and Declared by His Honor the President and Commander in Chief, by and with the Advice, consent and assistance of His Majesty's Council of this Province, and by the Authority of the same, it is hereby Ordained and declared, that from and after the Publication of this Ordinance, the following Species of Coin shall pass current throughout this Province at, and after the several rates herein mentioned, That is to say,

	dwt.	grs.		£.	s.	d.
The Johannes of Portugal weighing	18	17.	at	4.	16.	0
The Moydore	6.	18.	at	1.	16.	0
The Caroline of Germany	5.	17.	at	1.	10.	0
The Guinea	5.	4.	at	1.	8.	0
The Louis D'or	5.	3.	at	1.	8.	0
The Spanish or French Pistole	4.	4.	at	1.	2.	0
The Sevil, Mexico and Pillar Dollar	17.	12.	at	0.	6.	0
A French Crown or 6 Livre piece	19.	4.	at	0.	6.	8
The British Shilling			at	0.	1.	4
The Pistereen			at	0.	1.	2

And shall be so received taken and paid in the same proportion.

And it is hereby further ordained and Declared, that from and after the Publication hereof, the above Species of coin, or any of them reckoning the Dollar or piece of Eight at Six Shillings, and all the other Species in proportion, shall be deemed a legal tender in payment of all Debts and Contracts, that have or shall be made within this Province, where there is no special agreement to the contrary drawn up in writing, or before sufficient witnesses.

And in order to prevent the Importation of Copper Money in such abundance as to drain the Country of its Gold and Silver Coin, It is hereby further ordained and Declared, by the Authority aforesaid, that Eighteen British Copper Halfpence, or Thirty six British Copper Farthings or Forty eight Sols Marquis, whether old or new shall be deemed equal to and pass for, one shilling of the said currency of this Province hereby established. Provided nevertheless, that no person shall be obliged to receive of the said Sols marquis or other Copper Money, at any one payment, above the value of Five Shillings of the Currency hereby established.

Endorsed:—Copy of the Draft of an Ordinance for regulating and establishing the currency of the Province of Quebec.

In Mr. President Irvings Letter of 7 July 1766

No 4.

In the Lord's of Trade's, of the 3rd Septr 1766

[Q 3 p 202]

GENERAL GAGE TO GENERAL HALDIMAND

NEW YORK Decr 28th 1763

SIRS, Lieut Kemble brought your Letters of the 25th and 28th Octr for Sr Jeffrey Amherst which being on His Majesty's Service I took the liberty to open.

I have received no particular directions concerning the Forges of Trois Rivieres and conclude everything is to go on as usual. If anything is to be done in that affair, the Governor will of course receive orders from the Secretary of State.

I have removed all difficulties with Mr Barrow concerning your Draughts for the Service of your Government. He will give directions that you shall be supplied with such sums as are requisite to pay the extraordinary expenses or subsistence of the Troops under your Command.

I am now to acknowledge the receipt of your letters addressed to Mr Jeffry Amherst of the 22nd & 29th Novr with the several Returns enclosed which came into my hands yesterday I find the Companies from Quebec are arrived in the Montreal Government agreeable to the regulation you made with Governor Murray, & that Coll Burton has sent a Reinforcement to Fort Wm Augustus where it was much wanted You will have heard of the behaviour there of the Messengers. I hope the Inegatitsy Indians will bring back the Prisoners as it will be a proof of their good inclinations to keep quiet. I am satisfied that you will find great assistance from Lieut: Gugy, He is a very proper person for your Secretary as He understands both the English and French Languages. I hope the French Officers don't intend to remain in Canada, they will be very troublesome subjects & had better go back to their old master.

We certainly can't be too diffident of the Indians, and you have judged very right in securing your Detachment at St. François against every stroke of treachery.

You will have heard of the misfortune which happened to Major Wilkins' Detachment on Lake Erie, and that he was obliged to return to Niagara without being able to succor the Detroit. The Savages had luckily sued for Peace & given Major Gladwin the opportunity of getting Provisions into his Fort. He has reduced his force to 212 men, which he will be able to feed till June. He sent away the remainder to Niagara. Monsr de Neyon, Commander of the Illinois sent Monsr de Quiadre with letters to the Detroit, exorting the Indians to Peace.

He arrived there about sixteen days after they had demanded Peace, which strengthened their pacifick Dispositions & makes them throw all the blame on the French. You may remember the Examination you assisted me in two years ago. It's said that this Insurrection is part of the project we then heared of.

The Sincerity of the Savages is suspected, and we can't be certain of their real intentions till the Spring.

The news-papers say that Monsr Bigot is condemned to die, that the French Court will not allow him the honor of being beheaded but orders that he shall be hanged.

I am with great regard Sir Your most obedt humble Servant

THOS. GAGE.

Endorsed:—Genl Gage 28 Xhe 63 23 Jan 64.

[B 2-1 p 103]

MR. FRASER TO LIEUT. COLONEL CAMPBELL

ILLINOIS CASCASKIAS 20th May 1765.

SIR, I had the Honour of writing you from this place the 18th Inst Acquainting you of the Message the Shawanese Chief who came lately from New Orleans, had given to the Indians whom I had detained here to wait for Colonel Croghan. I complained to Monsr de St Ange* in a letter from this place giving the Message in the name of Monsr Obrie the present Governor of New Orleans as it seemed to make a very great alteration in the Disposition of all the nations here abouts I Desired that Monsr De St Ange would Contradict it as I could not suspect Monsr Obrie could be capable of advising the Indians to make war with us when we were on such good terms with his nation. But Monsr St Ange has not hitherto made me an answer to this though I had Letters from Him on other Subjects.

It is a great Encouragement to the Indians to continue the war, to see the vast Quantities of Goods that are come up here within these three weeks past.

*See appendix

The Indians would almost have made peace on our own terms before this Convoy came up, as they were in the greatest want of every thing, but the French who intended to quit New Orleans, as it is Credited to the Spaniards have sent all their Goods up here, and they are Eternally Spurring on the Indians to Continue the War thinking to dispose of it the sooner. The Shops and most of the houses in Town have already crowded with goods before the Arrival of a second Convoy here last night, which has brought a Considerable Quantity more. I have been insulted by some of the Traders here, and threatened in the plainest terms that I might assure myself if I made the least mention of them to the Indians that I should suffer for it.

I told them that their threats should not in the least alter my resolution of executing my General's orders & that if I should suffer that they should pay for it. They alledged that I had spoke to the disadvantage of the Inhabitants and wanted the Indians to cut their throats, I had no great difficulty in proving this Allegation to be false, & I told them that I saw plainly such Stories could never have been invented with any other design than to deprive me of my Life & I had seen some instances that confirmed my suspicions in a manner to be true.

I had sent away my men the night of the 18th as I proposed, but I thought best to stay behind myself till I should receive some news of Colonel Croghan I kept the Departure of my men so private that scarce an Inhabitant in the place had known of it till they were two days on their journey. Pondiach was the first whom I acquainted of it. I told him that my reasons were that I had no provisions nor Cloathing to give them, and that the Indians had always beat them when they got drunk. He told me it was very well, that I had done very right. But the Merchants who had threatened me the day before had him to dine with them, filled him Drunk, and soon afterwards I (as well as my Servant) was taken prisoner, He and his men fought all night about us he was reproached by them for having allowed my men to got off, they said that we would got off next day if they should not prevent our flight by killing us. Thus Pondiach would not do. All night they did nothing else but sing the Death Song but my Servant & I with the help of an Indian who was sober defended ourselves till morning when they thought proper to let us escape. When Pondiach was sober he made me an Apology for his behavior, and told me it was owing to bad Counsel he had got, that he had taken me, but that I need not fear being taken in that manner for the future. He told me if I chose to go to his village that he Expected to meet the Chiefs who had gone away there, and as they had promis'd to await the arrival of Mr. Croghan at that place, that after he would hold a Council with Him he would go with me & deliver me safe to the Commanding Officer at Detroit he begg'd I would let him know whether that should be more agreeable to me than going down the river.

I chose the later and he approved of it and beg'd I would give him a Letter to you Sir to acquaint you of his having saved my Life as well as those of my men several times. He told me if this nation on the Ohio had made peace (as I assured them they had) that he would make peace also how soon he would see them. I gave him some Presents and I intend to sett off in a day or two as I can learn no news of Mr Croghan, and that I have the General's Instructions for going down the river to meet Major Farmar. I think the Indians seem at present very well inclined to peace, and if Mr Chrogan has put matters on a good footing with the nation on the Ohio and comes to this country, I do not doubt but that he may fix a solid Peace with them, but as the French in this Colony are so capable of making them do what they please, I think Sir that you ought to be on your guard against them without shewing any Suspicion, as they are all unanimous they will begin the War again or make a General peace soon. Monsr St. Ange has held several Councils with them but I would not suspect him of any evil designs or giving them bad Counsels as he always spoke all he could for our Interests, when I was present. But Monsr Obries giving Permits for taking so much Goods into this Country at present gives reason to suspect what the Shawanese had told the Indians to be not entirely without foundation. If he had delayed the Convoy two or three days, one Monsr Gotterie a French officer could come along with it who is employed to settle a peace with the Indians in our behalf. The French say that the Arcansa Indians intend to take his presents from him, and send himself back.

I have the honour to be

Sir &c.

(signed)

Alexr Fraser.

[B 18 p 54]

GENERAL GAGE TO CAPTAIN BROWNE

New York Octr 5th 1766.

Sir, I have received your Letter of 1st Septemr by Major Bayard, and not a little Surprised at the Report you made of the very miserable state of your Fort, as the Engineer was ordered there in the Spring, to put the Fortification in some order; which must have fallen greatly in Ruin since the 46th Regt left it, to be in the Situation you represent it to be in.

I presume upon His Return from the Detroit, that the Engineer will imagine as you do, that it will be necessary to put in such Pickets as shall be wanting, As well to keep out the Indians as the Hogs, and this I hope is done by this time. With Respect to the Barracks, they are reported in the best order; and as for their furniture, Lt. Col. Robertson has forwarded a large Cargo for all the Posts, So Expect that you have been properly Supplied since you wrote.

I am Sir, your most obedient humble Servant

THOS. GAGE.

Captn Browne 2nd Battn. R. A. R
Niagara } turn over.

P. S.—You will be so good to see that Provision is forwarded in a Proper time in the Spring for Detroit & Missilimakinac that it is properly inspected and the very best Provision sent them. You will demand returns of the State of Provisions at Detroit, whenever the officer Commanding there has opportunities of writing, but will also be able to acquaint you of the state of the Provisions at Missilimakinac, that you may be a judge what it will be Necessary to forward.

T. G.

Genl Gage.

New York 6th Octr 1766

That Lieut Col. Robertson has forwarded a Large Quantity of Furniture for all the Posts. To demand Returns of Provisions from Detroit &ca.

[B 18 p 73]

GENERAL GAGE TO CAPTAIN TURNBULL

NEW YORK October 6th 1766.

SIR, I have received your letters of 25th August & 1st of September, and am very glad of anything I have done for your service has met with your approbation. Major Bayard brought down the return of Provisions & I hope you will have had a sufficient Quantity laid in as well to serve your own Garrison as to send some to Mitchilnakina early in the Spring. The Provision store must hold the Rum, if possible, the expenses increase more than I shall be able to procure Cash to answer.

With respect to the Inhabitants you will take care that no Taxes whatever are laid upon them. You will act for the best respecting the Wood, if your men are in such a situation of sickness as not to be able to cut it. Eight shillings per Chord may be given to the Inhabitants. As for the

King's Rights, I can by no means give them up, agreeable to the desire of some of the Inhabitants in a Memorial brought me by Major Bayard. It is not in my power to do it. I enclose you what they were in the time of the French, in same respect Different from, those in Canada, where the King had a Fifth of the Sales.

This account Major Bayard brought me obtained from Mr. Navarre, who may give you reasons why the conditions of the grants at Detroit differed from those in Canada. But you will see by the conditions that they are to keep up the stockades besides paying rent, &ca.

I repeat that it is not in my power to remit any one article of the King's Rights of which I shall write more fully hereafter. The People may not at once be able to replace all the stockades wanting round the Town, but they must do it by degrees and as soon as they can. I don't mean the Picketing ordered lately round the Fort, that must be done by the King as ordered;

After Mr Van Schack's proposals about the Cattle, I can make no Bargain about it, a contract is made at home to supply the troops, and I must keep up to it, and take the Provision from the Contractor. But I shall be very glad that Soldiers have an opportunity to exchange their Salt meat for Fresh.

I don't hear that the Works ordered were finished when Lieut: Colonel Campbell & Mayor Bayard left Detroit.

I shall hear more when Captain Sowers arrives. I hope they will be over by the winter, and you will send Lieut Brehm down to this place in the Spring.

I am Sir Your most obedt. humble Servant

(Signed) Thos. Gage.

To Captain Turnbull 2nd Battn. R. A. R. Detroit.

[B 27 p 105]

FROM GENERAL GAGE: UNADDRESSED.

New York 17th Novr 1766.

Sir, I received your's dated the 7th of September enclosing a memorial from the inhabitants of Detroit and am sorry that necessity has obliged you to think it necessary to build an Additional Guard Room, and could wish you had waited for Instructions before you had given such orders, I must desire that you will be as careful as possible for the future and that you will not put the Crown to the least expense without there is an absolute necessity.

I am verry sorry to find the Works of Detroit have gone on so very slowly, and are yet so very far from being finished, notwithstanding the great expense they have put the Government to.

In regard to Taxes you will find by a letter, which I wrote to you lately, that no kind of Tax is to be levied upon any account whatsoever, But that the King's rights to rents, Quit rents, and Fines of Alienation, or sales & exchanges are to be supported, and the Inhabitants of the Town agreeable to the conditions of their Grants, obliged to keep the Pickets in repair. I have wrote to His Majesty's Secretary of State representing the poverty & distress which the Inhabitants of Detroit have suffered, through the burden of quartering his Troops, and doubt not they will be exempted, from paying the Arrears due to the King on the above account, but the Inhabitants must expect to pay the King's dues for the time to come.

With Regard to the Trade & Traders at your Post you will consult with Mr Hay, the Commissary, who has orders relative to them & I no ways doubt you will join with him in preventing as much as possible any illegal Trade from being carried on, I am sorry to hear your Garrison, as well as that of Michilionackina are so sickly, and I am much surprised that Captn. Spiesmachers Detachment was so very ill provided with medicines.

I hope he has made you acquainted with his wants, and that you have given him all the relief in your power.

I am Sir your most obedt humble Servt

(signed)

THOS. GAGE.

P. S. As I expect a number of German Recruits over soon to complete the American Battalions, I am to desire you to discharge all the men of your Detachmt who are entitled to it and send them down as early in the Spring as the communication will permit you. And you will at the same time discharge & send with them all those who may be judged unfit. for the Service as there will be more Recruits than will be wanted to complete both Battns. You will take the earliest opportunity to acquaint Captn. Spismachen that he is also to follow these Directions, as there will be Canoes going from this Post to Montreal, I would have him send the Discharged men and those unfit for service by those opportunities, as the conveyance will be easier & attended with less expense, & I shall write to the Brigadier of the Northn District accordingly, who will give proper Directions about them when they arrive.

(signed)

T. G.

[B 27 p 108]

LIEUT. GOV. CARLETON TO SIR WM. JOHNSON, BT.

QUEBEC 27th March 1767.

SIR, I received the Favor of your Letter of the 27th of January, and shall allways think myself obliged to you for informing me of any irregularities committed by Persons from this Province, as by that Information I may be enabled to take such steps here, as may correct them for the future, and assist you in your Endeavours to prevent all Cause of Discontent to the Indians from hence: in Return I will communicate to you the complaints which I receive here, as I imagine this mutual Information must be of advantage to His Majesty's Service, whose Intentions are, that His Servants should promote the good of all His Subjects, as well as prevent any just cause of Discontent, to those under his Protection.

That the French who must allways be our Rivals in Trade, often our open Enemies, should take every opportunity of gaining the affection of the Indians, and of misrepresenting us, I expect as a Thing of course; it belongs to us to defeat their Endeavours, whether fair or fraudulent, and by wise Regulations, honest dealing, and by kind Treatment to attach them to us, and avail ourselves of those Extensive Channels of Trade, to enlarge our Commerce to the utmost.

Your complaints of the Canadians, by which name I distinguish the Subjects of the King our Master, acquired by the Conquest of this Province, are so general that I can only make my Enquiries, and speak to them in as general a manner; When I talk here of that Perfidy, false Stories, or views of exciting an Indian War, you complain of, they appeal to Colonel Gladwin, and all the rest of our officers, who were Spectators of the last, and are confident these will give Testimony of very different Dispositions in them at that Time, when such views might have been more excusable, than at present, and that even then some of them were utterly ruined by the Indians for their attachment to us; they very plainly shew me, that such a War must be very destructive to them, and in case of such a Misfortune, that they then did, and would again cheerfully take up arms, to reduce them to Peace, by Force. Ever since my arrival, I have observed the Canadians with an attention bordering upon suspicion, but hitherto have not discovered in them either actions or Sentiments, which do not belong to good subjects. Whether they are right or wrong in their opinion of the Indian Trade, I submit to those whom the King has appointed to direct and superintend the same, but the unanimous opinion of all here, Canadians and British, is, that unless the present Restraints are taken off, that Trade must greatly suffer, this Province, be nearly ruined, Great Britain be a considerable Loser, and

France the sole Gainer, as they must turn the greatest Part of the Furrs down the Mississippi, instead of the St. Lawrence, they compute that or very large Quantity of Merchandise, formerly passed thro' this Province to Nations unknown to Pondiac, and too distant to come to any of our Posts, and that so much is lost of the consumption of British Manufacturers. They say that their own Interest will allways be a sufficient Reason and Motive to treat these people well, and to use their utmost Endeavors to keep them in Peace, and the Canadians will engage to take some English in every Canoe, to acquire a knowledge of these Countries, and the Language, to shew they have no Jealousy at their becoming acquainted with this Trade. 'Tis imagined here, that the other Provinces, who are neither acquainted with these Countries, nor so advantageously situated for this Trade are the secret causes of their being so severely fettered; they presume to think each Province should be permitted to avail itself of its natural Situation, and acquired advantages, and that it would be as unreasonable in us to expect the Posts to the Southward should be shut up by Regulations, as long as ours are by a severe climate; that in this Respect all the King's Subjects should be considered as Brothers, or one Family, and that the Rivalship ought not to be between Province and Province, but between the King's Subjects and those of France and Spain; some have offered to prove, that two years ago, while they were confined to the Fort, the French or Spaniards from the Mississippi came within twenty Leagues of the Detroit, and carried of the very Furs, that were intended to clear off the Credit given the Indians the year before. They even assert 'tis impossible to prevent them from carrying off by far the greatest Part of that Trade unless those Restraints are taken off, they maintain that the only possible Means of preventing those Evils for the future, and of removing the Discontents of the Indians, for not being supplied with the necessaries of Life as formerly, is to permit them to go among them as was the Practice of this Colony, that thereby they will be enabled to undersell the Mississippi Traders, detect their Artifices, and be the means of bringing them to Punishment, as it is their Interest and Duty so to do; but supposing the worst of them, they hope the King's Subjects of Canada are as much to be trusted, as the French from New Orleans, and ought to have the Preference, considering they carry up the British Manufactures only.

I have also had many Complaints of the Partiality and Violence of some Commissaries, but as I find by your Letters to Lieutenant Colonel Massey, you are already informed of them, I will not trouble you with a Repitition, not doubting but they will be properly punished, if they are found Guilty, the British in particular request, that for the future these may all be obliged to give Security for their good Behaviour, while in that Employment, but should they commit any Injustice, Partiality, or Violence, they may know how to recover proper Damages in a regular course of Law, this they think the more reasonable, as they on their side give Bond to observe the King's Regulations, which, if they do amiss, subjects them to suffer for it, in the same way, and not to be left to the Mercy of a Commissary, or of those Indians he may Hulloo after them, they begged of me to let them have a Copy of those Regulations, they give Security to obey, and that I would not leave them to the Information of a Commissary in those distant Parts, of whose Partiality they have already seen many Proofs, by suffering many to go out and trade abroad, they suspect for Value received, while the rest were confined to the Fort, that whatever was the King's Pleasure, they would submit to, but still it became necessary to be apprised thereof, as they must considerably lessen the Quantity of Merchandise for these Parts, and not be obliged to leave them packed up, and lodged in a Warehouse without, willingly submitting to let all be confiscated, if they sold for one Farthing, rather than bring them to a small Market in the Fort, exposed to all the accidents of Fire this some of them preferred and practised at the Detroit. Had I those Regulations, I would have given them a Copy, but I am as yet uninformed of them.

General Gage acquaints me you complain to him of seven Persons who are among the Indians without Passeports, namely, Capucin, Lorain, La Motte, Pot de Vin, Bartholomé, Bergeron, and Richarville; the six last are Canadians, and have been settled among the Miamis and Onias from fifteen to twenty years, except Pot de Vin, who has been settled as long at Detroit, but I can give you no certain account of Capucin, who is also among the Miamis, it is supposed that is not his real name, but a fictitious one, to conceal that of his Family.

I have given some Presents to the Indians who came to see me at Montreal, as I find it was customary on the like occasions, and think that attention to them must have good consequences.

I am with Regard &c.

(signed) GUY CARLETON.

Endorsed:—Copy of Lieut Govr. Carleton's answer to Sir Willm. Johnson Bt. Super Int. &c 27th March, 1767. In Lieut Govr. Carleton's (No 4) of the 28th March 1767.

[Q 4 p 122]

MR. ROBERTS TO MR. JOHNSON

MICHILLIMACKINAC 20th Augt 1767.

DEAR GUY, New Scenes of Villany open every Day; last night a Quantity of Rum was conveyed out of the Fort about Midnight, I find that there is to be a Canoe loaded with Rum to go to La Bay [aes Puants] which will pick up all the Skins, and perhaps get all the Traders scalp'd.

Potter and the Major has quarrelled, he'll let me into the Secrets he knows; I have wrote to Capt. Claus to get Potter examined upon Oath, it is very certain and no Secret that he declares, he will go off in the Spring, and not empty handed, I am very much embarrassed, all the Traders begging me to fall upon some means for the Security of their effects and Persons, it is imagined there will be Bloodshed in some of the Outposts by some of his People trying to force away Goods these Representations are so frequent and strong, that I have been obliged to beg the assistance privately of Capt. Spiesmaker, that in case he should attempt to make an Excursion to stop him, which he has promised, he has Belts and Pipes from several Nations, which he only is to speak upon, and that in their own Villages. Think on my Situation, my Life, Effects, and Reputation is in danger, he has given the Indians so much that I can scarce keep them in good Humor, tho' I give them more than I fear will be agreable to you. There is the Nation of Cris or Christineaux, that had come down as far as the Grand Portage on their way here, by his Summons to his Council, they were very much dissatisfied last year by Captain Howard, he kicked their belt about and used them very ill, These have been stop'd by Canoes that set out from this after the account of my coming up arrived, T'was of very bad Consequence to the Service my being delayed so long at Niagara waiting Capt. McCleod.

I am told that a man that is gone out for Groesbeck, with whom they say Rogers is concerned, has carried Belts to the Northwest. Rogers says if affairs to the N West don't turn out luckily, he must go off and its thought Groesbeck wont stay behind.

I give myself very little Rest am always attentive to the Public affairs and hope by my vigilance to prevent any bad Consequences.

I am &c

BENJ. ROBERTS

To Guy Johnson Esqr.

[Q 4 p 308]

A DEPOSITION MADE BY POTTER LATE OF MICHILLIMACKINAC, TAKEN BEFORE THE HONORABLE WILLIAM HEY [HAY] HIS MAJESTY'S CHIEF JUSTICE OF THE PROVINCE OF QUEBEC, THE 28th DAY OF SEPR, 1767.

Mr. [Nathl.] Potter late of Michilimakinac maketh Oath upon the Holy Evangelists and saith, that about the Month of January in the Year of our Lord 1765 he became acquainted with Major Rogers,* who is now Command-

*See appendix

ant of the Fort of Michilimackinac, and that from that Time till this last Summer he has continued to be much connected with him, and employed by him in various ways. That he has several Times observed that the said Major Rogers was much dissatisfied with his Situation and expressed a distant Design of taking some extraordinary Methods to better it.

That the said Major Rogers sent the said Potter last Spring to Lake Superior, from whence he returned, about the latter end of last June—and in July last the said Major Rogers had a private conversation with the said Mr. Potter at the Fort at Michilimakinac, in which he explained his Designs to the said Potter in a fuller Manner than he had ever done before. He said he was much in Debt to several Traders, whom he was unable to pay, and that this gave him great uneasiness. That he was therefore resolved to apply to the Government of England to do something to better his Situation, and that he wished they would erect the Country about Michilimakinac into a separate Province, and make him Governor of it, with a Command of three Companies of Rangers, Independant of Sir William Johnson or the Commander in Chief of the Forces in America, that this would satisfy him and make him easy, and nothing else would: and he proposed to Mr. Potter to go to England to make these Proposals to the English Government in his behalf, and to let him know in the speediest Manner possible the success of his Negotiation, for that, if he did not meet with success he would immediately upon receiving notice of his Disappointment, quit his Post and retire to the French towards the Missisipi and enter into the service of the French where he was sure to meet with better Encouragement: That he had lately had a Letter from one Hopkins, who is now in the French Service in one of their West Indian Islands: That in that Letter Hopkins had offered him great Encouragement if he would embrace the French Interest and stir up the Indians against the English; That he was sure he would get great Riches and be a great Man if he was to go over to the French, and therefore he was resolved to do so if the English Government did not comply with his Proposals; and that he advised Potter to do the same as it would be much for his Interest; That upon Potter's expressing some surprise and Indignation at this Proposal, as being contrary to his Duty and Conscience, Rogers told him he was a fool; that he had hitherto taken him for a man of sense and his Friend that would join in any Scheme to serve him; but that now he found he was mistaken; But he said that for himself he was resolved to do so if his Proposals were not complyed with; and he added that if he did take that step and retire among the Indians and French, he would not go empty handed, but would in that Case get into his Hands, all the Goods he could both from Traders and others, by right or wrong, he cared not how; and he said that he had already made Preparations for such a step, by appointing people to meet him at a place called Louis Constant,* near a River that falls into the Missisipi.—When Potter refused to engage with Rogers in this Design, the latter flew into a violent Passion, and swore that he would never pay him a Farthing of what he owed him, and said that he supposed since he would not join with him in his Design he would go and reveal it, but that if he did he would certainly kill him. Potter answered him that he had allways served him faithfully, and wished to do so still, and had no Inclination to reveal anything that might turn to his Prejudice; but as he seemed to be so firmly resolved to take such a dangerous Step, that might be the cause of a new Indian War, or other dreadful Misfortune to the Interests of Great Britain, he apprehended himself to be bound in conscience and by Duty which he owed his Country to give intelligence of it to proper Persons; in order to prevent its taking Place. Rogers upon this took up an Indian Spear that was in his Room in which the Conversation passed, and pointed it at Potter, threatening him with instant Death, if he did not swear to keep this Matter secret. Potter seeing his Life in Danger, cried out for help, but was not heard; upon which he fell down upon his knees and begged Rogers to spare his Life 'till the next Day, when they might confer together upon the Subject again, he hoped with mutual Satisfaction. This made Rogers grow somewhat cooler, he then pressed Potter to give him up a Note of Hand for Fifty five Pounds, twelve Shillings Sterling, which he had given him in New York, and likewise to give him Discharges for Several Sums of Money, which he owed Potter, and which he knew Potter had set down in his Books of Accounts. But Potter did not comply with these Demands. Soon after Rogers opened the Door and went down one of the Steps that were before it; and Potter thinking this a good Opportunity to get out of his Company endeavored to push by him, and get out of the House; But Rogers would not let him go without Blows; He struck him and kicked him saying, "Damm you, you shan't come out yet; I'll Cook you, I'll Warrant you," besides other very foul Language. However by this Means Potter at last got out of the House, and went to his own Lodging. The People were all exceedingly surprised at this Behaviour of Rogers, as they had imagined that Potter had been a great Friend and Favorite of Rogers, as in Truth he had been 'till this extraordinary Conversation, which he did not at that Time communicate to any Body. The next day Potter went out to take a walk; and during this short absence, Rogers took from Potter's Lodging a Silver hilted sword worth six Guineas, a Fowling Piece, twenty Pounds weight of Beaver Skins, a Hat, and other wearing apparel. Potter upon his Return from his Walk met

*See appendix

Rogers on the Parade, who asked him what he thought of Things then, Potter answered that he continued in the same way of thinking as the Day before; which put Rogers into a violent Passion, and made him Swear that he would not let Potter go out of the Garrison. Potter went home and did not yet tell what had passed. The third Day Rogers again asked Potter what his thoughts were upon the Matters he had proposed to him, who again refused to join with him in his Designs; Whereupon Rogers knocked him down, and bid the Guard take care of him; But they, seeing that Rogers was in a violent Passion when he gave this order, did not obey it, and Potter was not confined, but went home strait to his Lodging. Then several Persons who had been Witnesses of the ill Treatment he had received from Rogers and were both surprised and shocked at it, went to see him; and amongst the rest Mr. Roberts the Commissary, who advised him to apply to Captain Spicemaker,* the Commanding officer of the Troops, for Protection. Potter did so and received the Captains Protection, and received no further Injury from Rogers after that Time. On the twenty ninth of August last he left Michilimakinac, and some Days, or the Day before, he acquainted Mr. Roberts the Commissary, with Roger's private conversation above mentioned, which had been the occasion of their Quarrel. Before he left Michilimakinac Rogers sent him word that, if he would not hurt him, he would pay him his Debt. Potter supposes that by the Expression *if he would not hurt him* Rogers must have meant, *if he would not discover the aforesaid private conversation.* Rogers never returned him the Sword, and hat, and Beaver Skins, and other things that were taken out of his Room. Potter says that Rogers is in Debt to almost all the Traders about Michilimakinac, to the amount of a hundred thousand French Livres, all which Debts have been contracted since he has been at Michilimakinac. He says that Rogers told him in the conversation aforesaid that he had sent eleven Canoes loaded with Goods to Lake Superior and Lake * [Michigan] * * and other Places of Indian Trade, Potter says that, Rogers seems to him to be cultivating an interest with the Indians in order to retreat to them, when he shall excute his Purpose of leaving the British Services; and he suspects that one Stoote and one Atherton design to go off with him.

Sworn before William Hey Esqr His Majesty's Chief Justice of the Province of Quebec at Montreal in the said Province this 29th Day of September 1767.

(Signed) Wm Hey* C. I.

(signed) Nathl. Potter

Endorsed:—Copy of a Deposition taken before Chief Justice Hey at Montreal the 28th Sepr 1767. In Lieut Govr Carleton's (No 14) of the 9th Octr 1767.

(Q 4 p 312)

*See appendix

EXTRACT OF A LETTER FROM CAPTAIN CLAUS TO BRIG. GEN. CARLETON

MONTREAL 1st October, 1767.

On my arrival last Sunday from Quebec I had a Packet at my Lodging from Lieut Benjn Roberts, Commissary for Indian Affairs at Michillimackinack, inclosing me a Letter to Guy Johnson Esq open, whereby he desired me to have one Potter late Clarke to Majr Rogers Commanding at that Post examined upon Oath, and send him to Sr. William Johnson for further examination, but finding that said Potter declined going down the Country on account of his bad state of Health, which he said would not allow him to travel by Land, and ready to embark for England, I found the nature of his Information to Mr Roberts such as to make application to the Chief Justice of this Province for having said Potter examined upon Oath, a copy of which Affidavit Mr Hey told me he was to send to your Excy. as well as one to Genl. Gage, and another I am to send to Sr. William Johnson, and thinking that a Copy of Mr. Robert's Letter to Guy Johnson might give your Excellency more Light into the Affair, I made out one and hereby inclose it.

Endorsed:—Copy of an extract of a Letter From Capt Claus to Brigdr. Genl. Carlton dated Montreal 1st Octr. 1767—In Lieut Govr. Carleton's (No 14) of the 9th Octr 1767.

[Q 4 p 307]

Information of Potter since writing the above.

"He says he has done so many things for Major Rogers, that he thinks he cannot answer for, that he left his Service, and had several times a great Inclination to write to Sir Willm. That the other day Major Rogers called him quietly into his office, treated him with a Pot of Porter, spoke very kindly to him, and wanted to engage him into his Service. he told me that the Major says, he has wrote by Major McDougal and others, that if he is not immediately given the Government of this Place separate from any Dependency, and two or three hundred Rangers under his own Command, that he will go immediately to the French, that he has great Encouragement from the French that very lately his Friend Captain Hopkins wrote him another Letter promising great things, and desiring he would keep up the Indians against His Majesty, that he would keep the Canadians disaffected, and engage a Party to join him, also try to get a Part of the Garrison to desert with him, that he will favour his designs, and that Major Rogers says he has a plan of Instructions sent him, that if he has no news to his Satisfaction in the Spring, he will go out and meet Athington, Fute and others who he has already stationed, that they have orders to get what they can into their Hands, that for his Part will take a Tour, and glean all the Coast as he goes, that he has one Stuart who is going out immediately to favour his Purposes to the Bay, and that they will all go by the way of the Missisipi full handed, that he intends to raise a damned Hubbub in the Garrison and then leave it.

Every appearance tally's so much with this Information, that I have desired Mr. Claus to send Mr. Potter to you to be further examined.

B. ROBERTS.

This instant an Information of 40 cags of Rum being lodged on an Island in the Way to La Bay. I detected Rum going out for this use last night by sd. Stuart, I have sent my Clerk, a Serjt and some men, and shall confiscate the Effects, seven Canoes are stopped by finding it, as they know they will have their Throats cut and Goods plundered if Rum goes among the Indians

a true Copy DANL. CLAUS

Endorsed:—Copy of a Letter and Infs from Comy. Roberts at Michillimackinack to Guy Johnson Esqre. 20th August 1767. In Lieut Govr. Carleton's (No. 14) of the 9th Octr. 1767.

[Q 4 310]

LIEUT. GOV. CARLETON TO MR. SUTTON

QUEBEC 9th October 1767.

SIR, The Bearer of this is Mr. Potter, upon whose Subject, by another Conveyance, I write very fully to Lord Shelburne, before whom he is desirous of laying some Matters of Consequence, which occasion his Voyage to Britain, and for which Purpose I am to request your introducing him to his Lordship.

I am Sir Your most obedient Humble Servant

GUY CARLETON

Richard Sutton Esqr

Endorsed:—Quebec 9th October 1767. Lieut Govr Carleton—R; S. R; 14th Novr—By Mr. Potter.

[Q 4 p 319]

FROM CAPTAIN SPIESMACHER UNADDRESSED

MICHILIMACKINAC the 30th of Jan. 1768—

SIR, The 6th Decr last I recd an Express from the Commr in Chieff who appointed me as commr. to this post, & orders to confine Major Rogers for High Treason, which was doen accordingly, by assistance & Deligancy of Lt Christie who we put under grat obligation to him an for his wachfulness &

care, the only oficier I had for duty. I his confinement we took much notice of his behavior, which was very suspitios.

The 30th of Jany last happily for us & this Post, cum in the Evening a Canadien born here & spoak the Indian languach, boren with natural Sence, told me he had a Secret of great importance to communicate to me and that it was now time to discover it, But wanted my Honour in Pledge, as he thought his Life was in danger by the Soldiers and others, if he was known to be the discoverer, I granted his request ——— He then informed me that Majr. Rogers had sent him several message by his formerly servant or orderly man David follerton 60 Regmt to doe what he could to save his Life and the Soldier told him, that the Majr. was in the Frens intrest, and would make his fortune. The Informer heard him with patiance, and told him he would see the Majr. soon, but wanted to know how many Friends he had in general to assis'd him, with his design in geting his Liberty, and what they were, David answer'd he was his Friend, and all the soldiers in general except 3 or 4. Lt. Christie's and one old German, 60 Regmt and one man of the artillerie Finsh.

The next night he went to the Major, who told him that his Designs was first to beg of him, to get the Savages in his Interest to decoy me & Lt. Christie out the fort, Ens'n Johnston diverting his time at the mission, a farm, was easy to git at, after this being throw to the mercy of the Savages, the rest the Major would undertaking, being assur'd the Sergeants would then Deliver him the Keys (:meaning when he had a number of Savages:) to awe the Soldiers, he then was determined to make a fortune before he joyn'd the French on Missisipie, and not go bear handet, for as soon the Fort was his, he should have Powder and Cannon plenty to Take Detroit, and after Ilinois, that his life or Death was in his hand, for without his help he would be shot or Hanged. He then told him, he did not now, but he would assis'd him, they then parted for that night tellen him he hoped to see him soon, the Informer Further told him that the Major had beg'd him to go hunting, by my leave, in order to better cloth his design, to get the Savages (namen several Lee Fourchi le Grant Sable & Mongamike, of Different nation, who he was certain was his Friends:) to make sure of me & Lt Christie, and also Frobisiere marcht from Montreal, then everything would be well, then the Frensh had You Battallion waiting for him at present Comdt by Col Hopkin, who had often wrot for him, I was siland, and the Informer believed I was in doubt, it is up my concence the truth word for word what I have declared, and to give you plain proof, com to morrow night at a place where you can hear and not be seen, where I will call David Secretly to be convinced of the truth, then I look'd on him to be satisfie', and told me Further you may give the Secret to Lt Christie who I look upon a vere good man & consult with him in an affair of sutch consequence to give his atvice.

I had made a scrole of the above showed it to Lt Christie who was Estonnished of sutch Villainas designs, we then consulted the best of our knoledge, to discover the whole in form, I then asked Lt Christie if he thought proper to take Mr. Frobisiere with me, who understoot Frensh (while the Conspiration was carry'd on in that Languech;) he answered to better, and a gentleman we can trust upon, accordingly we went in the Evening Secretly, the Informer put us in a sort of store house in a place where we could not be seen, David did arrive, who we could see & hear their conversation, about the time as above mentioned from David, after this assurd of the truth we went to Lt Christie, atvised that David not should be confined, and still to do duty, we then conjunctly consulted ferder to get more certainety, Mr Frobisiere then proposed a sceam, that the Informer should one more goe to the Major to assure him his Friendship, and at the same time to now what the Major was to do for him, for so great an undertaking, he did as deseer'd and the same Evening he Return'd the 4 night of Febry. to our Joy he brought to me a promissing not, which he saw wrot and Signd, by Majr. Rogers now in my possession.

The words are wrot as follows

At Michilimakinac 4th Febry 1768

I promiss to pay M. Josph Ans annaly an hundret Pound for Five years successfelly to carry me to Mr Hopkins.

as witness my Hand

Robt: Rogers

The whole being this settled and found that all was truè and without doubt and discovert every things, and Different Oaths taken signd and Seald, Lt Christie untertook tho very unwell to keep a strick guard till Revaillee Beating, David being on guard, should be confined, at that time in my Room, until we should.............. the disposition of the two Companies of the ....and the man of the Artillerie, who we immagine to be in the interest of the Treaters, David was privatly brought to me Room, Burst into tears Beging his life, cursing Rogers and wife, and confes'd his Treacherous designs as above, Rogers and David are now in Irons and centrys over them and the guard in the majors Houss Res'd till the Vessel arrev'd to take them from this.

I am Sir Your obedt humble servt

T. Spiesmacher Capt.
in 60th Regt

P. S. Major Rogers had last Spring, wrot for Mr Ans, then at St Joseph, to come to this, and be his interpreter, but had declar'd since, that his real design was to have sent him to Missisipie to invite Capt. Hopkins, with a few men, and on his arrival, should Deliver this Fort into his hands.

T. Sp.

Endorsed:—Letter of Intelligence
G. from Michillimakinac,
C. relative to Major Rogers,
W. delivered to Lord Hillsborough
S. by Mr. Guinand, a
N. Merchant of London. A 24
H. S. C. Read by the King.
G. P.

[Q 5 part 2 page 607]

FROM GENERAL GAGE TO CAPTAIN BROWNE

New York 22d Feby 1768

Sir, I am to acknowledge the Receipt of your letter of the 25th Octr wherein you acquaint me you had Received my Letter of the 2nd Septemr relative to Mr. Blackburn's Contract, and the Steps you had taken in Consequence thereof, they were proper & I approve of them. As you observe there was a mistake in addressing your Letter, but as that which was intended for you, was to the same Purport as the one you Received, it was of no Consequence. I am very sorry to find that the Boats at little Niagara, were so bad, as to be all Condemned, a fresh supply must be sent to you in the Spring from Montreal, orders will be sent there accordingly that you may have them as early as possible. I am concerned for the loss of the Poor Men who were Poisoned, and I hope as the Root must now be well known, that no other accidents of this kind will happen. I hope the Seneca's will Continue quiet, but have reason to suspect their want of sincerity from some information which I have received from Sir William Johnson, however I hope we shall be able to discover their designs, & easily prevent them, in the mean time you will watch them narrowly, and be Constantly upon your Guard. Captn. Sowers has laid before me the State of the Works, and I hope all the Repairs that may be thought necessary, will be Compleated in the Course of the Summer.

Inclosed you have a Memorial from the officers of Detroit to me, wherein

Captn Brown or officer }
Comman'g at Niagara }

they represent the Harship of being obliged to pay for the Transportation of their Stores across the carrying place at Niagara; as it was not meant that they should be put to this Expense, you will be pleased to inquire into it, and for the future order, that the Stores belonging to the Officers of Detroit & Missilimakinac be Transported in the like manner as the Provisions for those Posts.

I am Sir Your most obedient Humble Servant

THOS. GAGE

P. S. Orders are sent to Captain. Maxwell at Montreal to send you five good Boats for the use of Niagara, by the very first Conveyance, when the Communication is open.

Let. from Genl Gage dated 22d Feby
1768 recd. 26th March & ansd 28th do. 1768.

That he has reasons to suspect the Senecas of a Memorial from the officers at Detroit, on the hardship of being obliged to pay for the Transportation of their Stores across the Carrying Place, that they shall be transported in like manner as Provisions for the Posts. Of the Badness of the Boats at Little Niagara, that five good ones are coming up from Montreal & ca.

[B 18 p 91]

PARAGRAPH OF GENERAL GAGE'S LETTER TO CAPT. TURNBULL 29TH AUGUST 1768. RELATING TO HOGG ISLAND GIVEN TO MR. McDOUGAL BY HIS MAJESTY & COUNCIL

As Mr. McDougal's occupying these Lands depends on the surfferage of the Indians who have claim thereto it will be necessary that those Indians shou'd be collected by the friends of Mr. McDougal, and publickly signify to you, or rather give a written acknowledgement of their consenting to the cession of these Lands in favour of Mr. McDougal.

You are to contract no expence upon this account the collecting and supporting of the Indians must be of the account of Mr. McDougal or his friends in his absence, you are only to acquaint them, that you cannot admit them to take possession till you are satisfied of the Indians Intention and acquiesence therein.

This must be a solemn act performed in your Presence by Indians concern'd in the property of these Lands to which you must sign the marks of their Tribes, and you will certify the same to be done by you under my authority and in your Presence. Their Permission at the same time must be had to People the Islands for cultivation, For every necessary Particular shou'd be mentioned in the writing for the cession of these Lands, and the whole fully and distincly explain'd to the Indians to prevent future claims or Disputes. You are likewise to attend to the nature of the Improvements carried on by Mr. McDougal and see that they are such (as may when call'd upon) serve to the Purposes intended of an easy and affectual support of the Garrison at Detroit.

A true Copy T. BRUCE

Commanding Detroit, &c.

By an order of His Majesty and Council Dated at St. James's May 4th 1768 transmitted to the Honourable Thomas Gage Major General and Commander in Chief of all His Majesty's Forces in North America &c. &c.

Ordering that he shall put Lieut George McDougal late of the 60th Regiment in possession of Hogg Island situate and lying in Detroit River, three miles above the Fort of Detroit, Provided that can be done without umbrage to the Indians and upon consideration that the Improvements projected by the Petitioner be directed to the more easy & effectual supply of His Majesty's Fort and Garrison maintained at Detroit, The Commander in Chief having transmitted the same to George Turnbull Esqr. Capt. in the 60th Regiment commanding at Detroit, that he shall see the same executed by being present when the said George McDougal shall receive a Deed from the Indians for the said Island &ca.

By Virtue of the above Order.

This Indenture made by & between Lieut George McDougal late of the 60 Regiment of the one part, and Oketchewandng, Couttawyin, Ottowachkin, Chiefs of the Ottawas & Chipawa Nations of Indians of the other part. Do for ourselves and by the consent of the whole of the said nations of Indians, Witnesseth the said Chiefs for and in consideration of Five Barrels of Rum three Roles of Tobacco three Pounds of Virmillion and a Belt of Wampum, and three Barrells of Rum and three Pounds of Paint when Possession was taken valued, One Hundred and ninety four Pound Ten Shillings current Money of the Province of New York to them in hand paid the Receipt whereof the said Indian Chiefs doth hereby acknowledge, Hath Granted, Bargained, Sold, allienated, and confirm'd, and by these Presents do hereby Grant, Bargain, Sell, alien and confirm, unto the said George McDougal his Heirs and assigns for ever the aforesaid Island that he may settle, cultivate or otherwise employ to his, and His Majesty's advantage as he shall think proper the aforesaid Island in Detroit River about three miles above the Fort, together with all the houses, out Houses and appurtenances whatsoever on the said Island, Messuage; or Tenement and Premisies belonging or in any ways appertaining, and also the Reversion and Reversions, Remainder and Remainders, Rents & Services of the said Premises and every part thereof and all the Estate, Right, Title, Claim and Demand whatsoever of them the said Indians, off, in, and to the said Messuage, Tenement and Premises, and every part thereof to have and to hold the said Messuage or Tenement and all and singular the said Premisies above mentioned and every part and parcel thereof with the appurtenances unto the said George McDougal his Heirs and Assigns for ever, and we the above mentioned Chiefs do hereby engage our selves, our Heirs, our Nations, Executors, Administrators and assigns for ever to warrant and defend the Property of the said Island unto the said George McDougal, his Heirs, executors, Administrators and Assigns for ever against us or any Person whatsoever claiming any Right or Title thereto—

[OTTAWACHKIN]

[COUTTAWYN]

Geo Turnbull Capt
2nd Battn 10th Regmt
Commandant

Witnesses { Danl. McAlpin Lieut 66th Regt.
John Amiel Ensn 60th Regt

[OKITCKEWANDONG]

(a true copy)

T. Bruce
Commanding Detroit &c.

Endorsed:—In Lieut McDougal's of 29 May 1770.

[Q 7 p 117]

PETITION OF SUNDRY INHABITANTS OF DETROIT

To His Excellency Mr. Carleton, Governor of the Providence of Quebec and Dependencies &c.

My Lord, We, Citizens & Inhabitants of Detroit, seeing the publication made and posted up the 14th May of the present year in the name of Captain Turnbull, Commandant of this place, by which we have learned that His Majesty, by the advice of his Council has given an order to Mr. Macdougal to possess, cultivate and enjoy Hog Island, seeing at the same time a prohibition of my said Mr. Macdougal to the Public from bringing there any animals & the order to take away all those which may be there under pain of a fine &c.

Having the honor of representing to you the notable wrongs which the public would sustain by such a cession, if they can have the ground; His Majesty as well as his council cannot be informed of the right which we, inhabitants of the country have in this Island. We pray you very respectfully to consider that the Island in question is a common ceded to the public by the late M. de la Motte, first Commandant of the Country, to keep the cattle in safety, that this right lasted until now without having been chalenged, then that Mr. de Tonty since become Commandant undertook to appropriate it, but a request of the Public forced him immediately to abandon it. Mr. De Quindre under the order of Mr. de Celeron on account of his family & his personal merit obtained also the ownership; but the earnest representation the public deprived him of the possession.

Wherefore we faithful subjects of His Majesty earnestly pray Your Excellency to support & make good our rights and perogatives preserved to us by our former Sovereigns, in order that they be continued to us under the present Government, we pray you at the same time to consider how hard it would be for the ancient Inhabitants and faithful subjects of His Majesty to see themselves stript of their rights and privileges in favour of a stranger come into this country.

We hope that in presenting our demands and supporting them with your credit we will obtain entire satisfaction on this subject & that the said Island will remain in common as it has been since the establishment of this Colony.

The Petitioners have the honor to assure your Excellency of the profound respect with which they are

Your very humble &c very obedient Servants

Detroit the 16th May 1769.

Denoyé	Calliere	Pierre St Auben
Muilyoux	Miny	Charles St Auben
Jeamose	Noel St Aubin	Bayer

Owlette
Bouron
Dusault
Beriné
Pierre Reaume
Gouyeau
Theophille
Lesperanse
C. Leblond
Girmar for himself & for all the Inhabitants of the Larger Point.
Gamelin
Bufert
Beaubin
St. Louis
Cabadsier
Gabriel St. Auben
Antoin Beauford
Etene. Jacob
Antoine Rivard
Bondy
La Jennesse fils
Baptiste Derouillard
François Lebeau
Veaudry Binaulte
André
François Prudhomme
Joseph Paré

Jaques Campeau
Louis Campeau
Simonnet Campeau
Binault
Bapt Meloche
François Meloche
Guilbeau
Peltier
Langloir
Joseph Poupar Laflam
Philipe Le Due
Simon Gendron
François Derouillard
Labady
Hipolite Campeau
C. Maran
La Violette
Pierre Robert
Capiché Meloche
Bergeron
Simon Derouillard
Bainault
Fayan
Entaya
Monnerg
Louis Savar
Francois Chavy
Charles Lafrance

Lauron
Jaques St Auben
Joseph Cardinal
Pierre Cardinal
Bapt. Campeau pere
Bapt. Campeau fils
Reaume
Grejar
Paré
Bonvoloir
La Grand
Toinon Robert
Barthé
Lesperance
Claude Campeau
St Bernard
C. Gouin
Pierre Prudhomme
Pierre Meloche
La Soye
Grenon
Reault
Baptiste Du four
François Rober
Charles Fontene
Proux
Jaques Charon
Jaques St Auben

I the undersigned certify that the above contents also that the signatures are a true copy of the petition which the inhabitants of Detroit presented on the subject of Hog Island.

Detroit the 27th May 1769.

(Signed) L. Dejeau Judge.

Endorsed:—Copy of a Petition of sundry Inhabitants of Detroit 27th May 1769. In Govr Carleton's (No 17) of 18th July 1769.

[(Q 6) p 78]

PETITION

To His Excellency General Gage Commander in Chief of His Majesty's forces in North America &c &c.

Sir, Jean Baptiste Chapoton your very humble petitioner has the honor to represent to Your Excellency, that, in October of the year 1764 he purchased from Mr Lottredge, merchant, at that time of Niagara, a thousand pounds of common powder in twenty small barrels marked T W remaining in the King's Magazin at Fort Ontario, as appears by the inclosed receipt from Captain Wilson officer of Artillery at the said Fort Ontario.

Mr Lottridge promised me that he would deliver it at the risk & expence to Mr Digonaique at Niagara, & then leave for Albany but by the unsettled state of his affairs he has not been able to send the said powder nor the rest as he had promised; therefore I remain until now unable to obtain what Mr Lottridge owes me, & for which I have given him my note on his word. This determined me last year to charge my attorney Mr Edgard of this post to pursue, if he had the means, Mr Lottridge & make him fulfil his bargain. The said Mr Edgard passing Niagara found that Mr Lottridge had not delivered at Niagara the powder & other effects in question. He was told by Capt Brocor Commandant of this Post that there was a quantity of powder belonging to private parties which had been transported from Fort Ontario to Niagara & deposited in the King's Store by order of Your Excellency, and as he cannot deliver the said powder without an order for the price from Your Excellency, permit me to observe that I (gave) made my note for the value of this powder & a quantity of lead & fusils, that the said Mr Lottridge delivered at Niagara. That my note has been sent to Mr Walker at Montreal who has sent to demand payment. As I do not know if the powder was delivered at Niagara according to agreement I have refused to pay, seeing that Mr Lottridge has not sent me my goods of which I know nothing except that Mr Walker has my note & now keeps from me nearly £140 which belongs to me, this is why I ask Your Excellency if you will be good enough to give me an order on which Captain Brocor will give me my powder under the mark.

I ask to have the honor to assure Your Excellency of my profound respect

Your very humble & very obedient Servant

(signed)

B. Chapoton.

Detroit the 12th August 1769.

[B 18 p 124]

ACKNOWLEDGEMENT OF CERTAIN PERSONS

We the subscribers do acknowledge the following was the Question put to the Inhabitants on the 13th October 1769 and answers made by Lieut. McDougal by order of the Honble. Major Bruce Commanding officer of Detroit & its Dependencies relating to a Memorial sent by the Inhabitants to General

Gage setting forth their claim to Hogg Island as a Common; The first Question put to the Inhabitants by Major Bruce was if they had any Writing to shew to prove their Pretentions, their answer was they had none, but they had liberty to put their cattle there for fifty or sixty years past, which they Imagined gave them a Right as a Common and that the Island was given to Mr Degnand in the year 1752, but on their Representation his Deed was disannull'd which strengthened their opinion and that they had wrote to Montreal & Quebeck to have the Records of that Province search'd to see if it was mark'd there but they had got no answer except a Letter from Mr. Baby acquainting them that he had caused the Rechords to be searched into but had found nothing relating to the Island in their favour, that it was Recorded to have been given to Mr. Degnands but scratch'd out again and no mention made of its being given to the Publick of Detroit; They also procured an answer of a Letter from General Gage wherein he promised every thing in his Power & that he had wrote to General Carleton to have the Records look'd narrowly into, and that if he should find anything to their advantage shou'd acquaint them immediately of it. Major Bruce asked Lieut. McDougal if he had anything to say to confute their allegation, He answered that any thing they had advanced did not merit an answer untill they produced a Grant of the Island as they pretended to have as they set forth in their memorial to General Gage, but with the Major's Leave he shou'd be glad to ask them some Questions, as it is well known here they never had a Right to that Island during the Time of the French, but they may make some false pretensions on purpose to give trouble Lieut McDougal asked them who gave Liberty to one Mr. Pilet & Mr. Campau to live & cultivate the Island during the French, about six or eight years before we took Possession of this Country, they imagined it was the Commandg officer;

Mr. McDougal told them it was very extraordinary he could give these people Liberty to cultivate the Lands of the Publick & if it was their Right why did they ask the Liberty of every Commanding Officer since the English had Possession of this Country to put their Cattle on the Island as proved by Mr. Hay the time he has been here, they answered they were new subjects and were afraid; Mr. McDougal asked them why they did not find fault with Lieut McDonald for Labouring the Lands on the Island in the years 1761: 2 & 3 they answered as above. He asked them why they did not produce their claim to the Commanding officer and stop him (Lieut McDougal) from Building a House clearing ground, and setting a family on the Island in the year 1762 & 3 which was but off during the last Indian War, they answered still as above, Lieut McDougal also asked them why they did not find fault with the Commanding officer for giving a Farm to Mr. Bondy behind the

Fort in the year 1764, which they claim an equal Right to as the Island, their answer was, the Commanding officer was Master; he also asked them why they did not find fault with giving two acres in Breadth and forty in Length to Mr. St. Martin Lands of the King's Domain which they say is their Right also as the Island, they answer as above, Lieut McDougal told them then that he understood them well, that the Commanding officer was Master to give what he pleased to the french, but they did not allow the King of England to have the same Liberty to give to an Englishman Lieut. McDougal also produced to the Major the order he had from His Majesty & Council, He also acquainted him that the General had given positive orders to the Commanding officer of Detroit that he should not permit him (Lieut. McDougal) or any of his friends, in his absence to take possession of that Island untill he should receive a Deed from the Savages for the same, and that every expence incurr'd on that head should be the sole acct of Mr. McDougal he had the Savages called together last spring in Council in presance of the Commanding officer and all the officers of the Garrison, at that time he Received a solemn Deed for that Island, which cost him very considerably both in Presents and Provisions, but it being the General's orders he obey'd this the Inhabitants knew nine months before it was done, and on receiving the Deed the Commanding officer gave him Possession of the Island in Form.

The Commanding Officer and all the officers of this Garrison at present, have been here this three years Declare that they always looked on that Island as the King's and that the Inhabitants never attempted to put their Cattle or cut Hay on the Island without leave from the Commanding officer, or cut wood on the Island on any account whatever.

Geo Turnbull Capt.
2nd Battn. 60th Regt.

Danl McAlpin Lieut 60th Regt.

The Commanding officer as mentioned above was Captn. Turnbull.

(a true copy)

T. Bruce
Commanding Detroit &c.

Endorsed—In Lieut McDougal's of 29 May 1770.

[Q 7 p 122]

MEMORIAL OF LIEUTENANT MCDOUGAL

To the Right Honorable the Earl of Hilsborough One of His Majesty's Principal Secretary's of State,

The Memorial of Lieutenant George McDougall late of the 60th Regiment now on half pay most humbly sheweth

That your Memorialist got an order of His Majesty and Council for Hog Island, situated and lying in Detroit River, Three Miles above the Fort of Detroit, provided that it could be done without giving umbrage to the Indians, and on consideration the Improvements projected by the Petitioner be applyed to the more effectual and easy supply of his Majesty's Fort and Garrison at Detroit. But as no absolute Grant could be given to your Memorialist (Detroit being out of the boundary laid down by His Majesty and Parliament in the year 1763. He was contented to accept of an order of Council judging it equally good as a real Deed; and that His Majesty and Council referred the same to the Commander in Chief for the time being, to put your Memorialist in possession of said Island, or not; according as he judged it equitable.

The Commander in Chief ordered the Commanding officer at Detroit to put your Memorialist in possession of the Island after fulfilling the General's orders. A copy of which I herewith transmit to your Lordship.

Your Memorialist had the Indians called together the fourth of May 1769 in council in presence of the Commanding officer and all the officers of the Garrison, at which time he received a Solemn Deed for the said Island; which cost him very considerably both in presents and provisions, it being the Commander in Chief's orders to have such a Deed from the Indians. The French Inhabitants knew I had an order from His Majesty and Council for the Island nine months before I received the Deed from the Indians, in which time they never made the least objection to my possessing the Island, and I even had almost finished my house on the Island before the Inhabitants made any complaint; On your Memorialist receiving the Deed from the Indians the Commanding officer gave him possession of the Island in form agreeable to the General's orders. A Copy of the Indian Grant I herewith transmit to your Lordship, also transmit your Lordship a copy of Questions put to the Inhabitants with their answers the 13th of October 1769, by order of the Hon. Major Thomas Bruce Commanding officer of Detroit on his arrival here, he having received orders from the Commander in Chief to do so.

When your Memorialist got possession of the Island he engaged an English family to settle with him, which they now are, & has made very great improvements which cost us very considerably, in clearing ground and Building tho' neither of us as yet has reaped the least benefit nor do expect for one year to come. Your Memorialist was not the first that petitioned for that Island, there was two Memorials before His Majesty and Council, two or three years before mine. One by Lieut Mant, who had got a Deed for the Island by Colonel Broadstreet in the year 1764 when the Colonel was here settling the affairs of the Indian War, and the other Memorial signed by

Lieut. Abbott of the Royal Artillery. Those Memorials I still believe lies at the Council Chamber. If your Memorialist had ever known that the Inhabitants of Detroit would have made the least claim to that Island, he never would have apply'd for it; but as he had made no improvements on said Island, and had lost so much by it, he thought in reason to have the said Island.

Colonel Gladwin was Commanding officer here from the year 1762 to the year 1764, who I am certain will declare that the Inhabitants (while he commanded) never pretended to have the least Title or claim to the Island in Question, it being his publick orders that they should not put their Cattle on the Island, without his liberty, nor should they cut wood nor Hay on the Island on any pretense whatever (he is now in England) Col Campbell 17th Regmt. who succeeded him in the Command commanded till August 1766 gave out the same orders; Capt. Turnbull, 60th Regiment who signs the Inclosed paper has commanded here upward of three years gave out the same orders; While none of the Inhabitants ever made any pretentions to said Island, nor did they ever so much as whisper that it was their property; for if they had, as I said before, Your Memorialist never would apply'd for it.

Your Memorialist humbly conceives that he has fulfilled the Intention of His Majesty & Council with the aprobation & order of the Commander in Chief to whom it was referred, therefore he looks upon the Island as his property agreeable to the order of His Majesty and Council. Otherwise your Memorialist never would have laid out so much money in Improvements. Your Memorialist is well informed that the Inhabitants (now claiming a right to that Island as a common) cannot produce any title thereto, or is any thing of the kind mentioned in the Registers of this place or Canada. Your Memorialist humbly Implores your Lordships protection and favour, and begs that Your Lordship will not press him to refer his property to arbitration.

Your Memorialist in duty bound shall ever pray &c. &c.

Endorsed:—In Lieut McDougal's of 29th May 1770.

[Q 7 p 112]

LIEUTENANT MCDOUGAL TO THE EARL OF HILLSBOROUGH

DETROIT 29th May 1770.

MY LORD, By a paragraph of a Letter from the Honble. General Thomas Gage Commander in Chief of His Majesty's Forces in North America, To the Honble. Major Thomas Bruce of the 60th Regmt. commanding at the post. I understand that His Excellency has given it as his opinion to your

Lordship, that the Grant given me of Hogg Island by His Majesty and Council, referred to and confirmed by the express orders of the Commander in Chief in a letter to Captain Turnbull then commanding at this Fort. A paragraph of which will appear at the head of the Indian Grant Copy transmitted herewith to Your Lordship, that I should in consequence of an ill supported claim, made by some Inhabitants of this place to the said Island as a Common give up my right and property to be decided by arbitration. I hope Your Lordship will be good enough to excuse me for declining to leave what I think my property, with the Improvements thereto. Agreeable to the Tennor of my grant, to such a decision.

My Lord from your well known abilities to distribute strict justice to every subject within the limits of your administration. I have great reason to hope my past service and the justice of my cause may in some degree intitle me to your Lordships protection. I hope your Lordship will pardon the liberty I have taken to trouble you with the enclosed.

I have the Honour to be with the utmost Respect My Lord

Your Lordship's most obedient & most humble servant

George Mc Dougall.

To the Right Honourable the Earl of Hilsborough one of His Majesty's principal secretary's of state.

Endorsed:—Detroit 29. May 1770 Lieut McDougal Rf 17 August.

[Q 7 p 110]

THE EARL OF HILLSBOROUGH TO LIEUTENANT MCDOUGAL

Whitehall 3rd October 1770

Lieut. McDougal

Sir, The Decision by arbitration of the matter in dispute between you and the Inhabitants of the Detroit concerning Hog Island appeared to me to be just and equitable, as such I suggested it to General Gage, but since you do not think fit to acquiesce in that mode, the matter must remain for the final Determination of His Majesty in Council.

I am &ca

Hillsborough

Endorsed:—Drat to Lieut McDougal 3d October 1770

[Q 7 p 196]

FROM GENERAL GAGE. UNADDRESSED

NEW YORK April 8th 1771.

SIR, Your letters of the 14th and 18th December are very full on the subject of Grants, & Lands at the Detroit. I am to explain to you that the King has not invested any Person whatever with the power of granting Lands in America, except to his Governors, within the limits of their respective Provinces, & under certain forms and restrictions, and where any Purchase is made of the Indians tho' within the limits of the Provinces they are not valid, unless permission is given so to do, & the Purchase made in presence of the Governor & His Majesty's Superintendant of Indian Affairs. From hence you will know the power of granting Lands at Detroit remains solely in the King, & that no purchase can be made of the Indians but with the King's permission & authority.

It may be needless after the above explanation to inform you that all grants made by Lieut: Colonel Gladwin, Major Bruce or any other British Commander are null & void & of no value.

As for the French Grants in general unless approved of by the Governor General of Canada & registered accordingly they were not valid but as for Monsieur Belestre's grants in the year 1760, they cannot be deemed any other than fraudelent, and are by no means to be looked upon as valid.

And as for the Indian purchases they were not allowed by the French, nor are they allowed by the English Government but under the Restrictions I have already mentioned.

Monsr Navarre's Declaration or Certificate may be in part true, but it is not the whole truth. The first settlers with Mr. Salvrevrés, were not perhaps enjoined to the conditions imposed afterwards, respecting their titles—The Govt was glad to get any people to begin the settlement. But Monsr Navarre's conclusion is vague & ill founded. I am well informed in those matters, was Three Years in possession of the Books wherein the Titles were registered & received information upon them—The very time in which Mr Bélestre's Grants were made sufficiently points out their being invalid & that they would not be registered when the whole Govt of Canada was on the point of surrendering to the King & the Capital possessed by his troops so early as September 1759. Monsr Béléstré was not ignorant of those circumstances and his grants are fradelent.

I am not to require of you, as soon as this is received annul & make word by Public Act every concession made by Monsr Béléstré in the year 1760, every grant made by every British Commander, without exception, and all Indian Purchases whatever or Indian Deeds not obtained by the King's permission and authority—And that you do not suffer any settlements to be made with the above Titles or any new settlements to be began on any pretense whatever, and that you pull down as fast as any Person shall presume to build up—And that you do seize and send down the Country all Persons who shall be endeavouring to settle among the Savages.

I imagine the Indians will be set upon to talk to you upon these subjects, you will answer them that the King is tender of their property & has made regulations to prevent their being cheated and defrauded. That His Majesty has been induced to make these Rules upon the frequent complaints of the Indians against the white People who have defrauded them of their lands by making a few of them drunk & getting them in that condition to give away their country to the great disgust of the rest of the Nation, and that by such means the Indians have represented that the White People have taken a great part of their hunting grounds.

This has happened to many Indian Nations & unless you stop it in the beginning at the Detroit, the same thing will happen there.

Mr. Grant has engaged to build two vessels for the King, in which business you will please assist him, and give him such help as your Garrison affords, whenever he shall demand it. As for the Merchants they may build what vessels they please, but you will not suffer Mr. Grant's Artificers or Sailors to be taken from him. You have acted very properly in that respect already. I understand there is very good Cedar to be had which Mr. Grant will make use of for the King's vessels, and if you find it necessary you will reserve the Cedar and suffer no person to cut it, but when it is to be used in the King's service.

I hope that you have received the orders about fitting out the old vessels for this years service.

You must continue to take every precaution against accidents from Fire, if Mr. Babie's Stables are so near the Magazine as you represent it must be deemed a nuisance & removed accordingly.

I am &c.,

(signed) THOS GAGE.

P. S.—The Merchants alledge that there is Cedar to be had in the greatest plenty. It that is the real case I can have no objection to their cutting as much as they want of it, and you will not obstruct them, on that or any other business not detrimental to the service.

T. G.

[B 27 p 184]

ROADS FROM DETROIT TO THE ILLINOIS BY WAY OF THE FORTS MIAMIE, OUIATTAMON AND ST. VINCENT WITH SOME REMARKS.*

	Miles.	Miles.
From Detroit to Lake Erie	18	
To the River Miamie	36	
To the Foot of the Rapids	18	
To the Top of the Rapids	18	
N. B. Part of the Ottawa & a few of the Hurons inhabit this part of the River. In the former when the water is low, Canoes cannot pass the Rapids, otherwise than by being dragged over the stones & frequently the Traders are obliged to carry their goods the whole eighteen miles.		
To the end of the Still Water [near Florida, Henry Co.]	24	
To the top of the next Rapids [4 miles below Defiance]	9	
To the grand Glaze, a river so called on the left going up [at Defiance]	6	
N. B. A few Ottawas live here.		
To the little Glaze, in the right [Tiffin River]	3	
To the King's Glaze on the right [a few Ottawas live here] [Platter Creek]	12	
To the Elm Meadow [Antwerp]	15	
To Sledge Isd [so called from a large stone resembling a sledge]	12	
To the Split Rock	6	
To the Wolf Rapid [Bull Rapids]	12	
To the great Bend	12	
To Fort Miamie	15	216
N. B. The Miamie Nation live opposite the Fort and consist of about 250 men able to bear arms. The Fort is inhabited by Eight or Ten French families.		
From Fort Miamie to Cold Fleet* where the old French Fort was	3	
The carrying place to the little River	9	
To the river a'Boite	6	
To the Flats	21	
To the little Rock [Bull Creek]	3	
To the Ouabache [near Huntington, Ind.]	6	
N. B. Between the Miamie & the Ouabache there are Beaver Dams which when water is low Passengers break down to raise it, & by that means pass easier than they otherwise would, when they are gone the Beavers come & mend the Breach, for this reason they have been hitherto sacred, as neither Indians or White People hunt them.		
To the River Sallammee on left going down [Salamanie]	15	
N. B. This River is navigable for Canoes 150 miles.		
To the Pipe River on the left	18	
To the great Rapid	3	
To the Erel River on the right [Eel River]	3	
To the little Rock	9	
To the Island of Garlic [at Delphi]	15	
To Richard's Coal mine on the right close to the river	9	
To the river Teippeccans on the right to the river [Tippecanoe]	9	
N. B. This River is navigable 150 miles for Boats	18	
To Ouiattanon Fort		183
This Fort is on the right about 70 yards from the River. The Ouiattanon nation of Indians is on the opposite side, and the Reccapories are round the Fort in both villages about 1000 men able to bear arms.		399

*See appendix

ROAD FROM DETROIT TO THE ILLINOIS—*Continued.*

	Miles.	Miles.
Brought over		399
From Fort Ouiattanon down the Ouabache to the River Vermillion	60	
N. B. This river is on the right & at some seasons is navigable for boats about 120 miles, a mile up it is a village of Peankshaw's of upwards of 150 men.	3	
To the Highlands or old Boundary between Canada & Louisiana [Terre Haute]	57	
To Fort St Vincent [Vincennes]	120	240
To the Illinois by Land, the road is chiefly through Plains & Extensive meadows		240
N. B. From Detroit to the Illinois		879
The above Distances are all compated.		
The Road from Detroit to Fort St Josephs by land and from thence to the Junction of the Illinois River with the Mississippi by water.		
From Detroit to the River Huron,* or Nandewine Sippy	40	
N. B. There is a village of Puttawateamees of six large cabans. The river at this place is about Fifty feet wide and the water is generally from one and a half to two feet deep, when there are Floods Travellers are obliged to make Rafts to cross it, the road in this place bad.		
To the Salt River or Wanadagon Sippy	12	
N. B. There is another village of Pittawattamees of five Cabans. This river is never so high as to prevent people passing it.		
To one of the Branches of Grand River or Washtanon that falls into Lake Michigan	60	112
There is another village of Pittawattamees of eight large Cabans.		
To Reccanamazo River, or Pusawpaco Sippy otherwise the Iron mine river	75	
N. B. There is another village of Pittawattamees of eight large Cabans, this river cannot be passed in Freshes on Rafts, at other time 1 or 2 feet deep.		
To to the Prarieronde	30	
N. B. There is a small lake of about ¾ of a mile wide and 11 miles long, abounding with several sorts of Fish, such as Maskenongi, Whitefish &ca		
To the Fort St Josephe	75	292
N. B. There is a few Puttawattamees near the Fort the road after you pass the River Huron is very good being mostly on a small height of land & little wood till you come to St Joseph's where you pass through about a mile long and another about six miles long.		
From Fort St Joseph's you ascend that River to a carrying place	12	
From carrying place to Recankeekee	4	
To the Junction of this River with the Iroquois R	150	
N. B. In this fork is a village of 14 large Cabans of Mascontains.		
To the Junction of this River with the Chicangoni river which forms the Illinois River	45	
N. B. At this fork there is a village of Puttawatamees of 12 large Cabans.		
To the Rocks or old French Fort called Pumetewee	90	
To the Mississippi	240	541
From Detroit to the Mississippi by way of the Illinois R		833

[B. 27 295]

*See appendix

FROM AID-DE-CAMP KEMBLE TO MAJOR ETHERINGTON

HEAD QUARTERS, NEW YORK, 3rd May 1772

orders—

As confusion was happened in Provision accounts by officers and men drawing in one Post large Quantities of Provision which they alledge to have been due to them in others and as such Practices render it difficult to ascertain the Quantity of Provision necessary to be deposited in each Post respectively it is the order of the Commander in Chief that no Provision is issued to officers or men at any of the Posts or other Places of Deposit but from the day of their arrival at said Posts, and no Commissary or Depy. Commissary is to issue by any order whatever any Rations commonly called Back Rations. As he shall answer the contrary.

STEPH. KEMBLE
Aid-de-Camp

To Major Etherington, or officer commanding the 2nd Battn. of the 60th Regt. at Detroit.

Endorsed: General order 3 May 1772. Rec'd 1 June, That no Provision be drawn for at the different Posts, but from the day of the arrival of the Troops at the Post.

[B 122 p 1]

FROM GENERAL GAGE TO LIEUT. COL. SMITH

NEW YORK, Sepr. 10th 1772.

SIR, Mr. Anthon's demand for taking Care of the part of your Regt. at the Detroit is too high, if your Surgeon makes him a reasonable allowance besides the Medicine Money, the Charge may be admitted in your Bill of Extraordinarys. And in case of Extraordinary Sickness amongst the Troops, the Surgeon may supply him with a Proportion of Medicines which will be returned to him again from the Stores of the General at this Place. I can't deal with Mr. Anthon as a Garrison Surgeon. You observe rightly of your Company at Oswegatchie, tho' I am at a Loss how to get them Relief, but will write to Lieut Col Templar to try to get some Person there capable of giving Assistance in Case of Accidents, without doing harm from Presumption and Ignorance. You will believe that a very skillfull Person can't be procured. The Reasons given in your Letter of the 8th of August for the Crew of the Vessel wintering at Niagara, may be sufficient to authorize the laying her up at that Post, and no great time can be lost. There is no doubt a Risk of Desertion from Oswegatchie and indeed its' the greatest Inconvenience of that Post. You will settle that matter as you judge best. No time should be lost in providing a new Cradle for the Carrying Place. If materials must go from hence, I will order the Chief Engineer to provide them without Delay.

I am with great regard, Sir

Lieut Col. Smith Your most obedient humble Servant

10th Regt. THOS GAGE.

From Genl. Gage Sept 10th 1772. Of the wintering the King's Vessel at Niagara. The Repairing the Cradle at the landing place and of Mr. Anthon's Demand for taking care of the sick at Detroit.

[B 18 p 144]

GENERAL RETURN

General Return of the number of Rations, of Provisions Issued to His Majesty's Troops in North America, under the command of His Excellency, The Honble Lieut. General Thomas Gage. Commander in Chief &c. &c. &c. Between the 25th June & the 24th December 1772.

Detroit

Royal Artillery,	10th Regt:	1 Batt. 60th Regt.	2d Batt 60th Regt:	Total.
2,240	22918,	40.	3408.	28806.

Michilimackinac—

Royal Artillery,	10th Regt.	2d Batt 60th Regt.	Total Rations
915.	13001.	1985.	15901.

(Signed)

FRANCIS HUTCHESON Capt
60th Regiment Acting for
Major WILLIAM SHERRIFFE
Dept Quarter Master
General

[B 34 p 26]

GENERAL ESTIMATE

A General Estimate of the Works Carrying on in the Engineer's Department at the several Forts and Posts in North America, in the year 1773.

	N York Curry.		
At Pensacola & Mobile	9001	13	2
St. Augustine—£122.2.6 Stg	209	7	1¾
Niagara	1878	6	8
Fort Erie	447	6	0
Detroit	1272	14	0
Michilimackinac	616	10	0
Quebec Province £1231. 12. ½ Halifax Cy	1970	11	4¾
Halifax £1477. 10. 0. do. Cy	2364	0	0
Total N Y Currency	17,760	8	4½

Sowrr
Commanding Engineer

New York
April 1773

End:—A General Estimate of the Works carrying on at the several Forts & Posts in North America in the year 1773.

£17,760 8 4½ N Yk Curry.

[B 17 p 284]

[New York Currency was about one-half sterling]

TO MAJOR BASSETT WITHOUT SIGNATURE

New York, June 15th 1773.

Sir, General Gage being sail'd for England I am to acknowledge the Receipt of your letter of the 29th of April; I am very sorry to learn that another Trader has been killed by the Indians & that before we have received any Satisfaction for the Loss of One, we have again to demand it for a further outrage; I am fully persuaded these Mischiefs arise from the Quantities of Rum that get amongst the Indians, & wish with you some means were fallen upon effectually to prevent it, but I despair, whilst such different Interests prevail in the several Provinces concerned in the Indian Trade, to find any proper measures adopted to prevent this evil, you doubtless have heard that it has been recommended to the several Legislatures of the Provinces by the King to form Laws and Regulations for the Government of the Traders, but it has proved hitherto ineffectual & they have come to no agreement concerning them; however I could not have you pass over this Insult, a demand should be formally made from the Nation of the Murderer. Sir William Johnson will be informed of this event & will give you further directions concerning what may be proper to be done therein.

Respecting the Domain you mention to be reserved to the King round the Fort of Detroit it certainly appurtains to the commanding officers, for the Time being to make use of as he shall judge proper, but I cannot consent to putting the Crown to any Expense about it; and indeed as the paling it in seems by your own Representation, to be a measure so disagreeable to the people I think it better let alone, and I can't think it would Answer the Expense to any Commanding Officer; from the General Rotation of Regiments that is now determined upon, that Command will not continue very long in the same hands.

The Bill you mention has appeared, and will be paid; I am sorry the Repairs of the Barracks go on so slow, and that you are in want of Artificers. The Engineer will inform you further upon this subject.

I am Sir &c.

To Major Bassett 10th Regt Commanding at Detroit.

[B 33 p 5]

GENERAL RETURN

General Return of the number of Rations, of Provisions issued to His Majesty's Troops in North America under the command of His Excellency the Honorable Lieutenant General Thomas Gage Commander in Chief &ca. &ca. &ca. Between the 25th December 1772 and 24th June 1773.

	Royal Artillery.	10th Regt.	Total Rations
Detroit	2,251	23,114	25,635
Michilimackinac	900	14,894	15,803

Endorsed Copy. Half yearly Return of the number of Rations of Provisions issued to His Majesty's Troops in North America between the 25th of December 1772 and 24th June 1773—

To John Robinson Esq. Secretary to the Lords Commissioners of His Majesty's Treasury January 5th 1774—E.

[B 34 p 49]

TO LIEUT. COL. BRUCE. WITHOUT SIGNATURE

New York August 10th 1773.

Sir, On the 23rd of last June I received your letter of 16th May with the several returns therein mentioned. I am glad to hear that the Store House was then nearly finished, and think very proper what you have done relating to the Nails, without which the Works could not have been carried on, or must have suffered a Considerable Delay; I also approve of the Precautions you have taken to secure your Post, and hope by this Time that the Necessary repairs are Completed, I cannot Omit this Opportunity of recommending to you the strictest Economy, and to undertake nothing which is not absolutely Necessary to the Preservation of your Post, without communicating it Previously to me.

I have since received yours of the 16th of June & must observe to you that so many various reports being constantly spread amongst the Indians & White People, it is Necessary to be very Cautious of giving always credit to them, and to take all possible precautions to have true Intelligence's and to come att the source of the Reports previous to Informations, which at this great Distance, might be attended with prodigious Inconveniences, taking at the same Time such Precautions as to prevent even an attempt similar to that which took place some years ago, at your present Post, I shall always be glad of all Informations you can procure concerning the Indian Nations & their Dispositions towards us and towards one another.

I have ordered the payment of the Account of the Expenditures to the Indians, and approve that their Interpreter should Continue to receive one ration per day, till further orders and hope he may by his Behaviour in his office merit the Continuance of it.

I am very sorry to see that Mr. Baxter has met with so bad Success in his Attempts of the Mines, I shall gladly hear your opinion of the causes of his Want Success, whither there are any mines about Lake Superior & in short all such observations, of either Natural or Political which at any Time, you may get from the Indians and others.

I am Sir &ca.

To Lieut: Colonel Bruce or officer commanding the Troops at Halifax.

[B 33 p 63]

TO MAJOR BASSETT WITHOUT SIGNATURE

NEW YORK, August 12th, 1773.

SIR, On the 24th Ultimo I received your Letter of the 14th of June last inclosing the Speeches of the Indians and your Answers thereto: I am sorry that the Jealousy that will ever subsist between the New & Old Traders should be the Source of Disorders, & I depend on your Prudence to Preserve as far as lays in your power, a proper Behaviour amongst them, and cannot but approve your refusing to grant Passes to any Traders going to St Joseph where being remote from any Checks, little Dependance can be made on the best of them.

I am very glad to find that the Indians are so well inclined to Live in Amity with us, otherwise they would not have brought in the Murderers of their Nation to be Prisoners & expose them to well deserved Punishment, I hope that under your Prudent Management of Affairs in that part of the World, few Instances of any more Murders will happen & that our Lenity will gain us their Attachment.

I have given Directions to Captain Sowers, the Chief Engineer, concerning Captain Strike succeeding Lieut: Abbott in conducting the necessary Repairs, but the system of Economy, so much recommended will not permit Employing him Constantly you will therefore confine the Repairs and Publick Works within the narrowest bounds & undertake nothing but what shall be absolutely Necessary.

With respect to Indian Presents, I must beg that you will avoid purchasing any without the utmost Exigency, likewise not to buy any kind of Stores; I see that you have purchased some Flints the accounts of which may be attended with Difficulty's from the Board of Ordnance, I will order such as are Necessary to be sent from the King's Stores.

I am with very great regard Sir &ca.

To Major Bassit 10th Regmt. or officer commanding at Detroit.

[B 33 p 69]

TO CAPTAIN VATTAS. WITHOUT SIGNATURE

New York, August 27th 1773

Sir, I have before me your letter of the 1st Ulto. received the 25th inst, I observe what you say concerning Hugh Boyle's Murder by his Engagé, who I suppose has taken care to procure Evidence of the Provocation he received, that whenever he is Try'd for it, he may be acquitted, if the affair is as you mention it. With regard to the two men of Mr. Todds it appears to me from what you say of their Effects being found that their Death must be accidental; and I have had accounts sent me relating Mr Ducharme.

You will be pleased to insist on Proper Satisfaction and the delivery of the Murderer which the Saaks had promised to bring in, I have little faith however in the observation of their promise, and as there appears to be a fermentation amongst the Indians at present, I cannot too much caution you to take all necessary precautions, for the preservation of your Post & all possible to take measures to be informed of the Disposition of the Indians towards us, acquainting me by all opportunities of everything material coming to your knowledge and exhorting the Traders to deal fairly with the Indians and to be upon their guard, without giving suspicion, and avoiding all opportunities of Quarreling with them.

I am with regard Sir Your most obedient humble Servt

To Captain Vattas or officer commanding at Missilimakinac

New York August 27th 1773.

Sent pr. Post under cover to Major Bassett to the care of Messrs. Phyn Ellice & Porteous Merchants in Schenectady.

[B 33 p 79]

UNADDRESSED AND WITHOUT SIGNATURE

New York August 27th 1773.

Sir, I received your letter of the 13th Ulto on the 25th instant, likewise the letters of the Masters of the two Vessels on the Lakes, I cannot but approve of the steps you have taken in supplying these Vessels with Arms & Ammunition, and cannot too much recommend to you to direct that the utmost care may be taken for their preservation, and as I shall soon send up a supply of such arms as may be useful for their Defence in case they should be attacked, you will likewise give the Masters of these Vessels strict orders to preserve the Ammunition and Arms intrusted to them.

The present ferment amongst the Indians makes it necessary to behave with the utmost caution with them, what has happened formerly must make you sensible of the Necessity of mistrusting them, at the same time not to shew any ill Timed Diffidence, so as to give offence. I need not suggest to you what measures to take with them, your own prudence & the experience we have of what they can do, must be your guides, and I must desire to be informed by all opportunities of every occurrence, and every material intelligence you will be able to procure.

The Traders and Militia are I suppose generally provided with Arms & some ammunition, I will endeavour however to send some stands of Arms for fear they might be wanted.

I am with great regard Sir, Your most obedient humble Servant.

[B 33 p 80]

(EXTRACT.)

NEW YORK 31st August 1773

MY LORD,

* * * * * * * * * * * *

From Michillimakinac, where everything was quiet the first of July last, I am informed that the persons who had undertaken to work some of the Copper mines about Lake Superior are now on the point of relinquishing the enterprise and that some of them have already abandoned it.

I have the honor to be &c.

Endorsed:—Right Honble Earl of Dartmouth 31st August, 1773

[B 35 p 31]

TO MAJOR BASSETT. WITHOUT SIGNATURE

NEW YORK Octobr 10th 1773.

SIR, I have before my your Letter of the 29th of August and observe the account you received from the Waubach, relative to the Murder of Four Traders. I received some information of that affair from other hands, and expect soon a more particular account of it from Sir William Johnson.

You will be pleased to be very watchful of the Savages, without giving them reason to suspect your want of confidence in them, & to continue to acquaint Sir William Johnson as well as me, when anything material happens relative to them.

With respect to the Provision Store I gave you direction in a former Letter to have such repairs on it, as will be sufficient to preserve the Provisions from being Damaged.

It is not at present in my power to make any alteration in the Establishment at your Post, untill I hear from General Gage, who will lay that matter before the King's Ministers, when something I hope will be determined.

I remember Mr Sterling to be a good man, and shall take notice of his Memorial when occasion offers.

Mr Maisonvill, Inhabitant of Detroit, having presented me the Inclosed Memorial concerning the Portage of the Miamis, of which he had a grant during pleasure from His Excellency General Gage, dated the 21st of January 1771, Mr Maisonvill having given several proofs of his Loyalty & attachment to the King's Service, you will be pleased to protect him in that priviledge, that he may reap the advantage the General intended for him, and render at the same time that Carrying Place usefull to the Trade in General.

I am with great regard Sir &ca.

P. S. I have charged Mr Maisonvill with a Letter to the Inhabitants of the Wawbash which he has some expectations of delivering himself, & procuring me an answer some time this winter.

To Major Henry Bassett of His Majesty's 10th Regiment of Foot or officer commanding at Detroit.

[B 33 p 114]

TO MAJOR BASSETT WITHOUT SIGNATURE

New York, 22nd November 1773.

Sir, I have to acknowledge the receipt of your Letter of the 15th ultimo, on the 20th inst. with Doctor Anthons Memorial therewith sent; not long ago I answered to your application in his behalf that I would send up early in the Spring a Supply of Medicines, and from the strong commendation you give him, I wish it was in my power to provide for him as he deserves but all I can do at present is to mention his case to General Gage, who being in England, may have in his power to obtain some settlement in his favor.

I am with very great regard Sir &c.

To Major Bassett 10th Regiment Commanding at Detroit.

[B 33 p 155]

TO MAJOR BASSETT WITHOUT SIGNATURE

New York 26th December 1773

Sir, By this opportunity you will receive my Answer of the 22nd ultimo to your Letter of the 15th of October since which have received yours of 30th September and 15th November, the former of which inclosing the Speech of the Pouteowatamys of St. Joseph.

Tho' sensible that you must be at some Extraordinary Expenses for Stationery, Postage &c., yet it is not in my power to afford you any relief in that respect, being determined not to introduce any innovations in the Mode of Transacting Money matters in this Country and bringing precedents which it seems General Gage has not thought proper to establish.

I am very glad to see by your Letter of the 15th ultimo sent by Mr. Andrews that there is a probability that the Indians about you will remain in their present Pacifick disposition, and I depend a great deal on your Prudence to preserve them in it.

As your Regiment is to be sent to England the next relief, the vessels on the Lakes will be ordered as early in the Spring as possible on that Service and you will be pleased to prepare everything necessary for the information of your Successor in that Command that your knowledge of the Country and of Indian Affairs will enable you to do.

I am Sir &c.

To Major Bassett 10th Regt: or officer Commanding at Detroit
[B 33 p 180]

TO CAPTAIN VATTAS WITHOUT SIGNATURE

New York 26th December 1773.

Sir, I had the pleasure of receiving your Letter of the 8th of September on the 13th Ultimo, containing the disagreeable account of the bad success which the Company who had undertaken the Copper Works, has met with, I am afraid that their want of Success is not so much owing to the mismanagement of their Agent as to want of foresight in providing the necessities requisite for such an undertaking, the want of which at that immense distance must have overturned their Scheme at once—I am very glad to see by your Account, that the Trade of Furrs has been so successful tho' the jealousy of the Traders would represent in another Light.

As your Regiment is to be sent to England next Summer, and that the relief will take place as Early in the Season as the Navigation of the Lakes will permit, you will be pleased to prepare all the informations for your successor in the Command which your knowledge of the Country & of Indian Affairs will enable you to do.

I am with great regard Sir &c.

To Captain Vattas 10th Regiment of officers commanding at Michillimackinac
[B 33 p 184]

INSTRUCTIONS

New York February 26th 1774.

Instructions for the Commanding officer for the First Division of the 8th of King's Regiment in his way to Detroit & Michilimakinac.

Sir, On your arrival at La Chine with the First Division of the 8th Regiment under your command you will take under your care the Number of Battoes, which the Deputy Quarter Master General is ordered to Furnish to your Division together with the usual Quantity of Provisions and other

Stores which it may be necessary to send at the same time You will afterwards proceed with all possible Expedition to your Destination—agreeable to the March Rout given you by the Deputy Quarter master General. Two Companies are to proceed as far as Michilimakinac and Relieve the Garrison of that place the three other to remain at Detroit in the place of those of the Tenth, the Commanding officers at Detroit and Michilimakinac will receive all instruction heretofore sent to those Posts and Exactly conform thereto; they are also to sign Receipts for the Stores of all kinds delivered to them in their Respective Posts.

[B 33 p 230]

TO MAJOR BASSETT WITHOUT SIGNATURE

New York, April 21st 1774.

Sir, I have to acknowledge the receipt of your Letter of 10th January on the 12th Instant and am very glad to hear that the Indians about your Post begin to be better disposed than they have been for some years past, at the same time I must beg you will acquaint your successor in command that little dependance should be placed on this shew of Friendship and not to abate in the least of the caution which is absolutely necessary in such Posts, you will also be pleased to give him every information which your experience and knowledge of the Savages may render useful to him.

By a letter which Colonel Cleveland of the Royal Artillery has communicated to me, it appears that Lieut Colleton and the men of that Regiment have been obliged to take their turn of the Common Garrison Duty, You will be so good for the future, to continue to make their duty as separate as possible, at the same time as it is not my meaning that they shou'd have no Duty at all, you will be pleased to proportion to them in such a manner as to give them a turn of Duty in proportion to the rest of the Garrison by making them to take their turn every third, fourth, or other number of Days, of the Guards and that by themselves or else to allot them a particular Guard or Post, to avoid any more complaints.

The Detachment of the 8th Regiment which is to relieve you, will probably be at Detroit the latter end of May or beginning of June, I must desire that you will take the necessary measures that the relief for Michilimakinac may proceed immediately that Captain Vattas may join your Regiment as soon as possible to prevent an unnecessary detention of the Transports at Quebec.

I am with great regard Sir &c.

To Major Basset 10th Regiment or Officer Commanding His Majesty's Troops in Garrison at Detroit.

[B 33 p 255]

TO MAJOR BASSETT WITHOUT SIGNATURE

New York, April 22nd, 1774.

Sir, By order of His Excellency General Haldimand I am to acquaint you that your Bill for the last half years Indian Expenses is Paid, but you have not transmitted the Receipts for the Payment of the Interpreters and Blacksmith for either this or the former account you sent which is necessary and you'll be pleased to transmit them as soon as possible, you will also be pleased to observe that all Bills, drawn on the Publick Account are to be at Thirty Days sight which mode you and your Successor in the Command are to adopt for the future.

I am with Esteem Sir &ca.

(signed) Frans. Hutcheson.

To Major Basset 10th Regiment Commanding His Majesty's Forces at Detroit [B 33 p 259]

TO MAJOR BASSETT WITHOUT SIGNATURE

New York April 30th 1774.

Sir, Having Judged it Expedient for His Majesty's Service to send Mr. John Hay to the Illinois, on a particular Service, you will be pleased to give him all the assistance in your Power towards promoting the success of his undertaking.

I herewith send you two Proclamations one in English and the other in French which with the extract of the King's Proclamation relative thereto you will order to be made as publick as the nature of them will admit, causing copies of them to be affixed in the most publick places and taking proper measures to convince the Indians of His Majesty's Gracious attention to their Interest and their future Peace.

You will observe to oppose any encroachments on purchases contrary to the meaning & intent of the Royal Proclamation, by such measures as will to you appear most consistent.

I am with great regard Sir &ca.

To Major Bassett 10th Regiment or Officer Commanding at Detroit
[B 33 p 262]

TO MAJOR BASSETT WITHOUT SIGNATURE

New York, June 21st 1774.

Sir, I have to acknowledge the favor of Your Letter of the 14th May, and as Captain Grant is going to your Post to Morrow, I have communicated to him that part of your Letter respecting Thomas Shaw, who he will see is brought to proper punishment.

As General Gage is returned to the Chief Command in America, on your Arrival at your Quarters in Canada, you will be pleased to communicate to him any Occurrence relative to your Post which should come to his knowledge, and direct your Letters to him at Head Quarters in Salem.

I am with great regard Sir &ca

To Major Bassett 10th Regiment Commanding at Detroit.

[B 33 p 294]

STATE OF HIS MAJESTY'S TROOPS

State of His Majesty's Troops in the Province of Quebec, June 24th 1775:

	Lt. C	L 1st;	L 2d	S.	C.	B.	G,	M,	F.	Dr.	T.
Detroit	-	-	-	1	-	1	2	6	-	-	10
Michelemakinac	-	-	-	-	-	1	-	2	-	-	3

Royal Artillery

[Q 11 p 204]

GENERAL CARLETON TO CAPTAIN DE PEYSTER

MONTREAL June 25th 1776

SIR, I received yesterday your Letter of the 13th Instant. The Rebels are driven out of this province & I am preparing to return their vissit.

You may stop the Indians from coming down here, at least for the present, provided you can do it without giving offence to them.

Your obedient servant

(signe) G. C.

To Captain de Peyster Michillimackinac

[B 39 p 32]

TO CAPTAIN DE PEYSTER WITHOUT SIGNATURE

CHAMBLY 8th July 1776.

SIR, Mr l'Eveque, one of His Majesty's Council of this Province having applied to the General for a letter of recommendation to you in favour of a

Mr Chavandreuil, who is going up to your part of the World to settle the affairs of Mr l'Eveque there. I have it in command to desire you will give M. Chavandreuil all the assistance that may be in your power in the business which is the object of his journey.

I am, Sir, &c

To Captain Depeyster.
[B 39 p 63]

TO LIEUT. COL. HAMILTON WITHOUT SIGNATURE

MONTREAL 19th July 1776.

SIR, I have received all your letters to the 10th of June. Altho' I am perfectly persuaded of your care & attention in the management of the expenses for the King's service, I immagine the Treasury would, at this time, listen to no other than such as may be clearly necessary for offensive or defensive War, in which I include the Indians who should be kept as strongly attached to the King's Interest as possible, and ready to act upon any occasion, when called upon: you must therefore defer all matters of building or of a like nature for the present.

The Ottawas & some other Indians to the number of 140, expecting to find the Rebels have come down to me, in order to assist in driving them out of the Colony; but as that work was already done, the Indians unprepared to pass the winter here and their place of residence at so great a distance, I have sent them home again, desiring them to hold themselves in readiness to coöperate with His Majesty's Arms next Spring.

We are preparing with all possible dilligence between the visit of the Rebels.

Mr. Bellestre is the son of a member of the council of this Province, and of a very good subject; he has already met with very ill treatment at Detroit which has occationed his throwing himself into the hands of the Spaniards; he came as far as that port now at my particular desire, I should therefore be sorry to found any fresh cause of disgust there, tho' if not I think he would have waited till he heard further from me.

I am Sir &c.

To Lt. Col. Hamilton Detroit.
[B 39 p 76]

TO CAPTAIN DE PEYSTER WITHOUT SIGNATURE

MONTREAL 19th July 1776.

SIR, The Indians whom you have sent down, being unprepared to pass the Winter, and living at so great a distance, I have dismissed them after giving them some presents, more of which shall be sent up to you, to be delivered them at your Post. I have desired them to hold themselves in readiness to join us early next spring in case the war should continue so long; but I shall give you notice of this in time, if we should want them.

I have ordered such a Belt as you described to be made for them, which will likewise be sent up.

I am &c.

To Captain Depeyster.
[B 39 p 79]

TO CAPTAIN DE PEYSTER WITHOUT SIGNATURE

CHAMBLY 21st August 1776.

SIR, I was prevented by business from being present at the last Conference with the Indians & therefore had not an opportunity of mentioning the subject of the peace between the Sotteus and the Sceios [Chippewas and Sioux]. I must desire you to use all the means in your power to reconcile these two nations & keep them in harmony together as necessary for His Majesty's affairs. I have recommended to them all to keep themselves in readiness to act in the Spring, as circumstances may require, & beg you to remind them of my desire on this head.

I am &c

To Captain Depeyster
[B 39 p 104]

TO CAPTAIN DE PEYSTER WITHOUT SIGNATURE

CHAMBLY 21st August 1776.

SIR, I have received your letters of the 6th & 28th June and ordered the sums to be paid which you acquaint me you have drawn for.

I am &c.

To Captain Depeyster
[B 39 p 105]

TO CAPTAIN DE PEYSTER WITHOUT SIGNATURE

CHAMBLY 24th August 1776.

SIR, I am commanded by His Excellency the General to acquaint you that it is his desire in case the Indians, whose places of residence be beyond your post should run short of provisions at their arrival there you supply them with what shall be necessary for the remainder of their journey.

The General likewise directs me to inform you, that the full quantity of rum as is usual has not been given to the Indians, & that there will be sent up to your post as much of that Article as will make up the deficiency among the Indians of your neighborhood; & His Excellency also intends ordering some presents to be sent to you for the Indians of the Abbays over & above what they have received here.

I am &c.

To Captain De Peyster
[B 39 p 111]

TO LIEUT. GOV. HAMILTON WITHOUT SIGNATURE

CHAMBLY 9th September 1776.

SIR, Mr. Hay came here too late for any of the offices about the army, but as it might probably be more agreeable to him to be employed in the country near his family I shou'd have no objection to his being appointed an assistant in the Indian department provided you find the service require it.

I mean to send up a large quantity of provisions, the first half I suppose is already arrived at the posts. I shall write to you more fully another time.

I am &c.

To Lt. Governor Hamilton.
[B 39 p 144]

LIEUT. GOV. HAMILTON TO THE EARL OF DARTMOUTH

MY LORD, Tho sensible that a multiplicity of affairs must engage your Lordship's attention at present, and that the importance of them ought perhaps to deter me from trespassing on your time, yet my Duty informs me, that I should not lose an opportunity of laying before your Lordship the state of this Post and Settlement. Particulars of it I have from time to time transmitted to His Excellency General Carleton, and am honored with a letter from him dated July the 19th 1776 at Montreal, by which I learn, that my letters to the 16th of June had been received. In obedience to His Excellency's orders, I immediately on my arrival here (which was on the 9th of November last) directed the putting in repair His Majesty's Vessels lying here. As soon as the severity of the Season would permit, they were ordered to their Stations, being fitted for the purposes of transporting Stores and Provisions, and also for defence. As soon as the Frost would allow, the Repairs of the Fort were undertaken, which went on but slowly, as the Garrison consisted only of two companies of the King's (or 8th Regiment) Had the Country people been employed as Laborers, they must have had provision from the King's stores, and the communication from Montreal being cut off by the Rebels, it could not be spared. The Savages who resorted hither in great numbers in the Spring, consumed a large quantity, and the Militia employed to reinforce the crews of the Vessels, encreased the consumption. At this present time there are not two barrels of Pork in the King's Stores, but one of the Vessels loaded with Provisions, is in the River of Detroit, and is expected to arrive to-morrow.

On the 29th of July I signed a contract for supplying the Garrison with fresh Provision, and the same day a Vessel arrived from the Post of Michillimackinac, with the news of the Rebels being driven out of Canada.

The Fort is in a tolerable state of defence at present, against Savages, or an Enemy unprovided with Cannon. A stockade of 1200 Paces in extent, fortified with 11 Block houses and Batteries, would require for its defence a larger garrison than two Companies, but as there is at present a Ditch with fraising nearly compleated on two sides of the citadel, some men could be spared to the weaker parts. The Stockades which are of cedar 15 feet high, are mostly new, and the artificers among the Soldiery and Inhabitants are employed in the construction of new Block houses and Batteries. The old were nigh rotten. The Virginians have been tampering with the Savages, and have threatened frequently to attack the place, but hitherto have not been able to succeed with the former, or undertake the latter.

As I have been very closely attached to the Fort since my arrival, and my time been much employed in attention to the Savages, it would be improper for me to attempt giving your Lordship any but a general idea of the state of this settlement. I hope to be able when the present troubles subside, to make some enquiries, and gain such Information as not to be entirely at a loss, should your Lordship honor me with your commands, I shall yet be apprehensive of failing in my desire to convey information to your Lordship, and tho' on the spot, shall be happy to have objects of enquiry pointed out to me.

The Industry and enterprising Spirit of the traders at this Post, so far outgo the Canadians, that I am persuaded the latter will in a very few years be dependants on or brought out of their possessions by the former—The navigating the Lakes in large Vessels, is entirely in the hands of the new Settlers, the new Settlers manage their Farms to the best advantage—The Canadians are mostly so illeterate that few can read, and very few can sign their own names. 'till the surrender of the country to the English the breeding of sheep was not known here and horned cattle were very rare, at present I am told there are about 2000 sheep and 3000 head of black cattle in the Settlement.

This backwardness in the improvement of farming has probably been owing to the easy and lazy method of procuring bare necessaries in this Settlement—Wood was at hand, the Inhabitants therefore neglected to raise stone and burn lime which is to be had at their doors—The straight (which at the Town of Detroit is 1000 yards over) is so plentifully stocked with variety of fine fish that a few hours amusement may furnish several families, yet not one French family has got a seine—Hunting and fowling afford food to numbers who are nearly as lazy as the Savages, who are rarely prompted to the chace till hunger pinches them. The soil is so good that great crops are raised by careless & very ignorant farmers, Wheat, Indian Corn, Barley, Oats, Pease, Buck Wheat yield a great increase—Yet there is no such thing as yet, as a piece of land laid down for Meadow, and the last Winter, indeed a remarkable severe one from this country to the Illinois several of the Cattle perish for want of Fodder—There are very extensive Prairies in the Settlement, but so many natural advantages have hitherto appeared rather to encourage sloth than excite Industry—The great advantage to be drawn from the management of bees, has never induced any to try them here, tho there are wild bees in great numbers, and the woods are full of blossoming shrubs, wild flowers and aromatic herbs—As to the Climate, tis by far the most agreable I have ever known.

The heat of Summer tho great, does not overpower, and is not attended with either the ruinous gusts of wind experienced to the Southward, or the unwholesome vapours complained of usually by those who live near Great Waters. The Lakes are as free from stagnation as the sea, and this vast straight, has a swift current yet knows scarce any difference as to the fullness of its Bed in Summer and Winter—The Inhabitants may thank the bounty full hand of Providence, for Melons, Peaches, Plumbs, Pears, Apples Mulberries and Grapes, besides several sorts of smaller fruits—several of these grow wild in the woods, those which have got a place in gardens are after being stuck in the ground committed to the care of the climate and soil, so are perpetually degenerating—Hemp & Hops seem natives of almost all America, they might be greatly improved here—There are Salt Springs at a little distance from this place, but I have not yet had time to visit them—

The number of Settlers whites, is about 1500. They build on the borders of the Straight, and occupy about 13 miles in length on the North, and 8 on the South side—the houses are all of Log or frame Work, shingled, the most have their orchard adjoining, the appearance of the Settlement is very smiling. On Holy days one would be tempted to think the Inhabitants were fond of cleanlyness, for they in general dress beyond their means, almost every one has a calash for summer and a cariole for winter. They use Oxen and Horses indifferently for the Plough. As to the Indian trade, all who chuse to engage in it may, without limitation; but here I must entreat your Lordship to excuse me if I should be guilty of great errors in my account, for at the time General Carleton thought proper to send me up, the Rebels had entered Canada, and I crossed the Island of Montreal in a Canadian dress, and got the fourth day in a wooden Canoe to Oswegatchy, unprovided with (I may say) every thing. I was exceedingly struck by the unmoved temper and Firmness of the General. Tho' deserted by the most ungrateful race under the sun, tho' a General without Troops, and at the Eve of quitting Montreal to give entrance to lawless Rebels, his mind appeared unshaken, and he gave me his last orders for the Posts with apparent unconcern, tho' most undoubtedly he was wrung to the soul. Tho' I had frequently seen in him instances of uncommon Fortitude, yet nothing of so trying and discouraging a nature had perhaps put his Resolution to tryal before, and I believe all who knew him rejoyce sincerely to see him rise superior to so complicated distress. Your Lordship will I hope pardon my digression. Regulations for the trade with the Indians are either not generally known, or not duly enforced, for Example, great abuses subsist in the Weights and Measures used by the traders, and for want of an office to stamp the Silver works which make a considerable article in the trade with the Savages, they got their trinketts so debased with copper, as to lay open a large field for complaint.

The number of traders not being limited, allows of many engaging in it, who have no principle of Honesty, and who impose on these poor people in a thousand ways to the detriment of honester and to the disgrace of the name of *trader* among the Savages, which usually means with them an artfull cheat, the distrust and disgust conceived for these traders occasions many disputes which frequently end in murder. This trade being lucrative engages several who have little or no capital of their own to procure credit, sometimes to a considerable amount, their ignorance dishonesty (or both) occasion frequent failures, the adventurers then decamp to some other post, where they recommence the same traffic, improving in art and villany, and finally become desperate in their circumstances, and dangerous from their connexions and interest with the Savages.

Silver badges given at a proper office to Engagés of good character only might correct many abuses—as it is, they are the most worthless vagabonds imaginable, they are fugitives (in general) from lower Canada, or the Colonies, who fly from their Debtors, or the Law, and being proficients in all sorts of vice and debauchery, corrupt the morals of the Savage, a far more estimable member of Society, and communicate to the wretches, disorders they might have continued untainted by, were it not for the intercourse with these Engagés—having contracted new debts, they fly to the more remote Posts, where they recommence the same Trade—[During the time of writing this far. I have at intervals been obliged to break off to meet the Savages who began a council upon some Belts sent to the Shawanese by the Virginians. This first of September makes the fourth day they have sat, and the conclusion of their deliberation is that the Virginians have imposed on them by stating the cause of dispute falsely, that they have misrepresented their own ability to cope with the Mother Country, that they are not really well disposed to the Savages, their actions contradicting their professions—having sounded the Chiefs, and found them disposed as I would have, I tore the Messages, letters and speeches of the Virginians, and cut their Belts in presence of two hundred Indians, deputies from, the Ottawas, Chippawas, Wyandottes, Shawanese, Senecas, Delawares, Cherakees, and Pouteowattamis—Hitherto I have restrained them from acting, not having had an opportunity of receiving orders from His Excellency General Carleton, but a letter from him dated 19th July 1776, informs me that he had sent back some Ottawas, who had offered their Services desiring them to hold themselves in readyness next Spring to coöperate with His Majesty's Forces. In consequence of this; I have told the Savages assembled at this Council, to content themselves, with watchfully observing the Enemy's motions, that if the Virginians attacked them, I should give notice to the whole confederacy, and that an attack on one nation should infallibly be followed by the united force of them all to repel or as they term it strike the Virginians—They all appear perfectly satisfied, but I am not to rely on their assurances, for as soon as the Council breaks up, I expect to hear of several small parties falling on the scattered settlers on the Ohio, and Rivers which fall into it—a deplorable sort of war, but which the arrogance, disloyalty, and imprudence of the Virginians has justly drawn down upon them]

My Lord, Before I conclude this (I fear very incorrect and tedious) letter, I must remind your Lordship, that I quitted London in too great a hurry to make those acknowledgements due to your goodness and condenscencion—since my arrival in this country, the confusion, hurry and precarious state of affairs have prevented me, I therefore am obliged to embrace this opportunity tho' late of returning my very humble thanks, for favors conferred on me—

My good friend Mr. Hey is primarily the means of my having been made known to your Lordship, which is one among many marks of his Esteem which I value at a very high rate—

Were I to enumerate the obligations my family owes to the Bounty and patronage of Lord Harcourt, I must consequently mention one person at least who cannot lay the smallest claim to desert, but with noble minds, the satisfaction of conferring favors on those who can only return thanks for them, exceeds any other compensation—my situation in this country is likely to be every day more and more pleasing and satisfactory—The climate is by far the most healthfull and pleasant I have ever experienced, and I am happy to owe my being so circumstanced to the favor, countenance, and Protection of the three persons I have last mentioned—

I have the honor to be with the most profound Respect

My Lord Your Lordship's most obliged and devoted Servant

Henry Hamilton.

P. S. on the other side.

My Lord, [Since I began this letter His Majesty's Schooner Gage is arrived with Provisions for the Post of Michillimackinac, and some for this place, but as I have already sent to the Ouabash for Cattle, and have contracted at this place for fresh Beef for the Garrison till New Year's Day, I trust there will be no danger of scarcity—

[An Englishman, a Delaware Chief, called Captain White Eyes, and with them one Moutons educated at Williamsburg, but a savage, had the insolence to bring a letter, a string, and a Belt, from the Agent for the Virginian Congress, soliciting the Confederacy of Western Indians to go to a Council at Pittsburgh. I tore their letters, and cut their Belt in presence of all the Indians and sent them off, telling them their coming in Quality of Messengers protected them, but that they must leave the settlement without delay. They had a Pennsylvania Gazette of the 25th of July containing a declaration of Colonies, by which they entirely throw off all Dependence on the Mother Country.

The Council is finished with the Indians at this place this Evening, they are all well pleased, and in two days some Chiefs and Warriors from the Ottawas, Chippewas, Wyandotts, and Pouteowattamis, are to embark on board the Gage, to join the six Nations at Niagara, under the orders of Lieutenant Col Caldwell, and I am persuaded will act as he would have them—their inclination is for War, but I hope the colonists will open their eyes, before the clouds burst, that hang heavy over their heads—Moutons could not avoid being in company with the other people I mentioned—he has brought me a great Belt of friendship, addressed to his Majesty by the Delaware Nation. I send it to Genl. Carleton]

Detroit—from August 29th to Sept 2nd 1776.

HENRY HAMILTON.

Endorsed:—Detroit 29th August & 2nd Sept 1776 Lieut Govr and Superintendt Hamilton to the Earl of Dartmouth R 18th Novr.

[Q 12 p 212]

TO LIEUT. COL. CALDWELL WITHOUT SIGNATURE

OFF POINT AU FER 6th Octr 1776.

SIR, Mr. Langlade being on his return to Michillimackinac to pass by your post I recommended him to your notice as man I have had reason to be very much satisfied with and who from his influence amongst the Indians of that district may be of very much use to His Majesty's affairs—I have authorised him to bring down 200 of them early next Spring.

I am just now upon the point of proceeding upon the Lake with our armed Vessels and boats in order to clear that place of the Rebels who are upon it with a considerable naval force. I fear the season is too far advanced for anything further this year. I should be glad you gave directions that all which can be spared of the 8th Regiment & all the Indians of your neighborhood be prepared to take the field early in the spring—

I beg to have all the Intelligence you procure from time to time—

I am & ca.

To Lieut. Col. Caldwell.

[B 39 p 201]

TO CAPTAIN DE PEYSTER WITHOUT SIGNATURE

OFF POINT AU FER 6th October 1776.

SIR, I think it necessary to acquaint you that I have been very much satisfied with the conduct of Mr. Langlade but quite the contrary with that of Anis & Gauthier who have shown nothing but deceit & have been attentive only to their own concerns, and personal interest. I have commissioned Langlade to bring me down 200 chosen Indians in the Spring, in which I beg you to give him every assistance in your power and to dispatch him as early as possible—I send you two medals and a Gorget for chiefs whom Mr. Langlade will inform you of. I am just going with the armed Vessels and boats to endeavour to clear the Lake of the Rebels who are upon it with a considerable naval force; but I do not expect to be able to accomplish more this season.

I am &c

To Captain Depeyster

[B 39 p 203]

EXTRACTS FROM LETTERS FROM THE UPPER POSTS

From Ar S. De Peyster dated MICHILIMAKINAC
February 1777.

SIR I am just honoured with Your Excellency's Letter of the 6th October by Monsieur Langlade.

You may depend upon it that nothing shall be wanting on my part to dispatch the Indians as soon as the nature of the service will admit.

I have already engaged such as wintered here with the small pox; and shall advise him to take such only as have had it.

The last fall I had deputy's from several nations to assure me they will be ready at call; I wish I may be able to subsist them all. The five nations have sent a large belt inviting those of this part to meet them at Niagara to settle an alliance in favour of His Majesty's arms; such as choose it shall have my leave to go, but it shall not interfere with Langlades Expedition

From Lieut. Governor Hamilton
dated DETROIT 6th March 1777.

We have had a report at this place lately, mentioning that a number of men to the amount of five thousand were to rendez vous in the neighbourhood of Pres queisle, and had built or were to build three hundred boats.

[Q 13 p 151]

From Ar. S. De Peyster
dated MICHILIMACKINAC 12th April 1777.

SIR, I have the pleasure to inform your Excellency that the season affords me an early opportunity of sending of provisions to meet Monsr Langlad's Indians at La. baye.

I have seen many Indians during the course of the winter who are all well inclined; the only fear I have now is the not being able to prevent the whole country from going down. Such as are prevented will take it ill, they must however be diverted from it.

(signed) AR. S. DE PEYSTER.

Endorsed—Extract of a Letter from A. S. De Peyster dated Michilimackinac 12th April 1777. In Sr G. Oarlton's lre of 3d July 1777.

[Q 11 p 312]

From Governor Henry Hamilton
dated DETROIT May 11th 1777.

SIR, Several bands of savages have lately arrived at this place from their wintering, they all have behaved very quietly and give me the strongest assurances of their being determined to act as I shall require them. Your

Excellency's orders will order my conduct, in expectation of which, I shall detain them from the time of their meeting in council, which may be about the 25th of this month, till letters arrive from Canada respecting their management.

As some of the delawares appear wavering I have given one of their Chiefs a belt, with a present to induce them to come to the Council, when I make no doubt they will be influenced as I would wish.

The King's vessels on these lakes, are put in the best repair possible, and the Timber for the new one is all cut, but naval stores and Iron are yet wanting to proceed with the building of her, on the arrival of these articles no time shall be lost in the building and equipping her.

I am &c.

(signed)

HENRY HAMILTON.

Endorsed—Extract of a Letter from Governor Henry Hamilton dated Detroit May 11th 1777 R; 3d Aug from Sir Guy Carleton (5).

[Q 13 p 275]

MEMORANDUMS RELATIVE TO TRADE IN THE UPPER COUNTRY

Memorandums relative to the Trade in the Upper Country as far as it is carried on by the Grand River, either to Michellimackinac, or La Grande Portage, collected from the opinions of different Persons concerned in that Trade and well acquainted with the nature of it—

It is a Trade carried on at great risk, Laber, and expense, as well to the person, as to the Property, of those who are immediately interested in it and therefore, it cannot be expected, that the Traders in General, are men of substance few of them are able to purchase, with Ready Money, such goods as they want for their Trade and therefore are indebted, to the Merchants of Montreal, from year to year till such time as a Return is made in the Furrs &c. the Merchants of Montreal import their Goods from Britain and many of them with respect to Capital are in the same predicaments as the Traders to whom they furnish goods, on credit, so that the consequences of that Trade being interrupted tho for a very short time will be considerably felt not only by the Merchants, of Montreal but those of London: It is the Staple Trade of the Province, and one year with anothe produces to Great Britain Returns, to the amount of £200,000 in furs of which one half at least from Michellimackinac, and its dependencies, the other half from Niagara, Detroit, the Lower and inhabited parts of the Province. This Trade would require, one year with another 100 canoes which are navigated by eight men and which considering the Cargo of English Goods and the charges incident to the Transportation from Europe and the Transportation to the Indian Country, may be valued at £700, Currency, each Independent of the men emploied, in the Transportation many families are supported and maintained by the necessary expenses and charges of making the goods into cloathing &c for the savages. Of the 100 Canoes above mentioned one third would be wanted, for the North West or La Grande Portage, the rest are necessary for the Lakes Huron Michigan and La Baye. Of the number of Canoes allowed for the last year that proportion was not observed; for the Traders to the North West had 70 Canoes whilst those to the Baye &c had only 20, by which means the latter who were mostly new Subjects could not bring down the Returns of their goods whilst those to the North West who are mostly old subjects had as many canoes as they had occasion for, both to carry up goods, and bring down their papers, and it has been alledged, that they even sent four canoes, laden with Goods to Michillemackinac, in order to be distributed about the Lakes Huron, Michigan and La Baye. This no doubt was owing to the greater degree of danger, which was apprehended, of the Goods destined for la Baye, falling into the hands, of the Rebells provided they should succeed in their designs upon Detroit or of being carried by ill intentioned persons to the Rebels upon the Illinois, than of those which were sent to La Grande Portage. To the suppose danger of the goods sent to La Bay, falling into the hand of the Rebels provided they should this summer make themselves Masters Niagara and Detroit, it is objected that the distance, being many hundred Leagues from Michillemackinac, it would be impossible for the Rebels to send parties into the different wintering places from whence the goods are sold to the Indians; and that the Traders would even have time to collect the return of Furrs, and secure them from the Rebels, with regard to the danger of evil minded persons carrying the goods to the Rebels, first with regard to Michilemackinac, it is allowed to be practicable, as Traders have been known some time to venture on the Route, it is by Lake Michigan, at the Southermost part of it, thence up a River [Chicago], leading near to the Illinois River, into which the goods may be conveyed by a Carrying place, of several Leagues, and by proceeding down that River, they may fall into the Messissippi, near a French Settlement the whole distance being near 700 Leagues with regard to goods being carried from La Baye by evil minded persons, to the enemy the difficulty is very great, as the distance is near 200 Leagues, more, and the danger of being stopped and plundered by the Indians very great as the savages of La Baye and those of the Illinois Country are constantly at War, with one another; with regard to the North West or La Grande Portage the difficulty is so great as almost to amount to an impossibility the distance is above a thousand Leagues and from the West End of Lake Superior nothing but small Indian Canoes can be carried into the Mississippi near its sources and whoever attempts to pass that way—must run the risk of perishing by famine, or the depridation of numerous Tribes of fierce Indians. If to these difficulties is added the consideration that the Rebels have no money to give in payment to danger of Goods being to them will be lessened, and it is likewise to be observed that the Governor may refuse Passes to suspected persons, and that every person is by Law obliged to find two Securities, renders in the Lower Posts of the Province that he or they shall in every respect conform to the Rules and Regulations of his Pass, in which (except for La grande Portage or North West there should be a clause inserted obliging the Person, or Persons, first to go to Michillemakinac, and put themselves under the Direction of the Lt. Governor or Commanding officer who may be instructed to permit the Traders to go into the interior parts of the Country, provided nothing has happened which, if known to the Governor, would have prevented him from granting Passes to Lake Huron Michigan or La Baye, as it is said that Indian Corn has been ordered to be brought up at Detroit (for the support of our Indian Allies whose Settlements had been destroyed last fall by the Rebels, it may perhaps be necessary that the Canoes for La Grande Portage should sett off this Year earlier than usual, in order to supply with provisions the People, who have wintered at the Place, and as the Traders to La Baye &c have their Furrs, which are bulky to bring down if it can be done with safety the sooner they have Passes granted so much the better likewise.

[B 99 p 179.]

TO THE OFFICER COMMANDING AT MICHILLIMACKINAC WITHOUT SIGNATURE

Head Quarters Quebec 18th May 1777.

Sir, In my letters written to you in the fall of the year I gave you Instruction to give every assistance in your power towards the sending down here a body of Indians of the upper country this spring; the time approaching in which I expect them to arrive I now only take this opportunity of expressing my hopes that no unforeseen accident has happened to prevent or delay them.

There goes up to your post one —— a Jew with a passport which was only granted him in consideration of his creditors, but it is particularly specified that he be restrained to the limits of the Fort. I desire therefore that you keep a watchful eye upon his conduct, which it is also highly proper you should extend to all the traders in general.

I am &c.

To the officer Commandg at Michillimackinac.

[B 39 p 493]

FROM CAPTAIN DE PEYSTER UNADDRESSED

MICHILIMAKINAC 4 June 1777.

SIR, Mr. Langlade arrived here with Sixty Indians from Labay. He says he expects more but I fear they will come to late, I have compleated him with the number required from this post. The nations here have accounts that Spanish Agents have been amongst their Neighbors; If it be true I suppose it is to draw off the Trade during these Troubles. The news however has made the Indians rather more difficult to move than I expected such is their curiosity and Fear, for I think I may affirm they are all well inclined. The Embarkation is now ready and will take place immediately. I must beg leave to refer you to Mr. Langlade for further particulars.

I have the Honour to be with great respect Your Excellency's most Hum' servant

(signed)

A. S. DE PEYSTER.

Endorsed—Copy of a Letter from A. S. De Peyster dated Michilimakinac June 4th 1777.—3; In Sr. G. Carlton's lre of the 3d July 1777.

[Q 13 p 313]

FROM CAPTAIN DE PEYSTER UNADDRESSED

MICHILIMACINAC 6 June 1777.

SIR, Since Mr. Langlades departure for the Island, I have received an Express from Monsr. Laurent, Ducharmes at Milwakee informing that the Chief Siginakee or Letourneau has received a Parole from the Spanish Commandant, to raise all the Indians between the Mississippi and the little Detroit of Labaye.

I am sensible we can undersell the Spaniards, but still I am lead to believe they can only have Views of Trade flattering themselves with gaining that advantage during our Troubles.

The inclosed Letter from a Trader, will at least confirm that the Spaniards rather favour the English Traders. I must however observe that my intelligence from Milwakee is dated the 15th May, Mr. Ducharme answers me, that he will be on the look out, and come off to me immediately, should anything happen to require it.

Yesterday arrived here a number of strange Indians, all fine looking men, without one Women or Child, they decline going down the Country, but proffer the greatest Friendship. I shall have a strict Eye upon them.

Monsr. Langlade has left me his Papers, when they can be digested into a regular account, I will forward them.

The 2776 Livres, refer'd to me by your Excellency's order, I have caused a Merchant to pay him, as he said he cou'd not do without it. I begin to perceive that he wants some looking after, I believe him to be strictly honest, and quite disinterested, but I see he retains all the French Customs nothing so easy given as a bon au Compt du Roy, In short he can refuse the Indians nothing they can ask, and they will loose nothing for want of asking.

The presents Mr. Langlade brought up for the Minomunies, he tells me have been Pillaged, and, believes before they left Montreal, whilst he was sick. I shall take the first opportunity to have them examined, and shall transmit him the Bill of Parcels, whether they have been rob'd or not, by the Bulk they appear to be more than they deserve, at present after so many of them shamefully leaving Langlad yesterday. They took a French leave of me or I shou'd have sent them after him, as I did a party of his Ounippigoes—as the wind is very high, I am in hopes this will find him in the Island.

I am with the Greatest respect Your Excellency's most Humble and obedient Servant

(signed) A. S. DePeyster.

Endorsed: Copy of a Letter from A. S. De Peyster dated Michilimakinac June 6th 1777. R 3d Aug. from Sir Guy Carleton.

[Q 13 p 273]

FROM MAJOR DE PEYSTER UNADDRESSED

Michillimakinacn 13th of June 1777.

(1)

Sir, Since the departure of Mr. Langlade the Pottawatamies arriv'd here from St. Joseph's fifteen in number who are all either chiefs or chiefs sons totally ignorant of Bark Canoes. I am therefore oblig'd to send them in a Return Canoe, I hire for that purpose as Mr. Langlade assured me you was very desirous of seeing some of that nation their behaviour here has been Remarkably good they came under the conduct of Monsr Le Chevallier a man spoken very ill of at Detroit. I however perceive by the great attachment those Indians have to him that he had better be caressed at present than otherwise—Charlot Lassossissay the Iroquois came also with them and conducts them to Montreal. This Indian speaks good french and is a good subject Mr Langlade sent him with Therry to St Josephs to raise the Pottawatamies where he fell sick, but nevertheless was indifatigable in bringing over those Indians at another time those gentry would require a good Let down for past offenses and some very recent ones but at Present no nation requires more tender treatment their coming in I hope is a step towards future good behaviour.

Gautier is this instant arriving with the Saucks and Raynards I must therefore hurry them off before they see each other as a meeting will be rather inconvenient at Present and may greatly protract this Voyage.

Gautier it seems has been employ'd by Mr Langlade to bring those Indians in here I can count in the Canoes to the number of thirty two.

I am &c &c &c

(signed) A. S. De Peyster.

P. S. I have enclosed the examination of the Minominies goods to Mr Langlade by which then appears to have been a most Scandalous Imbarrelment.

Endorsed:—Copy of a Letter from Major Arrant Schuyler Depeyster dated Michilimakinac 13th of June 1777. In Sir Guy Carletons (No 28) of 9th July, 1777. (4)

[Q 13 p 327]

FROM LIEUT. GOV. HAMILTON UNADDRESSED

Detroit 15th June 1777.

I have the honor to inform your Excellency, that the Ottawas, Chippawas, Pouteowattamis, Hurons, Miamis, are come to this place and are to meet in Council on Tuesday next. There are also some Shawanese, Delawares, Quashtanows, but a few in Number.

I shall keep them together as long as possible in expectation of your Excellency's orders. Tho' the Majority should return home I make no doubt of being able to assemble a Thousand Warriors in three weeks, should your Excellency have occasion for their services.

I have the honor to be most respectfully Your Excellency's most devoted & most humble servant.

(signed) Henry Hamilton.

Endorsed—Copy of a Letter from Henry Hamilton dated Detroit 15th June 1777—In Sir Guy Carleton's (No 31) of 15th July 1777 (1).

[Q 13 p 342]

MAJOR DE PEYSTER TO GENERAL CARLETON

(2)

MICHILIMACKINAW 17th of June 1777.

SIR, The Sawkes and Raynards or Ottagamis arrived as I have already observed to your Excellency under the conduct of Monsr Gautier who Mr Langlade had employ'd to raise them.

It appears from the report of every creditable Trader, and even from Gaulter's enimies that he is the only person could have affected it in the critical situation he found things in the Mississippy his indefatigible industry to stop the reble belt and to divert that of the Spaniard, shows that tho he may have been guilty of an Imprudence below He still is a good subject at heart which I hope will appologize for my letting him go down as in so doing I comply with the earnest request of the Indians who declare they cannot do without him as he speaks their Language and is thoroughly acquainted with their customs manners &c &c.

I am informed that upon Gaultier's hearing that his conduct had been sensured he immediately sold off his goods even at disadvantage in order to Devote himself to the Service, part of which Langlade took for the Indians.

Every report confirms that the rebels have drawn to Batteau load of powder from the Mississippy by the Wabash under a Guard of a hundred men.

This report alarm'd the Indians here till I prov'd to them that it must go hard with them when driven to such a necessity.

The rebel belt was forwarded from Detroit by the Ottawa Chief, Itowagifhikee and the Spanish belt was in the hands of Monsr Hubert, and inhabitant of new orleans formerly in the frenit Service the true nature of the latter is Perhaps still a secret, Hubert said it was to invite the Chiefs of the different Nations to assemble at the Spanish fort and hear what their Father had to communicate Gaultier there upon told Mr Hubert that the Indians on this side the River knew of only one Father and therefore must not listen to his Message several Traders joined him in opposing Hubert who accordingly retir'd, the Spaniards may perhaps want to settle a peace between our Indians and theirs but any talks with them at present would greatly alarm the Indians in this Quarter especially as the rebels have so lately appeared in their Dominians.

I am &c &c

(signed) A. S. DEPEYSTER.

To his Excellency Sr Guy Carleton.

Endorsed:—Copy of a Letter from Major Arant Schyler Depeyster dated Michilimakinac 17th of June 1777. In Sir Guy Carleton's (No 28) of 9th July 1777. (5)

[Q 13 p 324]

TO MAJOR DEPEYSTER WITHOUT SIGNATURE

HEAD QUARTERS QUEBEC 14th July 1777.

SIR, I have received you Letters by Mr. Langlade and others on the subject of the Indians sent down from your neighbourhood.

Being sensible from the prudence & discretion with which you have conducted yourself in the command of your post that your leaving it in the present conjuncture would be attended with considerable inconvenience to the King's service, it is my intention that you continue at Michillimakinac, notwithstanding your appointment to the majority of your regiment, till further orders; of which Lt. Col. Bolton is made acquainted.

I am &c.

To Major Depeyster Michillimakinac
[B 39 p 585]

TO MR DAY WITHOUT SIGNATURE

QUEBEC The 16th Sep. 1777

SIR, I am ordered to acquaint you that it will be necessary if it is not already done that you send them to Niagara & Detroit consigned to the commanding officers there as to the quantity the Commander in Chief desires you will consult Brigadier General Maclean, Colonel Butler and Mr. Goddard the rum being chiefly intended to be distributed as the Commander in Chief shall judge proper, To the Indians from time to time.

I am Sir &c

Mr. Day.
[B. 40 p 12]

TO MR. CRAMAKE [HECTOR T. CRAMAHE] WITHOUT SIGNATURE

MASKINONGEE 21st Sep. 1777.

SIR, I have just received intelligence by express that the Rebels appeared on the 18th inst, and that they had succeeded at the Portage, Sugar loaf Hill and made the best part of four companies of the 53 Prisoners and summoned the Garrison in Mount Independence and its feared the Craft upon Lake George have all fallen into their hands.

I must desire that you will acquaint Lieutenant Governor Hamilton that it is my desire to repair immediately to his post, I shall order Cap Lamault [Lernault] there as soon as possible which will settle all matters that have been in dispute.

I am Sir &c

Mr. Cramake
[B 40 p 18]

GENERAL CARLETON TO LIEUT COL. BOLTON

St. John's 24th September 1777.

Sir, I learn from private intelligence that the Vessels upon the upper Lakes are not manned and armed, particularly the Seneca, agreeable to my former directions; altho' this is what I do not entirely give credit to, yet I think it necessary to repeat my orders, that nothing be suffered to navigate the Lakes, which is not compleatly man'd and armed, and in the King's Service; and I depend upon your exerting your utmost diligence in seeing, that these directions so important to the safety of the Upper Posts, and the security of the Trade, be strictly and expeditiously carried into execution, in every instance where they have not already been complied with.

As I understand that a disagreement has happened at Detroit, between the officer who has commanded there in the absence of Captn Lernoult, and the Lieut Governor, which must be attended with bad consequences to the King's Service. I am to desire you will order Captn Lernoult to return and take the Command of that Post, on whose judgment and discretion I can thoroughly rely to put an end to those animosities. I make no doubt he will be aiding and assisting to Mr. Hamilton in all things in his department, and in forwarding every thing else which may tend to the public good.

I am, Sir, Your most obedt humble Servant

(sign'd) Guy Carleton

Lt Col. Bolton

[B 18 p 179]

TO MAJOR DE PEYSTER WITHOUT SIGNATURE

Montreal The 6th of Octobr 1777

Sir, Application having been made to the Commander in Chief by the Merchants who carry on the trade at the Grand Portage for an officer and twelve men to be sent there for the time they take to transact their business there every year and for the purpose of preserving order and regularity among the people who resort to that place, I am directed to acquaint you that it is His Excellency's pleasure that an officer & 12 men be furnished from your post, on these occasions yearly & that it be a standing order untill countermanded.

I am Sir &c.

To Major DePeyster Michilimackinac

[B 40 p 64]

GENERAL CARLETON TO LIEUT. COL. BOLTON

Whereas His Majesty's Service has required the Establishment of a Naval Armament upon the Lakes Ontario, Erie, Huron & Michigan, and I have accordingly by Commission under my hand & seal appointed officers to serve in the several Vessels employed therein, for the reward and encouragement of whom I have thought proper to fix their pay at the rates as follows:

Vizt.	£.	s.	d
To the officer appointed by Commission to command on the Lakes aforesaid pr diem in Sterling money	0.	15.	0
To Masters & Commanders in the Naval Armament	0.	10.	0
To Lieutenants appointed by Commission under the Commander in Chief to Command Vessels	0.	6.	0
To First Lieutenants	0.	4.	6
To Second Lieutenants	0.	3.	6

And I do direct that you pay to the officers Serving in the Naval Armament aforesaid according to their Ranks their pay as it shall accrue from the dates of their several Commissions, at the rates aforesaid drawing upon me from time to time for the Amount, as in cases of other incidental disbursements at the post under your command.

Given under my hand at Quebec
this 20th day of Octobre 1777

(Sign'd)

GUY CARLETON

Lieut. Colonel Bolton of His Majesty's 8th Regt. of Foot, or officer Commanding at Niagara and Dependencies.

[B 18 p 181]

MR. FOY TO GENERAL CARLETON

WOODSTOCK STREET 10th March 1778

The Posts upon the Upper Lakes which hitherto for want of hands to employ the Garrison having been so small little could be done to, require the greatest attention, it being upon these that the importance of the possession of Canada depends principally, in regard of its commerce, and with respect to the check which that Province must prove upon the other Colonies both at present and hereafter. The Post at Oswegatchie has been extremely ill-chosen and in a ruinous state, it requires either being removed to an Island near it where the French had a work or to Deer Island at the entrance to the Ontario Lake. Niagara and Detroit require fortifying with care and judgement, being the most important from their situation on the back the Colonies. Michilimackinac should be put into a very respectable state, were it not for the impression necessary to make on the numerous Tribes of distant Indians resorting there. The commerce of this back country has extended lately to a very great degree; the Merchants last year found it necessary to apply for & they obtained of General Carlton a Detachment of soldiers to be sent during the summer months to the Grand Portage on the Lake Superior where the Trade has been carried on to a great amount. It is probable that the fur Traders, confined for the future, in all circumstances to the channel of Canada, well digested Regulations, & the Posts well attended to & put entirely under the control of the Governor General of Canada, resources may be found from it, that may amply repay the expenses attending all the arrangements necessary to make for the Canada Department.

I am Sir your most obedient humble servant

E. Foy.

Knox Esqr. under Secretary of State.

[B 46 p 65]

GENERAL CARLETON TO LIEUT. COL. BOLTON

Montreal March 14th 1778.

Sir, Your letters of the 31st January, 4th Feby. and likewise your note by the Savage have all come to hand.

The necessary directions are given for an ample supply of Provisions to be forwarded to you as soon as the navigation opens, and in order to secure the Transport I have directed a Subaltern & twenty men from Oswegatchie to take post at Deer Island, which with a Captain, Subaltern & forty men from your Garrison, you will order to repair there as soon as practicable, will prove a sufficient Detachment for the purpose.

My Intentions first were to send a party from hence, but recollecting that an additional quantity of Provisions would be required for their support, I thought it best for the present to adopt the last measure.

Your having only mentioned in general terms that seamen were much wanted; the number which may be required can only be guessed at, I have however at a hazard, ordered two officers and thirty men from the Naval Armanent at St. John's to join you as soon as it can be effected.

The labourers and Artificers you mention to have been employed at Detroit, prior to the orders you received from me, must necessarily come under the cognizance of Lieut. Governor Hamilton, or that of the persons who hired them. Captain Lemoult being under your Command will of course give you every assistance he can, in arranging and settling matters, as well in the Naval as in the other Departments.

You will please to direct the Captains of the Vessels which carry the Merchant's Effects, to take receipts as formerly ordered for the quantity and quality of goods they receive on board; which receipts are to be lodged with you, in order to be sent down here, with those of last year.

I cannot but be satisfied with the attention you pay to the Service: and entertain that opinion of the King's Regiment, which their good behaviour entitle them to.

I am Sir Your most obedient Servant

(Sign'd) Guy Carleton

Lt Colonel Bolton

[B 18 p 185]

DISPOSITION OF THE COMPANY OF ROYAL ARTILLERY TO BE STATIONED AT THE DETROIT & NIAGARA & PRESQ. ISLE

Captain's Name.	Places.	Captains.	Do. Lieuts.	1st Lieuts.	2nd Lieuts.	Lt. Firew'rs.	Surgeons.	Serjeants.	Corporals.	Bombars.	Gunners.	Mattrosses.	Fifere.	Drummers.	Total.
Captain Hay.......	The Detroit.	1	....	1	....	....	....	1	2	3	6	22	1	1	38
	Niagara.....	....	1	....	1	1	....	1	....	1	4	10	....	1	19
	Total.....														57
of McLeod's Com'y at Pittsburgh.	Presqu Isle..	....	....	....	1	....	....	1	....	1	3	8	....	1	15

Disposition of the Company of Royal Artillery to be stationed at the Detroit & Niagara & Presqu' Isle.

[B 18, p 189.]

MR. MACLEOD TO CAPTAIN MCKEE

Detroit 6th Aprile 1778

Dear Sir Permit me to express my happiness for your leaving Fort Sackville the Seventh February, by which you have escap'd sharing the unlucky fate of the Lieut. Governor Major Hay and Lieut Schiefflin who was made prisoners fifteen days after your departure with twenty of the 8th & the two artillerymen with the loss of four men killed & 6 wounded we hear the Volunteer Company refus'd to fire a Shott at the Enemy, for which reason Lamothe & them are prisoners at Large—

I am Heartily sory for the Governor and am much afraid he will be ill treated by the populace, The return of the vessel sent to Fort Erie last week is daily expected by whom Capt. Lemoult [Lernoult] expects a reinforcement Our Garrison at present consists of one Hundred & twenty Officers included and our New Fort is carried on briskly under the directions of Lieut Duvernet three Bastions is almost finished—I hope to have the pleasure of seeing you soon in this place—

I am Dr Sir

NORMD MACLEOD.

To Capt McKee Shaweness Towns.

N. B. You'll please receive all the things you Wanted from Mr Sulpten.

[Indian Papers M. G. I.]

ORDER FOR STORES

MICHILIMACKINAC 15th April 1778

You are hereby Directed & required to Issue out of His Majesty's Engineer Store the undermentioned particulars to Sergeant Langdown for the use of the Kings Works carrying on here and the Grand Portage. Viz

Twenty four penny nails lbs 38
Ten penny do. lbs 44

A. S. DE PEYSTER.

To John Pattison Bombr in charge of Engineer's Store.

[B 97 1 72]

RECEIPT FOR STORES

MICHILIMACKINAC 15th April 1778

Received out of His Majesty's Engineers Store from John Pattison in charge thereof, the undermentioned particulars for the use of the King's Works Carrying on here and at the Grand Portage viz.

Twenty four penny nails lbs 38
Ten penny do lbs 44

A. LANGDOWN Serjt.

[B 97 1 p 72]

LIEUT. GOV. HAMILTON TO CAPTAIN MCKEE*

DETROIT, Apl. 23d 1778.

SIR, I heartily congratulate you on your escape, and shall be happy to see you here, where you may be sure of finding Friends & sincere ones.

The sooner your convenience can admit of your coming to this place, the better as I wish to confer with you on several points 'tis impossible to touch upon in a letter. The news papers you sent, were very acceptable, they shall be forwarded to Sir Guy Carleton, whom I have made acquainted with your happy release. The Council to be held at this place and which I expect to be very full, will meet on or about the 15th of May, till when matters will remain as they are—nothing can exceed the good temper and tractable behaviour of all the Indians. The Bearer is a very spirited young fellow, is trusty and I hope by good behaviour will deserve to be put on a good footing.

The Six Nations are more than ever attached to Government & zealous in the cause against the Rebels—Considerable reinforcements expected to Canada this year.

I am Sir your very humble Servant

HENRY HAMILTON

To Capt. Alexander McKee.
[Indian Papers M. G. I.]

MR. HAY TO CAPTAIN MCKEE

DETROIT April 23d 1778

SIR, Permit me to congratulate you on your escape from Fort Pitt, I was in hopes last Fall of having the pleasure of seeing you, but your situation was such that I suppose put it out of your power to make the attempt. The bearer Edward Hazel setts off immediately to meet you, he tells me you desired him to bring you some refreshments which I should have been happy to send, but he goes by Land and says he can not carry any thing not as much as a Keg of Wine, provision I hope you will not want as there is people at Sandusky, and the Miamee River who can and will supply you. I have given him a little silver Works & Vermillien to purchase me a good Horse or two, but if you have the least occasion for them pray make use of them.

I wait with impatience your arrival, and assure you I am Sir

With truth Your most humble Servant

JOHN HAY.

To Alexr. McKee Sandusky.
[Indian Papers M. G. I.]

*See appendix

MR. CHEVALLIER TO MAJOR DE PEYSTER

SIR, The kind reply which you have honored me with, flatter me, the more so as I have received them from a man for whom I have a respectful esteem & an entire submission to his orders.

The watch which you propose to keep open on all the merchants of Eau de vie (brandy), or rather, according to your expression, D'au de mort, goes to show how great is the interest which I take in the success of our gracious monarch.

The surrounding savages, as I think I have notified you, have left to the number of forty to go to the Illinois. Notice was given to you of the hour named for the departure, but having come to see me I told them that that step would be fatal to them, in fine that their Father would be very angry to hear that his children had gone to see the enemy. These words made an effect I did not expect, for that instant they promised me not to go, & to reward their submission I have made them a present of a barrel of eau de vie (brandy) with the entire satisfaction of having rendered myself useful to the state, & to oblige if I can say also that to which I have the honor to be

The most humble & most obedient servant,

LOUIS CHEVALLIER.

At St. Joseph, the 20th July, 1778.

Addressed: To Major de Peyster,

Commandant of the Post of Michilimakinac at Michilimakinac.

Endorsed:—From M. Louis Chevallier, of St. Joseph, to Major De Peyster, 26th July, 1778. Enclosed in his letter of 15th August.

[B 97-1 p 38]

PETITION FROM CERTAIN PERSONS OF MICHILLIMACKINAC

The Inhabitants, Merchants, and Traders of Michillimakinac have the honor of representing to your Excellency the considerable injury which the want of a Missionary occasions to the said place, for too long a time deprived of all spiritual help. The profaneness and impiety, in the critical time would have taken a reigning power if our wise commandant had not always opposed the authority which your Excellency has so justly committed to him.

Gifted with all the rare qualities which distinguish persons of an honorable rank, the Honorable Major de Peyster by his love of justice, his severe exactness for military discipline, his indefatigible zeal to make peace & good order reign among a people so different in state, condition and character, prove to all, the advantages of which they would feel the full effect if a zealous priest would come to finish what is neither his state nor his office.

May our venerable Bishop then cease to alarm himself about the inconvenience, which might have happened to a priest in a country without regular rule. The Honorable Major De Peyster, favorable to our request, forbad public gambling, which his successors consider it a duty to maintain. We have made a subscription sufficient for the wants of a true minister of Christ.

Our brothers in Canada agree in complaining that in many places they have only found a priest for two parishes. His Highness deaf to their unjust complaints lent a favorable ear to the piercing cries of a people, which like a flock of sheep, have been a long time in the meadows without a shepherd & found themselves exposed to the fury of the wolves, make application to the Episcopal palace to obtain his help in this present distress, more than his character as a Christian give him the right to claim.

May it please your Excellency, whose eminent Benefits towards the Canadians, give a just right to their hearts & affections, to receive favorably our humble request & to prove to us in this, what we dare not hope for.

Continuing our wishes for your health and prosperity, we have the honor to be, Sir,

Your Excellency's most humble and obedient servants,

M. Linctot, Laurent Ducharme, G. Cotté, Marchessan, J. B. Guillon, Laurent Durocher, Etne. Campion, John Mcnamara, Laurent Bertrand, Guillon.

Addressed: To His Excellency Monsieur Guy Carleton, General & Comandant in Chief of Canada.

Endorsed.—No. 65. Petition from the Merchants of Michilimakinac to His Excellency Sir Guy Carleton applying for a Missionary for that post, dated 23rd July, 1778.

[B 97-1, p 31.]

TO THE MERCHANTS, &C., &C., OF THE POST OF MICHILLIMAKINAC AND DEPENDENCIES

Gentlemen, The honor of your Letter, which has been delivered to me by Monsieur Oreillat) praying me to favour you with my recommendation, your application to His Excellency to obtain a Missionary resident in this Post.

On this point, I have to answer you, Sir, that I took the first occasion to write to His Excellency on the affair in question, assuring you that he will be, as much as depends on me, favorable to your request.

I am, thanking you for the good opinion you express to have of my watchfulness for the public good

Sirs, your very humble & obedient servant,

A. S. De Peyster.

At Michillimakinac, 23d July, 1778.

Endorsed:—No. 67. Letter from Major De Peyster to the Merchants at Michilimackinac in answer to theirs dated 23d July, 1778.

[B 97-1, p 29.]

SUBSCRIPTION OF RESIDENTS AT MICHILLIMACKINAC

At Michilimakinack, this 25th July, 1778.

The Subscription of the Merchants, Inhabitants & Traders at Michilimakinac, whereof the collection shall be for the maintenance of the Missionary who shall be sent to the said Post:

M. Oskin, during the time his family shall be at Michilimackinac for each year 300
Etienne Campion 50
Ampte 200
Marchessaux 24
Jean Villat .... 100 francs.

The Doctor of Michilimakinac undertakes to furnish the necessary attention & remedies, gratis.

D. Mitchell.

John Macnamara 100
Laurent Ducharme 18
fr. Pepiss 6
proulle Crepe 18
Alexis Campion 12
Robert Ariez, during the time he shall be at Michilimakinac per annum 12
Deuruner 24
Benjamin Lyon 50
Jean Marie Cousolle 24
Mattw Lessey 30
Frans Clerc 12
D. Ducharme 24
frougeville, + his mark, Ducharme witness........ 12

Alexis Reaume 25
Ignace Petit 20
Ducheneau, + his mark, signed by Al. Reaume, witness. 6
C. Harche 25
Arers Auge 12
his sister 25
Sh. Biron 50
Jas. Hamelin 50
Charles Sanginet 50
D. L. Bomdasafiles 20
P. Anton Tabeau 24
Laurent Bertrand 25
J. Reaume 24
Amable Augé 24
J. Chevallier, + his mark, Jean Arillat witness...... 24
Jean Bte Guisé 24
Blondall 20
Louis desenchel, + his mark, Jean villat, witness.... 24
Parltemis Ozon 30
Joseph foutigny 12
fr. Marchand 12
Nr. Chenney 12
Jean Baptiste Sigmiez, called La Rose, + his mark, John oreillat, witness 12
Guillon, 12 francs in money.
Alessis amalair, in money 24
Joseph haliberté, his + mark, Jean oreillat, witness.... 12
P. Nurtebise 12
Louis Douvelle, + his mark..
Charles Gingras, + his mark 12
J. O. P. L. ferort, + his mark, hurtebise, witness...... 12
Jean Baptiste Datien ....francs 6
Jan Batiste Geno, his + mark, Guillon, witness........ 12
Laurent Durocher promises to pay 25
Josif Noy, his + mark, Guillon, witness............. 15
B. Augt. Chaboillez 48
L. Baby 24
C. Catin 24
P. Chaboillez 24
The mark of francs +

Le partegin, ... 24
Ch. Janginet, witness
prève le ceure 24
Bte Tabeau for ten years 30
Christian Burgy ....in money 50
Chr. dbr. Juss ....in money 20
Rode ....in money 12
Bt. Le fourbre ....in money 12
Antoine soumande 12
Joseph Howard, twenty-four livres................ 24
Charles Morison ....livres 12
Henry Bostwick 24
G. Cotté 60
William Grant while he shall be trading at Michilimaki-
nac 50
Ezekiel Solomon 50
J. B. Guillon 100

Amounting altogether to ....2398 annually without counting many other absent who would subscribe and give necessary presents.

Endorsed:—No. 65. Subscription of the merchants at Michilimackinac for a missionary for that post.

[B 97-p 34].

GENERAL HALDIMAND TO SECRETARY ROBINSON

(Extract.)

QUEBEC 28th July, 1778.

Since my arrival here Bills have been presented me, from Detroit for £30,298.7.5½ New York curr'y, as these were expenses incurred before my time, I applied to Sir Guy Careleton for an explanation of the matter and you have enclosed, copies of the letters that passed upon the occasion, the expense I own at first appeared to me heavy, upon consideration however upon the number of Indians collected by Lieut. Govr Hamilton at the settlement, I do not think it extraordinary, there is an absolute necessity of keeping these People in good Humor, and 'tis not a little will do it.

I have the pleasure of informing you of the safe arrival of the "Howe" victualler from Cork, by whom I received your letter of the 28th of April, she arrived the 25th Inst, & in her passage beat off one of the American Privateers.

As Lord North seemed anxious to have Sir Thos. Mill's accounts settled, I was desirous of entering into an examination of them, but so much other business of a more pressing nature crowded in, the King's service & the situation of affairs in America requiring, my most immediate attention should be given to preserving & securing this most important Province—I am obliged to put off this Business to a moment of more leisure, when the same shall be taken up and reported upon.

Mr. Parkhurst, one of the Deputy Commissioners General having represented to me that he was in a bad state of Health and requested my leave to go Home, for the recovery of it, you will please to acquaint their Lordships, I thought it reasonable to grant him this Indulgence, which I hope will meet with their Lordships approbation. I am, etc., etc.,

(signed) FRED. HALDIMAND.

[B 54 p 311]

GENERAL REPORT OF THE MILITIA AND OF THE COMPANY OF VOLUNTEERS OF DETROIT, 30TH, AUGUST, 1778

Distribution.	Major.	Captains.	Lieutenants.	Adjutant.	Serjeants.	Corporals.	Soldiers.
Militia.							
Present for service	1	6	18	1	15	4	423
Absent with permission							60
Total of the militia	1	6	18	1	15	4	483
Company of Volunteers.							
Present					3	3	31
Absent with permission at Montreal		1					5
Deserter, 22nd September, 1777							1
Total of volunteers		1			3	3	37
Total of volunteers and militia	1	7	18	1	18	7	520

William Lamothe Captain absent with permission.

HENRY HAMILTON,
Lieut. Govr and Lieutenant.

Endorsed:—General Report of the Militia and Volunteers of Detroit, 30th August 1778.
Enclosed Lieut. Governor Hamilton's Letter without date but suppose to be the beginning of September, and recd the 27th at Sorel, marked Detroit, No. 13.

[B 22 p 129]

General Return of Stores and Provisions received, forwarded, issued, condemned, &c., and remaining in store in Detroit from the 25th of Decem'r, 1777, to the 31st of August, 1778, both days included.

	Flour.	Fresh beef.	Salt beef.	Pork.	Mutton.	Butter.	Oyl.	Pease.	Corn.	Rice.	O. Meal.	Salt.	Rum.
	lbs. oz.	lbs. oz.	lbs. oz.	lbs. oz.	lbs. oz.	lbs. oz.	lbs. oz.	Galls pts.	Gallons.	lbs. oz.	lbs. oz.	lbs.	Galls. pts
DR.													
Remained in store the 24th of December pr. general account forwarded	4,765.15	4,033	16,473.8	71,261	....	6,700.3	395.13	63.4	127	99.5	9,274	2,682	906.1
Received at sundries from Lieut. Gov'r Hamilton, advanced by Messrs. Macomb	168,055	38,143.8	....	9,119.8	3,472	....	....	680	10,292	....	....	8,968	4,471.6
Received from Fort Erie since the 24th of June last	199,640	....	....	123,552	....	13,056	....	8,820	....	....	13,300	....	....
Total	372,460.15	42,176.8	16,473.8	203,932.8	3,472	19,756	3,395.13	9,563.4	10,419	99.5	22,574	11,650	5,377.7
CR.													
By provisions forwarded to Michilimakinac	70,760	....	....	40,558	....	3,904	....	3,104	....	....	5,964	....	....
By packages issued as charg'd to this store p. sundry accounts and vouchers Forwarded to Mr. Day to the 24th of August & yet to forward to the 1st Sept	191,244.15	42,176.8	9,004	79,106.8	3,472	4,892	169	1,323.4	7,619	19.5	1,839	3,050	3,485.7
By provisions condemned	4,351	....	1,846.8	1,768	....	357.8	....	32	....	....	1,181	....	....
By remain the 1st Sept., 1778	106,105	....	5,623	82,500	....	10,602	226.13	5,104	2,800	80	13,590	8,600	1,892
Total	372,460.15	42,176.8	16,473.8	203,932.8	3,472	19,756.3	395.13	9,563.4	10,419	99.5	22,574	11,650	5,377.7

N. B. Detroit flour is much preferable to that sent from Montreal, as the latter is somewhat coarser, and has received damage in transportation.

SAM. FLEMING,
Deputy Commissary of Stores & Provisions.

HENRY HAMILTON,
Lieut. Govr & Superintendent.

[B 122, p 141.]

Deduct one eight part for damages & defect, there will remain the 1st September—

Flour	92,841 lb.
Salt beef	4,920 lb.
Pork	72,187 lb.
Butter	9,276 lb.
Oyl	198 b.
Pease	4,466 galls.
Corn	2,450 gls.
Rice	70 lb.
Oatmeal	11,891 lb.

Endorsed:—General Return of Stores & Provisions at Detroit, from 25th Dec'r, 1777, to the 1st September, 1778, inclusive. Enclosed in Lieutenant Governor Hamilton's letter without date, but supposed to be the beginning of September & recd the 27th at Sorel, marked Detroit, No. 13.

PRESENTMENT OF GRAND JURORS

City and District of Montreal.

At His Majesty's Court of King's Bench Holden in the City and for the District of Montreal and Province of Quebec, on Monday the seventh day of September, in the year of our Lord one thousand seven hundred and seventy-eight.

The jurors for our Sovereign Lord the King for the body of the District of Montreal do present that whereas by certain testimonies and evidences to them offered it hath appeared that one Philip Dejeau, of Detroit, in the district aforesaid, hath at divers times during the year of our Lord one thousand seven hundred and seventy-five, one thousand seven hundred and seventy-six, and one thousand seven hundred and seventy-seven, at Detroit, aforesaid in & under the Government and command of Henry Hamilton, Esqre, the Lieutenant Governor of Detroit aforesaid, acted & transacted divers, unjust & illegal, Terranical & felonious acts & things contrary to good Government and the safety of His Majesty's Liege subjects. The jurors aforesaid upon their oath aforesaid are Bounden to present further to this Honorable Court that it may be stated & represented to His Excellency His Majesty's Governor in Chief in and over this Provence that the said Henry Hamilton hath not only remained at Detroit aforesaid and been witness to the several illegal acts & doings of him the said Philip Dejeau but has tolerated suffered & Permitted the same under his Government guidance

& direction & as Commission as Proven upon oath before this inquest hath authorized the said illegal acts & doings of the said Philip Dejeau.

Wherefore the jurors aforesaid Present that the said Henry Hamilton be charged, heard & adjudged, if the said acts & doings of Him the said Henry Hamilton done in the Premises contrary to the peace of our said Sovereign Lord the King his crown and dignity and further dealt with as the Law and Justice shall pertain.

MONTREAL, 8th September, 1778.

(Signed)

Thomas Burn	James McGill, Foreman.
Per. Guy	Richard Dobie
Per Fortiz	J. Grant
J. B. Disiez	John Lilly
Willm. Kay	—— Poudret
A. D. Birthellier	Chas. Robertson
P. Pillet	Richd. Pollard
A. D. Hemar,	Alegdr Ellice
P. Bouthellier	Richrd. MacNeal
La Croix	Geo King

I do hereby certify that this & the preceding page contains a true copy of the Original Presentment delivered into Court and now remaining filed in the Crown Office.

(signed)

DAVID LIND.
acting C. Crown.

MONTREAL, 17 September, 1778.

Endorsed:—Copy of Presentment of the Grand Jurors for the District of Montreal, dated 8 of September, 1778, transmitted in the Letter to Lord Geo. Germain of 25 October, 1778. (No. 10.)

[B 42 p 36]

MR. MONFORTON TO MR. CIRES

DETROIT, 22nd Sept., 1778.

To Mr. Cires at the Illinois:

SIR, Before leaving Michilimackinac I have done myself the honor of writing to you; uncertain if my letter has found you I repeat by this the part which I have taken in your disgrace, which prevented me from being true to you, I feel warmly & I share all the pain of the bad treatment which, with M. de Rocheblave you have experienced on the part of those who treat as enemies the persons whom honor & religion held submissive and faithful to their Prince.

I am a Frenchman, what in this capacity only, I owe to M. de Rocheblave —besides his rank & his merit impress me with respect & veneration and my gratitude for the marks of good will I have seen on the frequent occasions that I have been with you—interest me equally in his fate and I also deplore the fatal moment in which, without help, he has been surprised and taken, which is reported of a fury which was less to intimidate than to provoke those whom Captain Lord had confined under his care.

Could Captain Lord have chosen a successor who was more worthy of this favour for by his love of justice, his zeal for the public good and his disinterestedness he has justly merited this title from the Inhabitants of the Illinois, whose fate would have been truly deplorable if Providence had not sent prompt assistance to them to help to shake off a yoke which under the appearance of a visionary independence they went to impose on them. What advantages can they draw from this independence?

The conduct of the Americans in their invasion of Arkansas & other defenceless posts, their contraventions of the rights of men in respect to M. de Rocheblave whose sole motive was to render himself useful to a people, among whom a long frequentation had rendered him dear, has unfortunately felt the effects, whilst the Inhabitants of the Illinois are promised more real advantages than those which they could procure from the British Government.

They have not enjoyed them, I acknowledge, under the command of Colonel Wilkins, but the proofs that they have given of their attachment to Captain Lord, the regret which they testified at his departure seem to have destroyed the false ideas which his predecessor raised in their minds and if, like myself they have occasions for knowing the spirit and character of the English nation they would be fully convinced that the change with which they are threatened can not be fatal in its consequences.

You know, Sir, the events and circumstances which have given rise to their prejudices, which, although founded under an Institution as embarrassing, do not fail to divide the minds and opinions in such an unhappy conjuncture. France, it is said, has made a treaty of commerce with the Americans, consequently, war will be declared & people flatter themselves on knowing that Canada must be submissive to its laws.

The profound and obscure ignorance in which a country so distant scarcely permits wars to arrest the different news which the different interests spread among the public. I cannot nor do I wish to penetrate the secrets of the Cabinet, & it belongs to me still less to penetrate the political reasons of France.

I suppose that in the interest of its commerce they have judged proper to make a treaty with the Americans. Have they pretended to engage them to commit hostilities in Canada? If in declaring war she has the intention of rendering herself mistress and that success respond to her enterprise Is it in her interest that the Americans have established a dominant power there?

Why then alas! Too lavish of their own blood have they come to spill that of so many innocent? The good faith, the honor, the oath, the religion & the authority of their Prince oblige them to oppose their incursion, if they have believed themselves to have any reason to withdraw themselves from their obedience to their Sovereign. The Canadians naturally submit, and, in good faith, can he imagine any pretext to acknowledge them & follow their example without rendering himself guilty of perjuring himself as well as of blacker ingratitude?

Has the British Government neglected anything which might contribute to the happiness of this people? Their wise precautions in the choice of those to whom they confided their authority, their foresight in establishing justice when the administration was always given to those who were judged equally upright and enlightened, their encouragement for the advancement of commerce, which in so short a time has become so flourishing. Is that not a sure guarantee to the Canadians of their happiness?

Can the Americans not enjoy the same perogatives which had they been followed by the taxes which according to them, were onerous would have let them have a glimpse of the advantages preferable to those which they hoped for from an independence which they anticipated to purchase by the infusion of blood and for which the most distant posterity would justly reproach them.

This idol to whom they have sacrificed many innocent victims has oppressed only too many idolitors in this part of America among whom is counted Pere Floquet. If he is guilty of such treason he is doubtless more dangerous as his correspondence has been for a long time secret. In this case those who have any knowledge of the Institution of the Society of Jesus ought to know the difference between a complete Jesuit and a Jesuit Frank & the conduct of Mr. Carleton on that subject is a well authenticated proof that I wish to give to you of the mildness of Government. His Excellency has not taken any other step in a juncture so delicate, than to recommend to his care His Excellency the Bishop.

The zeal with which his Excellency with his respectable clergy have been moved to encourage the faithful, reassure the wavering & call back the misled leaves nothing more to be feared by His Excellency with respect to Pere Floquet & must doubtless destroy in all minds the unhappy prejudices which he has sown in the minds of a credulous and ignorant people and of whom a good part have been preserved by the striking example of the nobility of the right-thinking men of Canada, which honor alone has armed for the defence of their Prince.

I do not pretend, Sir, to set myself up here nor to give to anyone the lessons that a faithful subject owes to his Prince, I am neither in a position nor in an employment which would engage me to this. Those of your friends of my acquaintance to whom you may communicate the part which I took in your disgrace & of my sensibility of the unfortunate State of things which afflicts us equally have need of encouragement to follow your example if any opportunity presents itself to establish you in your rights, from which they were fallen as much as you, if under the auspices of Mr. de Rocheblave you had the least help.

I ask you, Sir, in the answer which I hope you will honor me with to learn his fate and the place where he is detained, impatient to receive his news and yours I have the honor to be

Very sincerely, Sir, your very humble and obedient servt,

MONFORTON.

Endorsed:—Copy of a letter from M. Monforton at Detroit to M. Cires at Kaskaquias dated 22nd September. Enclosed in Lieut. Govr. Hamilton's Letter of the 4th October. Received 29th, marked Detroit, No. 18.

[B 122 p 161]

SPEECHES BROUGHT TO DETROIT BY MR. BEAUBIEN

Sept. 27th, 1778.

The 21st September there arrived at the Miamis a man of that nation coming to the river a l'Anguille (Eel River) with the speeches of the Chicasaws, Peans & Virginians.

The words of the Chicasaws addressing all the people of the Ouabach as well as the Miamis:

My beloved brothers!

We have long desired to see you but the Virginians have occupied us, & we know that they intend to go to you. We pray you not to receive them but tell them to withdraw from your lands, &c. If you would defend yourselves we will help you—we are worthy of pity, we are not in the enjoyment of an inch of ground for hunting, and if you give them your hand you will be also like us obliged to work the land for a living. We tell you in the name of all the nations our neighbors,

You know that for a long time we have worked, that all the brown skins should act as a single man to preserve our lands. We have made peace with all the nations; you are the only ones who will be deaf, you see now, however, that we only work for a good thing; we hope my brothers that you will listen to us.

End of the speech.

A white metal collar accompanied by two branches.

The words of the great Chief of the Peans, and of the son of Tabac.

You other Miamis and all the people of the Ouabache:

I leave you masters of these words of the Chicasaws. I only tell you that we join ourselves to them and that we would have already struck the Virginians, but we waited your reply. It is our feeling that they should be sent home & not to let them pass.

The Loups, the Illinois and the Ottawas think as we do.

End of the speech by four branches of black porcelain.

Speech of the Virginians:

My children! We wait for you with great impatience and we invite you to come promptly for at the end of the other moon we will set off to go to see your English Father who is at Detroit.

Come now to look for what you want and you will find all that is necessary for you. We are not doing like your father giving you a little rum; with us it is as water, we make it ourselves.

You may believe that we are numerous and that we will make an end of your father, who is at Detroit. We regard him as a fish which we are about to take on the end of a line.

As for the Indians who are with him we regard them as nothing, we will sweep the roads with their bodies, and we will make a passage for you to supply your needs. Hasten to come because we will go with you as far as the Miamis.

End of the speech by four branches of white porcelain.

Endorsed:—Speeches brought by Mr. Charles Beaubin to Detroit the 27th Sept., 1778. A faithfull copy.

HENRY HAMILTON.

1778.

Come inclosed in Lieut. Govr. Hamilton's letter of the 22nd Sept. to the 3rd October. Recd 29th, marked Detroit, No. 17.

[B 122 p 196]

REMARKS ON A LETTER OF LIEUT. GOV. HAMILTON

Four letters written by Mr. Hamilton to Mr. Cramahe, the one without date, the second and the third of the 12th August, Hogg Island, and the third of the seventeenth in which he demands some orders.

August 11th. A letter sent by express from Niagara to inform me of the taking of the Illinois, received the 8th September.

September 9th. A long letter without date received the 27th September, gives a detail of Detroit of the difficulties that the Lt. Govr. encounters there, especially in the exercise of justice, it appears that this is the 1st letter which he has written me, this letter should be answered article by article.

September 9th. When there shall be time he shall send a copy of all the orders received to the quartermaster general.

Of the 9th acknowledges the first letter which he has received from me.

Of the 16th & 17th Sepr with an enclosure from M. Celoron of the Miamis, he acknowledges the receipt of my letters of the 26th & 27th August and says that he will fulfil my intentions concerning the Rebels who have taken post Vincennes, he will accompany the Indians. Capt Lernoult gives him all the assistance possible. He gives notice of his intention to Major de Peyster and asks him to engage his Indians to coöperate with him by the River Illinois. He believes he can set out the 1st of August and asks me to address my letters under cover to Captain Lernoux.

As he sees that the Indians do not look upon the Virginians with pleasure but that the French appear to favor them, there is no time to lose, he will try to anticipate my views in preventing the Rebels from settling themselves solidly at the Illinois.

Concerning Bently, Papers have been sent here which render him guilty. He has recalled all the Traders of Sandusky, because he was informed that they were trading with the Rebels.

From the 1st of June to the 17th of September the Indians have made 34 prisoners of which they have delivered seventeen to the Lieut. Govr, they have adopted several who are not included in this number. They have taken 81 scalps without committing any cruelty from the 22nd Sept. He says that the Batteaus are ready for his expedition and that in spite of the severity of the winter he hoped to be able to take Post and to maintain it until a reinforcement arrives, a naval engineer and a light cannon would be very useful.

He will try to engage the Western Indians to act at the Ohio.

He believes it will be a favorable time to found a fort at the meeting of the Mississippi with the Ohio.

He thinks that the Rebels are building at the Falls of the Ohio, the mouth of Teakiky and that of the Missouri, &c.

The Spaniards are weak and hated, the French frivolous and without leaders, the Rebels brave and enterprising but wanting resources; the Indians can receive their supplies only from us.

The French at Detroit have set a very good example & the arrival of the reinforcement of 80 men from Niagara has produced a very good effect.

Major Hay and the other officers of the Militia whom he has named and whose commissions he sent more than a year ago have not yet been confirmed at Quebec.

These gentlemen of the Detachment will serve under the grade given them. Lieut. Duvernet of the artillery will be of the party and will make remarks in the same manner as the Lieut Govr. The list of these officers will be sent in the letter dated the 23d.

He has reassembled the Indians and told them that his hands were tied by my orders and that he was no longer a simple village leader and all these preparations showed to them that he was going to war, he perceived that an attempt had been made to disgust the Indians, and seeing that two Lieutenants of Militia appeared not to be marching willingly he deprived them of their rank and put them on the roll of the corvées; the one is Irish and the other French.

He made the Militia take the oath, &c., and gave a fete to the Indians.

He received notice that Mr. Clark is at Fort Vincennes with 86 Rebels.

The Indians of the Ouabache are timid. He asks to be supported in his design of breaking authoritively the sale that the Peankakass Indians have made of their Lands without the permission of the King.

Mr. Gibault the priest has been very active in favour of the Rebels.

Mr. Celoron remarks that Jean Baptiste Chapoton (who has been Captain of Militia at Detroit), Bosseron, the younger, and M. Le Gras are on the best possible footing with the Rebels at St. Vincennes. The latter had received many favors from the English, Chapoton also is ungrateful.

He intends to leave as soon as possible, Captain Lernoux has sent him some reinforcement in order that the time employed in council with the Indians can be used to fortify the storehouse which he wishes to make at the Miamis.

He proposes to send from time to time an express to Niagara.

He thinks that we can send troops during the whole winter by the South Coast.

Good arms are wanting.

He will do all he can to correspond with Mr. Stuart, but he thinks difficulties will arise concerning the Post of the Miamis.

He wishes to build there a redoubt to protect his Provisions and ammunition, calculated on the number of Inhabitants.

He hopes that Captain Lernoux will send him a Detachment to put it in security.

He strongly recommends M. de Maisonville & hopes that when they shall be at the Illinois he will render to him a great service in the cause of his enterprising genius. He sends an express to Chicachaw to forward a message to Mr. Stuart.

The pay of the Volunteers, although it appears large, is only half what they could earn if they staid in America.

4th October. He recommends M. Monforton as a good subject & sends me the letter which he has written to Caskaskias.

7th October. He continues his journal from the 1st October and sends the speech which the Rebels have delivered to the Ouabash Indians with four Coliers.

It is plain that Mr. Celoron is inconveniently frightened in leaving for the Miamis, the effect of the indulgence of these gentlemen is that they cannot be depended upon.

Two men called Rainbault have gone with some goods of the Miamis to Post Vincennes against the most express orders which were given them & the oath which they have taken.

They say that M. Bellestre who has been among the Spaniards marching with 100 Rebels of the Illinois to Post Vincennes.

The 6th. They have struck their tents before day, when 3 Hurons coming from Sandusky brought very circumstancial Intelligence of the approach of the Rebels by different roads, that their advance guard consists of 800 men and that they had artillery intending to attack Detroit, and giving many particulars calculated to discourage the Indians.

He said to the messengers that having promised the Ouabache Indians to assist them he wished to keep his word, to which the Indians consented with a good grace.

7th. The reinforcement of 80 men of Niagara commanded by Capt. Bird arrived.

Capt. Lernoux has given him 1 off. 2 serjts. and 30 men of the 8th Regt. to accompany them.

The force of the Detachments will be in accordance with the list which he has sent and another of 70 Indians mostly Chiefs.

Endorsed:—Remarks on some letters of Lieut. Govr. Hamilton in 1778.

[B 122 p 205]

LIEUT. GOV. HAMILTON TO GENERAL HALDIMAND

Sir, I take this opportunity of advising your Excellency that I have drawn upon you in favor of Messrs. Alexander and William Macomb for Fifteen thousand five hundred and forty three pounds 2-6 N. Y. C. being for sundries in the Indian department, as per account herewith transmitted, and have the honor to be with most profound respect

Sir your Excellency's most devoted and
most obedient humble Servant

HENRY HAMILTON.

DETROIT 5th Octr 1778.

His Excellency Lt General Haldimand &c. &c. &c.

Endorsed:—Detroit No 19 1778. From Lieut Gov Hamilton advising of having drawn for £15,543, 2-6 New York C'ry and enclosing the amount of the disbursements of that sum for the Indian department of the 5th Octr. Recd. 9th Novr

[B 122 p 204]

GENERAL HALDIMAND TO LIEUT. GOV HAMILTON

Head Quarters SOREL 7th of October 1778—

Sir, I have received your letters of the 9th 16th & 17th Sept. The great Expence and difficulty attending the Transport of Provisions to the Upper Posts, make it much to be wished that effectual means could be fallen upon at them all for raising a supply within themselves that might relieve them from their inconvenience and sometimes distressful dependance upon what is sent them from below, and at the same time ease Government of part of the heavy charges to which it is now subject on this account. I am informed that the price of Fresh Provisions at Detroit is regulated chiefly by the Quantity of those of the King's sent up. If this be the case, much having been forwarded this year, it may be presumed that the Price will fall, of which it would be right to avail yourself, and therefore to purchase such a quantity from time to time as circumstances may require in order to spare the salt Provisions and reserve them for time of need. Besides these expedients I should be glad to know whether there are not Lands near the Fort where part of the Garrison might not be employed to cultivate grain & even raise cattle for the use of the Post, and in time by their own Labor raise their own subsistence. It is a consideration well worth your attention and that of the officers commanding the King's troops there, being likely to produce great advantages as well to the settlement as to the Troops who should have a reasonable allowance made them for what they raised & I hope if the attempt shall appear practicable that every step be immediately taken that can promise to render it successful.

(signed) I am Sir &c

F. H.

P. S. In answer to what you have mentioned to me concerning Mr. Bellefeuille—I think it may be necessary to let you know that the design of my recommendation in his favour was to engage your good offices towards him in the course of the Business that he should follow there, but I should not approve of new creation of offices.

Lt. Govr Hamilton or Capt Lernoult Comdg officer of the Detachment of the King's Regmt at Detroit.

Endorsed:—Copy No 6 1778 To Lieut Govr Hamilton of the 7th Octr from Book of General Entries Letter A fol 74 Entd Book B No 2 fol 7

[B 122 p 215]

FROM LIEUT. GOV. HAMILTON UNADDRESSED

Rocher de Bout Octr 14 78.

Sir, I have the honor to acquaint your Excellency that the little force under my command arrived at this place yesterday, having found the water higher than usual at this time of year. We have this day got up the greatest part of the provision brought by Capt Grant in a small sloop to the foot of the rapids. A Detachment of the King's Regiment of one Subaltern one Serjeant, & 31 Rank & File joined us at point des chésnes the 11th inst, but an unlucky accident has deprived us of Lieut Showrd who commanded it; his fuzee going off accidentally has broke his leg & I was under the necessity of sending him back to Detroit with the Surgeon in a batteau. The Indians join as we proceed and there is amongst us all the best temper that can be wished. this evening late, a trusty Savage arrived whom I had sent forward for intelligence. He brings an account that the propositions of the Rebels to the Savages at St Vincennes have been rejected & tho' they have not been apprized that the Indians of the lakes were coming to their assistance, they have answer'd then with a spirit that leaves me no room to doubt all will go well. Mr de Celoron has acted in a manner very unprecedented & which I hope for the honor of human nature will never be followed. Treachery ingratitude & perjury are heavy charges to lay to the account of a man reputed a man of honor, but I am bold to say it can be but too well supported.

He had the affrontery to repeat to me by word of mouth, & in hearing of the people of my batteau, that the Rebels were at the Miamis, tho' they had not arrived at the Ouiat, when he had precipitately left it, bringing with him however some Packs of Peltry, he ranged about for three days among the Indians in the mouth of the Miamis River spreading this report, which, however, they did not credit. I shall have the honor of writing to your Excellency more particularly from the Miamis town.

We have been highly favored by the Weather, else we must have suffer'd great delay in arriving thus far.

Any intelligence of moment shall be forwarded to Detroit by every accasion that presents.

I have the honor to be with the highest regard, Sir,

Your Excellencys most obedient & most humble servant,

HENRY HAMILTON.

(B 122 p 217.)

GENERAL HALDIMAND TO LORD GEORGE GERMAIN

(EXTRACT)

QUEBEC 25 October 1778.

MY LORD, Inclosed herewith your Lordship will receive some presentments of the Grand Jury at the Court held at Montreal in September last which I am induced to trouble your Lordship with at this time as some of the gentlemen, who were members of it are now going home

Copies of these papers have been transmitted to Lieutenant Governor Hamilton to which there is no possibility now of obtaining any answer before the next year; This Gentleman may have been irregular in some of the proceedings alluded to in these presentments but I am well convinced he acted with the best intentions for the King's Service & the security of that part of the Provence committed to his immediate charge. When the communication from this lower Part of the Provence to the Upper Parts was entirely cut off. Lieutenant Governor Hamilton's situation must have been particularly difficult surrounded by numerous Tribes of Indians, doubtful, and perhaps with too much reason of the disposition of the Inhabitants of the settlement it might be necessary for him to assure an authority, and exert Powers not so proper for more settled or peaceable times: The security of that settlement was undoubtedly to be the first object of his attention

— —

I have the honor to be
with great respect
My Lord Your Lordship's &c

(signed) FREDCK. HALDIMAND

Endorsed:—To Lord George Germain Secy of State 26 October 1778 No 10 Entered Book, letter C folio 5

(B 42 p 32)

ARTICLES RELATIVE TO THE ESTABLISHMENT OF A GENERAL STORE AT MICHILLIMACKINAC

Major DePeyster, Commandant of this Post having given to us the idea that a general Store would be very useful in a time as critical as the present & which would be the true means for the safety of the Upper Country & the way most agreeable to His Excellency Frederick Haldimand Governor General & Commandant of all Canada & its Dependencies; in virtue of which & to prove to him our zeal by our obedience on the following terms to ensure success, to-wit:

1st Article. The Company shall commence the day the articles shall be signed & shall end the 31st day of July next, unless the undersigned shall find it convenient to continue it longer.

2nd. It is agreed between the undersigned to put all their merchandise in a general Store for trading with the savages.

All persons who shall have any goods can add them to the general Store & shall share in the proceeds obtained by the Company in proportion to their stock as also of what shall remain unsold.

3rd. All goods shall be put in the General Store at a price fixed upon by 4 persons named by the subscribers.

4th. In case any persons desire to put any goods which are not suited for the trade nor profitable for the Company they shall not be received except with the approbation of a committee, chosen by the general vote, to admit the said goods & to settle the price.

5th. All the expenses which may be incurred on account of the society shall be charged before any division shall be made.

6th. All the subscribers promise & oblige themselves, each individually, not to make any private trade with the Indians, nor any other person, which can harm the interests of the Company, under the penalty of losing all their goods, without any return.

7th. If any difficulties arise touching the Company or any disputes, of whatever nature, they shall be decided by the Commandant & six persons of this post named by the majority of the votes of the subscribers.

8th. The Merchants who have refused to join the proposed Company shall have, after the publication of this act, six days allowed for reflection, after that time expires they shall be totally excluded & cannot be received into it.

9th. As it shall be indispensably necessary to choose qualified persons to trade with the Indians, as well as other persons judged necessary for the success of the Company. We are of opinion that these persons should be chosen by the general vote of the subscribers & approved by our Commandant. All the persons thus chosen are obliged to go where the Commandant shall permit us to send them so as to execute all the orders which shall be given in consequence, both for the interest of Government & the Company.

10th. Any one of the subscribers who shall be in want of any goods for his own private use shall be at liberty to take them at the price put upon them by a committee named for the purpose; they shall be charged to his own private account & he shall be bound to pay the amount from whatever share he may be going to have.

11th. Every Individual who shall have men employed during the winter shall be obliged to join them to the society, when the committee shall find them capable, the same committee shall be authorized to settle the accounts for advances which may have been made to those employed.

12th. Every person who shall have given credit to the Indians this year, before the present agreement, shall be at liberty to collect payment for them, provided that the committee have been notified before hand of such collection. If it be proved that any one has acted otherwise, or given merchandise, liquors or anything else whatever he will lose in general all his advances.

13th. That the clerks, interpreters, & engagés necessary for the interest of the Company shall be appointed by the Committee.

14th. If the Committee find it necessary to make any other arrangement in the interest of the Company, which we cannot now foresee, they are authorized to do it.

15th. As Mr. Askin wishes to avoid every dispute or blame for the future, he warns all the subscribers that he has interests at Sault St. Marie; therefore the 6th Article shall not be put in execution against him.

16th. As we have no intention of preventing the inhabitants of this place from having grain, as much for themselves as for their animals, we are agreed that they are to have the necessary quantity & that the general store obliges itself to furnish to them, at the price which they obtain from the Indians for the goods, for their use only, provided that their goods are assorted as usual.

17th. It is allowable for each one of the partners to sell the whole or a part of his right in the general store, provided allways, that he to whom it is sold be of good character, in that case, he shall enjoy all the priviledges and advantages of the store in the same manner as he who sold to him, in proportion to the stock he holds.

18th. We have named besides the Messrs. Jean Marie Ducharme, Henry Bostwick, Pierre hurtubise, Benjamin Läyne, to fit out the departments as it may please our Commandant to grant us leave & we shall approve of what they do for the profit of the said society.

20th. We shall give full & entire power to Messrs. John Askin, Joseph Louis Ainé, David Rinkin, Matthew Laissé, Augt. Chaboyer & Macrai to act fully in all which they judge right & necessary to do for the good and in the interest of the Company of the General Store. We shall approve entirely of the contents of the meetings, hereby joined, having consented with one accord at Michilimackinac. We have appointed Messrs. Sanguinet, Augé, Lessey, & McCrae to receive the goods into the general store, we authorize them to that effect & promise to approve of all the receipts which they shall give concerning the said Company at Mackinac.

The 1st 7th 1779. Robert Ord,
Made Duplicate. Et. Campion,
L. Ducharme,
W. Gasse, J. B. Guillon, David McCrae, & Co.
Ezekiel Solomons, Henry Bostwick, Augt. Chabilley,
A. Dubuc, B. Tabeau, Louis Chevallier,
John Macnamara, A. Campion,
Gamelin X his mark, G. Cahu & Co.,
Benjamin Lyon, J. Sanguinet, William Grant,
M. Auge, Matthew Lessey, J. G. Zanelius,
P. Chaboillez, Theodore & Grahame, James Bird.

Endorsed: Articles Relative to General Store formed at Michilimackinac.

[B 97-I-p 203]

LIEUT. GOV. HAMILTON TO CAPTAIN LERNOULT

Sir, As Mr. Cournailler propose to go to Detroit for his private affairs I request of you to permit him to return when he shall have transacted his business—I believe him to be deserving of this indulgence or should not have given you this trouble,

I have the honor to be Sir your most obedient humble servant

Henry Hamilton
by permission of Ck Clark

St. Vincennes March 8th 1779

Capt Lernoult Commd of Detroit

Endorsed:—Copy of G. Hamilton & Jehu Hay's letter in favor of Mr. Cournailler who brought them to Detroit.

[B 122 p 297]

FROM MR. ORILLAT, MERCHANT AT MONTREAL UNADDRESSED

Sir, I have the honor to inform your Highness that the Merchants of Michilimackinac & those of this place who usually carry on trade have made some just observations on the indispensible necessity of having a Missionary in this place, they applied to the Honorable Major De Peyster, Commandant, to obtain his approval & recommendation to the Governor General of this Province; thereupon he has sent them his subjoined answer of the 23rd of July last, & they have sent the subjoined letter to His Excellency Sir Guy Carleton, whom he thought then Governor, & which has not (as is said) any other object as Your Excellency can see; and the same day made the petition also subjoined, for the said General, signed by a great number of the Merchants; and the 25th July last made the inclosed subscription intending to support the said Missionary, whom I am charged to ask you for them & I hope that your Excellency will have the goodness to give them their demand for the reasons given in the said request and I shall have in my private capacity Sir, an infinite obligation to be interested in the said Michilimakinac.

I shall be exceedingly obliged to your Highness to send me back the subscription favour of the Missionary, to hand it to him, if your Excellency will deign to grant me the wishes & sollicitations of this place.

I have the honor to observe to your Excellency that I arrived here only the 1st of October & that, but for many inconveniences that I have suffered, I would have been to Quebec to assure your Excellency of my respect but, as I still continue to be unwell I flatter myself that Your Excellency will excuse me.

I have the honor to be in the name of the said Merchants (as well as my own) with the most profound respect

Sir, Your Excellency's most humble obedient Servant

Jean Orillat.

Montreal the 13th March 1779.

Endorsed:—No 65 1779. From M, Orillat Merchant at Montreal of the 13th March 1779.

[B 97-1 p 92]

COL. CLARK TO CAPTAIN LERNOULT

Fort P. Henry St. Vincent March 16th 1779.

Sir, As many of the gentlemen that fell into my hands at this Post, left letters at their departure for their friends at Detroit I have enclosed them to you hoping that you will expedite them to the persons directed to. As a few of the inhabitants of this town with a number of your own people have permits to go to Detroit on their lawful business, I hope you will not detain such as should want to return, as you may be assured that I want no Intelligence from them.

You have one Mr. Bentley, Inhabitant of the Illinois a prisoner among you, I would fondly exchange one for him of equal rank, if agreable. I learn by your letter to Govr. Hamilton, that you were very busy making new works, I am glad to hear it, as it saves the Americans some expences in building.

My Compts. to the Gentlemen of yr. Garrison.

I am yours &c

G. R. Clark

Capt. Lernoult: The officers of Fort Post Henry solicit Capt Lernoult to present their compliments to the officers of his Garrison.

Endorsed: Copy of a letter from Col Clark to Capt Lernoult dated March 16th 1779.

[B 122 p 301]

MAJOR BOWMAN TO CAPTAIN LERNOULT

Fort P. Henry St. Vincent March 20th 1779.

Sir, In justice to my countrymen Mr. Thos Bentley who has been detain'd in Canada almost two years as prisoner to the ruin of his business & distraction of his family. I hope you will therefore consider the lenity shewn to the Prisoners that fell into the hands of Colonel George Rogers Clerk at this Post, who upon application obtained permission from the Colonel to return to their familys at Detroit & that you will also apply to the Commandt in Cheife in Canada to obtain the permission of the said Thos. Bentley, in order that he may once more return to his family which suffer much by his absence.

I am Sir Yr. most humble servant

Jos Bowman Major

in Coll Clarks Battalion.

on public service

Captain R. B. Lernoult Esqre

commandt at Detroit

[B 122 p 299]

FROM LIEUT. COL. BOLTON UNADDRESSED

Niagara 24th March, 1779.

Sir, I received a letter from Capt. Lernoult some days ago, a copy of which I take the liberty of laying before your Excellency, &c. The 3rd of february. Simon Girtie Interpreter who was employed by Lieut Governor Hamilton to watch the enemies motions near Fort Pitt arrived with strings from the six nations, Delawares, Chawanese and Wyandots & informed him that 2500 men commanded by a General McIntosh advanced from Fort Pitt late last fall as far as Tuscarawa, three days march from St Dusky with six pieces of cannon, the largest only a six pounder, that they have built a stockaded Fort there, after which the main body retired back to Beaver Creek leaving 250 men in that Fort under a Colonel Gibson—Beaver Creek is 28 miles from Fort Pitt where they have a strong fort & a Depot of Provisions.

That he was informed the main body was to move toward Detroit the latter end of March & that when he left St Dusky part of the six nations Delawares Shawanese &c. to the number of 7 or 800 men were assembled at the upper town, determined to strike the fort at Tuscarawa & drive of or destroy the cattle & if any of the main army attempted to go to their assistance they were resolved to attack them in the night & to distress them as much as possible.

Capt. Lernoult writes that he has done everything in his power to encourage them, has sent them a large supply of ammunitions & cloathing also presents to the chiefs warriors. The Indians are displeased of the Governors attending to so distant a part when so large body of the enemy threatened their Lands so near hand, and have also he says given him a *sallade* for not sending his Warriors to their assistance, according to their Father's promises, now the enemy approach them. They also assure him they were told by two Delawares lately come from Niagara that neither the commanding officer or Col. Butler were informed of their situation or they were certain some troops or White people would have been sent to their assistance, in short they were so pressing & Capt. Bird so anxious to go with some few volunteers to serve with the Indians that he was forced to comply with their request notwithstanding the weak Garrison under his command, he also sent some ammunition &c. along with him to pave his reception & to keep the Indians in the disposition they are in to oppose & harrass the Virginians. Several Ottawas & Chippawas are setting off for St. Dusky & many more he thinks will follow when they arrive from their hunting.

The Indians in those parts he says are greatly in awe of the six nations, therefore hopes a belt from them to spur them on to act with spirit may be sent him.

He wishes much for the Governor or Mr. Hays return having no one to advice with him in this critical time when it requires great caution and attention to keep the Indians in good humour, & preserve their friendships, when every artifice is made use of by the enemy to draw them away. February the 16th William Tucker whom he sent out early in January last to reconoitre with five Chippawas—is returned this day and bring intelligence which corresponds with Girtie & further that some few Wyandots & Mingoes surprised three Virginians going Express from Tuscarawas towards Fort Pitt killed two of them & brought the third a prisoner to St Dusky with a Pacquet of Letters that the chief there opened the Letters & had them read to him by a white man.

That it appears by a Letter of Col. Gibson Commandant at Tuscarawa to a Capt. O'Hara at Fort Pitt, that he was apprised of the Indians design to attack that Fort, requested Provisions be sent him & a part of the army without delay having little provisions & only 190 men fit for duty in the Place. This Capt. Lernoult says is a lucky hitt, which the Indians will (he makes no doubt) take advantage off.

Capt Lernoult acquaints me that Detroit is capable in peaceable times to supply the Garrison with Provisions, but at this time the inhabitants are so much employed in Conveys & probably will continue so that they have not been able to thresh last years corn, & the great number of cattle furnished for Governor Hamiltons Expedition as well as for Detroit with what have been consumed by Indians have reduced the numbers so much that a pair of oxen cannot be purchased for less than 1000 Livres & then reckoned a cheap bargain, in order to save the salt provisions, he has fed the Garrison & Indians with fresh during the winter, but the scarcity & extravagant rate they are now at besides the poorness of the cattle at this season obliges him to deliver salt provisions.

Flour is 60 Livre a hundred & every article very dear. I have now only to acquaint your Excellency that some time before I received this Letter a large Belt with a Speech was sent by the six nations to their Western Bretheren encouraging them to fight to the last man & to drive the enemy out of the country. I am &c

(signed) Mason Bolton

[B 96-1 p 254]

SURVEY OF THE SETTLEMENT OF DETROIT TAKEN 31ST MARCH 1779

This survey was taken by order of the Command'g officer & each inhabitant put upon oath in presence of Mr. Thos Williams acting Justice of the Peace Capt. McGregor of the Town Militia & Mr. Sampson Fleming D. C. provision

as witness my hand R. B. Lernoult
Captain Command'g

A Roll of the Inhabitants of Detroit.

Inhabitants' Names.	Men.	Women.	Lodgers hired or young men.	Lodgers hired or young women.	Boys.	Girls.	Male slaves.	Female slaves.
Nicholas Litsenberger	1			1	1			
Antoine Goulette and wife	1	1						
John McPherson	1		2					
Alexr Helaire and wife	1	1			3	2		
Nicholas Patnotte and wife	1	1			1	5		
Antoine Miney and wife	1	1			2	2		
Francois Tremblé and wife	1	1						
Petite Claire	1				1			1
Michael Yacks, Senr, and wife	1	1	2		3			
Francois Dechesne and wife	1	1	2	2	1	6		
Jean Bte. Crittic and wife	1	1		1	2			1
Charles Grimaure	1		1		2	4		
Joseph Saucier and wife	1	1						
Ambroise Tremblé	1		4		3			
Isidore Moran and wife	1	1			4			1
Louise Tremblé and wife	1	1			2	2	1	
Jacob Harsen and wife	1	1		1	2	2		
Louis Renan and wife	1	1			4	2		
Ignace Thibeau and wife	1	1			5	1		
Jacques Lawson and wife	1	1		1	1			
Charles St. Aubin	1		1	1		1		
Joseph Tremblé	1		1		2			
Jean Bt. Chavin and wife	1	1				3		
Jean Crispé St. Jean and wife	1	1			7	1		
Joseph Laderoute and wife	1	1	1	1		2		
Michael Yacks, Jun	1		2		1			
Capt. Campeau and wife	1	1	2	1	1	5		
Jean Duprat and wife	1	1	1			3		
Gajetan Laderoute and wife	1	1	1	1	5			
Widow Marsac		1	1			1		
J. Bt. Marsac and wife	1	1				3	1	
Paul Marsac	1		2				2	1
Pierre Cardinal and wife	1	1	1	1	4	1		

Grain, Flour, and Cattle taken 31 March, 1779.

Pounds flour.	Bushells of wheat.	Do. for seed.	Bushells Indian Corn.	Do. for seed.	Bushells pease.	Do. for seed.	Bushells oats.	Do. for seed.	Oxen.	Cows.	Steers.	Hoggs.	Horses.	Sheep.
.....	.....	.....	.....	.....	.....	.....	.....	.....	.....	.....	.....	.....	1	.....
.....	.....	.....	.....	.....	.....	.....	.....	.....	.....	.....	.....	.....	.....	.....
.....	20	20	5	1	.....	.....	.....	.....	7	13	18	11	9	.....
200	.....	.....	.....	.....	.....	.....	.....	.....	.....	.....	.....	.....	.....	.....
.....	.....	.....	1	.....	.....	.....	.....	.....	.....	.....	.....	.....	.....	.....
.....	.....	.....	.....	.....	.....	.....	.....	.....	.....	1	2	6	1	.....
100	.....	4	.....	.....	.....	3	.....	.....	.....	3	.....	5	1	.....
200	.....	.....	.....	.....	.....	.....	.....	.....	.....	.....	.....	.....	.....	.....
.....	15	.....	.....	.....	3	.....	.....	.....	2	4	6	15	3	.....
100	10	10	.....	.....	1	.....	.....	4	.....	5	3	9	3	.....
500	10	8	.....	.....	2	.....	.....	.....	.....	4	2	2	2	.....
.....	20	30	.....	.....	.....	.....	.....	20	4	5	1	6	3	.....
100	25	15	.....	.....	.....	.....	.....	15	2	5	4	12	4	.....
.....	2	2	2	1	.....	.....	.....	12	2	4	.....	3	1	.....
.....	10	.....	.....	.....	.....	.....	.....	.....	.....	3	.....	4	6	.....
100	.....	40	.....	.....	.....	60	.....	.....	2	8	19	19	8	5
.....	.....	.....	.....	.....	.....	.....	.....	.....	1	7	1	.....	3	.....
.....	.....	.....	.....	.....	.....	.....	.....	.....	.....	1	.....	.....	1	.....
.....	.....	.....	.....	.....	.....	.....	.....	.....	.....	2	5	3	1	.....
.....	.....	.....	.....	.....	.....	.....	.....	.....	.....	1	2	5	1	.....
.....	30	.....	.....	.....	.....	.....	.....	.....	.....	2	.....	4	3	.....
1,800	64	16	.....	.....	.....	.....	15	10	4	4	5	5	6	.....
.....	15	10	.....	.....	.....	.....	.....	.....	1	2	1	4	2	.....
.....	.....	7	.....	.....	.....	.....	.....	.....	2	6	.....	4	1	.....
600	15	.....	.....	.....	.....	.....	.....	10	2	3	2	3	3	.....
.....	30	10	.....	.....	.....	.....	.....	15	.....	1	2	5	4	.....
.....	.....	25	.....	.....	.....	2	.....	20	2	9	6	6	7	.....
1,600	25	15	.....	.....	.....	.....	.....	.....	3	6	5	11	3	.....
.....	60	20	.....	.....	.....	.....	45	15	4	6	7	12	3	.....
500	30	20	.....	.....	.....	.....	15	15	4	8	5	10	4	.....
400	70	15	6	2	.....	8	.....	12	6	4	10	18	10	20
200	54	16	.....	.....	.....	2	10	20	4	5	9	14	7	12
.....	20	30	.....	.....	.....	.....	.....	.....	2	4	1	12	4	.....

40

A Roll of Inhabitants.

Inhabitants' Names.	Men.	Women.	Lodgers hired or young men.	Lodgers hired or young women.	Boys.	Girls.	Male slaves.	Female slaves.
Joseph Cardinal	1	....	1	1	4	3	....	....
Pierre St. Aubin and wife	1	1	1	....	....	....	....	....
Bazil Campeau	1	1	2	....	....	....	....	....
Jacques St. Aubin and wife	1	1	4	2	....	....	....	....
Louis St. Aubin and wife	1	1	1	2	3	1	....	....
James Casety and wife	1	1	2	....	....	2	2	....
Simon Meloche and wife	1	1	....	....	3	1	....	....
Charles Chavin and wife	1	1	1	2	6	1	....	....
Antoine Morau and wife	1	1	....	....	2	1	....	....
Guillairme Bernard and wife	1	1	1	1	4	3	1	3
Antoine Bogert and wife	1	1	1	....	....	....	....	....
Louis Beaufait and wife	1	1	....	....	1	3	1	....
Jean Bte Chapoton and wife	1	1	4	1	1	3	2	2
Jean Bte Pellier and wife	1	1	3	2	9	1	....	....
Francois Meloche and wife	1	1	1	1	4	3	....	....
Amable Letour and wife	1	1	1	....	1	....	....	....
Robert Jean and wife	1	1	....	1	2	4	....	....
Francois Letoure and wife	1	1	....	....	1	....	....	....
Jean Benoa and wife	1	1	1	....	....	....	....	....
Simon Campeau and wife	1	1	....	1	4	3	3	2
Antoine Robert Censé and wife	1	1	1	1	1	1	2	....
Jean Bte Campeau, Jun., and wife	1	1	1	1	4	2	3	3
Jacques Campeau and wife	1	1	....	1	6	....	1	1
Hippolite Campeau and wife	1	1	1	2	....	....	....	....
....	....	....	....	....	....	....	....	....
Ignace Boyer and wife	1	1	....	1	1	1	....	....
Noel St. Aubin and wife	1	1	1	1	....	1	....	....
Pierre Meney and wife	1	1	4	....	1	1	....	....
Alexis Cuillerie and wife	1	1	....	....	....	3	....	....
Antoine Cuillerie and wife	1	1	4	2	....	2	....	....
Charles Gouin and mother	1	1	3	3	....	2	6	3
Jean Bte. Rivaure and wife	1	1	....	....	7	2	....	1
Captain Morau and mother	1	1	2	2	3	3	....	1
Pierre Durand and wife	1	1	2	....	....	....	....	....
Jean Bte. Beaubin and wife	1	1	6	1	2	2	....	....
Jean Bte. Barthe and wife	1	1	1	....	....	....	....	....
Joseph Reaume and wife	1	1	2	....	3	3	....	....

Grain, Flour, etc.—CONTINUED.

Pounds flour.	Bushells of wheat.	Do. for seed.	Bushells Indian Corn.	Do. for seed.	Bushells pease.	Do. for seed.	Bushells oats.	Do. for seed.	Oxen.	Cows.	Steers.	Heggs.	Horses.	Sheep.
500	....	15	....	....	....	....	....	....	4	3	7	4	14	....
....	....	....	....	....	....	....	....	....	....	2	1	3	4	....
....	....	....	....	....	....	....	....	....	....	....	....	....	....	....
....	....	....	....	....	....	....	....	....	....	2	....	....	2	....
....	....	....	....	....	....	....	....	....	....	2	1	5	3	....
100	2	....	....	....	....	....	....	....	3	14	8	12	9	10
....	18	12	10	....	....	....	....	12	....	3	4	6	3	....
....	....	....	....	....	....	....	....	6	....	6	3	4	2	....
300	....	....	....	....	....	....	....	10	....	4	3	4	3	....
....	30	18	....	1	....	3	....	15	4	7	6	12	3	....
200	24	....	....	....	....	....	10	20	6	....	....	3	1	....
700	10	15	5	....	....	....	....	10	4	8	4	11	5	....
....	75	25	....	....	....	6	30	50	4	12	3	15	10	12
1,900	....	20	6	....	....	4	....	8	4	4	3	10	2	....
....	30	20	....	2	....	3	....	10	4	4	9	10	5	....
2,000	162	3	20	....	....	3	....	24	4	8	7	12	4	....
....	....	....	....	....	....	....	....	....	....	2	....	....	1	....
....	....	....	....	....	....	....	....	....	....	....	....	....	1	....
100	....	....	....	....	....	....	....	....	....	....	....	....	....	....
1,000	....	25	....	1	....	3	....	20	4	5	1	6	2	....
1,400	....	10	....	....	....	....	50	....	6	4	4	11	6	15
900	....	....	....	....	....	....	....	....	....	4	2	4	1	....
1,600	....	30	50	....	....	6	40	30	3	10	5	13	3	....
2,500	116	22	60	....	10	....	....	....	9	15	17	8	8	23
....	....	....	....	....	....	....	....	....	....	5	....	....	1	....
100	....	....	3	....	....	....	....	....	....	1	....	3	1	....
....	35	12	25	....	....	3	16	14	2	3	....	7	3	....
....	25	10	3	....	....	4	15	10	4	6	4	8	3	....
100	....	....	3	....	....	....	....	....	....	2	....	....	1	....
....	....	....	....	....	....	....	....	15	....	5	4	4	5	....
....	7	18	....	....	....	....	15	30	4	7	6	7	5	....
400	40	30	3	....	....	6	....	3	4	14	18	20	3	....
3,000	....	....	....	....	....	....	10	....	3	8	16	11	7	....
....	....	....	....	....	....	....	....	....	....	1	....	....	1	....
2,400	9	21	3	....	....	2	15	25	4	8	6	9	9	....
4,000	....	....	338	....	....	....	....	....	....	....	....	....	1	....
200	....	....	....	....	....	....	....	....	....	2	....	2	2	....

A Roll of Inhabitants.

Inhabitants' Names.	Men.	Women.	Lodgers hired or young men.	Lodgers hired or young women.	Boys.	Girls.	Male slaves.	Female slaves.
James Thompson	1	1		4				
Daniel Garret and wife	1	1						
Captain McGregor and wife	1	1			1		1	
William Sterling and wife	1	1			3			1
Thomas Williams	1		1				1	
William Tucker and wife	1	1			1	2		
Mr. Thorn		1				1		
Thomas Cox and wife	1	1	2				1	3
Mr. Cornwall, Jun., and Miller	2			1				
William Edgar	1		2				1	
Bernard Lafontaignet and wife	1	1						
Jean Bte. Sanchagrin and wife	1	1	1	1	2	2		
Greverat and Visgar	2		2		2			
John McPherson	1		1					
William Forsith and wife	1	1	3	1	6			2
Thomas McCrae and wife	1	1			3			
Mrs. Fleming		1			1	1	1	
James Cochran	1		1					
Teller and Grosbec	2		2					
James Ranken	1		1		1	2		
Thompson and Williams	2						1	
Andrews and Meldraun	2		2		3			
McWilliam Martin and Trimble	3							
Macnamara McLeod and wife	2	1	4			1		
Forsith Dyce and Macintosh	3		1				1	
Wright White and Lyons	3							
Mrs. Adhemar		1	1		1	2	1	1
Isaac Williams and wife	1	1	2			2		
James Abbott and wife	1	1	2		2	4		2
Edward Riddy	1		2					
Mrs. Hay and Mrs. Lamoth		2			3	3		2
Sarah etinnse		1					1	2
Margaret Scott		1				3		
Jean Bte Rocourt and wife	1	1			1			
Thomas Smith	1							
Pierre Provincal	1	1						
Louis Thebeau and wife	1	1	1	2	1			

Grain, Flour, etc.—Continued.

Pounds flour.	Bushells of wheat.	Do. for seed.	Bushells Indian Corn.	Do. for seed.	Bushells pease.	Do. for seed.	Bushells oats.	Do. for seed.	Oxen.	Cows.	Steers.	Hoggs.	Horses.	Sheep.
3,000			2		1					1			1	
										4	1			
4,700			189		6					1			1	7
													1	2
300	12		8		1								1	
										2			2	
150										1			1	
										1			1	
										1			1	
700													1	
													2	
800		7	14		2				3	11	12	14	4	
300														
										4			1	
100			9		1									
			5		1			10					1	
400			10							2	5		6	
			1		1			2			1		1	
1,000			10										1	
100			24										2	
1,200			8										1	
			56										1	
										2			1	
100			5							1			1	
3,500			30				10			2			1	
200			105										1	
										3			2	
100										3			4	
200														
													2	
600										1			1	

A Roll of Inhabitants.

Inhabitants' Names.	Men.	Women.	Lodgers hired or young men.	Lodgers hired or young women.	Boys.	Girls.	Male slaves.	Female slaves.
Pierre Desnoyer and wife	1	1	....	....	1	....	....	....
Pierre St. Cosme and wife	1	1	2	1	....	....	....	....
Mrs. Dejeau	....	1	1	....	2	....	1	1
Joseph L'Enfant and wife	1	1	2	1	1	4	4	....
Philip Belanger and wife	1	1	1	....	1	1	....	....
William Brown and wife	1	1	....	....	1	2	....	....
Joseph Gobielle and wife	1	1	....	....	2	....	....	....
Jean Bt Creste and wife	1	1	2	2	....	2	....	....
Mrs. St. Martin	....	1	....	....	....	1	....	....
Joseph St. John	1	....	3	....	....	....	....	....
Mrs. Chatlain	....	1	....	....	1	1	....	....
Isaac Gagine and wife	1	1	1	....	....	1	....	....
Charles and Andrew Lefleur and mother	2	1	1	....	1	....	....	....
Prisqué Cotté and wife	1	1	....	....	2	1	....	....
Richard Whittle	1	....	1	....	....	1	....	....
William Shaw and wife	1	1	2	....	....	....	1	....
George Anthon and wife	1	1	....	1	1	1	1	1
Pierre Boamy and wife	1	1	1	1	1	....	....	....
Antoine Cattan and wife	1	1	....	....	....	2	....	....
Joseph Vallad and wife	1	1	4	1	1	3	....	....
Martin Levril and wife	1	1	2	....	2	1	....	....
Gland Solant	1	....	1	1	2	....	....	....
Pierre Labady junr and wife	1	1	1	....	2	3	....	....
Renac Porlier	1	....	2	....	....	....	....	....
Joseph Bourdeaux and wife	1	1	....	....	2	6	....	....
Louis Bellaire and wife	1	1	....	....	....	....	....	....
Alexis Campeau and wife	2	1	....	....	1	4	....	....
Godfroy Robert and wife	1	1	1	1	3	3	....	2
Alexis Delisle and wife	....	1	1	1	6	....	....	1
Mrs. Chesne	1	1	1	1	....	2	1	1
Jean Bt Couture and wife	1	1	1	....	4	3	....	..
Louis Benoa and wife	1	1	1	....	....	....	....	..
Robert Navarre jr. and wife	1	1	....	....	7	2	1	1
Charles Campeau and wife	1	1	....	....	....	....	....	....
John Edgar and wife	1	1	....	....	....	1	....	....
John McErgan and wife	1	1	....	....	1	4	....	....
Gerard Bercelon and wife	1	1	....	1	2	....	....	....

Grain, Flour, etc.—CONTINUED.

Pounds flour.	Bushells of wheat.	Do. for seed.	Bushells Indian Corn.	Do. for seed.	Bushells pease.	Do. for seed.	Bushells oats.	Do. for seed.	Oxen.	Cows.	Steers.	Hoggs.	Horses.	Sheep.
.....	.....	.....	.....	.....	.....	.....	.....	.....	.....	1	.....	.....	.....	....
.....	.....	.....	.....	.....	.....	.....	.....	.....	.....	1	.....	.....	2	....
.....	.....	.....	.....	.....	.....	.....	.....	.....	.....	1	.....	.....	1	....
100	.....	.....	.....	.....	.....	.....	.....	.....	.....	3	4	1	1	....
.....	.....	.....	.....	.....	.....	.....	.....	.....	.....	1	.....	.....	1	....
600	.....	.....	.....	.....	.....	.....	.....	.....	.....	2	.....	.....	3	....
.....	.....	.....	.....	.....	.....	.....	.....	.....	.....	2	.....	.....	2	....
100	.....	.....	.....	.....	.....	.....	.....	.....	.....	1	.....	.....	.....	....
.....	.....	.....	.....	.....	.....	.....	.....	.....	.....	.....	.....	.....	.....	....
.....	.....	.....	.....	.....	.....	.....	.....	.....	.....	2	.....	1	2	....
.....	.....	.....	.....	.....	.....	.....	.....	.....	.....	.....	.....	.....	.....	....
.....	.....	.....	.....	.....	.....	.....	.....	.....	.....	.....	.....	.....	.....	....
.....	.....	.....	.....	.....	.....	.....	.....	.....	.....	.....	1	.....	3	....
100	.....	.....	.....	.....	.....	.....	.....	.....	.....	1	.....	.....	2	....
.....	.....	.....	.....	.....	.....	.....	.....	.....	.....	.....	.....	.....	.....	....
.....	5	.....	1	.....	.....	.....	.....	.....	.....	1	.....	.....	1	....
200	.....	8	30	.....	.....	.....	.....	13	2	11	6	12	12	40
.....	.....	.....	.....	.....	.....	.....	.....	.....	.....	.....	.....	.....	1	....
150	6	6	.....	.....	.....	.....	.....	.....	.....	3	.....	4	2	....
160	26	.....	.....	.....	.....	.....	.....	.....	5	4	1	3	3	....
.....	6	6	.....	.....	.....	.....	.....	.....	2	3	4	2	2	....
.....	4	12	.....	.....	.....	.....	.....	.....	2	.....	.....	.....	.....	....
.....	.....	.....	.....	.....	.....	.....	.....	.....	2	6	5	1	2	....
100	40	50	90	.....	.....	.....	.....	.....	4	12	.....	2	2	....
.....	.....	.....	.....	.....	.....	.....	.....	.....	.....	1	1	.....	1	....
.....	.....	.....	.....	.....	.....	.....	.....	.....	.....	.....	.....	.....	.....	....
300	15	15	.....	.....	.....	2	.....	25	2	10	6	4	2	....
.....	.....	.....	.....	.....	.....	.....	.....	.....	2	5	1	7	3	....
1,000	.....	20	.....	1	.....	.....	.....	20	2	7	8	6	5	....
200	.....	.....	.....	.....	.....	.....	.....	.....	2	3	2	5	2	....
.....	.....	.....	.....	.....	.....	.....	.....	.....	.....	2	1	.....	.....	....
.....	.....	.....	.....	.....	.....	.....	.....	.....	.....	1	.....	.....	1	....
400	50	10	.....	.....	.....	.....	.....	12	4	7	7	5	6	21
.....	.....	.....	.....	.....	.....	.....	.....	.....	.....	1	.....	.....	1	....
.....	.....	.....	.....	.....	.....	.....	.....	.....	.....	1	.....	3	1	....
.....	.....	.....	.....	.....	.....	.....	.....	.....	.....	.....	.....	.....	.....	....
150	.....	.....	.....	.....	.....	.....	.....	.....	.....	.....	2	.....	1	....

A Roll of Inhabitants.

Inhabitants' Names.	Men.	Women.	Lodgers hired or young men.	Lodgers hired or young women.	Boys.	Girls.	Male slaves.	Female slaves.
Ambrois Reopel and wife	1	1		1	3	3		
Jean Bt. Cicot wife and mother	1	2			2	4	2	5
Louis Visier and wife	1	1		1	2	3	1	2
Joseph Cabasy and sister	1	1	2				2	2
Beaugrain and Gilbeau	2		3	1	3			
Mrs. Drouillard		1				1	1	
Claude Campau and wife	1	1	1	3	3	1		
Robert Navarre Cenr. and wife	1	1	1		1		1	1
Etienne Hyvernois	1		1				1	1
Pierre Descompte Labady and wife	1	1	2	1	2	3		
Joseph Gamelin and mother	1	1	3		1	2	1	1
St. Jean	1							
Joseph poupar Lefleur and wife	1	1	1				2	
Francois Cadorel and wife	1	1				1		
Thomas Finchley and wife	1	1	1		2			
Charles Chasne and wife	1	1	1	1	3	2		
Francois Berthelet and wife	1	1			1			2
Widow Menard		1		1	4			
Louison Roberdoux and wife	1	1	2	2	4	2		
Gerard Cochran	1		1		1			
Mrs. Pike		1		1	2	1		
Mrs. Baby		1			3	5	1	3
William and Alexr. Macomb and wife	2	1	1	1	1	3	1	2
Mrs. Langton		1						
William Park	1							
Victor Moriseau and wife	1	1						
Jacques Besere and wife	1	1	1		1	1		
Josette Politte		1		1	1			
Charles Bermier and wife	1	1	1		2	2		
Francois Leblanc and wife	1	1	1		1	1		
Jean Saliot and wife	1	1			1	1		
Louis Montmine and wife	1	1			4	2		
Jean Bte Reau and wife	1	1			1	1		
Antoine Melsche and wife	1	1			3	1		
Jean Bt Antiya and wife	1	1			3	1		
Jean Bt Giginac and wife	1	1				1		
Thomas Pagotte and wife	1	1	1		1	5		

Grain, Flour, etc.—CONTINUED.

Pounds flour.	Bushells of wheat.	Do. for seed.	Bushells Indian Corn.	Do. for seed.	Bushells pease.	Do. for seed.	Bushells oats.	Do. for seed.	Oxen.	Cows.	Steers.	Hoggs.	Horses.	Sheep.
100	23	20	.....	.....	.....	.....	.....	15	.....	4	2	6	2	....
200	32	12	.....	.....	3	.....	26	18	4	8	6	6	4	....
800	.....	10	.....	.....	.....	.....	.....	.....	2	5	2	3	2	....
300	.....	10	3	.....	.....	.....	.....	10	3	4	8	9	3	14
100	.....	18	.....	.....	.....	.....	.....	.....	2	.....	.....	.....	.....	....
300	.....	.....	.....	.....	.....	.....	.....	.....	.....	.....	.....	.....	2	....
800	50	12	.....	.....	.....	.....	40	40	4	5	.....	10	7	....
500	28	7	25	.....	.....	.....	10	15	.....	4	11	4	4	....
800	.....	10	.....	.....	.....	.....	.....	20	4	7	5	3	2	....
.....	38	12	.....	.....	.....	.....	10	20	4	2	8	8	7	....
800	.....	15	.....	.....	.....	2	.....	22	4	6	6	5	6	....
.....	.....	.....	.....	.....	.....	.....	.....	.....	.....	.....	.....	.....	.....	....
200	18	.....	.....	.....	.....	.....	.....	.....	.....	3	.....	.....	.....	....
.....	.....	.....	.....	.....	.....	.....	.....	.....	.....	1	.....	.....	1	....
.....	.....	.....	200	.....	.....	.....	.....	.....	.....	2	.....	.....	1	....
.....	.....	.....	.....	.....	.....	.....	.....	20	.....	3	2	6	7	16
1,500	.....	20	.....	.....	.....	6	.....	20	2	5	6	10	6	15
.....	.....	.....	.....	.....	.....	.....	.....	.....	.....	.....	.....	.....	.....	....
.....	.....	.....	.....	.....	.....	.....	.....	.....	.....	.....	.....	.....	.....	....
.....	.....	.....	15	.....	.....	.....	.....	.....	.....	.....	.....	.....	2	....
.....	.....	.....	6	.....	.....	.....	.....	.....	.....	.....	.....	.....	.....	....
150	.....	.....	60	.....	3	.....	.....	.....	.....	5	.....	.....	3	20
500	.....	.....	.....	.....	.....	.....	.....	.....	.....	15	.....	.....	2	9
.....	.....	.....	.....	.....	.....	.....	.....	.....	.....	4	2	9	.....	7
8,893	.....	.....	619	.....	.....	.....	.....	.....	.....	.....	.....	.....	.....	....
.....	.....	.....	10	.....	.....	.....	.....	.....	.....	1	.....	.....	1	....
.....	7	5	2	.....	.....	.....	.....	.....	.....	2	2	3	1	....
.....	.....	7	3	.....	.....	.....	.....	.....	.....	2	.....	2	.....	....
.....	20	20	.....	.....	.....	.....	10	20	2	4	2	6	4	....
150	.....	.....	.....	.....	.....	.....	.....	.....	.....	.....	.....	.....	.....	....
.....	8	.....	.....	.....	.....	.....	.....	.....	.....	1	2	.....	1	....
.....	.....	15	.....	.....	.....	.....	.....	10	2	1	.....	4	2	....
.....	.....	.....	.....	.....	.....	.....	.....	.....	.....	.....	.....	.....	.....	....
.....	.....	10	.....	.....	.....	.....	.....	15	2	1	.....	3	2	....
.....	30	30	10	2	.....	.....	.....	20	4	4	1	6	6	....
.....	10	20	.....	.....	.....	.....	.....	.....	.....	1	.....	2	1	....
.....	92	15	2	.....	.....	.....	24	30	4	2	4	4	4	....

A Roll of Inhabitants.

Inhabitants' Names.	Men.	Women.	Lodgers hired or young men.	Lodgers hired or young women.	Boys.	Girls.	Male slaves.	Female slaves.
Francois Langlois and wife	1	1			3	3		
Louis Lajoy and wife	1	1			4	2		1
Antoine Boufare and wife	1	1	1		2	1		
Charles Reneau and wife	1	1			2	1		
Etienne Lavoilette and wife	1	1	2		2	3		
Francois Choisi and wife	1	1			1	3		
Charles Fontaigne and wife	1	1			3	2		
Jean Beaushomme and wife	1	1			1			
Augustin Toranjeau and wife	1	1	1		1			
Pierre Proux and wife	1	1			1	1		
Pierre Charon and wife	1	1			1	1		
Pierre Campeau and wife	1	1				1		
Antoine Rousseau and wife	1	1	2			1		
Etienne Jacob and wife	1	1			3	3		
Louis Ceazore and wife	1	1	1		2	4		
Madame Bissounette		1	2	1	3	2		
René Cloutier and wife	1	1			4	4		
Locariah Cloutier and wife	1	1				1		
J. B. Begras	1							
Micheal Roy and wife	1	1	1		1			
Pierre Bellaire and wife	1	1	1		3	3		
Louis St. Louis and wife	1	1	1		1			
Jean Lajiness and wife	1	1	4	1	1	3		
J. Bt. Toranjeau and wife	1	1	2			1		1
J. Bt. Bertrand and wife	1	1		1	5	3		
Joseph Drouillard and wife	1	1	1		1	2		1
Joseph St. Etienne and wife	1	1	1					
Simon Drouillard and wife	1	1			5	4		
Pierre Meloche and wife	1	1	2	2	6	1		
Joseph Bellperche and mother	1	1	2	1	3	4		
Jacques Peltier and wife	1	1			2	2		
J. Bt. Peter and wife	1	1			1	1		
J. Bt. Drouillard and wife	1	1	4	1				
Joseph Boudy and wife	1	1	2		4	4		
Pierre Coquilard and wife	1	1	3	1				
Jean Bt. Parry and wife	1	1	2	2	2	1		
Noel Chavin and wife	1	1	2	1	4	3		

Grain, Flour, etc.—Continued.

Pounds flour.	Bushells of wheat.	Do. for seed.	Bushells Indian Corn.	Do. for seed.	Bushells pease.	Do. for seed.	Bushells oats.	Do. for seed.	Oxen.	Cows.	Steers.	Hoggs.	Horses.	Sheep.
		15	16	7						1		5	2	
									2	2		4		
2,000	20	30	50					20	2	2	1	4	2	
	10	15						4	2	1		1	1	
	15	18	3	1					2		4		1	
	10	15	20						2	2	1	5	2	
	15	20	3						2	1	1	5	2	
		17								1	1	2	2	
								12	2	2		4	2	
		10	12					6	1	4	6	5	2	
										1			1	
150		16	60					8		1	4	4	1	
									2	1		2		
1,000			50						2	2		3	1	
	50	30					20	20	4	6	5	6	3	
100										2		4	2	
									2	2	1	4	2	4
	30	15							2	2		3	1	
	10	27						20	2	2	2	4	1	
		15							2	3	1	5	3	
	18	12	5						2	9	11	6	1	
200	20	10							2	3	4	6	2	
100	25	25	6					15	2	1	5	4	2	
		40	8					15	4	3	5	10	7	
										1		2	1	
900	144	8							2	1	8	7	3	
500									2	2		3	1	
		10						6	4	4	4	8	5	
	30	20	20				15		2	4		13	2	
100		18	1					30	8	3	8	5	4	
	20	30					25	15	4	4	6	3	2	
										5	2	10	1	
200									4	2	2	4	2	
200		7	320			3		8	4	11	10	6	3	14
	25			1				8	2	1	4	4	2	
	6							2		4	1	3	4	
										2	1	3	3	

A Roll of Inhabitants.

Inhabitants' Names.	Men.	Women.	Lodgers hired or young men.	Lodgers hired or young women.	Boys.	Girls.	Male slaves.	Female slaves.
Theophil Lamay and wife	1	1	1	....	2	3	....	....
J. Bt. Reaume and wife	1	1	1	....	3	3	....	1
Etienne Robidoux and wife	1	1	1	....	2	1	....	....
George Knaggs and wife	1	1	....	....	3	2	1	....
Pere Pothier	1	....	1	1	....	....	....	....
Francois Marentete and wife	1	1	2	....	5	1	1	....
William Monforton and wife	1	1	2	1	3	1	....	1
Jaques Parent and wife	1	1	1	....	3	....	....	....
Laurent Parent and wife	1	1	1	....	3	1	....	....
Mrs. Janess and son	1	1	....	....	2	1	....	....
Claude Reaume and wife	1	1	1	....	5	1	1	....
Philip Leduc and wife	1	1	....	....	5	2	....	....
J. Bt. Leduc and wife	1	1	2	....	1	2	....	....
Francis Sordillier	1	1	....	....	2	2	....	....
Widow Malont	....	1	1	1	2	....	....	....
Joseph Valcour and wife	1	1	....	....	2	1	....	....
J. Bte. Violette and wife	1	1	2	....	3	1	....	....
André Benetteau and wife	1	1	1	1	3	3	....	....
Charles Bourond and wife	1	1	1	1	4	3	....	1
Dominique Labrosse and wife	1	1	3	....	....	1	....	....
Pierre Reaume and wife	1	1	2	1	1	....	....	1
Nicolas Lenoir	1	....	1	....	....	....	....	....
William Gayeux	1	....	....	....	1	2	....	....
Vittel Demouchelle and wife	1	1	....	....	3	2	....	....
Louis Ganyeaux and wife	1	1	1	....	2	1	....	....
Jacques Charon and wife	1	1	1	....	....	1	....	....
Joseph Lesperance	1	....	....	2	1	....	1	2
Julian Parent and mother	1	1	....	3	1	....	1	....
Nicolas Langlois and wife	1	1	3	1	3	2	....	....
Pierre Labute and wife	1	1	3	2	....	3	....	....
Hyacinthe D. hetre	1	....	1	1	2	2	....	1
Michael Cattin and wife	1	1	....	....	....	....	....	....
Charles Delisle and wife	1	1	1	....	....	....	....	....
Antoine Langlios and wife	1	1	2	....	1	2	....	....
Joseph Dechesne and wife	1	1	....	....	2	1	1	....
Paul Campeau	1	....	....	....	1	1	....	....
J. Bte. Beaubien, Jr., and wife	1	1	....	....	1	1	....	....

Grain, Flour, etc.—CONTINUED.

Pounds flour.	Bushells of wheat.	Do. for seed.	Bushells Indian Corn.	Do. for seed.	Bushells pease.	Do. for seed.	Bushells cats.	Do. for seed.	Oxen.	Cows.	Steers.	Hoggs.	Horses.	Sheep.
...	5	...	...	...	...	...	21	...	...	3	4	3	3	...
600	20	10	...	...	...	...	...	...	2	4	6	6	4	...
...	...	20	...	...	...	...	...	...	4	8	5	5	2	...
...	...	10	10	...	...	...	...	...	6	18	8	17	4	...
...	12	...	8	...	...	...	14	...	...	1	...	1	...	...
2,000	...	30	...	...	...	5	30	30	6	7	6	15	8	24
...	...	...	...	...	...	...	...	...	...	...	...	...	...	...
...	15	20	12	...	...	5	...	15	2	4	6	3	3	...
800	...	10	...	...	...	3	...	20	2	3	5	6	2	...
600	...	15	...	...	...	...	...	20	2	2	1	6	2	...
...	30	17	...	...	...	...	6	14	16	3	5	10	3	...
...	30	15	...	...	...	2	...	15	2	4	2	7	2	6
200	30	20	4	...	...	...	15	...	4	3	2	8	2	...
200	...	...	...	...	...	...	...	...	...	1	1	5	1	...
...	20	20	...	...	...	...	...	10	4	3	2	4	2	...
...	...	...	...	...	...	...	...	10	...	...	...	...	2	...
...	...	20	...	...	...	...	...	20	...	4	2	7	4	...
100	...	...	...	...	...	...	...	...	...	1	...	3	3	...
...	20	20	...	...	...	...	...	30	4	5	2	5	3	...
1,000	...	18	...	...	...	...	...	18	5	2	...	6	3	...
4,000	50	30	...	...	...	...	...	...	4	6	6	10	4	...
...	...	...	...	...	...	...	...	...	...	...	...	...	...	...
200	25	30	...	...	...	5	...	20	2	2	...	10	4	...
300	30	16	26	...	...	...	...	15	3	2	4	8	3	...
800	40	...	...	...	...	...	...	...	2	2	...	7	2	...
...	10	30	...	...	...	4	...	12	...	1	4	7	4	...
600	20	24	...	...	...	...	...	...	2	2	2	8	7	...
600	10	30	...	...	...	...	25	25	4	3	2	6	3	...
...	30	...	...	...	...	...	...	...	2	...	2	6	2	...
...	100	50	150	...	...	...	...	...	...	...	6	14	8	...
...	20	31	...	...	...	...	...	...	...	...	...	...	...	...
...	...	...	...	...	...	...	...	...	...	1	...	...	1	...
600	...	20	20	...	...	...	...	...	4	2	2	6	4	...
700	...	30	...	...	...	...	...	15	6	4	3	9	3	...
...	...	...	...	...	...	...	...	...	...	1	1	2	1	...
...	...	...	...	...	...	...	...	...	...	...	...	...	...	...
700	7	20	...	...	...	...	15	25	4	2	1	3	3	...

A Roll of Inhabitants.

Inhabitants' Names.	Men.	Women.	Lodgers hired or young men.	Lodgers hired or young women.	Boys.	Girls.	Male slaves.	Female slaves.	Pounds flour.	Bushells of wheat.
Joseph Beaubien and wife	1	1	2	1	1			1	150	23
Alexis Maisonville and wife	1	1	3	1	2		3	3	1,800	250
Louis Labady	1				4	2	1	1		110
Bonaventure Reaume and wife	1	1			3	3				100
Joseph Gaudet and wife	1	1	1			3			200	20
Joseph Bertiaume and wife	1	1	1		2	1				25
André Peltier and wife	1	1			4	4			200	
Francois Drouillard and wife	1	1	1		3	3				
Alexis Argute and wife	1	1			2	1				
Vittal Depelleau and wife	1	1				1			700	
J. Bt. Laperle and wife	1	1			2					
J. Bt. Parrey and wife	1	1			4	2				
Francois Compary	1		2		2	1				
J. Bt. Lecoursier	1				1					
William Laforet and wife	1	1			2	2				
Laurent Griffaur and wife	1	1			1	3				
Louis Griffaur and wife	1	1			3	3				
Basil Belanger	1									
Jean Thoulouse and wife	1	1			1	2				4
Nicolas Thé and wife	1	1			3	2				
Coxes Wind Mill									2,464	41
Garrison and navy	239	34			30	28		1		
Extras, prisoners, etc	500								49,750	
Totals	1,011	265	253	100	484	402	60	78	141,517	5,273

Endorsed:—Survey of the settlement of Detroit taken 31st March 1779 upon oath. Recd 9th June 1779

[B 122 p 318]

Grain, Flour, etc.—CONTINUED.

Do. for seed.	Indian Corn.	Do. for seed.	Pease.	Do. for seed.	Oats.	Do. for seed.	Oxen.	Cows.	Steers.	Hoggs.	Horses.	Sheep.	Pounds pork.	Pounds beef.	Pounds oatmeal.	Pounds butter.
11					15	10	2	4	5	5	3					
					15	25	8	18	18	4	10	27				
40	40				20	20	10	8	6	7	13					
45						10	2	4	2	9	4					
20						8	2	1	2	7	2					
25						12	2	2	2	1	2					
12	4						4	4		5	2					
							2		1	7	1					
										6						
6	6				10	8	2	2	2	4	2					
							2	2			1					
							2	5	5	4	3					
								3	2	5	1					
							2									
								2	1	3	1					
								2	2	4	1					
1								2		3	2					
							2	2	2	2	2					
8						4		10		4	1					
											3					
	194		737										91,790	570	17,000	7,700
2,126	3,177	20	772	71	744	1,505	413	779	619	1,076	664	313	91,790	570	17,000	7,700

FROM CAPTAIN LERNOULT UNADDRESSED

NIAGARA April 2nd 1779

SIR, I have received an Express from Capt Lernoult by the felicity a copy of his Letter I beg leave to lay before your Excellency

DETROIT March 26th 1779.

SIR, I had just received copies of the several Letters taken by the Indians near Fort Laurance, & the extracts of Governor Hamilton's & Mr Hay's Letter when one Isidore Chaina (an Interpreter) & two Hurons arrived from Post Vincent with the unfortunate news of that place having been retaken by a Colonel Clarke the Governor & whole Garrison made prisoners, except himself who made his escape with difficulty. This most unlucky shake with the approach of so large body of Virginians advancing towards St Duskie has greatly damped the spirit of the Indians.

The Chiefs from St Duskie are come in here with John Montoine to claim Governor Hamilton promises to assist them. They declare If a large detachment of with cannon are not sent without delay from below they must go out of the way, being not able to fight the enemy alone. As the loss of this Post opens a new road for the Virginians to this place by the Miamis River, I hope a strong reinforcement will be sent here from Niagara by return of the vessels at least what they can convey, as the New work is not yet defencible requiring many hands. The Canadians exceedingly assuming on our bad success & weakness not one of them will lend a hand, spades shovels, &c. are much wanted also ammunition as per inclosed return above 30,000 lbs of flower of last years allowance not as yet sent here, with other species in proportion, the enormous quantity consumed in the last unfortunate expedition has reduced us greatly pray forward it, for the Indians insist on having provisions sent to them or they must starve.

The loss of Governor Hamilton is a most feeling one to me, I find the burden heavy without assistance, it requires I confess superior abilities & a better constitution, I will do my best however.

I beg leave to repeat to you the necessity of a reinforcement being sent as the consequences may be fatal.

I send the Felicity with this Pacquet which with the Angelica already down will convey part of the Troops as some of the Indian chiefs wait the return of the vessels to see if any notice is taken of their distress or prove me a liar. A letter to His Excellency's address I send you, it came some days before the unfortunate affair from Post Vincent by Lieut. Du vernet who is returned. All the Canadians are Rebels to a man, I shall wait your orders with great impatience.

I am &c

(signed) B. B. LERNOULT

[B 96-1-p 258]

GENERAL HALDIMAND TO LIEUT. GOV. HAMILTON

QUEBEC, the 8th April 1779.

SIR, I received your several Letters, previous to your departure from Détroit, the suddeness of your Resolution to march against the Rebels that had Invaded the Illinois, made it impossible for me to give you any orders; but, from my Knowledge of you & the Spirit your Letters breathe, I am persuaded you have executed what appear'd to you best for the King's Service, & in that Light the measure you had pursued was stated to the Secretary of State in my Letter of last Fall.

I have since by your Dispatches of the 18th Decemr last which came to hand the 19th of March with their several Enclosures, learned that you have taken Possession of Fort Vincennes, long before this reaches you, you will have been satisfied whether the Rebels seriously intended an attack upon Detroit, and acted in consequence, or seen what further could be done for the King's Service in those parts, with the force at present with you; my anxiety for the safety of Niagara & Detroit has induced me to send there Captain Brehm, my aid de camp, who has my directions to consult Captain Lernoult, & forward you from thence upon an exact view of the state of things in those parts, his opinion upon the further measures most proper to be taken by you.

By accounts which bear every mark of authenticity, His Majesty's Arms have been attended with success to the Southward, the Province of Georgia once more reduced to obey their lawfull Sovereign and great Hopes are entertained of the Royal Forces being able to penetrate further that way; it is likely this will engage the Southern Indians to make such a Diversion on their Part, as may tend in future to facilitate your operations.

In the uncertainty of all things here, uninformed how far this War may spread, it is impossible for me at this distance to give you orders & directions respecting the further measures to be pursued by you; of the possibility or practicability of those you embrace, you must be the best judge and on your doing what is best for the King's Service, I must & do fully rely.

Before you undertake anything considerable I must recommend your weighing well the difficulty & expense that must attend the transport of every article you are to be furnished with from hence, & whether they are likely to be compensated by the advantages expected to arise from such an undertaking.

When you write this way I should be glad to receive the best information you can procure in regard to the most likely measures to be pursued for conciliating the Indians, preventing the Rebels designs & securing the Upper

Country, that when my Spring Dispatches reach this I may be enabled to judge of what is best to be done for those purposes.

I am &c

(signed) FRED. HALDIMAND

Endorsed:—Entd Detroit No 7 Copy Letter from His Excellency General Haldimand to Lieut Gov. Hamilton, dated Quebec the 8th of April 1779. Copy Book B (No 2) fol 8.

(B 122 p 931)

GENERAL HALDIMAND TO CAPTAIN LERNOULT

QUEBEC 8th April 1779.

SIR, It is with real satisfaction I have received from Lt. Col. Bolton an account of the active and proper dispositions you have been making to receive the Rebels. Whatever their designs may be, it is happy for the King's Service, a Post of such importance as that of Detroit should be entrusted to so careful and diligent an officer, I hope and doubt not, that you will continue to exert your best Endeavours for the security and preservation of that settlement.

Anxious to be informed as soon as practicable of the true state of things in the Upper Country I send Captain Brehm my Aid-de-camp as far as Detroit and it is my request, you would open yourself to Him with the utmost freedom as to a Person, in whom you may safely confide, upon all matters, which concern the Kings Service in those Parts. Captain Brehm is directed to give you my orders respecting your Post, which He is to deliver you in Writing, signed with His Own Hand, and to which you will in every Part thereof, exactly conform yourself.

Capt. Brehm has received my directions to consult with you in regard to what may be done respecting the Post of Vincennes & the further steps advisable for Lt. Govr. Hamilton to take, upon which he is to write to him from your Post; for at this distance & without Information of the actual state of things in the Upper Country it is impossible for me to point out to the Lt. Govr the Measure he ought to pursue.

By this conveyance, I desire Lt. Col. Bolton to favour the Transport of goods, belonging to Mr. McComb of your settlement, as I understand he is the Person employed by Lt Govr Hamilton to furnish the articles wanted for the Indians.

I am &c

(signed) FRED. HALDIMAND.

Capt Lernoult

Endorsed: Copy 1779. To Captain Lernoult at Detroit—April 8th Entd in Book Marked B No. 2 page 11

[B 122 p 334]

LORD GEORGE GERMAIN TO GENERAL HALDIMAND

(EXTRACT)

WHITEHALL 10th April 1779

Sir Henry Clinton has acquainted me that he has transmitted to you the information he has collected of their designs. Their building Battoes at Still Water indicates a design of entering by the Mohawk and perhaps attempting Niagara & Detroit, if they are able to force their way to them; but I confess I am not apprehensive of their being able to effect any thing material on that side whilst the Six Nations continue faithful, and the judicious measures you have taken to succour them in case of an attack, and the supplies you will be enabled to send them, will, I hope, prevent their being frightened into a neutrality—The great importance of Niagara & Detroit and the navigation of the Lakes which depends upon them, must however, always render them objects of particular attention, and I was very happy to find you had reinforced the garrison & given orders for strengthening their defenses, as well as for repairing the armed Vessels and augmenting their Crews.

The astonishing activity and success of Joseph Brant's Enterprizes and the important consequences with which they have been attended, give him a claim to every mark of our regard and which you think will be pleasing to him. What has occurred to me as most likely to gratify him, has been done, and enclosed herewith you will receive a commission signed by His Majesty appointing him a Colonel of Indians and on Board the Three Brothers Store ship is a box with prints taken from Lord Warrick's picture of him which he was particularly pleased with, some of which you will send into his nation, and dispose of the others as you think most honorable for him, as a memorial of his services.

Major Butler and his son appear also to have done good service and you will acquaint him that their care to prevent the Indians from molesting the unarmed Inhabitants is much approved by the King.

I flatter myself Lieutenant Governor Hamilton has succeeded in his Expedition to the Illinois Country. The destruction of the settlements of the innocent inhabitants by the Rebel Banditti that professed themselves of that Country calls for the severest chastisment, and the orders you gave to Mr. Hamilton and Col. Bolton on that occasion were very proper & you will see by the inclosed extract of my letter of the 2d Dec'r to Colonel Stuart that he has orders to support the Ouabash Indians in effecting the services you have directed them to be employed in.

You will see by the enclosed extracts of my letters to Sir Henry Clinton that it is intended in the course of the summer to attack the sea costs of the revolted provinces wherever their posts or Inlets are accessible to the King's land or sea forces. These operations will of course prevent them sending any considerable detachments of the Militia from the lower Parts of the Provinces to join those upon the back Frontiers in an Expedition to Canada, or even to strengthen Mr. Washington's army. And as Sir Henry Clinton will after supplying these Expeditions have a large Force remaining with him with which to act in the Field as opportunities may offer, verry important results are expected to be brought about before the close of the Campaign. The Cooperation of Detachments of your Troops & parties of Indians on the Frontier must greatly contribute to the hoped for success. The attack intended upon the Province of Main must be particularly assisted by a detachment penetrating by the Chaudieré, and if a communication were opened with the Troops, which may be ordered to effect an Establishment on the Kennebec river, I should have little doubt of recovering to the King's obedience the whole of the Province.

I am therefore to signify to you the King's commands that you give particular attention to this important object.

The loss of your last Dispatches has deprived us of your Demands you proposed to send to the several Departments for supplies to be sent out this Spring. That respecting the ordnance branch which is the only one received has been fully complied with, as you will find by, the returns of what is shipped on Board the store ships that sail with this convoy, and we have done the best we could to furnish you with the other necessaries which were supposed to be wanting. A large assortment of goods, arms, and ammunition for presents for the Indians has been provided, and the inclosed Extract of my Letter to the Lords Commissioners of the Treasury will shew you what other articles were ordered to be sent out, & I have the satisfaction to find that everything ordered has been shipped in proper time. The Cloathing & other necessaries sent for 2000 Provincials is meant to enable you to supply the Canadians corps you are authorized to raise as well as those already on foot. The Battalion of Col McLean's regiment in Canada is not included in that estimate, for that regiment is included in the British Establishment and is to be considered as a regular Corps—The Major of that Battalion has lately been appointed a Lieut: Colonel by Brevet, and as Colonel Maclean is now going out to Quebec he will be able to account to the officers for the Major's absence or order him to join the Battalion.

Enclosed is the embarkation return of an additional company of Hanau chasseurs which are arrived at Portsmouth. The recruits for the Brunswick and Anhalt Zerbty Regiments are hourly expected & if they arrive in time will also proceed with this Convoy. I could have wished to have sent you a further reinforcement from Europe, but in our present circumstances all that could be spared has been sent to Sir Henry Clinton. I am, however, not without hopes your Force will be augmented by the return of the whole or at least a considerable part of the Troops of the Convention of Saratoga, Sir Henry Clinton having had orders to receive them in Exchange as Prisoners of War & upon their release to send them to Quebec.

Your Commission of General in America was signed by the King on the 17th of last September, but in order to give you rank agreeable to your former commissions the date of it was carried back to the first of January preceeding. Your agent to whom it was delivered put it on Board the Warrick Man of War and it was brought back with my Dispatch; but I hope you will receive it safe by this conveyance.

The Extract of my Letter of the 3rd of March to Sir Henry Clinton will inform you of the encouragement he is authorized to hold out to the Inhabitants of the Country they style Vermont, to induce them to return to their allegiance; your situation may enable you to have a more ready access to them; and it is the King's pleasure that you should endeavor to open a negociation with them upon the same ground & you will instruct your Agents to correspond with Sir Henry Clinton also and act in concert with such as he may employ in this Business.

I am Sir your most obedient humble Servant

George Germain.

General Haldimand.

P. S. Intelligence from France mentions that there is an Intention to send some Troops, with some ships of War up the St. Lawrence this summer with a view to promote a rising among the Canadians and assist an Expedition meditated by the Rebels; and I think proper to acquaint you of it that you may pay proper attention to the safety of Quebec tho' I cannot say they will venture, in my opinion, to carry the project into Execution.

Endorsed:—Duplicate No 10—1779. should be No 14 From Lord George Germain 16th April recd. 3d October.

(B 43 p 114)

LIEUTENANT BIRD TO CAPTAIN LERNOULT

[EXTRACT.]

Dear Sir, Tho' the situation I am in deprives me of power to detain the Vessel yet it appearing necessary for your information & the good of the Service that I should do it in the present case, I have taken upon me that authority at Aruntundis & the chiefs requests who are return'd from Warr

& by the message sent (by one of their chiefs) to me, they seem to have something of importance to communicate or resolve upon. They promise positively to be here on the 11th. Capt. Graham as been so anxious to return ever since the first day of his arrival that its with the utmost difficulty I have prevailed with him to remain. 13 March. The chiefs arriv'd yesterday, have considerably reinforced the Fort at Tuscarawas. The Savages are very uneasy, would fain Council, I refus'd anything to do with th' affair and beg'd they would send their determinations to you, which they conclude to do. Knives, flints, fuzees and tomahawks are wanting.

H. Bird.

To Capt Lernoult
Commandt of Detroit &c—

Endorsed: Extracts of Letters from St Duski from Lieut Bird to Capt Lernoult Recd. 17th April 1779 For Col Bolton

[B 122 p 336]

FROM LORD GEORGE GERMAIN UNADDRESSED

Whitehall 16th April 1779.

Sir, Soon after Mr. Livins's arrival in England he presented a memorial to the King, complaining of his having been removed from his office & praying that Sir Guy Carleton might be required to assign the reasons for his removal, and that they might be enquired into, and His Majesty was pleased to refer the matter to the Board of Trade for their consideration.

Their Lordships after a full examination of the charges contained in Sir Guy Carleton's correspondence, and the minutes of the Legislative Council, to which Sir Guy Carleton referred, reported their opinion to H. M. that there did not appear to the Board good & sufficient reason for Displacing Mr. Livins—But H. M. desirous that a matter of so much importance to the welfare of the Province, as the removal or restoration of the Chief Justice, should undergo the fullest examination before a final decision was made, their Lordships report was by H. M., command laid before a Committee of the Privy Council for Plantation affairs, and Sir Guy Carleton had notice to attend the consideration of it if he thought fit. The report of the Lords of the Committee which recites the report of the Board of Trade at full length, and the confirmation of it by the Privy Council is continued in the enclosed order of His Majesty in Council in the 29th of last month which I send to you by H. M. commands, and in obedience to which Mr. Livins has been restored to his office as Chief Justice of Quebec, and I have signified to him

His Majestys Pleasure—that he do immediately return to the exercise of his Functions & he Embarks in this Fleet accordingly.

The Two additional Instructions which the Lords of the Council recommended to be sent to you, have been prepared and approved by H. M. & I Enclose them likewise herewith by H. M'rs command for Your Guidance and Direction.

One of these Instructions will fully explain to you that it is H. M'rs Intention that all the members of the Legislative Council are to be considered as equally Members of the Council of State, and the other, that every Instruction respecting their conduct as a Legislative Council is to be communicated to the whole Body & entered in the Council Books, according to the Directions given in your standing Instructions for it was certainly the Intention of Parliament & H. M'rs gracious purpose in constituting the Legislative Council, that they with the Governor should exercise every Power of Legislation authorized by the act of Parliament for the further Regulation of the Government, & that the Inhabitants should by that means enjoy the advantages of making their wants known to a Body consistent to Relieve them, and if living under Laws suitable to their Local circumstances.

The regular & impartial administration of Justice is an object that Deserves the most serious attention, and as I understand, there has not yet been any act passed for Establishing an easy method for the recovery of small Debts, it is proper you should recommend a measure so necessary for the convenience of both Debtor & Creditor to the consideration of the Legislative Council.

The appointment of Magistrates in the several Parishes or Districts for the preservation of good order & prevention of Injuries, by the speedy apprehension of offenders, would be a very proper exercise of the Perogative you are Intrusted with,—But as their assembling at certain times & holding Courts of Sessions for the trial & Punishment of petty offenders may require the Interposition of the Legislative Council you would do well to make that also a subject of their consideration.

Many other matters of Domestic arrangements will naturally suggest themselves to you, or arise out of the Deliberations of the Council upon the state of the Province when they are assembled, which it may be proper to Digest into the Form of Acts, but as mistakes in Legislation are productive of much evil, and cannot be immediately remedied, I must recommend it to you to be extremely careful not to multiply Laws without evident necessity, and to guard as much as possible against passing any upon misinformation, or misapprehension of the subject to which they apply.

The Law Servants of the Crown are bound in duty to give you their best advice and opinion in all such cases, and I have great pleasure in acquainting you that Mr. Livins has given me the most solemn assurances that he will give you every assistance in his Power, & conduct himself in such a manner as a Member of the Council as will give you entire satisfaction of his Disposition to render your administration easy & honorable to yourself & beneficial to the Public.

The Presentments of the Grand Jury at Montreal against Lieut. Govr Hamilton & Mr. Dejeau are expressive of a greater degree of Jealousy than the Transaction complained of in the then circumstances of the Province appeared to Warrant.

Such stretches of authority are however only to be excused by unavoidable necessity and the Justness and fitness of the occasion & you will therefore direct the Chief Justice to examine the Proofs produced of the Criminals Guilt, and if he shall be of opinion that he merited the Punishment he met with, tho' irregularly inflicted, It is the King's Pleasure that you do order the Attorney General to grant a nole prosequi, & stop all further proceedings in the matter.

I am &c &c.

(signed) Geo Germain.

[B 50 p 22]

CAPTAIN BIRD TO CAPTAIN LERNOULT

Upper St Duski June 9th 1779.

Dear Sir, After much running about, some presents to Chiefs, we had collected at the Mingo Town near 200 Savages chiefly Shawanese—When lo! a runner arrived with accounts of the Shawanese towns being attacked by a body from Kentuck, they burn'd five houses, kill'd one Indian & wounded the Chief badly—lost their own Commander *Heron* or *Herington*—they carried off 30 Horses, were pursued by 50 Shawanese, the Shawanese were beat back with loss of five or six wounded—News flew that all the Towns were to be attack'd & our little body separated in an Instant past reassembling—confusion still prevails—much counselling no resolves—many are removing—more for Peace.

The Delawares make it dangerous travelling. By this opportunity Davison & Cook return sick—Girty is flying about—McCarty stays with me with some Ottawas. These unsteady Rogues put me out of all Patience. I will go with him in a few days, if nothing material occurs—see the Enemy that I may not be laugh'd at then return,—The Rebels mean I believe to destroy the villages & Corn now up—the method they bring their little Armies into the field as follows:

Every family on the Borders receive orders to send according to their strength (one or two men) to the place of Rendezvous at a time appointed (on pain of fine or imprisonment) with fifteen or twenty days Provisions, they immediately receive their Ammunition & proceed quickly to Action—I am credibly informed, by various means, that they can raise in that manner three or four thousand in a few days from such excursions—I was obliged to kill four more cattle for the Indians at the Mingo Town. They are always cooking or counselling.

I have nothing more to inform you off. if anything material occurs, which I really expect in a day or two, I will inform you by Express.

I am &c.

Henry Bird

To Capt Lernoult
[B 122 p 351]

CAPTAIN BIRD TO CAPTAIN LERNOULT

June 12th Upper St Duski

Sir, Couriers after Couriers arrive with accounts of the Rebels advancing to destroy the Savage Villages now all their Corn is planted.

Ondeonquat & Orontondy are now here, they say if their father, according to his promises will assist them, they and the Shawanese are determined to defend their country whilst they have a man; if you will now assist them in the time of need they shall remember it, if not they must abandon their grain & habitations.

These are the words I send you by their request. I believe there is some truth in the report, the Delawares think so; they are abandoning there Towns near here.

I am &c

H. Bird.

To Captain Lernoult.

P. S. I beg to recommend Macarty to you as an Interpreter—he is a steady fellow—speaks Delaware & Ottawa—he has kindly attended me on my little excursions & protected us, by means of the Ottawas from insults, which would have been offered by Rebel Delawares. I am sure, Sir, you will find him an excellent acquisition.

Endorsed:—1779. Copy of Letters from Capt Bird to Capt Lernoult Upper St Duski, June 9th.
(B 122 p 352)

GENERAL HALDIMAND TO CAPTAIN LERNOULT

QUEBEC 13th June 1779.

SIR, Having certain Intelligence that many of the Inhabitants in your Neighborhood are not only disaffected to Government, but in the present critical situation of Public affairs, may possibly prove dangerous Enemies to the King, I have judged it necessary for His Majesty's Service, hereby to authorize you to apprehend any Person or Persons whom you may have cause to believe is in any manner directly or indirectly aiding or abetting the Rebels or their allies, either with Provisions, Intelligence, or otherwise, and that you immediately send them to Niagara, to be detained there or forwarded to Carleton Island as Lt. Col. Bolton may judge best for the Public service.

And it is also your duty to require and obtain from all Persons of doubtful character, such Hostages as may effectually prevent them or any part of their Family from taking an active part against His Majesty's Government, or the Troops under your Command.

I am &c

(signed) FRED. HALDIMAND.

Capt Lernoult

Endorsed:—No 2. 1779—Copy to Captain Lernoult at Detroit June 13th. Entered in Book marked B. No 2 Page 12.

(B 122 p 354)

ORDER—RECEIPT

DETROIT, 23d June 1779.

£122.. 19.. 5 N. Y. C.

Please to Pay to Messrs A & Wm Macomb or Order One Hundred & Twenty Two Pounds 19s 5d New York Curry. being the Balance of your Account with

ABBOTT & FINCHLEY

Mr. Alexr McKee

Rec'd the within in full

A. & W. MACOMB

[Indian Affairs M. G. IV]

CAPTAIN LERNOULT TO GENERAL HALDIMAND

DETROIT June 25th 1779.

SIR, I take the liberty to draw on your Excellency for the several sums due me for command money, in favor of Messrs Alexr & Willm Macomb, amounting to three hundred and eighty-five Pounds two shillings & six pence sterling, sixty days after sight, which please Honor.

I am Sir with respect Your Excellency

most obedient & most humble servt

His Excellency General Haldimand.

Endorsed:—on His Majesty's service His Excellency General Haldimand governor & commander in Chief of the Province of Quebec, 1779. From Captain Lernoult, 25th June, recd 14th July.

[B 122 p 362]

CAPTAIN LERNOULT TO GENERAL HALDIMAND

DETROIT June 26th 1779.

SIR, I have the honor of your Excellency's letter by Captain Brehm, and entertain a most gratefull sense of the favorable opinion you are pleased to place my humble efforts to protect this Post. I beg leave to assure you I will exert every nerve in carrying on His Majesty's service to the utmost of my abilitys as I have always done (thro' inclination as well as duty) for these Thirty three years past.

In justice to the officers under my Command I take this occasion to mention the cheerful assistance I have experienced at their hand and particularly Lt. Duvernet of the Royal Artillery who has been of great service in directing the works as Engineer.

Conformable to your Excellency's wish I have unbosom'd myself without reserve on all matters relative to the service at this Post, to Captain Brehm, which makes it unnecessary to trouble you with a repetition, except laying before you a copy of Sir Guy Carleton's order for my return to take the command of this Post, after serving on the expedition to Fort Stamoix.

I beg leave to mention to your Excellency that notwithstanding a very just remark in a letter of Captain Brehm's relative to the company Mr. Baby frequents, I have from every other part of his conduct and good character, reason to be pleased with his attachment to Government & with his method of managing Indian concerns—

I have the honor to be with great respect

Your Excellency's most obedient & most humble servant

R. B. LERNOULT.

H. E. General Haldimand

Endorsed:—A. 1779. From Captain Lernoult 26th June. Recd 10th July.

[B 122 p 363]

CAPTAIN LERNOULT'S ANSWER TO THE HURONS OF ST DUSKI

Children, the Hurons of Sandusky.—

I return the Mingoes thanks for the Prisoner delivered to me yesterday thro' you, that in your manner of delivering them, the want of that duty which is due from a child to his parent wipes out any acknowledgement I have to you. Now children I desire you to listen with attention to what I am going to say to you, on the Commencement of the present war, your conduct I confess justly merited the approbation of your Father and the care that has been taken to supply all your wants from time to time has left no room for you to complain. The attention also paid to you by your Father & the Six Nations has in a manner placed you at the Head of the Western Nations they have depended upon you to act with that prudence & zeal against their & your Enemy with which you embarked in this cause, upon the success of which I can assure you depends the future happines of your Women & Children, for tho' you may hear fine speeches from the Rebels, they are only calculated to deceive you, the Breach of their Engagements with many Indians on different occasions & the late one with the Onondagoes is sufficient to warn you of the Danger of listening to them. And you must know it is not their Interest to be your Friends as your Land is what they depend upon to defray part of the Expenses of their War. Those things I mention that you may be upon your Guard against the return of some of your People who I understand are gone to Council with the Rebels. And particularly against Montour whom I hear is now acting like an open enemy to you & me. This my Children is your fault for when it was in my power to prevent them from doing harm, You took him away & engaged yourselves for his Good Behaviour. I wish you may not suffer yourselves to be imposed upon by more such Persons as him.

I am surprised to hear Your Complaints for necessaries, after the ample supplies I sent you this Spring, if there has been any unequal distribution of them among Yourselves, the fault cannot be charged to me. I took care to send you plenty & then was in hopes You would have been able to do something in Conjunction with the officer that went out to attend you against the Enemy, but the Evasions you made from time to time untill it was too late with your dispersing the Shawnese after they had collected in a Body at the Mingoe Town to accompany you against the Enemy gives reason to think you had no intention of doing any thing, for at that time I heard that most of your warriors instead of preparing for War set out to follow their Hunting and left your Father alone, those actions my Children do not correspond with your boasting desire of going against the Enemy, As to my children on this side of the Lake, I can assure you that many parties of them are now out against the Enemy and from their repeated professions to me I believe they will afford you all the assistance in their power, The reason of my not giving you more assistance must be very obvious to you. The Strong Work I have now nearly Compleated to defend the Supplies sent to us by Your Father the King.

Endorsed:—Speech in answer to the Hurons of St Duski July 2, 1779.———1779. Captain Lernoult's Answer to the Hurons of St Duskey 2nd August Recd 23d August by Capt Brehm.

[B 122 p 365]

MR. GAUTIER TO GENERAL HALDIMAND

MICHILLIMAKINAC 7th 11th 1779.

SIR, I beg of you to accept my very humble civilities which I address to you & my offer to you with all the respect possible the continuation of my slight services. Allow me also to beg you to give me still the honor of your protection.

I venture to promise you on my part, that I shall do as I have always done all which depends on me in order—to deserve always to be

Sir Your very humble & very obedient Servant

C. GAUTIER.

addressed To His Excellency General Haldimand Governor General of all Canada In Canada.

Endorsed:—1779 From Monsieur Gautier 11 Sept received 16th Oct

[B 97-1-p 221]

MR. MCKEE TO GENERAL HALDIMAND

SIR, Upon my arrival at D'troit last year, I did myself the Honor then to acquaint your Excellency of it, with the manner of my release from the Enemy and as I wish'd to render some service to His Majesty's Interest during my stay here was desirous of directions from your Excellency to inable me thereto, and having likewise been long detained a Prisoner was thereby unacquainted with the situation of the Indian Depart. or the officers thereof which induced me to trouble your Excellency upon this head, as the same motive lays me under the necessity of doing at this time, having never received any answer thereto. Soon after my arrival at this place was informed of an Expedition to be carried on by Lieut. Govr. Hamilton down the Wabash and I accompanied him on that Enterprize, there being a prospect at that time of uniting the Western & Southern Indians and engaging them in His Majesty's Service which would have been undoubtedly effected had not his unfortunate fate prevented it, This unlucky event has not only discouraged many tribes well disposed, but inclined others who were wavering, to stand neuter, so that a Force to act in conjunction with them appears necessary to engage them again to act with vigor against the Enemy as I understand that Colonel Johnson who was at the head of the Department I served in is expected at Quebec, my affairs make it requisite for me to see him, which I have thought my duty to acquaint your Excellency of & I have to pray your Excellency's directions in what manner to draw my salary as I wish to discharge my Expenses in the service I have been on

I have the honor to be with the greatest Respect

Your Excellency most obedient & very humble Servant

ALEXANDER MCKEE.

D'TROIT July 16th 1779.

His Excellency General Haldimand.

Endorsed: A 1779. Mr. McKee Detroit 16th July Recd 23rd August.

[B 122 p 370]

MR. LORRAINE TO CAPTAIN LERNOULT

MIAMIS TOWN 18th July 1779.

SIR, I have just learned by M. Gamelin that Colonel Clarke is certainly going to Detroit they have 1400 Bostonians and six hundred French men; all their provisions were sent to Post Vincennes. Colonel Clarke left, like M. Gamelin, the same day with all the Artillery to come to the Post, they have seven pieces of heavy cannon and four mortars, two of fifty pounds & two smaller. Mr. Linctot has left for the Illinois with 200 men they passed through the Country, they are just returned to the Onias, they are to buy some horses wherever they can find them. They have 200 Oxen with them and they expect to collect horses to the number of 200.

M. Gamelin assures me that they will be here in the beginning of August, he said to me that they will make a fort there to serve them as a store house, he left 50 Bostonians and 50 French men, the 7 deserters of your Post have just returned to the Miamis, you know by the Indians the reason why they keep them.

Sir, this is all the news that I know at present.

I have the honor to be

Sir, your very humble servant MICH'L LORRAINE

Capt Lernoult rec'd July 22nd 1779 endorsed:—Intelligence from the Miamis Town, 18th July 1779. Copy.

[B 122 p 372]

DEPOSITION OF HENRICK IAGO

Henrick Iago recruit in Captain Caldwell's Compy of rangers is willing to depose upon oath, that he being servant to James Cassedy, farmer at Gross Point, has often heard the said James Cassedy together with one Wm. Boslick, speak in a very rebellious manner against Government—And particularizes, that when he (Henk. Iago) wanted to purchase a farm the said James Cassedy advised him against it saying that he was very certain the Virginians would be at Detroit in a short time; & that on their arrival he would get him a farm for nothing; likewise that the said James Cassedy & Wm Boslick, used often to make mention of a quantity of Leather, which they said they were tanning for the use of the Virginians & that on *their* arrival they would make a great deal of money by it Hen'k Iago further say'th that the above James Cassedy declared that the Commanding officer dare not send any Person whatever down the country, that it was too late as the Americans were so near, & that some time before the depondent left James Cassedy's house—whenever the said James Cassedy & Wm. Boslick began to converse in a rebellious manner, they sent the depondent out of the room—telling him he could not keep his tongue silent

Detroit July 20th 1779.

(sign'd) H. Iago.

Sworn before me this 21st day of July 1779

R. B. Lernoult Commandt

Witness Andw Parke Capt King's Rgt

[B 122 p 381]

DEPOSITION OF JOHN LANGHTON

John Langhton Naval store keeper at Detroit is willing to declare upon oath that being in company with James Cassedy farmer at Gross Point has heard the said James Cassedy speak many threatening & abusive speeches against Government—Particularly that Detroit would be in the hands of Col. Clarke in less than 6 months & that the Government of it would be given to himself the said James Cassedy and further declared himself a Rebel & that every officer in the Fort knew it—and dare not touch him—that he knew the Country was in the possession of the Americans—& that his wife's brother was a Genl. & his two sons appointed Capts under Genl. Mixon their uncle & that in less then a twelvemonth his sons would give Law—to the settlement of Detroit—with many other threats against Government to tedious to mention, and which John Langton is willing to particularize upon Examination.

JOHN LANGTON
Naval Store keeper

Sworn before me on this 21st day of July 1779.

(signed) R. B. LERNOULT Commt

Witness (signed) Andw. Parke—Capt King's or 8th Regt

[B 122 p 379]

DEPOSITION OF WILLIAM MILLER

William Miller Ship carpenter at Detroit is willing to declare upon oath that being in company with James Cassedy farmer at Gross Point has heard the said James Cassedy declare that New York was in the hands of the Americans—and that as the country was entirely in their Possession the Commanding officer of Detroit dare not send any Person down the Country and further declares that he has heard the said James Cassedy with one Wm Boslick drink success to the Congress & the American Arms—that Coll. Clarke would soon be in possession of Detroit & that he & the abovementioned Wm Boslick had a Quantity of Leather which they were then a tanning & which they would not sell untill Coll Clarke's arrival at Detroit.

WM MILLER

sworn before me this 21st day July 1779.

(signed) R. B. LERNOULT Commandt

(signed) Andw. Parke Capt King's Regt.

[B 122 p 378]

DEPOSITION OF JOHN CORNWALL

John Cornwall is willing to declare upon oath that being in Company with James Cassedy farmer at Gross Point, the said James Cassedy asked him many Questions concerning Col. Butler & the Corps of Rangers under his command & their transactions during the last campaign to which he (Cornwall) relating the particulars—which proving much to the disadvantage of Rebels, the said James Cassedy reply'd that what he (Cornwall) had been saying was all a damn'd lie & that Col. Butler with his scalping crew would soon meet with their deserts, that he knew the Col'l to be a damn'd coward & no soldier & that he would turn hangman for him, & the whole Indian

Department the said James Cassedy further declared that there were many in Detroit who wore cockades in their hats, who thought themselves very great people—but that when Col'l Clarke came they would be no better than himself —We know added he all the damn'd Raskels there & they will soon meet with what they deserve with many other threats against Government which the said Jam's Cassidy made use of & which John Cornwall is willing to declare upon Examination.

JOHN CORNWALL

Sworn before me on this 21st July 1779.

R. B. LERNOULT Command't
Witness ANDW. PARKE
Capt King's Reg't.

[B 122 p 380]

GENERAL HALDIMAND TO CAPTAIN LERNOULT

QUEBEC the 23rd July 1779.

Captain Lernoult

SIR, I have received your Letter of the 26 June in answer to mine by Capt. Brehm. I have been informed and am well convinced of the zeal you have always manifested for the good of his Majesty's Service & of the particular attention you have paid to it in your present situation, and it is no small satisfaction to me to have a Post of such consequence and so well commanded.

I have acquainted Colonel Bolton of the impossibility of forwarding the Cannon required for Detroit & Michilimackinac this season, owing to the more pressing necessity for Provision & have told him, that if necessary you are to take what Guns you may have occasion for from on board the Vessels where there is but little probability of their being wanted.

I observe with great concern, the astonishing consumption of Rum at Detroit amounting to the rate of 17520 Gallons per year. The expense attending this article cannot possibly be born.—I must therefore recommend to your most serious attention a material diminution of it—at Niagara, where the expense of it is very considerable 10,000 Gallons is the most that ever has been expended—the men employed at the works have no allowance of Rum except upon very particular occasions, & then never more than a Gill per Day—indeed more must be hurtfull to their health, independant of the Expence to Government.

Your Letter without a date, inclosing an account & Bill for the Command money due to you is come to hand. I am sorry that the mode which has always been observed for the Payment of that money, & which does not come at all under my direction, prevents my being able to receive it—a general return every six months of the officers commanding at the different Posts should be transmitted to me to certify & a duplicate of the same should be forwarded to the Agent of the Regt by the commanding officer.

I am &c

(signed) FRED: HALDIMAND

endorsed:—Copy 1779 To Capt Lernoult commanding at Detroit 23rd July Extract Ent'd in Book marked B No 2 Page 13

[B 122 p 382]

FROM SECRETARY MATTHEWS. UNADDRESSED

QUEBEC 24th July 1779.

SIR, I am commanded by His Excellency General Haldimand to acquaint you that he has received your letter of the 22nd June, enclosing Mr. McBeath's receipt for £460 5 4 New York Currency your Bill will be duly honored. His excellency recommends to you the greatest Oeconomy possible in that article so enormously charged for by the Traders, untill the supplies he has forwarded reaches you

(signed) R. M.

[B 96-1-p 105]

DEPOSITION OF JOHN CORNWALL

John Cornwall deposes upon oath, that by the desire of Jeremiah Cockran Hatter at Detroit, he slept one night at his house and some days afterwards going into a Tavern he met with the said Cockran one Wiggins a Trader & Touché a French man from Post Vincennes. A little time after he sat down the abovementioned Wiggins (who he had never seen but once before) took the Deponent by the Hand and told he was sure he was a friend to their cause which he (Cornwall) not understanding Wiggins replied a Friend to the Americans or else he never would have slept at Mr. Jeremiah Cockran's house. He said Wiggins then got up & drank success to the Thirteen United States & said he hoped the Virginians would soon be in Detroit & added I am sure of it—which Cornwall asking him why he thought so—Wiggins replied that at Post Vincennes where he came from, they held a correspondence with them. The deponent further says that Wiggins spoke very disrespectfully of the officers of the Garrison at Detroit & told him if he had an opportunity he could inform him of a good deal more news—some time afterwards the deponent left the Town & Cockran followed him & beg'd he would not take notice of what Wiggins had been saying as he was a crazy kind of a fellow and would hurt nobody.

John Cornwall.

Sworn before me this 28th July 1779.

(signed) R. B. Lernoult
Commandt.

in the presence of Andw. Parkes Capt King's Regt.

N. B. Mr. Fouchet is the Person who gave the Rebels notice of the approach of the King's Troops towards Post Vincent last Fall, R. B. L., & employ'd Indians to convey goods out of the Fort without leave telling them he intended to carry them to Post Vincent, and would slip away in the night.

[B 122 p 384]

CAPTAIN BREHM TO CAPTAIN LERNOULT

Niagara, July 29th, 1779.

Sir, His Excellency the Commander in Chief having thought it necessary for the good of His Majesty's service, the Protection of Trade and His Majesty's loyal subjects & their effects to empower you to hold General Court martials for the punishing of all offenders and transgressors (of all descriptions & degrees whatever) according to the nature of their offences as they shall appear upon trial before the same.

Which you are hereby empowered and authorized to assemble as often as you shall see occasion agreeable to the rules & orders for the better Government of the Forces employed in foreign parts. Provided never the less that if from the circumstances of your remote situation the number of officers stipulated by the said rules & orders for the better Government of the Forces employ'd in Foreign Parts, cannot be had, you are in that case empowered & are hereby directed to summons as many officers as the situation of your Post will admit off, to compose the same, and according to their Judgements you are to cause sentence to be pronounced against the Person or Persons so offending, either on Pains of death, or such other Pains or Penalties as shall be thought fit to be inflicted by the said General Court Martial which Sentence or Sentences you are to cause to be put in execution or to suspend the same as you shall see cause—Power being hereby given you to Reprieve any

Person under my sentence 'till you receive further instructions from His Excellency the Commander in Chief of Canada for the time being. This Power to take its force after the Declaring of Martial Law on the approach of an Enemy to attack your Post or any Part of the Settlements under your Command.

(signed)

D. Brehm

Aid de Camp.

To Captain Lernoult, Commanding His Majesty's Troops at Detroit.

Endorsed:—Copy of a Power given to Capt. Lernoult, Commanding at Detroit to hold general court Martial &c., 29th July, 1779.

[B 122 p 386].

MR. ARUNDEL TO CAPTAIN LERNOULT

Lower St. Duski 31st July 1779.

Sir, the other day three Delawares arrived at the Upper Town, & had a Council with the Wyandots there, upon the originals of the enclosed copies which Dunquat (the half King) lent me the day after the Council and told me the answer he gave them was "He would send them to the Chiefs at Detroit, & what they thought fit to do, would be his rule"—

Mr. Baptiste Drouilliard has a printed paper that was given him by the Blacksmith at the upper Town, its a declaration made by Count D'Estagne by the French King's authority.—Mr. Drouilliard chusing to deliver you the paper personally; I thought fit to fold it up & have sealed it with an oval seal forming a D. reversed.

Thinking it my duty to inform you of the above circumstances

I am Sir, Your very humble Servt

Wm. Arundel.

To Captain Lernoult

[B 122 p 388]

NECESSARY PART OF THE COUNCILS HELD BY MR. BENNET WITH THE PONTAWATAMIES AT ST. JOSEPH

August 3d 1779.

On the 28th of July (three days after the arrival of Mr. Bennett at St. Joseph the Pontawatamies of the first village were assembled to listen to the words of their father. The Counsil commenced by an account of the causes which had brought them on to the Lands. He said to them, that the welfare of their children interested him too much not to help them, having heard it said that they were in danger of loosing themselves, he added, that he hoped to find them disposed to second the designs to which his fondness for them had prompted him, in short he pressed them, by all that could touch the heart of an Indian, to show themselves grateful. Determined also by the invitation of the Ottawas & Sauteux & also by the words of their father, after two days of deliberation, they declared that they would follow the example of their brothers. After having smoked with them their pipes of peace & received their belts they all agreed to be of one mind.

Satisfied with their answer, their father said to them I do not doubt that you are my good children also I know that you are some of the new comers of whom it is said that they have good hearts.

Having reported the extreme distress of the Americans & the prodigious progress of the Royal Arms in the Colonies & showed them the falsity of the pretended declaration of war between England & France for which design the Grand Couteaux (Big Knives) spread these false reports, he sent them back loaded with favors & asked them to remember their words.

Four days after—the Pontawatamies of the three villages assembled & held the following Council.

Grand Council held on the 6th of August by Mr. Bennet outside the intrenchment.

The Pontawatamies of the large village & of Terre Coupe & of the little Pilormeau being assembled, the following speech was made by a War Chief named Le Petit Bled.

My father, I do not come here with a mouth full of flattery & deceit, I do not come into your presence to hide my sentiments, on the contrary I come to tell them to you, many which are in my heart my mouth cannot speak.

I am surprised, my father, that you are come to disturb the peace which reigns in our lands. I am pleased however to see you with the pipe of peace which you offer us today instead of the tomahawk.

It is him who troubled the peace which we joined, it is him who made the division among us It is him that we will make unhappy. It is he who is the subject of my surprise & of this speech.

You vainly try, my father, to make us lift our heads from the pillow to listen to you. It is folly to present us with this load which is too heavy for our hands, a mat would be better, & it is that you should offer us, but we will ask it of you.

This belt (which I am only going to show) engages us to make this demand. It is from our French Father & represents his members & bones scattered here & there but which seem to-day gathered together & united against thee. Our Ancient Father, on giving it to us, said to us, "My Children, this belt is the knot which should bind and tie your hands, except for us, remember never to untie for your enemies, if they are conquerors, content yourselves with giving them the pipe of peace & living peaceably with them, until the day that we reappear on your Lands."

"I carry again the pipe of peace in the mouth & I invite you to smoke it, it is filled with nothing that can be repugnant to your hearts, it is good to smoke it, & there is nothing bitter in it, on the contrary, it is sweet, very different from thy pipe of peace which my chiefs as well as myself have, to-day, rejected as a mortal plague."

This Speach he addressed to the Ottawas & Sauteause.

I do not come to break the alliance between us, my brothers, I only come to show you my way of thinking in the same way that I have showed it to my father.

I confess to you that the red pipe presented to a party of my nation has been a poison to them as fatal as that of the venomous animal, this smoke has obscured the beautiful light & painted to us the shadow of death.

It is in virtue of our union that they received your words and swallowed the poison. Their error has preceeded yours, deceived yourselves by the choice of a pipe, they have allowed themselves to be deceived. I repeat to you, my brothers, that this red pipe should never have been presented to us, but that which is instead of our alliance & which you have left among us by a misunderstanding (he here gave four branches of porcelaine) nevertheless I had notice to give it to you, in giving you this porcelaine it is not to over throw our lands. Take care at the same time of raising a mob. Keep a ready eye on those whom I have told you of. Cease to be fools, be prudent and wise.

The speaker turned himself to his father, I have the same thing to say to my father, change thy plans, renounce thy projects which have been formed with neither prudence nor wisdom, if you are stubborn & despise my counsils you will perhaps repent, believe me my father and do not go farther.

The speaker holding the branch of porcelain in his hand.

Our lands peaceable until to-day refuse to carry men who would destroy the peace which has reigned so long, they also refuse to carry thy enemies, my father, & be persuaded that if my ears are deaf to thy voice they are also deaf to the Grand Couteaux (Big Knives) unless they say to me, "Keep quiet & be a spectator of our quarrel but do not mix in it." If you have the same thing to say to me, my father, I am ready to listen.

He gave the four branches of porcelain & finished the speech by telling to his father all that the Grand Couteax (Big Knives) had said to him, he assured him that their desire to be peaceable was the only motive which had brought him to speak in this way & that it was not hate; he added that the esteem which he had for his father compelled him to show him his danger as the enemies were the most numerous, he being (by comparison) but one mouthful for them.

Then he finished by saying to him that Governor Hamilton had given him a pipe of peace, which he still keeps, however he broke it in his engagement to take the tomahawk, that His Excellency had made him many promises which have not been executed, still he hopes that his father will accomplish them.

Mr. Bennet's answer to the Poutawatamies—

Your father at Michilimackinac having heard it said that his children the Pous [Pottawattomies] were in great fear of the Grand Couteaux (Big Knives) he is eager to send you help, accepted by some of your chiefs but which you refuse to-day. Go, this good father has said to me, go, throw off fear my children by offering them your arms & those of all who accompany you. I flatter myself, if they second your plans that they will recover their security & peace by destroying the principle of their terror.

I am here, my children, charged with this office. I appear on your Lands Tomahawk in hand & this club, made for some men but which you see with less horror, do not offer your regards to-day because they will serve as a reproach to the perfidy of your chiefs, & the truth broken by their false words. They were intended for your hands, but I dispense with you, my children, because you ask me to give into your hands an arm which cannot be taken except by a warrior's hand.

However I know your good will has revealed your sentiments, for I have neither pretence nor imposture.

I also come to declare mine to you with the same liberty with which you declared yours, before I was obliged in the capacity of your father to prescribe your duty to you by two comparisons, so that you cannot lay on me the blame of your unhappiness which is only according to your ingratitude.

I cannot see you made to tremble by the threats (for instance of the Grand Couteaux) nor your minds beguiled by the falsehoods prepared as they have been, what I have said to your chiefs is the pure truth. I cannot convince you more by a long argument, of your obligation to be faithful subjects.

I will not show you the perfidious designs which the Grand Couteaux (Big Knives) formed on the conduct which they would have made you keep, as what I have come to say includes all.

I ask you Poutawatamies which of the two fathers do you prefer? The one who attentive to your wants has laid a heavy hand on you, is watching your safety & taking care of your days or he from whom you have received no favors, who does not even know you except by the evils which he is watching to make you feel.

And you Chiefs & Nations what would be your amazement if the youths of your village carried away by a fanatical ardor, scorned your councils, hunted you from your lands, what part would you take?

Go, my children, go and ponder in drinking these drops of sweet milk, which I will willingly give you, what you will say to your father, above all, remember do not change your resolution neglect your fields but gather together with care & thrift every grain of wheat as for us we are resolved to go where duty honor and glory calls us.

This little mouth can perhaps choke those who dare to bite.

Two days had already passed without discovering what effect was produced on their minds by this answer when it was discovered that respect & clemency are not always the most proper means to bring them back to their duty, indeed the chiefs of the first village followed by their young men convinced by the last words of their father, came near him to seek preservation from the evils which he had predicted for them.

I am ashamed, in thy presence my father, said the first chief of the village, after having been a member of a council which one of my nation has held for the misery of the others. I have however forgotten what I had resolved to say to you but I still declare that none of us have gone there nor taken part. I still assure you that instead of entering into their sentiments I am resolved, on the contrary, to execute punctually the words which I have given you in presence of all my people.

I can not easily persuade myself to answer their father, that you be dignified by taking the name of my children for without your words of assurance, received in your general assembly I should not have known of your eagerness to second my intentions.

And thou Chiefs! if as I value to-day, your design in regard to me as your father & in this capacity you will conform to my will, why have you not risen up against the perfidy which offended me & declared in my presence that you have not participated in this perfidy?

This was excused because of the coarseness or rather ferocity of his nature. Their father continued in these terms.

I have a good heart my children, it is open to every one who will take a place there, but your conduct towards me has rendered access difficult, you can now only come by two paths I will show them to you, & if you banish them from you, you will not find them again. You only deserve the name of children, when you regard me as your good father, but your brothers are unworthy to participate in the favors of him who is at Michilimackinac. I counsil you to go to him & tell him your wants, he will help you, he will provide for the needs of as many as remain faithful & grateful to him. I still consider that a part of you should accompany me on the road to Detroit if I undertake it, there are only two courses which you can take & these I propose to you.

Having consulted among themselves as to the party they would take, such was the result of their deliberation.

You cannot doubt our fidelity, the War Chief has let you know satisfactorily by his song thy good will & ours, we pray you to observe that not being accustomed to go on the lake & not having the necessary carriages it is impossible for us to follow your advice, as for the latter we can easily execute it.

These difficulties are nothing my children, you will have all that is necessary for this road, it is absolutely necessary for your interests that you take it. I can do nothing, your father at Detroit cannot relieve your wants, he who is at Michilimackinac is the only one who can concern himself with you. Finally if I had not feared to show myself to you, do you fear what I will do to you?

These last words lifted the obstacles which appeared insurmountable to them & determined them to follow the advice of their father.

Some Miamis of a village called Coeur de Cerf (Heart of a Stag) present at this last council appeared also to have the same sentiments.

Endorsed:—Indian Council St Duskey.

[B 122 p 391].

ACCOUNT OF GOODS

Account of Goods belonging to Laventure Toucher & Brother taken at Detroit 3 August 1779 by Thomas Williams, Esqre agreeable to Captain Lernoult's order commanding at that time at Detroit aforesaid.

		£	s.	d.
2 Nests Blue Hair Trunks	200s	20	0	0
1 Best Pelham bridle	12s	0	12	0
2 ps Russia Sheeting	160s	16	0	0
1 ps Red Stroud	260s	13	0	0
2 ps blue do	260s	26	0	0
4 ps $2\frac{1}{2}$ pt Blankets	32s	6	8	0

Item	Rate	£	s.	d.
2 ps blue & white Callicoes	140s	14	0	0
3 ps dark Grd do	140s	21	0	0
3 ps Linen	293s 10d	14	13	10
5 yards Linen	4s	1	0	5
6 yds 6–4 Muslin	14s	4	4	0
8¾ yds Do striped	24s	10	10	0
26 Callico shirts	12s	15	12	0
3 Linen do	10s	1	10	0
4 doz black silk Handkf 2 @ / & 2 @	100s / 126s	22	12	0
4 Single Pieces Christian ribbon cut	12s	2	8	0
2 do whole	30s	3	0	0
2 do Indian cut	10s	1	0	0
6 ps Silk ferrits	15s	4	10	0
1 doz white Silk Hdkfs	156s	7	6	0
2 doz checht Linen do	42s	4	4	0
2 ps striped Callimancoes	84s	8	8	0
6 Red malabar Hkfs	6s	1	16	0
7 Blue do	6s	2	2	0
4 Gro. Rings	18s	3	12	0
1 do Thimbles	18s	0	18	0
6 framed Looking Glasses	4s	1	4	0
1 Doz paper looking glasses	18s	0	18	0
2 doz box wood combs	12s	1	4	0
24 doz Morris bells	24s	2	8	0
1 doz Horn Combs	9s	0	9	0
1 doz 10 Ivory do	20s	1	16	8
1 lb sealing wax	20s	1	0	0
5 packs cards	2s	0	10	0
2 Balls cotton Wick	2s	0	4	0
13 scalping knives	1s	0	13	0
13 clasp knives	1s 6d		19	6
9 small pewter Basons	2s	0	18	0
2 pr Boy's shoes	8s	0	16	0
12 fans	4s	2	8	0
4 plain Irons / 2 pr men's silk hose / 1 pr do We. thread — did not belong to Mr. Ridley who will return them on demand				
6 Wool Hatts	8s	2	8	0
2 Castor do	16s	1	12	0
1 pr leather breeches—does not belong to Mr. Ridley				
3 lbs 12 Worsted	12s	2	2	0
13 prs men's shoes	16s	10	8	0
7 Gimblets	9d	0	5	3
6 Bridles	7s	2	2	0
13 quire Writing paper	3s 6d	2	5	6

Item	Rate	£	s.	d.
2 doz scalping knives	18s	1	16	0
7½ lbs Vermillion	20s	7	10	0
25 lbs Beads	5s	6	5	0
6 prs blue strouds	260s	78	0	0
1 pr We Molton	140s	7	0	0
36 yds embossed Serge	4s 4d	7	16	0
35 prs Blankets	32s	56	0	0
14 prs do	24s	16	16	0
1 Large Hair Trunk	40s	2	0	0
New York Currency [about ½ Sterling]		£446	10	2

[B 122 p 402]

FROM GENERAL HALDIMAND UNADDRESSED

QUEBEC August 17th 1779.

SIR, I enclose to you a copy of instructions I have given to Cap. Sinclair as Lieut Governor & Superintendent of the Posts of Michilimackinac which you will peruse, and afterwards deliver to the officer who will succeed you in the Military Commands

(signed) F. H.

[B 96. 1. p 105]

DEPOSITION OF JOHN HIGGINS

This day Personally appear'd before me Thos Williams his Majestys justice of the Peace for Detroit.

John Higgins, who made oath on the Holy Evangelist of Almighty God, and saith that when they were going off, John Edgar furnished them with bread, ammunition, & knives & told them to steer a S. W. Course, this Deponent further says, after he was taken at the Miamis Town, Israel Ruland persuaded him to go along with him to the Ouias, that if this Deponent return'd to Detroit he would be hang'd and that Israel Ruland had several Letters directed to Colonel Clarke that said Israel Ruland promised this Depondent if he would go with him he would answer he should not be hurt, this Deponent further says the directions of the said Letters were in English, and that the said Rutland was employed by Colonel Clark at a Dollar per day.

sign'd JOHN HIGIN.
witness Andw Parke

Sworn before me 23d of August 1779.
I. Williams
a true Copy R. B. Lernoult Commandr
[B 22 p 262]

DEPOSITION OF WILLIAM HUMPHREYS

This day personally appeared before me Thomas Williams his Majestys Justice of the Peace for Detroit.

William Humphreys, who made oath on the Holy Evangelist of Almighty God, and saith, on the third day of July last past, Israel Ruland trader told some of this Deponents, comrades, if they would desert, he would supply them with three Fuzees, next day being Sunday they went down to John Edgars house and received the Arms accordingly, and that John Edgar gave them four loaves of Bread, Powder lead, and some Sugar, as likewise Breech Clouts & Leggins, and went part of the way, to direct them in the course they should steer, directing them to leave their Cloaths, and he (John Edgar) would take care of them, a Coat, a pair of Breeches, shoes and stockings left by the Deponent.

Israel Ruland told this Deponent that Colonel Clark had employ'd him to endeavour to get the Prisoners off, and told them if they could reach the Miamis River he would take care they should be supplied with Provisions; this Deponent further declares that after they were retaken at the Miamis Town, Israel told them to get off if possible.—This Deponent further saith, that John Edgar furnish'd one Fusil, to one of the three Prisoners who deserted last Spring.

his
WILLIAM + HUMPHREYS
mark

Witness Andw Parke
[B 22 p 263]

SECRETARY MATTHEWS TO CAPTAIN LERNOULT

QUEBEC 28th August 1779.

SIR, I am commanded by His Excellency General Haldimand to acquaint you that in consequence of your long & good services he has determined to confer on you the rank of Major—and before long I hope it will be in my power to inform you of something more to Your advantage.

I am Sir your most obedt & most humble Servt

Captain Lernoult R. MATHEWS.

Endorsed:—1779. To Capt Lernoult 28th August.

[B 122. p 405)

FROM GENERAL HALDIMAND UNADDRESSED [DE PEYSTER]

QUEBEC, August 28th 1779.

SIR, This letter will be delivered to you by Capt. Sinclair to whom you will give up the Command of Michilimackinac as Lt Govr & Superintendent of the Post. From a Letter of Lord George Germain to Capt. Sinclair wherein he stiles him commandant of the Posts, He conceives he is entitled to the Military Command, which is not expressed in his Commission, it being exactly similar to that of Lt. Govr. Hamilton's he therefore goes to his Government, vested with the same powers, & which are specified in my instructions to him, of which you have a copy. I shall write upon this Subject to Lord George Germain, & hope soon to have the line of those Commands finally determined. In the mean time the utmost Harmony and mutual Acquiescence is necessary to carry on His Majesty's Service with that spirit which I am convinced Capn Sinclair's zeal for it & that of the officer you will leave with him will dictate, for nothing can more conduce to the Reputation of officers than to relinquish little personal considerations when necessary to promote the public service.

(signed) F. H.

[B. 96-1 p 105]

GENERAL HALDIMAND TO CAPTAIN LERNOULT

QUEBEC 29th August 1779.

SIR, Upon Major Depeyster's arrival at Detroit you are to deliver up to him the Command of that Post, and after having made him fully acquainted with every particular relative to the command of it, the management of the settlement and Indians resorting to it, you will repair, without loss of time to Niagara.

I am Sir &c.

FRED: HALDIMAND.

Captain Lernoult.

Endorsed:—Copy, To Captain Lernoult at Detroit 29th August.

[B 122 p 406]

FROM GENERAL HALDIMAND UNADDRESSED

QUEBEC 29th August 1779.

SIR, After having given Lt. Govr. Sinclair every information your power relative to the Post of Michilimackinac agreeably to my letter of the 28th Inst. You will repair to Detroit without loss of time, and take upon you the command of that Post Captain Lernoult having my orders to give it up to you & to give every necessary information relative to it.

(signed) F. H.

[B 96. 1. p 106]

FROM GENERAL HALDIMAND UNADDRESSED [DE PEYSTER].

QUEBEC 30th August 1779.

SIR, From Captain Lernoult you will receive my instructions and every information relative to the inspection and management of the Publick Accounts of the different departments under your command at Detroit which I have to desire you will consider as a very material part of your duty, to inspect into in the minutest manner, studying, by every possible means to contract & diminish as far as may be consistent with the good of the service the expenses incurred in said Department I have thought proper to direct that in future you may draw Bills upon me for the different amounts observing the regulations you will receive for that purpose, and transmit them with the accounts to Lt. Colo. Bolton who will forward them to me.

Lieut. Governor Hamilton not having had authority to empower him to appoint a Town Major at Detroit Mr. McLeod cannot be admitted as such, there being no establishment of the kind for the Upper post, which is the only reason for my discontinuing Mr. McLeods of whom I have had a very favorable character.

(signed) F. H.

[B 96. 1. p 107]

ACCUSATION BY CAPTAIN AUBREY

DETROIT 30th August 1779.

Ensign Hamilton of the 47th Regiment, ordered under an arrest by Captain Aubrey, for having countermanded his orders.

(signed) THOS. AUBREY, Capt.
47th Regmt.

endorsed:—Copy] Capt Aubrey's accusation against En Hamilton both of the 47th Regt 30th August 1779.

[B 122 p 407]

CAPTAIN LERNOULT TO GENERAL HALDIMAND

DETROIT 5th Sept. 1779.

SIR, I have taken the Liberty to draw on your Excellency favour of Alex'r & William Macomb in four bills at sixty days sight for the sum of thirty eight thousand seven hundred & ten pounds four shillings & two pence New York Currency, for Expenses incurr'd at this Post, in His Mejestys Service as p'r Abstract & Vouchers which will be herewith delivered you, which I beg your Excellency will honour.

I am with respect
Sir, Your most obed't & humble servant
R. B. LERNOULT
Command't

His Excell'y Gen'l Haldimand Gov'r & Commander in Chief Quebec

endorsed:—1779. From Cap't Lernoult 5th Sept. advising of a bill for £38,710, 4, 2, Y. C. Rec'd 25th.

[B 122 p 408]

GENERAL HALDIMAND TO LORD GEORGE GERMAIN

QUEBEC 13th Sept'r 1779.

Lord Geo. Germain

MY LORD, The situation of His Majesty's affairs in the Upper Country requires that I should represent it to you, and it is with much concern, I must observe to Your Lordship that notwithstanding the amazing sums that have been expended, the unremitting united endeavours of the officers who command at the Posts, with those who have had the Direction of Indian affairs, it is much to be apprehended that our Indian allies have it in contemplation to desert us, those of the Western Nations in the neighborhood of Detroit particularly, their former attachment to the French, the Pains that have been taken by their Emissaries to reclaim them, together with the unfortunate miscarriage of Lieut Gov'r Hamilton have strongly served to alienate their affections, & although they continue to profess their attachment to the King, they frame excuses for not going to War, & discover upon all occasions an indifference which indicates their intentions to forsake us.

It is not so with the Six Nations, the Onidas & a great part of the Tuscaroras excepted, who from the beginning have strongly espoused the Interests of the Rebels, their attachment is as fixed as ever, but the regular advances made by the Rebels into their country in force, & the impossibility of their resisting them unassisted has alarmed their fears, but not shaken their fidelity.

The inclosed copies of Letters & Indian Speech will give Your Lordship a perfect idea of their situation. Their conduct the moment they declared for Government has been spirited & uniformly good, they have long requested assistance & it has been faithfully promised these three years past, but a want of Provisions, the difficulty of Transporting them to such a Distance, & the prodigious consumption owing, not only, to the necessity of feeding the Indians while collected, but supporting Entirely all Women & Children of the Mohawk, Cayaya, and many of the Onondaga nations, whose villages have been destroyed by the Rebels, & who have taken refuge at Niagara, has rendered it totally impossible for me to afford them any, although so much the object of my wishes. From the inclosed letters I have not a doubt that unless a well timed assistance may prevent it, they will be forced into a neutrality, which with Indians is little better than a Declaration of War against the weakest Party, thus situated I have been obliged at all risks to order a Detachment from this Province to their assistance of about 400 of the best and most active Troops, besides a large body of the Seven Nation Indians of Canada & some Mohawks who have resided here since their Country was destroyed (under the Command of Sir J. Johnson whose natural influence with the Six Nation, joined to the zeal & strong attachment he has upon all occasions manifested for His Majesty's service will I trust produce an happy effect.

Detroit is likewise menaced by the Virginians, they have made great advances & have established Posts of communication in that Country. From every information that has been received it would appear that an expedition against Detroit is certainly intended under the command of a Col. Clarke, who retook Post Vincennes. I have reinforced Detroit & the forwardness of a most useful work now erecting there will I hope ensure the safety of that Place, unless the Rebels should find means to make their way to it in great Force, which the growing slackness of the Western Nations may perhaps enable them to Effect.

Retaining the Indians in our Interests has been attended with a very heavy expense to Government but their attachment, has, alone, hitherto preserved the Upper Country, & the Devastation they have made upon the Susquehanna and Mohawk Rivers has distressed the Enemy prodigiously, their settlements in those parts have been entirely broken up, their stock of every kind destroyed & the Inhabitants driven for subsistence into the interior parts of the Country.

Major Butler's Rangers and the Indians have been constantly employed since the beginning of the Campaign, and have effected many good strokes Scouts from this Province towards the Enemy's Frontiers have likewise been continually employed & have rendered essential service.

Since I received the enclosed letters from the Indian Country, I had an opportunity of writing to Sir H. Clinton, I communicated their contents to him, & at the same time forwarded to him a Letter from Gen'l Washington upon the subject of the cruel Treatment shown to Lieut Gov'r Hamilton & the Prisoners with him, together with the Extract of a letter from Major Butler—Copies of which I transmit for your Lordships perusal.

I have the honor to be &c &c.

(signed) F. H.

[B 54 p 144]

GENERAL HALDIMAND TO LORD GEORGE GERMAIN

QUEBEC 14th Sepr 1779.

Lord Geo. Germain

MY LORD, I have this moment received an express from Major Nairne, commanding at Carleton Island, Enclosing a Copy of a letter from Lieut Col. Bolton which I send for Your Lordships Information of the situation affairs are in, in the Upper Country, which unless the arrival of Sir John Johnsons reinforcement given a fortunate turn to, will, I much fear terminate fatally. Every assistance in my Power to give, I have already informed Your Lordship has been afforded, and that not without much risk & inconvenience in this part of the Province.

By the same opportunity I have received accounts from Detroit concerning the slackness of the Indians, and the Defection of many of the Inhabitants in the quarter—I enclose to your Lordship a Declaration of Count D'Estaing which was sent me from Detroit, copies of which are distributed all through the Illinois & Miamis Country, & which have had a very bad effect amongst French Indians there.

I have the honor to be &c. &c. &c.

(Signed) F. H.

[B 54 p 150]

GENERAL HALDIMAND TO LORD GEORGE GERMAIN

QUEBEC 25th Sept. 1779.

I beg leave to represent to Your Lordships that if it is intended to preserve the Upper Country & Fur Trade 1000 or 1500 men with a necessary supply of Provisions distinctly for that Service alone, must be employed as early in the Spring as the River becomes navigable—half the number some time ago might have been sufficient, The Barracks at Oswego were, until last Autumn left standing, the remains of the Works were likewise in such a state, as to be rendered in a little time very Defensible. The Rebels have now destroyed the whole & every thing must be begun. The present state of Provisions in the Province & my pressing letters upon that subject, will point out to your Lordship, the impossibility of undertaking any operation of the kind, altho the salvation of the Province were to depend upon it (which I think in a great measure does) without very early supplies from Home, both of Troops and Provisions.

I have many years regretted that measures were not adopted such as to prevent the safety of those Posts depending upon supplies from Home, so very distant, the Transport so extremely precarious & attended with so heavy an expense to Government, all which might be obviated, The Troops infinitely better provided & the Different Posts be in perfect Security, by raising Grain & all kinds of Stock at Detroit, which from its critical situation could very well supply both Detroit and Michilimackinac.

The same Plan is very practicable at Niagara and there is nothing wanting but a beginning, it will necessarily be attended with some expense, the first two or three years, but would even in as many more amply repay it. In these times nothing can be vigorously undertaken, but should this unfortunate War speedily terminate, it should immediately be carried into execution & in such case I should be happy to receive Your Lordships approbation of, and commands to undertake what I am convinced would produce the most salutary effects for His Majesty's Interests in those Parts.

I have information, which I have reason to think authentic, that the Rebel Fleet consisting of several ships from 20 to 30 Guns and many smaller (which has blocked up General McLean at Penobsiot, sailed from Boston for the purpose of cruizing in the Gulf and mouth of this River & intercept our Victuallers—Should they succeed in this attempt we shall experience the greatest distress for Provisions before the Spring Fleet can possibly arrive. The probability of these misfortunes happening, independent of what Trade suffers every year by the very defenseless state of the River, urges me to repeat my wishes to Your Lordship that some means may be fallen upon to prevent them, either by sending out the Newfoundland Fleet early enough to cruise in the above stations to protect the Ships in the Spring, and to remain for the return of the Fall Fleet, or such others as Your Lordship shall think most expedient to effect this important end.

I have the honor to be &c. &c.

(signed) FRED. HALDIMAND.

[B 54 p 185]

ACCOUNT OF DELIVERY

MICHILIMACKINAC 4th Octr 1779.

Delivered into His Majesty's Engineer stores to the Care of John Pattison in charge thereof, the undermentioned particulars

Viz

Feby 18th 1780 by Lieut Mercer } Felling axes 34. Shovels 100
Broad do 3 Spades 17
Small Crow Barrs 2.

[B 97. 2 p 306]

RECEIPT

MICHILIMACKINAC, 4th Octr 1779

Received into His Majesty's Engineer Store from on Board His Majesty's Sloop the Welcome, the undermentioned particulars.

Viz

Feby 18th 1780 by Lieut Mercer } Felling axes 34. Shovels 100
Broad do 3 Spades 17
Small Crow Barrs 2.

JOHN PATTISON

[B 97 2 p 306]

ORDER FOR ENGINEER'S STORES

MICHILIMACKINAC 20 Octr. 1779

You are hereby directed and required to Issue out of His Majesty's Engineer Store the undermentioned particulars to Serj. Landon for the use of the King's Works, Carrying on Here and on the Island

PATT SINCLAIR Lt. Govr

Viz

Iron lbs	329	Spike nails lbs	3½
Steel lbs	56	Files	13
Old Iron lbs	27	Old Felling axes	9
Twenty four Penny nail	108	Old Broad do	3
Ten penny Do lbs	60	Old Pick do	1
		Shovels	8

To John Pattison in charge of Engineers Store.

RECEIPT

MICHILIMACKINAC 20th Octr 1779.

Received out of His Majesty's Engineer Store from John Pattison in charge thereof, the undermentioned particulars for the use of the King's Works carrying on here & on the Island—

Iron lbs	329	Spike nails lbs	3½
Steel lbs	56	Files	13
Old Iron lbs	27	Old Felling axes	9
Twenty four penny nails lbs	108	Old Broad do	3
Ten penny Do	60	Old Pick do	1
		Shovels	8

A. Langdon Serjt.

[B 97 1 p 256]

ACCOUNT OF DELIVERY

MICHILIMACKINAC 20th Octr 1779.

Delivered into His Majesty's Artillery Store To the Care of John Pattison in charge thereof the undermentioned particulars—viz.

Copper Powder Measures of sorts.......7

[B 97-1 p 252]

RECEIPT

MICHILIMACKINAC 20th Oct 1779.

Received into His Majesty's Artillery Stores from N. McKay master of the Sloop "Felicity" the undermentioned particulars—viz

Copper Powder Measure of sorts.......7

JOHN PATTISON.

[B 97-1-p 252]

THE CHIEFS & PRINCIPAL WARRIORS OF THE MINGOES, HURONS, DELAWARES & SHAWNESE. TO THEIR FATHER CAPTAIN LERNOULT COMMANDING AT D'TROIT.

UPPER SHAWNESE VILLAGE, October 20th 1779.

Father,

We are now returned home from puting your advice into Execution against your Enemies.

The Great Spirit has favored us with some success & it was our intention to have paid you a visit upon it; but having received some Information which gives us strong reason to believe that a large Body of Virginians are preparing to come against us from Fort Pitt, has determined us to stand upon our guard; requesting that as soon as you receive this Speech you will rise & come to our assistance you have promised to support us from time to time since the beginning of this War therefore we can't doubt your complying at this critical juncture your failing will entirely destroy our hopes hereafter. But Father be strong & comply with our desire. Detroit can never be in danger whilst you stand with us between it & the Enemy for in assisting us you defend it, we hope therefore that your dispatch will be so great as to reach us before the Enemy, in all probability the next account you have from us will be their being in our neighbourhood. The Cooshawking Indians are more than ever in their interest, they have help'd to shed the Blood of our friends to Northward which makes us the more anxious for your sending as many troops as you can spare if only to protect our Women & Children, while we harass the Enemy; we hope to see a day that those injuries will not pass with impunity even from those of our own Colour. We have also to request that you send us as soon as possible some supplies, we are in much need & the season advancing we hope you'll be so good as send them to Sanduskey by Water in a small Vessel where we can receive and divide them ourselves. In testimony of our sincerity we present you with this War Belt which will strengthen you in complying with our request as it is of our own manufacturing & so soon as you have fully considered its contents hope to see it returned pr Bearer to our satisfaction.

A Black Belt 8 rows.

endorsed:—No 9. Copied 30th October 1779. Speech from the Shawanese Village to Major Lernoult 20th Octr. Recd 24th Novr.

[B 122 p 424]

STATEMENT OF WORK

MICHILIMACKINAC 22nd October 1779.

Statement of the works which I have done for the King by order of Major De Peyster Governor at Michilimackinac.

1780 January 8th Five horse collars at 50" each.................... 250

March 5th For having pulled down a house of twenty four feet long by twenty deep and having transported it six leagues on rollers of white wood, having furnished the necessary wood for repairs and having put the key of the said house into the hands; the said house for the great Chief of the Sauteaux named Macquiquiovis for the price and sum of 4500 Livres of expense................ 4500

For having been down the river besides the house of the Chief Macquiquiovis to examine & find the pineries of red and white pine to make a saw mill & to examine the different sorts of wood and land for the good of the King........................... 250

For having been detained six months to conduct a party to the Illinois in the capacity of guide and promised one dollar per day.. 1080

That in order to induce me to abandon my interests he would bring down any one hundred and twenty Packets at the Expense of the King for which I was obliged to pay the sum of........... 5400

11,480

P. DURAND.

[B 98 p 284]

STATEMENT OF GOODS

Statement of the Goods which I, Durand, have left in charge of Baptiste Pointe Sable (naigre Libie) [free negroe] at the river Du Chemin [Calumet] which Mr Bennet Commandant has given orders to take

viz

1	New Canoe decorated with plumes	600
1	Covered kettle weighing 15 lbs at 10c	150
1	Large axe for use	20
10	Measures of Wheat lessive	500
3	" " Flour	150
15	lbs of Gum @ 2	30
500	lbs Flour and four sacks	1000
220	lbs Pork and three Barrels	660
10	Barrels of Rum containing each 20 gls	5280
3	Bench Lines Bundles 15	45
4	Bear Skins 15	60
2	Cotton Shirts 18	36
2	prs French Shoes & Buckles 30	60
1	Barrel of Sugar	90
1	Horn full of Powder	12
1	Sponge	12
	Total	8705"

[B 98 p 285]

MEMORIAL AND PETITION

To His Excellency Frederic Haldimand Governor in Chief of the Province of Quebec and Commander in Chief of all the Troops of His Britannic Majesty in Canada &c &c &c.

The Memorial and Petition of the Merchants joined in a General Company by the desire of Government in the year 1779 for themselves and the others who sign this Petition.

Representing very humbly that during this partnership in which they are engaged without hesitation and heartily for the good of the service of His Majesty they have sustained considerable losses and been much hindered in trade.

That on the dissolution of the said Company they had goods at St Joseph to the value of thirty thousand Livres.

That the following persons Messrs Lyons, Bostick, Campion, and Reilhe each sent goods to the amount of eight thousand Livres cost price at Montreal through the recommendation of Major De Peyster and at the request of Lieutenant Governor Sinclair in order that the Poutewatamies should not be turned from the interests of Government.

That at the risk of their lives they have frustrated the intention of the first robbers by repressing them.

That a second band of greater force deprived them of all their goods at that place and all the fruits of their industry for the season.

Wherefore they very humbly ask Your Excellency to take their losses into consideration and indemnification be made to them such as Your Excellency finds proper.

A Reilhe
for himself

Mattw Lessey
Henry Bostwick
Benjamin Lyon
John Macnamara
for the General Company

Henry Bostwick
Benjamin Lyon
Etne. Campion
for themselves

Endorsed:—Memorial of the Merchants of Michilimackinac to be presented to His Excellency General Haldimand.

[B 98 p 313]

COLONEL* CAMPBELL TO CAPTAIN LERNOULT

SHAWNEY TOWN Oct'r 23rd 1779.

SIR, I hope my Misfortune will be my Apology for troubling you, with a few particulars relative to myself and as your Ears have been often open to the Complaints of unfortunate Captives like myself you will attend to my particular case as there is something in it out of the common path of Indian Captives in which light I do not consider myself tho' I am detained by them, the particulars of which I will endeavor to relate as brief as possible.

On the 27th of last month, I set off from the Falls of Ohio on board of a Batteau with an Intention of going to Fort Pitt the Crew consisting of nine persons who were passengers worked their Passage & found their own Provisions & seven of the prisoners that were taken last winter at Post St. Vincents with Governor Hamilton a negro Wench & myself in company of two other Boats in the Service of the State of Virginia under the direction of Mr. David Rogers who had sundry clothing & other things on board which they brought from the Mississippi & on the 5th Inst. about three miles below the little Miami River we fell in with a party of Senecas, Wiandotts, Delawares & Shawneys at the crossing place of the Ohio Mr. Rogers with a party of men from the Boats attacked the Indians who were superior in number to the party he had with him he was obliged to retreat & two of the Boats fell into the hands of the Indians, but previous to the Indians taking possession of my boat I surrendered her and myself with two others & the Negro Wench to Serg't Samuel Chapman & the others choosing to be a prisoner to British Troops rather than trust to a savage enemy, this surrender would have been of little service to me if it had not been for the humane interposition of the White men who were with the Indians who have heretofore saved my Life tho' it was often in danger but since my arrival here I understand the Indians mean to detain me some time longer tho' I am & wish to be consider'd as a prisoner to British Troops I hope for your interposition to have me delivered up at Detroit as soon as possible that my sufferings in Captivity may be among a people of the same Language, Religion & manners & whom till within these few years, I looked upon in a different light from that of Enemys.

In the Compas of a letter it is impossible for me to relate minutely every particular relative to this affair. Serg't Chapman I make no doubt will inform you of all the particulars to whom I request to refer you & am

Sir Your most obed't humble Serv't

JOHN CAMPBELL.

Captain Lernoult Commanding Fort Detroit

*See appendix

Since writing the above I have heard of a speedyer conveyance than Serj't Chapman & therefore took the liberty of sending by the earliest.

endorsed:—Richard Beringer Lernoult Esq're Capt. in the 8th Reg't & Commandant at Detroit from Col. J. Campbell Rec'd 24th Nov'r

[B 122 p 426]

ORDER FOR ARTILLERY STORES

MICHILIMACKINAC 26th Octr 1779.

You are hereby directed and required to Issue out of His Majesty's Artillery Store the undermen-tioned particulars for Garrison and Navy Service viz.

PATT SINCLAIR
Lt Govr

For the Garrison.

Musquet Flints 74
Musquet Cartge Paper Quires.................................. 3

For the Navy.

Powder lbs....................	31	Common Cartridge Paper Quires	½
Loose Case Shot lbs...........	75	Musquet do do................	½
Musquet Ball lbs..............	18	Slow Match lbs...............	2
Musquet Flints................	36	Sheep skins dress'd..........	½

RECEIPT

MICHILIMACKINAC 26th Octr 1779.

Received out of His Majesty's Artillery Store from John Pattison in charge thereof, the undermentioned particulars for the use of the Garrison & Navy Service

For the Garrison

Musquet Flints 74
Musquet Cartridge Paper Quires............................... 3

For the Navy

Powder lbs....................	31	Common Cartridge Paper Quires	½
Loose Case Shot lbs...........	75	Musquet do do do.............	½
Musquet Ball lbs..............	18	Slow Match lbs...............	2
Musquet Flints................	36	Sheep Skins dress'd..........	½

WM BLUNT
Serjeant

[B 97-1-p 259]

MAJOR DE PEYSTER TO GENERAL HALDIMAND

DETROIT the 1st Novr 1779.

SIR, Agreeable to your Excellency's orders, I have relieved Major Lernoult, and have the pleasure to acquaint you that he sets off with the accounts of Simon Girty, his Brother and Mathew Elliot having defeated a Colonel Rogers on the Ohio, a stroke which must greatly dis-concert the Rebels at Pittsburg.

The papers relative to this affair & those found upon the Rebels, I enclose to Lt. Coll Bolton to be forwarded.

The demands of the Indians are great If Captain Caldwell's Light Compy was here, I would comply with their request, that not being the case, I have it not in my power to assist them with troops but shall send them a supply of Goods & ammunition in a small vessel & write to Capt McKee to see it properly divided.

Lt Govr Hamilton's Messenger Kissingua is returned from Pensacola with some Cherokees, & Letters from the Commissioners for executing the office of Superintendant which I also transmit.

By the Cherokees, I shall return answers to the Commissioners & shall write to Govr Chester inclosing him a copy of the Spanish Govrs letter.

I have the honor to be
with great respect
Your Excellency's
most humble & obedt Serv
At. S. DE PEYSTER

To His Excellency the Commander in Chief

Endorsed:—A 1779. From Major de Peyster 1st Novr Recd 24th

[B 122 p 430]

MAJOR DE PEYSTER TO CAPTAIN MCKEE

DETROIT, the 2nd Nov. 1779.

SIR, Your letter to Capt. Lernoult was delivered to me by W. Surphlet. Capt. Lernoult relieved by me, set out this morning for Niagara.

I heartily congratulate you on the success Messrs. Girtys and Elliot, on the Ohio. The Shoke will no doubt be severely felt at Pitsburg.

I am sorry at not having it in my power to comply with the demand of the Indians in sending troops to the Shawnee town, was Capt. Caldwells Rangers here It should be done. I shall however Comply with their request in what relates to Clothing, ammunition and for what purpose I will dispatch the Adventurer, with a cargo to be divided amongst the Wiandots, the Shawanese, Delawares and Mingoes—which I must request of you to see divided, at least the Proportion to the different nations, in order to prevent jealousy.

I send strings of Wampum, which I most earnestly request of you to cause to be delivered to the Monsey Indians desiring them to bring in, or to deliver up to you, a Woman named Peggy West, she was taken above a twelve month ago within twelve miles of Fort Pitt, the other side of it, near the Widow Miers her husbands name was Isaac West, you will please to send the other string to the Delawares for her daughter, a girl of about Eleven years of age, named Nancy taken at the same time. The circumstances will be remembered by the Indians, as the Father was Killed, and the Mother and two Daughters divided, one of the Girls of Twelve Years old lived with a Delaware whose name she thinks is Noughboughhallen this latter was lately brought in and delivered up to Capt. Lernoult, she is now with my wife.

If Sir! It be possible to find the Mother and the other Sister, I will not spare Expense, please therefore to employ some active people to go in search of them, assuring the Indians of a good Price, and my grateful acknowledgment.

The news lately received from Niagara is, that Sir John Johnson, Gl. Guy Johnson and Major Butler, with one Thousand Indians, and a body of Troops with Artillery are gone to attack the Enemy at Theoga.

The Western Nations about Michilimakinac are all well disposed, and will act with vigor against the Illinois.

The Hurons &c are returned from Niagara Sasterratzcé has brought belts from the five Nations, for the Cherokee, Chacklaws &c, desiring them never to make peace with the King's Enemies untill his Majesty shall require it. Some Cherokees being present, are charged with more belts.

I shall dispatch the Sloop for Sandusky in four days at present.

I am Sir
with due regard
Your most huml.
& obedt. Servt.

To Capt McKee
Shawanese Towns

AT. S. DE PEYSTER
Major

Indian Affairs
M. G. III

MAJOR DE PEYSTER TO CAPTAIN MCKEE

DETROIT the 5th Novr. 1779.

SIR, I take the opportunity of two Shawanese to acquaint you that Capt. Caldwell is returned from Theoga to Niagara and reports that Sullivan and his army abandoned that Fort with the greatest precipitation on receiving an Express from Washington. A rumor prevails that their Grand Army has been beaten by Sr. Harry Clinton. The Rebels left above Eight hundred head of Cattle at Theoga which the five nations will secure.

The Inclosed paper will give you pleasure as well as to all his Majesty's faithful Subjects with you. It is an undisputable fact.

Excuse the hurry I am in, the Indians on the point of going off, and many affairs crowding upon me.

I am Sr. Your most obedt. Servt.

AT. S. DE PEYSTER.

To Capt McKee.

Indian Affairs M. G. III.

FROM MAJOR DE PEYSTER UNADDRESSED

DETROIT the 20th Novr 1779.

SIR, I have the honor to acquaint your Excelly that I have just received the secret intelligence forwarded by Lt. Col. Bolton. I am sorry to say that the Indians are obliged to stand too much on their guard against the Virginians & Indians in their interest, to make it possible to get them to attempt anything whilst thus threatened, more than to endeavour to prevent the further incursions of the enemy into their country. I have received accounts from different bands of Indians, that the Rebels are with the consent of the Cashote Indians building a Fort at their Village, & I wait in daily expectation for Letters to confirm or contradict this report.

On my arrival here I found the Wabash Indians quite inactive, I therefore sent Belts & speeches to them to point out the necessity of their not suffering Clark to erect a strong Fort & Village at the falls of the Ohio, or at twelve miles down the river as he observes.

If I should succeed in bringing those Indians to act against Clark, it will take off his attention from the Illinois Country whilst Lt Governor Sinclair directs the Indians who have promised to strike at the Illinois in the Spring, to cross the Missippi, as if going to war against the Osages of the Missourie & thereby surprize Fort Louis at Pincour. I shall send off an Express by Land to Mr. Sinclair offering my opinion on the subject.

Your Excelly's Commission appointing Mr. Thomas Williams a Justice of the Peace, is come to my hands, but as the Dedimus is particularly directed to Capt. Lernoult & as I have not been legally qualified I can do nothing in it more than to lay it by till you may please to authorize Mr. Macomb to qualify both Mr. Williams & myself & Major Lernoult persuaded me that from Capt. Schanks having informed him of my being included in the Commission, that his & Mr. Macomb qualifying me, would be sufficient, but I now see that more ceremony is required.

I send off Mr. Jno. Campbell Col. of Militia (who was lately taken by the Indians) by this opportunity.

I have the honor to be with great respect Sir,

Your Excelly's most humble and obedt servt

AT. S. DE PEYSTER

His Excelly the Commander in Chief

endorsed:—1779. From Major De Peyster the 20th Novr recd 29th Decr

[B 122 p 434]

MAJOR DE PEYSTER TO CAPTAIN MCKEE

SIR, I wrote to you some time ago acquainting you with the Rebels having abandoned their fort at Theoga with great precipitation, and that Lt George Collier had destroyed the rebel fleet &ca. I now take the earliest opportunity to acknowledge the receipt of your Intelligence by the Cherokee, for which I am much obliged to you, I dispatch it to morrow for Niagara, when I shall strongly represent the necessity of some light troops in this neighbourhood.

I make not the least doubt but you will do Your utmost to baffle the designs of the Enemy upon all Occasions—

The General will no doubt regret the loss of so able a person as you to this Upper Country, and I daresay would be glad if you would change your mind with regard to your voyage to Europe for some time longer.

Please to excuse the brevity of this letter, being afflicted with a severe pain in my side.

I am Sir Your most obedient Huml Servant

AT S. DE PEYSTER

2nd Jany 1780

To Capt McKee

Indian Affairs

M. G. III

DOCTOR ANTHON TO CAPTAIN BREHM

DEAR SIR, A few days after your departure from hence, Captain Schank Commissioner for the Lakes arrived here, when I waited on him he informed me, that he had His Excellency General Haldimand's Instructions, to oppoint me Surgeon for the Naval Department here, at the same time desired me to give in my Proposals, which I did by desire to Capt Lernoult, both for the Garrison & Navy & presented them to Capt Schank who promised me to lay them before his Excellency at his arrival. Some time after I received His Excellency's commission appointing me Surgeon's Mate to this Garrison; in the year 1761 I was apointed by Lord Amherst Surgeon's mate in His Majesty's Hospital, and it is very hard after 19 years service to be under the direction & be commanded by a Mate from the Genl. Hospital who has got his appointment some time before my last commission, as would certainly have been the case, had not Capt. Lernoult & Major Depeyster settled it for the present.

May I beg the favour of your Interest to get me an allowance for my attending the Naval Depart. I had formerly a small sum subscribed by the Seamen for my trouble & Medicines which is now at an end since the new arrangement of the Navy has taken place.

Mrs Anthon & your acquaintance joyns with me in their respectful compliments to you & I am with respect

Your most obedt. & most humble servant

Geo. Anthon

Detroit 5th Jan 1780

Endorsed:—1780 from Doctor Anthon at Detroit to Captain Brehm of the 5th January. Naval Depart Rd to M. L. & Ct Schank

To Captain D. Brehm Aid de Camp. To His Excellency General Haldimand Quebec.

[B 122 p 459]

MR. MACLEOD TO SECRETARY MATTHEWS

Detroit 6th January 1780.

Sir, A few days after Major Depeyster's arrival at this place: he read me a paragraph in a Letter from His Excelly General Haldimand, wherein he says, Whereas Lieut. Governor Hamilton made an appointment of Town Major which he had no authority to do, that he could not continue Mr. MacLeod notwithstanding he heard he was a good man, as there was no appointment as yet made for the Upper Posts, on which I reply'd that His Excellency never continued me, he then desir'd I would explain myself, I told him that as I found that Generals Carleton and Haldimand had not approved of said appointment, that I never took the pay that was drawn for me, altho' offer'd repeatedly, & beg'd he would do me the Justice to acquaint His Excellency therewith. But being fearfull that he may forget, I make bold to give you that trouble & depend much upon your friendship.

If ever such an appointment should take place, that you will lay in my claim, if faithfull services from the beginning of the year one thousand, seven hundred & forty seven in Holland Brabant & North America to the end of the year one thousand seven hundred and sixty four should merit any prefferences with his Excellency.

I am Sr with great Esteem
Your most obedient & very humble servant
NORM'D MACLEOD.

Capt Mathews.

endorsed:—Capt. Mathews Secret'y to His Excellency Gen'l Haldimand Quebec 1780, A from Mr. Norman MacLeod 6th Jany. Rec'd 17th May.

[B 122 p 461]

MAJOR DE PEYSTER TO GENERAL HALDIMAND

DETROIT the 6th Jan'y 1780.

SIR, Mr. Alex'r Macomb who has hitherto supply'd the wants of Government at this post, having represented to me that he has a great quantity of goods laying at Montreal, which he would be glad to get up early in the spring.—I take the liberty to request that your Excelly. will grant his Correspondent a Pass for the number of Batteaux required to bring up all his Effects, as I think him entitled to such indulgence from the great recommendation I have had of him from my predecessor, as well as from my own observations.

I have the honor to be with great respect,
Sir, Your Excelly's most humble & obedient servant
AT. S. DE PEYSTER.

To His Excelly Gen'l Haldimand &c &c

endorsed:—1780. From Major de Peyster 6th Jan'y. Rec'd 20th May.

[B 122 p 463]

Dr. Laventure Toucher & Brother in account *Current with Ridley & Bennet* *Crs.*

Date	*New York Curry*	£	s	d	£	s	d	Date		£	s	d
1779								1779				
July 11	To balance due Ridley & Bennet as pr Acct settled this day				280	4	3	Octr 20	By amount of sundry Goods particulars as pr account annexed taken back at Detroit by Thomas Williams Esqre for the account and use of Ridley and Bennet sole creditors of the said Laventure Toucher & Brother by Permission of the Commandant Capt Lernoult	446	10	2
13	To 2 pieces Indian ribbon 20s	2										
	36 yards ribbon 2s 6	4	10									
	64 yards, do 2s 6	8										
	1 ps dble sattin black do 20 yards 1s 10	1	16	8								
	20 nutmegs 4		6	8								
	2 Gallons spirits 32s	3	4		19	17	4					
20	To 4 pieces Ribbon 20s	4	0	0								
	Cash	2	0	6								
	2 Gallons spirits	3	4		9	4	6					
25	To 2 Gallons do				3	4	..					
Augt 3	To cash pd Hire of cart bringing goods to Fort				......	10	..					
15	To pd Carta & baleing the goods when put into the King's Store				1	4	..					
	To cash paid Thomas Cox for Laventure's note in his favor				10	7	10					
1780	To interest on Cash advances £80 1s 0 for about 4 months nothing charged				......							
Jany....	Balance in favor of Laventure Toucher and Brother to be paid them in Goods at the same terms & prices as those already placed at their credit in this account											
	New York Currency				£446	10	2		New York Currency	£446	10	2

Detroit January 1780

[B 122 p 464]

GENERAL HALDIMAND TO MAJOR DE PEYSTER

QUEBEC, February 12th, 1780.

SIR, I have received your Letters of the 1st Octr. 1st & 20th Novr. and have honored your last bill from Michilimackinac.

The Expenses attending the Indian Department at that Post this last year have been enormous.—I shall be glad to be more fully informed what they have been doing to & on what particular services and account they have been incurred. I hope you have cautioned Governor Sinclair to moderate as much as possible the Expense of that Department.

Your account of the success of the Scout upon the Ohio together with the Papers that were taken have been forwarded to me by Colonel Bolton. I hope that stroke will have a good effect with those Indians whose affections seem declining—much depends upon their steadiness at this interesting period, and I am persuaded nothing in your Power to preserve their attachment will be wanting.

I very much approve your Plan of employing the Wabash Indians, & hope they will succeed in preventing Mr. Clark from establishing himself at or near the Falls of the Ohio, otherwise the Indian country will be open to their continual Incursions & safe communication will be formed between Fort Pitt & the Mississippi, if Lieut. Governor Sinclair should not be quite so successful as is wished, his striking at the Illinois will be well timed, & if not too late may (in some measure) favor the proposed operations towards that Quarter.

I am &c.

(signed) F. H.

Major De Peyster

endorsed:—Copy No 1, 1780. To Major De Peyster of the 12th of February. Copy Entered in Book marked B. No 2. Page 13.

[B 122 p 465]

MAJOR DE PEYSTER TO CAPTAIN MCKEE

DETROIT the 17th Feb. 1780.

SIR, The Shawaneese, Mingoes, and Delawares having asked for Troops to act in conjunction against the Enemy, lays me under the indispensible necessity of requesting that you will defer your voyage to Europe till some more favorable opportunity, knowing that the uncommon Influence you have with those Nations, particularly the Shawaneese, will be a great means of furthering His Majesty's Service, and preventing Cruelty to Prisoners, many instances of which you have already given much to your honour.

I will be glad to see you to morrow morning when we can speak more fully upon this Subject.

I am Sir Your Most humbl & obedt Servt

A. S. De Peyster.

To Capt McKee.

Indian Affairs M. G. III.

LIEUT. GOV. SINCLAIR TO SECRETARY MATTHEWS

Island of Michilimackinac 24th Feby. 1780

Sir, I enclose you a List of Medicines which are greatly wanted at this Post, for Artificers, Laborers, & others.

I am Sir your most obedt & Humble Servt

Patt Sinclair Lt Govr

Captain Mathews Secy.

[B 97-2 p 292]

MAJOR DE PEYSTER TO GENERAL HALDIMAND

Detroit the 8 March 1780.

Sir, I think it necessary to send this Express by Land, to acquaint your Excellency with my having received a Letter, from Mons Louis Chevallier of St Joseph's (brought by his son Aimable) acquainting me with the Rebels having totally evacuated the Illinois country. Thirty Indians also arrived from the Omat, and Post Vincent, in consequence of my Invitation, they are now on their way back, having promised that the Rebels shall not recross the Wabash.

Lieut Caldwell of the King's Regt Capt McKee, Mr Elliot, the three Girtys, & about fifty Indians, consisting of the principal chiefs of the Mingoes, Shawnese & Delawares are also arrived, who reports that the Rebels failed in their attempt to establish a Fort at Cooshocking, but that they had quite surrounded the Indian Hunting ground of Kintuck, by having built small Forts at two days journey from each other as will appear by the Indian Map of that country.

The Indians further say that the rebels intend to cross the ohio in the spring, & build a fort at two days journey from their principal Village on the Little Miami. They therefore require of their Father to fulfill the promise made by former Commandants who assured them that when the Enemy should approach their Villages, Troops should be sent to their assistance, they produced Lt. Governor Hamilton's Belt and other strings to this effect, as a proof of their assertion, saying that it was now time to fulfill the promise, or they would be shortly under the disagreeable necessity of falling back and thereby become a burden to their father, or else quit their ground & go to the Southward.

The principal Chiefs of the Hurons, Pottawatamies, Chippawas, Ottawas, Ouiattons, Miamis, Ouiats and the Pirorias, with the Keekapoos, being present in Council declared, that if I would send a few Soldiers, 'till a larger body could be spared, they would all rise & assist their elder brothers, and act in conjunction in future for the good of the King's Service. I see the necessity of sending some soldiers & I therefore propose to send one Capt. one Lieut. & about fifty men with two small pieces of ordnance to help them to knock down the Pickets of the first Fort.

To this party I shall add all the Indian officers and as many volunteers as may offer from the Settlement—this may for a while keep up the spirits of the Indians, 'till your Excellency's pleasure is further known.

Their route shall be up the Glise and down the Great Miamis to the Ohio. I flatter myself that this early movement, if accompanied by the great number of savages I expect, will facilitate Lt. Gov'r Sinclair's partys in their enterprises down the Mississippi, divert the attention of many from Niagara & be of some use to B. Gen. Campbell, if he has not already taken New Orleans.

The Wabash Indians & some from Michilimakinac have promised to amuse Mr. Clark at the falls. I wait 'till the mouth of the Miami is clear from ice to send of this Party.

An Express is arrived from Michilimackinac, which I have the honour to forward.

I am Sir, with great respect

Your Excellency's most humble & obed't Serv't

At. S. De Peyster

To His Excellency the Comm'd in Chief.

endorsed:—A 1780. From Major De Peyster 8th March Rec'd 17th May By Express

[B 122 p 467]

MAJOR DE PEYSTER TO GENERAL HALDIMAND

Detroit the 10 March 1780.

Sir, By the last Express I acquainted you that, Capt McKee was desirous of going to Europe when he could obtain your Excelly's permission. Seeing that the King's Service must suffer much by the absence of so valuable a man I have prevailed upon him to return into the Indian Country, and assist in the intended enterprise & promised that I would represent his situation to you. He has now been two & twenty years in the service, and had lately the offer of one of the Provl Battallions to be raised by Lord Dunmore in the neighborhood of Pitsburg, but the Commissions & Instructions were intercepted by the Rebels. He observes that should he be so unfortunate as to be taken by the Enemy, he has no rank to protect him from Insult.

Mr McKee appears to be a sensible man, & much of the Gentleman, his influence with the Shawnese nation is beyond conception.

They solely confide in him.

As this Gentleman's losses are very considerable, could something be done for him to induce him to continue in the service; it would be of very great advantage.

I flatter myself you will not think me troublesome in writing upon the above subject, as I can have no other view, than the real Good of His Majesty's service in so doing.

I have the honour to be with great respect, Sir,

Your Excell'ys most huml & obedt Servt

At. S. De Peyster.

To His Excellency the Comm in Chief.

Endorsed:—A 1780. From Major de Peyster 10th March Recd 17th May By Express.

[B 122 p 472]

FROM MR. CHEVALLIER UNADDRESSED

I do not know by what prodigy, Sir, the Poutawatamies have suddenly come out from a Sloth or rather a lethargy, that three years of want have not been able to cure, they have risen ashamed of a sleep which the voice of their Father and mine could not awaken them from; they have resolved to open their ears to this voice. Scarcely have they heard your words, calling to remembrance all those which they have received and given, than they have taken immediately the tomahawk. First holding themselves on the defensive but having learned from some chiefs, come from Detroit that the Five Nations invited them to the War, they set out the 12th of May to the number of 24, I believe now there are fifty or sixty for they are coming from all sides to swell the party. I am doing myself the pleasure of equipping them & of giving them proper instructions for the good of the Service. The Party is not composed only of those who have always given hopes but of those on whom they cannot rely. At the same time I am giving ammunition to the other party composed of Indians of Terre Coupé, the most obstinate and false of all. The Petit Bled was at the Illinois last autumn, with all his young men. He was there to receive the presents which Linctot promised to him in writing, or to avenge himself for the bad faith if he is deceived. That is what he explained to his nation there-by hoping to find favour with his true father. Whilst I am sealing your letters this, that I add is just handed to me. I send it to you that you may persuade yourself that if the Rebels have all the Indians, as it appears, against them, it is improbable that they can penetrate to their land. I have given you a true picture of the disposition of the Poutawatamies, I desire that it should last as long as they have been in showing it.

L. Chevallier.

St. Joseph, 13th March 1780.

The Warriors of Terre Coupé have left to-day, 14th March, singing the death song.

Endorsed:—M. L. Chevallier Letter from St Joseph dated 13th of March 1780.

[B 97-2 p 297]

MR. PAPIN TO MR. REILHE

St Louis the 23rd March 1780

Dear Comrade,

I have acquitted myself of all your Commissions, send me some goods if you have the power to do it. I exhort you to this if you will do me the pleasure. I am deprived of every thing even the necessities; they refuse here all passes for the Mississippy especially for carrying provisions; there has been published on the part of Kaos, an order which forbids the sending away of any money. They say that Irland is revolted; Jamaica taken by the Count D'Estaing; Admiral Biron well beaten by the same; New York blockaded by the same & by the Americans; the Prince of Monfacon in the River St. Lawrence for the seige of Quebec; the Natches, Mamchauks at Mobile & Peinsacole have been taken by M. Galvez Governor of New Orleans; the United States send Colonel Clark to establish a considerable stone fort at the entrance of the Belle Riviere [ohio] & another at the Cahoss. The Empress of Russia appears surprised that England had boasted that she would assist, the Empress adds that as Great Britain had called herself victorious & mistress of the sea she is not in want of my help; besides I do not wish to mix myself in any of her troubles which she can manage alone. The inhabitants of Artois have furnished to the King of France a vessel of the line of six guns, with promise of a large reward to all the crew from the captain to the lowest sailor, if they take another vessel with even one man & one gun more.

Adieu dear friend. I wish you well and believe me for life.

Your good & sincere friend

J. Papin

Our wives salute you & my big boy who is two months old waits to fight you.

endorsed:—Letter from J Papin an Indian Trader at St Louis to Mr. Reilhe another Trader at Michilimakinac of the 23rd of March 1780. Received the 11th June inclosed in Lt. Gov. St. Clair's Letter of 29th May.

Addressed:—To Mr. Reihle at Michilimackinac

[B 97-2 p 299]

FROM MADAM ROCHEBLAVE UNADDRESSED

Sir, As I think that you have not forgotten that my husband was taken prisoner by the Rebels & imprisoned at Williamsbourg, [then Capital of Va.] being in the service of His Britanique Majesty, I therefore recommend myself to you for his exchange which I hope will take place as soon as possible as I have learned that Mr. Henry Hamilton has been very ill in the prison and in chains; I am led to believe that Mr. Rocheblave has the Town for his prison, I do not know if I can believe this. Trusting also to your humanity to procure me an idemnification sufficient to put me in a position my family & also of Mr. Lord whom I have with me. It is absolutely necessary that I pay for what I require; I have not even the necessities of life, all my property has been stolen & I have only debts left me.

I have the honor to be with consideration,

Sir, Your very humble servant

Marie Michel de Rocheblave.

at Caskias the 27th March 1780

I would have sent you a letter which my husband wrote to you but I have not found occasion to put it in your hands.

[B 97-2 p 303]

CERTIFICATE OF EXPENDITURES

I do hereby Certify that the undermentioned Michilimakinac Artillery Stores have been expended by my orders in carrying on the Different Services, as undermentioned, between the 1st October 1779 and the 31st of March 1780, Inclusive and the Acting Conductor of Stores is hereby Discharged thereof.

PATT SINCLAIR.

Species of Stores	Quantity	For what Service Expended
Powder lbs	107½	Firing Salutes & for the Navy Service
Cartridges 6 Pounders	16	
Slow Match lbs	3	
Musqt Cartge Paper Quires	3½	
Common Cartge Paper Quires	½	For making Squib Cartridges for two Compy of the King's (or 8th) Regmt at this Post & Navy Service For Coating the Sponges belonging to ordnance & Navy
Musquet Ball lbs	18	
Musquet Flints	110	
Loose Case Shott lbs	75	
Sponge Tacks	100	
Sheep Skins	2	

[B. 97-1 p. 257]

CERTIFICATE OF EXPENDITURES

I do hereby certify that the undermentioned Engineer's Stores have been expended by my orders in carrying on the different Services as undermentioned between 1st Octr. 1779. & 31st March 1780. Inclusive and the Acting Conductor of Stores is hereby Discharged thereof.

PATT SINCLAIR
Lieut Govr.

Species of Stores	Quantity	For what Service Expended
Iron, lbs	125¼	For making & repairing Fillings & Broad axes & other Tools & making Fish Hooks, and large Spikes for the Block Houses & shoeing his Majesty's Horses by the Blacksmith
Steels, lbs	1	
Old Iron	27	
Twenty four penny nails lbs	7	
Ten penny do	12	
Spike do lbs	3½	Converted into other uses for the Kings Works By the People at work
Files	2	
Old Felling Axes	9	
Old Broad do	3	
Old Pick do	1	
Shovels	8	

Expended on the Island of Michilimackinac

Iron lbs	$203\frac{3}{4}$	For making a new Wharf Building New Houses and other Works for His Majesty's Service
Steel	55	
Twenty four penny nails lbs	101	
Ten penny do lbs	48	For the Blacksmiths, Carpenters Sawyers &c
Files	11	

[B 97-1-p 253]

Return of Engineers Stores Issued and Expended at the Garrison and Island of Michilimackinac, between the 1st October 1779 & 31st March 1780. Inclusive as per Vouchers.

Date, 1779.	To whom and for what Service	By order of	Species of Stores	Quantity S.	R.	U.
Octo. 20th.	To Serjeant Langdown for the use of the Kings Works.	Captain Patrick Sinclair Lieut. Govr. of Michilimackinac & Its Dependencies.	Twenty four penny nails, lbs...	2	....	....
			Ten penny nails	4	....	....
26th.	To do. for making & repairing, Filling axes & shoeing the King's Horses.		New Iron lbs	$3\frac{1}{4}$	....	....
			Steel lbs	1	....	....
			Files	2	....	....
			Twenty four penny nails..lbs	5	....	....
30th.	To do. for use of the King's Works.		Ten penny do	4	....	....
Decr. 8th.	To do. for erecting a Block House & other of the King's Works.		Spike nails lbs	$3\frac{1}{2}$	....	....
			Ten penny do lbs	4	....	....
30th.	To do. for making Fish Hooks & Spike Nails for the Block House.		Old Iron lbs	27	....	....
			Old Pick axe lbs	....	....	1
Feby. 7th.	Converted into other uses for the King's service.		Old Felling axes	....	....	9
			Old Broad do	....	....	3
9th.	To Seargt Langdon for making Felling Axes & other King's Works.		New Iron lbs	$121\frac{1}{4}$	....	....
	Expended on the Island		of Michilimackinac			
Novr. 8th.	To Sergt Langdon for the use of the King's Works.		Iron lbs	$127\frac{1}{2}$	....	....
			Steel lbs	55	....	....
			Twenty four penny nails lbs	98	....	....
13th.	To do. for use of the King's Works.		Ten penny nails lbs	30	....	....
			Files lbs	5	....	....
15th.	To do. for use of the King's Works.		Iron lbs	$76\frac{1}{4}$	....	....
			Ten penny nails lbs	18	....	....
			Files	4	....	....
Feby. 12th.	For the use of the King's Sawyers.		Twenty four penny nails..lbs	3	....	....
	Expended by order of between the 1st of October 1779 and this present date, Inclusive.		Files	2	....	....

[B 97-1-p 255]

Return of Ordnance Stores, Issued & Expended at the Garrison of Michilimackinac, between 1st Oct 1779 & the 31st of March 1780 inclusive. As Per Vouchers.

Date.	To whom and for what Service	By order of	Species of Stores	Quantity S.	Quantity R.	Quantity U.
1779						
Oct 4th....	For the arrival of Lieut Govr Sinclair..	Lieut. Gov. Sinclair Superintendt of Michilimackinac &c. &c.	Powder lbs..................	4	....	....
			Cartridge 6 Pounders.........	2	....	....
Oct 15th...	For Departure of Major De Peyster from this Post.		Powder lbs..................	12	....	....
			Cartridge 6 Pounders.........	6	....	....
Oct 25th...	In Honor of His Majesty's accession to the Throne		Powder lbs..................	16	....	....
			Cartridge 6 pdrs.............	4	....	....
Oct 26th...	issued out of His Majesty's ordnance Store for the Navy Service		Loose Case Shott lbs.........	75	....	....
			Musquet Ball lbs.............	18	....	....
			Common Cartridge Paper—Qrs	½	....	....
1780						
Jan 12th...	To Serjt Blunt for making Squib Cartridge		Cartridge Paper Quires.......	1	....	....
			Musquet Flints..............	50	....	....
Jan 18th...	In Honor of Her Majesty's Birthday..		Powder lbs..................	12	....	....
			Cartridge 6 Pounders.........	4	....	....
Feb........	For the Arrival & Departure of Indian Chiefs at different times		Powder lbs..................	32½	....	....
Feb 29th...	To Serjt Blunt for making Squib Cartridges		Musquet Cartridge Paper Quires....................	2	....	....
			Musquet Flints..............	24	....	....
	Expended by order of between 1st Octr 1779 & this present date, Inclusive					

[B 97-1 p 258]

Return of Engineer's Stores taken at Michilimackinac 31st March 1780

	Serviceable.	Repairable.	Unserviceable.	Deficiencies.		Serviceable.	Repairable.	Unserviceable.	Deficient.	Expended since last return.
Blacksmiths Tools:					Cooper's Tools:					
Bellows Pairs					Jointers	2				
Anvil	1				Hawling Knives	1				
Sledge Hammers	1				Stave do	2				
Hand do	2				Truss Hoops of Sorts	7				
Bench Vices	1				Intrenching Tools:					
Hand do	1				Pick Axes	28				
Screw Plates			1	1	Spades	54		13	13	
Nail Tool			1	1	Shovels	92		30	30	
Hardie			1	1	Hows	9				
Files of Sorts	41		43	43	Iron Crows	4				
Steel lbs					Hand Bills	22				
Iron lbs	122¼				Wheel Barrows	4				
Twenty four penny nails lbs	202½				Hand do	2				
Ten penny nails lbs					Iron lbs					392
Spike do lbs					Steel lbs					56
Sawyers Tools:					Old Iron lbs					27
Whip Saws	6				Twenty four penny nails					108
Cross cut do	9				Ten penny do lbs					60
Saw Setts	3		2		Spike do lbs					3½
Iron Dogs	2				Files					13

Hand Saws	4		1	1	Old Felling axes					9
Tennett do	2				Old Broad do					3
Felling axes	50				Old Pick do					1
Broad do	9				Shovels					8
Adzes	8				Cross Cut Saws	1				
Clawed Hammers	3				Hand do	1				
Long Planes	3		1	1	Adze	1				
Jack do	2		2	2	Spade	1				
Rabbit do			1	1	Shovels	2				
Iron Squares	3				Augur	1				
Chissels of Sorts	21		5	5	Gouge	1				
Gouges	11		2	2	Pick Axes	1				
Augurs	14		4	4	Hand Bills	2				
Compasses Iron Prs			2	2	Trowel	1				
Gimletts	13		15	15	Gimlets	2				
Drawing Knives	4				Clawed Hammers	1				
Grind Stones	1									
Masons Tools:										
Stone Hammers:	8									
Lathing do	2		1	1						
Trowels	5									

[B 97-2 p 304]

PATT SINCLAIR, Lt GOVR.

Return & State of Ordnance Stores taken at Michilimackinac 31st March 1780

	Serviceable.	Repairable.	Unserviceable.	Deficient.
Ordnance:				
Heavy Six Pounders Iron	2			
Light Six Pounders Brass	2			
Ambuzettes Brass Blown in 7 vents	4			
Mortar do 4 2–5 mounted	1			
Wall Pieces	2			
Carriages:				
Travelling six Pounders	2			
Garrison six do	4			
Garrison Ambuzettes	4			
Ladles for Six Pounders	2			
Spunges for do	6			
Wad Hooks of sorts	4			
Drag ropes with pin setts	2			
Hand Spikes Traversing	2			
Aprons of Lead	9		9	
Hand Spikes pinching	10			
Searcher, Pricker & reliever of each	1			
Leather Pouches	4			
Tube Boxes	4			
Slow Match lbs	17			

	Serviceable.	Repairable.	Unserviceable.	Deficiencies.	Expended since last return.
Live Shells with damaged Fuzees			25	25	
Empty Shells	29				
Sheep Skins	3				
Sponge Tacks	420				
Empty paper Cartridges 6 Prs	284				
Thread lbs	4				
Musquet Balls lbs	947				
Tann'd Hides	1		1	1	
Nave Grease lbs	2				
Harness:					
Mens setts		2			
Horse do		3			
Cartridge Paper:					
Reams	3				
Quires	6½				
Tonners:					
For Musquet Cartridges	4				
For Carbine do	2				
Flints:					
Musquet	5046				
Carbine	780				

Linstocks	4			
Portfires				
Portfire Sticks	5			
Tin Tubes	270			
Priming Horns	4		2	2
Priming wires	4			
Vent Punches	2			
Vent Spikes	10			
Corn'd Powder lbs	947			
Copper Measures measures of sorts	7			
Round Shot on the Bastions	403			
Round do with cartridges fill'd & fixd	38			
Case do do do do do	60			
Round do fixd to Bottoms only			31	31
Case do do do do do			122	122
Case do 1½ & 1 oz mixd lbs			15	15
Grape do for Ambuzettes round			24	24
Round Lead in shot for Ambuzettes rounds	41			
Cannon Cartridge paper quires	19½			
Fuzes 4 2–5	100			

Iron Beams with weights & scales setts	1				
Garrison Colours setts	2				
Powder lbs					107½
Paper Cartridges					16
Slow Match lbs					3
Musquet Cartridge Paper Quires					3½
Spunge Tacks					100
Sheep Skins					2
Common Cartridge Paper Quires					½
Case Shot loose 1½ & 1 oz mixd lbs					75
Musquet Balls					18
Musquet Flints					100

N. B. Two of the Ambuzettes on Board His Majesty's Sloop "Felicity."

[B 97-1 p 250]

PATT SINCLAIR Lt Governor.

TO† MAJOR DE PEYSTER WITHOUT SIGNATURE*

QUEBEC the 16th April 1780.

SIR, Having long thought it would be expedient to remove the Fort, &c, from its present situation to the Island of Michilimakinac, & being encouraged to this undertaking by advantages enumerated by Lt Governor Sinclair, that must result from it, & the earnest desire of the Traders, I have given directions that necessary Preparations, by collecting materials &c. be made with as much Expedition as the strength of that Post will admit of. You will therefore please to purchase four good draught mares (not too old to breed) & two Stallions & send them to Governor Sinclair by the first opportunity.

I am persuaded it is unnecessary to recommend to you to furnish him every other assistance he may require & that Detroit can afford, in forwarding this work, further than by giving you my sanction for the same, which I do, in the fullest manner.

I am, Sir your most obedient & most humble servant

P. S. I wish you also to send 4 pair of strong cart wheels to Michilimakinac, eight setts of Harness for that Post, will be sent for you to forward by the very first Vessels.

MAJOR DE PEYSTER.†

endorsed Copy 1780, to Major de Peyster of April.

[B 122 p 477]

* [The accompanying cuts and descriptions were undoubtedly submitted to General Haldimand by Lieut. Gov. Sinclair some considerable time previous to the date of the letter here given, but as this is the first reference found in the manuscripts to the removal of Fort Michillimackinac it seemed advisable to insert the drawings at this point.—Ed.]

† The correspondence published in vol. IX shows this letter to be from Gen. Haldimand to Major De Peyster. Sinclair claimed that De Peyster treated the above instructions with unfriendly neglect and many accrimonious letters were exchanged. The letter from Sinclair to Brehm remitting the following plans for a new fort may be found on page 523, vol. IX.—Ed. Sec. Edition.

This elevated Plain is rich loam, mixed with Limestone Gravel, some of that kind of stone loose, and in some few places fixed rocks of it—It is a very soft kind of stone when not exposed to the sun, and when sought for deep is found to be easily crumbled to resemble marl. The Island produces Oak, Beach, Elm, some Ash & Poplar—on the N. W. side there are some Pines, but not fit for use. The other woods are good—In the middle of the Island there is a small lake, apparently recruited by exhalations & not able to bear any drain from it—

There is no Stream of water on the Island.—Good situations for a Wind Mill.

A vessel can winter here with safety from the weather, or an Enemy when fortified at the Point marked thus * and on the ridge dotted. . . . .

Appearance from Isle bois blanc dist one mile and a Quarter.

People can fish at all seasons & with the worst weather without danger from this Island.

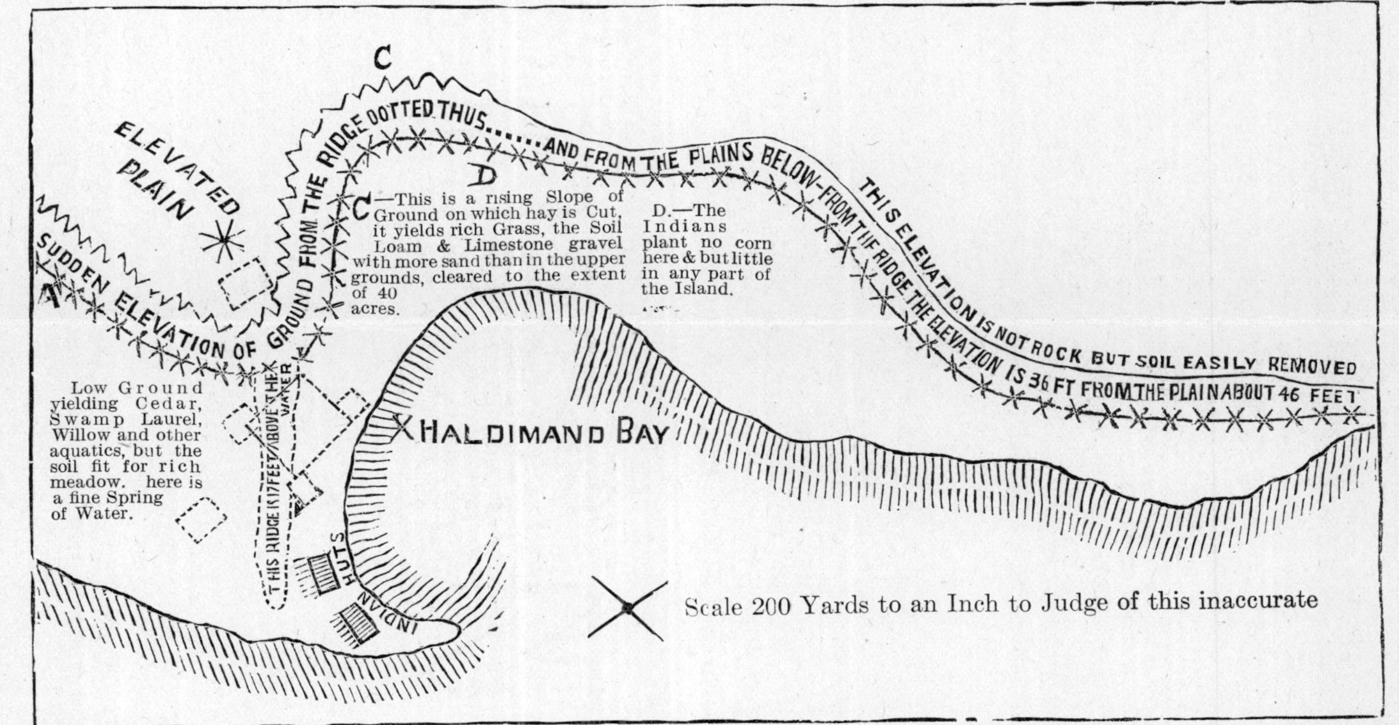
C
ELEVATED PLAIN
SUDDEN ELEVATION OF GROUND FROM THE RIDGE DOTTED THUS...... AND FROM THE PLAINS BELOW—FROM THE RIDGE THE ELEVATION IS 36 FT FROM THE PLAIN ABOUT 46 FEET
THIS ELEVATION IS NOT ROCK BUT SOIL EASILY REMOVED
D
C—This is a rising Slope of Ground on which hay is Cut, it yields rich Grass, the Soil Loam & Limestone gravel with more sand than in the upper grounds, cleared to the extent of 40 acres.
D.—The Indians plant no corn here & but little in any part of the Island.
A
Low Ground yielding Cedar, Swamp Laurel, Willow and other aquatics, but the soil fit for rich meadow. here is a fine Spring of Water.
THIS RIDGE IS 17 FEET ABOVE THE WATER
HUTS
INDIAN
X HALDIMAND BAY

Scale 200 Yards to an Inch to Judge of this inaccurate Sketch by * * * * The two lines so marked are to express the sudden Elevation of Ground from the ridge which is dotted, & from the Plains near the Bay, it rises almost perpendicular 36 feet above the ridge.

*A Fortification here would command the whole Bay & would overlook all the accessible part of the Island from that side, it would flank the ridge & any work erected on it, & it is not commanded by any ground behind it.

N. B. I send its appearance from Round Island as I wish you to draw a Sketch of the whole, before you show it to the General, & to urge that so respectable & valuable a situation may be early seized upon.

It will give no offence to the Proprietors who wish for it—The Ottawas may be a little jealous at first. then our Fort is to be built upon the Chippewa ground. The present Fort is partly on Ottawa and partly on the Chippewa ground which the only apparent good policy in the first choice of their situation—

From this Fort to Haldimand Island is only 8 miles but convenient for St. Mary's route, Grande River, Huron and Michigan Lakes as this dangerous Traverse will be thereby avoided—The Vessels can unload within 6 yards of the Beach and may be drawn within six feet of the shore in the winter at the part of the Bay marked X but every ...re within it is a great depth of water tho' the bottom is a little hard in some places, there is a fine sand & a ... marl in this place.

It is not improbable that the Fort of Michilc. was placed in its present bad situation for the convenience of the Mission of St. Ignone, and the St. Hawas who were found the Earliest Prosylites of Christianity.

A. Fort or work at * would protect a Vessel laid up at X in the Bay but must always leave the Enemy two natural approaches from under the Banks A & C & therefore would be better at C, if afforded equal protection to a vessel laid up opposite by Commandr. both banks towards C & D, but upon the whole an Engineer should be sent up, as it being impossible to fix the spot for a Fort by a sketch, as greatly depends upon distances & heights which are better discovered upon the very Spot. If a Block House could be sunk at the point * and another at the side of the Ridge C, so as to be covered by the same from one side and a Raised Rampart from the other, or even sunk into the very Ridge itself, thesame angular connected with one another so as to contain all the Trader's Hutts, or House & the stores, it would afford a better Defence than the proposed two Half Bastions—as Block Houses are the only works which afford a self defence without eed of annother work to flank them & at the same time may serve as Barracks or guard room.

This Island is nearly 2400 yards distant from the other.

Part of little White Wood or Round Island placed here to show in what manner it shelters Haldimand Bay & leave it but a very little open to any wind, & that blows over 3 Leagues of water it is then only open to about tons or from the wind E. N. E. Easterly this Island runs further to the nor thward than Paper will admit of.

but nothing of all that can be done without being on the Spot for reasons above mentioned and none others.

[B 97 1 p 243]

LIEUTENANT PHILIPS TO LIEUTENANT CLOWES

La Praire du Chien 27th April 1780

General Wabasha was well contented with his commission & believe me his Warriors are nothing inferior to regular Troops in regard to Discipline in their own way, it being their first & principle care to examine their arms in the morning, by drawing & drying their Powder and always fresh loaded at Sun Sett—

To Lieut Clowes Commanding the Detachment of the King's (or 8th) Regiment Michilimackinac

[B 97 2 p 322]

FROM LOUIS CHEVALLIER UNADDRESSED

St. Joseph the 30th April 1780

Sir, The same inconveniences which are opposed to the sudden execution of your orders, still detain me, but the desire which I have to execute them, at least partly, has made me endeavour to collect them.

One of our Canoes has left to be loaded with provisions, after its return I shall embark for your post where I shall personally justify the conduct that I have been obliged to observe, perhaps contrary to your intentions.

I am about to inform you of all that is happened, to my knowledge, concerning the good of the service, which forms the subject of this letter.

Although the facts contained in this, which is addressed to me from Post Vincennes, of which I send you an extract, could have influence only over minds ill-disposed or destitute of good sense, yet they have had enough over the minds of the Indians, to relax the zeal, with which they appeared to have been filled, for the glory of their father.

To conclude. Jamaica has been taken by the Count D'Estaing, he has left a garrison there of 8,000 men, but another expedition calling from elsewhere, his absence has occasioned a revolt on the part of the English. Having been informed of this he has returned to condemn the authors of the revolt to be hanged.

The Governor of New Orleans found some orders in an English frigate, armed with 800 men, taken by a Spanish vessel, to destroy Pointe Coupée, kill the French and hang the negroes. This refers to the war between England & Spain. Immediately the Governor of Spain sent an expedition to Manchauk, which has been taken by assault, with 500 men, after having sustained 900 shots from cannon. Baton Rouge & the Natchez have been taken; he is working now for Pensacola & by a postcript I am informed, that 1500 men of Fort de Quesne are coming & that 500 are coming down by the Cheraquois River.

It is not, however, the chimerical rumors which has stopped the Poutawatamies in their route. A Frenchman met them on their road &, recognising them as warriors going to war, he said to them. Have you become enemies of France & Spain? Do you not know that it is they who are making war just now? Return to your Villages or if any one doubts the truth, let him follow me & he shall see with his own eyes. The War Chief held a council immediately, not to seize the French who spoke with so much impudence but to send them back.

It is, however, agreed with me, that he was humiliated for he had believed the false reports & the more so having to return without the author of it.

As in such cases the Poutawatamies are divided, twenty warriors of different Villages detached themselves & are gone to follow the French, who offered to lead them to the head man who was a Chief named Iuoiqueperman, this is the same man who took the letter which I communicated to you. They went to Post Vincennes ashamed of allowing themselves to be deceived, being allowed to speak, the Chief invited by the Americans spoke first & told him all that his feeling inspired him with, told him also that he was English, that he was to be regarded as such, that he had already come to kill him & that, if he had not been deceived, he would yet see his tomahawk dyed in his blood. The Americans, instead of being annoyed by the tone in which he spoke, compared him to a man making a crime of lying; he then assured him of the truth of the Declaration of war of France & Spain against England & dismissed him after he had given him a white flag on which are laid two little pieces of blue cloth in the form of a knife.

I have found it useless, said the chief to me, making a stroke, although the number of Rebels does not exceed 30. They are so much on their guard that he has not been able to surprise them.

He has reported again to me that Petit Bled has taken 3 scalps & a prisoner, one of the scalps is of a Frenchmen & the 2 others of Americans, & that the prisoner is escaped.

This stroke is a good omen, a poutawatamie has struck this is enough, the others are leaving to strike also. I hope Quamciose, followed by 24 warriors, will show his zeal; evidence of the return of the Poutawatimies & of his cause, he has not any regard either for the one or the other which makes me believe he will have success.

This is in a few words what I have been informed of & I believe it my duty to send you an account for your convenience principally, with much fidelity I am

Sir Your Excellency's most humble & most obedient servant

LOUIS CHEVALLIER

Whilst sealing your letter I am informed that an Ottawa, who is among the Poutawatamies of the Post has received two strings of wampum, which those of his nation who are at the large village had given him to assure his Chiefs that the French & Spaniards were really come & to ask them to remember, that they have never been their enemies but on the contrary they have always been their benefactors & friends.

Endorsed:—L No 15 Mons'r Chevaliers letter of the 30th April 1780

[B 97-2 p 326]

GENERAL HALDIMAND TO MAJOR DE PEYSTER

QUEBEC 8th May 1780.

SIR, The very enormous Expense attending the purchasing of Indian presents at the several Posts in the Upper Country, owing to the avidity of the Traders who supply them, has determined me to attempt a diminution of it by supplying them from England. I must therefore desire that with the assistance of the Indian officers and such other Information & remarks as you shall be able to obtain from the necessary Expenditure of the late years, that you will make out & transmit to me an Estimate of the different articles and Quantities of each that will be wanted at your Post, for twelve months, in order that you may be from time to time punctually supplied I hope at a more moderate Expense to Government.

I do not expect your Calculations to be perfectly just, I know it is impossible it should, as the demands fluctuate with the times, but it can be brought so near as to leave very little to be purchased from the Traders, you will in the mean time buy as few things from them as possible and calculate your wants allowing for the stock you may have in store.

I am &c.

signed FRED: HALDIMAND

N. B. a copy of this Letter sent to Lieut Governor Sinclair at Michilimackinac.

Major De Peyster

Endorsed:—Copy No 2 1780 To Major de Peyster commanding at Detroit of the 8th May N. B. A copy of it sent to Lieut Governor Sinclair at Michilimakinac Copy Entered in Book marked B. No 2 page 14.

[B 122 p 480]

GENERAL HALDIMAND TO MAJOR DE PEYSTER

QUEBEC 8th May 1780.

SIR, As the death of the late Captain McDougal will necessarily occasion an arrangement of his affairs, & as his Executors may in this Business, comprehend as Property & offer to sale L'Isle aux Cochons—I must desire that you will not permit the same to be disposed of, it being my Intention to reclaim it for the use of the Crown & Garrison of Detroit.

Mrs McDougal need not be alarmed at this notice which you will give her, as she must be persuaded from what I have already done for Captain McDougals Family that my Inclination leads me rather to assist than to distress her.

I am Sir &c

(signed) FRED: HALDIMAND

Major De Peyster

Endorsed:—Copy No 3—80. To Major De Peyster at Detroit 8th May Copy entered in Book marked B No 2 page 14.

[B 122 p 482]

MAJOR DE PEYSTER TO CAPTAIN MCKEE

DETROIT 8th May 1780.

DR. SIR, I must request of you to give the Inclosed a place in your Pocketbook for fear of accidents. You will please to inform every one in your Department that I expect they will pay the strictest attention to orders,—and exert themselves upon every occasion. They must know that taking a few scalps is not the object of the present enterprise.

If W. [Matthew] Elliot is with you please to give one Comp'y to him, also remem'r me to the Chiefs and Warriors.

Mrs. D. P. and your friends here desire to join in comp'ts to you, wishing you success, and a speedy return.

This letter will be followed in two days by Egoustwa and a large band of Ottawas, one of Chippawas, and one of Pottawatamies.

I have the Honour to be Sir Your most obed' Serv.

AT. S. DE PEYSTER.

Alex. McKee Esq

Indian Affairs M. G. III.

MAJOR DE PEYSTER TO CAPTAIN MCKEE

Sir, In case of any unforseen accident happening to Capt Bird, so as to prevent his commanding the expedition—This is to Order the Officer who may succeed him in the Command of the Troops, not to undertake any enterprise without Consulting you, and first obtaining your concurrence therein.

Given at Detroit this 8th day of May 1780.

At S De Peyster Commanding

To Alex McKee Esqr Agent for Indian Affairs &c &c &c &c.

Indian Affairs M. G III.

MAJOR DE PEYSTER TO CAPTAIN MCKEE

Every person employed in the Indian Department upon this enterprise, are hereby ordered to obey such orders as they shall occasionally receive from you, Undertaking nothing of themselves or by any other orders unless they come from Capt Bird.

As there is no time for Counselling, I have no other Speech to make to my friends, and children, the Indians, than to assure them of my friendship, and to desire that they will loose no time in showing the way to some of the Forts, in order to give my Cannon the opportunity of levelling the Pickets.

Give me leave to add my best wishes for your health and success.

I am Sir Your most humbl & obedt Servt

At. S. De Peyster

Major the King's Regt. Commanding Detroit

To Capt Alexr McKee

Indian Affairs M. G. III

MAJOR DE PEYSTER TO GENERAL HALDIMAND

Detroit the 17 May 1780.

Sir, I have the honor to acquaint you that by Letter just received from Captain Bird, he expected to have passed the carrying place by Tuesday last, after which he has down the stream all the way to the Ohio. My intentions however to amuse the Rebels at the Rappids have in some measure been baffled by a ridiculous circumstance.

A Canadian Trader meeting with the Pottawatamies and Grand River Indians, near to Post Vincennes, asked them if they were mad, to go against their old friends the French, of whom there were 4000 in Garrison in Post Vincennes, with all the Artillery Count D'Estaing had taken at Jamaica & the Govr of New Orleans upon the banks of the Mississippi, who he said, had taken the Natches &c & was actually laying siege to Pensacola.

They unfortunately listened to those extravagances, & returned to their homes except a few, who proceeded to satisfy their curiosity when to their great mortification they found only 23 Virginians in the place—too late to recall their friends. Mons. De Quindre, who I had ordered with the St. Joseph's Indians would have prevented the imposition, had he not fallen ill on the way. Such is the dependance on Indians without Troops to lead them on. The Delawares and Shawnese are however daily bringing in Scalps & Prisoners, having at present a great field to act upon.—those unhappy people being part of the one thousand families who to shun the oppression of Congress are on their way to possess the country of Kentuck, where if they are allowed quietly to settle, they will soon become formidable both to the Indians & to the Posts.

I should be glad your Excellency would order what you would have done with the Prisoners who are daily brought in. They may in time become troublesome—Tho' at present ev'ry thing is quiet here & no talk of an Enemy. Clark is really gone to establish a settlement at the Iron Mines on the Mississippi below the Ohio.

By Letters just now received from the Master of the Windot, she is on shore on the east side of Lake Huron, Crew & Cargo all safe. The vessel will be got off, for which purpose we dispatch Capt Burnett this day.

I have the honor to be with great respect Sir, Your Excellency's most obedt & most humble Servt,

At S. De Peyster

To His Excelly the Commr. in Chief

Endorsed:—No 1 Entd 1780. From Major De Peyster at Detroit of the 17th May Recd 3rd June inclosing a Letter from Mr. Louis Chevallier of St Joseph.

[B 122 p 484]

MAJOR DE PEYSTER TO GENERAL HALDIMAND

Detroit 17th May 1780.

Sir, The bearer of this letter, Mons. Perault of Pincour, was taken with C. Campbell last fall on the Ohio, when on his way to Virginia to recover debts due to his Father. Sickness occasioned by ill treatment received from the Indians prevented his leaving this before. He is a well bred young man and is Nephew to Madame Peraut of Quebec.

I have the honour to be with great respect

Sir Your Excellency's most humble & obed't servant

AT S. DE PEYSTER

To His Excellency the Commander in Chief &c. &c. &c.

Endorsed:—A 1780. From Major De Peyster 17th May.

[B 122 p 486]

FROM LIEUT. GOV. SINCLAIR UNADDRESSED

MICHILIMACKINAC 29th May 1780

The bearer of this *Monsieur St Germain,* having letters for His Excellency the General. It is expected that no Canoe coming from Montreal will refuse a guide or men should he stand in need of either, and that the Post Master of Montreal will furnish him a Carriage to Head Quarters.

The Crew of his Cannoe are six men taken from the Mississippi & are to remain where the officer Commanding the Troops at Montreal will direct suited the General's pleasure is known relative to them.

PATT SINCLAIR

Lt Gov'r

The Crew of the Cannoe to be victualled for a few days.

[B 97-2 p 358]

LIEUT. GOV. SINCLAIR TO GENERAL HALDIMAND

SIR, The Enclosed Letters which I have the honor to put under cover for your Excellency are No 1, on the state of the Post. No 2 on the subject of My Lord George Germain's Circular Letter & No 3 on the state of affairs dependant on the Post.

Mons'r St. Germain will have the honor to deliver them, & to relate the particulars of an unhappy accident in Lake Superior.

I can hardly suppose that Passes will be granted for that Lake, or Lake Huron, independant of this Post after the irregularities of this and Last winter.

I have the honor to be Sir, with Respect

Your Excellency's most obedt. humble Servant

PATT SINCLAIR

Lt Gov'r

Michilc. 29th May 1780.

Monsr. Parent
Monsr. St Chie
Monsr. Le Compt
Ignace Ebere
Louis Dodier
Simon St Amant
} Prisoners

To Mr. Mitchel Dy. Commissary

[B 97-2 p 359]

Sir You will please to victual the above six Persons as the Troops are victualled commencing this day 2nd June. PATT SINCLAIR Lt Gov.

LIEUT. GOV. SINCLAIR TO CAPTAIN BREHM

Dear Brehm,

I put under this cover a Letter from the Illinois addressed to His Excellency with several others brought by Mons'r Groselier also the Pass mentioned in one of my other Letters. I hope you will pardon the incorrectness of all of them as I write with Indians on every hand, & whispering in each ear, Rum or Bread.

I am with sincere regard
Dear Brehm Ever Your's

PATT SINCLAIR

[B 97-2 p 411]

MAJOR DE PEYSTER TO GENERAL HALDIMAND

DETROIT the 1st June 1780.

SIR, Since the last letter I had the honour to write to your Excellency arrived a Michilimakinac Chief from the Ohio with the Scalps of four men. Two of them were officers going Express from Williamsburg to Mr. Clark. I herewith Enclose two original Letters taken. They were many private letters & grants for land.

The Pottawatamies who returned from near Post Vincennes came here with all those of St. Joseph to have their Hatchet sharpened; they are now on their way to the Post where there are but thirty Virginians under the command of one Dalton; From thence they are to reconnoitre the rappids of the Ohio. The Canadians at Post Vincennes are the worst enemies we have.

There are now about 2,000 Warriors fitted out from this place to reconnoitre the Ohio & Wabash.

Monsr. Dagneaux Du Quindre of St. Joseph's came in with the Pottawatamies at my request and has engaged that they shall behave well, if I give him the leading of that nation agreeable to their own request. I have taken him into the Indian Department for this District, and promised to write to know what rank and pay you will please to allow him. He was formerly a Lieut. in the French Service.

I have the honour to be with great respect

Sir, Your Excellency's most humb'l & obed't serv't,

At S. DePeyster.

To His Excelly., the Comm'r in Chief.

Endorsed 1780, From Major De Peyster, 1st June, Rec'd 22nd.

[B 122 p 487.]

MAJOR DE PEYSTER TO GENERAL HALDIMAND

Detroit the 8th June 1780.

Sir, I have just received Your Excellency's letter of the 12th February, by which you desire to be more fully informed what occasioned the enormous Expenses, attending the Indian department at Michilimackinac, the last year. To which I hope the following remarks will be satisfactory.

Partly by reconciling the Chippewas of the bay de Noque with the Menomenies, & the Chippewas of the plains with the Scioux, in order to make those nations useful in case of being wanted. A large present sent to the Scioux in order to make them keep the Sacks & Reynards in awe.

By Lieut Governor Hamilton's Expedition, in which I was required to give him ev'ry assistance in my power. To which purpose I sent to raise the Indians of the Grand River and the Dog Plains, [Prairie du Chien] which could not be done without taking up a quantity of Goods and provisions in the Indian country, with every accumulated Expence thereon, as will appear by Messrs Langlade & Gautier's accounts & Vouchers sent to Mr Dunn's office.

By Clothing & Arming a body of Canadians, and by raising the Indians a second time, to march & oppose the Rebels who threatened Detroit. My design was to harrass Mr Clark on his way up the Wabash, and to put a body at St. Joseph's sufficient to oppose Linctot, with his cavalry from the Pey. Few of the Indians proceed further than St Joseph's, but I am nevertheless persuaded that the noise of their assembling after Mr Hamilton's defeat, so contrary to rebel expectations, did in a great measure oblige them to retire and, to lay aside their Expedition, especially as they were also informed that the Scioux were to fall upon the Habitations of the Creoles, if they marched with Clark against Detroit.

The familys of all the Indians were by agreement taken care of & clothed. Canoes were not only furnished for the Warriors, but also for their familys to return home with; those they came in, by the time they reached the Post, were rendered quite unfit for future use. Numbers of strange Indians resorted to Michilimackinac that year, whose friendship it was my instructions to cultivate, The Expence of which gave me great uneasiness of mind, & the extraordinary trouble I took proved equally grievous to the body, having almost exhausted myself with fatigue, in order to see the Indians pleased, by delivering them every article in my presence, whereby I saved Government some thousands, which would otherwise have been expended without giving satisfaction in the critical juncture affairs then stood.

I am sorry to say Sir, that the Indians are now come to such a pitch, as to make their own demands, and that the refusal of a trifle, if not done with caution, may turn a whole war party. I lately had an instance of this kind, by being obliged to refuse a keg of rum, we had not to give.

I have the honour to be with great respect Sir, your Excellency's most humbl & obedt servant

At. S. De Peyster

To His Excellency the commr in Chief.

Endorsed:—A No 2 1780 From Major De Peyster Detroit 8th June. Recd 28th Copy in Book marked B No 3 Page 5.

[B 122 p 489]

CERTIFICATE OF SUPPLIES

Michilimackinac, the 13th June 1780.

Supplies which Mr. Jh. Ainssé has furnished for the King, by order of Governor Sinclair to be sent to St Joseph.

Viz.

4 Barrels rum 1200

I certify that Mr. Jh. Ainssé has furnished the above mentioned articles at Michillimackinac.

The 6th April 1780.

Dugay.

[B 97-2 p 513]

MR. DE QUINDRE TO LIEUT. GOV. SINCLAIR

St. Joseph, 14th June 1780.

Sir, I do not know if, by assuring Your Excellency that it has not been in my power to respond more promptly to the honor which you have overwhelmed me with by your letter, I can thus deserve pardon, but I flatter myself to recover the favour which you accord to faithful subjects, since I make effort to render myself worthy, by resembling them. It is not for me to publish that I have sought to signalize my zeal uninvited, & less still as I have been judged capable of filling the charge I have been lately gratified with, but I can protest to you, Sir that I am about to put all to work in oder recognise the honorable rank, which they have raised me to.

Although my instructions bind me to inform Your Excellency, above all of that which has reference to the service, this time I am about to contravene them, but Monsieur Chavallier, who is preparing to visit you, will act for me in this letter.

It is to his capacity & to his labours, Sir, I am indebted for the success that I have over the minds of the Poutowatamies, & consequently it is for him to render an account of it.

I give him this testimonial before you because he has too much dignity to claim it himself. I am happy if I can gain your favour & happier still if I can always merit to be

Sir, Your Excellency most humble & most obedient servant,

Dagniau de Quindre.

addressed to His Excellency Lt. Govr. Sinclair of Michillimackinac at Michillimackinac.

Endorsed:—1780. Letter from Mr. de Quindre To Lieut. Govr. Sinclair St Josephs the 14th June.

[B 97-2 p 362]

GENERAL HALDIMAND TO MAJOR DE PEYSTER

Quebec 18th June 1780.

Sir, I have received your Letters of 8th & 10th March, acquainting me with your Information, by Mr. Chevallier, of the Rebels having evacuated the Illinois Country and of the return of the officers & Indian Chiefs from St Dusky, with an account of the Rebels having possessed themselves of the Hunting Grounds of Kentuck & their intention of crossing the Ohio & establishing themselves near the principal village on the Little Miami River—I cannot but approve of the steps you have taken to cheque their advances & have no doubt that if the detachment sent are faithfully & vigorously supported by the Indians, they will effect their purpose, and facilitate other operations as suggested by you.

The success I would fain anticipate of this Enterprise will I hope quiet the pressing sollictations of the Indians (at least for the present) for a Reinforcement of Troops, which situated as I now am both for Troops & Provisions it is impossible I can comply with besides, the great uncertainty of what Turn the War may take this Campaign in this part of the Continent, suspends for the present my intended efforts to strengthen the Upper Posts.— Arrivals which cannot be very distant will I flatter myself enable me to do something for them; what you have already undertaken will or ought to convince the Indians of our Inclinations to support them, and altho' your Garrison will be in some measure weakened by reinforcing that of Michilimakinac, the Company of Rangers which has before this time joined you, will enable you to send out some White men with very considerable Scouts of Indians, those Scouts, if the Indians do their duty by defending their own Country with any degree of resolution, will be sufficient to repel any Incursions of the Enemy, which are not in such force, as cannot be opposed in the Field upon the present Scale of affairs. In all Events your Fort is in perfect Security against any attempts in their Power to make, every measure for its defence, and an unremitting Œconomy of provisions are the Chief objects to be considered, the uncertainty of procuring, & the difficulty of conveying the latter oblige me to recommend it to your most serious attention.

From your Representation of Mr. McKee's influence with the Indians, his zeal for the Service, & the disadvantages that would result from his quitting it at present, I cannot think of permitting him to go to Europe and at the same time it would give me pleasure to reward & encourage his Services; I am at a loss in what manner to accomplish it. You mention in your Letter his desire to obtain Rank, in order to protect him from Insult should he be so unfortunate as to fall into the Enemy's hands. In the line of his Department, there is no Rank beyond that he has, except the Superintendant's who has no Rank in the Army. Please to inform me in your next Letter what his wishes point to, and what you think might be done to serve him at Detroit, but do not take notice of my desire to him, least it should not be in my Power to gratify his wishes.

Your several Letters, Accounts &c are received, but time will not permit me to answer them by this opportunity.

I am Sir &c

(signed) FRED: HALDIMAND

Major De Peyster.

Endorsed:—Copy 80. To Major De Peyster at Detroit 18th June

[B 122 p 495]

PROPOSALS TO SUPPLY GOVERNMENT AT DETROIT WITH MERCHANDISE & RUM BY MACOMB EDGAR & MACOMB.

Macomb Edgar & Macomb will engage to furnish what merchandize may be wanted for the use of the Indian Department at Detroit at 25 per cent advance on said Merchandize, supposing them to cost at Montreal 50 per, the whole delivered at Detroit at their risque.—They will furnish the Rum wanted yearly for Government, delivered at Detroit at 18s New Yk. Cy. per gallon, paying for the Casks. Provided that thirty Batteau load of their Effects be transported yearly from Carleton Island to Detroit at the expence of Government, and all their Goods &ca. be ordered to pass at the different Posts a they arrive, in their turn with King's Stores.

Should this proposal be agreeable to His Excellency General Haldimand, Messrs. Macomb & Co will undertake it as long as it may be found necessary to continue Expenses for Government, (unless prevented by any unforseen public event the consequence of war or otherwise in which case they shall not be bound to fulfill this proposal) and they will advance their money as usual for the payment of the other departments.

They are assured that Government by adopting this method will save a very considerable sum every year, neither will it be subject to a change of prices which can happen only to the disavantage of Government, and Messrs Macomb & Co, being on the spot, and acquainted with every necessary article, will take care to have a sufficient quantity always ready for the necessities of the place.

MACOMB EDGAR & MACOMB

Quebec 19 June 1780.

Endorsed:—1780 Mr. Macomb's Proposals to furnish Government with Goods at Detroit Recd 19 June.

[B 122 p 498]

TO GEN. HALDIMAND

Mr. Rose presents his Compliments to Sir Fred Haldimand and acquaints him that the holders of the Bills drawn by Lieut Governor Sinclair from Michilimackinac are renewing their application to the Lords of the Treasury for the payment of them stating (among other reasons) that Mr. McBeath's conduct could not give Displeasure to General Haldimand as he was continued in his situation at Michilimackinac till he left Canada three years after the Bills were refused acceptance. Mr. Rose will therefore be obliged to Sir Frederick Haldimand to inform him of the reasons that induced him to continue Mr. McBeath in the employment for so long a Period, and as Mr. Rose is to see the Merchants on the subject at 11 O'clock to morrow, he begs the favor of an answer before that time.

Treasury Chambers 22d June 1780.

[B 52 p 48]

MAJOR DE PEYSTER TO CAPTAIN MCKEE

DETROIT, the 22nd June, 1780.

DEAR SIR, I am favored with your letter of the 4th June. It gives me pleasure to hear that the Indians were assembling so fast and in such numbers.

There certainly must be some mistake with regard to the Hurons, as I am confident there does not remain any either at Sandusky or here except the aged, and part of them are gone to war, but the Hurons have taken a different route, towards Fort Pit, which perhaps will be of as much, If not more service to Capt Bird than If they had joined you.

The deputation from the Six Nations arrived Safe here. Kayashota seeing that no General Council could be held on account of the Nations being gone to war, left the belt and Speech with the Hurons, to deliver to the different nations as Occasion should offer. It consists of 4 Belts containing 24 thousand wampun, requesting all the Indians to hold firm to the General Alliance with the King of Great Britain, denouncing bad luck to such as shall separate therefrom.

Mrs. De Peyster and the Gentlemen of the King's Regmt. join in compts. to you and all friends.

I must request that you will remember me to my Indian Children & assure them that they shall find me a good friend If they go thro' with the work in hand with becoming patience and fortitude. The old story of Humanity to Prisoners, I am convinced you will loose no opportunity to initiate.

I am D'r Sir

Sincerely your humb'l & obed't serv't

AT. S. DE PEYSTER.

To Alex'r McKee Esq.

Indian Affairs, M. G. III.

AGREEMENT

We the undersigned agree & promise to furnish as many Corvés et help as we can to establish the Village of Michilimakinac

The 24th June 1780

Augt. Chaboille

Sr. Marcotte his + mark

Mr Auge

P. Chaboillez

Mr. La Fontain his + mark

Jas Gamelin

Endorsed:—No 20 Sundry opinions of people attached to the post who oblige themselves to assist by this inclosed cover expressing an obligation so to do. A similar obligation remains here—All of them will be permitted on sufference only until His Excellency's pleasure is known.

[B 97-2 p 369]

STATEMENT

St Joseph June 1780

Statement of the Merchandise delivered, for the Kings Service, to Mr Joseph Ainssé, charged with orders from Lieut. Governor Sinclair.

7 cotton shirts .... at	18	126
1 bundle bench lines	12	12
2 doz large knives	12	24
5 lbs nails	4	20
2 doz awls	6	12
5 bags wheat	50	250
12 bags do	50	600
2 large fat pigs	300	600
2 two year old bulls	300	600
	Total	2244

I certify to have delivered to M. J. Ainssé, charged with orders from Lieut. Govr Sinclair, the goods above mentioned for the Service of His Britannique Majesty.

Louis Chevallier

[B 97-2. p 515]

MR. AINSSE TO LIEUT. GOV. SINCLAIR

Mon Gouverneur,

Circumstances oblige me to send a canoe to inform you of the news which has arrived to-day in this place. Three parties of Poutougatemy left to kill the Rebels, two to attack Chatre & the other to strike at Post Vincennes. The Miamies oppesed them & killed four men & wounded three and five are missing. Their arrival has caused much distress in the Village, but I flatter myself, at the same time, I can assure you that it is an evil for good. They are enraged they ask you by sixteen branches of Porcelaine, which I have charged La Fourche to hand you, to assist them, also the Outogoy & Sottu. They wait with impatience for your answer. They will find 300 warriors but this is not sufficient to attack Post Vincennes & the Miamie. They request you to send them some ammunition & musquets. La Fourche has answered them that he has always tried to do your will. I have rendered eleven canoes useless at the entrance to the river & I think with twelve others, bark as well as wood, to reach Michilimackinac with every one excepting the two who you ordered to keep watch over the rest of the baggage. If they are not sent to look for the goods of these poor unfortunates, they will be entirely ruined. They recommend themselves to Your benevolence, there are the cargoes of two vessels at the entrance of this river, without counting what we bring ourselves. La Fourche & all the other Savages have behaved as faithful subjects of His Majesty.

You will find that I am a long time on the way, when the canoes are rotten, like those you sent me, it is not possible to execute your orders, according to your desire. If it is possible to send me 50 gun, by a little Indian canoe, without that God knows when I can get off. You will find enclosed the census of all the inhabitants of this place. Nothing more.

I have the honor to be with Respect.

Mon Gouverneur

Your very humble & very obedient Servant

C. Ainse

St Joseph the 30th June 1780

Endorsed:—Letter from M. Ainse to Lt Gov Sinclair 30th June 1780.

[B 97-2 p 370]

CENSUS

Census of every woman, child & slave resident at the Post of St. Joseph. viz.

In the house of M. Chevalier:

Mr. Chevalier,

Daujinné,

Gibaut,
Pieniche,
Youtra Junior,
Mde Chevalier,
Md Youtra, her daughter
Raby Tany,
Lizette Panize,
Angelique panize & his child.

In the house of Seur Marcot:

Marcot,
Mad Marcot & four children,

In the house of Mad St Germain:

Mad St Germain her daughter & her son.

In the house of Sieur Morin:

Morin,
Md Morin three children boys.

In the house of Mr. Caron:

Mr Caron,
Md Caron,
Marianne Panize & her child.

In the house of M. Pre Hurtebize and his employees:

Mr Pre Hurtebize,
Rolle,
Lognon,
Gervais.

In the house of Pieniche Chevalier:

Prche Chevalier, in war,
His wife & three children.

In the house of Sieur Rode:

Rode,
His wife & child.

Names of private persons each one in his house.

Joseph Hurtebize,
Youtra,
Dursan,
La Douceur,
Langloy,
Duchenan,
Counol.

[B 97 2 p 573]

FROM LIEUT. GOV. SINCLAIR UNADDRESSED

Sir, I have the honour to put under this inclosure for Your Excellency Monsieur Durrands Bond, with some Papers, which were reported to Captain Brehm.

Monsr. Durrand has behaved with propriety during his stay here, but appears to have been involved in the general Defection of the Illenois—

I have the honour to be Sir, Your Excellency's most obedt & most humble Servant

Patt Sinclair Lt Govr.

Michilimackinac 3rd July 1780.

[B 97 2 p 381]

GENERAL HALDIMAND TO MAJOR DE PEYSTER

Quebec, July 6th, 1780.

Sir, I have received your Letters of the 16th & 17th of May and of the 1st ultimo by Mr. McComb & Mr. Perault, covering a Bill in favor of the former & intercepted Letters to Colonel Clark & Todd and reporting the measures you had taken to cheque the advances of the Rebels upon the Ohio, and to dispossess them of the Post at St. Vincennes.

It gives me pleasure that you have viewed the dangerous encroachments of the numerous People said to have taken refuge from the oppression of Congress in the Country of Kentuck in so proper a Light & that you have provided against the consequences, in which it is my desire that you vigorously persist, as well to prevent their becoming formidable in the Vicinity of our Posts as to secure to the Indians their natural right to that Country, confirmed to them by Treaty, which Justice as well as Policy requires we should attend to.

I hope the Indians will heartily take part in a measure so intimately connected with their Welfare, and that those who accompanied Captain Bird will act faithfully and with such Vigor as must effectually ensure his success—but it is distressing to reflect that notwithstanding the vast treasure lavished upon these People, no dependance can be had on them, and that the most trifling circumstances, altho' ever so false or absurd will divert them from a Pursuit of the last Consequence, as in the Instance, mentioned in your Letter of the French man's report to those on their way to Post Vincennes, by which a good opportunity & much time has been lost, besides the Expence of a new Equipment to the War Party. You no doubt represent in Council the absurdity of this conduct, & paint the evil consequences that cannot fail to result from it. You would do well ever to remind them of it, and if your agreements can be strengthened by expressing my knowledge of the affair, my astonishment & displeasure at their conduct, I would have it done. It is unfortunate that French man could not be taken hold of, to be made an example of. As these are the most dangerous Enemies we can have, do not hesitate, where you have well founded suspicion, to seize them & send them here in Irons, giving me your Reasons in writing, I hope those of that description at Post Vincennes will be taken proper notice of.

In regard to the Prisoners who multiply so fast with you, should you find it necessary, a Part of them must be sent to this part of the Province, although we are equally at a loss to find room for them. The infamous Behaviour of the Rebels to our Prisoners, in variety of Instances, particularly in the case of Lieut. Governor Hamilton & the Troops taken with him, who are still confined to a dungeon upon scanty & bad Provisions, and their obliging many (even in the character of Gentlemen) to work for their Maintenance would sufficiently justify a Retaliation I wish to forbear, but if the number of your Prisoners become inconvenient, you will please to employ as many in the works as you can with safety trust abroad at a time—to work under a Guard if necessary, giving them a Ration of Provisions, and allowing them the same Pay as your Labourers have, which must be applied to cloathe them. The air and exercise will preserve their Health, and there is no doubt of their being treated with proper tenderness. Those who will not comply, you will please to send down in close confinement.

The list of Indian officers is at every Post so long & the expense so very great, that I rather wish to diminish than augument their numbers. But if Mr. du Quindre is so very useful a man, he must of course be employed and I should imagine as a Lieut. upon the usual Pay of a Dollar per Day.

His services may hereafter entitle him to something more.

I have accepted your Bill for the amazing sum of £64,035 8s 8½d. The appearance of such drafts in so regular & so quick a succession, naturally laid me to reflect upon their fatal consequences to the nation, the Difficulty (not at present thought of) that will be experienced in getting them passed at Home. I am far from attributing this Evil to indifference, or unhandsome conduct of the officers under whom the Expence is incurred, yet I cannot help being persuaded, from Comparison, that a stricter & earlier attention to this essential circumstance, would have prevented Evils, which it is now very difficult to repair—and long habit of Indulgence has created wants with the Indians, which otherwise they would never have experienced, such as fine Saddles & many Luxuries carefully exhibited to their view by the all grasping Trader. I think it would be cruel to deny these poor people who are employed by us, such marks of our attention & regard as are necessary to their comfort—every shilling beyond that is superfluous to them & a loss to Government, nor is it in a Political view necessary, for however they may threaten to forsake us, we must know it is impossible they can exist without our aid, the Rebels not having necessaries sufficient for their own wants, and consequently unable to supply theirs. I am likewise satisfied that the expense has been greatly increased by permitting persons in Government Employ to become Traders, few of whom have virtue enough to consider the characters independently of each other. I must therefore desire your particular attention to the conduct of such as may be at present in that Predicament, which the Times make it necessary still to employ, and that in future, upon no account whatever to suffer any Person under your command to be even *concerned* in Trade while in any appointment of the Crown. I should likewise think it possible in a great measure, to curtail the Indian Presents by representing to them the impossibility of gratifying their unnecessary demands, from the enormous expense attending it. That they shall be supplied with every article that comfort requires, but not with Superfluities. I am very sensible that the persecution which a commanding officer at one of those Posts must go through from the Indians continually exciting by the avidity of the Trader, to demand, is very great—but as in those Situations, the most Essential part of their Duty is to attend to the Expenditure of the Public Money, I am pursuaded it will be cheerfully borne.

I have received your Letter accounting for the expenses at Michilimackinac. Particular Notes and Remarks of the kind, specifying Services, &c from Time to Time will be satisfactory to me, and may hereafter be useful. I must therefore desire you will by way of Journal, note them in such manner as to refresh the memory should it be necessary to refer to them.

I am Sir &c.

[signed] FRED: HALDIMAND.

Major De Peyster.

Endorsed: Copy No 4 To Major De Peyster at Detroit July 6th Copy entered in Book marked B No 2 Page 14.

[B 122 p 506.]

LIEUT. COL. MONTGOMERY TO MAJOR DE PEYSTER

SIR, Mr. Philip Dejeau having at the Instance & through the Intercession of Mr. Bentley obtained permission from the Governor & Council of this State to come to this Country on his Parole, & applying to me to go to

Detroit, I offered to comply with his request on his taking the oath of neutrality which he did not think proper to do. Notwithstanding which as he is extremely anxious to have his family with him until a Cartel takes place for the Exchange of Prisoners & well knowing the Disposition of the State of Virginia under which I have the Honour to serve that it is not their intention by any means to oppress, but as far as in them lay to alleviate all such Persons as the fate of arms shall deliver into their hands. I have therefore at his particular requisition granted him a Party under my Protection to go to Detroit in order if you should think meet to conduct his family to this country. I hope they will be properly received, begging leave to assure you that I am inspired thereto by no other motives whatever than those of humanity, in which I have no doubt from your known character but you will most readily concur with me.

I have the honour to be Sir, your most obedt & very humble servt.

JNO. MONTGOMERY

Lt Col. Commant Fort Clark at Kaskaskias in the Illinois Country 6th July 1780.

Art. Schuyler De Peyster Esqure.

[B 122 p 513]

FROM GENERAL HALDIMAND UNADDRESSED

QUEBEC 7th July 1780

SIR, Having naturally reflected upon the vast experience uncertainty and difficulties attending the Transports of Provisions to the Upper Posts, and for the better accommodation and support of His Majesty's Loyal Subjects, who driven from their homes, take refuge at Niagara, I am come to a resolution to reclaim the land granted by Messessagua to Sir William Johnson for the Crown, situated on the south west of the river opposite to the Fort, directions of which will be communicated to you by another letter, which Land will be divided into several lots, and distributed to such Loyalists who are capable of improving them, and desirous of procuring by industry a comfortable maintenance for their families until such times as, by peace, they shall be restored to their respective homes, should they be inclined to quit their situation at Niagara.

As the above mentioned grant of land will be reclaimed at the Expense of Government, and of course remain at all times the sole property of the crown and annexed to the Fort, Those who settle upon it are not to consider that they have the smallest right to any part thereof, the produce alone being their property. They will hold their possessions from year to year, which will be granted to them by the Commander in Chief for the time being according to their merits. If at any time they should remove, either from inclination or by order of the Commanding officer they are to have permission to dispose of their crops, stock of cattle &c and a reasonable allowance will be made by them for their improvements. For their further encouragement no rent will be required of them. They will be allowed a reasonable quantity of provisions for the space of twelve months after they are put in possession of their Lots Steel Mills, Ploughs and other implements of Husbandry will be furnished them gratis, and you will please to afford them every assistance, whether of horses or otherwise as shall be in your power to those whose sobriety Industry and good conduct may entitle to such Indulgencies.

Some part of the land being cleared, and all of it being fertil it is expected that in a short time the produce will be considerable. The settlers are therefore to understand that the produce of their farms over and above their own consumption is not to be removed from the Post, but disposed of the Commanding officer for the use of the Troops, and not to Traders or accidental Travellers

I am &c

(signed) F. H.

[B 96 2 p 145]

GENERAL HALDIMAND TO MAJOR DE PEYSTER

QUEBEC July 13th 1780.

SIR, Having maturely reflected upon the vast Expence, uncertainty & difficulty attending the Transport of Provision to the Posts, and the evil consequences that may attend the Kings Service from being limitted in that so necessary an article I am come to a Resolution to cultivate a sufficient Quantity of Ground at each, which I expect will in a short time produce, if not enough for its consumption, sufficient, considerably to diminish the Transport. I have therefore to desire you will immediately reclaim for His Majesty's use, the Ground commonly known by the name of Hog-Island and appropriate it to the above mentioned Purpose, *exactly* upon the same *Terms* and *Footing* with those at Niagara, agreably to the enclosed Articles. If you have not any Persons who are fit for this undertaking Lieut. Colonel Bolton will probably be able to supply you from Niagara.

I am the more desirous to employ Loyalists, as well as because it is a present relief for them, as that they are in general expert Farmers. It will not be necessary to send to Detroit as to Niagara the necessary implements of Husbandry as they are to be procured there. You will therefore provide them in the same Proportion, and give every assistance your Garrison will admit of to forward the success of so essential an object. As I wish to make Mrs. McDougal a reasonable Compensation for what Houses &ca. may be found upon the Island, you will please to appoint proper Persons to apprise them and transmit to me their Report. In doing this, you will observe, that it is not intended an Estimation should be made of what money may have been laid out on Improvements, Fences &c. at present gone to decay, for which it is supposed Indemnification has been had by Rent & Returns from the Land, which can have no connection with the present appraisement.

I am Sir, &c

(signed) Fred: Haldimand.

Major De Peyster.

Endorsed:—No 5 Copy. To Major De Peyster at Detroit 13th July. Copy entered in Book marked B No 2 Page 17.

[B 122 p 514]

SECRETARY MATTHEWS TO LIEUT. GOV. SINCLAIR

Quebec 16th July 1780

Sir, An Express Just setting out for Carlton Island gives me an opportunity of obeying His Excellency the Commander in Chief's Commands by Transmitting to you the Enclosed Letters, one of which is left open for your Perusal, the other is a Duplicate—

I am, Sir, &c.

(signed) R. Mathews

Lieut. Gov'r Sinclair

[B 97-2 p 406]

MAJOR DE PEYSTER TO GENERAL HALDIMAND

Detroit the 19th July 1780.

Sir, I have the honor to acquaint your Excellency that Captain Bird has been successful against the Forts on Licking Creek. Copys of his Letters & Mr. McKee's, I forward to Lt. Col. Bolton to which I beg leave to refer you for particulars.

I have the honour to be with great respect,

Sir, Your Excellency's most humbl. & obed't serv't

At S. De Peyster

To His Excellency the Comm'r in Chief

Endorsed:—A 1780. From Major De Peyster 19th July. Rec'd 2 Aug't.

[B 122 p 516]

MAJOR DE PEYSTER TO CAPTAIN MCKEE

21st July, 1780.

Dr. Sir, This is only to acquaint you that Mr. Sulphlet and Shehée takes my boat to meet you at Roche debout, with them I send six half barrels of Pork, and fifteen bags of flour to be sent up to Roche debout for Capt. Bird till I can send a Vessel. This exclusive of what provision they take for you, &

As I shall soon see you I shall defer my Congratulations till that happy moment.

I am, Sir, Your hum'l serv't,

At. S. De Peyster.

To Capt. McKee,

Indian Affairs, M. G., III.

MAJOR DE PEYSTER TO SECRETARY MATTHEWS

Detroit the 25 July, 1780.

Sir, Major Lernoult commanded here at the time Fanchett's effects were seized, and, being convinced that the goods he was then in possession of had been taken from Mr. Riddley, (by what I can learn) ordered them to be returned to said Riddley, who has stated his account with Messrs. Fanchett, which I herewith enclose and beg you will let Monsr. Fanchett have it, so that he may know what to depend upon.

I am, Sir, Your most huml. & obed't servt,

At. S. De Peyster.

Capt. Mathews.

Endorsed 1780, From Major De Peyster 25th July, Rec'd 16th Aug't., concerning Touchet.
[B 122 p 517.]

RETURN

Return of Ordnance required for the Defence of the New Fort of Detroit, July 1780.

18 Inch Howitzer,	demanded
ditto Royal ditto	May 28th, 1779.

From Conductor Iony's Spare Cannon at Oswegatchie, demanded July 30th, 1779.

Cannon, &c.	Number.	Nature.	Length.		Weight.		
	"	prs.	Feet	Ins.	F.	Grs.	Lbs.
With a Large Proportion of Ordnance Stores.	13	18	11	..	48	..	..
	1	9	8	6	26	..	..
	2	9	8	6	27	..	..

Iron Trucks.	18 Prs.		12 Prs.		9 Prs.		6 Prs.		Total.
Demanded July 30, 1779.	Hind.	Fore.	Hind.	Fore.	Hind.	Fore.	Hind.	Fore.	
	2	2	4	4	4	4	8	8	36

HENRY DUVERNET, Lieut. R. R. A.

Endorsed return of Ordnance required for the defence of the Garrison of Detroit, July, 1780.
[B 122 p 518.]

ACCOUNT

The 6th AUGUST 1780.

Expenses incurred by Louis Jos. Ainssé of Michillimackinac in coming to Montreal to bring back the families of St Joseph which he came to find by order of Governor Sinclair.

Viz.

15 measures of wheat	at 50	750£
2 canoes	300	600
300 lbs of biscuit	150	400
for plumes for the canoes		200
for a guide		100
for steersmen for the same		300
		2350£

All the rest of the men were passengers.
[B 97-2-p 514]

GENERAL HALDIMAND TO MAJOR DE PEYSTER

QUEBEC 10th August 1780

SIR, I have received your Letter of the 27th June covering an Estimate of Indian presents necessary for 12 months. The Indians have been accustomed to receive so very liberally, that now their Demands are quite unlimited. I have always thought the Presents too generally distributed, and am of opinion that Discrimination would not only diminish the expence, but materially forward the Service. You have now a good opportunity to make a trial of it, by distinguishing those Nations or Individuals who were most hearty in support of Captain Bird, and most attentive to the Execution of his measures and by retaining or lessening the presents of the others.

It evidently appears that the Indians in general, wish to protract the War, and are most happy when most frequently fitted out—it is impossible they can draw resources from the Rebels, and that absolutely depend upon us, for every Blanket they are covered with— I am far from wishing to curtail the advantages, these poor People ought to deserve from their Services, but to cloath & feed the Idle & undeserving, it is certainly if it can be avoided, improper.

Their conduct with Captain Bird is highly reprehensible, they have incessantly reproached the Commanding officer for not sending Troops to assist them in preventing the Incursions of the Rebels, and when with great Expence and at a very inconvenient time, you fitted out an Expedition for that purpose, they grew refractory, & instead of complying with & supporting the measures of their conduct, by which success must have been ensured, they abandoned him, followed their wild schemes, and by wantonly contrary to their Engagement, killing the Cattle, rendered it impossible for him to prosecute the Intention of his taking the Field.

Lieut. Governor Sinclair in one of his Letters says that "Major Gamble writes me from Detroit that many complaints are sent against me." I fear there are Persons at Michilimackinac or its Dependencies who convey Reports from thence to Detroit prejudicial to him, & tending to create Jealousies & Discontents between the Commanding officers of these Posts.—I am persuaded that your zeal & wishes for the King's Service are equally strong, having both the same object, only in view, there can be nothing wanting but a perfect confidence in each other, joined to the abilities you possess, to give success to every measure undertook in that Country; for I am persuaded you both think too liberally to suffer any little difference of opinion, (if such there is) to lead you from that sense of duty, which distinguishes the perfect officer from the lukewarm croud. You would therefore do well at once to lay open to Lieut. Governor Sinclair whatever reports of the kind may have reached you, whether by Letter or otherwise, with the name of those who have circulated them, and I shall desire him to do the same for your Information, by which means, these mean disturbers of Tranquility & of the Public Service, will be brought to light and discouraged.

Altho' I consider St. Joseph's from its situation naturally more dependent on Michilimakinac, & of course more immediately under the direction of Lieut. Governor Sinclair, yet, as the Indians of that place sometimes resort to Detroit(and always expect an answer to what they may have to propose) you and Captain Sinclair should mutually inform each other of what passes & perfectly coincide in whatever is to be recommended to them to regulate their conduct—

Whatever has been hitherto the custom in regard to trading to Saguenant Bay, or other Places in the Vicinity, either from Michilimakinac or Detroit, I would have punctually observed, subject at all Times to whatever changes the Exigencies of the Service may require. These matters cannot possibly be determined except by you & Capt. Sinclair, who, there cannot be a doubt will cordially unite, in whatever measures are best calculated to promote the King's Service.

Messrs Finchley & Fisher are from their conduct & connections very unfit Persons to trust at a Distance, & where there is any possibility of holding any kind of Intercourse with the Colonists—I should therefore think it very unsafe to permit them to winter from Detroit, or in the summer to give them a Latitude of which they can take advantage—the former was disarmed by Lieut. Governor Hamilton, much suspected by Major Lernoult & other officers at Detroit & the other has always born a doubtful character independent of his connections.

I am &c

(signed) Fred: Haldimand

Major De Peyster.

Endorsed:—No 6 Copy 1780 To Major De Peyster commandt at Detroit of the 10th August Copy entered in Book marked B No 2 Page 17.

[B 122 p 519]

GENERAL HALDIMAND TO MAJOR DE PEYSTER

Quebec 10th August 1780.

Sir, I have received your Letter of the 19th ultimo reporting Captain Bird's success against the Forts on Licking Creek, the particulars of which were forwarded to me by Lieut. Colonel Bolton.

I recommend to your attention to paint to the Indians in the strongest terms the distressing and evil consequences of their perverse conduct in not supporting the measures planed for the effectual destruction of their Invaders & the difficulties they have thrown in the way of any future attempts for that purpose.

I have wrote more fully to you upon this subject in a letter of this date.

The Barrack Master at your Post having represented that the Straw necessary for Bedding for the Troops, is not only extravagently dear, but very difficult to be procured. You will please to give orders that the Troops shall be supplied with that article by the Inhabitants, at the rate allowed by Government, this they cannot think hard, as the Troops are not quartered upon them & kept there for no other purpose than to protect them.

I am Sir &c

(signed) FRED HALDIMAND.

Major De Peyster.

Endorsed: Copy, To Major De Peyster at Detroit 10th August.

[B 122 p 523]

BOMBARDIER HOMAN TO CAPTAIN BIRD

HON'D SIR, Three days after the departure of Mr. Lorimer, I received Intelligence of the Rebels approaching to Cheteekothee, upon which I purpos'd to take the five horses belonging to Mr. Lorimer, and transport the Ordnance to the Ottawa Village and to conceal the loose Shot & Shells in the Wood—and in case of a close approach of the Enemy, before I could remove the fix'd ammunition, to destroy it. We sought for the Horses & could find but four—and when we came to harness them and were preparing to go: an Indian who resides here came & took two away in lieu as he said, of two that Mr. Lorimer had borrowed of him to come to Detroit, and also took a young horse that had not been used to work, as he pretended through friendship to Mr. Lorimer, least we should spoil him, so I was reduced to only one, with which & our assistance we drew the Gun a considerable way into the Wood, not near any Road and digged a hole & buried it so securely, that no one could even suspect of such a thing being concealed there.

The smaller Ordnance, loose shot and shells &c we concealed in different parts of the Wood. I am afraid you'll say I might have conquer'd the Indian, so perhaps we might have killed the whole, he having two or three more with him; but I could not tell what might be the consequences of beginning a War with the Indian—I beg pardon for running on thus, I ought to have left those remarks to your superior Judgment.

The 13th Instant—Silver heels (an Indian Chief) came here & informed us of the Rebels having evacuated the Indian Country, after having destroyed Cheteekothee & the Pickawee Towns. They left it on the night of the 9th inst. Their sudden departure was owing to the desertion of the Frenchman you gave in charge of Delaware Jack to bring to Detroit, whom he took to the Pickawee Town and kept him at his house: He informed the Rebels of Mr. Lorimer's taking the man from thence in order to bring to Detroit; they had supposed the man to be dead in the Bush. The Indians got this intelligence from a Rebel Prisoner they took, whom they afterwards burnt. They also killed all the male Prisoners that were able to desert and give intelligence—it was at those two towns only that they killed the Prisoners. The Indians in the different skirmishes, had six men killed and one man & one woman taken Prisoners. What losses the Rebels sustained is not known, but the prisoner informed them of two of the Colonels being killed, and Silver heels has forgot their names. Rogers the Prisoner was missing when the Chief came away; but they harbour too good opinion of him to think he is deserted. The Rebels killed the Woman by ripping up her Belly & otherwise mangling her—they also opened the graves of the Indians that had been buried several months, and scalp'd them.

I have sent to Roche de bot for two Bags of Flour & two Cags of Pork, which is more than a month's provision; but it will be an even load for the horses—I am not suffered to take more than two.

Please to let me have the honour of hearing from you soon.

I am Sir, Your most obliged obedient humble servant

(signed) Wm Homan Bombr. Royel Artillery.

Lormier's House Augt 15th 1780.

To Captain Bird.

Endorsed:—Copy of a letter from Wm. Homan Bombr at Lorimer's House to Capt. Bird at Detroit dated August 16th, 1780. Copy B entered in Book marked B No 3 Page 8.

[B 122 p 523]

MAJOR DE PEYSTER TO GENERAL HALDIMAND

Detroit the 18th August 1780.

Sir, Mr. Alexr. McKee arrived here on the 4th of August with Captain Bird. He left this again on the 16th upon our hearing that the Rebels were advancing into the Indian country in hopes to be in time to assemble the Indians to act in a Body, giving them assurances of soon being supported, by Capt Hare with his detachment of Rangers, and Captain Chabert's Canadian Volunteers.

During Mr. McKee's short stay here, I conversed with him upon the subject of his expectations when he gave me to understand that Lord Dunmore had ordered two Battalions of Provincials to be raised in the Vicinity of Fort Pit.

That the command of one was given to a Mr. Connolly who on his way to Fort Pit was taken Prisoner, and actually has his Pay & Rank at Philadelphia where he still remains confined. That a commission of Lt. Colonel of the other Battalion was made out & sent to him, Alexr McKee, which commission was taken on its way to Fort Pit, and destroy'd by which means he never received it, and finds himself thereby deprived of the rank intended for him, after having made some disbursements on account of said Battalion. I know of no way to serve Mr. McKee here unless a small provincial corps of loyalists were to be raised for the defence of the frontiers of Detroit.

I have the honor to be with great respect Sir

Your most humb & obedt servt

AT. S. DE PEYSTER.

His Excellency General Haldimand.

Endorsed:—A 1780 From Major De Peyster at Detroit of the 18th August Recd 16th Sepr with enclosure.

[B 122 p 527]

SPEECH OF THE DELAWARES AND SHAWNESE ASSEMBLED AT THE UPPER SHAWNES VILLAGE, TO THEIR FATHER MAJOR DE PEYSTER COMMANDANT OF DETROIT. AUGT 22ND 1780.

Father! This belt we now present you with is that which we have spoke to you twice before upon; and as our words then made a proper impression upon your Heart; we are now induced to send it to you a third time.

Father! Upon the first certain Intelligence we received of the Virginians design to strike our Village, we sent in a deserter from them, who we thought would have given you sufficient information to have afforded us your timely assistance. The person he was charged with had also a string of wampum accompanied with a piece of tobacco to those of your children who were round you to inform them of our danger and excite their support; as all the force we were able to collect was too small to withstand their number; And now Father we have to inform you of the destruction of Four of our Villages by them, and though the loss we have met with of our Friends in the resistance we made against them is not considerable, yet our distress is no less, on account of our women and children who are left now destitute of shelter in the woods or Food to subsist upon. Our warriors have not now even Ammunition to hunt for, or defend them; And we have received certain advice that another Army of our Enemies (are preparing to come from Fort Pit) of two thousand men, and are destined to strike you at Detroit as well as us in their way; therefore we desire all your children to continue in the same mind of coming out here to meet them, tho' those who have done us mischief are gone. Father! Here we have determined to make our stand, and wait to hear from you. It is needless for us to say more than this to you, we have represented our situation, from which you must be sensible how far it is incumbent on you to assist us, being mutually engaged in the same cause.

Whatever you are pleased to send let us be acquainted thereof, and we will send our horses to the Miamis for it. we beg your answer may be speedy and that this Belt be returned with it.

A Black Belt of eight Rows.

[B 122 p 533.]

CERTIFICATE OF MERCHANTS

The undersigned, being assembled at the house Mr. W. Gulpin, in consequence of a notice from Captain McNamara, declaring that have never suffered any tyranny, oppression nor restraint in business since the Lieut Governor has commanded this post.

Given at Michilimakinac this 22nd of August 1780

David McCrae.	Etne Campion.
Matt Lessey.	A. Reilhé
Marechepac.	John Macnamara.
John Kay.	Henry Bostwick.
James Aird.	M. Augé.
Benjamin Lyon.	Grignond.
John Sayer.	Guillon.
Shaw & McDonald.	Jas. Bullony.
George Skeech.	

Endorsed:—Certificate of the Merchants of Mackinac.

[B 97-2 p 470]

MR. CALVE TO GENERAL HALDIMAND

MICHILIMACKINAC The 23rd August 1780

To M. Frederick Haldimand Governor General & Commander in Chief of North America &c. &c. &c.

SIR, Pardon the liberty I take in addressing the present to you, which is only caused by the reception which the Sacqs, Renards, & the Aimaiois as well as myself had from Lieut Governor Sinclair, Commander of Michilimakinac, on the return of our campaign, which surprised me extremely as I had no reason to expect it. After all the pains and trouble I have taken to maintain the nations in the true intentions of Government & to manage, in all things the interest of His Majesty, I cannot then penetrate what are the causes of this sad return unless I may judge that it is from false reports made by the Commandants & Interpreters of this district. In consequence I have thought it my duty to prove that my conduct has been irreproachable, I have applied many times to Lieut. Govr Sinclair, for this purpose, without having had the advantage of being listened to, it causes me much grief to be thus treated without reason, wherefore I pray you to be convinced of my assurance that no one can be more respectful than he who has the honor to be

Sir Your very humble & faithful subject

J. Calve.

Addressed:—To His Excellency Frederick Haldimand Governor General & Commander in chief of North America &c. at Quebec

Endorsed:—1780 From M. Calvé Indian Interpreter Michilimakinac 23d August Recd 23rd September.

[B 97-2 p 485]

FROM LIEUT. GOV. SINCLAIR. UNADDRESSED

Sir, I have the honor to send Your Excellency this my letter of advice for the Sum of Two Hundred & thirty Eight Pounds N. Y. Currency, drawn in favour of Lieut. Mercer of the 8th Regmt.

To support the Credit of Promissory notes issued for carrying on the Works, I have been obliged to draw without Printed Bills, the necessity of which I pray Your Excellency to consider.

I have the honor to be with the most perfect respect.

Your Excellency's most
obedient Humble Servant

Patt Sinclair
Lt. Gov'r

Michilimackinac 23 Aug't 1780—

[B 92-2 p 494]

LIEUT. GOV. SINCLAIR TO MAJOR DE PEYSTER

(No Date)

Sir, I have memorialed his Excellency the Com'r in Chief for the recovery of the perquisites of my appointment of Lieutenant Governor of Michilimackinac from the 1st day of May 1775, in which I promise myself much candour on your Part—

I am, Sir,
Your most obedt. humble Servant
(signed) Patt Sinclair
Lt Gov'r

Major De Peyster
[B 98 p 306]

MAJOR DE PEYSTER TO GENERAL HALDIMAND

Detroit the 31 August 1780

Sir, I am honored with your Letters of the 6th & 13th July to which every attention shall be paid, as soon as possible: being at present so involved in business that I scarce know which way to turn me.

The Rebels I hear have left the Shawanese country, after having destroyed the corn & burnt the Villages. The wretched Women and Children are beginning to come in for Provisions, as at Niagara.

The Enemy I am told threaten a visit to the Wiandotts at Sandusky, some reports say that 1200 men are actually in march for that place.

Captain Hare with the Rangers & Canadian Volunteers, tho' little can be expected from the latter, are moving to oppose them with all the Indians Mr McKee can muster. At this instant, accounts from Capt. Mompesson, advise that 200 Pirogues with Creoles, are on their way to Michilimakinac to revenge the stroke lately made upon them. I however am inclined to think, that no force from that country will attempt that Post at a season, when they have so strong a Militia and that their Expedition must be against the Indian country only. At any rate in the present situation of affairs here, I cannot pretend to weaken this Garrison having so lately sent off considerable detachments & having six & thirty sick, with the New Fort in the condition lately reported. I am not yet called upon, & it is hoped the news like much of the like nature may prove false, by the time it is confirmed, the Rangers may be back, when I shall not hesitate to send of a Detachment to their assistance.

Monsr. Du Quindre is just arrived from St. Joseph's with 200 Pottewatimies & one Scalp, taken near the falls of the Ohio, by a few who followed him that far, his main body left him on hearing that the Piankishaws had killed some of their people.

Still those Scoundrels have the Impudence to come in a body & require a reward for their Services. I have positively refused them any presents, have given them a severe reprimand, and have made them promise to bring in the traders who infest the Pee, & who have hitherto given them such bad Council, before they shall taste of the King's Bounty.

They are setting off for that purpose, but I fear the Michilimakinac news when it comes to their knowledge will stop them.

Please Sir, to excuse the hurry of my letters, being cooped up in Council from morning to night, often obliged to dispatch business amidst a confusion of languages, and in thick fumes of sickening smoke, which is the case at present.

I have the honor to be with great respect Sir,

Your Excellency's most huml & obedt servt

AT S. DE PEYSTER

His Excellency the Commr in Chief

Endorsed:—No 3 Enterd 1780. From Major De Peyster 31st August Recd. 27th Sepr. Copy in Book marked B No 3 Page 6.

[B 122 p 537]

FROM MAJOR DE PEYSTER UNADDRESSED

DETROIT 31 Augt 1780.

DEAR SIR, I received your Letter, and thank you for the contents—I now must beg leave to address you upon a very dry subject, which is that you will please to make my most respectful Compliments to Genl. Haldimand & tell him that I have lately heard that the Justices of the Peace here, have no power to meddle in money matters—whereas we thought they had a right to decide small differences, not exceeding ten Pounds, as used to be in the Colonies. Now if some such power, & for a greater sum too, is not given, this place will go into confusion, as it will hardly do, to summons People to appear at Montreal, for such trifling affairs, &, if they are not, there will be no recovering small debts. The Dedimus which came up for Captain Lernoult to swear in Mr. Williams is laying here. I wrote to have one come up to impower Mr. A Macomb to qualify both Mr. Williams and myself but none came, please at a proper season to mention these matters & write me something satisfactory about them, keeping this hurried scrawl out of the sight of those who cannot make favourable allowance for the hurry I am at present in.

I am dr. Sir your humble & obedt. servt.

A. S. DE PEYSTER.

P. S. Please acquaint His Exy. that the first 96 Barrels of Rum arrived here the 24th Inst.

[B 122 p 540]

MAJOR DE PEYSTER TO GENERAL HALDIMAND

SIR, The inclosed letters were brought from the Ouiat by Express, I shall make no answer to them, till I have your commands for so doing.

I have the honor to be with great Respect, Sir,

Your Excellency's most huml. & obedt. servt.

AT. S. DE PEYSTER.

To His Excelly Genl. Haldimand.

Endorsed: A 1780. From Major De Peyster at Detroit no Date. Recd. 16th Sept. with inclosure.

[B 122 p 541]

Return of Ordnance required for the Defense of the Garrison of Detroit Sept. 3rd 1780.

1 Eight inch Hawbitz	demanded May 28th 1779
1 Royal Hawbitz	ditto ditto
with proportion of Stores—for the above	

Cannon demanded July 30th 1779.	Number.	Nature.	Length.	Weight.
		prs.	Feet Ins.	C.
From Conductor Jones's	13	18	11.1	48
Return of Spare Cannons	1	9	8.6	26
at Oswequatchi	2	9	8.6	27

Iron Trucks demanded July 30th 1779.	18 prs.		12 prs.		9 prs.		6 prs.		Total.
	Hind.	Fore.	Hind.	Fore.	Hind.	Fore.	Hind.	Fore.	
	2	2	4	4	4	4	8	8	36

HENRY DU VERNET, Lt. R. R. A.

N. B. A large proportion of ammunition required for the above, with 50 barrels of Powder.

Endorsed:—Return of Ordnance required for the defence of the Garrison of Detroit Sepr. 3rd 1780.

[B 122 p 542]

MAJOR DE PEYSTER TO CAPTAIN MCKEE

Detroit the 8th Sept 1780

Dear Sir, I did myself the pleasure of writing to you by George Girty's Companion the young Delaware, sending back the belt with a Speech.

Nothing material has occurred since, yet I cannot let slip this favorable opportunity of assuring you of my good wishes.

If it is possible to obtain C Riddles wife, and the remainder of his children you will do me an infinite pleasure.

Mrs. De Peyster and the Gentlemen join In Compliments to you and the Gentlemen with you.

I am Dr. Sir Your Huml. & obedt. Servt.

At. S. De Peyster

To Alexr McKee Esq.
Indian Affairs M. G. III

FROM MAJOR DE PEYSTER UNADDRESSED

Detroit 8th Sepr. 1780.

Sir, I have this day drawn on Your Excellency favor of Messrs. Macomb, Edgar & Macomb four Bills at 60 Days sight for Forty two thousand seven hundred & fourteen Pounds, seven shillings & eleven pence ½ New York Currency being for disbursements for His Majesty's Service in the different Departments at this Post as pr. Accounts herewith transmitted which I hope Your Excellency will honor.

I am Sir, Your Excellency's most humbl & obedt servt

At. S. De Peyster,
Major to the King's Regt. Commanding.

Endorsed:—1780, From Major De Peyster 8th Sept. Recd 27th.

[B 122 p 544]

MAJOR DE PEYSTER TO GENERAL HALDIMAND

DETROIT, the 9th Sepr. 1780.

SIR, In complyance with your Commands I have had the Buildings on the Island appraised by two able Master Carpenters whose report I herewith Inclose.

I propose to settle Mr. Riddle's family, with three other Families on the Island, as soon as possible, reserving part of the meadow ground for the grasing of the King's cattle.

I have the honour to be Sir, Your Excellency's most huml & obedt servt

AT. S. DE PEYSTER.

His Excelly Gen Haldimand

Endorsed:—1780. From Major De Peyster 9th Sepr., Recd 27th.

* * * * * * * * * *

Enclosure

Appraisement of the Buildings on Hog Island the 5th September 1780 by Nathan Williams & Jean Batiste Craite, Sworn appraisers

one Dwelling House	£250	0	0
one do do	40	0	0
one do do	10	0	0
An old Barn without a Top	18	0	0
a Fowl House	6	0	0
Some timber	10	0	0
New York Curry	£334	0	0

Appraised by us the fifth day of September 1780

NATHAN WILLIAMS
J B CRAISSTE.

[B 122 p 543]

SPEECH TO THE SHAWANESE, MINGOES &C.

UPPER SHAWANESE TOWNS Sepr 15th 1780.

Speech sent by a frenchman in the Rebel service at Fort Pitt to the Shawanese, Delawares, Mingoes, Hurons, & the nations in alliance with them.

CHILDREN, Once more I desire you to listen to me, upon my arrival last spring at Cooshawking, I then spoke to you and out of pity, endeavoured to represent the miseries that were likely to overtake you, pointing out at the same time the means that you might avoid them, to which I received no answer, not discouraged at this, about Harvest I spoke to you again upon the same subject, still anxious to save you from destruction, but you have rejected all my proposals for promoting your peace and tranquility, therefore all I had to say on that head is at an end; and perhaps what I am now going to say may be more agreeable to your inclinations as you seem determined to prosecute the warr, be strong, you shall have enough of it.

Children! All you who have struck the Virginians & continue to do so, strike your ancient Father the French, you strike the Spaniards & you strike six Towns of my dutyful children, who have joined me to punish those who persist in being disobedient; therefore all who have refused to embrace peace must prepare to fight, for be assured you will have all those nations to encounter, & in twenty days from the date hereof, they will approach your towns. I have now forewarned you of your danger, & if you still prefer listening to the English to peace, you will not only find the Virginian's Hatchet as sharp as theirs, but your antient Father the French have an ax as sharp as theirs, the Spaniards have one equally so, & the six towns of my children have a hatchet tho' small as sharp as theirs. Now my Children what is your dependence: inevitable ruin must be the fate of all who are found beyond Kooshawking.

A large White Belt, 12 rows with two rows of black wampum in the center, a square at one end & the figures of two Hatchets at the other.

Message from Colonel Broadhead commanding the Rebel forces at Fort Pitt to the Delawares of Whitstone.

Brothers, I call you by that name, but it is only those who listen to me, as I am convinced there is still some Indians of that Village who deserve my pity, I desire them to rise and come out of danger, I am now upon my feet and ready to strike all my Enemies in that Country, all beyond Kooshawking, I deem as such therefore you shall have twenty days to repair to that place, where I expect in that time to take all by the hand who comply, even those who have struck me upon appearing there as Friends shall be forgiven, but all who delay it longer must prepare to receive the discharge of my Guns.

2 small strings black & white Wampum.

The above messengers say they were informed that the Enemy are to come by four different ways, Expresses being sent to Kentucky to join an army coming by the Kenhawa at the Shawanese Villages. That Col. Broadhead with the main body is to march the road by the Tuskarawas to Sanduskie & to detach three hundred horse and eight hundred foot to cut of Whetstone village, the whole to form a rejunction at the Huron Villages, & from thence go against Detroit Eleven days is to come of the time allowed the Whetstone Delawares to go to Kooshawking. The Delawares, Shawanese & Mingoes present having considered the above speeches & Intelligences unanimously agreed to stand their ground and oppose the Enemy & to enable them to call for the assistance of their father the English & nations of Indians in their alliance, their chiefs speaking to the following Effect.

Friends & Brother Warriors! You have now heard the speech brought us in the name of the french, whom we formerly called father, accompanied with one from our Enemies the Virginians. We thought they were our only Enemies, but now find the french & Spaniards have joined them, therefore we must determine to defend ourselves like men against all who are their friends; they threaten us with immediate destruction, but friends the great Spirit who has placed us here has not made us for their disposal at will, & on him we must rely *& on him we must rely* & on the engagement of our father the English & their children, for it was for this purpose all the Indian nations made themselves one with them the better to enable them to oppose any Invasion of our Country, these Belts and Speeches shall be immediately sent to Detroit for our Father's consideration accompanied by this Belt, that has passed between us and which he knows has never spoke false he is wise and will soon send us an answer. In the meantime let us take courage, & watch our Enemies motions, tho' they have drove us from our Cornfields, our hearts are firm & we can never be conquered while our father the English and the six nations are upon their feet.

A Black Belt 7 Rows.

A twist of Tobacco was then sent to inform the Indians of Sanduskie of the above Intelligence & to enjoin them to watch the Enemy & another twist was delivered to call for the assistance of the Miamis.

Endorsed:—Speech sent by a Frenchman in the Rebel Interest at Fort Pitt, to the Shawanese, Delawares, Mingoes, &c.

Rec'd 28th at night.

[B 122 p 553.]

CERTIFICATE

Detroit the 18th September 1780

I do hereby certify that this account was presented to me at Michilimakinac, and that my Reason for not including it in my draught upon His Excellency the Commander in Chief was that a Rumour then prevailed that Mons'r Durand had made Lampoons upon the King which were sung at the Caskakias

signed A. Depeyster

Endorsed:—Memoire des Effets que Durand a laissé en Garde a Baptiste Pouite Sable, neigie Libe, à la Riviere du Chemin, dont M' Benet a donne ordre de prendre.

[B 98 p 286]

REASONS OF LIEUT. GOV. SINCLAIR

There appears to me an improbability that the Indians bordering on the Mississippi can be entirely prevented from visciting this Post annually, notwithstanding they are forbid to come, and were they disgusted by too severe treatment, or bad reception, after their arrival, the Traders in this country would suffer, *particularly those,* who have had merit in attaching them to Government and engaging their services when they were wanted—and if Traders amongst them who can be depended upon, are totally restrained from making any presents in their wintering grounds, a communication of Intelligence with the Post and between the Traders would be interrupted entirely, & there would be no means of employing an Indian untill he came first to the Post and thereby the opportunity of his service lost.

Endorsed:—Gov. Sinclairs reasons against discouraging totally the Mississippi Indians from coming to the Post, or against refusing them Presents.

[B 98 p 315].

GENERAL HALDIMAND TO LORD GEO. GERMAIN

QUEBEC 17th Sept 1780.

Lord Geo. Germain

MY LORD, The 27th Ultimo, I had the Honor of writing to Your Lordships by a Brig bound to Guernsay, which was unfortunately cast away, the Crew were saved & my letters returned, which I suppress, having now the Honor, by a vessel going north, about to make a second attempt to acknowledge your Lordships dispatch by the Danae Frigate, containing a secret letter dated the 8th of April—Letters no 23—24 & 25—

Their several contents I shall have the Honor to answer more fully by the first safe opportunity.

Your Lordship will have heard long before this can be received, that the Trade Fleet was dispersed at Sea, and that many of the ships are taken, it is I fear but too certain that the "True Briton" is of the number, but this misfortune happened so early, I hope it was known in time enough to be in part repaired this season.

There are but 14 ships of the Trade Feet arrived, and it is now too late to expect that any more of them will appear—The Rebel Papers are crowded with the Reports of their being carried in by their Privateers— I am however happy to acquaint your Lordship that "Ocean, Bridgewater, Argo & Hercules" Victuallers escaped, and that the "Nancy, Isabella, Weir, Sophia, Spring & Holmton" which sailed after, are safely arrived. the "Amphitrite" is lost in the Straits of Bellisle—The Convoy Frigates, with the "Hind" & Provincial armed vessels are cruizing to protect the Gulf—They have sent up three Rebel Privateers & it is reported that the Newfoundland Fleet have sent six into St. John's.

For the better security of the Trade & Posts in the lower part of the Province, I purchased a fine Vessel carrying 22 Guns, 6 & 9 pounders, which with two smaller Vessels well fitted out, I put under the command of Captain Young— I have lately had the mortification to hear that the former the "Wolff' is cast away upon the Island of St Peter's, owing entirely to a thick Fog & Tempestuous weather, The "Hind," very narrowly escaped the same fate, her Provisions, Guns & a great part of her rigging were saved.

By His Majesty's Sloop, "Swift," which sailed for New York on the 12th of July, with the return Transports, I had the honor of addressing Your Lordship to report the arrival of a reinforcement from the Southern Army, and that nothing of any moment had occurred in the course of the Winter, —I think it unnecessary to send a Duplicate of my Letter, having since received advice of the return of a Detachment from Detroit to opposes the advances of the Virginians upon the Ohio (who are successfully encroaching upon the most valuable Hunting Grounds of the Indians) three Forts were taken & destroyed, near 400 were made, many of them Women & Children, and a considerable number of Cattle killed. The Superiority of the Indians to the inconsiderable number of Troops that could be spared from the Garrison, their natural Fickleness & obstinacy, prevented sometimes more being effected,—The uncertainity which turn affairs might have taken in this part of the Province, & Provisions not having arrived in time for that tedious Transport, prevented my sending more Troops into that Distant Country, I am the more easy on this account, as the Posts of Niagara & Detroit are in a good state of defence. If the Western Indians were more attached & more interested, they might originally have prevented, & still may, the advances of the Enemy, but it is their interests to protract the War, that they may live in Indolence, receiving Presents which were at first indispensably necessary, & cannot now, with safety, be withheld from them, particularly as the Spaniards are become Masters of the Mississippi & can by that Channel supply their wants.

Joseph Brant & the Five Nations in general have been very active upon the Frontiers, the former has lately destroyed a very extensive settlement upon the Mohawk River, a considerable number of Cattle, Horses, Sheep &ca & a quantity of Grain.

I have lately received two Expresses from Sir H. Clinton, the first by Halifax, about six weeks on the way, advising me that Monsieur De Ternay was expected at Rhode Island, and that Canada was still supposed to be his object. His last Despatch informs me of the arrival of the French Fleet & Army at Rhode Island, & that from the lateness of the season & other circumstances their views appeared to be changed from this Province, against him, I nevertheless employ every possible endeavour in preparing for whatever may happen, I shall continue to do so, in expectation that they will undertake it in the Spring. In order in the mean time to divide the strength that may be brought against Sir H. Clinton, or to favor any operations his present situation may induce him to carry on, as well as to destroy the Enemie's supplies from the late plentiful Harvest, and to give His Majesty's Loyal Subjects an opportunity of retiring to this Province, I have fitted out two Parties of about 600 men each, besides Indians to penetrate into the Enemy's Country by the Mohawk River, & Lake George, the former being chiefly drawn from Niagara & to rendezvous at Oswego is already marched under the command of Sir J. Johnson, the other I shall send across Lake Champlain so as to appear at the same time. I flatter myself these movements will answer the purpose for which they are intended.

Sir H. Clinton has not mentioned the arrival of Admiral Graves, but reports affirm that he has blocked up the French Fleet at Rhode Island, this will render an attempt against Canada this year Impossible, yet, from the preparations formerly made by the Rebels and Monsieur De la Fayette, it is probable they may invade it by Land, for I have every day more reason to be confirmed in the opinion, I gave Your Lordship in my letter of the 14th of last September, and I have undoubted proofs that they have Emissaries in this Country, but more particularly at present.

I have the Honor to be &c &c &c

(signed)

FRED. HALDIMAND.

[B 54 p 324]

ACCOUNT

Amount of Lieut Governor Hamilton's Bills for my pay from the 24th September 1778 to the 24th April 1780 as Lieutenant to the Detroit Volun-

teers and Miter Indian Department at nine shillings sterling per diem £253 11
from the 24th April to the 24th September 1780........... 71 11

sterling £325 2

Governor Hamilton had assured those officers that had followed him on that unfortunate Campaign, his intercession with His Excelly. the Commander in Chief for the allowance of Batt & Forage.

Mr. Schieffelin prays that the above be paid him, if His Excelly. should think him entitled to the same agreeable to his appointments under the administration of His Excelly. the Commander in Chiefs' Predecessor (the 22nd June 1777 the date of his Commission)

Endorsed:—Lieut Scheflin.

[B 122 p 557]

GENERAL HALDIMAND TO MAJOR DE PEYSTER

QUEBEC 30th September 1780.

SIR, I have received your Letters of the 16th Ultimo with the several Enclosures.

Mr. Dejean's request of having his family removed to Post Vincennes, I by no means think it prudent to comply with, considering the disposition of the People there, & the Intercourse & Intimacy that would unavoidably follow—You will therefore please to acquaint him, that from the probability of these Troubles soon ending, his being but in part disengaged from his confinement & still subject to experience a Breach of Faith, so common with the Rebels in Regard of Prisoners, together with the Difficulties & Inconvenience as well to his family, as to the service, in transporting it thro' the Indian country. I cannot consent to its leaving Detroit at present.

I am &c.

(signed) FRED: HALDIMAND

Major De Peyster

Endorsed:—Copy 1780. To Major De Peyster commanding at Detroit of 30th Sepr sent 2nd Octr.

[B 122 p 560]

MAJOR DE PEYSTER TO GENERAL HALDIMAND

DETROIT 1st Octr 1780.

SIR, I am honoured with your letter of the 10th August, wherein you think the Presents are too generally distributed, and that discrimination would diminish the Expence. I can assure your Excellency that no goods are given to people who are altogether inactive, and that I have ever made a distinction according to the several merits, in the donation of the Goods, intended for the promotion of His Majesty's service, & I think I may safely affirm that in the treatment of Indians, I have hitherto stretched the cord to its utmost extent, whosoever shall hereafter give it another pull, must inevitably break the chain of alliance so necessary to subsist betwixt us & the Indians.

The Expences therefore do not arise from any Injuditious management, (having lately sent away 200 Pottawatamies empty handed till they perform a service pointed out to them) But from the number of Indians resorting to this Post since my arrival nearly double to what were ever here before. The Western Indians follow me, notwithstanding my endeavours to prevent them and I have brought over several wavering Nations.

Believe me, Sir! That, notwithstanding the enormous Indian account from the great attention I pay to the service taking nothing from report, which I may possibly in person attend to—I have & shall yearly save the Crown, great sums, even to the prejudice of my health which I shall ever do cherfully whilst your Excellency honours me with your confidence.

I have the honor to be with the greatest respect Sir

Your Excellency's most humbl & obedt servt

At. S. De Peyster

His Excellency Gen. Haldimand

Endorsed:—No 4 Entrd F. H. 1780. From Major De Peyster Commands at Detroit of the 1st October Recd 25th Copy in Book marked B No 3 Page 10

[B 122 p 561]

MEMORIAL OF LOUIS JOSEPH AINSSE

To His Excellency Frederick Haldimand General & Governor in Chief of all the Province of Quebec & Dependencies in America, Vice Admiral of the same, General and Commander in Chief of His Majesty's Troops in the said Province & Frontiers &c. &c. &c.

May it please Your Excellency.

The most humble memorial of Louis Joseph Ainssé formerly employed as Indian Interpreter at the Post of Michillimakinac.

The Petitioner has the honor to represent that he has served at the said Post in the said capacity, under the orders of different commanders, during the space of two years, with all the zeal & fidelity of which a good servant can be capable—from whom he has certificates which justify his advances

That last autumn, by agreement with Major De Peyster, he went to Montreal with his family to arrange his private affairs there, but under a promise which he made to the Commandant, to return to the said Post that year in the early spring having judged that his presence would be necessary to the service. Mr. Sinclair who had then arrived at the said post expressed his satisfaction to know that he would return to it.

That the 12th May last the Petitioner, to keep his promise, with the consent of Lieut Colonel Campbell equipped a canoe, the expense of which he advanced, to take him to Michillimakinac and took with him six Indians Foxes who were returning to their village. The expenses for this purpose according to the statement subjoined 2224 Livres of 20 sous.

When he arrived at the said Post Mr Sinclair received him favorably and immediately gave him orders, in writing, to go to St Joseph to bring with him to Michillimakinac, all the Canadian families who were settled there, viz Mr Chevallier his uncle. However delicate was his mission through the consequences which might result the memorialist passed over the difficulties &, animated by his usual zeal for the service, he accepted it without reply nor objection.

He left with six canoes in each of which were three canadians, he placed in each of the said canoes twenty Courtoreiller Indians, chosen by him. These Canoes were completely provided with the necessaries for the voyage by the general association with the exception of four barrels of rum which the petitioner furnished, according to the certificate subjoined by Dugay authorised to this effect by Mr. Sinclair £1200 currency of the said Post.

The Petitioner went to St Joseph happy enough to succeed & execute there punctually the orders with which he was charged. He placed in his canoes all the inhabitants with a part of their baggage & brought them to Michillimackinac. The expenses incurred by the Petitioner for this voyage, according to the statement subjoined, amounted to 2244 Livres of 20 Sous.

On arriving at Michillmackinac Mr Sinclair expressed to him all the satisfaction possible with his conduct he retained him during four days for services towards the Indians but on the fourth day the Petitioner believed that it was his duty to give notice that the Indians of La Baye [des Puans] having testified some discontent that other warriors who had done less at war were better treated; it was a matter of consequence to extinguish this jealousy. According to orders the petitioner presented them, they opened proceedings with Mr Sinclair by demanding two barrels of powder for their Village, at this demand he was excited & said to them, showing his hands that he would give them two handfuls. On this answer the Chief of the Foxes left & the next morning went away with his band very discontented.

That the fifth day Mr. Sinclair sent S. Gauthier, Interpreter, to find the Petitioner, he was much surprised on arriving at Mr. Sinclair's to hear him say these words: "Sir, I order you to stay in the Fort & I forbid you to leave it." He then perceived that, far from rendering him justice, he was looked upon with suspicion & a striking contrast also in the conduct of Mr. Sinclair in this respect, without any real foundation, & it grieved him beyond expression.

That the Petitioner seeing himself thus treated desired to obtain his permission to descend to Montreal & at the same time settle his accounts with Mr. Sinclair. He charged the said Mr. Dugay with this settlement, but on the presentation of his accounts, the answer of the Lieut. Governor was: "That Mr. Ainssee, Askin & Chevalier were rich enough to pay their own expenses, that besides he had only to apply to His Excellency."

On this report the Petitioner hazarded going to him, to inform himself of the truth of the Matter. His answer was: "That Dugay had misunderstood him," that he had not said these words to him & as the Petitioner would enter into the matter, he turned his back to him; on which he judged it convenient to retire.

That the Petitioner had in Merchandise at the said Post 2700 Livres of twenty sous, cash price at Montreal, he wanted to take them down, he asked permission & it was refused him; but Mr. Sinclair had told him that, if he left them at the cash price in Montreal, he would take them.

The Petitioner consented although he feared loss, & when they knew his adhesion, he required still a reduction of £700, to which the Petitioner would not consent, rather preferring to loose everything. Mr. Sinclair has had them placed & the Petitioner has neither the power to descend nor to dispose of them otherwise. He was then under the necessity of leaving the Post, to which he had gone only to render himself useful to the Service. Obliged to let horses, goods & cattle & to abandon the effects which he could then have disposed of with advantage, if he had not found himself covered with such disgrace. But to crown his unhappiness the permission to go is given him under the humiliating condition of giving a security of some considerable amount for his good behaviour and also on condition that he would take with him Mr. Chevalier, his family and as many other persons as would be possible. To this effect he fitted out two canoes, & was obliged a little beyond Michillimackinac to take a third, having ascertained that they were not sufficient to transport the people & their baggage.

This Expense according to the subjoined account amounted to 2350 Livres of twenty sous.

That the Petitioner having sacrificed his youth in the Upper Country, where he was engaged in Trade, believed that he could there some use his industry & his talents, in short, after having honored his engagements, he found himself with a little capital which he has employed here in landed property on which he can live with economy, and there is the great fortune with which Mr. Sinclair wishes to pay the expenses of the King.

That the Petitioner, convinced of the justice and integrity of your Excellency trusting also to the justice of his cause, & his good conduct in all respects, comes with a firm confidence to implore his assistance and protection.

1st. To obtain his reinstatement in the distinctif character of a good and faithful subject to his Majesty & the discharge of the outrageous security which Mr. Sinclair has laid him under.

2d. To ask your Excellency to take into consideration and examine the statements and certificates of expenses sub-joined amounting all together to the sum of 8018 Livres of twenty sous in order if the judges right to warrant the payment to the Petitioner.

3rd. To order likewise that the goods which Mr. Sinclair has detained at the said Post shall be paid for according to the price which like goods would sell for there. And finally the Petitioner believes himself to have grounds to demand an indemnification or remuneration in consideration of his journey & his services; but he shall be always content if your Excellency would grant well to him for this purpose, and on the whole he will not cease to endeavor to show his gratitude and to pray to the All Powerful for the safety and prosperity of your Excellency.

AINSSE.

Montreal the 5th 8th 1780.

Endorsed:—Memorial from Louis Joseph Ainssé with sundry accounts relative to Michillimakinac 5th October.

N. B. Copy of all which sent to Lt. Gov. Sinclair 9th Oct. 80.

[B 97 2 p 517.]

* * * * *

Expenses incurred by M. Ainssé at the Lake of the Mountain

Mainard steersman	300
Portatamies Guide	500
Lamaroche middleman for the canoe	200
Gum for canoe	130
Man for canoe	200

1 canoe for M. Beaubin	500
5 Packets	5
24 lbs Gum for	24
1 Long pole	3
3 oars for	9
4 Pairs leather shoes	12
3 Blankets for the equipment of the men	36
3 Cotton shirts	36
1 sail for	40
6 Packages screw nails for repairs	18
9 lbs Tobacco at	27
200 lbs Biscuit	136
100 lbs Flour	48
	2224

I certify to have delivered the above mentioned articles for the service of the King at the Lake of Two Mountains to enable me to go to Michillimakinac.

JH. AINSSE.

Endorsed: Accounts belonging to Joseph Louis Ainsse accompanying his memorial of the 5th Oct. Copy of which transmitted Lt. Gov. Sinclair the 9th Oct. 1780.

[B 97-2 p 516.]

PETITION OF LOUIS CHEVALLIER

To His Excellency Frederic Haldimand General and Governor in Chief in all the Province of Quebec and Territories depending thereon, Vice-Admiral of the same, General and Commander in Chief of the Troops of his Majesty in the said Province and Fronties. &c. &c. &c.

May it please Your Excellency,

The very humble address of Louis Chevallier, formerly Merchant at St. Joseph & successively employed for a number of years by Messrs. the Commandants of Michilimackinac to maintain the Indians in their duty and fidelity towards his Majesty.

The Petitioner has the honor to represent that for about thirty five years he was settled at St. Joseph, where by his conduct and behaviour under the two Governments, he ventures to flatter himself to have obtained, there, the confidence and esteem of those who were the trustees of authority; that having made himself beloved by the Indians in this district, he has profited by the ascendency which he has over their minds only to keep them in their duty and fidelity towards His Majesty and His Government, since the conquest and cession of Canada.

That for some years, there having been no Commandant nor Garrison at St. Joseph the different Commandants had chosen him as the King's man in this district. Honored with instructions to this effect & with the execution of their orders to which he has always conformed in the character of a true and faithful subject of His Prince.

That last year Mr. Barmer [Lieut Bennett] with a Detachment came to St. Joseph to endeavour to pacify the Indians, to encourage the good, reassure the weak, and bring back, if possible, the bad to their duty (your Excellency has been informed of the result of this step) the Petitioner accompanied this officer on his return to Michilimackinac, he was well received there by Major De Peyster and on his departure that Commandant gave him an order to continue his care and to give his attention to carry out the desired purpose.

That the Petitioner had the consolation of seconding the views of this wise officer, by succeeding in bringing back their principals, so that all the nations of his post and the surrounding district, appeared, at the moment in the interest of the King. It was necessary to perfectly assure them that they approved of their proposal to go and strike at the Post of Vincennes, and at the Belle Riviere [Ohio]; they consented to this unanimously. Then it was necessary to equip them, which was done partly by the advances made by the Company and partly by the Petitioner who advanced 6000 Livres of twenty sous, and the petitioner was authorized by Major De Peyster to incur these expenses. One party composed of twenty two men went towards Post Vincennes, another of one hundred and twenty men having with it M. DuQuindre and three Canadians went towards La Belle Riviere. The first party having doubtless been too much engaged was quickly met and repulsed by the enemy. There were six killed and four dangerously wounded. The rest of this party arrived at St. Joseph on the 24th of June last, nearly naked and all tattered; there has not yet been news of the second.

That the 25th of the same month, that as the Petitioner set himself to console the afflicted & to cloathe them, M. Ainsse having received orders from Mr. Sinclair, with a detachment of Indians and Canadians, appeared at St Joseph, they were notified by him that, either voluntarily or by force, he was to bring all the Inhabitants of the Post to Michilimackinac. The Petitioner began to obey the others did so led by his example, sixty eight years of age his wife of seventy having all his fortune in the neighborhood, ten houses, good lands, orchards, gardens, cattle, furniture, utensils and debts, of which he has made an entire sacrifice to obedience.

That being arrived at Michilimackinac he presented himself to the Lieutenant Governor who received him politely at first, but afterwards sent to search his boxes, he opened them in his presence and took all the papers they contained, which were all the letters of the Commandants & their orders, he promised to return them which he has not done. Then after that he confined him a prisoner in the Fort and forbad him to leave it.

That after this treatment, which was as hard as unexpected, the petitioner asked for permission to go down to this Town, which was accorded him only after having furnished security to a large amount for his good behaviour.

That as the conduct of the Petitioner is not blameable that he is as he has been and will always be faithful to his Prince; he has good reason to claim the protection of your Excellency which is never refused to the weak unjustly oppressed by the strong and in consequence he humbly hopes himself authorized to ask it.

To pray 1st To discharge him from the security which he has given, having been unjustly considered as a suspected person at the same time that he went to show his fidelity in the most striking manner.

2nd To order that the advances which he has made by order of Major De Peyster be paid to him.

3rd That he shall be permitted to return next spring to St Joseph to gather together the remains of his fortune and to order that his papers be sent to him.

He is led to expect all these things from the justice of your Excellency for the preservation of whom he will never cease to pray.

LOUIS CHEVALLIER.

Endorsed:—Request of M. Louis Chevallier formerly Merchant at St. Joseph.

Copy of this transmitted to Lieut. Governor Sinclair the 9th October 1780.
[B 98 p 151]

MAJOR DE PEYSTER TO GENERAL HALDIMAND

DETROIT 10th Oct'r 1780.

SIR, Agreeable to your Excellency's desire I have fixed loyalists upon Hog Island conformable to the terms prescribed in your letter to Lt. Col. Bolton. The Island is however sufficient for two substantial families only, there being much meadow Ground & swamp on it & it being absolutely necessary to preserve a run for the King's Cattle, being the only place of security— I have sent your Excellency a sketch of the Island which is only 768 acres. If I had placed more families there, it would have augumented the Expenses and not have been cultivated so much to advantage of Government. The remainder of the prisoners (having mostly taken the oaths of allegiance) I shall employ at King's Work having built a small Barrack for them in a convenient place, some time hence they may if your Excellency should desire it be placed upon adjacent Lands, which the Indians have from time to time, ceded to Inhabitants who would be glad of the opportunity of fixing them upon their Lands at their own Expence, But in the present disposition of the Indians, towards the people who are brought from Kentuck, it would rather be hazarding the lives of the Prisoners—If however there had been other Lands here belonging to the Crown I should have proceeded as the prisoners are very desirous themselves of running all risques.

I have the honour to be with great respect,

Sir Your Excellency's most hum'l & obed't serv't

AT S. DE PEYSTER

His Excell'y Gen'l Haldimand

Endorsed:—A 1780. From Major De Peyster dated Detroit 10th Oct'r. Rec'd 2nd Dec'r.

[B 122 p 563]

ORDER FOR STORES

MICHILIMACKINAC ISLAND 20th Octr 1780.

You are hereby directed & required to Issue out of His Majesty's Engineer's Store, the undermentioned particulars to Mr. Phelan, for the use of the King's works Carrying on here, vizt.

Steel	48½ lbs
New Iron	469 lbs
Old do	100 lbs
Nails	3 casks
Horse Harness	4½ setts
Files of sorts	32
Grind Stones	2
Bellows	1 pair

JOHN MOMPESSON

asst Engt.

To James Davidson in charge of Engineer's Stores.

[B 98 p 17]

RECEIPT

MICHILIMACKINAC ISLAND 20th Octr 1780.

Received out of His Majesty's Engineer's Stores from James Davison in charge thereof, the undermentioned particulars for the use of the Kings works carrying on here, vizt.

Steel . . . . 48½ ℔s
New Iron . . . . 469 ℔
Old do . . . . 100 ℔
Nails . . . . 3 casks
Horse Harness . . . . 4½ setts
Files of sorts 32
Grind Stones 2
Bellows . . . . 1 pair

WM. PHELON

Conductor of the Kings Works on Island Michilimackinac.

[B 98 p 17]

ORDER FOR STORES

MICHILIMACKINAC ISLAND 24th Octr. 1780.

You are hereby directed and required to Issue out of His Majesty's Artillery Store, the undermentioned particulars for the Different Services of the Garrison, vizt.

Musquet Ball Cartridges 2317
Copper Hoops 3

To James Davidson in charge of the Artillery Store.

[B 98 p 14]

MR. HARMON TO MR. DUCHARME

SIR, I give myself the honor of writing you the present to ask for the continuation of your perfect health & as you have made me good offers of service I hope that you will let me have, at Michillimakinac, the bill which I send you if possible. I will pay you or your agents in raw furs, that is to say beavers, lynxes & others.

The memorandum contains the following

6 Pieces linen rapeé Viz.

6 ditto

6 ditto
6 Pieces coarse cotton
2 pieces calico blue ground all the same pattern
100 Blankets 2½ pts
50 ditto 2 pts
30 ditto 3 pts
25 ditto 1½ pts
1 doz cardboard snuff boxes
6 Pieces blue cloth
200 lbs. powder
150 lbs lead shot
600 flints
3 doz cotton shirts
10 lbs vermillion
2 gross large knives
3 or 4 doz large buckles
1 gross small spring knives
½ gross case knives
6 Traps 2 gross of Pipes
18 Blanket hoods 6 pieces blue borderin
6 ditto black 6 pieces pretty ribbon
100 needles 2 cases of pins
12 doz common scissors 18 steels
100 ½ doz ducks
2 Pieces of cotton 5½ blue
doz assorted stockings ½ gross of womens
4 Bundles of bench lines
1 doz double cloaks

I hope, Sir, that you will charge your brother Dominique with the presents & that you will give him 2 doz black Plumes; you may rely on my designs of paying nobly him who you will charge with your orders & whilst you will be well satisfied, you would render them a service. I will not send deer skins, anticipating that they would not be worth the expense. I hope you will answer that I may make other arrangements & am

very truly your servant

Send me three doz black skins, 2 doz. women's gloves & eight dozen handkerchiefs black as well as blue.

A. Harmon dit sans facon

Addressed:—To M. Jean Marie Ducharme Merchant at Michillimakinac.
[B 97-2 p 583]

SPEECH OF CERTAIN INDIANS.

Speech which the Indians have made to M. Ainsse, bearer of His Majesty's orders, to write to their Father at Michillimakinac.

Father, We have just received a stroke, which has made us too ill to avenge ourselves.

You have always said to us that if any one did evil to your children it was done to yourself. We have received this stroke for having done your will, we hope that you will not leave us in the fires that the Miamis have kindled & that you will help us quickly, as well as our brothers the Court aureille and Sauteus, which we ask immediately if possible & a great number to extinguish their fires which are spoiling our ground. We wait with impatience for your answer for we can do nothing without your assistance. We are faithfully

Your children the
Toutegatemy
Mahaquoy By
Nogyalousy

All the other chiefs are at war with the Rebels.

This council was held yesterday it sends you sixteen branches of Porcelaine.

I have dried up their tears with a barrel of rum & six fathoms of tobacco.

I could not help giving something to the widow from you.

[B 97-2-p 572]

GENERAL HALDIMAND TO LORD GEORGE GERMAIN

(Extract)

Quebec 25th October 1780.

The article of Provisions has considerably augumented these Expenses, particularly of late, since the Five Nations in the District of Niagara, & the Shawnese, Delawares, Mingoes, Munsies, & depending Tribes along the Frontiers, in that of Detroit, have been driven with their Families from their Villages into those Posts, for refuge & subsistence, in so much that, at the former from 3000 to 5000 Indians were victualled all the last winter, and about £18,000 New York Curry. paid in the latter in that Period, on the same account, notwithstanding the numbers of War Parties continually kept abroad to lessen the consumption. Add to these the Families who are, or call themselves Loyalists, continually coming in, in large Parties, naked & starving with Hunger & who must be received.

I am nevertheless persuaded that these expenses are greatly increased by the avidity of the Merchants in that country who taking the advantage of the times, have raised the Prices of their goods, particularly Rum & those in demand for the Indians, to a most exorbitant & shameful height, nor is this the only evil attending their conduct, the Inhabitants who depend upon them for their little wants are obliged to raise the price of their Stock in proportion, which puts it totally out of the Power of the Troops to purchase many little things of comfort they would otherwise enjoy, while the Farmer is sure of a market from the want of Provisions for the Indians, all which centers with the Merchant, nor is there the least reason to doubt that they urge the Indians to make Demands, not only of greater quantities than are necessary but many articles they would themselves never think of, nor is there the Power of the Commanding officers is continual prosecution is not to be conceived but by experience, to refuse materially their Demands, the alternative being too serious a consequence for them to risk—or for me to authorize unless I am empowered to do it.

I have the Honour to be &c &c

(signed)

FRED HALDIMAND

[B 54 p 343]

GENERAL HALDIMAND TO MAJOR DE PEYSTER

QUEBEC 27th October 1780.

SIR, Lieutenant Scheifelin of the Volunteers who accompanied Lieut. Governor Hamilton upon his Expedition & acted as Secretary to the Indian Department, having found means to effect his escape from the Jail at Williamsburg returns to Detroit, and will deliver this Letter. In consideration of Mr. Schieffelin's Endeavours for & sufferings in the King's Service you will continue to him his Pay as Lieutenant until further orders & if you have occasion for his services in his other capacity, you will please to employ them, with the Pay he before enjoyed which he informs me was four shillings sterling per Day.

I am Sir &c

(signed) FRED: HALDIMAND

Major De Peyster

Endorsed: Copy 80—To Major De Peyster at Michilimackinac, 27th Octr Detroit

[B 122 p 567]

STATE OF THE SETTLEMENT OF DETROIT, TAKEN THE 1st OF NOVEMBER 1780.

394	Heads of familys	Exclusive of them employ'd in the King's Service.
374	Married & young women	
324	Young & married men	
100	Absent in the Indian Country	
455	Boys from 10 to 15 years	
385	Girls	
79	Male Slaves	
96	Female do	
772	Horses	
474	Oxen	
793	Cows	
361	Steers	
279	Sheep	
1,016	Hogs	
13,306	Bushels of Wheat	
5,380	ditto Indian Corn	
488	ditto Pease	
6,253	ditto Oats	
3,580d	Flower	
2,028	Bushels wheat sown last Fall	
2,885	Bushels Potatoes	
828	Barrels Cyder	
12,083	Acres of Land under Cultivation	

[B 122 p 568]

MEMORIAL OF JOHN KAY AND DAVID McCRAE

To His Excellency Frederick Haldimand Esqr Captain General, Governor and Commander in Chief of the Province of Quebec &c. &c. &c.

The Memorial of John Kay & David McCrae Merchants in Montreal—
Humbly Sheweth—

That your memorialists have for several years past carried on a pretty Extensive Trade in this Province in sending goods from Montreal to the Upper Country to Traffick with the Indians, particularly in the Spring 1778, they sent up to Michilimackinac Eight Canoe load of Goods—

Upon the arrival of your Memorialists at Michilimackinac, Major Depeyster having no Information of the Rebels, being at the Illenois granted them a Pass for that Country for Five of the aforesaid Canoes, which Canoes were under the conduct & in the charge of a certain Charles Gratiot, unfortunately for your Memorialists the said Gratiot upon his arrival found the Rebels in possession of that Country, the said Gratiot has ever since remained amongst the Rebels to the great detriment of your Memorialists, Trading upon the aforesaid Property, without ever having made any remittance to your Memorialists excepting about seven or eight hundred Pounds, Halifax Currency value in Furs, the Spring following—

In April last the aforesaid Gratiot sent off from the Illenois under a Spanish Pass a large Boat loaded with Furs, Provisions &c. (the produce of the aforesaid Goods) a list of the Loading is here enclosed with orders to the Conductor of said Boat to proceed up the Mississippi, as far as a Place called La Prairie du Chiens, and there to dispose of the Cargo if possible and return immediately to the Illinois—

The Boat in coming up the Mississippi was seized by Lieut Alexr Kay of the Indian Department, Brother of the aforesaid John Kay your Memorialist) and sent in to Michilimc.

Part of the Peltry, all the Provisions, Tobacco, Rum, &c. has been made use of at La Prairie du Chien by orders of Lt. Govr. Sinclair by a Party of Canadians & Indians at that time on their way to attack the Illinois—the remainder is at present at Michilimackinac & the Boat Employed in the service of Government.

Your Memorialists have already made application to Lieut Governor Sinclair concerning the aforesaid Boat & Loading—He has referr'd them to your Excellency (which is the reason your Memorialists take the liberty of troubling you at present) with a promise at some time of giving Your Excellency a particular account of that affair which they flatter themselves he has done.

As your memorialists are conscious of having on their part always behaved themselves as good & faithful subjects of His Majesty, & convinced that your Excellency will always show that Clemency & Indulgence lies in your power to those that behave so, they flatter themselves that the circumstance of their affairs with said Gratiot, by whom they are losers of at least Four Thousand Pounds, Halifax Currency, will draw your Excellency's attention.

Your Memorialists therefore humbly beseech Your Excellency to take their circumstances of their Case into Your Consideration & that your Excelly. would be pleased to order the Goods seized and made use of as aforesaid to be paid for, & those that remain at Michilimackinac to be delivered up to your Memorialists, being in reality their property, procured by said

Gratiot in Lieu of the goods intrusted to his Care, as aforesaid, & your Memorialists will as in Duty bound ever pray.

DAVID MCCRAE,
for self &
JOHN KAY.

Quebec 13th Novr. 1780.
[B 97-2 p 533]

MAJOR DE PEYSTER TO GENERAL HALDIMAND

DETROIT the 16th Novr. 1780.

SIR, I have the honour to acquaint your excellency that a body of Canadians, commanded by Colonel La Balm,* were defeated on the 5th inst, by the Miamie Indians near their village. The Colonel and between thirty and forty of his men were killed, and Monsr. Rhy who stiles himself Aid-de-Camp taken Prisoner—He relates that they left the Cahokias on the 3rd Octr. with 41 men. That a larger body were to follow them to the *Ouia,* from whence Colonel La Balm proceeded to the Miamie with one hundred & three men, & some Indians without waiting for the Junction of the Troops expected, leaving orders for them to follow as well as those he expected from Post Vincent.

His design was to attempt a coup de main upon Detroit, but finding his troops which were to consist of 400 Canadians & some Indians did not arrive, after waiting twelve days, they plundered the place & were on their way back, when the Indians assembled & attacked them.

I have sent the Colonel's Commissions Papers & a Volume of his Works to Brigadr General Powell, There are many other Papers which might have been of consequence but they are quite defaced by water &c.

Those I have sent will sufficiently serve to show your Excellency the dispositions of the Canadians.

Had this little army arrived here compleat, & Joined by soo many more, they would under such an enterprising officer, have given us a deal of trouble.

As the enemy came from the Ouia in four days, on horseback, it will account for the Miamie Indians being surprised to see them at their village before they had any accounts of their coming, and, it so happened that my scouts were just returned from that Country. But what astonished me was, that they were near twelve days at the Miamie, before we got the accounts of it here.

---

*See appendix

The Indians say that the few then at the village were surrounded, and did not dare stir till the Enemy retreated, at which lucky period war parties arrived, which gave them heart & strength to follow them.

Upon the whole I believe it was the thoughts that I would allow no more goods amongst them—if they did not defend those they had—be it as it will, the Chiefs make a merit of being faithful allies, and I must improve the lucky moment, therefore, least the Party expected should endeavour to revenge the affront, I sent off the Rangers to take post at the Miamie Town to act in concert with that Nation, which now is fairly entered.

Your Excellency will see the necessity of continuing them a Trader, who I propose shall be Monsr. Beaubin (whom the people of Post Vincent wish to hang) ordering all others in to Detroit.

It will also be necessary to make those Indians a handsome present for this signal mark of their loyalty.

I have the honour to be with the greatest respect, Sir,

Your Excellency's most huml & obedt. servt.

AT. S. DE. PEYSTER.

P. S. I send down the Colonel's Aid-de-Camp who is a very intelligent young Gentleman. I forgot to observe that the Indians retook great part of the Goods, & lodged in Monsr Beaubins store again.

His Excelly. Genl. Haldimand.

Endorsed:—No 5 enter'd. From Major De Peyster 16th Novr. Recd 2nd Decr. Copy in Book B No 3 Page 11.

[B 122 p 569]

FROM GENERAL HALDIMAND UNADDRESSED

QUEBEC 3rd December, 1780.

My Lord,

I retarded the Sailing of the last Vessel from this Post in Hopes of the arrival of an Express from Halifax with the dispatches which were on Board the Garland Frigate for me, and with a view to give your Lordship accounts as late as possible from this Country.

The Vessel would have sailed Yesterday had it not been aground from want of precaution of the Master in not bringing it to the proper Wharf. The Weather has Set in so very Cold, and the Ice forms so fast that there is a Risk of the Vessel not getting away, however its Stay has given me Time to Receive this day Letters from Detroit & Niagara, which Confirm the Loss of the Armed Ship, the Ontario, upon the Lake of the same name; Inclosed is a Return of the Officers and others who perished on that occasion. I likewise send Your Lordship a coppy of a Letter from Major de Peyster of the 8th Regiment who commands at Detroit; I consider this attempt of Colonel La Balme as in part of the Execution of that Plan which the Enemy has formed. I am Sorry to find that the Canadians in the Upper Country and So lost to a Sense of their Duty and are so much inclined to favor the Plan of the Enemy. The necessity of a strong Force, in order to guard so extensive a Country is evident. Your Lordship will likewise observe how very incumbent it is upon the Commanding officer at Detroit to take Care what kind of men he allows to go as Traders into the Indian Country. The present is not the time for pushing commerce, it is that of defence, and nothing will more tend to keep the Indian allies to their Duty than to make them feel a Dependance upon the King, their Father, for such goods as have now become in Some Measure necessary to their Existence. I know that the Traders, either Ignorant of the necessity, or indifferent to every Consideration except that of Interest, will not fail to Complain against the Command'g officer as being influenced by Partiality in the choice of the Traders whom he sends here, but such is the Misfortune in this Distant Country, that an officer who does his duty must suffer the abuse of Popular Clamor till such time as Experience will discover his Motives and justify his Conduct.

I have the Honor, &c., &c.

(signed) FRED. HALDIMAND.

[B 55 p 36.]

MAJOR DE PEYSTER TO GENERAL HALDIMAND*

DETROIT Jan'ry 8th 1781

SIR, I have the honour to acquaint your Excellency that since the affair at the Miamis Town, something similar happened at St. Josephs—A detachment from the Cahokias, consisting of sixteen men only commanded by a half Indian named John Bablest Hammelaine, timed it so as to arrive at St. Josephs with pack Horses when the Indians were out on their first hunt, an old chief and his family excepted— They took the Traders Prisoners and carried off all the Goods consisting at least of fifty Bales and to the rout of Chicagon —Lieut. Dagneaux Du Quindre who I had stationed near St. Josephs, upon being informed of it immediately assembled some Indians and pursued them as far as the *Petit Fort* a days journey beyond the River *Du Chemin* [Calumet] where on the 5th Dec'r he summoned them to surrender, on their refusing to do it he ordered the Indians to Attack them—Without the loss of a man on His side, he killed four, wounded two, and took seven prisoners, the other

*See appendix

three escaped, in the thick woods—Three of the Prisoners were brought on here, amongst whom is one Brady a Superintendant of Indian Affairs—The rest he suffered the Indians to take to Michilimakina—I look upon those Gentry as robbers and not Prisoners of War having no commission that I can learn other than a verbal order from Mons'r Trottier and Inhabitants of the Cahoes. The Rebels having long since quit all that country—Brady who says he had no longer a desire of remaining in the Rebel Service, therefore did not follow them, informs me that Colonel Clarke was gone down to Williamsburg to Sollicit a Detachment to join with a Spanish Colonel in an expedition against this place—When the heavy Cannon and Ammunition arrived, which I have returned wanting—I shall be ready to give them a warm reception, should they be rash enough to attempt it—Our workes are However yet in a shatter'd state—

I am just informed that the Rangers are safe arrived at the Miamis Town.

I have the honour to be

Sir Your Excellency's most obedient

& most Humble Serv't

AT S: DE PEYSTER

His Excellency Gen'l Haldimand

Endorsed:—A 81 Major de Peyster of January the 8th Rec'd March 21st.

Copy In Book marked B no. 3. Page 14

[B 123 p 5]

MAJOR DE PEYSTER TO GENERAL HALDIMAND

DETROIT January 8th 1781

SIR, I have this day drawn on Your Excellency in favor of Messrs Macomb Edgar & Macomb, Four bills of Exchange amounting to Forty four thousand nine hundred and sixty two pounds six Shillings & one penny half penny New York Currency, being for Expences incurr'd at this Post for His Majesty's Service, as per account and Vouchers which will be deliver'd herewith, and to which your Excellency will please to honor.

I am Sir Your Excellency's most obedient & humble Servt

AT S: DE PEYSTER,

Major King's Regt Commanding.

His Excellency General Haldimand Governor & Commander in Chief Quebec.

Endorsed:—A 1781 From Major De Peyster 8th Jany Recd 21st March.

[B 123 p 7]

MAJOR DE PEYSTER TO CAPTAIN MCKEE

DETROIT February 1st 1781.

DEAR SIR, Since the affair at the Miamis something similar happen'd at St. Joseph's—the prisoners brought in are all Canadians except one Brady who stiles himself a Superintendent by the Commission of Helm. Brady says that they were sent by the Creoles to plunder St Josephs & they inform me there is not a Virginian in all the Illinois Country, nor even at Port Vincents. The Snake has been here a considerable time, waiting he says for you. He took his leave about a week ago but returned here for some provisions which gave me the favorable Oppy of Charging him with Joshuah Stile and John Harrison the former a Delaware & the latter a Shawnese who had been tampering with the prisoners and a number of the Sailors to carry them off to the Rebels. I was under the necessity of Confining these two men till I could come at the Truth of the Matter. This rash step of the prisoner obliges me to confine all except these who have families. A drunken Indian named Washington attempted to stab the Snake but luckily miss'd him and stabbed his son, he immediately after that stabbed a squaw. I hope it is nothing extraordinary keeps you out as I heard once you was coming in to Detroit. I shall be glad to hear from you when ever an Opportunity Offers provided you are not coming in your self. I have been laid up this fortnight with a sprained ancle and not likely to get the Better. Mrs. DePeyster and the Genl of the Kings desire their Compliments to you.

I am dear Sir your most obedt Servant

AT S. DE PEYSTER.

To Capt McKee.
Indian Affairs M. G. III.

LIEUT. GOV. SINCLAIR TO GENERAL HALDIMAND

MICHILIMACKINAC 12th February 1781.

SIR, I have the honor to draw for the sum of twelve hundred and Forty Four N. Y. C. in favour of Monsr. Ettienne Campion for expenses incurred in the Indian Department, the Vouchers for which are herewith sent.

I have the honor to be Sir

Your Excellency's most humble and most obedient Servant

PATT SINCLAIR Lt Govr.

General Frederick Haldimand.
[B 98 p 7]

LIEUT. GOV. SINCLAIR TO SECRETARY MATHEWS

MICHELEMK ISLAND 23rd February 1781.

SIR, I am at a loss to answer the complaints of Messrs. Chevalier & Ainse. The accounts of last year prove them in part false, as his Excellency would observe from the necessity of all Bills being drawn in favour of the General Store. If it is requisite their Agents here, who are men of character, shall contradict every other part of their Complaint Excepting the hardships of lodging within the Stockade instead of without.

I am Sir Your most obedient Servant,

PATT SINCLAIR Lt Govr

Captain Mathews Secretary
[B 98 p 8]

LIEUT. GOV. SINCLAIR TO CAPTAIN MOMPESSON

SIR, Depositions are offered to me respecting William Hipworth's treatment since he was first delivered by you as a Prisoner to Ensign McDougal. As they appear to me serious I will delay them for a little, until you have time to consider of them.

I am, Sir, Your most humble Servant,

March 8th, 1781. PATT SINCLAIR, Lt. Governor.
To Captain Mompesson.
[B 98 p 56.]

INDIAN COUNCIL

At a Council held at Detroit 11th March, 1781, with the Pottewatimies from St. Josephs, Terre Coupe and Coeur de Cerf.

Assimut speaks with 4 Strings of Wampum

FATHER, I am hired by the Pottewatimies at and near St. Joseph's, to acquaint you with the Reasons of having suffered the Enemy to carry off their Traders. They came to St. Joseph's at a time that all the Indians were yet at their hunt, excepting a few young men who were not sufficient to oppose one hundred white People and Eighty Indians led by *Seguinack* and *Nakewine,* who deceived them by telling them that it was the Sentiment of the Indians in general to assist the French and Spaniards—had we assembled in time, we would nevertheless have given them such a stroke as we gave those who came to St. Joseph's a few moons before. We therefore hope our Father will take pity on us and not leave us to the Mercy of the Enemy, who threaten soon to come and destroy our Women & Children.

Wawiaghtenou, Chief of the Pottewatemies of Detroit speaks in behalf of his Nation, the Ottawas and Chippewas, &c., with six strings

Father, I rise to speak in behalf of the Pottewatemies of St. Joseph's, I desire in the Name of our Nation, the Ottawas and Chippewas that you will not abandon them to the Mercy of the Enemy. I am convinced they were no ways in concert with the Enemy and therefore hope you will have pity on them.

Major De Peyster's answer,
with six strings of Wampum.

Children, (You see I still call you children since it is the request of the Nations present)—I have at different times said so much to you on the subject of the Traders and Goods entrusted with you, by the Governor of Michilimackinac, that it is needless to say any more at present—My words have proved true, you have lost your Traders and I have only to pity you—open your ears and attend now to what I am going to say—The Spaniards tell you they are in alliance with the Virginians and the French, They therefore offer you their Hands, or threaten to destroy your Women and Children—Believe me,—they can never destroy them until you are simple enough to shake hands with them—If you adhere to your alliance with the King of Great Britain and his Indian Friends, nothing can hurt you. The Spaniards in the time of your Ancestors, by fair word when they failed by force of Arms, got possession of an Indian Country the other side of the Mississipi, where they Killed Thousands of the Inhabitants to get the stuff that those Bracelets and Gorgets you are now wearing are made of—You have no such Clay in your ground at St. Josephs, but you find fertile Lands which will produce abundance of corn. If therefore you listen to those sugar-mouthed Spaniards, what would you Spirits of your ancestors say if they knew that their Burrying Grounds were to be levelled by Ploughs, and their Bones disturbed for the Spaniards and Virginians to sow Corn, &c. Whilst you their decendants tamely came to Detroit to beg a little piece of Land from the Ottawas to hide yourselves, which must be the case soon unless you are determined to stand firm as the Oak which grows upon your Land—do not be afraid to trouble the Lands because there are Indians foolish enough to join them—If you are afraid, I am not—Therefore to prevent yourselves the affront, return to St. Josephs and bring me the chiefs *Seguinac* and *Makewine,* or I will find others from Michilimackinac to do it. Do you not know that they are the outcasts of their Nations—I once bought those Runnagade Chiefs off in hopes that they would return to a sense of their duty—I am now determined no longer to spare them—Whilst some of you look out for your Enemies, let others fresh cover the Graves of your Ancestors, and raise the earth so high over them that no plough can level them. Mr. Baby will furnish you with ammunition and such things as are absolutely necessary—You must not expect ornaments or conveniences till you show yourselves thoroughly deserving of them.

Children—the English always have treated you well, and the Indians on the other side the Mississippi are so sensible of the goodness of an English Father, that they have invited him to send his troops to drive the Spaniards out of the country. They are now about it, and are helping those Indians to revenge themselves upon their enemies. Tell *Nanaquoibe* and *Betagushach* their old Michilimackinac Father speaks to them. He begs they will also attend to what they soon will hear from Him who is at present at Michilimackinac, as they may expect to hear from him soon.

Wawiaghtenou speaks

Father! In calling to mind the Bones of our Ancestors, you draw tears from me. have pity of them, and I'il engage they will raise Mountains over their graves.

(Signed) At. S. De Peyster.
Commanding.

Endorsed:—A Council with the Pottewatemies of St. Josephs. Detroit 11th March 1781.
[B 123 p 10.]

DEMAND OF SUPPLIES FOR THE GARRISON OF DETROIT—17th MARCH 1781.

Vizt.

Fuzes fixt— 4 2-5 Inch		100
Shells Empty 4 2-5 Inch		100
Musquet Ball—Ton		1
Musquet Flints		5000
Match Slow—lbs		50
Powder W. B.—C. H.		50
Lanthorns	Muscovy	3
	Tin	3
	Dark	3
Portfires—Doz		6

Round Shot	18 Po'r	150
	9	300

[Signed] AM DU VERNET
L't R'l Artillery.

Endorsed:—Demand of Supplies of Ordnance Stores for the Garrison of Detroit, 17th March 781.

[B 123 p 14.]

PETITION FROM MERCHANTS OF DETROIT

To Arsent Schuyler De Peyster Esqr Major of the 8th Regiment and Commrs of Detroit and its dependencies, &c &c.

SIR, We beg leave to lay before you the unhappy situation of ourselves and others residing at this place, for want of some mode, to oblige those who are able and yet unwilling to pay their lawful debts.

From Experience we Can assure you there are many who avail themselves of this, and unless some Method is fallen on we will suffer Considerably. To you alone we look up for relief, until our superiors establish some plan for the administration of Justice at this Place (which we request you will Recommend). Your constant Protection and encouragement of Trade here, and at Michilimackinac makes us hope you will take our Situation into Consideration and Grant Redress where you may see it Just & necessary.

We are with Esteem & Respect, Sir, Your most obedient Humble servants

Detroit 28th March 1781.

(Signed)

David White
George Lyons
Isaac Williams
Tellier & Groesbeck
Alexr Dyer
Nathan Williams
John McPherson
Tho Cox
John Shipboy
Obediah Robins
Thomas Finchley
James May

Macomb Edgar & Macomb
James Rinkin
Robt. McWilliams & Co
Colin Andrews & Co
Allott & Saunders
William Park & Co
James Thomson
Richard Wright
Edward Ridley
William Pawling
William Hands
Chapman Abram

Endorsed:—Petition from the Merchants at Detroit to Major DePeyster of the 28th March, 1781.

[B 123 p 15]

CERTIFICATE OF EXPENDITURE

I do hereby Certify that the undermentioned Michitim Island Artillery Stores, have been expended by my orders in Carrying on the different services as undermentioned, between the 1st October 1780 & the 31st March 1781 Inclusive, and the Acting Conductor of Stores is hereby Discharged thereof.

Patt Sinclair Lieut Govr

Species of Stores.	Quantity	For what Service Expended.
Powder lbs	66½	For Firing in honor of Her Majesty's Birthday & to the miners in the Engineer's Depart.
Musqt Ball Cartridges	2317	For the use of Troops in Garrison.
Copper Hoops	3	For Bushing Ordnance.

N. B., The Ball Cartridges are chiefly used in loading for guard, what Balls are not used in Firing &ca, are Return'd and Consequently not Reckon'd in the Expenditures.

[B 98 p 12]

CERTIFICATE OF EXPENDITURES

I do hereby certify that the undermentioned Michitim Island Engineer's Stores have been expended by my orders in carrying on the Different Services as undermentioned Between the 1st Oct'r 1780 and the 31st March 1781 Inclusive. And the Acting Conductor of Stores is hereby Discharged thereof.

Patt Sinclair
L't Gov'r.

Species of Stores.	Quantity	For what Service Expended.
Steel lbs	48½	For different Services at King's Works.
New Iron lbs	469	
Old do lbs	100	
Files of Sorts	28	
Bellows, pairs	1	
Files	4	
Nails, casks	3	To the Carpenters &c. for the King's Works.
Grind stones	2	

[B 98 p 15.]

RETURN OF STORES

Return of Engineers Stores Issued and Expended at the Garrison of Michilimackinac Island between the 1st October 1780 & 31st March 1781. Inclusive as per Vouchers.

Date.	To whom & for what service	By order of	Species of Stores.	Quantity. S.	R.	U.
From Oct. 24th to Mar. 24th.	To Mr. Phelan for the King's works.	Patrick Sinclair, Esqre., Lieut. Govr. & Commandant here.	Nails of sorts Cast....	3	....	....
	To the King's Blacksmith.		Steel..............lbs	24½	....	....
			New Iron..........lbs	469	....	....
			Old do............lbs	100	....	....
			Files of sorts.........	28	....	....
			Bellows prs...........	1	....	....
	To Mr. Phelan.		Hand Saw Files.......	4	....	....
	To Mr. Hepworth Carter.		Horse Harness Setts...	4½	....	....
	For the Lieut. Govrs. chimney.		Steel..............lbs	24	....	....
	Taken by Mr. Phelan.		Grind Stones.........	2	....	....
March 31st	Expended by order of between the 1st of October 1780 and this present date, Inclusive.					

[B 98 p 16]

RETURN OF STORES

Return of Ordnance Stores, Issued and Expended at the Garrison Michilimackinac Island between the 1st October 1780 & the 31st of March 1781 inclusive. As per Vouchers.

Date.	To whom & for what service.	By order of	Species of Stores.	Quantity. S	R	U
From Oct. 24th. to March.	To Serjeant Langdown for 2 companys of the King's (or 8th) Regmt in garrison here.	Patrick Sinclair Esqre Lieut Govr. and Commandant here.	Ball Cartridges..........	1,389	....	....
	To Serjeant Donaldson for do. do.		Ball Cartridges..........	538	....	....
	To Serjeant Haldimand for a detachment of the 84th Regiment.		Ball Cartridges..........	390	....	....
	In honour of Her Majesty's birthday.		Powder lbs.............	15½	....	....
	Issued to miners in the Engineers Dept.		Powder lbs.............	51	....	....
	To the Kings Blacksmith for Bushing ordnance.		Copper Hoops..........	3	....	....
Mar. 31st.	Expended by order of between 1st Octr 1780 & this present date, Inclusive					

[B 98 p 13]

Return & State of Ordnance Stores at Michilimackinac Island 31st March 1781

	Serviceable.	Repairable.	Unserviceable.	Deficiencies.		Serviceable.	Repairable.	Unserviceable.	Deficiencies.	Expended since last return.
Ordnance:					Live Shells			25		
Light Six Pounders Brass	2				Empty do	29				
Heavy do Iron	2				Round Shot for Six Pounders	403				
Swivels do	3				Round do filled and fixed	38				
Howitzers do 3 in	2				Round do. fixed to bottoms only			31	31	
Ambuzettes Brass	4				Case do. filled and fixed	60				
Mortar do 4 2–5	1				Case do. fixed to bottoms only			114	114	
Wall Pieces	2				Grape do. for Howitzers	24				
Carriages:					Grape do. for Ambuzettes	24				
Travelling six Pounders	2				Round lead shot for ditto	40				
Garrison do do	1				Cannon Cartridge Paper Quires	15				
Garrison for Swivels	2		1		Fuzes 4 2–5	100				
Garrison Howitzers	2				Sheep Skins	1				
For Ambuzettes	4				Sponge Tacks	300				
Ladles of sorts	4				Empty paper Cartridges	591				
Spunges of do	10				Thread lbs	2½				
Wadhooks	5				Musquet Balls lbs	180				
Junk Wads	415				Tann'd Hides	1				
Drag ropes with pins (setts)	2				Nave Grease lbs	2				
Hand Spikes Traversing	4				Harness:					
Hand do punching	14				Mens setts		2			
Aprons of Lead	11				Horse do		3			

Leather Pouches	4			
Tube Boxes	4			
Match Slow lbs	5			
Linstocks	4			
Port fires				
Port fire sticks	5			
Tin Tubes	270			
Priming Horns and wires	4			
Vent Spikes	10			
Vent Punches	4			
Spears	38			
Corn'd Powder lbs	261			
Copper Powder Measures	7			

Cartridge Paper Quires	12				
Formers:					
For Musquet Cartridges	4				
For Carbine do	2				
Spare Copper Hoops	29				
Iron Beam weight & scales setts	1				
Garrison Colors do	1				
Musquet Ball Cartridges	10,530				
Flints:					
Musquet	4,874				
Carbine	780				
Carbine Ball lbs	190				
Expenditure:					
Powder lbs					66½
Ball Cartridges					2,317
Copper Hoops					3

N. B. Two of ye Ambuzettes on Board the Sloop Felicity.

PATT SINCLAIR Lt Governor.

[B 98 p 19]

MAJOR DE PEYSTER TO GENERAL HALDIMAND

DETROIT 3rd April 1781

SIR, I take the liberty to trouble your Excellency with the enclosed petition from the Merchants of Detroit, I sincerely wish that some method could be fallen upon to oblige the Inhabitants to pay their just debts without the parties being obliged to go down the country for the recovery of every trifling sum. Formerly summons were issued by the Justice and decisions given, but since we have learned that they have no such power, that mode has ceas'd—I am confident that many wish for a Revolution in order to wipe off their scores, who otherwise would be very easy under the present Government. This is greatly the case at Detroit & Will I hope Apologize for my troubling you.

I have the honor to be with great respect,
Sir Your Excellency's
Most humble & obed't Servt.

AT S. DE PEYSTER

His Excellency Gen'l Haldimand

Endorsed:—From 1781 Major Depeyster of the 3d April Rec'd 19th Inclosing a petition from the Merchants of Detroit.

[B 123 p 17]

INDIAN COUNCIL

At a Council held at Detroit April 5th 1781 with a Deputation of Principal Chiefs of the Shawanese, Delawares, & Cherokees.

PRESENT

Major De Peyster—Commandr of Detroit & its Dependce
Major Gamble 47th Regt.
Lieut. Du Vernet Royal Artillery

Captain Bird Lieut. Pepyat Lieut. Saumarez Ensn Frey	Kings (or 8th) Regiment
Lieut. England Lieut. Ford Ensn Hamilton	47th Regiment

Alexr McKee Esqr. Dep't Agent Colo. Johnsons Dept.

Monsr Duperon Baby Monsr Chesne Simon Girty James Girty	Indian Dept.

Wry Neck, Chief of the Shawanese speaks in behalf of the Ohio Confederacy.

Father, We return the Great Spirit thanks for permitting us to meet you this day in our Council House, but I am sorry that several nations of your Children are absent—vizt.—the Ottawas, Chippewas & Pottewatimies, equally concerns, but we suppose the season has prevented them, & shall therefore proceed to inform you of my Errand.

Father, I am now to acquaint you that after the destruction of our Villages by the Enemy last Fall. Our chiefs have been in constant Councils and early this spring whilst they were engaged in one, Simon Girty with a party of Hurons and some of our own Nation, delivered us a prisoner they had taken from the Enemy who confirms their designs against us as early as possible this year. He was brought for the purpose of giving us and you Intelligence, therefore we now deliver him to you, in hopes that what he'll tell you will convince you of the danger with which we are threatened by the Enemy.

Delivers Richd Rue a Prisoner.

Father, Notwithstanding the misfortunes that have happened to your children of our Confederacy. We can assure you they are not cast down, but that they still hold up their Heads & are determined to revenge themselves upon the Enemy—therefore I am come to speak to you in their behalf on business of importance to you and us both.

With 3 Belts.

Father, This is the Council Fire at which you and the different Nations of your Children were united, those are the Belts that bind us together and make us one flesh and Blood, and you must remember the Promises of assistance.

Whenever we should be in danger, the time that we received them, therefore it is needless for us to say more than that the Time is now come that we must demand your assistance for the Enemy are now in readiness to strike us again. Be strong Father & rise up with us to oppose them. Collect all your Warriors as speedily as possible, for the latter end of this month or the bgeinning of this month will bring them into our country. A few warriors will not be sufficient to oppose them, for they now make a more formidable appearance than ever. Therefore not doubting your assistance, We take you by the hand and lead you to the front of our Villages that lay next to the Enemy. We hope you'll be strong and encourage your children the Lake Indians to rise with you.

Delivers 3 Belts.

Father, We are yet sick with the blow we received from the Enemy, but hope with your help to take revenge, and this Tobacco which we received from the Great Spirit, I now present you with, when you come to smoak of it, it will induce you to grant us our requests when you consider that what we desire, is for our mutual Benefit.

Delivers a small quantity of Indian Tobacco tied up in a remnant of Linen.

Father, Now we have acquainted you with our danger hoping that you will acquaint your children the nation round you as soon as possible.

Wry Neck continues with 5 Belts in his hand.

Father, These belts are addressed to our younger Brethren the Ottawas, Chippewas, and Pottawattimies putting them in mind of the league made by our forefathers in which they mutually agreed to support each other; They must now see us their elder Brethren in danger and that we are under the necessity of looking towards them for assistance as they are numerous—We see ourselves weak and our arms feeble to the force of the Enemy. 'Tis now upwards of Twenty years since we have been alone engaged against the Virginians—Exert yourselves now and join our Father to help us; and we now deliver these Belts and Strings to our Father that he may acquaint the Nations they are addressed to, with the contents—We likewise deliver for them some, Tobacco received from the Great Spirit.

5 Small Belts

The Swan, Chief of the Cherokees Speaks—

Father, My business with the Shawanese (amongst whom I reside at present) is to support the general League of Friendship, between you and your Indian Children, which I do from the bottom of my Heart.

Holding in his Hand a Hatchet Belt and scalp affixed to it.

Father, This Belt I rec'd four years ago from Gov'r Hamilton, and I now show it to you to convince you that I have adhered to what was said to me upon it, and that I have also communicated the contents of it to the Southern Nations. The good effects of it begin already to appear as they have commenced Hostilities against the Enemy.

The Snake Shawanese Chief speaks for himself and the Shade, another Shawanese Chief

Father, You are now acquainted with the resolutions of our Nation from our Chief, Wry Neck, and now Father you will listen to me who left our Villages some time after him. This piece of Tobacco that I present you with overtook me on my way here, and was to desire me to make all the haste I possibly could to this Place, to acquaint you that the Enemy were in motion and coming, and that no delay should be made in coming to their assistance, as they are too weak to withstand them. Here is a piece of their Flesh taken from them when in actual motion towards us.

Delivers a piece of Tobacco with a fresh Scalp tied to it.

(Signed) At S. DEPEYSTER.

Endorsed Copy (15.) A Council held the 5th day of April, 1781, with some of the principal Chiefs of the Shawanese, Delawares & Cherokees at Detroit.

[B 123 p 18.]

GENERAL HALDIMAND TO MAJOR DE PEYSTER

QUEBEC 10th April, 1781.

SIR, I have received your letter of the 8th January, reporting the defeat of a party of Rebels from the Cohokias who had seized upon the effects of the Traders at St. Joseph's—the conduct of Lieut. DuQuindre and the Indians was very meritorious. Whatever may have been the Motives of the Latter. This attempt Should Serve to Convince the Traders of the impropriety of permitting Large Quantities of Goods to be carried into Remote Quarters where they cannot be protected by the Kings Troops. I should suppose you have but little to apprehend from Mr. Clark's success in Collecting a Force at Williamsbourg to attempt Detroit. The Enemy having Sufficient Employment in that Quarter, besides that the late cheques at the Miamis & St. Joseph's & the Effect Clark will know they must have had upon the Indians, will make him cautious how he returns to that country. I doubt not however that you will have the Breach in the New Work repaired with diligence & take every step that may be necessary for the defence of your Post.

I am, &c.,

(Signed) FRED. HALDIMAND.

A Letter of the 12th April to Captain Robertson commanding at Oswegatchie is here inserted by a P. S., it relates a convoy of 70 Sleighs. Sent from Schenactady to fort Stamoix, Major De Peyster.

Endorsed copy, 1781, To Major DePeyster, of the 10th April.

[B 123 p 23.]

GENERAL HALDIMAND TO MAJOR DE PEYSTER

QUEBEC 10th April 1781

SIR, I have received your letter of the 8th January advising me of your having drawn Bills upon me to the amount of £44,962 York Currency, which I have since honored—The Frequency of these Amazing demands is a matter of very serious Concern to me, knowing how ill they are received at Home, and how very trifling the Services that can be urged in Support of them, I therefore cannot help repeating to you my earnest desire, that you make a

Diminution of these Expences in the Indian Department an object of your first attention—the Indian Presents, and the expensive articles that compose them are enormous, I am not a stranger to the Persecution Commanding Officers are subject to at the Posts from the continual Requisitions of Indians prompted by the avidity of the Traders, but it is so essential a part of their duty to evade all Demands that are not indispensably necessary, that I persuade myself the Inconvenience will be chearfully submitted to, and a little firmness in refusing to Indians what their real wants do not require, will make them more reasonable in their demands.

I am Sir &c

(Signed) FRED. HALDIMAND

Major De Peyster

Endorsed:—(Copy) 8, To Major De Peyster at Detroit 10th April Copy, Entered in Book marked B no 2 Page 20

[B 123 p 24]

MEMORIAL

To His Excellency Frederick Haldimand, Governor General of the Province of Quebec & dependencies Commander in Chief of the said province &c. &c. &c.

SIR, Philip Rocheblave has the honor to state to you, that, as a punishment for his attachment to Government, the Americans took him prisoner in 1778 at the Illinois on the Mississippi where he commanded for the British Government. They plundered him in such a way as to leave nothing either for himself or his wife & family. He has undergone a long & cruel captivity during which he has been obliged to have recourse to ruinous means of living and clothing in a country where distress was general, Whilst in addition his wife who was living at the Illinois with the children was forced to use the same means, producing a mass of debts, which, since his return he has tried in vain to pay by means of his industry. In consequence of his attachment to Government he has refused to return to the command of the Illinois for the Province of Virginia, though they have proposed to him since his captivity to indemnify his losses & shown the advantage that it would be if he would take their part. Your Excellency is a witness of his zeal in the cause of the King for whom he has already incurred a great expense last year in bringing part of his family. The rest with the mother are presently to return to Michillimakinac on their way here where he hopes to settle under the protection of the British Government, for this purpose he needs land. He asks your Excellency to accord him in the name of Government 1,000 acres in the place called the Rideau River below the last Gallop in mounting the River Cataraquouy, that the said Rideau River is only an overflow of the first which takes place in a low part of the north bank opposite Levi Island which water is lost in the River which flows on the north of Michilimakinac, known here under the name of the Grand River into which it flows over a considerable fall. His plan would be to form a useful & constant settlement there and form a store house. That by the favor of the climate they could leave a month sooner than from here & diminish by so much the advantage which our neighbors have over us on account of their climate. Hoping, Sir, you will give him a grant held under the Crown, if it is possible, if not, on any condition you like. He will not cease to make his prayers for the prosperity and preservation of Your Excellency. Montreal the 12th April 1784

(signed) PHILIP ROCHEBLAVE*

Endorsed:—Memorial of Mr de Rocheblave of the 12th April. Recd the 15th
[B 123 p 438]

FROM CAPTAIN MOMPESSON. UNADDRESSED

MICHILIMACKINAC ISLAND 15th April 1781.

SIR, According to your Message delivered to me by Mr. Cotes respecting Cardinal and La Roche being sent for from this Post, I hereby inform you that the reason I had for sending those two people prisoners away from this Post, was on account of their characters being too bad for them to be enlarged with the rest of the people brought from the Illinois, they having been in Irons in the Guard house, for some time past, before I arrived at this Post, and as upon enquiry of their characters, whilst you was ill and incapable of transacting Public Business, I found they could not be trusted from the sight of a Sentry—I judged it most advisable to send them down the Country Prisoners, of which I wrote Major de Peyster, mentioning particularly of Cardinal to him, Besides the Soldiers of the Guard had frequently represented to me the inconvenience they were put to by having the above mentioned prisoners continually in the Guard House with them, they being full of Filth and Vermin, and cooking their Victuals at the Guard House fire, caused altogether an insufferable stench for people in health to be in. These above mentioned considerations was the cause of my sending them away Prisoners to Canada—Where I imagined a more suitable lotment would be found for them.

I am, Sir, your most obedt Servt.

JOHN MOMPESSON.

[B 98 p 21]

*See appendix

Dr.—*Monthly Returns of Liquors & Provisions received & Delivered at Michili-*

Date.	From whom received.	Rum.		Salt Provisions Received.									No. of Vouchers.
				Flour.	Pork.		Pease.		Butter.		Oatmeal.		
		Galls.	½ pts.	lbs.	lbs.	oz.	Galls.	pts.	lbs.	oz.	lbs.	oz.	
M'ch 25..	Remaining in Store......	3,084	6	124,572	64,629	6	3,828	2	3,235	7	2,293	15	34 35 36 37 38 39 40 41 42 43 44
April 24.	Purchased from ye troops	......	......	....	127	...	......	...	......	...	......	...	
	Received....................	3,084	6	124,572	64,756	6	3,828	2	3,235	7	2,293	15	
	Delivered....................	208	10	10,954	5,813	15	570	7	572	2	489	14	
Remaining in store April 25.........		2,875	12	113,628	58,943	9	3,237	3	2,663	5	1,804	1	
	Rationed....................			1 lb.		97		3–7		6–7		11–7	
	No. of Rations....................			113,628	103,145		60,802		49715		25536		
	Victuals 100 men................			days. 1,136	days. 1,031		days. 608		days. 497		days. 255		

mackinac Island between 25th March & 24th April, 1781, Inclusive—Cr.

Date.	To whom Issued and to whom sent.	Rum.		Salt Provisions Issued.										Rations.
				Flour.		Pork.		Pease.		Butter.		Oatmeal.		
		Galls.	½ pts.	lbs.	oz.	lbs.	oz.	Galls.	pts.	lbs.	oz.	lbs.	oz.	
April 24.	Lieut. Govr......	......	....	31	....	17	11	1	5	1	10	2	3	31
" "	Royal Artillery....	......	....	62	....	35	6	3	2	3	5	4	6	62
" "	8th Regiment.....	......	....	2,077	....	1,187	....	111	2	111	4	148	8	2,077
" "	84th Regiment....	......	....	403	....	230	4	21	4	21	9	28	12	403
" "	Interpreter.......	......	....	31	....	17	11	1	5	1	11	2	3	31
" "	Brrk Master......	......	....	31	....	17	11	1	5	1	10	2	3	31
" "	Indian officers....	......	....	93	....	53	2	4	7	4	15	6	10	93
" "	Navy.............	27	2	651	....	217	....	13	4	27	2	27	2	434
" "	Artificers.........	85	4	2,046	....	682	....	42	5	85	4	85	4	1,364
" "	Labourers.........	17	7	558	....	318	13	19	7	29	14	39	13	558
" "	Sundry uses.......	78	13	3,563	....	1,879	2	170	2	98	1	53	4	3,206
" "	Commissary.......	......	....	31	....	17	11	1	5	1	10	2	3	31
" "	Cooper...........	......	....	31	....	17	10	1	5	1	10	2	3	31
" "	Blacksmith........	......	....	31	....	17	11	1	5	1	10	2	3	31
	Rejected..........	......	....	1,225	....	1,033	...	184	....	141	....	83	....	......
	Lost by Transp. Diff in wt. & Issuing..	......	....	90	....	54	....	......	....	40	....	....	....	......
	Total issued...........	208	10	10,957	....	5,813	13	570	7	572	2	489	14	8,383

David Mitchell,
Acting Commissary.

[B 98 p 26]

Return of the Number & Denomination of People victualled at Michilimackinac Island between the 25th March & the 24th April, 1781.

	Lieut. Governor.	Artillery.	8th Regiment.	84th Regiment.	Interpreter.	Barrk. Masr.	Indian officers.	Navy.	Artificers.	Labourers.	Indians, &c.	Commissary.	Cooper.	King's Black-smith.	Total.
No. of each..................	1	2	69	13	1	1	3	14	44	18	103	1	1	1	272

Provisions Issued per Contra rationed.

	Flour.	Pork.		Pease.		Butter.		Oatmeal.	
	Pounds.	Pounds.	oz.	Galls.	pts.	Pounds.	oz.	Pounds.	oz.
Issued at the Garrison as pr ration	2,821	1,612	......	151	1	151	2	201	8
Rationed at....................	M	....	9 1-7	......	3-7	....	6-7	....	1½
No. of Rations in all Species...	2,821	2,821	......	2,821	......	....	......	2,821	......

[B 98 p 24]

Return of the Barracks, with their Bedding, Furniture and utensils taken at Michilimackinac Island 24th April 1781.

	Chords of wood.	Pounds of Candles.	Guard Rooms.	Barrack Rooms.	Iron Stoves.	Tables.	Forms.	Buckets.	Prs. of Tongs.	Prs. of Handirons.	Trundles.	Iron Kettles.	Brass Kettles.	Panes of Glass.	Bed Cases.	Bolster Cases.	Ruggs.	Blanketts.	Prs. of Sheets.	Candlesticks.	Axes.	Fire Shovels.	Grind Stones,
Total.	25	80	1	13	8	10	12	17	20	17	12	19	3	611	98	115	41	165	125	5	29	10	1

A. Langdon,

Acting Barrack Master.

N. B. The Furniture, utensils & Bedding very much worn.

To Richard Murry Esqr

D. Barrack Master Genl at Quebec.

[B 98 p 23]

Return of His Majesty's Garrison at Michilimackinac Island 24th April, 1781.

Detachments.	Officers present.							Effective Rank & File.							Royal Artillery.		
	Commissioned.				Staff.												
	Lieut. Govr.	Captain.	Lieut.	Ensign.	Surgeons Mt.	Serjeants present.	Drummers present.	Present fit for duty.	Sick in quarters.	Sick in Hospital.	On command.	Recruiting.	On Furlow.	Total.	Corporal.	Matrosses.	Total.
8th Regiment	....	1	1	1	1	3	2	67	4	2	....	....	....	73	1	1	2
84th Regiment	1	1	....	....	....	1	....	28	....	....	1	....	....	29	....	....	....
Total	1	2	1	1	1	4	2	94	4	2	1	....	....	102	1	1	2

PATT SINCLAIR,
Capt 84th Regiment.

[B 98 p 23]

GENERAL HALDIMAND TO MAJOR DE PEYSTER

QUEBEC 20th April 1781.

SIR, I have received your Letter of the 8th January, advising me of your having drawn Bills upon me to the Amount of £44,962 York Currency, which I have since honored—The frequency of these Amazing Demands is a matter of very serious Concern to me, knowing how ill they are Received at Home, and how very trifling the services that can be urged in Support of them.

Having so often expressed my anxiety to You on this important Subject, and convinced of your paying every possible attention to it, I forbear enlarging thereon. The Exhorbitant Charges of the Merchants at the Posts have determined me to send up Supplies for the Indians from hence, and I have given orders immediately to purchase and forward an Assortment (from your Estimate) least any Accident should happen to retard the arrival of the goods from England, and I hope you will have no occasion, or will be able to avoid purchasing any more goods, particularly Rum—until this Supply reaches you. But this measure must not be divulged least the Traders should in the mean Time take advantage of it.

I am Sir &c

(Signed) FRED HALDIMAND

Major Depeyster

Endorsed:—(Copy) 81 To Major De Peyster at Detroit 20th April.

[B 123 p 25]

INDIAN COUNCIL

At a Council held at Detroit the 26th April 1781, by Major de Peyster Commanding Detroit and its Dependencies, with the several nations.

Present.

Major De Peyster Commanding Detroit &c
Major Gamble Commandg the Detacht 47th Regt
Alexander McKee Esqr Depy Agent

Captain Bird	King's (or 8th) Regt
Lieut Bennet	
Lieut Mercer	
Lieut Pepyat	
Lieut Saumarez	
Ens Frey	

Lieut Du Vernett—Royal Artillery
Lieut Hamilton—47th Regt

Duperon Baby for the Shawanese		Sworn Interpreters.
Isidore Chesne	" Ottawas &c	
Pierre Druillard	" Hurons	
Wm. Tucker	" Chippaweys	

INDIAN CHIEFS.

Six Nations.	*Hurons*	*Ottawas*
Ca, ya, Shu ta,	Andesherry	Chaminatawa
Captain Brandt	Sunhusagaya	Wiwishgay
Alias The, yain, de, ne, ga	Mandoron	Nianega
	Sundinon	Kewitchiwini
	Shugenesse	Egonshewey
	The na towat	Nitanweykisik
		Nigick
		Chimanduck
		Attawackey

Chippoweys	*Potewatamies*
Quokock	Pemomoketack
Mishiash	Chibins
Wiannockeum	
Tuckaweygassi	
Soushgoyné	
Shabokgoy	
Washemang	
Muckey dewassen	

Miamis

Key ta ga yan and a great number of the Warriors of the several Nations.

Children (the Shawanese &c, that compose the Ohio confederacy.

Your Belts and Strings were delivered to be the other day in council, their contents were made known unto me, you desired they should be delivered to your Brothers the Ottawas, Chippeways, and the other Nations who were then absent, requesting in the name of your Confederacy, immediate assistance to repel the Rebel force which were making their appearance in your country; as you are now present in this General Assembly of which I am rejoiced that you see with your own eyes, part of a Nation, who for a long time were absent (Ouidas) and our Friends the six Nations, who are come to your aid. I now desire that you repeat the Contents of your Embassy to your Brothers present.

Sastaritsi, then spoke on 4 Strings mix'd Wampum.

Father! I pray you to attend as also my Brothers from nigh and afar to what I am now going to relate.

Brothers—You have heard of the arrival of one of our Fathers Vessels from Niagara, in her came our Brothers the Six Nations—Two of their Chiefs addressed themselves to me, and said that they hoped their Brethren would now open their Ears and attend to what was good—here is one of them (Cayashutta) that has animated us, and that from us he looked for assistance, after that of his Father.

The Snake, Shawanesse Chief speaks on a Belt and several strings of Wampum.

Father, You see that your Children of the Confederacy on the Ohio are here assembled—some days elapsed since we met you in Council; informing you that we were under great apprehension from being harrass'd continually by our Enemies the Rebels, that we prayed the assistance of you our Father & that of your Children—These Strings and Belt we left with you to deliver to e-y Ottawas, Chippawas, & the rest of our then absent Brethern.

Brothers, We brown skins are all of one blood & I who speak to you am sent by the Confederacy of the Ohio to inform you of the Accounts received by a Prisoner, which alarmed us not a little—we thought it our Duty to communicate the same to our Father and his Children our Allies—no sooner we saw our embarrassed Situation we immediately recollected the antient Friendship which subsisted between us, we were told that the Enemy were numerous and encroached our Country—we then thought it most advisable to come in unto you, who are the great Body, and with your assistance be enabled to drive them from out of our Country, Brothers, How could you plead ignorance to our situation, we applied to you last Fall but had no relief—We now make this declaration before our Father, and you our Brethern who compose this great assembly, in order that you may no more, in future, appear ignorant.

Brothers,—holding Indian Tobacco—

You now have heard what we have had to say to you, we now present you this herb which we have received from Heaven: we pray you to give us your immediate answer, to smoake therefrom as a few whiffs of it induces us to grant the request that may be made upon it.

He then held up a Scalp with a piece of Tobacco thereto, and repeated much the same as in Conference of the 5th instant—and added

Father, What I've now said is no more than what I delivered to you the other day in Council, praying your assistance—as a delay may be of great consequence, but if we get up in time we may meet the Enemy ere they be upon us.

Major De Peyster then spoke,

Children—The Shawanese, Delawares, and the rest of the Nations that are of your Confederacy—I am now going to address myself to the Ottawas, Chippawas, and the Nations who were absent at the time I met you in Council, when you made your request respecting your Embassy, where you required Assistance—I told you that I would supply you with Ammunition and necessary Clothing as much as I can spare—as to men the number I have, are employed for the defense of this Post, to keep it in security that I may receive my Children from time to time with open Arms—I pitch upon St Dusky for a Depot, and I request that you and your Brethern the Warriors in general to attend there. I can almost answer for your Brethern, that it is unnecessary to press them on to meet the Enemy, it was with difficulty I could prevail on them to remain here untill the great Council met, as they were continually proposing to send off small Parties of 10 and 15 men to War—I am of opinion that it would be much better that my Children gather & collect themselves into a great Body, by which means they will be able to frustrate the designs of the Rebels, ere they penetrate into the Indian Country, you now see that my wishes coinside with yours and that I am ready to support you in defeating their attempts—

Children, I have last received a letter from a Trader at Rocher de bout* which informs me that the Enemy have taken possession of Kuskackin, and are inclined to get to St Dusky—for my part, I don't put an implicit confidence in the report, as I cannot imagine them to be so far advanced—if true, we need not cry for the loss of that place, as we may then be assured that the Indians of Kushackin are Enemies to the Rebels—

*See appendix

Cayashutta great war Chief of the six Nations then speaks on 4 Strings white & black Wampum, and addressing himself to the several Nations present.

Brothers, I now greet you all and am much rejoiced to see you all assembled at our Fathers Council Fire.—you have heard that we brown skins are one Body, and I now tell you that we the Six Nations are come here for to open your Ears to hear what is good, and to attend to whatever our Father may say—

On which delivers the 4 Strings

The, ya, en, dinega (alias) Capt. Brandt, addressed himself to the several Indian nations, and said.

I am pleased to find that you are ready to assist your Brethren the Shawanese—You see me here, I am sent upon Business of importance to your several nations, I shall follow you and your Father to the camp that it is to be formed at St. Dusky, at which place I shall deliver you the Speeches of the Six Nations in presence of the Ohio confederacy who will be there, I hope when you are acquainted with the contents of my Embassy it may furnish means to unite you more strongly in the cause we are mutually engaged, and continue our Friendly intercourse as the meeting will be general.

Major De Peyster, holding a War belt.

Children; This Belt is sent to you from the Six Nations, in order to sharpen your War Hatchets from St. Dusky.

Delievers the War Belt to Cayashutta, who sings as is usual, and says—Take Courage, Brethren, this is our Fathers Hatchet, we will make a good use of it.

Onishacheré a Wyandotte Chief sings the War Song, and then says—

Father, I sing because I am disposed to meet my Brethren at your Council Fire, which is to be held at St. Dusky.

Egnshewey, Ottawaa War Chief takes the War Belt and sings, after which he says—

Father, you see your children are prepared to meet the Enemy, don't let us see but a few of your own colour, let us see you get up with a number of them—

Mashquiash Chippowey Village Chief takes the Belt & Speaks—

Father, you see here your Children & speak well to them, you have a Strong Arm, why don't you arise and go with us where you direct—

Negig, Ottawaa War Chief

Father, Why should I not take this War Hatchet, when it is presented from you and my Brethren.

The Council was then closed with the following Speech by Major De Peyster.

Children, I have already told you that this Belt is delivered for to sharpen your Hatchet on, and that I shall give you all the support that is necessary—You seem to hint that I should go with you to War; my reasons are already assigned which prevent my going out with you, and I hope when you reflect on them, that it appear to your satisfaction—You say I sit still, but don't you see that I am not idle—have I not raised the ground and made this place strongly fortified against any attempt whatever, that I may be able to protect my children and supply them with the necessaries. Don't suppose that your Father the King does nothing because he sits still, who has as many children as the sands of the Sea to supply. I now conclude with assuring that the officers &c belonging to your Department shall be ordered to be in readiness to attend you. (Signed)

At S. DePeyster, Major.

Extracted from the Council Book, J. Schieffelin Secr. Ind'n Dept.

* * * * * * * * * * * *

Memorandum

On Thursday the 26th April 1781. P. M.

After closing of Council, arrived a young Indian in three days from St Dusky and reports that the Children of the Chief from that place (Du, you goud) report that they saw the Virginians at the Village of Kushackin—that they divided their Army in two Parties, each of which took a different rout, one by St Dusky and the other by the Shawanese side.

The Indian Women of St Dusky have dispatched this runner with this message on four Strings of Black Wampum and a piece of Tobacco tied thereon, praying that their Father Major DePeyster to send them immediate relief, that seven days are elapsed since the Enemy left that place—50 men from St Dusky departed immediately in search of them. The Indians of Kushackin retired with great precipitation towards St Dusky, half naked, being surprised by the Enemy. Simon Girty is gone on to the upper St Dusky to get what news he can from a Rebel Prisoner, who was taken by the half Kings Son.

Endorsed:—Copy, 16 Indian Council held at Detroit 26th April 1781.

[B 123 p 27]

GARRISON ORDER

MICHILIMACKINAC 28th April 1781.

A Vessel will sail in the beginning of next week for Detroit. Any person wishing to send their Letters in one Packet to Detroit, Niagara, Carleton Island, Montreal, Quebec and Europe may deliver them to Serjeant Langdon before twelve monday forenoon.

[B 98 p 56]

GENERAL HALDIMAND TO LIEUT. GOV. SINCLAIR

QUEBEC

SIR, The season for the departure of the trading Canoes bound up the Grand River being arrived, & the Traders become very solicitous for their Passes, I am obliged to gratify their wishes, although I should have been glad to have heard from the Indian Countries, before they set out, which the Backwardness of the Season has prevented, I have however taken the necessary precaution of laying on them the strictest Injunctions of submitting implicitely to such restrictions as from circumstances unknown here, and the Good of His Majesty's Service, you may see fit to lay them under, and I must earnestly desire that you will pay the utmost attention to the respective destinies of these Traders, who I cannot help thinking under a pretext of exercising the *Furr Trade* abuse the Indulgences granted them, for that purpose, and do many things injurious to the King's Interest, & likewise to the Reputation of Trade, I am not so well informed of the complicated circumstances attending that remote Trade as I could wish, or as it is necessary I should be, I enclose to you a few hints & memorandums upon that Subject & I request you will, with your Leisure correct them & suggest to me all such as your long experience and knowledge of that Country, and your late observations may have furnished you with that I may be the better enabled to give that Encouragement, I wish to so essential a Branch of Trade, but at the same time carefully avoid giving Latitudes which in the present situation of affairs might tend to prejudice what we most wish to preserve. Altho' it is practicable to convey supplies to the Enemy, by way of Lake Superior into the Mississippi, the vast labour & difficulties that must attend such an undertaking, makes it rather unlikely that it should be attempted, I am therefore desirous to give every proper encouragement to the North West Trade. Their views however will be better perceived by you, than here, and the officer you send to St. Mary's (should you find that necessary) will be still a further Cheque upon their Conduct.

I send you likewise a Copy of a Memorial from the French Traders in your environs, who, from my apprehension of supplies falling into the Enemies hands, were not permitted to carry up their usual proportion of Goods last year. From reports of affairs upon the Mississippi, these apprehensions are not lessened, but so heavily do the Traders complain of the Losses they have sustained, that to content them I have given Passes for 100 Canoes upon the conditions I have already mentioned to you, and that whenever you see the least prospect of danger, you will not suffer a single article to be sent. Altho' the observations upon the Trade to Detroit do not concern the Trade of your Quarter, Yet, their being in some measure connected has induced me to let them accompany the others—I wish you to be particular upon the subject of persons employed in the Service of Government, being permitted to Trade, as things are now situation, I fear the evil cannot be removed, men who make Hundreds yearly, would relish being reduced to their Ten or Five shillings per day—this evinces the impropriety of suffering upon any pretence whatever, the smallest relation of good order, these people's service having been improperly rewarded by indulging them with carrying up small quantities of goods, from Time to Time, until they at last become professed Traders.

I am Sir, &c

(signed) FRED HALDIMAND

Lieut. Governor Sinclair
[B 98 p 92]

SIMON GIRTY TO MAJOR DE PEYSTER

UPPER ST DUSKY May 4th 1781.

SIR, We sent to Cushoking* twenty of our men, sometime ago, and this day have returned with the following news—20th April Col. Brahead, with 500 men, burn'd the Town & Killed 15 men, left 6 Houses this side of the Creek that he did not see, likewise took the Women & Children Prisoners & afterwards let them go. He let 4 men go that was Prisoners that showed him a paper that they had from Congress.

Bradhead told him that it was none of his faults that their People was killed, but the Militia that would not be under his Command, likewise he told them that in 7 months that he would Beat all the Indians out of this Country. In six days from this Date, he is to set off for this place with one

*See appendix

Thousand men—and Colonel Clark is gone down the Ohio River with one Thousand men.

There was 120 of the Wyandotts that was ready to start off with me, till this news came. Your Children will be very glad that you will send those people you promised to send to their assistance, likewise send the Indians, that is about you, to assist us. The Christian Indians has applied to us to move them off before the Rebels comes to their Town.

I have 160 Indians at this place, their Provisions are all gone, and they beg that you will send them some.

Mr. Sevéyer when he heard that the Rebels were in the Indian Country, He went off to the Lower Town where there was not a man but himself, and told the women & Children that the Rebels was close by. He ran off in the night without giving notice to the Chiefs, or me. He minds Trading more than Kings Business.

I will be much obliged to you Sir, if you send me a little Provisions for myself, as I was obliged to give mine to the Indians.

I am, Sir, Your most obedient and humble Servant

(signed) Simon Girty.

To Major DePeyster Commanding Detroit

[B 98 p 33]

MAJOR DE PEYSTER TO MR. ASKIN

Detroit 10th May 1781.

Sir, In answer to your Letter of this date wherein you put several Questions respecting your behaviour whilst under my command, during 5 years at the Post of Michilimackinac—I have to say, that it was ever my opinion, in every respect you fulfilled the Duties of a Faithfull and Attentive Deputy Commissary and Barrack Master—As to your Loyalty I have experienced it upon several essential occasions, & I cannot but repeat here, what I said to you in a Letter soon after my arrival at this Post, viz, that the Service has often been greatly forwarded by the assistance you had in your power to give, which you always did most cheerfully, and with disinterestedness.

You certainly never excited troubles at the Post of Michilimackinac during my command, nor ever troubled me with disputes relative to private property—On the contrary you have often been a Mediator in differences between seditious persons rather than I should be troubled with them—And, in all your Dealings, I have ever found you, and know you to be esteemed an Honest man.

This much I believe will serve to answer your several questions, give me leave to add, that I have long entertained a friendship for you, and your family, and, as yet see no reason to alter those sentiments—

I am, sir, with great regard & esteem
Your Humble Servant
AT. S. DE PEYSTER

To Mr Jno Askin
[B 98 p 34]

FROM LIEUT. GOV. SINCLAIR WITHOUT SIGNATURE

SIR, The dog work of the new Fort is raised platform high as described in the rough sketch sent to you which shows what is picketed for the present to secure the Troops Stores &c.

The two Vessels which were reported by some mistake, have been put in nearly the same repair as when they arrived. One sailing from Detroit in April & the other has been employed for some weeks past in transporting Bricks Boards Planks &c from the old Fort. The Garrison Boats which were drove away by one accident or other, I found & repaired also. The Trader's servants will receive every encouragement to compleat the works. The enclosed order to the Commissary of the Post will shew that the Prisoners were not treated with inhumanity as to Provisions, & their present allowance of pay will not afford them the same quantity of cloathing which they received from the Indian Store.

In obedience to His Excellency's Command I send all the information I can gather relative to Cardinal, excepting that he is a runaway Bankrupt from Detroit & that he was employed as a Guide by the Rebel Col. Clark.

The Bearer Monsieur Campion very fortunately was at the Post of St. Joseph's to repell the first attack of the Pillagers from the Illinois, His Business called him to Michilimackinac when the second attack was made & the Traders plundered.

I beg to be honored with the Generals orders relative to the conduct to be observed towards those mauraders & to any indulgence hereafter to be shewn the Pottawatamies who still solicit for Traders amongst them.

Inclosed is the Indian Deed for this Island, which may, if not fully comprehensive, be altered to His Excellency's Pleasure.

By the return of Mr. Sarayen of the Indian Department, I am glad to find that the Traders towards the Mississipi have been much protected by the Indians in their neighbourhood, who prevented a like accident to that of St.

Joseph. All the nations to the Westward appear well disposed, and propose coming to this Post to know from me, why they are hindered from going to war to get rid of the People who menaced them & their Traders. I shall make them no answer until I receive a return of this Express.

A Batteau from Detroit with letters for Captain Mompesson mention that no vessel can be sent here for some months, We are in want of Iron Tools and everything but wood, stone and Lime for finishing the officers and men Barracks.

I hope that Mr. Campion's reception will be such as he deserves from his readiness to give every aid to forward the service, of which he gave proofs heretofore as well as here.

I am, Sir, Your most obedient and most humble Servant

PATT SINCLAIR

Lieut Governor & Commandant.

MICHILIMACKINAC 12th May 1781.

[B 98 p 38]

SECRETARY MATTHEWS TO LIEUT. GOV. SINCLAIR

QUEBEC 14th May 1781.

SIR, I am commanded by His Excellency General Haldimand to transmit to you the enclosed Memorial laid before Him by Messrs. Key and McCrae, and to signify to you his Desire that you will consider the merits of it, (to Him unknown) and render such Justice to the Parties concerned as you shall think equitable.

I am, Sir, &c

(signed) R. MATTHEWS.

Lieut Governor Sinclair.

[B 98 p 43]

MAJOR DE PEYSTER TO GENERAL HALDIMAND

DETROIT 27th May 1781.

SIR, I am honoured with Your Excellency's letters of the 10th and 20th April. It gives me great concern to find that I have been under the indispensible necessity of Purchasing a large Quantity of Indian Goods, it was evident to me at the time I purchased, that the goods ordered from England, could not arrive soon enough: not aware that Your Excellency would have

61

purchased in Canada. But at all Events such was the alarm amongst the Indians, on the Report of the Enemys determination of entering their Country and penetrating to Detroit, that it became necessary to answer the demands of the several Nations, who were invited to assemble here, besides the Supplies to be sent into the Shawanese Country and the Quantity requisite to secure the Wabash Indians who were very high and insolent upon the Occasion, till they found that Linot* failed in procuring the troops he expected by the Mississippi—What remains in store, after having endeavoured to satisfy the different nations will serve to cloathe the warriors on their Return who are always Naked, the Squaws never failing to tear off everything from their backs, before they enter the Fort, when they must be Equipd anew and also rewarded for their Exploits however trifling——

Mr Baby has joined me, with his utmost Endeavours to lessen the enormous expences at this Post and its dependencies, I am therefore extremely sorry that at the time we expected in some measure to bring about Your Excellency's Wishes, the exigencies of the times should have obliged us, to pursue the old plan of Pleasing the Indians at all Events——

I am sensible of the Justness of Your Excellency's Remarks that the Services which can be urged, are trifling in Support of the Expense. The following possibility however may be admitted.

The Rebellious disposition of the Canadians of this upper country, including Post Vincents and the Illinois joined to the Natural Liking the Indians have for them in preference to the English might in Case the French & Spaniards found means to push goods and Ammunition up the Mississippi draw the Indians to listen to them, and if not to act against us, at least to remain Neuter. In either case His Majesty's Troops with this present garrison would be confined to the Limits of a small fort till your Excellency could enlarge it.

It was the goods and the goods only that made the Miamies & the Pottewattimies strike LeBalm & the Creoles. Some Extra Presents have also been well applied by Mr. Baby in defence of our Provisions, by dispatching the Indian families otherwise our provisions would not have lasted so as to have had a Sufficiency in Case of Emergency a supply could not have been had.

I am in hopes that in a month the Fort will be in a State of Resistance against any force they can possibly bring, notwithstanding that our other Works accumulate fast. On the 23rd Instant, our Powder Magazine in the Citadel fell in.

We have nothing new from the Camp at Sandusky, since the account of Broadheads having cut off the Delaware Villages, and Clarke gone down the Ohio to Kentucky to raise the Militia there, with what numbers I am not

*See appendix

well informed. The reports of a thousand men I can by no means credit, but I know the Militia of Kentucky exclusive of two hundred Soldiers at the Falls will amount to eleven Hundred men.

Your Excellency need not be under the least apprehension of the Transport being stopp'd on Account of the Schooner Hope, on the contrary it will be greatly forwarded; had she undergone a slight Repair she must have been laid up in August, supposing she had weathered it out till then. Now it is expected she will be ready to sail in July, and thereby gain one month of Transport at a season when there will be most need of it, the Master Builder tells me he must take out two hundred Timbers which are quite decayed, when Repaired he says she will last four years.

I have the Honour to be Sir

Your Excellency's most obedient & Most Humble Servant

AT S. DE PEYSTER.

P. S. Just as I was closing my letter, an Express arrived from Sandusky with a letter from Captain Jos. Brant and Monsr. Isidore Chesne, which I Herewith Enclose.

His Excellency General Haldimand

Endorsed:—No 7 Entd From A. 1781 Major DePeyster 27th May Recd 16th June Copy In Book B No 3 Page 14

[B 123 p 42]

ACCOUNT

Account of Sundry Goods for Indian Presents sent to Detroit addressed to Major De Peyster commanding there. Lachine 28th May & 6th June 1781.

		£	s	d
1200 Pair 2½ Point Blankets at 15s per pair	£	900	....	....
24 Pieces Scarlet Cloth 638 yards @ 16s 8d		531	13	4
30 Pieces Crimson and Scarlet Strouds 180s per piece		270	....	....
72 Pieces Blue Strouds 140s		504	....	....
43 Pieces Moltons sorted 75s		161	5	....
10 Pieces Bath Coating 348 yards @ 7s 6d		130	10	....
10 Pieces Ratteens 282 yards @ 6s		84	12	....
52 pieces Callimanco 50s		130	....	....
1000 yards Tinsel Lace 1s 6d		75	....	....
1000 do 2s 4d		116	13	4
1080 Yards Callico 4s 6d		243	....	....
42 pieces Linens 1575 yards 2s 4d		183	15	....
53 groce Gartering 20s		53	....	....
500 lbs Vermilion 10s		250	....	....
4 Nests Copper Kettles 162½ lb 3s 9d		30	9	3
4 Nests Brass do 320 lb 2s 6d		40	....	....
10 groce Butchers Knives 60s		30	....	....
10 Groce Indian Awls 8s 4d		4	3	4
10 Groce Gun Worms 7s 6d		3	15	....
10 do Fire Steels 16s 8d		8	6	8
3 do Spring Knives 50s		7	10	....
1 Groce Scissars		2	10	....
375 Fusils 36s		....	....	....
91 Half Axes 4s 2d		18	19	2
300 Small Do 2s 6d		37	10	....
1111½ lb Carrot Tobacco 4s		222	6	....
36 Doz Pocket Looking Glasses 7s 6d		13	10	....
57 Pieces Ribbons 20s		57	....	....
100 Brass Smoking Tomahawks 4s		....	....	....
195 Hoes 5s		48	15	....
John Campbell Supert. Ind. Affairs	£	4158	3	1

Endorsed:—Account of Sundry Goods for Indian Presents sent to Detroit, 6th June 1781.
£4158 3 1.

[B 123 p 47]

INVOICE

Invoise of Sundry Goods for Indian Presents sent off in Batteaux's from Lachine addressed to Major de Peyster, commanding at Detroit, marked and numbered as per margin.

Ind: †Dt. Detroit.	
No 1 a 24	24 Bales cont. 950 pair each is 1200 pair 2½ point Blankets
25 a 27 / 69 a 72	7 do do 102 pieces Stroud or 2142 yards
68	1 do do 24 pieces Scarlet Cloth or 638½ yards.
28 a 29	2 do do 43 pieces Moltons sorted or 1290 yards
30	1 do do 10 pieces Bath Coating or 348 yards
31	1 do do 10 pieces Ratteens or 282 yards
32	1 Trunk do 30 pieces Callimancoes & 2000 yards Tinsel Lace
67	1 do do 60 pieces printed Callicoes 18 yards each
33	1 Case do 42 pieces Linens or 1575 yards
34	1 do do 53 groce Gartering
35 a 36	2 Boxes do 250 lbs Vermillion each
37 a 38	2 Baskets do 4 Nests Copper Kettles
39 a 42	4 do do 4 Nests Brass do
43	1 Box do as follows
	5 groce Butchers Knives
	10 groce Indian Awls
	4 groce Gun Worms
	2 groce Fire Steels
44	1 Box contg. as follows
	5 groce Butchers Knives
	3 " Spring "
	1 groce Scissors
	8 groce Fire Steels
	6 do Gun Worms
45 a 59	15 Cases do 25 Fusils each
60 a 62	3 Boxes do 25 Half Axes & 100 Smaller do each
1 a 3	3 Casks do 1111½ lb Carrot Tobacco

Indn †Dept	
No 73	1 Box Contg 36 Doz. Pocket Looking Glasses & 114 Half Rs. Ribbons
74	1 do do 100 Brass Smoking Tomahawks 30 Hoes and 16 Half Axes
75	1 do do 78 Hoes
76	1 do do 87 do.
77	1 Bale do 22 Pieces Striped Callimanco or 616 yards

JOHN CAMPBELL
Superdt Indn Affairs

Endorsed:—Invoise of Indian Presents Sent to Major De Peyster Detroit May 1781.

[B 123 p 45]

GENERAL HALDIMAND TO LIEUT. GOV. SINCLAIR

QUEBEC the 31st May 1781

SIR, Captain Brehm has communicated to me your Letter of the 12th Instant. I am pleased that the New Fort upon the Island is in such Forwardness. I am persuaded that you will employ to the Best advantage the working Season, in order to Compleat and occupy the new Post as soon as possible. Iron and Tools such as could be procured are forwarded to you.

I am glad to hear that the two Vessels reported by Brigadier General Powell to have been much damaged, are repaired, & navigating and that the Batteau which were dispersed by accident are recovered & repaired.

Particular attention should be had to the place and manner in which all Boats & Canoes are drawn up, that the Prisoners employed in the works may not have an opportunity to escape in them—

In regard to sending Traders to St. Josephs you must be the best Judge how far the conduct of the Potowatamy Indians merit Indulgence, and you may permit Traders to go, or restrain them, just as you find it necessary—

The Potowatamies and all other Indians at Trading Posts, may be informed that if they ever again permit the Enemy to Pillage the Traders they may rest assured that a Trader will never be permitted to return to them—their being on their Hunt, or any other evasive argument will not be any more admitted as an excuse. If Traders are sent amongst them at their Request, it is their duty to protect them, and they must never leave their Villages defenceless, if they keep out proper Scouts & support that Intercourse with each other which the Times require—they can never be surprised—much credit should be given to the Indians towards the Mississippi, who have so faithfully protected their Traders—The good Disposition of the Indians to the Westward affords me much pleasure, I by no means wish to prevent their going to War against their and our Enemies who almost surround them & I recommend that it may be done immediately for their Villages, to enable them to which, reasonable supplies will be allowed them—but their resorting always to Michilimackinac to fit out, must consume Time & swell the expense already so enormous.

I leave & recommend to you to reward the Services of Monsieur Champion, and all other Traders who have manifested their Zeal for the King's service to the Prejudice of their Private Interests, either by giving them the Preference of others, who have not deserved so well of Government by placing them in the most advantageous Trading Posts, or in such manner as you shall see fit.

A Memorial signed by many of the Traders at Michilimackinac has been laid before me representing their sufferings by the late misfortune at St Josephs, & Praying Indemnication thereof, not to mention the Impropriety of Complying with this request, it would be opening a Door, for endless unreasonable applications—if Monsieur Champion or any other Individuals have actually sustained Losses by their being employed in the King's Service (and not having appointments) it is but Reasonable their Losses should be made up to them, but I imagine that the Traders rather solicit, than wait for orders to be sent to a Post, and that those in question were well pleased with their situation, if any Judgement can be formed by the regret with which others left it.

In regard to Cardinal, I cannot as Civil Governor refuse to hear the Complaints of the Kings Subjects—his being sent Prisoner, in Irons and detained as such demanded an explanation—in the mean time you will perceive by the enclosed Extract, that I paid no more attention to his Representations than Common Justice required, and if I had been at first supplied with the Charges now produced, I would never have admitted him to Bail, which I have now recalled & remanded him to Prison—

Whatever Prisoners have been and may hereafter be taken upon such Incursions as the late one at St. Joseph's, are to be allowed Provisions, such as other Labourers, and made to work, Comfortable Cloathing must likewise be provided for them.

Your letters advising of your several Bills dated the 12th & 21st Feb'y, and 12th May, amounting to £38,026, 10, 10 are honoured.

I am Sir

your most obedient most humble Servant

(signed) FRED HALDIMAND

To Lieut. Gov'r Sinclair

P. S. The Bill advised in your Letter of the 12th Feb'y for £1244, N. Y. Curry. in favour of Mr. Champion is also honored.

[B 98 p 46]

SECRETARY MATTHEWS TO LIEUT. GOV. SINCLAIR

QUEBEC 1st June 1781.

SIR, Mr. Joseph Parrant who was taken Prisoner at La Prairie du chien having laid before His Excellency a Memorial requesting Permission to return to Detroit and Michilimackinac, and being well Recommended for this Indulgence, by Mr. Champion, I am directed to acquaint you that His Excellency's him to accompany Mr. Champion to Michilimackinac and leaves it to you to let Him proceed to Detroit or not, as you shall think fit.

The General is informed that there is very good stones for Mills & Grind Stones on the Island, he begs you will give him your opinion of their Quality, and if possible send him a Sample of them, as Hee purposes erecting a Wind Mill on the Island, and at other Posts, he therefore wishes for the best Information and Remarks.

I am Sir, &c &c

(signed) R. Mathews

Lieut Governor Sinclair
[B 98 p 50]

SECRETARY MATTHEWS TO LIEUT. GOV. SINCLAIR

Quebec 1st June 1781.

Sir, Your Letter of the 23rd Feby. reporting for the Information of His Excellency, the Commander in Chief, the Incursion of the Party from the Illinois under Hamelin, upon the Post of St Joseph's, & their Repulse by the good conduct of Mr Champion, I have had the Honor to lay before His Excellency the Commander in Chief, and I am Commanded to acquaint you that His Excellency has signified to you in a Letter of yesterday his approbation of Mr Champions Conduct, & his authority to you to reward his merit as you shall see fit—

The other part of your Letter respecting the New Fort is likewise answered by His Excellency—

I am Sir &c

(signed) R. Matthews—

Lieut Governor Sinclair
[B 98 p 51]

SECRETARY MATTHEWS TO LIEUT. GOV. SINCLAIR

Quebec 1st June 1781.

Sir, I have had the honor to lay before His Excellency General Haldimand your Letter of the 23rd Feby. respecting Messrs. Chevalier & Ainse and I am commanded to acquaint you that it will be necessary to produce Reasons (which will be good in Laws) to justify his not paying them the money; they affirm to have advanced for Government, particularly in the case of the former, who represents that the expense incurred was by order of Major De Peyster (to whom a copy of his Memorial is sent for Information) the General is likewise at a loss how with propriety to Refuse him, the Permission he requires, to return for the purpose of arranging his Affairs, which he represents to have been left in great disorder, and his Private Papers detained—but he would nevertheless for the present defer it, if his presence there would influence the Indians, or in any respect militate against the King's Service, of this, the General wishes he had had early information, but he hopes it is not yet too late to have your opinion respecting it, & the other circumstances contained in his & Ainse's Memorials, as he earnestly wishes to conclude all Intercourse with them, I have some doubt that I omitted sending you a copy of Chevalier's Memorial, I therefore enclose one now—

I am, Sir, &c.

(signed) R. Mathews

Lt Gov Sinclair

[B 98 p 53]

SECRETARY MATTHEWS TO LIEUT. GOV. SINCLAIR

Quebec 1st June 1781.

Sir, Having laid your Letter of the 24th February concerning a List of Medicines wanted for the Post of Michilimackinac before His Excellency the Commander in Chief, I am directed to acquaint you that orders were sent to the General Hospital to provide the Medicines, agreeable to your Requisitions, the Vinegar excepted, which will be sent from Detroit (and they have been forwarded accordingly—

I am Sir &c

(signed) R. Mathews

Lieutenant Governor Sinclair

[B 98 p 52]

LIEUT. GOV. SINCLAIR TO BRIG. GENERAL POWELL

Sir, The termination of disputes was perfectly consonänt to my wish and —as I shall clearly make appear, it has been the object of my attention.

The first part of the Letter you have honored me with upon that subject refers to my interference with the internal Œconomy of the Naval Department. The state in which the vessels were in, laying aside the hasty reports made of them, required some interference, & General Hadlimands letter, received since, directs the very steps which were taken to render them serviceable.

Captain Mompessons complaints shall be answered to very fully, & I beg leave now to trouble you with some Information respecting them, It will be difficult to find out why He should bring in as a complaint my deferring a publication of His Majesty's decision on the rank of Lieut Governors, as any Rank in the Army with the charge given to me by the Commander in Chief placed him still in the same situation in which he now stands.

The enclosed paper No 1 is a copy of my letter to him relative to Hipworth—No 2 is a Copy of the order 28th April—Phillips has done no duty in the Indian Department, or in any other but that in which he was placed by Captain Mompesson, Serjeant Langdon is D. Barrack Master and does the same Regimental Duty as he did in Major DePeyster's Time, & since I have been at the Post Serjeant Dodymead was detached all Winter, and he was put in orders to oversee the Workmen, when he was called in—I am at a loss to conceive how any of these matters can be tortured into Complaint.

Whatever the representations against me may be, or whatever weight they may carry with those to whom they are made, my attention during my stay here shall be, as it has been, invariably directed to the good of the King's Service & the Establishment of the Post.

I have the honour to be Sir,

with respect Your most obedient and most humble Servant

(signed) PATT SINCLAIR Lt. Governor.

Michilimackinac 22nd June 1781.

Brigdr General Powell

[B 28 p 54]

GENERAL HALDIMAND TO MAJOR DE PEYSTER

QUEBEC 24th June 1781.

Major De Peyster

SIR, I have received your Letter of the 27th Ultimo, Covering Copies of Letters from Joseph Brant & Mr. Chêne—Notwithstanding the Reports current in the Quarter where they are, & the Vicinity of Detroit I cannot see a possibility of any thing being Effected the least alarming either against Detroit or even the Indian country. Virginian Troops we are certain cannot be spared to act in Conjunction with the Settlers upon the Frontiers, who alone are the Enemies to be apprehended in that Quarter and their views are merely by taking advantage of the Times to establish themselves, in good settlements, which, if the Indians suffer them to do (and surely they can prevent it) they will find it difficult, after they have tasted the sweets of their Situation to remove them.

The Body of Indians assembled at St. Dusky, if Vigilant and Enterprizing have it in their power to Repel all attempts that can be made, but it is to be apprehended that as long as these people are supplied with Provisions &c. from Detroit, they will not be very desirous of leaving their Camp, but patiently wait for Events—Should this happen, the Expence to Government will be increased, and the active Season wasted, while the Enemy are effecting their purpose and by degrees Establishing themselves in the country—It is unfortunate that the service could not permit so short a delay as the waiting for Indian goods—Expected from here would have occasion the more so, as the alarm of the Indians (perhaps fabricated for the purpose) have turned to nothing, and the Evil consequences which might follow their being supplied by the French and Spaniards from the Mississippi, altho' very probable yet too distant to be alarming—I have determined in future, to supply the wants of the Indians, as mentioned to you in a former Letter, from England, or this place, and to Transport the Goods at the King's expence—This last resource will, I hope in some measure have the desired Effect, assisted as I expect, and am persuaded it will be by you and the officers under your Command.

To which end, it will be necessary, not only to observe a strict Œconomy in the Distribution of Presents, but to make such arrangements in the Indian Store as shall be continually under your immediate Inspection. Inclosed you have an Invoice of Presents already forwarded to you.—on the arrival of a further supply daily expected from England, your Estimate shall be compleated, which will so amply supply every possible want of the Department, that I have directed Brig'r Gen'l Powell to Publish at the several Posts under his command my order of this date, prohibiting the purchasing in future, Rum or Indian Goods, upon any account whatever at the Posts—The former must always be received from the King's Store; and if it should at any time happen that the quantity in store shall be expended before a supply can be procured, it will not be admitted a Reason for Purchasing a Single Gallon from the Traders residing at the Posts. In the Consumption of this Essential Article, I should think it will be much in your Power, by means of the most Pendent of the Sachems to make a dimunition essential at the same time to the object of Expence, to the Punctual Execution of service and to the Healths and well being of the People. I have now by me Speeches lately made in Councils by Chiefs, returning thanks for the happy Consequences of withholding Rum from their People reproaching it as the cause of all their Distresses and hoping that for the time to come it will be distributed with a sparing hand.

You would do well to take the most early & most publick occasion to signify to the Indians, the attention I have had of their wants, by ordering from England a sufficiency to supply them, of the best Quality, and at the same time acquaint them with the Restrictions I have laid you under concerning Rum. Inform them, it is not for the Paultry consideration of its value, that I withhold it from them, it is for the Pernicious Effects it has upon their Warriors & young men, & the poverty and disease it brings upon their Families.

It is because I wish to preserve to the former, the Character of a Brave & Warlike People so long enjoyed by their ancestors, and to the latter, the happiness resulting from Sobriety and Industry—This is the duty of a Father who loves his Children and consequently mine—to the King's faithful Allies—Inform them of the Wisdom of their Brethren mentioned above, and in the Private Council, Work upon the minds of the most respected Sachems & Chiefs, to follow their Example by a Public Approbation of my prohibiting to excess the use of Rum.

(signed) F. H.

P. S. Captain Schank has applied to me to send up money by this opportunity for the Payment of the seamen Employed in the Naval Armament upon the Upper Lakes, but as a more convenient one than the present will soon offer I shall defer it until then.

F. H.

[B 121 p 16]

GENERAL HALDIMAND TO BRIG. GENERAL POWELL

Quebec 24th June 1781.

Brig. Genl Powell

Sir, Having long but in vain attempted to restrain within moderate limits the expences incurred at the several Posts in the Upper Country in the Indian Department, I have at length been able to accomplish an effort which I hope will have a good effect. It is to supply from England or purchasing here the Necessary supplies of Indian presents having by the latter means provided for the present wants of Niagara Detroit and Michilimackinac agreeably to the largest Estimates transmitted to me from these Posts, I have thought fit to prohibit future purchases to be made upon any account whatever you will herewith receive my orders upon this subject which you will please without loss of time to issue and transmit to the several commanding officers and I must desire that for the more effectual execution of them you will inform yourself of all arrangements that shall be made in consequence thereof and give such orders or advice as you shall think most conducive thereto.

The Sums Expended in this Department collectively amounting to a considerable part of the National Expence, and the Services performed by it, being so very inadequate thereto cannot fail of attracting the serious observation of the King's Ministers and ought to command the most unremitting attention of every officer concerned to an object of so great importance.

I am Sir

(Signed) Fred Haldimand

[B 96 2 p 2 34]

SECRETARY MATTHEWS TO MAJOR DE PEYSTER

Quebec 24th June 1781

Sir, By Command of His Excellency General Haldimand, I transmit to you a copy of a Memorial laid before him by Mons Chevalier, late of St Josephs, who was sent down here by Lieut. Governor Sinclair—One of the demands he makes upon Government for Disbursments, appearing to have been made by your order. His Excellency desires You will explain the same, in order that it may be paid, if incurred by sufficient authority, and not in Opposition to the Regulations of the Post.

I am Sir &c.

(Signed) R. Mathews

Major Depeyster

His Excellency is pleased to direct that you will send to Michilimackinac by the first opportunity two Barrels of Vinegar for the use of that Post.

R. M.

Endorsed:—(Copy) 81 To Major De Peyster at Detroit 24th June

[B 123 p 48].

MAJOR DE PEYSTER TO CAPTAIN MCKEE

DETROIT 25th June 1781.

DEAR SIR, I received your letter inclosing mine directed to Capt Thompson—I hope by the time you receive this he will be at Laurimiers—Here are a number of letters for his division which I have thought best to forward to you as you will soon have an opportunity of sending to him—Your Ships arrived from England from the 12th to the 20th May they confirm the news from Virginia and the accounts of the Dutch—Genl Clark is coming to Canada with some troops it is not known how many he is to succeed to Mr Cramahe—

Your friends here all join in Compliments to you

I am Sir Your Humbl & obedt Servt.

AT. S. DE PEYSTER

torn that to Chenes
returned from Fort Pitt
they saw nothing stirring

Indian Affairs M. G. III
To Capt McKee

FROM MR. ASKIN UNADDRESSED

QUEBEC June 28th 1781.

May it please your Excellency,

Mr. Day the Commissary General has been pleased to make me acquainted with Your Excellency's pleasure, respecting my Pay & other matters. Permit me to assure Your Excellency that I ever will retain a due sense of these obligations.

I have much to say however dare not Intrude on Your Excellency's Time, further than to beg your Excellency will be pleased to peruse the inclosed papers which will shew, what Major DePeyster's sentiments of me always have been, and what Lieut Governor Sinclair lately were.

There is but one thing wanting, to make me full amends for my long & expensive Voyage, & that is, to have the Honor of waiting on Your Excellency, that being the great & principal Proofs to strangers that I havent Incurred Your Excellency's Displeasure. If after your Excellency has perused the within papers, you find no Impropriety in my request, I shall be happy to attend your Excellency's leisure, after which, with you Excellency's permission I will return to my Family I hope that eleven years faithful service, tho' not in a high Station, will recommend me to this mark of Your Excellency's favour.

I have the honor of being with all possible respect

Your Excellencys most obedient & very humble Servant

JOHN ASKIN.

[B 98 p 57]

FROM LIEUT. GOV. SINCLAIR UNADDRESSED

SIR, Since my last letter by Monsieur Champion we have raised the old Provision Store, the Soldier's Barracks, with stone chimnies, the Powder Magazine Stone work, both partly cut stone, & have kept raising the defences of the Fort which receive our rubbish. The foundation of the officers Barracks will be laid in a few days. I detained the men of the King's Canoes for one week & allowed the Labourers four York Shillings per week and the oarmen six.

The distant Indians were arrived in greater numbers than usual before Mr. Carey arrived with the King's Canoes, their stay was rendered more tolerable by the supply of Indian Corn which the last favourable season furnished us with.

They appear firmly attached & have given up their French & Rebel Medals with assurances that they will not listen to the tales with which they have hitherto been abused by the Enemy & that they will be answerable for the Safety of our Traders.

The Conduct of the Indians near the Mississippi deserve confidence.

I have the honor to be, Sir, Your most obedient & most humble Servant

PATT SINCLAIR Lt. Governor

MICHILIMACKINAC 8th July 1781

[B 98 p 59]

FROM LIEUT. GOV. SINCLAIR UNADDRESSED

SIR, A few Carpenters, some Iron Spades, & Picks Axes are much wanted at this Post as early as they can be conveyed.

I have made requisitions to Brigdr General Powel and to Major DePeyster for them which probably are wanting on the communication.

I am Sir, your most obedient humble Servant.

PATT SINCLAIR Lt Governor

MICHILIMACKINAC 8th July 1781.

[B 98 p 58]

INVENTORY

Inventory of Merchandize for Indian Presents remaining in the Kings Store, Detroit the 17th July 1781

834 plain shirts of Linnen
503 fine Ruffl'd Shirts
28 small ditto,
174 Calico ditto,
85 Striped Cotton ditto
57 Russia Sheeting ditto
111 Callimanco Bed Gowns
37 lined do with flannel
76 Calico Coats,
33 Scarlet Coats, Laced
3 pieces Strip'd Cotton
222 Capotts
525 yards Tinsel Lace
16½ doz Gun Locks
12⅔ Doz Spurs
18 Groce finger Rings
38 Groce Morrice Belts
5 Groce Jews Harps
7½ Doz Watch chains
450 Stretching Needles
11½ Groce Brass Thimbles
8½ Doz Tobacco Boxes
2 2-12 Doz Snuff Boxes
3 2-12 Doz Ink Stands
38 Pair Cotton Trousers
44 Pair Stroud & Ratteen ditto
9 Pair Russia Sheeting ditto
20½ pieces of Muslin
51 Doz Scalping Knives
85 Doz Clasp ditto
30 Speers
13 8-12 Gro. Gun Worms
13¼ doz worsted Caps
17 Pieces & 7 yds. Russia Sheeting
37 7-12 doz. small Pewter Basons
73 Pair 1 pt Blankets, & 1½ pt.
7 pieces & 3 Yards Calico
6 Saddles
125 lbs Woorsted
44½ doz Combs
145 Briddles,
10 Pieces of Embos'd Serge
2 pieces of white Flannel
17 Tents,
161 Pair Shoes,
11 2-12 doz. pair Shoe Buckles,
8½ pieces Irish Linnen
309 Smoked Skins
74 Pair Mokasins
38 Beaver Traps
87¼ doz Looking glasses
470 Cotton Handkerchiefs
81 Linnen ditto
33 Black Silk ditto
5 Large Fusils
4 Pair Pistols
83 Riffles
44 lbs Brass wire
52⅔ Pieces Strouds
3 Pieces Scarlet Cloth
12 yards Ratteen
26 Hatts
92 Pieces Strip'd Callimanco
6 Pair Saddle Bags
4 lb Coarse Thread
5600 Needles
7 Pieces Blanketting
15 Nests Gilt Trunks
18 ditto hair ditto
57 small kettles
1 Nest Copper ditto
2128 lb Tobaco
29 oil cloths and Sails
3 cases of Beeds
198½ Pair 2½ pt. Blankets
119 Pair 2 pt. ditto
100¼ Gro. Gartering
10½ Gro. Narrow ditto
8 pieces Ribbon
7¼ Gro. Ferretting
11 Crooked Knives
2 8-12 Gro. Awls
2½ doz Scissors
55 Wampum
2300 lb Shott and Ball

[B 123 p 103]

INVENTORY

An inventory of Merchandize received from Montreal 18th July 1781.

† Indn Dept. Detroit			
No 1 a 24	24 Bales Contg 50 pair each is 1200 Pair 2½ Point Blankets		
25 a 27 / 69 a 72	7 ditto	do	102 Pieces Strouds 2142 yards
68	1 ditto	do	24 Pieces Scarlet Cloth 638 yards
28 a 29	2 ditto	do	43 ditto Molton's assorted 1290 yards
30	1 ditto	do	10 ditto Bath Coating 348 yards
31	1 ditto	do	10 ditto Ratteens 282 yards
32	1 Trunk	do	30 ditto Callimanco & 2000 yards Tinsel Lace
67	1 ditto	do	60 ditto Printed Calico 18 yards each
33	1 case	do	42 ditto Linnens 1575 yards
34	1 ditto	do	53 Groce Gartering
35 a 36	2 Boxes	do	250 lb Vermillion Each
37 a 38	2 Baskets	do	4 Nests Copper Kettles
39 a 42	4 ditto	do	4 Nests Brass Kettles
43	1 Box	do	as under
		"	5 groce butcher knives
		"	3 do spring do
		"	4 do Gun Worms
		"	2 do Fire Steels
44	1 ditto	do	as under
		"	5 groce butcher knives
		"	3 do Spring do
		"	1 do Scissors
		"	8 do Fire Steels
		"	6 do Gun Worms
45 a 59	15 Cases	do	25 Fusils in each is 375 Fusils
60 a 62	3 Boxes	do	25 half axes and 100 Smaller do. each
1 a 3	3 Casks	do	1111½ lb Carrot Tobaco
No 73	1 Box containing 36 Dozn Pocket Looking glasses 114½ Pieces Ribbon		
74	1 ditto	do	as under
		"	100 Brass Smoaking Tomahawks
		"	30 Hoes
		"	16 Half axes
75	1 ditto	ditto	78 Hoes
76	1 ditto	ditto	87 ditto
77	1 Bale	ditto	22 Pieces Callimanco 28 yards each

AT. S. DE PEYSTER

Major King's regt. Commanding Detroit & its Dependencies.

Endorsed:—Inventory of Merchandize for Indian Presents remaining in the Kings Store Detroit the 17th July 1781—and an Inventory of Merchandize received from Montreal the 18th July 1781.

[B 123 p 105]

MAJOR DE PEYSTER TO CAPTAIN MCKEE

DETROIT the 21st July 1781.

DEAR SIR, I am favoured with your letter by Surphlet who seems very impatient to get back to you. The Hurons left this yesterday and in two or three days Mr Chene will move with the Ottawas Chippaways Pottawatamies &c. I shall send the little sloop adventurer to roche de Bout with provisions & some cloathing for the Warriours—

Mr Laurimus I am told spares you one thousand wt of powder in case of necessity—

I am anxious to hear if the Intelligence you received of the enemy's motions are confirmed or not, If they are in motion the Indians may be assured from the news we have from below that they will have no enemy to oppose but the Inhabitants of Kentuck, unless Clark should bring 50 or an hundred with him—

I make not the least doubt but you recommend strongly to the Indians to stick together. The Little war is by no means the thing—Please to give my Compliments to Capt. Thompson and tell him that I have sent Provision to the roche de bout of which his people will have a share, they must however land for it there—I am so very ill with the Head Ache at present that I have it not in my power to answer his Letter—

The man you mention coming with Letters from Post Vincent to this place has not yet made his appearance.

Wishing you and the Gentlemen with you health and success—

I am Dr Sir Your humble & obedt Servt

AT. S. DE PEYSTER

Alexr McKee Esq

Indian Affairs M. G. III

FROM LIEUT. GOV. SINCLAIR UNADDRESSED

MICHILIMACKINAC 21st July 1781.

SIR, I am to acknowledge the receipt of a second copy of Monsieur Chevaliers memorial to which I am equally at a loss how to give answer as when I received the first.

He represents to His Excellency his services at St. Joseph's for a number of years without mentioning the Period of their commencement or ending. This length of Establishment at that Post very particularly. His conduct & Deportment under the two Governments which had it under rule. His authority given to Him by the officers commanding at Detroit and Michilimackinac, with many other claims to General Haldimand's attention.

Mr. Ainse troubles the General with representations equally ill supported, as neither had any right to produce an account in which all the Traders were not concerned. They being so bound by their general agreement, I shall however examine with attention their accounts and take the opinion of men in commerce here as the equity of their charges in part or in whole—being at a loss to produce the reasons you demand for supporting in Law a refusal of their payment. The enclosed certificates may in some measure account for their being unpaid hitherto, and as no account from either was tendered to me I am not to blame for the trouble which they give to the General. I delivered Mons'r Chevaliers Papers to Mons'r Gautier & offered them to Mr. Ainse last year.

I am, Sir,

Your Most obedient and most humble Servant

PATT SINCLAIR

Lt. Governor

[B 98 p 62]

ACKNOWLEDGMENT OF CERTAIN PERSONS

The Merchants of Michilimackinac being engaged in a General Company and joined since the Month of August 1779 till the 30th July 1780.

Messrs. Louis Chevallier and Pierre Hurtibisse were employed by the Company at St Joseph & were forbidden from trading privately as well as all the others concerned in the said Company.

To annul all unlawful demands, we the subscribing proprietors and trustees of the said Company confess to have received payment in full of all the advances made by us for the Crown at the Post of St. Joseph, in payment of the services of the men employed by us at that Post during that time.

Signed this 21st of July 1781

J. H. Biron J. B. Guilley
E. L. Reilhe Etne. Campion
C. Catine M. Augé
Bte Tabeau Pre Hurtebise
C. Larehe J. Sangréune.

[B 98 p 60]

SECRETARY MATTHEWS TO LIEUT. GOV. SINCLAIR

QUEBEC 23rd July 1781.

SIR, Having had the Honor to receive and lay before His Excellency the Commander in Chief your Letter of the 8th Instant representing a Want of Carpenters, some Iron Spades, and some Pick-axes, I am directed to acquaint you that two of the former, if the Works at Detroit can Possibly admit, will be immediately forwarded, to you, the other articles are long since sent off, and I hope safe arrived with you.

I am, Sir, &c. &c.

(signed) R. MATHEWS.

Lieut. Governor Sinclair

[B 98 p 64]

INDIAN COUNCIL

Speeches of the principal Huron Chiefs in council with Major De Peyster, Commandant of Detroit &c. 29th July 1781.

Tiockouanhown speaking with some branches of porcelaine.

My father, I pray you to give your attention to my words they are those of the chiefs, warriors, women & children who use my mouth to implore your help in the sad state in which we find ourselves. It is of the greatest consequence to us.

By a belt.

The death of our pious missionary Pere Gortier has thrown an inconceivable trouble on our minds, since then the ignorance with which we are surrounded has darkened & holds us in a pityful state, which solicits your fatherly compassion in our favor; we ask you to join with us to obtain from His Excellency General Haldimand his help in getting us a new missionary; condescend also to acquaint him with our words.

Showing a belt

This belt is the symbol of our adoption of the Christian Religion & of the chain which binds us, we hope to obtain to-day a spiritual leader such as was first given us.

By a belt addressed to Gen. Haldimand.

We pray Your Excellency, who represents His Britanic Majesty to us, to give his attention to the demand which we would make of him.

By another belt to the same.

My father, deign, if you please to consider the sad state of our nation since the loss of our missionary, we lamented our present unhappy state & have come, without knowing to whom to apply, that is why we ask Your Excellency, our most solid support near His Excellency the Bishop of Quebec, to have another missionary given to your children the Hurons of Detroit.

By an other belt to Monseigneur Briant Bishop of Quebec.

My father, in the name of God & of all the Huron nations, help us in our present need of a missionary, the loss of Pere Poitier has left a general desolation in our villages, which will only cease when he is replaced by another. Instructed from infancy in the principles of the Christian religion, we follow them faithfully under the direction of our spiritual leaders; but to-day what have we become? The souls of our warriors will tremble henceforth at the thought of death which follows them every moment, the blood of our old men & of our women will freeze at the approach of the last moment of their lingering lives, the mothers are distressed at the state of their children, finally your charitable zeal should say more for us & urge you in our favor, we ask you to consult it & the pressing want in which we stand, that you may undertake to avoid all delays as every moment is precious in the present affair—We pray God to be favourable to us in the demand which we make of you & for the preservation of Your Excellency.

By another belt addressed to His Excellency General Haldimand & His Grace the Bishop of Quebec.

My fathers,

Hoping to obtain your goodwill in our demands for a missionary which we have asked you to give us. This belt is for him as soon as you have fixed your choice, to show him the road which will take him to our village & to assure him in advance of our filial affection & the respect of our nation.

By another belt addressed to the Hurons of the Loretto at Quebec.

My brothers,

You are of the same nation & religion as we are, that is why we ask you with confidence to join with us to obtain a new missionary to replace Pere Potier who died on the 16th of July. You will know the right way to take to obtain such a favor, we ask you then to take every way to obtain this favor from our father the General & our Bishop. We salute you all.

Names of the principal chiefs present.

Tiockouanorhon	Jorihoha
Toienthet	Isononcainen
Cimrathon	Tharatohat
Tihockeres	

With the principal women of the Nation.

Endorsed:—(17) Speech of the Chiefs of the Hurons at a Council held at Detroit 29th July 1781
[B 123 p 107]

MEMORIAL

A Memorial from Captain Thomas Aubrey of his Majesty's 47th Regiment to his Excellency General Haldimand, Commander in Chief &c &c.

As your Memorialist thinks that he has been extreemly ill treated, & hardly used, not only, by your Excellency having allowed a Majority to be purchased by a younger Captain, than him, & by your having given a Majority to another, whose commission was likewise of a later Date, than your Memorialists; but by his having been ordered with part of a Detachment of e-y 47th Regiment to relieve a Detachment of e-y Kings Regiment at Michilimackina, on account of the Disputes, & Disagreement that have happened there betwixt Governor Sinclair & Captain Mompesson, & your memorialist is to be at that Post under the Command of a junior officer; at which, with the other treatment Your Memorialist has undeservedly received from Your Excellency, He is much distressed, & exceedingly mortified, He has therefore memorialed your Excellency for Leave to go to England in the fall, which Request he is in Hopes will be granted to,

Your Excellency's Most obedient humble Servant

THOS. AUBREY.

Detroit 30th July 1781

Endorsed:—A 1781, Memorial Capt Aubrey 30th July for leave to go to England.
[B 123 p 111]

FROM LIEUT. GOV. SINCLAIR UNADDRESSED

SIR, The new Fort is a good deal advanced from the labour of the Canadians who have not uttered a single complaint here—The Tools & Iron have not yet arrived nor any Barrack stores for this year—If three or four large Crow-Barrs with as many large Sledge hammers could be forwarded this year they are much wanted—We can purchase no Iron of that size, I hope to have all the Timber, drawn in this winter which will be needed—

I raise the work at present as we fill in with Earth, that part done in the Winter will be very troublesome to get filled in—& is no more than a Wall of Squared Loggs equally inaccessible outside & inside, I mean hereafter to make alterations in it & am at present obliged to continue the side next the Bank, with Logg work to receive the earth raised out of the foundation of the officers Barracks—

All the Troops & Stores will be within the works in October if the Season is favourable—One half of the Garrison is there now & Provisions for one year for the Hundred men—I wish the men who come up in the Kings Canoes may know to be the General's Intentions that they may remain as long as the Season will permit—

I am, Sir, your most obedient and most humble Servant

Patt Sinclair

Lt. Governor

Michilimackinac 31st July 1781

[B 98 p 68]

FROM LIEUT. GOV. SINCLAIR UNADDRESSED

Sir, Should it be Your Excellency's pleasure to give permission for the early departure of the Cannoes to the N West & to this Post for the next year, on condition of giving their assistance here it will greatly forward the Works.

The Canadians have cheerfully contributed to it this year—

I am Sir Your Excellency's most obedient

& most humbl Servant

Patt Sinclair

Lt. Governor

Michilimackinac 31st July 1781

[B 98 p 70]

FROM LIEUT. GOV. SINCLAIR UNADDRESSED

Sir, I have the honor to advise Your Excellency of my having drawn in favour of Mr. Macnamara & Coy, for the Amount of Forty nine Thousand, five Hundred and three Pounds, twelve shillings & four pence N. Y. Currency, a charge against the Indian Department. The late arrival of the Indian Presents by the King's Canoes, with the unusual number of Indians at the Post have swelled the Accounts very much. The Provisions from Europe have been Spared by the quantity of Corn & Grease which has been purchased, still the Indians are more expensive when inactive. In order to lessen, if possible, the charges brought in by the Traders from their wintering grounds, I have given to the Interpreters, Roque, Calvé & Blondeau and to Mr. Campion and other Traders each several Bales of Goods to give to the Indians in behalf of the Crown.

I am Sir, Your Excellency's most obedient humble Servant.

(Signed) PATT SINCLAIR, Lt. Governor.

Michilimackinac 31st July 1781.

[B 98 p 66]

MAJOR DE PEYSTER TO MAJOR LERNOULT

DETROIT 31st July 1781.

DEAR SIR, The bearer of this Letter, Monsieur Pongée, is deputed by the Inhabitants of the Parish of Lassomption, &c., to carry their Petition, requesting the Indulgence of a Priest in the room of Pere Pottier who was killed the last week by a fall which fractured his skull. The Hurons also address His Excellency in a Speech and Belts, which they have requested may be presented to His Excellency by you. Immediately upon my receiving the accounts of the old man's death, I sent and had an Inventory taken of his Papers, among which are many volums of Manuscripts, chiefly copies, and nothing of any consequence.

Mrs. DePeyster and the lads are well and desire to join in Comps. to you & our friends at Quebec.

I am Dr. Sir, Your Humble & obedt. Servt.

AT S. DE PEYSTER.

Major Lernoult.

Endorsed:—From 1781, Major DePeyster, of the 31st July, to Major Lernoult.

[B 123 p 112]

LIEUT. GOV. SINCLAIR TO GENERAL HALDIMAND

SIR, The late arrival of Mr. Sayer from his Wintering Ground, Agent to a Mr. Howard Merchant in Montreal afforded me so late an opportunity of advising your Excellency of my having drawn in favour of Mr. Howard for one Thousand, four Hundred & Forty Three Pounds, eleven shillings N. Y. Curry. a charge against the Indian Department for the year 1780. I am persuaded of the Justice of the principal parts of the claim & believe the others to be proper charges against Government. Mr. Howard's Agent represents many other losses sustained which cannot be admitted to the same consideration.

I am, Sir, with respect
Your Excellency's most obedient humble Servant

PATT SINCLAIR
Lt Governor

Michilimackinac 6th August 1781
General Haldimand
[B 98 p 72]

ACCOUNT—RECEIPT

MACKINAC ISLAND, 6th August 1781.

Goverment Dr. to Joseph Howard For the following articles taken from his Effects in the year 1780 by a Party of Canadians & Indians sent by Lt. Governor Sinclair against the Illinois

vizt.

	Livres	Sols Decimo.
5000 Wht Flour at 200 lb per Ld	10,000	00
600 wt. Tobacco at 8 lb. per lb	4,800	00
58 Bushls Salt at 12	600	00
22 lb Pork at 3	66	00
13½ Galls Taffia at 60	810	00
7 Fusils at 140	980	00
100 wt. Powder at 12 lb	1,200	00
50 wt. Shott at 6	300	00
58 Baggs Corn at 50	2,900	00
	£21,656	00

Equal to £1443 11 N. Y. Curry.

Received the above from Lt Governor Sinclair by a Bill of Exchange on His Excellency General Haldimand at Sixty days sight, which when paid will be in full of all Demands

Mackinac Island 6th August 1781.

JOHN SAYER for
JOSEPH HOWARD.

[B 98 p 71]

MAJOR DE PEYSTER TO SECRETARY MATTHEWS

DETROIT the 8th August 1781

SIR, I received your letter of the 24th June inclosing Monsr. Chevalliers petition to the Commander in Chief respecting a sum of money amounting to 6000 Livres advanced for the Indian department.

You will please to inform His Excellency that Mr. Chevallier had my orders to equip those partys of Indians, which I found necessary to send towards the Wabash, and Ohio. That I look upon the sum expended to be moderate, considering that agreeable to custom he found himself under the necessity to clothe those Indians afresh who had been defeated and returned quite naked. My intentions in sending the above partys were in order to make a diversion, and to secure the alliance of the Pottawatamies.

Their defeat answered the purpose of securing their alliance, they have returned to the same place, and have met with another drubbing, being just returned with the news of having left nine dead in the field, three of which were Principal Chiefs sons, whose Bones their nation will not fail to visit often.

I am Sir

Your Humb & Obed. Sevt.

AT. S. DE PEYSTER.

Capt. Matthews

Endorsed:—From A 1781 Concerning Chevalliers Acct. Major De Peyster Recd. 28th Aug.
[B 123 p 113]

INDIAN COUNCIL

At a Conference held at Detroit the 11th August 1781 by Major De Peyster, Commanding Detroit and Dependencies with the Pouttiauwatomies from the Terre Coupe.

PRESENT.

Major A. S. De Peyster Commandant
Duperon Baby Sworn Interpreter
Pierre Druilliard ditto

Pe, tau, you, shin Spoke on two scalps

Father, We the Poutteauwatomies have been out against the Enemy and have taken these two Scalps which I present to you in performance of our promise.

delivers the two Scalps

he then speaks on four Strings—

Father! I thank you for having yesterday given me the opportunity of drowning my Sorrow—I now come to speak to you and beg you may extend your charity towards our men, Women and Children, particularly to the family of my son who lost his life in the late action.

Father The Qui, qu, a, pous Saac, Renerd, and Sue Nations have sent us word, that they mean to assemble at St. Josephs to speak to us, we have not given them our answer, as we conclude to inform you first of their intention, not wishing to do anything without your concurrence.

Father! I thank you beforehand with respect to the request I made you in behalf of my people, "that you may extend your charity towards us," as I assure myself that you will comply therewith.

A War Chief from the Terré Coupé speaks.

Father! I have made use of your ax at the time Pe, tau, gou, shins Sou fell and I intend to return immediately and revenge his death as I am extream angry against the Rebels. I pray you to wipe away the Tears from the face of our chief. Your manner of treatment I know will do it.

Father! We have performed your will and now beg of you to be generous and order us to receive Saddles, Rifles and everything that is most precious.

Delivers 4 strings wampum.

A Poutteauwatomie from Cœur de Cerf, speaks.

Father! You have heard what the people from Terre Coupé have had to say. I now pray you to listen to the absent. the loss of our Brother's blood gives us spirits and with tears in our Eyes we pray of you to give us a war belt to enable us to revenge his death. we need not hint to you what is most necessary for us. we expect you will treat us as the other warriours. when I leave this I shall proceed for my village where I raise my warriours.

Delivers 4 Strings Wampum.

Major De Peyster then said:

Children! When I first heard of the death of Pe, tau, gou, shins Sou, it gave me pain as I had a good opinion of him. As these accidents are common to all, I have to recommend to you to bear his loss with that fortitude which is necessary on such occasions. I am ready to relieve the distresses of my children who have acted agreeable to my orders. several bands of your Nations have been here and have received necessaries for the same purpose, but I am happy I have retained somethings for you, which you will receive.

Children! Your father, the General at Quebec having sent a quantity of goods to be given from time to time, to his children as I shall find them deserving—from the great numbers of Indians who draw supplies at this place, it becomes necessary that care be taken the same be equally divided. with respect to the article Rum, your father the general desires you should be informed that the Nations in Canada request it may be withheld as it destroys more of your people than the Enemy. with regard to the other articles you mention, you shall be served with a portion and if anything should be wanting you must rest contented as I cannot look elsewhere for them.

As some of your Nation are desirous to go to war towards St. Vincennes and the Falls of the Ohio [Louisville] they shall be equipped accordingly, and I expect whatever discoveries they make, that immediate information be made to me.

Extract from the minutes.

J. Schieffelin,
Sec'ry.

Note. Major De Peyster added.

Children! With respect to the Saac Renerd and Sue Nations, who say they mean to assemble at St. Josephs, they ought to go to their father at Michilimackinac, as they belong to his district.

Endorsed:—No. 18. Extract of a conference held at Detroit the 11th August 1781 by Major De Peyster Commanding Detroit &c with the Poutteauwatomies from the Terre Coupé &c.

[B 123 p 114]

FROM MAJOR DE PEYSTER UNADDRESSED

Detroit the 17th August 1781.

Sir, I am honoured with your Excellency's letter respecting Indian Presents with the orders forwarded by Brigadier Genl. Powell. I am confident that everything has been done which the nature of the service would admit of, to manage the property of Government at this Post, and, many are the difficultys we have had to struggle with: still desirous to contribute my mite, I shall spare no pains, in order to execute your Excellencys commands in the most pointed manner—Happy should my endeavors meet with approbation.

I have wrote to the several Traders, and Indian Officers, to close their accounts and to regulate themselves accordingly. The order will greatly alarm them, in as much as they must expect Ill treatment, should they refuse to comply with the demands of the Indians—to avoid which, I shall proceed to contract the trading posts, and prepare myself to stand the brunt of constant upbraidings from the Indians in Council.

Your Excellency desires me to have the Indian stores, so arranged as to have it under my immediate inspection: I ever have had a proper attention to it, putting a necessary confidence in Mr. Baby, without whose aid it would be a difficult matter to carry on that part of the service.

I am to acknowledge the receipt of the Indian goods, sent from Montreal. The inclosed list will be necessary to make it a compleat assortment with what remains in store, to last till Christmas When the Warriors return, the men, women and children will expect something, which will clear the store! I therefore also hope it will be convenient to forward the assortment this fall, agreeable to the list I had the honour of transmitting to your Excellency.

I am with the greatest respect Sir

Your Excellency's Most Huml. & most obt. Servt.

At. S. De Peyster.

Endorsed:—A 1781. From Major De Peyster 17th Augt. Recd 5th. Copy In book marked B no 3 Page 16.

[B 123 p 188]

SECRETARY MATTHEWS TO LIEUT. GOV. SINCLAIR

Quebec 25th August 1781.

Sir, I am to acknowledge the favour of your Letter dated the 21st ultimo, Covering a Certificate by many of the Merchants respecting their accounts with Government as a Collective Body in which Messrs. Chevalier & Ains ever considered.

The present claims I should imagine will turn (or rather the Decision of them) upon the necessity of their furnishing their Private Goods & their authority for so doing, for which Information His Excellency waits your report after the examination of their Accounts, and taking the opinions of men in Commerce as you propose doing, and likewise the answer of a Letter to Major De Peyster as far as He is Concerned in that affair.

I have the honor to be &c. &c. &c.

(signed) R. Mathews.

Lieut Governor Sinclair

[B 98 p 74]

MAJOR DE PEYSTER TO CAPTAIN MCKEE

Detroit 7th Sept. 1781.

Dear Sir, The two Squas heare delivered me your dispatches. I am extremely glad to hear of Brant's Success, and If the report brought in this morning by a young delaware prove true, You have given Mr. Clarks second Division a good Check. I wait with great anxiety to hear from you upon the occasion.

I fear that after this stroke the Indians will want to disperse but am confident you will do your utmost to keep them together, least Clark should attempt to revenge the blow when he can assemble the Militia.

Please to tell my Children that there is nothing like striking the Iron whilst hot.

Mrs. De Peyster & your friends here join in compliments

I am Dr Sir with the greatest Esteem

Your huml & obedient

At. S. De Peyster.

To Alexr Mckee Depy. Agent for Indian Affairs Shawanese Country

Indian Affairs M. G. III.

MAJOR DE PEYSTER TO GENERAL HALDIMAND

Detroit 11th Sept 1781.

Sir, Having got in the several accounts from the Indian Country &c—I have ordered Messrs Macomb & co to make up the general account of Expenditure at this Post, which they now transmit to their Correspondant with my letter of Advice, I however think it necessary to acquaint Your Excellency that Mr Alexr McKee whose Account could not finally be got in, may have some small demand on his return from the Indian Country. The enclosed letter & intelligence received from him, I take this opportunity to forward, since the receipt of which a Delaware Runner is Just arrived in nine days from the Ohio, who reports that Clarke's second division have fallen into our Hands, that he was present at the Action & saw a Colonel and seven other officers taken prisoners, with a number of men & thirteen large Boats. I expect to hear from Mr. McKee in a few days, and shall detain a small Vessel, in order to give Your Excellency more certain accounts of this affair, which is confirmed, tho' Clarke has escaped, will put a stop to his further progress this Campaign.

I have the honour to be Sir,

Your Excellency's Most Obedient & most Humble Servt.

At. S. De Peyster

His Excellency Gen. Haldimand

Endorsed:—From A 1781 Major DePeyster at Detroit of the 11th Sepr. Recd. 29th with enclosures.

[B 123 p 120]

MAJOR DE PEYSTER TO GENERAL HALDIMAND

DETROIT 12th Sepr 1781.

SIR, I herewith enclose Your Excellency an inventory of Indian Presents remaining in Store on the 17th of July last with a return of the Quantity received the 18th from Montreal, both on the same sheet; I also enclose a return of the Quantity of Rum in Store on the 24th of Augst last and an estimate of what more goods will be wanting to supply the Indians to the 20th Augt 1782

Should a Supply not come up this fall, I shall then be glad to receive Your Excellency's further directions how I am to proceed when the Goods in Store are expended least the service should suffer, through my determination literally to comply with the last order received concerning Indian presents.

I think it my duty to observe in time that the Goods in Store cannot with the strictest economy last longer than till next December at which time I shall be able to give you an account of the Nations that have been Supplyd and of the Services render'd—

I have the honor to be Sir Your Excellency's most
obedient & most humble Servant
AT S. DE PEYSTER

His Excelly General Haldimand

Endorsed:—From A, 1781 Major De Peyster 12th Septr Rec'd 6th Octr.
[B 123 p 122]

MAJOR DE PEYSTER TO GENERAL HALDIMAND

DETROIT 12th Septr 1781

SIR, I have this day drawn on your Excellency four Bills of Exchange in favor of Messrs Macomb Edgar & Macomb amounting to Thirty Five Thousand Two Hundred & Twenty five Pounds thirteen shillings & 6¼d New York Currency being for sundry Expenses incurred in the different Departments at this Post for His Majesty's Service, as per Vouchers herewith transmitted, which Your Excellency will please honor.

I have the honor to be Your Excellency's
Most obedient & very Hble Servant
AT. S. DE PEYSTER
Major King's Regt Commanding Detroit
& its Dependencies

His Excellency General Haldimand
Governor & Commander in Chief Quebec

Endorsed:—From Major De Peyster at Detroit of the 12th Sepr Advising of a bill of £35,225, 13, 6¼. N. Y. C.
[B 123 p 121]

MAJOR DE PEYSTER TO CAPTAINS THOMPSON AND MCKEE

DETROIT 13th Sep. 1781.

GENTLEMEN, I have received your letter of the 29th Augt. it gives me great pleasure to hear of Capt Brants success, tho' I much regret the Indians not taking your advice, if they had, we certainly should have made a noble Coup. It is to be hoped however that they will see the necessity of keeping together yet awhile, as it is most certain that Clarke as soon as he can get a reinforcement from Kentuck, will endeavor to avenge this affront. I am sure you will not fail to instill into their minds that if they beat Clarke, which they certainly will do, if he makes a Stand or advances towards them, they will recover their Hunting Grounds, and their descendants will bless their memory, otherwise should he escape this time, the next army will make them repent their folly. I had the opportunity immediately after the receipt of yours to transmit it to the General, convinced that this prelude of your success Will make him extremely happy.

I have the honour to be gentlemen, Your most obedt Servant

AT S. DE PEYSTER

Capt Thompson & Alexr McKee Esqr Indian Country.

Indian Affairs M. G. III.

MR. MACOMB TO COLONEL CLAUS

DETROIT 14th Sep 1781.

DEAR SIR, By letter from Captains McKee & Tomson dated 29th August 1781 Camp near the Ohio, we have the agreeable news of Captain Brants having on the 26th ultimo, with about one hundred whites & Indians, taken fourteen Boats with Troops, provisions &ca part of Colonel Clark's Army on their march from Fort Pitt to St. Duskey, the whol amounting to one hundred and one. He on this occasion as usual, behaved with so much good Generalship, that not one of the whol party escaped, & without the loss of a man on his side.

Colonel Lockey,* Commandant of the party, six officers & thirty privits were killed in the action—A Major Craigenafts, with eleven other officers of difrent ranks & fifty two privits prisoners. He is so particular in his return that he mentions the name & style of every person. When the Express left the Camp, McKee & Thompson were pushing forward to join Brant with about seven hundred, who was then not more than three miles from the rear of

*See appendix

Clarks Army, which the prisoners said did not exceed five hundred, but expected a reinforcement from Kentucky—I communicate this intelligence to you because I think it will be pleasing to Sir John & you and I hope it will make some amends for my not saying something to you before since my arrival here.

Mrs. Psister is well & joins in best wishes to Sir John's family & your's & do you believe me.

Dear Sir Your Sincere friend & Humble Servant

Colonel Clause JOHN MACOMB.

Indian Affairs M. G. IV.

MAJOR DE PEYSTER TO GENERAL HALDIMAND

DETROIT 16th Sept'r 1781

SIR, I have the Honor to enclose your Excellency an estimate of Merchandise wanting for Indian Presents to commence on the 21st August 1782 agreeable to orders, this estimate varys in a few articles from the one I sent last year, particularly in the silver Works which will thus, turn out to better advantage, I shall send the Duplicate & Triplicate of this Return by the next Vessels—

I have the honor to be sir
Your Excellency's Most
Obed't Humble Serv't

AT S. DE PEYSTER

His Excellency General Haldimand

Endorsed:—From A 1781 Major De Peyster 16th Sept'r Recd. 6th Oct.

[B 123 p 123]

ORDER FOR STORES

MICHILIMACKINAC ISLAND 20th Sep'r 1781.

You are hereby directed & required to Issue out of His Majesty's Engineer's Stores, the undermentioned particulars to Mr. Phelan for the use of the King's works carrying on here

vizt:

New Iron ....1819 lbs
Steele . ... 68 lbs
Nails sorts, casks 5

To James Davidson
in charge of the Engineer's Store

[B 98 p 81]

RECEIPTS FOR STORES

MICHILIMACKINAC ISLAND September 20th 1781

Received out of His Majesties Engineer's Stores from James Davidson in charge thereof, the undermentioned particulars, for the use of the Kings Works carrying on here.

vizt:

New Iron ....1819 lbs
Steele . ... 68 lbs
Nails sorts casks 5

[B 98 p 81]

MAJOR DE PEYSTER TO GENERAL HALDIMAND

DETROIT the 24th Septr 1781

SIR, I have the honor to enclose a Triplicate of the estimate of Indian presents, wanting for the year 1782.

I am with great respect Sir Your Excellency's
Most Humbl & Obedt Servant
AT. S. DE PEYSTER

His Excellency General Haldimand

Endorsed:—From A 1781 Major De Peyster 24th Septr Recd. 8th Octr.
[B 123 p 124]

LIEUT. GOV. SINCLAIR TO GENERAL HALDIMAND

MICHILIMACKINAC 26th Sepr 1781.

SIR, I have the Honor to Enclose an Estimate of the Goods requisite for Indian Presents at this Post, and to be sent out with Interpreters to the Different nations, who from their force & consequence in the Scale of Commerce, deserve & expect attention.

It is necessary to remark to your Excellency that the greater part of the Expenses for the Indian Department has arisen from the charges made by the Trader unauthorized so to do in their Wintering Grounds. Some of those charges were requisite. The scanty supply sent by the Kings Cannoes, and always too late for the Post, will be scarce sufficient to stop that Practise.

The Indians cannot be deprived of nearly their usual quantity of Rum, however destructive it is, without creating much discontent, nor can they be detained at the Post to await the arrival of Presents without dissatisfaction, and a waste of Provisions greater in value than the presents they Receive.

I shall only add that I make no purchases from Traders, when the necessary articles are in Store, and that I scarce make the Provision necessary for Casualties aiming at a Reduction of the Expense as far as my duty of Superintendent will allow, and in as far as I have been frustrated Your Excellency can trace the Cause.

I am, Sir, Your Excellency's most obedient humble Servant

(signed) PATT SINCLAIR Lieut Governor

General Haldimand

Copy of a Letter from Lieut Governor Sinclair to His Excellency Genl Haldimand dated Michilimackinac 26th Septr 1781.

[B 98 p 75]

CAPTAIN THOMPSON TO MAJOR DE PEYSTER

CHETICOTHY, 26th Septr. 1781

SIR, I am favoured with a letter from Mr. Frey by your desire & shall observe the Contents, The 5th instant we arrived at the Mouth of Kentucky River, no appearance of Clark, we then held a Council with the Indians to know their intentions, the major part of them were of opinion that a stroke should be made at Boons Fort, we disuaded them from that notion by convincing them they had nothing to fear from that quarter, and that we ought to keep in a Body & move down the River if we did not meet Clark we should strike at the Falls and by those means disable the Enemy from making any further attempts upon the Indian Country this fall. They agreed to send a Scout which returned soon after with two Scalps but no news.

The 7th we proceeded and arrived within 30 miles of the Falls on the 9th inst. Where the Indians after holding a Council sent off another scout who arrived with two prisoners soon after. They informed us that the result of a large Council that Clarke held with the Principal officers in those parts was that no Expedition was to be carried on this Season against the Indians, who when they heard what the prisoners said, got entirely out of the notion of going any further. The Shawanese who had the directions how we were to proceed gave it over. We then got Capt. Brant & the Mingoes to take their place. The Indians who broke of very fast in small parties, some going home, others going after Horses which they had done all along so that we were Reduced to a small Number, not able to attack the falls—Being four days without provisions induced me to return during which we had nothing to subsist on but two Bears that luckily fell in our way. Capt. Brant and the Mingoes moved a little further down to see what number would follow—Captain McKee likewise follow'd with intention of being with me the next morning—But finding two hundred (more than he expected) induced him to strike at Boons Fort or Lins Fort. On their march they fell in with a Colonel Cloyd whom they killed and destroy'd most of His party with the loss of three Hurons and one Miamis. Captain McKee is returned, but part of his Indians left him before he fell in with Cloyd. I have waited here 5 days by desire of the Indians and intend staying two more as an Indian reported the enemy were advancing. We do not believe this news as all the prisoners confirm that Clarke is not able to raise a sufficient number of men to make another effort this fall. The day after to-morrow I move with my people for Detroit (as they are much in want of cloathing, and nothing here to eat but Green Corn) unless I may receive your further orders on the march.

I am Sir

Your most obedt. Servant

(signed) A. Thomson.

Major De Peyster

Endorsed:—1781. Copy of a letter from Captain A. Thomson of Col Buttler's Rangers to Major De Peyster, Septr. 26th.

[B 122 p. 135]

CAPTAIN MCKEE TO MAJOR DE PEYSTER

Upper Shawanese Village, Sept'r 26th 1781.

Dear Sir,—I returned to these Villages yesterday and take the earliest opportunity of informing you thereof. My letter of the 26th ulto. dated in the Miamis near the Ohio, with the several papers accompanying it would inform you of everything material to that time. Here the Indians seemed to think that their success two days before against the Second Division of Clark's Army would ensure them peace for some time in their Villages imagining that this would disable him from any further attempt this year. I endeavored to convince them that as there was so large a Body of them then collected, that it would be prudent to watch his motions some time longer and to send Scouts towards the Falls and endeavor to gain some certain accounts of his future intentions in consequence of this we fell down the River some miles where I found again that it would be difficult to keep them together long, therefore advised our proceeding towards the Falls keeping out scouts continually before us, and that if the Enemy did not advance, that we should attempt drawing them into an action in the neighbourhood of the falls where their main body lay, and by a further success totally destroy their designs of carrying an Expedition into the Indian country. They were reluctantly brought into this measure till we arrived at the mouth of Kentucky, where we waited the return of our Scouts who joined us the next day with two officers' scalps taken the day before at the Falls. as nothing material was learned by this of the Enemies Intentions yet we prevailed upon them still to keep on towards this place, and to keep out other Scouts who could meet us upon our way, but to my surprize they stopt within 25 miles of it for them. they returned the third day in the Evening with two prisoners whos account was that Clark had called a General Council of the Field Officers of the several Counties, that the result thereof was not then made Public but that it was the general opinion of the country that they could not assist him in carrying on an Expedition this Season. this Intelligence increased the indifference of the Indians about attacking the Enemy and many of them began to turn back others dispersing into small parties to plunder Houses. The Rangers also finding their provisions exhausted returned from this. However a number of Indians still inclining to go forward determined me to following them as far as there was a probability of getting them to do anything. the same evening we arrived within 15 miles of the Falls and not finding ourselves in numbers sufficient to put in execution our first plan it was here agreed to cross the country and attack some of their small Forts, or infest the Roads. the second day we arrived near the waggon Road leading from the Falls to the upper Forts here we met a party of Miamis who had been separated from us two days and who a few hours before upon this Road had fallen in with a party of the Enemies light horse escorting a number of Families who were flying from the upper Forts upon being apprised of our being out. they killed a number and dispersed the rest. This Intelligence induced us to take Possession of the Ground they had drove the enemy from and to wait their coming to bury their dead. accordingly they came next morning but before the Indians were posted to receive them owing to their being busied in collecting the plunder found upon the field. The exchanged a few shots with the Indians in front and fled, however greatest part of them were killed & taken with some officers of rank. We lost three Hurons amongst whom was their principal warrior one of the best Indians with us and a great loss to our party, after this we retired to our Baggage in order to consult what could be further done. the Lake Indians would listen to no proposals and thinking they had prisoners and Scalps sufficient did not even halt upon this Ground. here again we proposed to them taking Boons Fort in our way and endeavour to draw them out, destroy their cattle and otherways distress them as much as was in our Power but the Hurons discouraged by the loss of their Chief and likewise being left by their younger Brethren that the whole might return home which was agreed to by the other Nations—we ware never able to ascertain our numbers being constantly left by small parties who's View was only to plunder, many of those are not yet returned. Upon the whole since our first setting out from the best computation I am able to make there has been near to two hundred of the Enemy killed and taken amongst whom are near thirty officers some of considerable Rank but how far it may effect their future operations it is hard to say however should they still attempt any thing we are certain their numbers will not be so great, particularly as we understand the General clamour of the Country is against Clarke for his ill-treatment of the Militia. It would be good policy however to watch him till the Season is further advanced if the Indians could be possibly prevailed upon, perhaps if they ware informed that the Supplies intended for them would be sent out it would prevent their returning to Detroit. Mr. Elliot return'd also yesterday from the Moravian Towns and informs me that the party he accompanied to that place ware detained there a long time and amused by the Moravians who were secretly sending Intelligence and endeavoring to bring the Enemy upon them to cut them off which at length they discovered and then fell upon them and are bringing them away by force the Hurons are disposed I understand to place them at Upper Sandusky where they will still be too convenient to correspond with the Enemy, and tho' they may not be even concerned for the future yet from this Situation they will be blamed for it. However a Message with your advice to the Indians upon it may alter this matter there is Six of their Teachers taken with them, the principal appears to be a Jesuitical old man and if I am not mistaken employed by the Enemy tho he denies it, if the whole of those white people can be removed from the Indians it will be so much the better for it is not likely they will be our friends whilst they have such Teachers. Messengers are arrived from the Southern Indians by whom we learn that they are all still heartily engaged against the Enemy and prosecuting the War with vigor, they have not as yet delivered their Speeches so soon as they do shall inform you of them should there be anything material, in the mean time am with respectful Compliments to Mrs. DePeyster and Gentlemen and with great respect

Dear Sir, Your most obedient & very Humble Servant

A McKee

Major DePeyster 1781 Septr 26th To Major DePeyster

[B 123 p 129]

LIEUT. GOV. SINCLAIR TO GENERAL HALDIMAND

Sir, I have the Honor to represent to your Excellency, that it will forward the Establishment of this Post, to grant Papers early, for the next year, to the North West on condition of their working so many days here.

I am, Sir, Your Excellency's
most obedient humble Servant

Patt Sinclair
Lt. Governor

Michilimackinac 30th Sep'r 1781
General Haldimand
[B 98 p 82]

CERTIFICATE OF EXPENDITURES

I do hereby Certify that the undermentioned Michilc. Island Engineers Stores have been expended by my orders in carrying on the Different Services as undermentioned between the 1st of April & the 30th of September 1781, Inclusive—And the Acting Conductor of Stores is hereby discharged thereof.

Patt Sinclair,
Lt. Governor.

Species of Stores.	Quantity.	For what Service Expended.
New Iron	1819	For Different Service at the King's Works.
Steel, lbs	68	
Nails, sorts, Casks	5	To the Carpenters, &c., for the King's Works.

[B 98 p 79]

Return & State of Engineer's Stores at Michilimackinac Island 30th September 1781

	Serviceable.	Repairable.	Unserviceable.	Deficiencies.		Serviceable.	Repairable.	Unserviceable.	Deficiencies.		Serviceable.	Repairable.	Unserviceable.	Deficiencies.	Expended since last Return.
Blacksmith's Tools:										Cooper's Tools:					
Bellows, pairs	2				Files of sorts	216		72		Jointers	2				
Andvils	2				Tongs, pairs	4			1	Hauling knives	3				
Sledge Hammers	5				Punches	3		3		Staves do				1	
Hand do	9				Drills	1				Truss Hoops of sorts	32				
Riveting do	2				Spring Vices				2	Broad Axes	1				
Bench Vices	3				Buttress	1				Adzes	4				
Hand do	4				Burnisher	1				Tap Borers	4				
Screw Plates	1				Soldring Copper				1	Screw	1				
Nail Tools	4				Brazing Pipe			1		Cramp	1				
Hardies	1				Hinges of Sorts	48				Gousse	1				
Mason's Tools:										Gage	1				
Steel lbs.	250				Nails of Sorts					Hammers	1				
New Iron do.	100				Keggs	26				Intrenching Tools:					
Old do do.	60				Barralls	1				Pick Axes	39			11	
Store Hammers	16				Chissels	2				Spades	27		69		
Lathing do	7				Iron Wedges	2				Shovels	6		92		
Trowels	7				Iron Ladles	2				Howes	16			3	
Picks	8									Iron Crowes	2			7	
Carpenter's Tools:										Hand Bills	14			8	
Hand Saws	20			3	Grinding Stones	2				Hand Barrows	4				
Tennet do	3			3	Plane Irons	49				Wheel do	6				

Natching do	2				Bench do	3				Horse Collars	5				
Broad Axes	24				Moving Gouges	6		4		Horse Harness Setts	4½				
Felling do	30		35		Nippers	2			4	Fuzees			40		
Half do	48		1		Rasps	4		8		Scythes	11				
Adzes	9		3		Chalk lines & wheels	3				Scythe Stones	4				
Clawed Hammers	20			1	Hand Chisels	2				Expenditure:					
Long Planes	7				Punches	2				New Iron lbs.					1819
Jack do	11				Two foot rules	6			1	Nails of sorts, Casks					5
Smoothing do	7			1	Compass Saws	2				Steele lbs.					68
Moulding do	2		23		Glue Pots	2									
Squares	3			6	Iron Brace				1						
Chisels of sorts	34				Haulling knives	1									
Gouges of do	36				Trunk for Tools	1									
Augurs of do	57				Jointing Planes	3									
Compasses, pairs	9				Moulding Stocks	3									
Gimlets of sorts	38		15		Turn Screw	1									
Drawing knives	15				Bevel	38									
Grooving Irons	4				Locks, sorted										
Sawyer's Tools:					Boulting machine & steel mill	2									
Whip Saws	13				Saws setts	6									
Cross Cut do	10				Iron Doggs	1									

[B 98 p 78]

RETURN OF STORES

Return of Engineer's Stores Issued & Expended at the Garrison of Michilimackinac Island, between the 1st of April & 30th September 1781, Inclusive. As per vouchers.

Date.	To whom & for what use.	By Order of	Species of Stores.	Quantity. S.	R.	U.
June 18....	To Serjeant Dodymead, for use of King's Works.	Patrick Sinclair Esqre. Lieutenant Governor & Commandant here.	New Iron.................lbs	440	....	....
			Steele.....................lbs	18	....	....
July 8.....	To Serjeant Dodymead for use of King's Works.		New Iron.................lbs	486	....	....
Augt 21....	To Serjeant Dodymead for use of King's Works.		New Iron.................lbs	60	....	....
			Nail Casks................lbs	2	....	....
Sept. 4.....	To Corpl. Huson for use of King's Works.		New Iron.................lbs	833	....	....
			Steele.....................lbs	50	....	....
			Nails of sort..........casks.	3	....	....

By order of between the 1st of April & 30th Septr. 1781.
[B 98 p 80]

MAJOR DE PEYSTER TO CAPTAIN MCKEE

DETROIT Oct'r 4th 1781.

DEAR SIR, I am favoured with your letter & am glad to hear of your successes, but could have wished that the Indians had stayed a little longer in that neighbourhood as I think it probable that Clarke may yet visit them. I approve much of your scheme & now send you some things with which you will endeavor to stop the Shawanese & Delawares from coming to Detroit, by assuring them I will send off a Vessel with Goods to the Roche de Bout as soon as I hear from you that they will consent to send there for them, or at Sandusky if you should think it more convenient. I leave you to make the speech which you think best calculated for the occasion I shall only give you one Hint which is to tell them that I have Stopt the Rum nor will further give or suffer one drop to leave Detroit till I am convinced that Clarke has given over all thoughts of entering their Country, this I shall do out of regard for the Indians for whom only I can fear. If the Goods are to be sent please to let me know who will be at Roche de Bout or elsewhere to make the distribution, it must be some person acquainted with their number & Language.

I send some things which you will please to forward to the Hurons requiring them to bring in the six Teachers and a few of the Principal Chiefs of the Moravians only—the article of provisions prevents me objecting to their scheme of keeping the Moravian Indians at Sandusky. It would be best however if they contrived to settle them between the two Huron Villages, all which I must leave to your prudent management, You will therefore please to frame such speeches as you think are most proper for the occasion.

The Indians must not expect any provisions from me, we are hard pushed ourselves for that necessary article and have not the means of procuring it by hunting.

We have no News from England as yet the Hope is at the Rivers Mouth & has sent up word that the Gage has the Packett, they parted in a storm, all we know is that the fleet is armed. All your friends Beg leave to join in Compliments to you—

I am Dear Sir with
great Esteem & Friendship
Your most obedt. & Humble Servant

At. S. De Peyster

Alex'r McKee Esq.
Indian Affairs M. G. III.

MAJOR DE PEYSTER TO GENERAL HALDIMAND

Detroit 5th Oct'r 1781

Sir, I have the honor to inclose letters just received from the Indian Country, which will give your Excellency an Insight into the State of affairs on the Banks of the Ohio. I have sent to have the Moravian Teachers brought in here. The Indians I must leave to the management of the Hurons, as their residence here, would occasion to great a Consumption of provisions. Some time ago I acquainted your Excellency that there did not come up any ammunition with the Indian Presents, since which, I have borrowed all the lead the Merchants can spare, I am now at a loss what to do for that absolutely necessary article.

I have the honor to be with great respect Sir,
Your Excellency's Most Huml & obedt Servt

At S. De Peyster

His Excellency Genl. Haldimand

Endorsed:—From A 1781 Major De Peyster of the 5th Octr with enclosures.
[B 123 p 138]

GENERAL HALDIMAND TO MAJOR DE PEYSTER

QUEBEC October 6th 1781.

Major de Peyster

SIR, I have received your Letter of the 11th and 2 of the 12th Ultimo, containing a Report and Confirmation of Captain Brant's Success, and giving me hopes of his pursuing it with still greater Effect against Mr. Clark, should his Efforts be faithfully supported with the force you mention, there can be little doubt Mr. Clark's dispirited army will be totally dispersed & discouraged from future attempts in that Quarter.

Joseph's persevering and spirited Conduct will furnish the Indians in that Country, with an Example worthy their Imitation, and you, with an opportunity representing to them the facility of defending their Country against any Incursion in the power of the Rebels to make, provided they are determined mutually to oppose them, and it is painful to reflect that by their obstinacy, or unsteadiness, so favourable an occasion of Extirpating that army has been lost, of which, the Success of inconsiderable a Party is too evident a proof.

The Bills for £35,225 13s 6¼d, agreeable to your Letter of Advice have appeared, and I have accepted them, but I cannot help expressing my surprize, not only at the astonishing amount of those Bills, so soon following the last, but at so great expence being incurred at all, after you were made acquainted with my intention and were given to expect an immediate supply of Indian presents from hence. I am &c.

(signed) F. H.

[B 121 p 71]

GENERAL HALDIMAND TO MAJOR DE PEYSTER

QUEBEC October 8th 1781

SIR, I have received your Letter of the 12th & 16th Septr. Covering an Inventory of Indian Presents remaining in Store on the 17th July last, with one of those Received from Montreal, and also a Return of Rum in Store, and an estimate of the goods which will be wanted for the ensuing year, and for the year 1783.

I have given orders to forward to you Immediately, if not the whole, such part of the Goods received from England as will Carry you thro' the winter, In these, and in the Article of Rum, I must Recommend to you a very rigid economy least any accident should interfere with the Transport of the former, and because the latter has risen to so extravagant a Price that I have Determined not to purchase any until it falls considerably, which may not happen for a long time.

I am &c

(signed) FRED HALDIMAND.

Major De Peyster

Endorsed:—(Copy) 1781 To Major De Peyster Commandg. at Detroit of 8th October [B 123 p 146]

CAPTAIN MCKEE TO MAJOR DE PEYSTER

DEAR SIR, My last Dispatch informed you of everything material relative to the Indians, since which matters still remain quiet several small parties of Indians are come in since our return from Kentucky and a prisoner they have brought confirms the account of the Enemies not being able to carry on an expedition into the Indian Country this Season, but that their Intention is to take Post at the mouth of Kentucky and Salt Creek where it empties into said River the design of this is to cover their small Forts advanced from the inroads of the Indians as they would otherwise remove into the Settlements. A meeting was held here yesterday by the Chiefs of the several nations at which they returned thanks to the Six Nation Deputies for the amiable speeches delivered by them in the names of the English & Six Nations giving the strongest assurances of their always continuing to adhere to their advice—they also thanked those Deputies for the attention shown by them to their Interest during the Summer whilst threatened by the Enemy with an Invasion and they likewise told them by a large belt that as they had given them reason now to expect their assistance, that nothing would be so satisfactory to them as to see the Six Nations turn their attention towards Fort Pitt as the source of all the Enemy's capability to distress their Country and that whilst the enemy are in possession of this door into it they can never live in either ease or safety that therefore as their arm when joined to that of their Fathers the English was strong and sufficient to accomplish what they would undertake, they now beg'd they would consider this matter of equal importance to the whole and that they will be always ready to join their small assistance.

I had an opportunity at this Meeting of mentioning to those Chiefs the necessity of watching the Enemy till the Season was so far advanced that they would not be able to come and with respect to the cloathing intended for them by their Father, I was certain in this case he would send it to them provided they did not crowd to Detroit—they were thankful and approved of the proposal much but said the Chelliothy Chiefs ware gone upon business to the Hurons and probably would visit their Father before their return but as to those of the Upper Villages they would remain as directed as it was agreeable to their wish. I was about closing this When your favor was delivered to me, this morning and I have just time to inform you that I shall observe the Contents with respect to those upper Villages you have their Sentiments already & notwithstanding their & my endeavours to stop the Indians from going in I am informed a number are gone however do they receive anything at Detroit they cannot expect out of that sent to the rest. Roche De Bout will be as agreeable to those Villages as Sandusky, the distance pretty near equal. I have not an opportunity of consulting the Indians of that place, but they will have very little further to go than from Upper to Lower Sandusky, the only inconvenience will be the want of a Shelter at the foot of the Rapids, so soon as I am informed of the Quantity of Merchandise that is to come out for them I can proportion to the different Tribes the carriages that may be necessary to each. Mr. Elliot will proceed to the place so soon as I am informed of it to receive them, till the division can be made for the Indians, which I must endeavor to if I find myself able, tho I have been ill with a Stab I rec'd in my leg. He also in the meantime sets off to the Hurons & Delawares of Sandusky with the Messages respecting the Moravian Indians and their Teachers.

I am with great respect Dear Sir

Your Most Obedient & very Humble Servant

A. McKee.

Upper Shawanese October the 10th 1781

Major De Peyster

Endorsed:—Copy of a letter from Captn McKee dated the 10th October 1781 from Upper Shawanese to Major De Peyster Commanding Detroit &c &c &c.

[B 123 p 147]

CAPTAIN MCKEE TO MAJOR DE PEYSTER

Dear Sir, I have just received a Message from the Lower Villages informing me that a Shawanese Indian who came from Post Vincent in the summer and suspected to be a Spie was gone off to that place again & taken with him a prisoner lad. And also that some small Parties ware returned from Kentucky and the Falls who report the Enemy to be in Motion there, having been joined by Militia and Indians from Post Vincent. We have already sent Parties down upon the Ohio to make discoveries should they bring a Confirmation of the above account shall inform you of it by express. in the mean time the Indians here are desirous their people gone to Detroit return with haste, as the account that will be carried by the above Shawanese & Prisoner to the Enemy of the Ind[ns] being dispersed may induce them to come. Mr. Elliot is returned from Sandusky and has delivered messages to the Indians agreeable to your desire, which they received with Satisfaction.

Captain Pipe & Winginum have undertaken to carry in the Moravian Teachers immediately. They are both sensible men & their activity upon the whole of this business merits some notice and I hope their satisfaction on their return from their visit to you may be such as will induce them to be as further useful as they are capable of being.

The Bearer of this Brice Ragen is one of the young men taken up by the Shawanese last spring upon the Ohio having deserted from the Enemy at Wuling [Wheeling] he is adopted into a principal family of the Shawanese who do not now lay much restraint upon him: having served as a Volunteer with us during the summer against the Enemy and behaved as becometh him I take the liberty of recommending him to you for a few cloaths.

I am with great respect Sir Your Most
Obedient & very Humble Servant
A. McKee.

Shawanese Village October 18th 1781.
Major De Peyster.

Endorsed:—His Majesty's Service At. Schuyler De Peyster Esqr. Major to the King's Regiment, Commanding Detroit and its Dependencies, Detroit 1781. From Mr. McKee to Major De Peyster Octr. 18th.

[B 123 p 150]

INDIAN COUNCIL

Detroit 21st October 1781.

At a Conference held with the Hurons from Saindooskey by Maj'r A. S. De Peyster Commanding Detroit & Dependencies &c &c &c.

PRESENT.

Major At. S. De Peyster Commandant
Duperon Baby, Isidore Chesne } Interpreters
Pierre Druilliard & Simon Girty }

Orotondy, the Snipe, Sindaton, Huron Chiefs. Sindaton Speaks

Father, Listen to what I'm going to say before you and the Six Nations present. I speak in behalf of the half King, who says he was formerly a Six Nation chief and therefore wishes they may Know his Sentiments, he says, he has taken the Moravian Delawares from their Villages as he found they were inclined to assist the rebels, however he has settled them in his Village where they are under his eye, this Step he has taken after the repeated requests of his Father the Commandant of Detroit. Our half King says he is sorry to find that there yet remains a few Delawares nigh and about Fort Pitt who are too headstrong to listen to his advice, he therefore looks upon them as Rebels and recommends to you to treat them as such.

delivers Six Strings wampum to the Six Nation

Indians—Sindaton says further.

Father! and our Brethren the Six Nations attend to what I have further to say in the name of the half King and the Hurons in General which is addressed to you the Six Nations in particular, we recollect that when the War Belt was first introduced amongst us, that you at the same time recommend that we should get up and be strong, we have done so, but are not pleased to find you are rather indolent and not as active as you ought to be. You know the Succours which the Enemy receive from Fort Pitt and that it is the Door on our Frontiers, we inform you that we are resolved if you join us with our Father, to rise up to a man and proceed in the Spring towards that Fortress in order to reduce it.

Delivers a number wampum Strings to the Six Nation Indians and then says—

Brethren, the Six Nations at the time lost our two young Chiefs the party made this piece of flesh (a prisoner) which we present to you, to dispose of him as you shall judge proper.

Delivers up the Prisoner

Major De Peyster then said

Children! With respect to the first part of your speech I shall communicate it to Col. Guy Johnson, who will intimate to me what the Six Nations have to say in answer thereto, and before Spring I shall have it in my power to inform you of their Sentiments in General. When I heard of the loss of the son of Orotondy, (the half King's Brother) took the first opportunity to forward Strings of wampum in order to condole with him for the great misfortune but since he is now present I shall take the opportunity to cover his departed son as is customary amongst you on such occasions.

Extract from the Minutes.

J. Schieffelin Secy

Endorsed:—Extract of a Conference held with the Hurons from Saindooskey by Major De Peyster Commanding Detroit &c &c Detroit 21st Octr 1781

[B 123 p 152]

LIEUT. GOV. SINCLAIR TO GENERAL HALDIMAND

MICHILIMACKINAC 22nd October 1781.

SIR, As Mr. Thiery the Conductor of the King's Canoes has brought up some articles not sent up in the Indian Presents, I have purchased them from him at the Price of the Post, in consideration of his great care of his charge on every occasion, & I have drawn for their amount Seven Hundred & Thirty two Pounds, New York Currency, a charge against the Indian Department.

I have the Honor to be Sir
Your Excellency's Most obedient & most humble Servant
(signed) PATT SINCLAIR
Lt Governor

General Haldimand
[B 98 p 83]

LIEUT. GOV. SINCLAIR TO GENERAL HALDIMAND

MICHILIMACKINAC 22nd Octr 1781

SIR, Your Excellency's Letter of the 25th August arrived here by the King's Cannoes on the 18th Instant, and gives me pain to find that, the Expenses of the Post seems to Your Excellency high beyond expectation, I beg leave to remark that the vouchers, for a considerable part of the sum drawn, for in the Bills mentioned, expressed that they were for expenses incurred in the year 1780, whether the expenses of this Post exceeds or keeps pace with the other Posts, it has been my care not to let it overstep the bounds of necessity, & that necessity was created by a variety of circumstances which I need not trouble your Excellency with at present.

The only Indians who were invited to come to the Post were a nation which had, after having been liberally supplied with the King's Bounty for years, delivered several of their English Medals to the Spanish officers at Pincour.

I feel with much concern the difficulty of retrenching the expenses, the risk of losing the good will & affection of the Indians & the appearance of giving your Excellency cause of Displeasure.

If presents for Indians are not assorted, they had better be withheld as they answer no purpose but to show them that we are studying to please them, without ability to accomplish it.

I believe Colonel Campbell can inform Your Excellency that the Presents which are sent by the last canoes will require to be assorted, and before that assortment can be sent from Montreal the Indians will be on their return from this Post next Spring.

The Vouchers have been regularly transmitted, & copies of them preserved, for all the money drawn by me at this Post.

I shall do my utmost to bring the Fortification, &c. to a close, early, the ensuing year.

I have the Honor to be Sir,

Your Excellency's Most obedient & most humble Servant

(signed)

PATT SINCLAIR Lt Governor

To General Haldimand

[B 98 p 84]

GENERAL HALDIMAND TO LORD GEO. GERMAIN

QUEBEC 23rd Octr. 1781

Lord Geo. Germain

MY LORD, I have the pleasure to acquaint Your Lordship that by a late Dispatch from Detroit I have an account of an advantage gained by Joseph Brant with 100 Indians over a division of Colonel Clarke's Army assembling on the Ohio for the Purpose of Destroying the Indian Settlements, & if successful in his Levies penetrating to Detroit.

Joseph having intelligence of his motions, waited for him at the mouth of the Miamis River where he passed in the night & with too great a Force for Joseph to attack him, but the next day he fell upon a Party of 100 men commanded by a Lieut Col. Lockery, 64 of whom he made Prisoners, 36, including the Colonel and 5 other officers were killed, a Reinforcement of a Company of Rangers and a strong Body of Indians penetrated as far as the Falls in hopes of pursuing the Blow with success, but Mr. Clark's Army were so discouraged by this early Defeat that they began to separate, & it is supposed here for this Season, abandoned their Enterprize.

Many smaller Indian Parties in that quarter have been very successful & some considerable strokes have been made upon the Mohawk River & Frontiers of Pensylvania, the vicinity of these and the perpetual terror & losses of the Inhabitants will I hope operate powerfully in our Favor with Vermont, who will experience the happy effects of having their Settlements Protected, & some Inhabitants of the neighbouring States begin to retire there for safety. It would be endless and difficult to enumerate to Your Lordship the Parties that are continually Employed upon the back Settlements.

From the Illinois Country to the Frontier of New York there is a continual succession. I must do Colonel Johnson & the officers who have the Direction of this Service the Justice to acquaint Your Lordship that they have paid great attention to it. Colonel Johnson has likewise made great progress in re-establishing the Indians whose settlements were destroyed in 1779, and from the pains and expence which have attended that undertaking, a great saving, both of Provisions & of Presents is to be expected. I likewise have the satisfaction to acquaint your Lordship that the Families I have placed upon Carleton Island, at Niagara & Detroit with a view to cultivation promise fair to succeed, & I have not a doubt will in a very few years materially contribute as well to the support as to the convenience of these Posts.

I am &c. &c.

(signed) FRED. HALDIMAND.

[B 57-11 p 359]

GENERAL HALDIMAND TO LORD GEO. GERMAIN

QUEBEC 23d October 1781.

Lord Geo: Germain

MY LORD, For Your Lordship's Information and satisfaction, I have the Honor to transmit a State of Provisions in Store in Canada, and to Express to Your Lordship the Pleasure I feel in the Reflection that while so amply supplied, no Military operations which may be found necessary can be impeded, at the same time I beg leave to assure Your Lordship that the Oeconomy which I have ever studied in that article shall not be remitted—

I beg leave in this Letter to Remark to Your Lordship, that the chief part of our Work this summer has been confined to Quebec, and I hope we are so well advanced as to Render what is done very useful, Should we be attacked next Year, if not, some more attention may be paid to other parts of our extensive frontiers—

I am &c

(signed) FRED HALDIMAND.

[B 55 p 103]

LIEUT. GOV. SINCLAIR TO SECRETARY MATTHEWS

SIR, I enclose Monsieur Ainse's account amounting to Two Hundred & ninety four Pounds, fourteen shillings & eleven Pence—New York Curry, with Monsr Chevalier's account amounting to one Hundred & Forty nine Pounds, twelve shillings N. Y. Curry to both of which I had no objection, but that which I made last year, vizt, that it was by General consent all the Trade of the Post should be General—

Monsr Chevalier's other account does not meet with the approbation of the Merchants & Traders here—

If more than this Certificate is necessary for admitting to Payment the Two enclosed accounts for the sums above mentioned I shall follow your Direction on that head—

I am, Sir, Your most obedient and
most humble Servant
PATT SINCLAIR
Lt Governor

Michilimackinac 24th Octr 1781
Captain Mathews
[B 98 p 86]

INDIAN COUNCIL.

DETROIT October 29th 1781

At a Conference held by maj'r A. S. De Peyster Commandant of Detroit & Dependencies &c &c &c with a party of Miamis just arrived from the Miamis Town.

PRESENT.

Maj'r At. S. De Peyster Commandant
Duperon Baby & Bobin, Interpreters.

A Miamis Chief speaks

Father! I am sent into you from our Chiefs in all haste for Powder & Ball, the Dry'd meat you see here (Seven Scalps) is the produce of our Warriours who desire it to be presented to you.

Father! Do not be surprised when you see but the young men before you, since we are sent by our Chiefs to address you in their names. Our Chiefs with about Seventy warriours were on their way hither in order to see you, but were obliged to return to our Village immediately, on having had the report from a runner detached from thence that the Enemy was advancing towards the Miami Town from St Vincennes. When we say the Enemy we wish you should know that it consists of French, Indians and Rebels—the courrier reports further, that on the arrival of the Rebel forces at St

Vincennes, a Qui, qu, à pous and a Oüiat Indian were confined, as they were at that place to ask presents.

Maj'r De Peyster then said

Children! Your Chiefs acted right in returning home on the report of the Enemies approaching towards your Village, I am happy to inform you that your Brethren the St Joseph Indians are prepared for them so I've sent officers from hence for that purpose the St Joseph Indians will never forget the Indians who struck on them last year. The ammunition you require shall be delivered to you immediately, and as soon as I find that the report proves true, I shall give my children the Miamis all the assistance in my power, as it will not look well to say anything till then.

A Miamis speaks on

strings of wampum

Father! as the Danger is evident our chiefs have recommended to us to be diligent & to look upon our journey hither as absolutely necessary, in short to apprize you of the future rout of the Enemy and the necessity of forwarding immediately ammunition in order to enable us to defend ourselves, as we are entirely unprovided and can do nothing without assistance.

Our Chiefs have recommended to us strongly to pray of you not to think anything too precious for the young warriours, but give them freely—which you will do to us a Deputies and warriors who have been this summer for the Kings cause ag't the Enemy, and after you have furnished us all with arms & precious clothing, we hope you'll be good enough to give us in profusion of that Shining Metal, an ornament which draws the attention of the Warriours, which is the true way of engaging them, their lives, and their blood to the King.

Father! We pray of you to do agreeable to our desires, and the Demands of our Chiefs by doing which, you'll conciliate their regard.

Extract from the minutes

J. Schieffelin Secr'y.

Endorsed:—Extract of a Conference held by Maj'r De Peyster Commanding Detroit and Dependencies &c &c &c with a party of Miamis sent from their Town with the Intelligence of the approach of the Rebels,—29th October 1781.

[B 123 p 155]

RECEIPT OF STORES.

Michilimackinac Island, 1st Nov 1781.

Received into His Majestys Engineers Store from Mr. McNamara the undermentioned particulars—viz:

	No.	lbs.
Kegs of Nails	10	1583
Iron Barrs	16	930
Steel do	27	196
Kegs of Paint	2	140
Decr. 5th Received from Mr. Meldram the undermentioned particulars:		
Barrs of Iron	14	560
Do of Steel	9	153
Brass Locks	12	....
Large case Stock Locks	2	....
Pad Locks	1	....
Decr. 9th Received from Mr. McCrae the undermentioned particulars:		
Squaring Axes	7	....
Felling do	51	....
Half do	10	....
Decr 17th Received from Mr. Coates the undermentioned particulars:		
Falling Axes	5	....
Decr. 22nd Received from Mr. Wm. Grant the undermentioned particulars:		
Whip Saws	2	....
Falling Axes	6	....
1782 March 20th Received from Mr. Leasy the undermentioned particulars:		
Blacksmiths Rubbers	1	....

[B 98 p 110]

FROM GENERAL HALDIMAND UNADDRESSED

Quebec 1st November 1781.

I have received your Letters of the 21st & 24th September, covering a Duplicate and Triplicate of the yearly Estimate of Indian Presents for the Post of Detroit, and likewise your letter of the 5th Ultimo transmitting copies of Mr McKees and Captain Thompson's Letters, from which it would appear that they have been obliged to abandon the pursuit of Joseph Brandt's success against Mr. Clarke, owing to the Caprice of the Indians in dispersing at the time their assistance was most wanted to give an ultimate Blow to the Enterprise and hopes of Mr Clarke in that Country. But this conduct has been uniformly their system, and notwithstanding the Treasure which has been, I must say from their conduct, thrown away upon them this year, it appears no more than *one hundred* could be brought to action, and those from the Influence and under the direction of Joseph, a Six Nation Chief, If even as many more and the Company of Rangers had joined that Party, Mr Clark's fate would have been decided, which now will be the Atchievement of another Campaign, & in the mean time, you will have perpetual demands for assistance, Equipments &c. to oppose Incursions upon the Indian Villages—This matter really merits being very seriously treated in Council, and those Indians who distinguished themselves with Brant should be well rewarded from the donations intended for those who have not so well deserved them.

You will 'ere this arrives receive a supply of Indian presents, in which is included the Shot you are so much in need of and other ammunition.

The greatest care has been taken in putting these Goods up carefully and an officer will see them delivered.

I am &c.

(signed F. H.

[B 121 p 73]

CAPTAIN MCKEE TO MAJOR DE PEYSTER

Sir, I have received the Invoice of Goods sent out for the use of the Indians and agreeable to it have made divisions suitable to the numbers of the Several Tribes and Nations which I have forwarded to Mr Elliot with directions to deliver them in Bulk as soon as the people to be appointed, go for them, and I have advised the Indians to send a few people from each Nation for their Shares and divide them here in their Villages to prevent too many of them going to that place who not being satisfied with the part they get will still be troublesome at Detroit.

There is an Englishman lately come into the lower Villages from the Enemy at the Falls who reports them to be only about one hundred & thirty strong these Continentals and that they have given up all thoughts of coming against the Indians this year all the proposals made by Clark for this purpose to the Inhabitants of Kentucky ware rejected their numbers being greatly diminished since last Year, and most of their Regular Troops returned into the Country as the times of their Enlistments expired.

He says also that the Artillery which Clarke carried down the River is sent back to be delivered to the Pennsylvanians from whom it was borrowed under the promise of being returned this Fall and that the party with it consists of only Sixty five men, I have been at the Lower Villages endeavouring to get the Indians to follow them, but they ware not to be prevailed upon alledging they ware to far past us to be overtaken, the above Deserter having miss'd his way and been near a fortnight before he reached this. He farther says "that Clarks Aid de Camp with the second in command is gone into Virginia to make application for two thousand men next Year to Support the Settlements of Kentucky which must otherwise brake up—and that a meeting has been lately held by Clark with about thirty of the Wabash Indians who went there to ask for Supplies—he gave them Six Kegs of Powder and a promise of cloathing next Year and sent an officer and Fifteen Men to Post Vincent.

I am with great respect Sir Your most obedient
and very Humble Servant
(Signed) A. McKee

Shawanese Villages November 2d 1781

Endorsed:—Copy of a letter from Captn McKee dated the 2d November 1781 from the Shawanese Villages to Majr De Peyster Commanding Detroit &c &c &c

[B 123 p 160].

MAJOR DE PEYSTER TO GENERAL HALDIMAND

Detroit, the 3rd Novr. 1781.

Sir, I am honoured with your letter of the 13th Sepr. and shall as far as is in my power pay due observance to its contents.

I must however repeat that the Goods sent up and received here last July, came unaccompanied with ammunition, I had powder remaining in store but have been obliged to borrow Ball, flints and paint, from the traders I have also exchanged other articles for Ball &c And we are now nearly at a stand. The Indians are greatly displeas'd with the small allowance they receive of those necessary Articles, at a time the Enemy are said to be in movement towards their country.

A large body of Miamis were on their way here, to receive their usual presents, but return'd upon receiving intelligence, that the Creoles join'd by some Virginians and disaffected Indians were on their march towards their Village, to revenge the death of La Balm. Whether this news be true, or false, it has given them a pretence to demand ammunition, which they have accordingly sent for.

Least none should arrive this fall, I shall rest in expectation to hear from your Excellency, by the Winter express, as the Indians and Volunteers will want to be equipp'd for the field long before a vessel can arrive from Fort Erie in the Spring.

Your Excellency may rest assured that I am not in the least over delicate with, or afraid of giving offence to the generality of Indians, but their necessary Wants must nevertheless be supply'd or we must give them up a prey to the enemy.

They cannot hunt to furnish themselves, whilst they have a part in the War. As to what your Excellency styles superfluities, I have had repeated Quarrels with them on that Head.

They say they are all provided with horses (canoes not being used by the Shawanese, Mingoes, Delawares, Potteuattimes &c) and having been accustomed to Saddles they cannot do without them. The Enemy use rifles, they therefore must have Rifles, to be on a footing with them, That the Fuzees we give them are only fit to make trammels of and in fact they give them to the Squaws for that purpose.

It would be tiresome, to repeat all their impertinences, but I must give Your Excellency some insight into the temper of those people. About a week ago Mr. Alexander, McKee Depy Agent, sent in an Indian named Morgan, who had not been in here for two years past, recommending him in the strongest Terms. I order'd Mr Baby to equip him handsomely to give him some articles for his family, and send him to me to receive a present of silver Works, with which I decorated him as fine as a Miamis.

"Morgan are you content? Yes father, but won't you give me a rifle, it will be well bestowed, I know how to use one. I gave him a Rifle. "Father you have only given milk at one breast, I would willingly have a Kegg to speak to the young men when I get home, in order to rouse their Spirits to Martial deeds." I gave him the Kegg. "Father my saddle was stolen last night You surely will give me a saddle? in consideration of his great services and what he still might be of, I gave him a conditional order to Mr Baby which he protested, not having any in store. Now my intentions were to have given him my own saddle and housing, rather than he should be discontented. But the first accounts that I heard of him, were, that on being refused at the store, he threw down his load in the street, mounted his bare backed horse and Rode off to his village. These are circumstances which will frequently happen, but I shall not in future trouble your Excellency with a detail of them, nor would I suffer them tamely had I a Regiment in this garrison, in which case, I would dictate to my children as they are pleased to call themselves.

I have the Honour to be with great respect, Sir,

Your Excellency's Most Humble & obedient Servant

AT. S. DE PEYSTER

His Excellency Genl Haldimand

Endorsed:—No 9 A Entd. 1781 From Major DePeyster 3rd Novr. Recd 2nd Decr. Copy Entd in Book marked B No 3 Page 17

[B 123 p 162]

INDIAN COUNCIL

In Council Detroit Novr 9, 1781.

PRESENT

Major At S. De Peyster Commandant
Messrs. D. Baby and P. Druillard, Interpreters
Capt'n Pipe & Win, gi, nam Delaware chiefs with a number of Warriors from the Shawanese Country.

Capt'n Pipe speaks

Father! As soon as Mr. Elliot had returned to the Shawanese Touns having executed your orders, in bringing away the Moravians the same was immediately communicated to you through Capt'n McKee, since which you have directed that they should be brought to you. in obedience thereto we have taken them by the hand and are come here to hear what you have to say. for my part I am happy that they are here with us and as they are our friends I hope you will speak nothing but what is good to them.—

He then speaks on 14 scalps

Father! You may recollect that eighteen years are now elaps'd since Sir William Johnson call'd a council of us Delawares. He then assured us that the English would never deceive us, but I find that they do.

On presenting the scalps he says—

Father! These were all your friends as well as mine, but as they used us ill we put our hands on their throats and choked them—You recommended to us brown skins to do your will we have done so, and we now expect that you will take care of all our people by providing for our men, women and children with cloathing and other necessaries for the winter. do not say you have not any because we know your store abounds with plenty and we hope you will give us in profusion.

Father! When your vessel came to the Miamis River I sent you some fresh meat (Prisoners), as I apprehended you would have said it was your flesh and would ask them from me. I therefore would not subject myself to that and sent them before me—

Father! on my arrival I went to visit our Uncles the Six Nations and found Thyandiuiga, I told him that the Six Nations composed seven fires, but I had a boy to present to them, whose voice shall apprize them all of his approach—I then gave him a scalp for each nation to shew them how we have acted—

A Mowhawk speaks on 3 scalps

Father! The last time you was here you recommended to us to be strong and espouse the King's cause, all of which we have done as you may see by these Scalps that we have seen the Enemy and that we mean to be firm in the Quarrel, we are thirty in our Band who pray you will provide us with cloathing and other necessaries.

Major De Peyster then said to Captn Pipe,

After having listened to what you had to say, I must now desire you and your people will pay attention to what I shall say—ever since I have presided amongst you it has been the universal Complaint of the Warriors who came into me "that the Moravian Teachers had always apprized the Enemy of our Manouvers by which means they were always frustrated, after repeated Informations of this nature I sent strings of Wampum to the Moravian Indians inviting them to come in to me, as I was desirous to speak to them, but they never came—I then sent Indian officers with Indians to desire them to come in, but no sooner had my Indian Children rec'd my orders, than they executed them, in bringing them and their Teachers in by force, before they had yet my Speeches, now as we are together and the Moravian Teachers before us, I request of you to inform me whether or not the report I have received respecting them be true and when I have your reply to this, I shall then speak further—

Captn Pipe then said—

Father! Tis very true what you have said, and as the Moravian Teachers are here present with us, we must take care that they send no more intelligence to the Enemy—You say, true, these people did write letters for the Kooshacking Delawares who were once my people but now at Fort Pitt—

Major De Peyster then put the following Interrogatories to the Moravian Teachers who replyed as under.

Q. How many are there of your mission?

A. Six.

Q. Where are you from?

A. Bethleheme in Pennsylvania and two sent to each Town—

Q. by what authority do you act?

A. By that of our Bishops at Bethleheme.

Q. How long have you been in the Indian Country?

A. I have been on the Muskingum River Since 1768 and many followed me.

Q. by what did you pass?

A. by permission of Congress.

Q. I suppose you must have rec'd instructions from the Congress.

A. not any of us—

Q. what correspondence could you have carried on with the Enemy, which I have been informed by my Interpreters that you have practised from time to time.

A. Being obliged to draw near to the Kooshaking Indians we were often importuned by them to write to Fort Pitt and after two years residence with them we found they were rather troublesome which obiiged us to quit their Towns and retreat to our former villages as we had long declined writing for them, we drew their resentment upon us, since when we have never wrote any.

Q. how many Indians are there who belong to your Mission?

A. Including Men, Women, and Children 350.

Q. have they ever joined in the War?

A. not any.

Q. Where are the Kooshacking Indians?

A. Dispersed every where, as they have deserted their villages.

Major De Peyster then spoke to Captn Pipe.

I wish to be informed whether the Christian Indians are desirous that their teachers remain amongst them?

Captn. Pipe replies.

Father! I can say nothing in answer to your question where the Christian Indians mean to place them, but I imagine it will rest intirely with you and if you have no objection we shall be glad to have them with us to instruct our people—

Major De Peyster then said—

Children the Delawares

Since it is your desire that the teachers remain with you, I agree to it, until the General in Chief's pleasure be known—My design in having them brought in was to learn whether or not they had been meddling with Public Matters, for if they had I should have witheld them, but since I find they were compel'd to do what they did I admit of their going back with your people, provided they behave themselves as good Subjects—

[The Moravian Teachers say they never rec'd any speeches from the Commandant of Detroit, or else would have made an answer—

Major De Peyster then continued his speech to Captain Pipe—

With respect to the particulars of your speech which concerns the Six Nations in General, I shall by the first opportunity intimate them—in your speech to me you observe I have goods, I do not deny but I have, altho' I sent you and your Nation some last summer, you shall receive cloathing necessary for the winter, but should there be anything wanting you must content yourselves as I now make it a rule to supply my children from my own store and not buy from every Trader. I shall take care that you be provided with such cloathing as will keep you warm.

The General at Quebec who commands throughout this Country desires me to inform his Indian Children that as the War may be of long duration and he has many children to support, that he wishes they content themselves with what is really necessary, as he promises to provide for his Indian Children as long as they are engaged in his war, but they must not open their hearts for everything which strikes their fancy but content themselves with what is useful, Your father at Quebec says further, "that your Brethren the Indians in Canada have requested that Liquor be witheld in some measure, for they find it is more destructive to their brethren than the Sword, he therefore recommends that you avoid drinking to that excess but be advised by your brethren below—as I understand that the Christian Indians are prevented by their religion from taking an active part in the war, I shall order something to be delivered to those who have come in to see me.

Major DePeyster then addressed the Mohawks telling them he was satisfied with their manner of acting and that they should receive the same treatment as the rest of his children who have done his will.

"Extract from the minutes

"J. SCHEFFELIN Secry

Endorsed:—No 21 Extract of a Council held by Major DePeyster Commanding Detroit &c &c &c with Delawares under Captn Pipe and Winginam their principal chiefs Detroit November 9th 1781.

[B 123 p 166]

MAJOR DE PEYSTER TO CAPTAIN MCKEE

DETROIT the 19th Novr 1781

DEAR SIR, In compliance with your request I now dispatch a party of rangers with a batteau loaded as pr Invoice sent by Serjt. Secord, I have thought it necessary to send some provisions and acquaint you that Serj. Fisher left four hundred of flour & thirteen half Barrels of Pork with Archbald McAlisters, Mr Cochren's Man, of which you may also take giving him your receipt.

I hope the Indians will be satisfied, as we have it not in our power to purchase any different articles—We have nothing more to communicate but as Mr Surphlet returns here I hope to send you some favourable news which I expect by the Hope.

I am Dr Sir Your Huml & obedt Servt

AT. S. DE PEYSTER

P. S. The Indians from this Quarter are of opinion not to go off from their wintering in small bands but wait to hear if they are wanted in a body—Your Indians being acquainted with it will account to them for the few partys they perhaps may see

To Alexr McKee Esqr.

Indian Affairs M. G. III.

INDIAN COUNCIL

In Council, Detroit 8th December 1781.

PRESENT.

Major At. S. De Peyster, Commandant

D. Baby }
J. Chesne } Sworn Interpreters
W. Tucker }

Buckagihitas with his band of 240 Delaware warriors, 70 women, and 90 children.

Buckagihitas Speaks on 16 scalps—

Father! Listen to your children the Delawares who are now come in to see you at a time they have nothing to apprehend from the Enemy and present you some dry'd meat as we could not have the face to appear before our father empty handed, its long since you have seen this part of your Children who were always engaged in doing your will, as we are fatigued and hungry we must beg of you to order us provision and as soon as we are refreshed I shall take the earliest opportunity to speak to you in behalf of my people which is the subject of my coming in and I would wish that a few principal chiefs of the huron nation were also present—

Major De Peyster then said

It gives me pleasure to see my children at all times, especially such as have executed my orders, I'm persuaded you would not have taken this Journey had you not something very interesting to communicate, but as you are fatigued, I shall order you wherewith to refresh yourselves and as soon as you are ready I shall attend to what you may have to say—

In Council Detroit 10th December 1781

PRESENT

Majr. At. S. De Peyster, Commandant.
Captain Caldwell, Corps of Rangers

Lieut. Bennett Lieut. Saumary Ensign Sheehen Ensign Pollard Ensign McDougal Ensign Frey	Kings Regt.

Lieuts. Butler & Clinch Corps of Rangers Delaware Chiefs, Captn Pipe and Buckagihilas

D. Baby W. Tucker P. Druillard Geo. Girty	Sworn Interpreters

Captain Pipe speaks on Wampum Strings.

Father! with your permission I'll speak to the Hurons (he then makes a long speech of condolence to the Hurons, in their usual form and then adds)

Father! I am going to proceed in the ceremony of replacing the dead (he then presents a large wampum Belt pendant on a red pole with a Scalp to the Hurons—unites the Hurons)

We the Delawares are extremely sorry for the loss you sustained this summer, and I return thanks to the Great Spirit who enabled us to wipe away your tears in our ancient manner by presenting you with this Belt of nine thousand nine hundred wampum which was collected amongst our nation for this purpose—

Captn Pipe speaks in favour of a Delaware to have payment for Corn which was taken from him for the use of the party under Mr. Eliott last summer, and the Warriours all join in the request that the Commandant order the same to be paid—

Major De Peyster then said, Since it was the request of all present, the corn should be paid for, but should any Indian in future make advances it will be necessary that they have certificates as vouchers for the receipt which alone shall entitle them to payment—

Captn Pipe.

Father! You have heard what I had to say to the Hurons and tomorrow I propose to shew you the war Belt which we received from our Father Govr Hamilton, at the same time I shall say a few words thereon.

In Council Detroit 11th December, 81

PRESENT

Maj'r At. S. De Peyster Commandant, and the Gentlemen who composed the Council on the 10th.

Buckagihitas Delaware Chief speaks on a War belt and sings the war song—

Brethren! I salute you all and pray you will listen to what I am going to say to our father, I could wish that our uncles the Hurons were present, that they might see this War Belt which they introduced amongst us Delawares and we were the first of our Nation who readily accepted it from their hands, after the Kooshacking Indians had refused it. It's sufficiently notorious that we have made use of our fathers ax ag'st the Enemy for these five years past as may appear by the blood we have made fly throughout the Frontiers and we now find that it has made in part this ax dull which has obliged us to come in to our father who alone is able to sharpen it for us, by supplying us all with Rifles and other Implements of War to enable us to continue the war.

Father! This War Belt is not only for war but serves amongst us brown skins as a token of alliance and amity—

Major De Peyster then said—

Children the Delawares It gives me pleasure to find that you have readily accepted from the hands of your uncles the Hurons my ax and that you have exerted yourselves for the Kings cause.—

Children! I'm extremely satisfied to see the zeal you shew to-day in presenting the ax before this assembly in order to renew the intent of its first presentation, and I assure you that your exertions are as necessary as ever, and I make no doubt from your past actions but they will be continued. It's now five years since I have taken you all by the hand and that this ax has united us together in the same cause since which every effort we have made against our Enemies has prov'd successful, but should any of us hereafter let any part of this ax go, we may not continue to be so—I well know that there are many bad birds who report amongst you fictitious stories, it's therefore proper you should attend to what I say as you will then hear the truth only. I now return the ax to you who have particularly distinguished yourselves as warriours and I assure you that your father the King is as strong as ever—the things you stand in need of shall be delivered to you.

Buckagihilas Speaks, after each Warrior had sung the war song.

Father! You see with how much alacrity we have hastened to sharpen your ax and its my duty to recommend to you to provide for my people good

Rifles which may kill at a distance, otherwise the Enemy would have the advantage over us, as they are well armed—we want good Kettles, Tomhawks and other necessaries for warriors—the Tomhawks we received formerly were of no use as they would brake to pieces not only on the heads of the Enemy but on the Smallest branch in the woods I therefore pray you will order us good strong Tomhawks.

Major De Peyster then said

Children! I have listen'd to your demands which are rather great however you shall receive your share as much as my store can afford I am sorry that my Kettles are small and my Tomhawks no use to you but I'm only authorized to give you such as are sent for that purpose. The General in Chief at Quebec writes me that this War has been of long duration and may continue longer, he wishes that his Indian Children be content with what he provides for them as they must know he has many to support, he says he never will abandon his children but send them up such things as are really necessary for them his motive in confining you to what is necessary only "i that he may be the better able to continue his Supplies—he says further that the Indians below with him desire that Liqur be restricted as they find it prejidicial to you because you drink to excess—the weather being severe I shall order a Sufficiency for your journey,—

Buckagihilas says

Father! I have one thing more to mention to you which is the surprize that my people and myself are in at your allowing the Moravians to return after having them brought in to you, for we know them to be our Enemies who try to do us all the injury they can. I therefore most earnestly request of you in behalf of myself and people that you send for them and keep them close—

Major De Peyster then said

Children! As soon as I had heard that the Moravian Teachers and their adherents had arrived at Saindooskey and that the Hurons had given them a spot of land in order to have them under their Eye, I immediately sent a belt to Captain McKee desiring him to send them in as I wanted to examine them. He informed me that Captain Pipe and Buckagihilas were bringing them in but sometime after Captain Pipe arrived with them. He told me that Buckagihilas could not come in with him. I examined the Moravians in his presence and could find no harm ag't them. He told me as they were with us they could do injury to the cause. he desired I would allow them to go back to take care of their families who were starving in the woods, on which I consented to their returning to Saindooskey on their behaving as good subjects until I heard the General's pleasure. If any one had appeared to accuse them, they should have been secured—Since I find you are against their being at liberty as you know them for Enemies I shall order them in here early in the Spring and send them to the General to be dealt with as he may please to direct.

Extract from the minutes J. SCHIEFFELIN
Secry.

Endorsed—No 22. Extract of a Council held at Detroit 8th 10th & 11th Dec'r 1781, by Major De Peyster Commanding with Delawares under Buckagihilas and Captain Pipe.

[B 123 p 174.]

MAJOR DE PEYSTER TO GENERAL HALDIMAND

DETROIT January 24, 1782

SIR, I have this day drawn on Your Excellency four bills in favor of Macomb Edgar & Macomb amounting to Seventeen thousand nine hundred & seventeen pounds, one shilling and sixpence three farthings New York Currency; being for Expences incurr'd for the different departments at this post for His Majesty's service, as per vouchers which will be herewith delivered, and which Your Excellency will please honor.

I have the honor to be Your Excellency's
Most obedient & humble servt
AT. S. DE PEYSTER
Major King's Regt Commanding Detroit & its Dependencies.

His Excellency General Haldimand Governor & Commander in Chief &c &c &c Quebec

Endorsed:—From A 1782 Major De Peyster 24th Janry Rec'd 5th May

[B 123 p 183]

FROM MAJOR DE PEYSTER UNADDRESSED

DETROIT Jany 25th 1782

SIR, I have the Honor to forward the annexed papers which will give your Excellency the best information of the dispositions of the Delawares, Shawanese, and Wyndotts, who in fact speak the Sentiments of the Indians in general the few Delawares excepted which are mentioned in the Half Kings Speech I have also forwarded duplicates to Colonel Butler to be Communicated to the Six Nations—

Having lately received information that some traders from the Illinois, having taken post at Chicagou, and, the forks of the Theakiké,* I have dispatched some trusty Indian officers to endeavour to dislodge them before they corrupt the Indians in that neighbourhood, as I am informed they have circulated Speeches through the different villages, I fancy this has not yet reached Lt Govr Sinclair as he can have little intercourse with that part of the country, in the winter season, tho otherwise much more contiguous to him—

Such sudden necessary movements will occasion some small Expenses which are unavoidable—The orders given to those officers are notwithstandg. not to take up any Goods on account of Government limiting them to the Expense of Provision only, In the Accounts which go down By this Express, Your Excellency will see some Charges of Goods which were unavoidably taken up by Captain Chabert and others before the orders reached the Shawnese Country, Mr. Clignancolne arrived here late in the fall with the greatest part of the Goods, as the ice had set in it was too late to send a Vessel back. I shall dispatch him to fort Schlosser early in the Spring for the remainder, when a proper Receipt shall be given for the whole—

I have the Honour to be with Great Respect, Sir Your
Excellency's most Humble & obedient Servant

At. S. De Peyster

Endorsed:—No 10 A Ent'd 1782 From Major De Peyster 25th Jany Rec'd 5 May Copy Entd. in Book marked B no 3 Page 19

[B 123 p 184.]

MAJOR DE PEYSTER TO GENERAL HALDIMAND

Detroit the 26th Jany 1782

Sir, I have this instant received Your Excellency's letter of the 1st Novr and I hope this will overtake the express which went off yesterday for Niagara—my motive is to have it in my power as early as possible, to inform your Excellency that the Chief reason which prevented the Rangers joining Brant, before Clarke passed, was owing to want of provisions, which neither proceeded from neglect in me, or those employ'd by me. Captain Chéne, an active officer had the transporting of the provisions, and was detained by a series of the heaviest Rains known in this Country, which rendered the roads impassable. The Rangers, some Volunteers and Indians, however, pursued Clarke to within a few miles of the Falls.

With regard to the Indians, in General, I am sorry they are not under

*See appendix

better discipline. I have wrought hard to endeavor to bring them to it, but, find it impossible altogether to change their natures. I assemble them, get fair promises, and send them out, but when once out of sight the turning of a Straw may divert them from the original plan. If too severe with them, upon such occasions they tell us we are well off that there are no Virginians in this Quarter, but such as they bring here against their inclinations.

The Treasure given to them, I must own is Immense, I cannot however think it altogether thrown away the last Campaign. The Indians in this Country must be looked upon as a large body of Irregulars, Fed, and cloathed, to prevent the inroads of the Virginians into this Country, and, who must be delicately managed, to prevent their favoring those rebels—in the execution of which, during Seven years application, I suffer myself to be flattered with having used some degree of judgment.

I have the Honor to be with Great respect, Sir,

Your Excellency's Most Humbl & obedt Servt

At. S. De Peyster

His Excellency Genl Haldimand

Endorsed:—No 11 A Ent'd 1782 From Major DePeyster 26th Jany Rec'd 5th May. Copy Ent'd in Book marked B No. 3. Page 19

[B 123 p 186]

LIEUT. GOV. SINCLAIR TO GENERAL HALDIMAND

Michilimackinac 5th Feby 1782.

Sir, I have the honor to acknowledge the receipt of Your Excellency's Letter of the 13th Septr. 1781. In my letter to Captain Brehm dated 20th Augt. I acknowledge the receipt of an order bearing date the 22nd of June, which was nearly on the same subject with that which Your Excellency mentions to have been dated on the 24th of June.

It was forwarded by Brigadier Powell and in compliance with it, I transmitted to Your Excellency an estimate of Goods with my Letter of the 26th September which I now beg leave to subjoin, and to recommend to your Excellency's attention as an infallible method of most strictly complying with Your Excellency's orders, if new difficulties such as we now experience are not created by badly supplying the Post with Provisions—

Michilimackinac 26th Septr 1781.

"I have the honor to enclose an estimate of the Goods requisite for Indian Presents at this Post and to be sent out with Interpreters to the distant nations who from their force and consequence in the Scale of Commerce deserve & expect attention.

"It is necessary to remark to your Excellency that the greater part of the Expenses of the Indian Department has arisen from the Charges made by the Traders, unauthorized to do so in their Wintering Grounds—some of these Charges were requisite—The scanty Supply sent by the King's Canoes and always too late for the post, will be scarce sufficient to stop that practise—

"The Indians cannot be deprived of nearly their usual quantity of Rum, however destructive it is, without creating much discontent nor can they be detained at the Post to wait for the arrival of Presents without Dissatisfaction, & a waste of Provisions greater in value than the Presents they require—

"I shall only add that I make no purchase from Traders when the necessary articles are in Store, and that I scarce make the provision necessary for Casualties aiming at a reduction of the expense, as far as my Duty of Superintendent will allow, and, in as far as I have been frustrated Your Excellency can trace the cause—

I have only to add my request of your Excellency's declaration to the Traders that they are not in future to expect payment at this Post for any assistance they may give to Indians—

I shall be always under a necessity of purchasing Canoes for them, in order to avoid giving them Provisions—

I have the Honour to be Sir Your Excellency's
most obedient & most humble Servant—
(signed) PATT SINCLAIR Lt Governor

[B 98 p 95]

FROM MAJOR DE PEYSTER. UNADDRESSED

DETROIT, the 6th Feby 1782.

DEAR SIR, Mr. Surphlet having just acquainted me that he is ready to leave this gives me the opportunity to acquaint you that six Onidas arrived here a few days ago to join Joseph [Brant] being his particular friends. They brought the letters which came by the last Vessel a crost Lake Ontario, but nothing new having been forty six days on their journey. One of the Papers mentions that His Majesty had knighted Admiral Parker on board of his own Ship for having beaten the Dutch fleet under Adml Soutman in the North Seas. There is a Paragraph mentioning that we have recovered all our Possessions in the East Indies—No letters for you. If the Express should return here before you pay us a visit I shall not fail to send your Letters. Mrs. De Peyster and the Gentlemen Desire to be remembered to you.

I am Dr Sir Your humbl & obedt Servt

AT. S. DE PEYSTER

Please remember me to my Indian Friends & Children

[Indian Affairs M. G. III]

INDIAN COUNCIL

In Council Detroit Feby 25th 1782

PRESENT

Major At S. DePeyster Commandant

Captain Henry Bird	
Lieutenants Saumarey, Brooks, Mercer; Ensigns Macdougal, Pollard, Sheehan, Frey	
Lieut. England 47th Regiment	
Captain Caldwell; Lieuts. Butler & Clinch	Corps of Rangers
Duperon Baby; Isidore Chesne; Charles Beaubien	Sworn Interpreters
Schoch, pi, my; Chin, Chack, quan, Le Grew	Mascontin's Chiefs
Pe, pa kick, coy, ya; Pick, co, nishi me	Qui, quabous Chiefs

Major DePeyster addressing himself to the Chiefs and warriours of the Mascontin and Qui, quabous Nations.

Children! Since it is my desire that I should call you my Children, it is this day I call you so as it gives you pleasure.

Two days are now elapsed since you told me you were in want of every thing and delivered over to me two of my people who deserted from the Enemy, you also informed me that the Rebels have deserted Post Vincennes, and were in the greatest want of every necessary of life.

You asked me for many things and asserted that you were entitled to a Supply of necessaries as some of your people were now at war against the Rebels towards the Falls of the Ohio—it is well that you commence following the example of your brethren by acting against the King's Enemies; You should have done so long since and I would have taken care to prevent your wants by maintaining the Miamis Town.

In order to render yourselves happy in future, you must on your return to your Villages send Deputies to your several nations that border Owabash and inform them that since the Rebels have deserted the Post you are determined not to let them return amongst you and send Deputies to this place to acquaint me with their sentiments. If I withhold Traders from amongst your people it is to avoid injuring you by putting an ax into the hands of the Enemy to strike at me and my Children, what I have recommended to you is not difficult on your part to perform which is to keep back the Enemy should they attempt to come up the Wabash or by land once more, the situation of your country admits of it, you see that the Delawares keep their Ground clear, for should the Enemy return hereafter and I get information thereof; I shall then naturally think that my Children in that quarter are a sleep, or wish to be so and it will then be out of my power to send them traders to supply them with their necessaries, you plainly see that the Enemy is too far distant that I should have anything to apprehend from them & that it is for your good only I give this advice and hope you'll advantage therefrom—that your People may not be ignorant of your English father being strongly united with the brownskins in general you see here Deputies from the Six Nations Ottaawas from Michilimackinac and others too tedious to mention who are always here to testify that the English and the Indian Nations are but one and why should not you the Mascontins and Qui, qua bous with those who border the Wabash follow their example—as you are come in to see me I shall order such things as is proper for you, but with respect to ammunition and necessaries for those who are absent I cannot allow of any unless I see them here, as it is seldom properly divided therefore whenever I hear you are sincerely engaged in the war and you shew yourselves in number I shall then take the opportunity to give such ammuniton and cloathing as is necessary for you.

Children! On your return I request of you to tell the Ouittanongs (that killed McCarty and made two prisoners last year) "that I do not approve of their manner of making war as I am informed that they had taken a french man in the same action and allowed him to return home again. this is not acting according to my orders, it is your duty to make all prisoners you can who appear in arms against the King your father—

(delivers several strings of wampum to each nation)

Captn. Jos. Brant, who being present with others of the Six Nations address'd himself to the the Mascontins and Qui, qu, abous—

Brethren! We are glad to see you before our father. we who address you are of the Six Nations who live on the other side of the Lake, you see here who we depend upon this is our father (the Commandant) who supplies us with our wants, we are pleased with what your father told you who we call brother, it is from him however that we brownskins should take the lead since we make one with him and those who are under him. We invite you Brethren by the few words which we now say "to attend to what your father has said and not listen any more to the Rebels, least that we who have not too much sense may fall out with each other should we not think with our father. We speak but little, as we are warriors therefore take the hint from us who know the dispositions of the Americans and of those from whom we come—

Themigassey an Ottawa from Mackinac

Brethren! the Mas-contins & Qui, qu, a bous

Listen to what I shall say, which is to recommend to you to pay a proper attention to what our father has said in your regard, Since you complain of your misery it is your duty to perform his will and assure yourselves of becoming happy—

Our father said true when he told you that he and his children the Brown Skins make but one, as he is the support of us, our wives and children—

A Qui, qu, abous Chief address'd himself to the Commandant, in the name of the Mascontins and Qui, qu, abous

Father! We are highly pleased with what we have heard from you, and the Sentiments of our elder Brethren the Six Nations in our behalf, we have to return you our thanks for the free manner you have made known yours to us, all of which we shall on our return communicate to our people & we expect to benefit thereby—

Extract from the Minutes

J. Schieffelin
Secry.

Endorsed:—Extract of a Council held at Detroit Feby 25 1782, by Majr. De Peyster Commanding Detroit &c with the Mascontins and Qui, qu, abous nations.

[B 123 p 193]

LIEUT. GOV. SINCLAIR TO GENERAL HALDIMAND

Michilimackinac, 9th March 1782.

Sir, The Abstract of Bills herewith sent gives a clear state of the expense of each Year, and my other letter under the same cover will explain how the Chief part of the Expense of the last proceeded from the year before—As the amount of the whole appears to your Excellency very large it cannot fail to do so where it will not be considered that Goods are rated at this Place as *Four* is to *One*—and that calculating the Canoes, Boats, Provisions, Arms, Ammunition, cloathing & gratifications sent down the Mississippi to amount to one Hundred Pounds per man, would not by computing the Expense with that consideration, Exceed Twenty Five Pounds for each Person.

Dissatisfaction was easily propogated amongst the people who were employed in that Service, and it is not yet stifled, notwithstanding the greatness of the Expense. The Last Bill drawn for the Indian Department was chiefly for articles of Provisions, & however strange it appears, Sugar is given and required with Indian Corn instead of Grease, or Pork, (which latter article cannot be spared.

I have the Honor to be, Sir,

Your Excellency's most obedt & most humble Servant

PATT SINCLAIR

Lt Governor.

To General Haldimand

I certify the above to be a true copy

Danl. Robertson

Captain 84th Regt

Michlc. 9th Feby 1783.

[B 98 p 98]

LIEUT. GOV. SINCLAIR TO GENERAL HALDIMAND

MICHILIMACKINAC, 9th March 1782

SIR, Your Excellency's Letter of the 29th Oct'r 1781 reached this on the 7th of March, the Estimate of goods for the Post of Michilimackinac was rated as nearly as possible to the exigencies of the District, and to the provision necessary to be made for the strict obedience of Your Excellency's orders to purchase no goods from Traders. As to the Remark in my Letter of 26th of Sept. "that the greater part of the charges in the Indian Department had arisen from Charges made by Traders, unauthorized to do in their Wintering Grounds."

A party of Canadians & Indians were raised early in the Spring 1780 in consequence of an order sent from this Post in the month of March in that year. They could not have been equipped from the Post had there been Government present sufficient for the purpose, therefore it is apparent to Your Excellency that they must have been furnished by Traders in the Country when they were assembled, to have restrained the Traders who did furnish, and to have confined them to what was only requisite, would have been impossible.

The Canadians & many of the Indians came to the Post the year after impatient for their Reward, and for their return to their Families, they were detained some weeks in expectation of the arrival of the King's Canoes, & the supply when arrived was certainly not adequate to the presents which they expect in years when they have no such claim. The remark was made with a view of stating these matters to Your Excellency.

I wish to withhold an explanation of the expenses since my arrival at the post.

The Interpreters are forbid to bring distant Indians here, and for that purpose (as I had before the honor to inform your Excellency), I sent presents for them.

Inclosed is an abstract of the Bills drawn by me. I am sorry that the services which gave rise to the expense were not greater, more essential & more to your Excellency's satisfaction. I submitted Mr. McNamara's claim for commission to your Excellency in a Letter which I had the honor of receiving an answer to without any remark upon it. it was then submitted by Certificate—

If the necessity for relieving, for clothing, rewarding or employing an Indian is allowed in any degree with me, I offered in my Justification to his Excellency "that I make no purchase from Traders when the necessary articles were in store—

Your Excellency's Letter of a Later Date than the order mitigated thus far its strictness—

I have the honor to be sir

Your Excellency's most obedient humble Servant

(Signed) PATT SINCLAIR,

Lt. Governor.

General Haldimand.

I certify the above to be a true copy—Dan'l Robertson, Captain 84th Regimt.

Michilimackinac, 9th Feb. 1783.

[B 98 p 99]

MR. GAUTTIER TO LIEUTENANT FORD

SIR, I have the honor to inform you that I have already entered in the King's store five hundred sacks of wheat fulfilling in part my engagement with Lieutenant Governor Sinclair for this article. I expect every day the rest of my Milwauky wheat to entirely fill my contract by which I am obliged to furnish all in the course of the month of July next.

I am Sir, with respect

CHA. GAUTTIER.

Lieut. Ford.

[B 98 p 121]

THE OUTLINES FOR A REFORMATION OF EXPENSES IN THE INDIAN DEPARTMENT

It has been a common custom it seems of late with the Indians on their return from Hunting to make an *Offering* to the Governor or Commanding Officer at the *Posts* of *Michilimackinac* & *Detroit* in particular of a part of the produce of their chace in *Furs* of different sorts, as likewise upon their getting in their Harvest for those of the Villages adjoining to these Posts—to make them a considerable Present of *Corn* & *Grease,* all which commodities these Gentlemen have considered as due perquisites of their places, to which by the tenor of their commission they are entitled, and which they have accordingly converted to Cash, in the most advantageous manner for their own benefit. What the quantum of these Presents is accustom'd to be I have not been able to ascertain, but understand from different authority that as the Indians expect on their parts *presents* in return, so their *generosity* is excited in *proportion* to *that* of these officers in this *respect.* Now from the above state of the case is it natural to Expect that the Indians should either be discouraged from coming to the Posts & putting us to the Expense of feeding them whilst there, which is always the consequence, or that an Oeconomy should be observed in the distribution of the necessities supplied by Government, or allow'd to be purchased as Presents to the Indians? Whether the *Power* of making these presents therefore & feeding the Indians, is committed to the hands of Lt. Governor's, & Commanding officers of these Posts—or to Deputy Superintendents or Commissaries of Indian Affairs, it matters not in the least I think to Government. Individuals will be more or less conscientious just as it may happen, and it is perhaps just as likely (if not more so) to find that degree of conscience not to push the abuse to excess among the Military Line, as amongst the class of People employ'd in the *Indian* Department, tho' the temptation under the circumstances describ'd as they stand at present, appears to me I confess too great to be thrown in the way of either. The only effectual remedy therefore in my opinion to keep the Indian Expenses within their just bounds, is in the first place to make the Salaries of your Lt. Governor's, Commanding officers or Indian Commissaries (*call* them what you will or lodge the management of this business with *which* you please) Ample respectable and sufficient for the situation taken in every fair point of view. Obliging them at the same time by the strongest instructions to that Effect & under the strictest penalty of disgrace & punishment, either to *bring* all *presents* of *whatever sort received from Indians* to the *account* of *Government,* or what would be striking at the root of the evil still more effectually, not *to accept* of *these presents* at all—which I am so far from thinking would be that Difficult matter to bring about such as it is in general represented, that on the contrary nothing would be easier effected if earnestly undertaken in a proper manner by these gentlemen themselves; Lt. Governor Hamilton (or I have much misunderstood it) having constantly refused accepting Presents during the whole of his command at Detroit, & from the explanation he entered into on the subject with the Indians without having given them any offence.

With a regulation of this kind & a proper attention to the characters & Capacities of the People at first employed under it, so as once to put a stop to the practices mentioned and to all the collusions with Traders &c. that at present attend upon them, wherever these practices prevail—a reduction of a long and seemingly unnecessary list of persons *paid* & victuall'd in the Indian Department at the several Posts. Such a provident precaution in sending up to the Posts timely supplies of Presents (upon proper & moderate calculations) so as to obviate totally the *pretence* for purchases which has set open another wide door for abuse, not only from combinations being enter'd into by the Traders to take advantage of this Public necessity, but from *those* finding an interest in it who ought not, as it has clearly appear'd that the greater the purchases & presents the more profits they ultimately produce. An exactness in requiring a most particular account of the disposal of all presents. Finally by establishing some *Check* upon the number of Indians at present *said* to be victualled at the several Posts—but the mode of this check I confess myself unequal just how to point out—with these regulations, or rather taking them as a rough outline for framing others. I repeat there can be little doubt of a most considerable reduction in the Indian Expenses, and this without bringing on any ill consequences from giving discontent to the Indians themselves, which perhaps the measure of striking off or reducing any indulgences granted them of late years (however unprecedented before) might occasion & which for the security of the Posts & communications under *present* circumstances it might be bad policy to risque the Friendship of the Indian Nations in general being perhaps to be depended upon no longer than whilst it is purchased. one circumstance only more appears, that upon any reduction or dismission of Individuals at present employ'd in any branch of this Department, care should be taken to remove them away from the Posts, and the power of giving impressions to the Indians out of pique & resentment, by a misrepresentation of facts, that might lead to troublesome consequence.

Endorsed Outlines of a Reformation of Expenses in the Indian Depart. given by C. H. private.
[B 98 p 308]

CERTIFICATE OF EXPENDITURES

I do hereby certify that the undermentioned Michilimackinac Island Artillery Stores have been expended by my order in carrying on the different services as undermentioned between the 1st October 1781 & 31st March 1782 Inclusive, and the acting Commissary of Stores is hereby discharged thereof.

PATT SINCLAIR,
Lt. Governor.

Species of Stores.	Quantity.	For what Service expended.
Powder lbs	21½	Used in Honor of Her Majesty's Birthday.
Musquet Cartridges	2	For making Squib Cartridges for the Troops
Paper qrs		to fire in honor of Her Majesty's Birthday.
Common do Sheets	8	For the use of the Governor.
Musquet Ball Cartridges	1506	For use of Troops in garrison.
Musquet Flints	34	For use of do.

N. B. The Ball Cartridges are chiefly used in loading for Guard. what Balls are not used in firing &ca. are returned & consequently not reckoned in the expenditure.

[B 98 p 104]

CERTIFICATE OF EXPENDITURES

I do hereby Certify that the undermentioned Michilimackinac Island Engineer's Stores have been Expended by my orders in carrying on the Different Services of the Garrison as undermentioned between the 1st Octo. 1781 and the 31st of March 1782. Inclusive—And the Acting Conductor of Stores is hereby discharged thereof.

PATT SINCLAIR Lt Governor

Species of Stores.	Quantity	For what Service expended.
New Iron—lbs	1601	For use of Kings Works carrying on here
Steel—lbs	136	For the use of Do. Do.
Kegs of Nails	4	For use of do. do.
New Hemp Traces—pairs	5½	For the use of do.
Large Case Stock Locks	2	For the Governor's House
Brass Locks	12	

[B 98 p 105]

RETURN

Return of Engineers Stores Issued and Expended at the Garrison of Michilimackinac Island between the 1st October 1781 & the 31st March 1782 inclusive. As per Vouchers.

Date.	To whom & for what Purpose.	By order of	Species of Stores.	Quantity. S.	R.	U.
1781 Oct 1	To the Engineers Blacksmith for use of works	Patrick Sinclair Esq. Lieutenant Governor & Commandant here.	New Iron lbs	1334		
			Steele lbs	78		
	To the Indian Blacksmith for use of works		New Iron lbs	182		
			Steele lbs	58		
	Issued to Corpl Huson for use of works		Nails Kegs	4		
	To the Carters for the use of do		New Hemp traces Pairs	3½		
	To John Lees for dragging Stone for the use of Works		New Hemp Traces Prs	2		
	To Mr. Phelan for the Governor's House		Large Case Stock Locks	2		
	For the Governor's Chimney		Brass Locks	12		
	To Serjt Hartimen for the well		New Iron lbs	40		
			Do. Do	45		

1782 March 31st Expended by order of between 1st Octr. 1781 & this present date Inclusive.

[B 98 p 106]

Return of Ordnance Stores Issued and expended at the Garrison of Michilm'c Island, between the 1st of October 1781 & 31st March 1782 Inclusive. As per Vouchers.

Date.	To whom & for what service.	By order of	Species of Stores.	Quantity. S	R	U
May 15	For making squib cartridges for the Troops to fire in honor of	Patrick Sinclair Lieutenant governor and Commandant here.	Corn'd Powder lbs...........	11	....	....
	Her M. Birthday...............		Musquet Cartridge paper Qrs.	2	....	....
18	Used in honor of ditto by the cannon......................		Corn'd Powder lbs...........	10½	....	....
20	Issued to Sergeant Hardiment of the 84th Reg't.................		Musquet Flints..............	34	....	....
	Issued to do.....................		Musquet Ball cartridge.......	120	....	....
Feb. 28	Issued to Sergeant Wilcocks of the 47th Regiment............		Musquet Ball cartridges.......	1386	....	....
Mch. 12	Issued for the Governor..........		Cannon Cartridge Paper sheets.	8	....	....

Expended by order of between 1st Octr 70 & the present date Inclusive.
[B 98 p 102]

Return & State of Engineer's Stores at Michilimackinac Island 31st March 1782.

	Serviceable.	Repairable.	Unserviceable.	Deficiencies.		Serviceable.	Repairable.	Unserviceable.	Deficiencies.		Serviceable.	Repairable.	Unserviceable.	Deficiencies.	Expended since last Return.
Blacksmith's Tools:										Cooper's Tools:					
Bellows, pairs	2				Files of Sorts	276		7		Jointers	2				
Andvels	2				Tongs, Pairs	4			1	Hauling Knives	3				
Sledge Hammers	5				Punches	3		3		Stave do	1			1	
Hand do	9				Drills	1				Truss Hoops of sorts	32				
Riveting do	2				Spring Vices				2	Broad Axes	1				
Bench Vices	3				Buttress	1				Adzes	4				
Hand do	4				Burnisher	1				Tap Boarers	4				
Screw Plates	1				Soldering Irons				1	Screw	1				
Nail Tools	4				Brazing Pipe			1		Cramp	1				
Hardies	1				Gouges of Sorts	48				Gousse	1				
Steel lbs.	521				Nails of Sorts					Gage	1				
New Iron lbs.	559				Boxes	1				Hammers	1				
Old do do.					Kegs	19				Pick Axes	39			11	
Mason's Tools:										Spades	27		69		
Stone Hammers	16				Chisels	2				Shovels	6		92		
Lathing do	7				Iron Wedges	2				Hows	16			3	
Trowels	7				Iron Ladles	2				Iron Crows	2			7	
Picks	8				Kegs of Paint	2				Hand Bills	14			8	
Carpenter's Tools:										Hand Barrows	4				
Hand Saws	20			3	Grinding stones	2				Wheel do	20				
Tennet do	3			3	Plane Iron	49				Horse Harness setts	3	3			

Hatching do	2			
Broad Axes	24			
Falling do	79		35	
Half do	58		1	
Adzes	8		3	
Claw'd Hammers	20			1
Long Planes	7			
Jack do	11			
Smoothing do	7			1
Moulding do	2		23	
Squares	3			6
Chisels of Sorts	34			
Gouges of do	36			
Augurs do	57			
Compasses, pairs	9		15	
Gimlets of sorts	38			
Drawing knives	15			
Grooving Irons	4			
Sawyer's Tools:				
Whip Saws	15			
Cross Cut do	10			

Bench do	3			
Moving Gouges	6		4	
Nippers pairs	2			4
Rasps	4		8	
Chalk lines & wheels	3			
Hand Chisels	2			
Punches	2			
Two foot rules	6			1
Common Saws	2			
Glue Pots	2			
Iron brace				1
Hauling knives	1			
Trunk for Tools	1			
Jointing Planes	6			
Moulding Stocks	3			
Turn Screws	3			
Bevel	1			
Locks, sorted	30			
Boulting Machine & Steel Mill	2			
Saw Sets	6			
Iron Dog	1			

Horse Collars, spare	2	3			
Fuzes			40		
Scythes	11				
Scythe Stones	4				
New Iron lbs.					1601
Steel lbs.					136
Kegs of nails					4
New Hemp Traces, pairs					$5\frac{1}{2}$
Stocks lock					2
Brass do					12

PATT SINCLAIR,
Lt. Governor.

[B 98 p 112]

Return & State of Ordnance Stores at Michilimackinac Island 31st March, 1782.

	Serviceable.	Repairable.	Unserviceable.	Deficiencies.		Serviceable.	Repairable.	Unserviceable.	Deficiencies.		Serviceable.	Repairable.	Unserviceable.	Deficiencies.	Expended since last Return.
Light Six Pounder Brass	2				Mortars Brass 4 3–5	1				Round Shot for six Pdrs	403				
Heavy do do Iron	2				Swivels Iron	4				do. filled & fixed	38				
Howitzers Iron	2				Hall Pieces	2				do. fix'd to Bottoms only			31	31	
Ambuzets stocks	4									Case do. filled & fix'd	60		114	114	
Traveling Six Pounders	2				Garrison for Howtzs	2				do. fix'd to Bottoms only	24				
Garrison do do	3				For Ambuzets Stocks	3				Grape do for Howtzs	24				
Do for Swivels	2									Do for Ambuzetts	40				
Ladles of Sorts	4				Drag Ropes with Pins set	2				Round Lead for do	100				
Tube Boxes	4				Wad Hooks of Sorts	5				Fuzes 4 2–5	100				
Match Slow lbs.	4				Junk Wadds	400				Common Cartridge paper	9				
Sponges of Sorts	10				Hand Spikes of Sorts	10				Sheep Skins	1				
Leather Pouches	1	3			Vent Spikes	10				Spunge Tacks	300				
Lint Stocks	5				Do Punches	4				Empty Paper Cartridges	590				
Port Fires										Thread lbs.	1½				
Tin Tubes fixed	270				Aprons of Lead	11				Musquet Balls lbs.	300				
Priming Horns	4				Spurs	38				Tannd Hides	1				
Corn'd powder lbs.	45				Copper Powder Measures	7				Nave Grease	2				
Live Shells	20				Empty Shells	29				Harness men's sets		2			
										Musqt. Cartridge Paper	7				
										For Musquet Cartridge Qrs.	4				
										For Carbine do	2				
										Spare Copper Hooks	39				

Iron Beam weights & scale	1	....	....	....	......
Garrison Collars setts	1	....	....	....	......
Musqt. Ball Cartridge	6032	....	....	....	......
Musqt. Flints	1799	....	....	....	......
Carbine do.	700	....	....	....	......
Expenditure:					
Corn'd Powder........lbs.	....	....	....	....	21½
Musqt. Cartridge Paper Qrs.	....	....	....	....	2
Musqt. Ball Cartridge	....	....	....	....	1506
Common Cart. Paper Sheets	....	....	....	....	8
Musquet Flints	....	....	....	....	34

N. B. Two of the Above Ambuzets on board the Sloop "Felicity."

Patt Sinclair
Lt. Governor

[B 98 p 109]

ORDER FOR STORES

Michilimackinac 31st March 1782.

You are hereby directed & required to Issue out of His Majesty's Artillery Store the undermentioned particulars for the different Services of the Garrison—vizt.

Patt Sinclair
Lt. Governor

Corn'd Powder lbs	21½
Musqt Cartridge Paper 2 rls	2
Cannon ditto Sheets	8
Musquet Ball Cartridges	1506
Musquet Flints	34

To James Davidson
in charge of the Artillery Store
[B 98 p 103]

RECEIPT FOR STORES

Michilimackinac 31st March 1782.

Received out of His Majesty's Artillery Store from James Davidson in Charge thereof the undermentioned particulars for the different Services of the Garrison vizt—

Corn'd Powder lbs	21½
Musquet Cartridge Paper qrs	2
Cannon do Sheets	8
Musquet Ball Cartridges	1506
Musquet Flints	34

[B 98 p 103]

ORDER FOR STORES.

Michilimackinac Island 31st March 1782.

You are hereby directed & required to Issue out of His Majesty's Engineers Stores the undermentioned particulars for the different Services of the Garrison—viz

Patt Sinclair
Lt Governor

New Iron lbs 1601
Steel lbs 136
Kegs of Nails 4
New Hemp Traces 5½
Large Case Stock Locks 2
Brass Locks 12

To James Davidson
In charge of the Engineers Store
[B 98 p 107]

RECEIPT FOR STORES

MICHILIMACKINAC ISLAND 31st March 1782

Received out of His Majestys Engineers Stores from James Davidson in Charge thereof, the undermentioned particulars for the different Services of the Garrison—vizt

New Iron lbs 1601
Steel lbs 136
Kegs of Nails 4
New Hemp Traces pairs 5½
Large case Stock Locks 2
Brass Locks 12

[B 98 p 107]

MAJOR DE PEYSTER TO CAPTAIN MCKEE

DETROIT the 3d April 1782.

DEAR SIR, I have waited in daily expectation to hear from you, especially as there has been a report spread in this place (which came from Fort Pitt) that Lord Cornwallis surrendered his little Army to Washington who besieged him in York Town and Gloucester Virginia. The Same reports say that the Six Nations have offered to make peace with the Americans & upon hearing this I spoke to Brant upon the subject, who says he'll forfeit his life it is not true, unless it has been done by some of the Indians in the Neighborhood of Fort Pitt, where he says there are a few families of the Six Nations who have been neutre during the war. We have had no Express from Canada yet therefore are in the dark of what is going on there. The Inclosed Speech will let you into what was the sentiments of the Indians at Niagara last fall. If the accounts from Fort Pitt concerning Lord Cornwallis be true it may make them alter their plans—You will be the best Judge whether to communicate the resolution to the Shawanese or not—I have thought best not to say anything to the Indians here till I hear further least we give the alarm to the enemy—

Mr. Laurimier will send you this letter to whom I now send for the Shells and Cannon Ball which was hid at the Glaize, we may have occasion for it in case of an expedition F. P.

Your friends here are all well & beg to join in compls. to you—

I am Dr. Sir Your most Humble & obedt. Servant

AT. S. DE PEYSTER

To Capt McKee

Indian Affairs M. G. III.

FROM GENERAL HALDIMAND UNADDRESSED

MONTREAL 21st April 1782

Private No 14

SIR, I embrace the first opportunity of communicating with you to acquaint you that I have lately received a dispatch from Sir Henry Clinton dated the 22d February an extract of which I send you, another dated the 10th March says that notwithstanding his former Intelligence, he has more reason to think that New York is the object of the Enemy's design, & not Canada.

If an attempt against Detroit was really an agitation I conceive it must have been upon the Original Co-operating plan, and if that is laid aside for New York they cannot I should think, spare a Force equal to so arduous a task as Mr. Clarke's is represented to be in all events, I think it must have reached the knowledge of Major DePeyster, and of course been communicated to you, my not yet having heard from you, confirms me in the opinion that everything is quiet in that quarter, you will nevertheless communicate the enclosed to Major DePeyster giving him orders to take every precaution possible for the safety of his Post, as well in regard to securing all the Provisions he can from the settlement should the enemy advance, as for the defence of the peace. In the great uncertainty I am of what may happen here, or the necessity I may be under to make a Diversion in favor of Sir Henry Clinton I cannot think of lessening my Force, already so inconsiderable should you therefore find it absolutely necessary to reinforce Detroit there is no alternative but with drawing one or two Companies of the Rangers from Oswego, which I hope will in a short time be secure from

Insult this will be the less felt as I purpose immediately to send to that place the remainder of Sir John Johnson's second Battalion I am but too sensible that the force at these posts should rather be augmented than diminished but we are governed by contingencies and not contingencies by us we must therefore act for the best.

It may not be amis to communicate the inclosed intelligence to Lieut Governor Sinclair, with directions to give what assistance may be in his power with such Indians as he can collect should the attempt be made.

I send you some news-papers they contain all in my power to tell you. You will please to forward them after perusal. You will herewith receive three Copies with Duplicates of Regulations for the Freights of goods over the several Lakes, for the Commanding officers of the Posts and Naval Commanders at Niagara, Detroit and Michilimackinac.

I am &c

(signed) F. H.

[B 96 2 p 174]

INDIAN COUNCIL

In Council Detroit 22d April 1782.

PRESENT.

Major At S. De Peyster Commandant
Messrs D. Baby & Ç. Beaubien, Interpreters
Misshikinackwaa, Chief from the Ouiat.
Kickatassia, Chief from the Eel River with a number of their Warriours.

Misshikinackwaa speaks on a War Belt

Father! Since I have undertaken to fight for the English I have received three War Belts and have been out against the Enemy three different times —I have been always successful but not quite to your wishes nor my own the great Spirit has ordered it to be so.

Father! You see here part of those who made the last Campaigne, who have done nothing but taking Prisoners and have not as yet spilt Blood, we are now desirous to know from the Indians in this Quarter how we are to act in future.

delivers the War Belt

Father! You see some of my people who with me think themselves entitled to demand of you a supply of cloathing and necessaries for ourselves, our Wives and Children as we are the only people from our Village who have acted for the King.

Some of our Chiefs and Warriours of our Village are now speaking with the Rebels having left the Village with that intent.

delivers several strings

Father! You see here the fruits of my Campaigne (two Prisoners) one of which I had adopted in lieu of a Brother as he is a Loyalist but as I know it will give you pleasure to have him I will therefore forego the happyness by giving him up to you.

Father! As there are some of our people who have skins with them I have to request of you to permit them to trade with the Traders.

Father! The long journey in the cold season we have had prompts us to pray of you to order us an ox that we may drink broth.

delivers several strings Wampum

Father! I shall say but a few words more to you which is to beg of you to dispatch us immediately homewards as we are bordering on the Enemies Gates—

Peck, cossia, spoke a long while on a smoaked skin and strings of wampum representing his and peoples misery having lost his son by the Enemy and therefore craves the assistance of his father the Commandant—

Kawiyachtaa speaks for Le Bornne

Father! What you have just heard is true and I now am going to speak to you not for myself but for my Chief though he has not been out to War himself he has sent his young men, as his disorder is such that it has prevented his going, but without your assistance what can we do, we have neither Powder nor Ball and are nigh the Enemies Gates Governor Hamilton was our friend for he provided for our wants we are anxious to know what is become of him in the mean time you are our father and we expect you will treat us as he did—I will now explain to you what the old man meant to say who spoke last it was to tell you that we had attacked a Pianquishaw and a frenchman between the Post, and the Fall of the Ohio, therefore have compassion on us for we have acted as good children in doing all in our power for your service.

Major DePeyster then address'd Mischikinackwaa the chief from the Ouiat and those who accompanied him.

Children! I return you my thanks for the Prisoners you have delivered over to me, it shews your attention to my orders "to take as many Prisoners as possible and avoid spilling the blood of Women & Children when Warriours meet you and they fall in action it is what they must expect and I should be pleased if this day I could hear that the Rebels have followed your example but by report from Fort Pitt I find that they have acted quite in a different manner and I begin to fear for your Chiefs who have imprudent enough to go and speak to them.

Children! I must continue to you to continue to avoid cruelties that the Great Spirit may give success to our undertakings, for be assured he does not take pleasure in them, it will yet turn out that the perpetrators of these acts of cruelty will suffer the vengeance they merit—with respect to your demands such as I am used to give to my children I shall order to be provided for you, I have to advise you to get cloathing ammunition or such things that may be necessary for you at home for the skins you have brought here to trade and avoid buying of that pernicious Liquor (Rum) which so often deprives my children of their reason, for such as carry from hence necessaries find the advantage when they arrive at their Village, while those who take rum perceive they gain nothing but indisposition—the General with the Indians below have requested that Liquor be withheld as they find that the Indians drink to excess and ruin their constitutions.

Children! Notwithstanding what I've said to you at this time I fear you may let the Enemy pass you unmolested, if you do, be assured that hereafter, you and those who are behind them will become a Sacrifice, should they come and you oppose them at your Village if you find them too strong you can retreat to the Miamis and if overpowered there then come in to me, united we shall be strong enough to defeat all attempts that may be made against us—

Children! I address this speech equally to you all with the distinction only that you who have produced Prisoners shall be treated with greater mark of Esteem than those who come here to trade only.

(Extract from the minutes) J. Schieffelin

Secry.

Endorsed:—No 24 Extract of a Council held by Major DePeyster Commanding Detroit with the Misshikinackwaa Chief from Oüiat and those who accompanied him. Detroit 22nd April 1782.

[B 123 p 206]

FROM MR. LAMOTHE UNADDRESSED

April 24th 1782

Plan of an Expedition against the Illinois, which I have the honor to present to your Excellency.

Leaving Detroit with a small army of & some neighboring Indians, Sauteux, Hurons & Misthey will come by land to St. Josephs a journey of eight or ten days. Then after having taken the poux [Pottawattamies] Nation, who are settled on this river they will come to the branch of the Chicagoust & the Quinquiqui to try to get the Indians of the small fort of Milanaquis & another village, who have appeared, till the present to give their services to the Illinois & lately conducted a party to St Joseph who took the Commandant placed there by Governor St Clair [P. Sinclair]. As the two villages are the refuse of all the malefactors of all the other nations of which the two chiefs are Dougurne Sauteux, the one named Segurnac & the other Macquivois who have their families near Michilimackinac & it would be easy for the leader of the party to send them with the belts & we would by these means keep back the intelligence which they would have given to the enemies. During this time we could bring the barges & ammunition & go to join the little army at the entrance of the Chicagous where is a portage of half a league in good weather, in this way we could come without difficulty to the Illinois. Another plan for the same Expedition & one which would have still fewer difficulties.

The small army would leave Detroit in the same way but instead of continuing their route by this same river, they would turn & pass La Baye where the Folles Avoines, Sacs, Foxes, Puans & the Aganvois have their villages established on the bank of the river which we would pass. In this way we would take a few of each nation so as not to create any Jealousy & to keep up a good feeling. The expenses of this expedition would be in presents for the nations, coats for the chiefs & some medals, belts & flags.

One field piece & four pieces which would be fixed on the barges would not fail to command respect for the little army, passing before these nations & would be a great resource if the Spaniards should make any movement. If his Excellency would honor me with his confidence, & give me an interest in this expedition I would prove to him that my zeal has no limits in defending King George's standard.

I would like that my company should be formed on arriving at Detroit & that I should be given permission to name my officers, knowing the brave subjects who have no fear of their lives when doing their duty.

If he fails to engage volunteers to complete my company we would choose a few men from each company of Militia & the rest of the small army would be filled by the corps of the nearest place & by some good militiamen. I ask Your Excellency if you will be pleased to allow my brother to accompany me on this Expedition, he is an officer in the Department, knows all the roads & places & I dare say all the Indians, as he has been among them for fifteen years. He is Seventy five (soixantect quinze) years in the service & is recommended & praised as a brave officer by his superiors.

I only ask Your Excellency to enquire of Major Carleton, Mr St Luc, Colonel Camperel & Capt Frazer, as to his conduct.

As there are among the people of Detroit, Niagara & Michilimackinac, men who could be trusted to do their duty, Your Excellency will have the goodness to send orders to the different Commandants to assist, as far as lies in their power, the good of the service.

If the Expedition succeeds in taking the Illinois, then the small army will embark & go to reduce the Post of St Vincennes & continue its route to come to Detroit by the Wabache.

(signed)

GUILHAUME LA MOTHE

Endorsed:—From 82 Mr LaMothe of the Detrois April 24th

[B 123 p 212]

LORD SHELBURNE TO GENERAL HALDIMAND

WHITEHALL 27th April 1782

SIR, Finding by the tenor of your correspondence that Lieut Governor Cramatré's character and time of Life is more adapted to other situations than what he now fills, and this being confirmed to me by different Persons here, as well as by considerations here, regarding the State of the Province in the Present moment, I have taken upon me to recommend Lieutenant Governor Hamilton, late Governor of Detroit, to succeed to the Lieutenant Governor of Quebec, & Major Kay to succeed to that Detroit. I have not the honor of knowing either of those Gentlemen personally; I have submitted their names to His Majesty, from their General Good Character, and the great hardships they have undergone, so strongly confirmed by your Letter, of the 8th of July last, in favour of Lieutenant Governor Hamilton. I have a very great personal regard for Colonel Caldwell, known how much he has distinguished himself in a Military Line, & make no doubt of his doing so —whenever he happens to be employed, but I flatter myself he will consider the preference given to Lieut. Governor Hamilton, as an act due to Humanity & Justice, and I trust that the service in General, will consider it as a Proof that Personal merit and distinguished Services are sufficient to ensure His Majesty's favor without any other Interest whatever.

I am Sir

Your most obedient humble Servant

SHELBURNE

General Haldimand

Endorsed:—No 2) 1782 From Lord Shelburene Of 27th April Received by the Dœdalus the 23rd June in Letter 17th July No 5 Ent'd Book B fol 55

[B 45 p 46]

TO MAJOR DE PEYSTER WITHOUT SIGNATURE

28th April 82

Sir, Captn La Mothe's sufferings with Lt Govr Hamilton, & the character I have heard of him as a zealous active officer, engaged me to continue him in Pay until the arrival of Mr Hamilton, and as he is acquainted with the country, & a good woodsman I send him to Detroit in Hope that you may find him useful in the Indian, or some other Line until such Time as I shall be enabled by the arrival of Lt Govr Hamilton to make some & permanent arrangement for that Post—He expresses a strong desire to be put under your orders & I hope will acquit himself well in whatever You shall have occasion to employ Him.

Endorsed:—To Major De Peyester 27th April 1782 Captn La Mothe
[B 123 p 216]

TO MAJOR DE PEYSTER WITHOUT SIGNATURE

28th April 82

Sir, This will be delivered to you by Monsr Rochblave, whose former situation & character is sufficiently known to you not to require my enlarging upon it—The confidence I am told Gr G. Carleton had in him, and his sufferings in the cause of Government have induced me to continue for the present, his former allowance as Condr of the Illinois. He has made urgent offers of his further Service, & I send Him to you in Hope that you may find Him useful—It is not in my power to point out in what particular Line, that must depend upon your further Knowledge of Him and the Situation of affairs with you—I have permitted him to take up a small cargo of Goods, in order, in some measure, to repair his Losses, & have directed it should not Pay Freights over the Lakes.

Endorsed:—To Major De Peyster 28th April Monsr Rocheblave
[B 123 p 217]

LIEUT. GOV. SINCLAIR TO GENERAL HALDIMAND

Sir, This Letter is conveyed by the Grand River to forward an Extract of a Letter from Major de Peyster received on the 20th of this months.

I have the Honor to inform Your Excellency that, having the Timber on the spot, with the aid of Horses and Carts belonging to Private Persons, the works are getting in forwardness.

Two Twelve and two six Pounders with their ammunition are much wanted as well as Two Royal Artillery Privates in addition to the Corporal & Recruit of that Corps now here.

As the latest accounts from the Traders towards the Mississippi assure that every thing has been quiet in their Quarter, notwithstanding the reports circulated in the beginning of Winter, I hope the Passes will not be retarded as the men are much wanted here.

I have the Honor to be, Sir, Your Excellency's most obedient & most humble Servant

Patt Sinclair
Lt. Governor

Michilimackinac 29th April 1782
His Excellency General Haldimand
[B 98 p 113]

FROM GENERAL HALDIMAND UNADDRESSED

Quebec May 6th 1782

Sir, Having already wrote to you by Capn. Brehm my aid-de-camp who will communicate to you from Detroit, my orders in general respecting the security of your Posts, I have only now to add that Lt. Col Campbell has my orders to send you by the great Rivers a considerable supply of Indian presents which I expect you will receive with this Letter and which I hope will for the present answer your demands for I perceive that the charge made by the Merchants in the upper Country are so exhorbitant that we must contrive to take as little from them as possible observing however not to delay the King's Service in any material point by our Oeconomy. a very large supply of Rum will also be sent to your post by Detroit, so as I think to avoid any expence this year on that extravagant article.

I am hourly expectation of the ships from England, and the proportion of the Indian presents, I shall receive by them, shall be sent immediately to your post.

(signed) F. H.

[B 96 1 p 91]

MAJOR DE PEYSTER TO GENERAL HALDIMAND

Detroit the 13th May 1782

Sir, The enclosed letter directed to the Rev'd N. N. Sohaukirch, which the Moravian Teachers wish to have forwarded, and the Letter from Alex'r McKee Esq'r D'y Ag't will give your Excellency an account of the horrid treatment the Christian Indians met with at Muskingum. The Nations in General as yet take it patiently, how it will operate when they have overcome the consternation this unparalled cruelty has thrown them in I cannot pretend to say. They daily bring in prisoners and beg of me to observe the different treatment they give their Enemies who acknowledge to have received kind treatment, and, I am bold to say, that except in cases where prisoners have been too weak to march, few people have suffered, and we have had many instances of the Indians having carried the Sick for several days.

The Half King* of Sandusky has lately informed the remaining Moravian Indians that it was by no means safe at Sandusky, and therefore obliged them to turn their faces towards the Shawanesse I have their Teachers Six in number, with four Women and two children at Detroit—They are very desirous to settle under my protection, and, the Chippewas have consented to allow them to cultivate a tract of Land upon the river Huron Lake St. Clair [Clinton]. I have therefore sent an Invitation to such of the Christian Indians as chuse to come, being sensible that those people must soon fall upon our hands for succour, it is therefore most prudent to put them in the way of raising stock to support themselves, and it is evident that by shewing them kind treatment it will insure us the confidence of the other nations.

I have the honour to be with great respect

Sir Your Excellency's

most Hum'l & obed't Serv't

AT. S. DE PEYSTER

His Excell'y Gen'l Haldimand Comm'd in Chief

Endorsed:—From A 1782 Major De Peyster 13th May Rec'd 26th

Copy

Entered in book marked B No 3 Page 20.

[B 123 p 218.]

FROM MAJOR, DE PEYSTER UNADDRESSED

DETROIT the 14th May 1782

SIR, An express this day arrived from Sandusky, informing that two of my scouting party fell in with the enemy on this side the Ohio opposite to Wheeling on their road to Sandusky. The Scouts had some of their men wounded and escaped with difficulty not having been able to ascertain their numbers. A deserter is also arrived who reports that he left the Enemy near

*See appendix

Wheeling consisting of an Thousand men intended against the Villages of Sandusky, and, that Mr Clark was still at the falls—

In consequence of the above intelligence the chiefs have requested the assistance promised upon the like occasions, assuring me that they will not make face to the enemy without receiving both ammunition and a detachment of men. I shall order off the Rangers with a few Canadian Volunteers and some Lake Indians, in order to keep up the spirits of the Wiandotts, least they retreat or otherwise listen to overtures from the enemy, which I am informed by a person of credit, they have in View should no succour arrive in time—It will however not be prudent to weaken this garrison much more, till I am satisfied that Mr. Clark is not meditating a stroke at this settlement by way of the Wabash.

Your Excellency may rest assured that I have, and shall take every necessary step to procure early intelligence of his designs, and endeavour to defeat them to the utmost of my abilities.

I have the Honour to be with great respect
Sir Your Excellency's Most Huml &
most obedt Servt

At. S. De Peyster

P. S. The Delawares have just delivered up some Prisoners which they took the 22d March navigating a large boat from Fort Pitt, loaded with three hundred Barrels of Flour, on its way from New Orleans. They report that several other boats were to follow, some of them larger, and all loaded with flour for the same Market.

Endorsed:—From A 1782 Major De Peyster 14th May Rec'd 27th Copy Entered in Book marked B no 3 Page 22

[B 123 p 220]

MAJOR DE PEYSTER TO SECRETARY MATTHEWS

Detroit 14th May 1782

Dear Mathews: Should His Excellency the Commander in chief think proper to deviate from the plan he once proposed of obliging the Indians so far as not to let the prisrs taken by them return to Virginia—I must beg you will put in a word for Captain Orr, who was taken when Col. Lochrey [Archibald Loughry] was killed, and has been upon his parole at Detroit ever since, where his behaviour has been so circumspect as to entitle him to a preference, he has a large family at home, and is ready to promise anything, tho' I firmly believe he will say no more than he will perform.

I am with great sincerity
Yours &c

AT. S. DE PEYSTER

Captain Mathews Secretary to His Excy,
the Commander in Chief Quebec

Endorsed:—From Major De Peyster 14th May Rec'd 12th June 1782
[B 123 p 222]

INDIAN COUNCIL

In Council Detroit 15th May 1782.

PRESENT

Major At S DePeyster Commandant Alexr McKee Esqr Deputy Agent Captain Caldwell, Corps of Rangers Lieut Brooks 8th Regt. Messrs Baby, Chesne & Druillard Interpreters Several Chiefs and Warriors of the Ottawaas, Wyandots, Chippowaas, and Poutteauwatomies.

Major DePeyster, address'd himself to the several Indian Nations and presenting the large War Belt from the Six Nations.

Children! This belt has been already shewn to you for to sharpen your War Hatchets as it was sent here by the Six Nations for that purpose, I shall not shew you again the Belts on which our alliances is founded, nor repeat to you that the King of England and his Indian Children are but one, I shall only present this Six Nation War Belt that you may all again sharpen your hatchets as it is necessary you should do so, and I hope you will not leave any of them dull—it is a good thing to have this belt by us to keep our hatchets always in order and enable us always to succeed, for those of my Children who were out last year return'd successful.

He then presents a small Belt

Children! This Belt is sent to you by the Shawanese, Delawares, & Mingoes, desiring of you their Brethren to arrise and come to their assistance, this belt originally came from you, with the promise to assist them whenever it was shewn to you, I now do so in their name.

delivers the Belt to ye Ottawaas he then speaks on strings from the Shawnese, Delawares, & Mingoes

Children! These strings accompanied the Belt to me, requiring ammunition and assistance—I have already sent them my answer which was, "that I should speak to their Brethren this day and send them immediately ammunition and assistance part of my Troops are already order'd for that purpose—

Children! You applied early in the Spring for leave to go to War against the Enemy and I have alway's stop'd you, my reasons were "that it was better to detain you until we heard of the Enemy's coming into the Indian Country that you might then be ready to meet them in a great body and repulse them—the Shawanese, Delawares & Mingoes add further "if our father and our Brethren send us assistance we beg that they come by the way of St. Dooskey, this is all I have to say to you in their names excepting a few words which I shall deliver to you when I close this days council.

Children! The day before yesterday I had an express from the Chiefs of St. Dooskey who inform me that they were out against the Enemy and saw them in number pass the Ohio opposite to Wheelin—a Deserter from the Enemy is now at St Dooskey who reports that their design is for St. Dooskey —the Gentlemen who are to represent me in the Indian Country are to set out in two days—

Children! These Strings are dry but I believe them wholesome as they are from your brethern the Shawanese, Delawares & Mingoes who desire that Liquor be withheld from going out into the Indian Country and I join them in that, as it is with Powder & ball we must drive the Enemy back, after this is done we shall then tap it with discretion.

Egushuvey, holding the War Belt

Father! How can you expect of us to sharpen our war hatchets when you give us no water (Rum) to do it with?

Majr De Peyster then said

Children! I have water to sharpen my ax with but I expect after it is sharpened that you will go and use it and not continue drunk in the Streets,

T' Sindatton a Huron Chief

Father! I arise to tell you that I want water to sharpen your ax and I shall sing the War Song although one half of my people are already killed by the Enemy—

"The several War Chiefs sang the War Song in their turn and made the same application as did Egushewey and T'Sindatton—

Major De Peyster then said

Children! The water (Rum) you ask for shall be provided for you to sharpen your war hatchets and I shall be glad to hear your sentiments as soon as possible, as I mean to acquaint the Six Nations therewith.

Children! I request of you to attend to what has been said and that no one make his appearance here with the view only of being provided for and then hide themselves if there be any who act in this manner I hope their Chiefs will mark them out—it is to your Villages the Enemy are coming against for they declared before they came from home that they are going to St Dooskey. Yet altho' I have nothing to apprehend from them I send my Indian Children assistance

(Extract from the Minutes)

J. SCHIEFFELIN Secr'y

Endorsed:—No 25. Extract of a Council held by Major De Peyster commanding Detroit & with the Ottawaas, Wyandats, Chippowaas & Poutteauwatomies of Detroit. Detroit 15th May 1782

[B 123 p 223]

GENERAL HALDIMAND TO MAJOR DE PEYSTER

MONTREAL 19th May 1782.

Major de Peyster:

on the 5th Instant I received your Letters of the 24th 25th and 26th January. I have accepted your Bills for £17,917 1s 6¾d including some Presents purchased for Indians, as my orders prohibiting such purchases had not reached your distant Quarters when that Expence was incurred. I am but too sensible that an Innovation so nearly affecting the Trader and the Indian will not fail to meet with every difficulty they can mutually throw in the way, and I regret, that in doing, what I consider to be my duty to the Public, additional Trouble and disagreeable circumstances should arise to the officers whose Lot it is to carry my views into Execution, but from the confidence I have in their zeal & constancy, I flatter myself that the step I have been obliged to take, to reduce an Expense so little understood & so ill received at Home will be attended with success.

I hope you have received the Remainder of last year's Presents from Fort Erie. A fresh supply was forwarded to you some days ago from hence, which I hope will answer your necessities until the hurry of the Transport will admit of forwarding a part of the Presents, I now look for from Home.—

Brigadier General Powell transmitted to me an Extract from your last Letter to Him, communicating the Intelligence you had received of Mr. Clarke's Intentions. You must have long since have heard from the Brigadier on that subject, and are informed how circumstances combine, to prevent my sending you that assistance I could wish, but still am inclined to think you will not have occasion for it. I observe with much satisfaction, from the Proceedings of the Councils covered by your Letters, that the Indians seem united in their professions to support their own and the rights of the Crown if they are firm in the Resolution, and will take the Field and stick together, Mr. Clarke's attempt must prove as fruitless as the former.

He may alarm the Indians, but to penetrate to Detroit with such a Force and preparation as to insure success is hardly probable unless the Rebels were in a situation to abandon other objects of infinitely greater consequence.

The reasons which prevent my sending you a reinforcement from hence, equally operate against the United wishes of the Six Nations and Delawares to reduce Fort Pitt, from which object you will endeavor to dissuade them—admitting it could be effected, it would be the business of a Campaign and when dearly purchased, we should, in our present situation, be obliged to destroy and abandon it.

Should circumstances alter, it is not impossible to gratify the Indians, that I hereafter undertake it, it may not therefore be amiss that you procure authentic Information of the state of the works, the numbers and natures of the Guns, strength of the Garrison, &c. &c.

I shall be glad to hear of the successful return of the officers you sent to dislodge the Illinois Settlers at Chicagou.

I am &c.

(signed) F. H.

Your Letter of the 3rd November was duly rec'd but want of opportunity prevented my acknowledging it before.

[B 121 p 74.]

INVOICE

Invoice of Goods sent to Michillimackinac, addressed to Lieut. Govr. Sinclair the 24th May, 1782.

200 Pairs 3 pt. Blankets
300 pr 2½ pt. do
58 pr. 2 pt. do
53 pr. 1½ pt. do
8 ps Scarlet Cloth
82 ps Blue Strouds
30 ps White & blue Molton
82 doz Linen Ruffled Shirts
62½ doz Callico do do
48 Scarlet Laced Coats
26 Green do Capots
109 Laced Hats
48 Feathers

56 Plumes
137 lb Vermillion
13 ps Callico
54 ps Ribband sorted
48 ps Silk Ferreting
192 Stript Callimanco Mantlets
12 ps Embost Serge
12 Large Flags
294 ps Gartering
16 doz. Gilt paper Looking glasses
8 doz. Fish Knives for chiefs
98 doz. Butcher Knives
44 doz. Spring Knives
18 lb Sewing thread
20 lb Coullured thread
4000 Needles
1080 lb Roll Tobacco
2160 lb Carrot Tobo
255 lb Net thread
216 Maitre de ray
72 doz. Fish Hooks
102 Pair Canadian spears
180 Crooked Knives
24 Large Axes
120 half do
150 small do
144 doz. Gun Worms
72 doz. Indian Awls
36 doz. Fire Steels
12 doz. Razors
144 doz. Brass Thimbles
11 Bundles Brass Wire
11 doz. Horn Combs
11 doz. Box Combs
26 doz. pr Scissars
120 Fusils
4500 Flints
2100 lb Powder
1440 lb Balls
480 lbs. Beaver Shott

480 lbs Duck do
480 lbs Pigeon do
120 Brass Kettles
108 Tin Kettles
192 Gallons Rum
250 Silver Armbands
250 Silver wristbands
500 Silver shirt buckles
500 Silver earrings with drops
50 Gorglets
24 Double Silver Hangers

JOHN CAMPBELL
Superrd &c Indn affairs

Endorsed:—Invoice of Goods for Indian Presents, sent to Michillimackinac addressed to Lieut Govr Sinclair 24th May 1782

[B 123 p 233]

CAPTAIN MCKEE TO GENERAL HALDIMAND

SIR, I beg leave to inform your Excellency that since my residence in this country I have done myself the Honor to write Your Excellency several Letters, And that during this time I have so fortunate as to meet with approbation in my endeavors to promote His Majesty's Service, tho I have not been able altogether to act in the Capacity I could wish in this situation have made frequent application some years past for leave to settle my affairs, which can not be done in this remote part of the World but the threats of the Enemy to invade the country has hitherto prevented. And as I had also an appointment at the commencement of the present war which occasioned my being at considerable disbursements, the Accounts of which have been long since lay'd before the Superintendent of Indian affairs & pass'd his inspection being the channel I was directed to pass them in, but to my disappointment I find they still remain unpaid which is disadvantageous to me having Interest to pay for a considerable amount & tho' I had authority to make expense yet it was difficult for me to preserve papers in the dangerous situation I was in.—I came here but a few days ago from the Southward where I have been several months past upon service, and as Intelligence is received of some designs of the Enemy to Invade the Indian Country am about returning again, And as soon as the service will admit me to return have to beg your Excellency's Permission to take an early opportunity of settling my affairs, and in the mean time that your Excellency will be pleased to give directions for the Payment of my Accounts which I flatter myself will appear just and reasonable—

I have the Honor to be with greatest respect your
Excellency's Most obedient and very Humble Servant

A. McKee

Detroit May 25th 1782
His Excellency General Haldimand

Endorsed:—From A 1782 Mr McKee 25th May Rec'd 19th
[B 123 p 236]

TO MAJOR DE PEYSTER WITHOUT SIGNATURE

31st May 82

Sir, A few days ago I received your letters of the 13th & 14th Instant communicating the Intelligence brought by your scouts who were engaged with a Party of the Enemy on their Route to St. Duskey, and covering a letter from Mr McKee reporting the Massacre of the Christian Indians at Muskingum. I hope the small Reinforcement forwarded from Niagara with the Canadian Volunteers You have sent out, will keep up the Spirits of the Indians, until B. Genl Powell shall be able to forward a detachment of Rangers to you for that Purpose and I hope the melanchoy Event at Muskingum will rouse the Indians to a firm and vigorous opposition and Resentment at St. Duskey or wherever they shall meet the Enemy. I am concerned that the situation of affairs will not admit of my sending you the ample succour I could wish, I am not in the least apprehensive for the actual safety of your Post, but the effect the distribution of the Indian Settlements May have upon their minds should it happen, may produce bad consequences. I depend upon your exerting your utmost Efforts and abilities as well to convince the Indians of the indispensible necessity there is for their resisting this shock with unanimity and Firmness, their future Existence as a people depending on it, as in taking every possible Precaution for the security of your Post in which I persuade myself I shall not be disappointed.

The Capture of the Boats with Flour will I hope encourage the Indians to be vigilant.

I approve the Measure you have adopted for the Relief of the remaining Christian Indians, and think it must have the wished for Effect with that People in general.

I have to acknowledge the Receipt of the Proceedings in Council accompanying your Letters—and the satisfaction with which I perceive the general friendly disposition of the Indians.

Commerce has long been an object by the Ohio to the Mississippi, and you would do well at the most likely seasons to send interupting Parties they will often prove successful.

Endorsed:—To Major De Peyster 31st May 1782. Copy entered in book marked B No 2 Page 25.

[B 123 p 231]

LIEUTENANT TURNEY TO MAJOR DE PEYSTER

Camp Upper Sanduskey June 7th 1782.

Sir, I am desired by the Wyandotts to return you thanks for the assistance you have sent them just in time of need, and they hope their Father will send them some Provision—ammunition and some cloathing, as they say they are quite naked, & beg, if possible, a few more men, and the half King a little rum to drink His Majestys health and the day on which he was born, as that was the Day on which they defeated the enemy, and they hope you will tell the Indians in General at Detroit to be ready to come to their assistance as soon as they send a runner which may be in a few days, as the Enemy is coming into the Shawnese Country—

I am Your most obedt Humble Servant
(signed) John Turney
Lieut of Rangers
Commat upper Sandusky

Major De Peyster
[B 98 p 114.]

THE MINGOES, SHAWNESE AND DELAWARES TO MAJOR DE PEYSTER

Upper Sandusky June 8th 1782—

From the Mingoes, Shawnese & Delawares.

Father, What we told you this Spring, it is needless to Repeat you granted it to us, your assistance came in good time, we have with your People defeated the Enemy. There is another Army coming against us from Kentuck, this we are certain of, not only from Prisoners, but from our Young men who are watching them—

Father, we hope you will again grant our request & let the Rangers remain at Lower Sandusky about 10 days & then March for our Villages—We hope if possible you will send some more of your People & Stores, such as are necessary for Warriours, with Canoes & Provisions sufficient to maintain the Indians you may send to us, this you cannot do too soon, as we are determined if the enemy does not come into our Country, that we will go into theirs, & we will give you all the assistance in our Power to transport your Provisions & what other necessaries you may send for your People. We hope Father you will not fail but send us all assistance possible.

Three Strings black Whampum

Captain Snake

Major De Peyster.
[B 98 p 115]

MAJOR DE PEYSTER TO CAPTAIN MCKEE

Detroit 11th June 1782.

Dear Sir, I am favoured with your letter from Upper Sandusky of the 8th Inst. the pleasure I rec'd from the defeat of the enemy would have been greatly heightened had Capt. Caldwell not been wounded. before this reaches you the Lake Indians will all have join'd and by the Gage I shall send a reinforcement of Pottewatmies from the Coeur de Cerf. Hazill and the Doctor will inform you of an accident which befell on the 10th Inst. which should require the utmost exertion of both the troops and Corveé men to repair—As this years Campaign was not begun upon the offensive plan, it would be too late considering the circumstances which attend us to send Cannon. If my Children are capable of defeating the enemy in the field we must content ourselves to let their Posts alone till a more favorable opportunity I shall send you more Ammunition by the Gage and shall take care to send provisions for the Rangers and Lake Indians as much as our present Circumstances will permit. My intentions are that the Rangers shall give every assistance to the Shawanese in their power and am in Hopes they will send us a small Reinforcement from Niagara. Please to acquaint the Snake with this, in ansr. to his Speech, and be so good as to assure my children that I wish them success which experience convinces, will ever attend them if they are unanimous and resolute.

I am Dear Sir Your most obedt. Humble Servant

At. S. De Peyster.

P. S. Mr. Du Quindre Mr. Le Clive and Chevallier will join you with the Coeur de Cerf Indians—

Alexr. McKee Esq.
Indian Affairs M. G. III.

LIEUT. GOV. SINCLAIR TO GENERAL HALDIMAND

MICHILIMACKINAC 12th June 1782.

SIR, I have the honor to acknowledge your Excellencys letter dated 9th May, mentioning refusal of Bills for the Post. Your Excellency desires that the names of Traders, who advanced for Indians in their Wintering Grounds may be transmitted. After the delivery of your Excellencys Letter of June 1780 by Niagara & Detroit numbers of the Traders stand in that predicament to the amount of Thirty thousand Pounds and upwards for that year. One of them in particular a Monsieur Ducharm was sent down, and as much as possible found fault with for incurring any expense but for Provisions & Canoes & for his bad conduct otherwise. As I am perfectly reconciled to the proper expenditure of the Public Money since I had a Garrison out of Mutiny, I wish for every opportunity of thoroughly satisfying Your Excellency on that Head.

I have the honor to be Your Excellencys
most obedient & most humble servant
(signed) PATT SINCLAIR
L't Governor.

His Excellency General Haldimand
[B 98 p 118]

MAJOR DE PEYSTER TO GENERAL HALDIMAND

DETROIT the 12 June 1782

SIR, During the command of Capt. Lernoult, he, purchased a small lot of ground, of half an acre in front, and one acre in depth, situate at a little distance from the Town, for the accommodation of Capt. McKee. The House thereon being very old and in danger of falling he is desirous to build at his own expense, paying the original sum of one hundred and fifty pounds N. Y. currency—However desirous I may be to grant his request, I do not chuse to take any steps in the matter without your Excellency's approbation.

The situation is very advantageous for him, and can be of little other use to Government.

I have the Honor to be Sir
Your most Huml and obedt. Servt.
AT. S. DE PEYSTER

His Excelly—the Command in Chief

Endorsed:—From A 1782 Major De Peyster 12th June Rec'd 10th Jly
[B 123 p 241]

MAJOR DE PEYSTER TO GENERAL HALDIMAND

DETROIT the 12th June 1782

SIR, I have the honour to transmit Copys of Letters just received from the Indian Country, which will serve to acquaint your Excellency with the success the rangers and confederate Indians from this Post, have had in repulsing the Enemy at Sandusky.

I have the honor to be Sir

Your Excellency Most Huml. & Obedt. Servt.

AT. S. DE PEYSTER

His Excellency the Comm in Chief—

Endorsed:—No 14 1782 From Major De Peyster 12th June Rec'd 10th July. (Copy Entered in Book marked B No 3 Page 23 Moravians.)

[B 123 p 242]

MAJOR DE PEYSTER TO CAPTAIN MCKEE

DETROIT, the 13th June, 1782.

DEAR SIR. The Gage was getting under way when I received yours of the 8th Inst. The Pottawattamies are very anxious to get off therefore shall only detain her till Mr. Baby can run up and send off the Blankets and such Cappots as he has made; and the Pack Saddles with which they are running down as fast as possible—Believe me Sir it is not in my power to send any Troops or even men to work the cannon so that it will be best not to send any. You certainly will agree with me that a pretty divertion may be made in the Enemy's Country, off hand, without the Incumbrance of Cannon, the loss of which would tarnish all our former success.

I am glad to hear that Capt. Caldwell is so well, and hope he will soon be able to stand, but he cannot flatter himself to be able to enter upon a speedy Campaign. My former letter will inform you that I hope they will consider us at Niagara. If they do not believe me we have enough upon our hands here. It has not cease raining one day since you left us.

I have been all this day in Council with a large band of Miamis, Ouiattonons, Piankeshaws, Meskonties and Peorias. they promise well but seem to come more on account of trading than otherwise. If however any can be moved to join you they shall follow.

Please to give my Compts. to Capt. Caldwell and the Gentlemen at Sandusky, & If possible make my Children sensible that it is not in my power to do more than send ammunition and Indians accompanied with proper officers.

I am Dr. Sir Sincerely Yours

AT. S. DE PEYSTER.

Serjt. Langdon will give you an account of all he brings. he is a careful good man.

H. M. S.

Alex. McKee Esq. Dy Agent Indian Affairs Sandusky.

Indian Affairs M. G. III.

INDIAN COUNCIL

In Council, Detroit 14th June 1782.

PRESENT.

Major At S. DePeyster, Commandt.

Lieut. T. Bennett Lieut. D. Saumarez Ensign R. Pollard Ensign Sheehan	8th Reg't.
Messrs. D. Baby C. Baubin I. Chesne	Interpreters.

About fifty Chiefs and Warriors of the Qui, qu, a pous, Mascontings, Ouiattanong, Pianquishaw, Miamis, and Peyaurias Nations,—

Major De Peyster address'd the several Nations—

Children! I desire to know from you whether you have received the strings which I sent pr. the Fleas, or not? as I desired him he should send them among your people. if you have received them I desire that one of your Chiefs may repeat what has been said upon them.—

A Chief then replies—

Father! Your Strings were just brought to my Cabin which was much to this purport "Take courage my childn, the Qui, qu, a pous. Listen to my speech and make it circulate among all the Nations who border the Ouabach, desiring them to shut up the Ouabach on the approach of an Enemy and that some of our people should go to reconnoitre towards the Falls of the Ohio, you said also, that you would open your Heart and your arms to receive us and those who live near us—this is all I can recollect.

Major De Peyster then said:

Children! Since you cannot recollect my speech, I shall repeat it over to you again. When your War Chief delivered over to me two of my People, they told me "that the Enemy had left the Post and were gone to the Falls, I said it was well, and that the Indians who border the Ouabach might then enjoy quiet, he asked me for Cloathing & Ammunition for his people, I told him he should have some for himself and party but for the absent ones I would not send any until I found they were enclined to act for the King of England—I gave him at the same time a few Strings to deliver to all the Indians Nations on the Ouabach telling them "that since the Enemy was gone from St Vincennes, it was in their power to prevent their returning again, and that I desired to know from them whether or not they were inclined to join me in hindering them from coming in to their country, as my speech is equally addressed to you all I directed that it should be made known to you, requesting an answer to be sent to me by a Deputation of Two Chiefs from each nation, that I would then receive you with open arms—

Children! I am not afraid of the Enemy as I am too strong for anything they can do,, it's for your good only that I give my advice that you may become happy and not listen any more to the Rebels, that by their fine speeches they may pass your River and destroy you, as I am well assured they seek your destruction only—

Children! As soon as you have given me Proofs of your Attachment to the British Government I shall then know how to confide in you. You cannot say that you were in want of wherewith to execute it, for I took care to provide a Trader for you at the Miami Town, I now give you these Strings and desire to know immediately if you are of these Sentiments which I have suggested to you?

delivers several strings

Major DePeyster then speaks to the Masconting, telling him as he was present at the time when he delivered his first speech with the Strings, he desired that he would therefore inform his Brethren present, whether or not, what he just said was not the subject of the Speech delivered.

The Masconting, answers, Father! Where is the necessity of repeating what you told us when we were here before, for what you now say is nothing but the truth.

Major DePeyster, tells Pe, can, the Miami Chief that he did not address him with the Strings but the Foreign Indians only he being fully satisfied with the Miami because they think as he does.

The Great Member, got up and told the other nations that altho' they were younger and not so great as he was, that he hoped they would speak their sentiments freely, as they were nigh the Enemies Gates it belonged to them to speak first and not to deceive their Father the Commandant—

La Mine de Plomb, a Ouiat speaks

Father! I salute you in the name of our nation and beg of you to listen to me, We have come a great way to see you and to return you our thanks for the favours we have received, hoping you'll continue them towards us—

Father! I gave us pleasure when we received your speech for by that we found you thought of us, for 'till then we were in obscurity, you can see by our faces the satisfaction it gave us—

(delivers 4 white strings)

The Great Member, speaks on a scalp

Father, You urged us to make War against the Rebels and bring you marks that we acted as Warriours, you see by this what we have done, I cannot say I made it, however, I hope you will accept of it from my hands as it came from my chiefs who sent you some time ago a great Pacquet of papers, I have told our Brethren to follow our example by doing which they would gain your favors—

(Delivers the Scalp)

—he then adds,

Father! It would be to little purpose to take too much of your time, let it suffice for me to assure you that the Ouiattanongs, all to a Man are ready to take the War hatchet for the King and do your will—

Ne, me, ka, a Qui, qu, a, pous [kickapoo] says—

Father! We the Qui, qu, a, pous with the several nations here present make but one and we have no other thought but yours—when your speech came to our hands, we all rejoiced, as we only wished to please our father—

—he then speaks on a Tobaccoe Pipe—

Father! This Pipe I deliver to you as a token of friendship and alliance, since you desire we should make known our sentiments, this will serve to tell you that we are inclined to do whatever you may desire from us and to keep fast hold of your hands that it may not slip from us—

(delivers the Tobaccoe Pipe)

—he then speaks on 8 Beaver Skins—

Father! We know your sentiments and you know ours, we now hope that you'll not shut your Gates upon us, but permit us to have access to your traders that we may get Goods for the skins we have brought with us—

(delivers 8 Beaver Skins)

Che, u, pi, nin, a Masconting speaks

Father! I remember when I was here before, you gave me a general invitation, telling me, that whenever I came here you would give me a welcome, I have therefore accompanied my Brethren hither—

a Pianquishaw Chief speaks on a large Tobacco Pipe.

Father! Our Chiefs and Warriours desires you will accept of this Tobaccoe Pipe which you may keep as a proof of our friendship and alliance to Great Britain, We have no other thought but yours and we shall no longer listen to the rebels as they were the cause that we, our wives and children ar misera-ble—

Father! We give you the strongest assurances that we shall execute your desires and we hope that you will fulfil ours as we now stand in need of assistance, we are the youngest of the nations present therefore want your advice to direct us—

Father! We pray of you to allow us to trade with your people as we have Packs for that purpose—

Father! Our Chief is greatly enraged against the Rebels for having deceived him he has lost some of his people in their services and they had not wherewith to cover them excepting the leaves of the Forest, so great is their poverty.

(delivers the Tobaccoe Pipe)

Le Marengoin, a Masconting speaks in the name of the Peyaurias

Father! Pray listen to me, I address you in the name of the Peyaurias and this man in particular (pointing to one) who's loss he yet laments since the time Lieut. Governor Hamilton was at St Vincennes, he begs of you to take compassion on him and his people and give them cloathing &c—

Father! The Peyaurias are of the same mind as the rest of your children and give you this Tobbacoe Pipe as a token thereof—

(delivers a Tobaccoe Pipe)

Major De Peyster then said,

Children! The Qui, qu, a, pous, Masconting, Oüiattanongs, Pianquishaws, Miamis and Peyaurias, I have listened with impatience, when I say impatience considering I have thrown away the Key of the Council House Door as I am thinking of nothing but war, I have a Vessel fitted out for that purpose which will sail immediately for St. Dooskey, if there are any among you who are disposed to go that way to assist your Brethern, let them declare themselves and prepare to embark in the Vessel, those who are here to trade I will allow them to do so, that they may return to their Village, to assemble together and oppose all attempts of the enemy should the come up the Ouabach or elsewhere, by doing which you will secure the lives of yourselves, women & children—

Children! I do not pretend to enforce your going to St. Dooskey, I should have ill used you did I not pay you the Compliment of inviting you to that Quarter—What I now do is for the good of the Brown Skins in General, as the Enemy seek their destruction and not mine,—

My Children the Oüiattanongs have already given me marks of their being out to War and I have rewarded them, I shall now do so to the person who gave me marks of that nature to day.

The beaver skins you have presented to me this day are marks for the women & not for Warriours, the Vessel being ready you can embark in her for St Dooskey where you may enable yourselves to procure such marks as will be acceptable from your hands.

(Extract from the Minutes)

J. Schieffelin Secr'y.

Substance of a Council held at Detroit 14th June 1782 by Major De Peyster Commanding Detroit and its Dependences &c &c with the

Qui, qu, a, pous
Mascontings
Oüiattanongs
Pianquishaws
Miamis and
Peyaurias

[B 123 p 243]

MAJOR DE PEYSTER TO GENERAL HALDIMAND

Detroit 15th June 1782

Sir, I have the Honour to enclose a letter just received from Captain Caldwell—I have also received Messages from the Indians, who persist in having Cannon and troops sent to them. Brigadier General Powell will have transmitted to your Excellency my reasons, for not having already comply'd with their request. I am sorry to acquaint Your Excellency that the badness of the weather has put us farther backward, than we were in the beginning of the Spring, and that we have not tools enough to supply the working men. Everything shall however be done that lays in my power to put the Fort in a state of defence, Superior to any Efforts the Enemy can possibly make against it. I this day held a Talk with a band of Cherokees from Schoté, and yesterday with a large Band of Miamis, Wyachtenous, Piankshaws Mascontins and Pioryas, who are come here to trade, whilst I am privately informed that their Brothers who remained, are called to a talk by the invitation of one

Boisseron at Post Vincents, to hear what he has to say to them in behalf of their French father.

I fear the excessive rainy weather will spoil our crops, which in the beginning of the Spring had a fair prospect.

I have the Honour to be Sir Your Excellency's most obedt & Most Humble Servt.

AT. S. DE PEYSTER.

His Excellency General Haldimand

Endorsed:—No 15 Entd 1782 From Major De Peyster 15th June—Rec'd 10th. Copy Entered in Book marked B No 3 Page 24.

[B 123 p 252.]

CERTIFICATE

MICHILIMACKINAC 19th June 1782

Jno. Coats has furnished the Quantity of Corn that he contracted for, viz. Five Hundred & Thirteen Bags, of which numbers twenty were delivered to Mr. Stove at old Mackinaw for the use of the Indians, & the remaining Four Hundred and ninety three Bags are now in the Indian Store.

JNO COATS.

[B 98 p 119]

MEMORANDUM

A Memorandum of the Corn still to be delivered to Government by John Macnamara & Co. as per Agreement—

357 Bags on the Church
100 Bags in our Store
258¼ Bushels in do.
2789 lbs. of Grease do.

MATT LESSY & CO.

[B 98 p 119]

FROM MR. GRANT UNADDRESSED

MACKINAC 19th June 1782.

SIR, As several of the Traders have not yet arrived from their Wintering Ground with whom I have Contracts for Corn I shall deliver immediately on this arrival the quantity I have contracted for with Lieut. Governor Sinclair to be furnished on or before the 10th of August next.

I am, Sir your Humble Servant

WM. GRANT.

[B 98 p 119]

FROM MR. GRANT UNADDRESSED

MACKINAC 19th June 1782.

SIR, I have already put in 50 Bags of Corn belonging to Mr. Hepolite Chaboelley but as he has agree'd with Lieut. Governor Sinclair for 580 more to be delivered in the course of the summer they shall be put in as soon as they arrive.

I am, Sir your obedt. Servant

WM. GRANT.

[B 98 p 120]

FROM MR MELDRUM UNADDRESSED

MICHILIMACKINAC ISLAND 19th June 1782.

SIR, Agreeable to the Advertisement, I here give you my reasons for not furnishing the quantity of Corn agreed for as the Commanding officer at Detroit in the Spring of the year gave a positive order for the non exportation of Provisions from that Place, which stops me from furnishing the quantity but should that order be contradicted shall deliver it on its arrival.

Sir your Humble Servant

GEORGE MELDRUM.

[B 98 p 121]

MR. MC CRAE TO LIEUTENANT FORD

SIR, The Remainder of the Corn which I contracted for with Governor Sinclair is not yet arrived from the Wintering Ground, when it does I shall put it in Store immediately.

I am, Sir Your most humble Servt

D. MCCRAE.

To Lieut Ford 47th Regmt.
Arrived 20th June 1782

SAML. FORD Lt 47th Regmt.

[B 98 p 122]

RETURN

MICHILIMACKINAC 20th June 1782

Return of the Indian Corn received into the Indian Store from the undermentioned Persons, vizt

Names.	No of Bags	No of Bushels
Mr. Coats	493	
Mr Gautier	500	
Mr Chabaille	50	
Total	1043	

[B 98 p 119]

MR. SMALL TO LIEUTENANT FORD

Lt Ford

SIR, Mr Visgar with whom I contracted for Corn arrived here the 26th Ulto, with two Boats Loaded which I understood is barely sufficient to answer the quantity Intended for the Grand Portage, his men were employed in the King's Works untill the 12th Instant when he was able to sett off for Sageneau with Three Boats. He likewise told me that he expected a Boat loaded in a few days as well as a small quantity in a vessel which Mr Berthe had sent. I think that the whole will be delivered in the month of July & will leave directions with a Person to deliver it in measure as it arrives.

I am Your Most obedt Humble Servt

PATT SMALL

[B 98 p 120]

MAJOR DE PEYSTER TO GENERAL HALDIMAND

DETROIT June 23d 1782

SIR, Your Excellency will see by the enclo'sd that the late acts of cruelty perpetrated by the Enemy at Muskingum, at the time the Indians were almost wean'd from it, have awaken'd their old custom of putting prisoners to most severe tortures by what I can learn the unhappy Victims were themselves at the Massacre of the Moravian Indians.—Nearly the same body of those Troops certainly were present and had similar intentions upon Sandusky.

A Shawanese Chief is just arrived, who informs me that some scouting parties have seen a large Encampment of the Enemy at Tuscarawas, if this is true I shall soon have it confirmed. In my last, I acquainted your Excellency that a great Number of Wabash Indians came here to trade, since which I have shipp'd sixty three of them on Board the Faith, and have sent them to join Captain Caldwell—

Lieutenant Sumander of the Indian Department is just arrived with part of the goods sent under his Care, the remainder is expected in the next Vessel

I have the Honour to be Sir,

Your Excellency's Most obedt and Most Humble Servant

At. S. De Peyster

His Excellency General Haldimand

℔ No 16 A Ent'd 1782 From Major DePeyster 23rd June—Recd 10th Copy Ent'd in Book marked B No 3 Page 25

[B 123 p 254]

LIEUT. GOV. SINCLAIR TO GENERAL HALDIMAND

Sir, On the 19th inst two Rebel Prisoners brought in report, their having left *Cross Creek, Mingoe Bottom,* with Five Hundred men under the command of Colonels [William] Crawford & [David] Williamson in May last, and that they were attacked by the Rangers & Indians near Sandusky on the 8th or 9th of June & obliged to retreat, that they were for the greatest part mounted & carried their own Provision & at their own expense.

One of them had been at Fort Pitt in April—He says that a General Irvin commanded there some Militia & the 13th Virginia Regiment.

The Indians of this neighbourhood are in readiness, waiting for accounts from Detroit.

I have the Honour to be, Sir,

Your most obed't & most Humble Servant

Patt Sinclair Lt Governor

Michilimackinac 25th June 1782

General Haldimand

[B 98 p 123]

LIEUT. GOV. SINCLAIR TO GENERAL HALDIMAND

Sir, Having received from Detroit the within copy's of Letters on the

26th Inst, I send all the Ottawas Indians (who have been in readiness) to receive Major de Peyster's commands

I have the Honor to be Sir,

Your Excellency's most obedient

& most humble Servant

PATT SINCLAIR Lt Governor

Michilimackinac 28th June 1782

General Haldimand

Endorsed:—L. No. 84. 1782. From Lieut Governor Sinclair at Michilimackinac of the 28th June inclosing the copy of three Letters from Capt Caldwell, Lieut Turney & the Mingoe Indians to Major de Peyster. Recd. 13th July

[B 98 p 125]

INVOICE

Invoice of Goods for Indian Presents sent to Michillimackinac by the way of Detroit Montreal the 3d July 1782—

225 ps Strouds each Cg 21½ yards, 4837½ yards

2½ point Blankets 480 pairs

3 point Blankets 160 pairs

JOHN CAMPBELL

Super'dt &c Ind'n affairs

Endorsed:—Invoice of Goods sent to Michillimackinac 3rd July 1782

[B 123 p 255]

LIEUT. GOV. SINCLAIR TO GENERAL HALDIMAND

Copy of a Letter to the Commander in Chief assigning reasons for incurring expenses in the Indian Department—

SIR, I beg leave to assure your Excellency that my endeavours will be joined to Mr McBeath's, in reducing the expenses of the Post—At present I humbly submit to Your Excellency my reasons from deviating from the Prohibition against Indian Charges in Accounts. It was at first difficult & expensive to arm, & so bring Indians to act, and it now requires attention to restrain them from their former ravages, or from joining loose people in & near their country to destroy the Commerce of the Province, added to these considerations, I beg the liberty of observing the hardships there would have been in sending back this year. Five Hundred families naked & without provisions after coming a great distance in expectation of receiving presents at a Post which they visited annually as friends, during the War, they are forbid to frequent the Post—It is possible that many will not return next year, but certainly numbers of the distant Tribes will not lay aside that practice all at once, to deprive them of Provisions or Presents necessary for their subsistence would be the same thing as to destroy them for they bring scarce anything with them to the Post—Laying aside the consideration of losing their attachment, it would appear severe when by degrees your Excellency will have every proof of the strict attention paid to Œconomy, so often recommended and at last commanded by your Excellency—

Another very considerable expense will unavoidably appear this year upon the return of the Ottawa's from Detroit, if Governments presents do not arrive before them, I must have recourse to Mr McBeath, for their being sent home, satisfied having promised it on conditions that Major De Peyster approved of their conduct.

I have the Honor to be

Michilimackinac July 5th 1782

Endorsed:—A Copy of Lieut. Gover. Sinclair's Letter of the 5th July 82 to Genl. Haldimand excusing his disobedience to orders, relative to the purchase & making Presents—and assigning reasons—No. 5—

[B 98 p 126]

MR FRY TO CAPTAIN MCKEE

DETROIT July 10th 1782.

DEAR SIR, I am sorry that all the endeavours of my friends to procure me the pleasure of making the Summers Campaign with you in the woods have proved fruitless. I nevertheless look upon myself equally obligated to them. The few troops that arrived in the two last vessels could never have come in better time. I believe the Major has at length pretty well convinced the Indians of the mutility of Cannon upon an occasion of this kind. The Rangers w't Captain Bradt will however put them in high spirits. We have the most authentic news of a Victory gain'd by Admiral Sir George Brydges Rodney over the French Fleet in the West Indies. I will endeavour to send you a true Copy of the Antigua Gazette which arrived at Quebec I believe the 11th June. There is the greatest reason to believe that a peace will succeed the Cessation of Arms, which has most certainly taken place, some of the American Vessels are actually fishing in the Gulph, with Licenses from Genl Carleton, who is Comr in Chief of the British Army to the Southward. Bergoyne Commr in Chief of His Majestys Forces in Ireland. Thus you see the Effects, caused by the Change of the Ministry, which has been total. We expect General Powell up here in a few days, who has orders to visit the

Upper posts once every year, at a Season when he can best be spared. enclosed you have the Copy I mention'd which I am convinced will afford you much satisfaction. I trust that you may meet with much success. Mr. McDougals Compliments to you. Please present mine to the Gentlemen with you.

I am Sir with much esteem

Your most obedt Humble Servant

P. R. Fry.

Alexr McKee Esq.
Indian Affairs M. G. IV

GENERAL HALDIMAND TO MAJOR DE PEYSTER

Quebec 11th July 1782

Sir, I have Received your Letters of the 12th 15th & 23rd ultimo with their several Enclosures, communicating the Defeat of the Rebels at St. Dusky by the Rangers and Indians under Capt. Caldwell circumstanced as Brigr. Genl. Powell would have informed you, affairs are, I regret the necessity of the Rencontre. While I very much Applaud the Conduct and Bravery of the officers and men who have so much distinguished themselves—It is unfortunate the affair was tarnished by the cruelties committed on Col. Crawford and the two Captains, and the consequences may be very prejudical should an accommodation be in agitation—I have not a doubt that every Possible argument was used to prevent that unhappy Event, and that it alone proceeded from the Massacre of the Moravian Indians, a Circumstance that will not extenuate the Guilt in the Eyes of the Congress—When you see a fit occasion, express in the proper Terms the concern I feel at their having followed so base an Example, and the abhorance I have thro' out the war at acts of cruelty, which, until this Instance, they have so humanely avoided

I am &

(signed) Fred Haldimand

Major De Peyster

In Regard to Mr. McKee's Request respecting the lot of ground, you did Perfectly right not to permit him to build until you first heard from me, those Indulgences resting entirely with the Governor of the Province—Send me down a Description of the Lot & its Extent, & I shall, as a mark of my approbation of Mr. McKee's Conduct possess him of it without the consideration proposed———

Endorsed:—No 15 Ent'd 1782 [Copy] To Major De Peyster of the 11th July. Copy Entered in Book marked B No 2 Page 26.

[B 123 p 257]

MEMORIAL

To His Excellency Frederick Haldimand, Governor & Commander in Chief of the Province of Quebec & its Dependencies, Vice Admiral of the same &c. &c. &c.

The undersigned merchants and inhabitants of Michillimackinac have the honour to represent to your Excellency that for want of a curé they are reduced to live without any outward exercise of religion; that those who finish their career in this country are deprived, at the last moment, of the consolations which they can procure for the dying. That the employees who arrive annually either from Canada or from among the Indians have need of being sustained by this powerful motive, which joined to the wise regulations of our Lieutenant Governor put the finishing stroke to this settlement, therefore we pray that you will give it to them, obliging them to provide what is legally necessary for him; take the liberty of claiming your protection and of assuring you of the respectful consideration with which they have the honour to be your Excellency's &c.

L. Gauttier—Marcot—P. Tromonteau—Joseph Caron—J. B. Barthe—L. Bertrand—Alexis Campion—Etne Campion—

Endorsed:—Request of the Merchants and inhabitants of Michilimackinac on the subject of a curé for that post. Recd 13th July '82.

[B 98 p 128]

MAJOR DE PEYSTER TO GENERAL HALDIMAND

DETROIT July 14th 1782

SIR, I have this day drawn on Your Excell'y four sets of bills favour of Messrs Macomb Edgar & Macomb amounting to Thirty thousand Three hundred and seventy eight pounds twelve shillings and eleven pence ½ d 3-7 New York Currency, being for disbursements in the different Departments at this post for His Majesty's Service as p abstract & vouchers which will be herewith delivered your Excellency, and which I hope your Excellency will honor.

I have the honor to be Your Excellency's
most obedient & humble Servant

AT S. DE PEYSTER
Major Kings Reg't Commanding Detroit
& its dependencies

His Excellency General Haldimand
Governor & Commander in Chief Quebec.

Endorsed:—From 1782 Major De Peyster 14th July, Rec'd 16th Aug't

[B 123 p 259]

ACKNOWLEDGMENT

The Traders from Michilimackinac being engaged in one Joint Concern & Interest from the month of August 1779, to the 30th July 1780. Messrs Louis Chevalier & Pte Hurtibise were employed by the company at St Joseph's, and they as well as others employed for or concerned in said Company were forbid all private Trade—To invalidate therefore all illegitimate Claims, We the subscribed Proprietors & Managers of said Company do hereby acknowledge to have received full payment from Government for all advances made by us for the Crown at the Post of St Joseph's, or for the services of People employed by us at that Post during that Period.

Signed this 21st July 1782

John Macnamara & Co
Henry Bostwick
William Grant
David McCrae

[B 98 p 61]

MAJOR DE PEYSTER TO CAPTAIN MCKEE

Detroit July 27th 1782.

Dear Sir, I have received your letter of the 23d and have in Consequence thereof ordered the few Indians present at Detroit to join you. M. Beaubin arrive here at 12 O'clock last Night from the Miamis Town whither I had sent him to get intelligence, he has brought in two Canadians from post Vincent whom he found there, they made no mention of an Enemy coming by the Wabash. A Speech from Le Gris assures me of the fidelity of the Miamis who have sent off thirty of their Warriours to join you. I shall dispatch Beaubin this afternoon to raise the rest of the Miamis and march with them to your assistance. I also expect a large Band of Chippewas from M. Makina who shall be forwarded immediately on their arrival. The Ottawas from thence, already gone forward I hope will have join'd, as well as Captain Bradts Detachment, before Captain Caldwell finds himself under the Necessity of attacking the Enemy. By this Opportunity I send some provisions and ammunition to be deposited at the foot of the Rappids of the Miamis. The same Vessel proceeds to fetch Serjt. Langdon with his Stores from Sandusky and to land them at the foot of the Rappids, from whence you are to receive your Supplies. Contrary winds have prevented my seeing Brigadier General Powell here before now, he is on his way to visit this part of his District, as soon as he arrives I will write you again and to Captain Caldwell to whom you'll please to show this letter, and assure him of my good wishes, in the mean time should be glad to hear from you both.

I am, Dr. Sir, your humbl. & obedt. Servt.

At S. De Peyster

Alexr. McKee Esq.

Indian Affairs M. G. III.

A SURVEY OF THE SETTLEMENT OF DETROIT MADE BY ORDER OF MAJOR DE PEYSTER THE 16 DAY OF JULY 1782.

Heads of Families.	Married Women.	Young & hired men.	Boys.	Girls.	Male slaves.	Female slaves.	Horses.	Oxen.	Cows.	Steers & heiffers.	Sheep.	Hogs.	Flour.	Wheat.	Wheat sown arpents.	Indian corn do. arpents.	Oats do. arpents.	Arpents of clear land.
François Prudhome															5			40
Charles Fontaine	1		4	2			2	2	1	2		3						40
Jacques Bissere	1		2	1			1	2	4	1		4			18	6		160
Antoine Soumande	1						3		1			2			57		14	120
Pierre Meloche Junr	1						1		1						20	2		40
Pierre Fouquerau	1	1	1	2			1			1					20			60
Ettienne Lavoilette	1		3	2			3	2	3	4		4		18	23	5	8	48
Joseph Cotté	1		5	1			2		1			2			10	6	5	16
Louis Montmorency	1		4	3			2	2	1			3			18	4	4	32
Antoine Meloche	1		3	3			5	3	2			10	250		22	6	4	64
Jean Baptiste Giginac	1		1				3	2	2			4		12	11	6	6	32
Jean Baptiste Antilliya	1		2	2			4	2	4	2		10		30	17			48
Thomas Pagotte	1	1	3	5			8	4	4	2		10		20	16	6	11	50
Charles Renaud	1	1	4	1			2	2	2			2			18	4		50
Jean Beaus Nomme	1		1	2			2		1						17			50
Pierre Prudhomme		1					3			2					10			55
Amable Gerard	1		2	3			3	2	1	1					20	4		60
Jean Louis Reveau	1	1					2					2			17	2	7	60
François Lesperance		2					3	2	2			4	300		18	5	8	60
Pierre Proux	1	1	1	3			2		2			4	300		18	5	16	55
Antoine Rousseau	1			1			2	2	3	2		12		5	18	5	8	55
Charles Bernier	1		2	1			3		3	1		3			9			
Antoine Boufard	2	1	5	1			3	2	4	2		6			30	6	6	100
René Cloutier	1	2	4	4			2	2	2	1		12			16	4	4	50
Zachary Cloutier	1		1	2			4		1			7			8	2½		
Michael Roy	1	1	2	1			2	2	1		11	5			18	3	5	100
François Mouton	1		1	4					1			5						
Ettienne Jacob	1	1	5	3			4	2	1			5			22	8		75
Louis Sousore	1	1	2	5			3	4	5		15	12			20	4		75
	27	14	58	52			75	39	53	21	26	131	850	85	494	93½	106	1,695

SURVEY—*Continued.*

Heads of Families.	Married Women.	Widows & Hired Women.	Young & Hired men.	Boys.	Girls.	Male Slaves.	Female Slaves.	Horses.	Oxen.	Cows.	Steers & Heiffers.	Sheep.	Hogs.	Flour, lbs.	Wheat, bushels.	Indian Corn, bushels.	Wheat Sown, bushels.	Indian Corn Sown, arpents.	Oats Sown, bushels.	Arpents Clear Land.
Mrs. Bissounette		1	2	3	3			10		4	1		6		25					
Jean Bap. Begras								2		2			1		6		10			40
François Belaire	1		2	2	4			6	2	5			7				20	3	5	60
Paul Campau	1		1	2	2			6	4	6	5		9				13	6	26	75
Louis Lajenness	1		2	1	5			5	2	4	2		10				25		10	240
Joseph Pouget	1		3	2	4			4	2	2	5		8				47	6	4	180
Jean Bte. Taureujau	1	2	4	2	1			12	6	6			4				5	6		120
Jean Saliotte	1		1	1	2			2					2				4	3	3	
Guillaume Monforton	1		1	3	2		1	3	2	5			4				16	6	10	120
Joseph Drouillard	1		1		3	1	1	7	2	2	1		10	1000	80	12	8	5		120
Jean Bte Lebeau	1		1	1	2			3	4	2			2				12	8	15	75
Pierre Campau	1		1		2			3					4	300			5	6		
Joseph Nattade	1			1	1			2					2				2½			
Simon Drouillard	1		2	3	4		1	6	4	5			12				8	8		120
Pierre Meloche	1		1	6	2			2	4	4	2		8	300		20	10	2	7	160
Jacques Belleperche		1		1				5	2	2			5				25½		4	120
Antoine Robert Junr	1			1	2			3	2				4				3			120
Louis Robidoux	1			3	3			10		2	1									120
Joseph Boudy	2		3	2	5		1	5	6	9	5	30	7		20	40	22	3		120
Jean Bte Drouillard	1			1				2												
Jean Bte Drouillard Senr	1		3					5		3	2		2	100			11			120
Pierre Cocquillard	1		2					2					3				8	3	6	120
Jean Bte Parrey	1		3	2	3			2		1			3				10			120
Augustine Toraujeau	1							2		1	5		2				7	5		120
Theophil Lemay	1		1	1	4			4		3	2		5				10	2		120
Charles Reaume	1		1	3	1		1	5	4	4			7		15		26	4	12	120
Louis Lajoye	1			5	2			4	4	4	2		4				23	4		120
	25	4	35	40	57	1	5	122	50	79	33	30	131	1700	146	72	331	80	102	2630

SURVEY—*Continued.*

Heads of Families.	Married Women.	Widows & Hired Women.	Young & Hired Men.	Boys.	Girls.	Male Slaves.	Female Slaves.	Horses.	Oxen.	Cows.	Steers & Heiffers.	Sheep.	Hogs.	Flour.	Wheat.	Indian Corn.	Wheat Sown bushels.	Acres of Indian corn sown.	Bushels of Oats Sown.	Arpents clear land.
George Knaggs	1			3	2			7	2	9			4				18	6		120
James Rankin				1	3		1	5	3	7	4						7	5		
François Pratt	1			3	1	1	1	4	2	2	1		3				5	2	6	160
François Marentete Gaudet	1	1	1	5	2	1	2	10	8	5		25	12	300			50		15	200
Charles Robidoux	1		1					1												
Jacques Parent	1		1	4			1	10	4	4			6	600			18	8	12	120
Laurent Parent	1		1	3	2			6	2	2	4		10	400			20	4	10	120
Claude Reaume	1			5	2	2	2	5	2	3	4		10	600			26	5	9	80
Joseph Mathieu			3	2				2					4				15		10	
Philip Leduc	1		1	4	1		2	9	2	2	1	10	12	200			30	4	15	120
Ettienne Robidoux	1			3	1			3		3										
Jean Bte. Leduc	1		1	1	1			2	4	2	1		6	400	10		26	3	8	120
Joseph Duchesne	1			4	1			2	2				4				8	2	4	
Joseph Maillou		1	1	2	1			4	4	4	1	3	6		8	5	30	3	6	120
François Janesse		1		2	1			5	2	3	3		10	500			25	3	15	120
Jean Ouillette	1	2	2	3	2			10	2	3	3		9		25	5	15	4	12	80
André Bennetau	1			3	1			1		1			2	200			12	1	8	
François Bennetau	1			1	3			1	2	1			6	150			10	1	8	80
Charles Bouroud	1		1				1	6	2	3			3	300			40	1	20	80
Joseph Larente								1		1				100						
Jean Bte. Tourneux	1		2		1			7	2	5			5	200			40	2½	15	120
Pierre Reaume			1				1	7	3	3	2		20	400	80		50		20	120
Ignace Duvalle	1	2	2	1	2			2	2				8				30	2½	12	120
Nittat Demonchelle	1		1	3	4			6		3	5		13		20		26	6	14	40
Louis Gouyou	1		2	3	1			3		1	3		8	300	35		32	4½	10	80
Jacques Charou	1		2	1	1			10		2	1		3	400			33		14	80
Joseph Lesperance		1	1	1	2		1	3	2		1		7				27	4	12	80
Julien Parent			1	1	2			5	4	3	2		15				40	4	20	80
Nicholas Langlois	1		2	3	2			6	2	1			10	800			70	4	30	80
	21	8	26	62	39	4	12	143	58	73	36	38	196	5850	173	10	703	79½	305	2320

SURVEY—*Continued.*

Heads of Families.	Married women.	Widows & Hired Women.	Young & Hired Men.	Boys.	Girls.	Male Slaves.	Female Slaves.	Horses.	Oxen.	Cows.	Steers & Heiffers.	Sheep.	Hogs.	Flour.	Wheat.	Indian Corn.	Bushels of Wheat sown.	Arpents of Indian Corn.	Bush's of Oats sown.	Arpents of clear Land.
Pierre Labute	1	1	1	1	2	2	1	6	4	3	3		10		100		65		33	160
François Gaudette	1							2		2			1				25		8	120
Hyacinth Dehetre		1	2	1	1			2					2				18		8	60
Charles Delisle	1			1				3	2	1	1		6	400	50		20		8	60
Antoine Langlois	1	1	1	5	2			4	1	3	3		5	800			30	5		120
Jean Bte Beaubien	1			2	2			3	2	2	2		6				22	1½	12	105
Joseph Beaubien	1	1	1	4	2		1	3	2	3	1		3	400	10		20	3	10	90
Joseph Cecire	1	1																		
Fontenay Dequindre	1		1	1	1			4		1			2				7	4	3	
Alexis Maisonville	1			4		2	2	11	7	7	8	44	15		300		104	5	37	280
Antoine L. Labady				3	3	1	1	17	4	3	13		12	2000	200		40	10	24	240
Bonavarture Reaume	1			4	3			5	2	3	1		7		50		36	3	10	80
Joseph Gaudet	1			1	2			3	2	1	4	3	4		20		18		11	80
Joseph Bertiaume	1		1	2	1		1	2	2	1	1		6		16		35	3	6	80
Pierre Reaume Jr	1				2			4	2	1			2	500	5		23		10	40
Jean Bte. Sauserainte	1		2	2	1			1					4							
François Meloche	1		2	4	3			5	4	3	5		11	400	14		25	5	20	150
Mrs. Levril			1	2	1			4	2	1	3			200			20	3	12	150
Pierre Geiron			1					2	2				4		8			8		15
Guillhaume Gouyou					2			9		1			5				4	1½		18
Nicholas Petit	1			3	4			1					3					1½		
André Pettier	1		1	3	5			4	2	4	2		10	400	10		23	4½	11	24
Jean Bte. Lapointe	1			2	3		1	3		1	1		3				13	5	7	20
Pierre Letrouneau		2	2	3	1			4		1			3				12	5	10	48
François Drouillard	1			4	3			2	2	3			10		30		18			33
Louis St. Louis	1		1	2				6	2	3	2		6				18			33
Pierre Leverseur	1			1	1			2	2	2	2		6	100			18			36
François Sourdellet	1			3	3			6	2	5			6				22	3	8	36
	22	7	17	58	48	5	7	118	46	55	52	47	152	5200	813		620	71	248	2078

SURVEY—*Continued.*

Heads of Families.	Married women.	Widows & Hired women.	Young & Hired men.	Boys	Girls.	Male Slaves.	Female Slaves.	Horses.	Oxen.	Cows.	Steers & Heifs.	Sheep.	Hogs.	Flour.	Wheat.	Indian Corn.	Bushels of wheat sown.	Arpents of Indian corn sown	Bushels. of Oats sown	Arpents clear land
Joseph Valcour	1			2	2			3	2	3	3		3				14	2	4	42
Jean Bte. Parrey	1		2	4	3			3	4	5	3		6	500			20		6	66
Joseph Beauchamp			1					2	4	2	4		2				13	4	5	66
Antoine Robert	1		3				1	4		3	1		5				16		6	66
Pierre Laperle								1		1										
A. Goulette & Litzimburgen	2			1				3	2	2	1		6		10		10	3		8
Pierre Yax								1												6
William Forsith	1		2	3		2	3	11	6	14	7	20	18	300	22	6	8	12	14	40
John Askin	1		4	1	2	4	2	7	5	7	3	19	14	3,200			6	5		52
Gregor McGregor	1		3	2	2	2		12	10	22	16		17		20	10	35	8	34	200
Julian Ferton		1		2	2			1					4	200			8		2	18
François Duchene	1			1				3		1	1		4				11	2	5	18
Nicholas Patnotte	1			1	6			2	2	3			2	300			16		7	18
Antoine Meney	1			2	4			2		3	2		6	200			9			21
François Tremblay	1		1	4	2			3		6	2		15	600			14	3	1½	21
Michel Yax	1	1	3					5	4	6	3		15	300			25	1	12	60
Claude Duchesne	1	2		2				3	2	2	1		5	200			13	4	15	20
Pierre Duchesne	1			2				1		1			5				10	4	2	10
Jean Bte. Crequi	1			2	6			4	4	2	2		2		10		16		6	40
Charles Grimaur				2			1	3	4	4	5		5	1000			23	10	8	45
Joseph Saucier	1		1	2	5			3	2	8	6		8	1500			27	4	14	72
Jean Bte. Lacoursiere			6					3	6	4	4		8	600			43	5	18	90
Benjamin Jones	1			4	1															
Laurent Griffaur	1			2	4			2		4			4				4	2		
Isedore Maurin	1			4				6		4			6							
Augustin Tremblay	1	1	2		1			1		1			7					1		
Louis Tremblay	1			4	3		1	12	6	14	7	21	20	4000	60		36	3	20	80
Jacob Harsen	1			3	3	1		2		9	3		12	800			19	3		30
Jean Champaigne	1		3	1	6			6					12				2½	1½		6
	24	5	32	51	52	9	8	109	63	131	74	60	201	13,700	122	16	398½	77½	179½	1095

SURVEY—*Continued.*

Heads of Families.	Married women.	Widows & Hired women	Young & hired men	Boys	Girls	Male Slaves	Female Slaves	Horses	Oxen	Cows	Steers	Sheep	Hogs	Flour	Wheat	Indian Corn	Bushels of wheat sown	Arpents of I. corn sown	Bushels of wheat sown	Arpents clear land
Mrs. Casety			1			2	1	5	3	8	10	5	10				18	30		180
Jacques Allard	1			1	1			2		3			4				10	1	3	12
André Skyaudis	1		1	1				3					3				10		10	9
Louis Griffaur	1		1	4	3			4	3	2			5				14	1	6	24
Jean Cripeit	1	1	1		2			4		2			6				8	1		18
Jean Thoulouse	1	1	2	1	3			4		1	2		4				22½			18
Louis Renaud	1			3	4			1					5				16	1		9
Ignace Thibeau	1			5	2			2		5	1		7				17	2		9
Jacques Lauson	1		2	3	2			2		2			2				6	1		16
Joseph Tremblay			1					6	4	2	4		2	1200	100		7		12	27
Jean Bte. Chauvin	1	1		4	3			2		2	2		3				7	1½	8	30
Jean Duprau	1		1	2	3			3	2	4	3		4	1000			12	1½	8	22
Gaetau Laderoute	1	1	1		1			4	2	6	10		6	1000			9		12	33
Mrs. Marsac		1	2	5	1			6	6	5	4		12	400			22		12	90
Joseph Laderoute	1		2	2	1			4	2	3	3		11	300			15		8	24
Michel Yax Junr			1					2	2	2	2		3				20	1	12	45
Jean Bte. Marsac	1			1	4			15	4	7	10	43	12	200			22		12	75
Thomas Cox	1	2	2			2	3	7	2	3			8				42		36	45
Joseph Perinier	1			5	2			2		1			3							
Jean Marie Dubaye	1			3	2			1		2			3					3		
Joseph Laperle	1			1	3			1		1			2					3		
Charles Chauvin	1	3	2	6	3			2		1	2		7				14		6	30
Jean Bte. Campau Junr	1		3		6	1		9	4	7	4		18				25	1	18	120
Pierre Cardinalle	1			4	2			2		2			6				30	2	14	45
Joseph Cardinalle		1	1	3	4			25	3	5	4		7	500	15		15			45
Jacques St. Aubin			4		1			5					3				20	1	10	75
Pierre St. Aubin	1	1	1					2		1			3				14			
Louis St. Aubin	1		3	2	3			3			2		9				20	1	6	45
Simon Meloche	1			2	1			4		1			5	200	10		16	1	10	30
Robert Jean	1		1	1	3			3												
	24	12	33	59	60	5	4	135	37	78	63	48	173	4,800	125	....	431½	53	203	1076

SURVEY—*Continued.*

Heads of Families.	Married Women.	Widows & Hired Women.	Young & Hired Men.	Boys.	Girls.	Male Slaves.	Female Slaves.	Horses.	Oxen.	Cows.	Steers & Heiffers.	Sheep.	Hogs.	Flour.	Wheat.	Indian Corn.	Bushels of Wheat Sown.	Arpents of I. Corn Sown.	Bushels of Oats Sown.	Arpents of clear land.
John Martin Franks			1					1												
Antoine Moras	1		3	2	1			3	2	4			4	200			20	1	8	45
Guillaume Bernard	1		1	5	5	2	5	2	4	6	6		10	800			48	2	16	100
Antoine Boyer	1	1			1			3	2	1			7	700			10		20	36
Nicholas Michel dit Lorrain	1	1	2			1	1		2			4								
Louis Benfait	1	1	1	1	3	2	1	6	2	6	7		19	1000			40		12	50
Jean Bte. Chapoton	1	1	6	1	3	2	2	14	6	5	5		20	1000			50	4	22	150
Jean Bte. Peltier	1		4	2				6	4	5	4		10	400			32	3	17	110
Pierre Durand	1		1					1		1								3		
Charles Lapalme	1	1	1	2	1															
Jean Bte. Meloche	1		1	1	8	1	2	5	4	6	6		9	1500	70		23	6	20	60
Philip Belangé	1	1	4	1	3		1	3	2	2	2		4	200		4	10		10	32
Mrs. Benoa			1					4	2	2	2		3	150			15	1	10	60
Simon Campau	1			4	6	3	2	8	3	7	4	26	16	1600			32	4	40	75
Jean Bte. Campau	1	1		5	3	5	2	7	4	6	4		8	600		10	29	5	32	75
Jacques Campau			2	6		1	1	6	7	14	19	18	19	8000	50	36	36		18	138
Hippolite Campau	1		3	1	1			3		2			4	300			6		8	30
Ignace Boyer	1		1		1			2		1			3				4	2	5	
Neol St. Aubin		2	2	1	2			7		4	2		8				20	1	14	80
Antoine Mency		2	2	2	2			6	2	4	2		2	600			20	2	8	40
Francois Gouin	1		1		1			2	2	3			3	200			10		6	27
Alexus Cueillerie	1		1	1	4			3		1										
Nicholas Gouin	1		1	2	1			1	2	1			3							
Charles Gouin	1	1	1	1	3	1	1	5	3	5	2		7	400			36		20	60
Amable Latoure	1		1		1			1		1			1							
Antoine Dequindre	1			1				3		2				2500					6½	
Robert Deninston	1				2															
Jean Bte. Revaur	1		2	7	3		1	5	8	12	18		10	2000	20	10	20	2	20	84
François Bellecour	1				1		1	2		2	1		3							
Charles Moran		1	2	2	4		1	12	3	4	8		10	400			48	1½	22	120
	24	14	45	48	60	17	21	122	62	109	92	44	187	22,550	140	60	509	37½	324½	1372

SURVEY—*Continued.*

Heads of Families.	Married Women.	Widows & Hired Women.	Young & Hired Men.	Boys.	Girls.	Male Slaves.	Female Slaves.	Horses.	Oxen.	Cows.	Steers & Heiffers.	Sheep.	Hogs.	Flour.	Wheat.	Indian Corn.	Bushels of Wheat Sown.	Arpents of Indian corn sown.	Bushels Oats Sown.	Arpents Clear land.
Jean Bte. Beaubien	1	2	8	1	3		2	9	6	5	3		13	1000			31		26	100
John Pike	1		2	2	2			2		2			2							
Joseph Lusier			7					6												
James Thompson		1	3					2		2				300						
Normand McLeod	1				1		1			2										
Pere Simple		1	2					2		4			2							
Thomas Finchley	1		1	3	1	1	1	2		1				1000						
François Billiet	1		2																	
Nathan Williams			2													20				
Ridley & Hands								1								5				
John McPherson				2				5						250		5				
Jean Morin				3				2												
Abbott & Saunders	1		1	2	4		2	1		2				1500						
George Lyons	1	1		1		1		2		1										
William Groesbeck			2					2						100						
Alexander Macomb	1	2	4	3	4	3	4	20		27	6	18	12	800			53	6	41	150
William Macomb	2			3	2	4	4													
Duperon Baby	2		4	3	5	1	1	4		4										
Thomas McCrae	1		3	5				4		1										
Gerret Greverat	1		6	3		1		4						4000						
George Anthon	1			1			1	6	1	4		20								
Jean Bte. Sanchagrin	2		1	1	3			1		1				6000						
George Cotteral	1		1		1			3		1										
James May	1					1		1		1										
John McKirgan	1			3	5															
Daniel Garril	1	1	1	2				1												
William Scott	1		4		3			1		3										
Pauling & Burrell			2			1	0	2												
Antoine Adhemer	1			2	2	1	1	1		2					2	20				
T. Williams	1		2	1	1	1		3		3	1		2	600	40	10				
	24	8	58	41	37	15	17	87	7	66	10	38	41	16,150	40	60	84	6	67	250

SURVEY—*Continued.*

Heads of Families.	Married Women.	Widows & Hired Women.	Young & Hired Men.	Boys.	Girls.	Male Slaves.	Female Slaves.	Horses.	Oxen.	Cows.	Steers.	Sheep.	Hogs.	Flour.	Wheat.	Indian Corn.	Bushels of Wheat Sown.	Arpents of I. Corn Sown.	Bushels of Oats Sown.	Arpents of Clear land.
Alexander Grant	1				4		2	3		4		24								
Thomas Reynolds	1			3	2		1			2										
William Tucker	1			2	1		1	2		2			2							
Simon McTavish			2											2800						
William Park			1	1		1		2		2		48		4900		6				
Andrews & Trimble								1	1	3		1	1	150		100				
Jacob Schieffelin	1			1		1		1		1										
Mrs. St. Corme			2					2		2				100						
Louis Thibeau	1		2		1			1		1				500						
Joseph Voyer	1		2																	
Augustine Lafory			1					3		1										
Patrick McGulpin	1		1	2	1			1		1										
Jean Bte. Roucourt		1		1																
Willson & Dolsin	1			1	1			3		1				200						
Sarah Ainsse							1	5		1			2	600		8				
Isaac Gagner	1		1	1	2	1		1		1				300						
Prisque Cotte	1			2	1			2		2			2							
Jacques Peltier	1		2	3	3		1	4		3	1						7½			
Amable Maillou	1		2					1												
Isaac Williams & Son	2			1	3			2		3			4							
Pierre Borgia	1		1	5																
Joseph Cire dit St. Jean		1	1	1		1	2	1		3				700						
Jean Bte. Craite	2		2		3	1		2		4	1		3							
Antoine Bernard	1		1					1		1										
François Gaubrelle	1		1	3				3		2	2									
Cornwall & Miller			4			1		1												
Pierre Drouillard	1	1	1		2	1	1	2		7			15				50		4	150
John Carbey	1							1												
Walter Goodfellow				1																
	21	3	27	28	24	7	9	45	1	47	4	73	29	10250	....	114	57½	....	4	150

SURVEY—*Continued.*

Heads of Families.	Married Women.	Widows & Hired Women.	Young & Hired Men.	Boys.	Girls.	Male Slaves.	Female Slaves.	Horses.	Oxen.	Cows.	Steers & Heiffers.	Sheep.	Hogs.	Flour.	Wheat.	Indian Corn.	Bushels of wheat sown.	Arpents of I. corn sown.	Bushels of oats sown.	Arpents of clear land.
Jean Bte. Petre	1			3	2			1		2			2							
Trudille & Charbouneau								2												
Joseph L. Enfant	1		2	4	3			1		4	1		4	1000		6				
Charles Chesne	1	1	2	2	1			8	2	1	4		4		50		30		19	51
Gabriel Hunot																				
Victorie Morriseaux	1			2				3												
Joseph Gamelin		1	1	1	1	1		12	1	6	4		4	900			25		15	50
Pierre Demasse	2		2	3	1			3		1			1	1000						
Dominique Labrosse	1		2							1										
Joseph Baron	1			3				1		1			1							
Alexis Labady	1		2	2	3	1		6	4	4	2		8		20		22		10	60
Pierre Labady	1		1					1												
Ettienne Hyvernois & Son	1			1		1	1	3	2	7	7		4	500			30		20	60
Robert Navarre & Son	2		2		2	1	1	4	4	8	2		4	1200	40		7	2	25	75
Pierre Robert	1		1	4	3			4		2			1							
Claud Campau	1	2	3		1			10		3	2		10				22		25	78
Joseph Poupar	1		1		2	2		1		1				300						
Registre Benoa		1	1					2		1										
Jean Guillebau			2					4												
Jean Marie Durand	1																			
Joseph Vermette	1		2		2															
Joseph Cabasy	1	1	2		2	1	2	2	2	4	3		7	600			29		12	50
Louis Couseneau	1		1	1	1			3		1			1							
Louis Vissiere	1			3	4	1	2	2	2	4	2		6	200			19		9	50
Jean Bte. Cecot	1	1		2	4	4	4	6	2	5		9	6				48		13	100
Ambroise Reopelle	1	1		5	4			4		4	2		11	200			25	2		50
Louis Tremblay	1				1			1												
Antoine & H. Laselle			2					1												
Simon Geudron	1																			
	25	8	28	36	37	12	10	85	19	60	29	9	74	5,900	110	6	257	4	149	627

SURVEY—*Continued.*

Heads of Families.	Married Women.	Widows & Hired women.	Young & Hired men.	Boys.	Girls.	Male Slaves.	Female Slaves.	Horses.	Oxen.	Cows.	Steers & Heiffers.	Sheep.	Hogs.	Flour.	In. Corn.		Bushels of Wheat Sown.	Arpents of Indian Corn sown.	Bushels of Oats sown.	Arpents Clear Land.
Gerard Bercelau	1	1	1	3	2			1		2			1	500						
François Chabert } Isidore Chesne }	2		3	2	2	1	1	5	6	5	3	8	7	1200			32		40	70
Alexis Delile	1	1	2	6	2	1	1	6	2	6	2		12	1000			15	1	20	34
Jaques Godfroy & Son	1		2		1		2	5	2	5	3		6				20	2		34
Charles Campau	1		1					4		1				200						
Robert Navarre Junr	1		1	5	3		2	6	4	4	7	26	5	1500			10	2	16	68
Jean Bte. Couture	1			4	1			2		1			3	300						
Pierre Labady Junr	1		1	3	3			3	1	5	3		2	200			9	1	6	50
Alexis Campau	1		1	3	4			3	2	5	3		5	200			15	1½	8	50
William Brown	1				1		1	10	2	3	5		4	800						
Claude Sloant			1	2				6	2	2	1		2	100			12	3	2	24
François Gamelin			1			1		4	2	3	4		2			10	20		6	24
Antoine Revaure	1		1	2	2			1		1							3			
Jean Bte. Reaume	1	1	2	2	4		1	6	4	3	6		4				18		15	45
Joseph Andre	1		1	2	2			3	2	2							20		10	36
Antoine Cattin	1		1	1	3			2		3			1				8	6		36
Joseph Bourdeaux	1		1	3	5			2	2	2	1						1½	3	2	6
Reverend McHubert				1				1		2			4	1300	50	7				
Amable Bigras	1		1		1			1		1			3							
	17	3	21	39	37	3	8	71	31	56	38	34	61	7,300	50	17	183½	19½	125	477

Recapitulation.	Heads of Families.	Married Women.	Widows & Hired Women.	Young & Hired Men.	Boys.	Girls.	Male Slaves.	Female Slaves.	Horses.	Oxen.	Cows.	Steers & Heiffers.	Sheep.	Hogs.	Flour.	Wheat.	Indian Corn.	Bushels of Wheat Sown.	Arpents of Indian Corn Sown.	Bushels of Oats Sown.	Arpents of clear land.
1st Column	29	27	....	14	58	52	....	....	75	39	53	21	26	131	850	85	....	494	93½	106	1,695
2nd do.	27	25	4	35	46	57	1	5	122	50	79	33	30	131	1,700	146	72	331	80	102	2,630
3rd do.	29	21	8	26	62	39	4	12	143	58	73	36	38	196	5,850	173	10	703	79½	305	2,320
4th do.	28	22	7	17	58	48	5	7	118	46	55	52	47	552	5,200	813	....	626	71	284	2,078
5th do.	29	24	5	32	51	52	9	8	109	63	131	74	60	201	13,700	122	16	398½	77½	179½	1095
6th do.	30	24	12	33	59	60	5	4	135	37	78	63	48	173	4,800	125	....	431½	53	203	1076
7th do.	30	24	14	45	48	60	17	21	122	62	109	92	44	187	22,550	140	60	509	37½	324½	1372
8th do.	32	24	8	58	41	37	15	17	87	7	66	10	38	41	16,150	40	60	84	6	67	250
9th do.	33	21	3	27	28	24	7	9	45	1	47	4	73	29	10,250	....	114	57½	....	4	150
10th do.	33	25	8	23	36	37	12	10	85	19	60	29	9	74	5,900	110	6	257	4	149	627
11th do.	21	17	3	21	39	37	3	8	71	31	56	38	34	61	7,300	50	17	183½	19½	125	477
Total	321	254	72	336	526	503	78	101	1112	413	807	452	447	1376	94,250	1804	355	4075	521½	1849	13,770

The Subscribers do hereby certify that the above is a true state of the Settlement of Detroit (exclusive of the absentees) according to the best information we could obtain from the several Inhabitants.

Detroit 30th July 1782.

T. Williams, I. P.
Gregor McGregor.

At S. DePeyster,
Major Kings Reg't Commanding Detroit.

Exclusive of the above quantity, Hog Island will produce this Harvest, one Hundred Bushels of Wheat, and Seven or Eight Hundred Bushels of Indian Corn. The small quantity of Wheat owing to the late heavy rains.

A. S. DeP.

[B 123 pp 266-272]

CENSUS

State of the Settlement of Detroit taken the 20th of July 1782—

321	Heads of families	Exclusive of them employ'd in the King's service and are in the Inian Country—say—100—
254	Married Women	
72	Widows & married women	
336	Young & Hired men	
526	Boys	
503	Girls	
78	Male Slaves	
101	Female do.	
1112	Horses	
413	Oxen	
807	Cows	
452	Heffirs & Steers	
447	Sheep	
1,370	Hogs	
29,250	wt Flour	
1,804	Wheat—Bushels	
355	Indian Corn do.	
4,075	Bushels wheat sown last fall	
521	Acres under Indian Corn	
1,849	ditto under Oats	
13,770	ditto under cultivation	
3,000	Bushels Potatoes supposed to be in the ground	
1000	Barrel Cyder ditto will be made	

[B,123 p 273]

Return of the Barracks, furniture, Beding, Iron Utensils &c, in the Barrack Master Generals Dept. at Detroit 31st July 1782.

	Gentmn officers Apartments &c.										
	Apartments.	Rooms.	Locks and Keys.	Tables.	Chairs.	Ashboxes.	Water Buckets.	Iron Potts and Bales.	Pairs of End Irons.	Pairs of Tongs.	Fire Shovells.
Total	14	16	25	12	43	12	22	9	19	18	18

	Serjeants Drummers Rank and File.														
	Numbr of Rooms.														
	Att 16 Men to each room.	At 20 Ditto.	At 24 Ditto.	At 28 Ditto.	At 50 Ditto.	Total Rooms.	Total Men.	Tables.	Forms.	Ashboxes.	Water Bucketts.	Hanging Shelves.	Racks for arms.	Berths for 4 Men each.	Berths for 2 Men each.
Total	12	1	1	2	2	18	392	22	42	20	37	18	15	62	75

	Beding.				
	Ruggs.	Blankets.	Pairs of Sheets.	Bed Cases.	Bolster Cases.
Total	171	305	..	254	320

	Iron Utensils &c.													
									Glass & Putty.		Boxes of Iron.			
	Iron Potts and Bales.	Pairs of Iron Trammels.	Cast Iron Stoves.	Pairs of Hand Irons.	Pairs of Tongs.	Fire Shovells.	Iron Candlesticks.	Axes.	Boxes of Glass.	Pounds of.	Square.	Flatt.	White Wash Brushes.	Grind Stones.
Total	60	69	5	25	35	32	35	75	....	3	....	3	2	1

N. B. The Sheets present, is in general bad, and have left that Column Blank—The Dep. Barrack Master General, writes, he will send a sufficient quantity of Sheets, and other Barrack Beding, for this Post this Summer--

(Errors Excepted) ABRAHAM ALBEY Barrk. Mstr.

To Brigadier General Henry Watson Powell Commandant of Niagara and its Dependencies &c. &c—

Detroit 31st July 1782 Return of the Barracks furniture, Beding, Iron utensils &c. in the Barrack Master General's Department at this Post—

[B 123 p 274]

Return of the Barracks at Detroit Specifying the Number of Rooms with the number of men each room may contain, Detroit 31st, July, 1782.

	Number of Rooms	Number of Births & Bedsteads		Number of men each room may contain	Total number of Persons
		for 4 men each	for 2 men each		
Citidal—Barracks—No 1, occupied by Serjts, Drum's Rank and file..	10	41	....	16	160
Ditto No 1, occupied at present by the Serjt Major & 2d M'r Serjt...............	1	....	1	16	16
Ditto No 1, occupied at present by the Drum Major & Band of Music..........	1	4	1	16	16
Ditto—New B'ks—No 2, occupied by Serjts, Drumrs Rank & file.....	2	10	....	28	56
Ditto-Blockhouse-No 3, occupied by Serjts, Drumrs Rank & file.....	2	7	11	1 @ 24 & 1 @ 20	44
Fort Lernoult B'ks-No 1, occupied by Serjts, Drumrs Rank & file.....	1	....	32	about 50	50
Ditto No 2, occupied by Serjts. Drumrs Rank & file.....	1	....	30	about 50	50
Totals..................................	18	62	75	....	392

[Errors excepted]

ABRAHAM ALBEY Bark. Mastr

To Brigadier General Henry Watson Powell Commandant of Niagara and its Dependencies &ca. &ca.

Detroit 31st July 1782—Return of the Barracks at this Post, specifying the number of Rooms with the number of men each Room may contain.

[B 123 p 275]

Return of Provisions in His Majesty's Magazine at Detroit July 31st 1782

Magazines.	Flour.	Pork.	Pease.		Butter.		Oatmeal.		Tallow mix'd with Bears Oil.	Indian Corn	Vinegar.		Rum.	
	lbs.	lbs.	Gals.	Pts.	lbs.	oz.	lbs.	oz.	lbs.	bushels.	Gals.	P's.	Gals.	P's
Fort Lernoult..	36,624	90,432	1,120	....	10080	...	11,600	...	....	....	.....	....	.....	...
Citadel.......	12,768	40,696	7,485	....	4,020	...	1,200	...	1,900	....	56	...	1679	...
Council House Cellar.......	....	....	.....	....	.....	...	....	...	....	....	369	...	6496	...
Total......	49,392	131,128	8,605	....	14100	...	12,800	...	1,900	....	425	...	8,175	...

THOMAS REYNOLDS
Assistant Commissary.

To Henry Watson Powell Esqr. Brigadier General Commanding the Posts on the Lakes &ca &ca—

Endorsed:—Return of Provisions in His Majesty's Magazine at Detroit July 31st 1782.
[B 123 p 276]

Return of the Militia of the Settlement of Detroit Augt 1st 1782

	Companies.	Present. Commission. Captns.	Lieuts.	Surgeons.	Rank & File.
Captains.	Mr. Gregors................................	1	4	4	112
	Maisonvilles................................	1	3	3	88
	Montfortons................................	1	2	3	72
	Campeaus................................	1	2	3	69
	Morans................................	1	2	3	57
	Gamelins................................	1	3	3	70
		6	16	19	448

AT. S. DE PEYSTER
Major King Regt. Commanding Detroit.

Endorsed:—Return of the Militia of the Settlement of Detroit August 1st 1782.
[B 123 p 277]

Return of Ordnance fitt for Service in the Garrison of Detroit 1st August 1782.

Natures				Quantity
Ordnance	Brass	Mounted on Garrison Carriages compleat	12 Pors	2
			6 "	1
		Mounted on Field Travellg. Carriages compleat	6 Pors	2
		Mounted on Grasshopper Carriages compleat	3 Pors	2
		Mortars with Beds	4 2–5 inch	4
	Iron mounted on Garrison Carriages with Beds, Coins & Side Arms Compt. to the whole.		18 Pors	1
			12	1
			9	4
			6	5
			4	4
			4 2–5 in. Mortr with bed	1
Ordnance Mounted in the Garrison		Field Service		4
		Garrison Do		17
		Mortars with beds		5
Total				26

N. B. The Proportion of One Hundred rounds a Gun in Flannel or Paper Cartridges with round and Case fixt Shott for all the Field Ordnance Compleat

CHRISTR. MYERS
Lieut. Commander Royal Artillery

August 1st 1782 Detroit

Endorsed:—Return of Ordnance fit for Service in the Garrison of Detroit 1st August 1782
[B 123 p 278]

A General Return of the Force & Burthen of His Majesty's Armed Vessels, etc., on Lake Erie, Huron & Michigan.

Vessels Names.	Commanders.	Force on Board.				Wanted to Compleat.							Dimensions.		Dimension.			Burthen.		Estimate of the No. of Troops that may be carried.			State & Condition.	
		Men.	Guns.	Swivells.	Musketts.	Men. For Current Service.	Men. For Actual Service.	Guns & Weight of Metal.	Swivells.	Musketts.	Pairs of Pistols.	Spears.	Range on Gun Deck.	Breadth, Feet.	Depth of the Hold.	Height between Decks.	Draught of water when laden.	In Tona.	In Barrels Bulk.	The Hold Fill.	Men.	Barrels.	When and where built.	State of the Hull, Riggings, etc.
Gage, Brig........	John Burnet........	27	14	....	25	3	78	....	..	25	15	..	70.9	22	8	....	10	154	400	80	160	200	Detroit 1772	Good.
Dunmore, Schnr..	Jas. Graham........	14	....	4	14	6	46	....	..	16	10	40	60.0	20	7.10	....	8	106	500	40	100	200	Detroit 1772	Good.
Hope, Schnr......	Henry Ford........	11	....	4	9	..	50	4 pts 6	..	20	10	40	54.4	18	6.8	....	7.4	81	275	40	80	70	Detroit 1771	Good.
Angelica, Sloop...	Jas. Underston.....	7	....	4	7	3	23	6	6	15	6	20	52.0	17.6	8.3	....	7.6	66	400	30	60	200	Detroit 1771	Good.
Felicity, Sloop....	Norman McKay....	6	....	4	6	5	25	....	4	15	6	20	57.6	16	6.	....	6.	55	200	20	40	50	Detroit 1774	Good.
Faith, Schnr.....	Geo. Andrews.......	48	10	....	47	..	..	....	..	..	15	..	56.0	15.6	6.4	....	6.	61	250	25	60	100	Detroit 1774	Good.
Wyandott, Sloop.	Wm. Gibson........	7	....	4	6	3	19	....	2	15	6	20	44.0	15.6	6.	....	6.	47	100	15	30	30	Detroit 1779	Good.
Adventure, Sloop.	Jas. Cunning........	8	....	2	6	2	17	....	4	15	6	20	44.6	13.	5.4	....	4.	34	100	12	30	30	Detroit 1776	Good.
Gun Boats.......	Joseph Williams....	11	1	4	..	..	..	....	..	..	..	..	....	....	....	....	....	....	....	....	....	....	....	......

N. B. Men sick on Shore—4—Left in the Dock yard 6.
The officers & men belonging to the Dock Yard are included in the above.
A new Vessel on the Stocks of one Hundred and Thirty Six Tons & pieced for 14 guns but no men or Guns for her.
Detroit August 1st 1782.

ALEXR GRANT,
Comd'g all His Majesty's Vessels on the Lakes Erie, Huron & Michigan.

Endorsed:—A General Return of the Force & Burthen of His Majesty's Arm'd Vessels &c., on Lake Erie, Huron & Michigan August 1st 1782
[B 123 p 279]

Field Return of the Troops at Detroit August 3rd 1782.

Regiments, &c.	Officers Present													Effective Rank and File							
	Commissioned						Staff														
	Colonel	Lt Colonel	Major	Captains	Lieutenants	Ensigns	Chaplain	Adjutant	Qr Master	Surgeon	Mate	Sergeants present	Drummers present	Under Arms fit for Duty	Fit for Garrison Duty Only	Unfit for Service	Sick Present	On Guard	Employ'd by the Engineer &c.	On Command	Total
Royal Artillery					1									12				1			13
King's (or 8th) Regiment			1	2	5	3		1	1			14	13	157	20	1	16	31	16	5	246
47th Regiment					1							4	3	44	4	4	2	17			71
Rangers																				120	120
			1	2	7	3		1	1			18	16	213	24	5	18	49	16	125	450

Endorsed:—Field Return of the Troops at Detroit August 25th 1782

H. WATSON POWELL Brigdr Genl

[B 123 p 280]

Return of Naval Stores in His Majesty's Dock Yard at Detroit—9 August 1782.

Group	Item	Quantity
Anchors	Wgt C 8-3-14	1
	C 7-3-24	1
	C 7-0-0	1
	C-6-0-0	1
	592 lbs	1
	540 lbs	1
	300 lbs	1
Arms & Accoutremts	Muskets	13
	Baynotes	7
	Seaberts for Baynotes	..
	Cutlasses	6
	Cartrage Boxes	14
	Belts for do.	12
	Musgloons	3
	Picks	..
Axes	Broad	16
	Felling	12
	Coopers	2
	Pick	1
Adzes	Foot	12
	Coopers	1
	Augers of Sorts	29
	Brimston Barrels	1
Brushes	Painting	14
	Tarring	21
	White Wash	5
	Scrubbing	27
Blocks	Careening setts	2
	Topsail sheets	2
	Snatch	1
	Tackle	6
	Sorted not pind or shiverd	20
	Shivers	173
	Bells Brass	1
Buckets	Leather	140
	Wood	....
Ps Bunting	Red	¼
	White	¾
	Blue	½
	Budge Barrels	1
	Barr Crows	..
	Bellows smiths	..
	Creepers	4
	Chain Rope	9
	Cringles	100
	Callipers	1
	Compasses carpenters	3
Chissells	Cold	..
	Mortice	1
	of Sorts	22
	Firmers	4
Compasses	Steering	8
	Pocket	4
	Cards for do.	3
	Glasses do.	2
	Chalk lbs	30
	Candles Boxes	28
	Cartrage casses—wood	4
	Cambouses—Iron	1

Group	Item	Quantity
Canvass Bolts	No 1	46
	No 2	35
	No 3	7
	No 4	35
	No 5	1
	No 6	26
	No 7	62
	No 8	9
	Rushea Canvass	7
	Rushea Canvass	36
Cordage Coiles	9 Inch	3
	7 Inch	1
	6 Inch	1
	5 Inch	4
	4 Inch	22
	3½ Inch	5
	3 Inch	..
	2¾ Inch	6
	2½ Inch	4
	2 Incn	15
	1¾ Inch	6
	1½ Inch	20
	12 thread Ratlin	16
	9 thread Ratlin	6
	6 thread Ratlin	7
	Fenders	2
	Files of sorts	37
	Froes	1
	Flints	200
	Fidds	2
	Fires false	17
	Gimblets of sorts	29
Glasses Watch	2 Hower	..
	1 do.	10
	½ Hower	4
	½ Minute	43
	¼ Minute	15
Gla s	Crown Pains	14
	Common do.	....
	Grind Stones	6
	Gouges of Sorts	27
Hooks	Fish	..
	Tackle	169
	Boat	..
Hinges	H	3
	Chist	2
	Door	..
	Garnet	..
Hammers	Carpenters	6
	Fedd	....
	Heads & Rammers	45
	Hanks Horn	71
	Hammocks	40
Iron	Bars	180
	Bolts	....
	Palms	28
	Iron Sheet	75
	Jarrs	11
	Jack Screws	2

[B 123 p 282]

Return of Naval Stores—Continued.

Knives.		Locks.							Hides Leather.			Lines.						Leads.						Mauls.		Measures.							Nails.													Casks.					Needles.			Ordinance Iron.				
Drawing.	Skinners.	Cannon.	Brass Knobs.	Cubbord.	Chest.	Padd.	Trunk.	Stock.	Pump.	Half Tand.	In the Hair.	Deepsea.	Hand.	Hamber.	Logg.	Chalk.	Marlin.	Hand.	Deepsea.	Lantherns of Sorts.	Ladles 6 Po'ds.	Ladles Pitch.	Lamp black Barrels.	Top.	Penn.	Gallon.	Half do.	Quart.	Pint.	Half do.	Magnets.	Match Slow.	Spikes 7 Inches.	Spikes 6 Inches.	40 Peny.	30 Py.	24 Py.	20 Peny.	12 Peny.	10 Py.	8 Py.	6 Py.	4 Py.	3 Py.	Pump.	Boat.	Sheathing.	Spunge lb.	Brads Casks of Sorts.	Sewing.	Ropeing.	Marling.			4 pondrs.	2 pods.	Swivels.
6	1	1	1	16	.	1	2	1	3	10	...	2	..	2	7	25	380	21	10	61	2	2	36	....	....	..	..	..	..	..	1	..	¼	..	4	5	7	6	2	6	3	1	1	3	..	½	½	1	3	105	96	14	..	..	4	..	..

N. B. Three Hundred and five Oak Plank from 2 to 4 inches thick & 27 to 40 foot long. two hundred & forty pine plank from $1\frac{1}{2}$ to 3 inches thick & from 24 to 40 foot Long. three Rafts of Pine Loggs one Raft of pine plank also 70 pieces of Ship Timber & 120 boats Timbers three Lower Masts & forty seven Spars for Yards & Topmasts &c.

J. LAUGHTON Naval Storekeeper Detroit.

Oil.					Paint.					Plane.										Saws.										Squares.														Twine.		
Linseed Galls Qts.	Train Galls Qts.	Sweet Do Do.	Potts Iron	Pitch Barrels	Red Kegs.	White do.	Yellow do.	Black do.	Planes Compt of Sorts.	Stocks.	Irons.	Paper Carth Quires.	Putty lb.	Pails Water.	Pincers.	Pasps.	Rosin Barrels.	Rules 2 feet.	Ruths Papers.	Whips.	Mill.	Cross Cutt.	Hand.	Tennant.	Turning.	Scrapers.	Spicks Marling.	Steel Barrs.	Stones Mettle.	Wood.	Iron.	Shovels Ballast.	Stilyards Pocket.	Scales Brass.	Spades.	Tarr Barrels.	Turpintain do.	Tallow do.	Travellers.	Thimbles.	Thread lb.	Trumpets Speaking.	Turpentain Spirits Gallons.	Sewing lb.	Ropeing lb.	Twine Seen lb.
10	40	....	24	1	7	5	5	2	3	....	16	..	4	..	1	..	½	2	2	18	4	3	12	4	1	39	....	8	13	....	2	....	....	1	....	44	20	2	7	20	½	1	3	360	120	118

Endorsed:—Return of Naval Stores in His Majesty's Dock Yard at Detroit 9 August 1782.

[B 123 p 283]

ORDER CONCERNING PROVISIONS

SIR, Judging it necessary for the safety of this Post, that no provisions of any kind shall remain without the Fort, but what is needed for the daily consumption of the People, residing here. I request that you will send a Commissioned, two non Commissioned officers & twelve Privates, six of whom are to carry their arms, to search all Magazines, Store Houses & Cellars, without Exception & to guard & conduct within the Fort every species of Provisions here—after described, informing the owners that they shall be placed under Lock & Key, their having access to them in the day time when necessary.

Flour, Corn, & Salt meat in Barrels are the articles to which this order extends. The officer will also see all the Picket Enclosures pulled down, agreeable to the intimation given in December last, to provide Post & Rail fence in their stead.

Endorsed:—Copy of an order which will bring to view all the Provision purchased from the Troops in the winter at 2 sh per Pound for Pork only. They never sell Bread.—*Perhaps much more.* The General's order respecting it will be looked for early, for the reason mentioned in my letter. Traders placing a Dependence upon it.

[B 97-2 p 575]

---

* * * * * * * * * * * *

As the Traders will not conform to Regulations Established for the last year recommended (as they were told by Major De Peyster) by His Excellency the Governor General, altho' their passes oblige them to conform to such Regulations.

It is not Judged necessary to stop Trade on account of the obstinacy & demerit of the Trader.

Therefore another scheme is proposed to them to avoid the Ruin of the most unworthy—

Goods will be permitted to go to a certain number of Wintering Grounds, Proper People will be chosen by the Lieut. Govr. for these Places. The others must lodge their goods in the Fort under a Proper Person also chosen by the Lieut Governor and they will be permitted to take an equal quantity out weekly, giving Bond that they will sell none but by Retail at the Post.

Endorsed:—Mr Burgy will publish the within.

[B 97-2 p 581]

SECRETARY MATTHEWS TO MAJOR DE PEYSTER

QUEBEC 5th August 1782

SIR, His Excellency the Commander in Chief in order to diminish the Vast Expense of all sorts of Goods and Provisions at the Post of Michilimackinac has established Mr George McBeath at that Post in order to provide those Articles for Government, at what is considered a Reasonable Profit, but as he will experience every difficulty in the Power of the Traders there to throw in his way particularly in the articles of Indian Corn & Grease (for which it seems there is a great Demand) I am directed to Signify to you His Excellency's desire that you will give Him every assistance in your power, and direct as much of both as can be procured in your Neighborhood to be purchased for the Crown, which Mr McBeath will receive and account for.

By some unpardonable neglect, or worse, the whole Rum in store at Makinac has been rendered useless. His Excellency therefore desires that you will by the first opportunity send such supply as you can spare & you shall think necessary to carry them thro' the winter and make a Requisition of the Like Quantity to Niagara.

I am &c.

(Signed) R. MATTHEWS.

Major DePeyster

Endorsed:—To Major DePeyster of 5th August 1782

[B 123 p 281]

MAJOR DE PEYSTER TO MR. MCKEE

DETROIT 6th August 1782

SIR, It having been reported to me by Isaac Zeans, that the Shawanese & Delawares push their retaliation to great lengths by putting all their prisoners to death, whereby if not prevented they will throw an odium upon their friends the English, as well as prevent their Father from receiving the necessary intelligence of the Enemy's Motions, so essential to carry on the service for their mutual interests; I must therefore reiterate my injunctions to you of representing to the Chiefs that such a move of War will by no means be countenanced by their English Father, who is ever ready to assist them against the common Enemy, provided they avoid Cruelties. Tell them I shall be under the necessity of victualling the Troops (who must be tired of such scenes of Cruelty) provided they persist and assure them that the Lake Indians complain much of their late treatment to the three prisoners taken near the Falls.

I am confident, Sir, that you and the Officers do all in your power to instill humane principles into the Indians; it is however a duty incumbent on me, to beg of you once more to speak to the Chiefs and assure them that Brigadr General Powell was greatly shock'd at hearing the report spread by Zeans, and strongly recommends that it may be stopp'd, he is however still in hopes that Zeans must have greatly exaggerated Matters, as I have not received a line from you upon the Subject. Some Lake Indians who arrived from Sanguina left this two days ago, they will no doubt spread a false report that the Sacks, on leaving Machilimakina, fell upon their Wives & Children. I have already desired Captain LaMothe to assure the Chiefs that I gave no credit to it, not having then received a line from Lieut. Governor Sinclair. And I now have the pleasure to inform that a vessel arrived this morning, in five days from Michilimakinac, assuring me that no such thing has happen'd, but on the contrary their Wives and families were all well and desire to be particularly remembered to them.—Please to present *La Fourche* and *Quoioigushkam* with the annexed Belt of Friendship which they gave me at Michilimakinac, and which will now serve to convince them that their old Father speaks truth—I request to hear from you and Captain Caldwell, as soon as You receive this Letter, Craig brought me the last accounts from You dated Wakitamikee the 22nd & 23d July 1782—please to shew this letter to Captain Caldwell, to whom I shall write by the next opportunity.

I am Sir Your most obedt & very huml Servt

AT. S. DE PEYSTER

Alexr McKee Esq

P. S. The four Belts are, one for the Hurons, Mingoes, Delawares, and Shawanese—Should any other nations be present you will please to add accordingly.

Indian Affairs M. G. III.

FROM BRIG. GEN. POWELL UNADDRESSED

DETROIT August 7th 1782

SIR, Some letters which have lately arrived here mention that Mr. John Hay has succeeded Lieut Governor Hamilton at this Post, and as he has only the rank of Lieutenant in the army. I am convinced it will be very disagreeable to Major De Peyster (who has commanded here a long time with great credit to himself and to the satisfaction of the inhabitants in general) to serve under an officer of that inferior rank.

I therefore beg to know if it will meet with your Excellency's approbation, should I give him leave to go down to Canada if he applys for it.

I am Sir &c

(signed) H. Watson Powell

[B 96-2 p 38]

CAPTAIN BIRD TO BRIG. GEN. POWELL

Detroit August 13th 1782

Sir, By this opportunity I have the honour to enclose to you the Plan of Fort Lernoult remarking (according to your desire) what Parts of the Body of the place are compleat, and what remains to be done towards putting the work in as formidable a state of defence as the nature of it will admit—Lieut. H. Duvernett (who is admirably skill'd in surveying & as a Draughtsman) has furnish'd the Genl with a plan & Sketch of the Fort Town and Country Adjacent. I need not remark that the utmost extent of my abilities at Plan drawing is to explain my Ideas.

The inside of Fort Lernoult as you must have observed Sir has suffer'd nothing from the weather. From the Angle of the South Bastion to the Flag-staff Bastion is also in a very good State. From the Flag Staff to the Angle of the Magazine Bastion chiefly suffer'd by the Deluge we had here; the whole exteriour face to the thickness of four or five feet having been wash'd into the Ditch—It is now intirely a new work to the thickness of ten feet intirely of clay, well beat and united every three foot by layers of Brush and cedar stakes, the sod being only six inches thick by way of coat. I am convinced what caused the works to suffer so much by the violent rains was owing to the Sods being five or six feet thick on the face—which turning to a rich and springy loam never united properly with the clay, but was separated by the Rains and slid down.

The Magazine Bastion is of new work & as far as the Sally-Port on the same plan. The rest of the Fort tho' now very defensible, becomes worse every shower and must be new faced with the same precautions.

The Counterssarf Gracis & covered way are ragged, being much channel'd by the floods—which were more violent than the oldest man in the place remembers to have seen before.

The Stone Magazine which was erected by the Major's order at the fort of the Gracis, is constructed exactly from the scale of Vanbars recommended by Muller—it is on the inside 30 by 20. The arch was turned by good English masons, and the materials prepared according to rule. The Angle of the Work intended for its defence is flank'd on both sides by the cannon of the Fort, at half musket shot the plan being approved by yourself Sir & Major DePeyster is already began, as is the Gallery of Communication, which must be a covered one, as the ground from the Stone Magazine to the Fort rises nine or ten feet. I think the enemy would suffer as much by an Assault on the Magazine work as on the Fort itself—Two guns from this work scower a hollow not commanded by the Fort—I have taken the heights round Fort Lernoult with exactness—there is no ground within eight hundred yards that is of equal height with the Terre Plein.

As Fort Lernoult was originally laid down by me—I account this a favourable opprtunity Sir of obviating some objections made to it respecting its form and size—or rather of giving some reasons why it was not form'd otherwise, and the whole larger—Late in the fall of 1778 we were alarm'd by the approach of the Enemy under one Broadhead, who with two or three thousand men had actually advanced as far as Tuscarawas about 90 miles from the Lake at lower Sandusky, and were employ'd in building a large Picketted Fort—Major Lernoult at a conversation with the officers at Detroit on the above alarm, concluded Detroit incapable of making a defence that might reflect honour on the Defendants, it being of great extent—only picketed—and in a manner under a hill—By his orders, on the same evening I traced a Redoubt on the Hill, the Plan was left to me—I at first intended only a square (our time as we imagined being but short for fortifying ourselves) but when the square was marked out it appeared to me so naked & insufficient that I added the half Bastions—imagining if the Enemy approached before the curtins were completed we might make a tollerable defence by, closing the Bastions at the Gorge—So perfect a work as one with entire Bastions for so small a number of Defendants, four or five six Pounders very ill furnish'd, and no artillery officers—and an attack expected in a few weeks was what I never would have engaged to have undertaken.

We began I think early in Nov'r and worked without intermission until Feb'y—At which time the Indians declaring an intension of attacking Col. Broadhead's Post of 400 then at Tuscarawas, I joined them—In the mean time Lt Duvernett return'd from Post Vincent, and was appointed Engineer —the work was then too far advanced for him to alter the form of it.

Some Gentlemen who are in a manner Engineers by profession have very gravely assured me that a square or Polygon with entire Bastions would have been a much more perfect Work than a half Bastions Fort—to which assurance I acquiess'd full as gravely.

I do not Imagine Sir this Post will ever have to sustain regular attacks—but rather (if attempted at all) it will be by a large Body of men with some

Field Artillery to dismount the Cannon of our Defences and then storm the whole face of the work. The Plan I have proposed for its defence according to the best of my judgment is conformable to that Idea—and meet with Major De Peysters approbation. The detaining the Enemy a considerable time beyond the foot of the Glacis and between that and the foot of the Parapet by means which cannot be ruin'd by the Enemies cannon I conceive to be the principal point of Defence for this place. The means proposed are good abbatis—small stakes drove thick in the ground & pointed by way of caltrops Picketts with a cuvette in front—fougasses—a cheveux de Fraize on the Berm, and fougades of small shells behind it on the faces of the Bastions—To Take our small garrison into the Body of the Fort or from all outworks incapable of withstanding an assault as well as the Fort itself—The outwork began by Lt H. Duvernett since discontinued, being only protected by a Glacis and requiring fifty or sixty men at least to defend it—might (I think) have been carried any night without much annoyance from the Fort, by an Assault in front, which was in form of a Swallow's tail and depended entirely on its own defendants—the destruction of whom would have greatly dispirited the Garrison within—Such are my reasons Sir for the form and sise of the Fort—I am less secure of those for discontinuing the out work and had not Major De Peyster approved them I would very readily have condemn'd my own opinions—as the Plan was Lt Duvernett's.

I had nearly forgot mentioning that the new raising the centirs has given me an opportunity of indenting them at the extremity at a on the plan—by which I have obtained a tollerable second flank for the angle of the Bastions. I have Major De Peysters permission to mount the Brass three Pounders on low & weighty field carriages—The platform very narrow which has a false top turning on the center so as to give the gun a horrizontal Motion of fifteen or twenty degrees—this top has grooves for the wheels & those who serve the gun using rope rammers may load under cover of the Parapet.

The Enemy are by all accounts retired--I am sure it is now too late for them to advance to Detroit and by the time they will be able to advance next year, every method proposed above for the defence of this Place will be employ'd.

I am with respect Sir

Your most obed't and most humble Serv't

A. Bird

Capt'n 8th Reg't Ass' Eng'r Detroit

Brig'r Gen'l Powel

Endorsed:—Capt. Birds Letter dated 13th August 1782 describing the state of the Works at Fort Lernoult.

[B 123 p 284]

VOLUNTEER ANTOINE CHESNE TO MAJOR DE PEYSTER

(Extract)

SANDUSKY 16th August 1782

SIR, Since my last to you a party of Puttewattamies came in here, they have been at Cross Creek but could not take a Pris'r and (as they say) on their return home on this side of the Big River they found a negro they think he was Horse Hunting.

The Negro was examined by Mr Arundel he says his Master's name was Epharaim Hart from whom he deserted, they lived about twenty miles up the said creek.

That General Irwin [William Irvine] is mustering men at Fort Pitt to come against Sandusky, and that they are to come fifteen hundr in number, they are not found in Provision by the Fort, but by the able Farmers, his master furnish'd Beef, this is what he heard at his Master's House, where all the meetings of the country are kept and where several hundreds of that place had already given in their names to join Gen Irwin at Fort Pitt or Col'l [David] Williamson at Fort McIntosh, the Rendezvous to be held all the month of Augst and the beginning of Septr they are to set off for this place, they are not to have cannon as the Expedition is to be carried on with all the Secrecy possible, and they intend it shall be as expeditious as possible, as their intention is to kill and burn all before them. As soon as this Matter was mentioned, there was four hundred rose and said they would go to revenge the Death of Colonel Crawfurd. He says Hannan's Town [Hannastown, Pa.] was burnt by some white People, and about two hundred Indians, they kill'd seven & took nine Prisoners, they killed all the Cattle there.

To Major DePeyster Commanding at Detroit

Endorsed:—Extract of a Letter from Volunteer Antoine Chesne dated Sandusky 16 Augst 8
[B 123 p 290]

MAJOR DE PEYSTER TO GENERAL HALDIMAND

DETROIT the 18th Augst 1782

SIR, I am Just honoured with your Excellency's Letter of the 11th July, approving the conduct of the officers in the affair at St Dusky, and regretting the crueltys committed by some of the Indians upon Col. [William] Crawford, desiring me to assure me of your utter abhorrance of such proceedings. Believe me Sir! I have had my feelings upon the occasion, and forseeing the retaliation the Enemy would draw upon themselves, I did everything in my power to try to reconcile them to the horrid massacre at Muskingum and believe I should have succeeded, had the Enemy not, so soon after advanced with the intent, as they themselves declared to extermenate the whole Wiandott Tribe—not not only by words but even by exposing Effegies which they left hanging by the heels in every camp.

I had sent messengers throughout the Indian Country previous to the receipt of your Excellency's Letter; threatening them that I would recall the troops If they did not desist from such horrid cruelty, I have frequently signified to the Indians how much your Excellency abhors all acts of cruelty,—the inclosed copy of my last letter to Mr. McKee will show you that I have also made use of the Brigadier's name and I shall to morrow dispatch a person I have great confidence in to carry your Excellency's fresh injunctions to the several Southern Nations.

We have been alarmed here lately with the accounts of a formidable Body of the Enemy (under the command of a Gen'l Hands) advancing this way, which occasioned my reinforcing Captain Caldwell, and sending Captain Grant to the Mouth of the Miamie with the armed vessels and Gun Boat. Our scouts now report the Enemy retired—Captain Caldwell remains Encamped on the banks of the Ohio, and Captain Grant arrived here yesterday.

I have now to request as a singular favour of your Excellency, that in case Mr. John Hay is appointed Lieut. Gov'r of Detroit and is to winter here, I may be allowed to leave the place, either before, or immediately after his arrival, I shall ever be happy to serve my Gracious Sovereign in any station, that, under Mr. Hay excepted, for various reasons—I have already spoken to the Brigadier upon the subject, who promised me he would write to your Excellency for discretionary leave, which I hope will reach Niagara before this reaches Quebec.

I have the Honour to be with great respect, Sir,

Your Excellency's Most Hum'l & most obed't Servt.

At. S. De Peyster

His Excellency Gen. Haldimand

Ent'd, 1782 From Major De Peyster 18th Aug't Rec'd 11th Sept'r. Entered in Book marked B No 3, Page 25.

[B 123 p 292]

VOLUNTEER ANTOINE CHESNE TO MAJOR DE PEYSTER

Sandusky Augst 19th 1782

Sir, A few days ago the Puttewatimies left this with a letter for you informing you of the news we have here, since which a party of Delawares is arrived from a Scout and says that the Enemy is assembling at this side the *Big River,* of which Captn Brandt at the Shawnee Towns is inform'd so there's no time to loose to send the assistance of this place. I would have sent you this Account before, but could not get Abm Williams to go, as he says he quits the Service, & the Indians from here are going off on a Scout to see the Enemy, & beg'd I would let you know, hoping you'll be so good as to give them all the assistance you can this time, as you were pleased to do before, and they are in good hopes they'll meet with the same success.

I am Sir, Your humble Servant

(Signed) ANTNE CHESNE

To Major De Peyster
commanding at Detroit

Endorsed:—Copy of a Letter from Volunteer Chesne dated Sandusky 19th Augt. 1782
[B 123 p 294]

MR. EDGAR TO CAPTAIN MCKEE

DETROIT 19th August 1782.

DEAR SIR, I have the pleasure to acquaint you that His Excellency General Haldimand (In Consequence of Major Depeysters Representation) has promised to make over to you the house & lott.

I take the earliest opportunity of letting you know this, that if you Intend building &c you may in time prepare materials &c.

You will have the means I suppose from the Commanding Officer & I am sorry to say there is a probability of our loosing him this fall, as our friend Mr Hay is appointed Lt Governor of this place in the room of Governor Hamilton who succeeds Mr Cramahe as Governor of this Province—

I hope & wish to see you here soon—

and am Dear Sir Your Huble. Servt.

WILLIAM EDGAR.

Addressed:—To Alexr McKee Esqr.
Indian Affairs M. G. IV

MAJOR DE PEYSTER TO CAPTAIN MCKEE

DETROIT 19th August 1782.

DEAR SIR, You must be sensible that I have lost no opportunity to request that you would recommend Humanity to the Indians, It has ever been the Principle that I have acted upon, and I am convinced that no task is more agreeable to your wishes. Upon my arrival here I found the Indians greatly civilized from the good advice they received from you and my Predecessors, in which disposition through our earnest Endeavors we continue them till the imprudent step of the Enemy at Muskingum called up their Savage ferocity which I am convinced, but for the timely Interposition; would have gone to greater lengths, I see they still hold their prisoners formerly taken in mild Captivity, whilst their resentment only shows itself upon those newly taken looking upon them as a part of the People who imprudently declared by words & signs that they were come to exterminate the Wyandott Tribe.

The Inclos'd copy of a Letter from His Excellency the Commander in Chief will give you his sentiments upon the cruelty lately committed upon Col'l Crawford and the two Capts. such parts thereof as you see necessary to the Purpose you will please to communicate to the Shawanese, Delawares, Mingoes & Wyandotts & you will further endeavor to convince those Nations that by persisting in acts of retaliation they will in the end draw Mischief upon themselves & upon their Posterity, but on the contrary if they make Warr agreeable to the Example set them by their Father & Brothers the English they will always find themselves supported against their Enemy.

Capt. Chesne who will deliver you this dispatch, will on his return speak to the Miamis, Potawatamies &c.

I am Sir Your most obed't hum'l Serv't

AT S. DE PEYSTER

To Alex'r McKee Esq. Dep'y Agent.
Indian Affairs M. G. III.

MAJOR DE PEYSTER TO CAPTAIN MCKEE

DETROIT the 22nd Aug't 1782.

DEAR SIR, being much hurried when I sent Mr Chene off, I either put a wrong letter under cover to you, or must have closed my letter without putting any one in it, for this morning in looking for a Letter wherein His Excell'y approves of my having called in the Moravians to Settle near Detroit, I found the Inclosed which should have been sent, Please to send me the other back by the first favourable opportunity and you'll oblige your Hum'l Serv't

AT. S. DE PEYSTER

Mr. Alex'r McKee
Indian Affairs M. G. III.

ESTIMATE OF MERCHANDISE WANTED FOR INDIAN PRESENTS AT DETROIT TO 20TH AUGST 1782.

80 Pieces strouds blue
16 do. Red Strouds
9 do. Crimson do.
9 do. Scarlet do.
2600 Pairs $2\frac{1}{2}$ pt Blankets
1000 Do. do. fine do.
300 do. 3 pt do.
400 Do 2 pt do.
400 Do $1\frac{1}{2}$ pt do.
840 Pieces linnen
85 Do. Striped Cotton
1500 lbs Vermillion
30 Pieces Muslin
96 Doz Black Silk Handkfs
180 Pieces Ribbon sorted
180 Groce Bed Lace
50 Do Gartering
20 Pieces embossed Serge
51 Do Rateen Blue & Brown
450 Felt Hats
100 Caster Do
50 Beaver Do
94 Saddles
250 Bridles
120 Fusils
120 Rifles small Bore
40 Pairs Pistols
60 Coteaux de chasse
50 M. Gun Flints
45 Groce Scalping Kinves
18 Do Scissors
100 pieces hambre lines
100 Do Mackral Do
500 Salmon Hooks
30 Dozen Spurrs
10 Groce Morrice Belts
30 Groce Brass Thimbles
6 pieces Red Serge
10 Do White Do
6 Do Blue Do
300 in Black Wampum
100 in White Do
5 Boxes Soap

10 Groce Looking Glasses
10 do. Razors
1 Groce Gun Locks
20 do. Fire Steels
30 do. Awl Blades
20 do. Gun Worms
10 do. Jews Harps
20 do. Finger Rings
300 Tomahawks
300 half Axes
100 Hoes
300 lbs Thread Sorted
20 Pieces Spotted Swanskin
10,000 lbs Gun Powder
35,000 lbs Ball & Shott
5,000 needles sorted
10,000 lbs Tobacco
300 lbs Beads
290 Pieces Callico
25 Groce box Combs
5 Groce Ivory Do
12 Nests Brass Kettles
15 Do copper Do with covers
20 Do Tin Do
30 Nests hair Trunks
200 ls Pewter Basons
60 Beaver Traps
500 Powder Horns
3 Groce Tobacco Boxes
80 Do Clay Pipes
300 large red, Blue & Green feathers
300 Black Ostrich feathers
100 pairs of shoes
1 Groce Buckles
Silver Works vizt
400 Large Gorgets
400 Do Moons
400 Arm Bands 3 Inches broad french manufacture
400 Ear wheels
10,000 large Broaches
5,000 small Do
1,000 pair large Earbobs

ESTIMATE—*Continued.*

5 Barrels White Wine	1,000 pair small Do
5 Do Shrub	Some Medals chiefly large
5000 lbs Iron	An assortment of for armourer & Black Smith.
1,000 lb Steel	

(signed) AT. S. DE PEYSTER

Major King's Regiment Commanding Detroit and its Dependencies.

Endorsed:—Estimate of Merchandize wanted at Detroit for Indian Presents to the 20th Aug. 1782

[B 123 p 295]

MAJOR DE PEYSTER TO BRIG. GEN. POWELL

DETROIT the 27th Augst. 1782

SIR, Immediately upon receipt of your Letter of the 15th Instant, I dispatched an Express to Captain Caldwell and Bradt, and one to Mr Alexr McKee, ordering them not to make any incursions into the Enemy's country, but to act on the defensive only. I hope the courier will be in time to stop Captn. Bradt, who is on the point of setting out for the neighbourhood of Wheeling, but I fear Capt Caldwell has already passed the Ohio, in order to be satisfied of the enemies motions, in which case he will strike some stroke before he returns—my endeavours however, shall be to turn their attention towards Sandusky to which place i am informed by a deserter the Enemy are determined to march, from one thousand to fifteen hundred strong. When the deserter left them, in the beginning of this month, they were assembling in the Neighbourhood of Wheeling, and Fort McIntosh, under the command of the blood-thirsty Col. [David] Williamson who so much distinguished himself in the Massacre of the Christian Indians, at the Settlement of Muskingum, which cruel proceedings have been the cause of the late retaliation of the Delawares, and Shawanees, on the persons of Col. [William] Crawford, and the two Captains, and the three prisoners taken near the Fort of the Falls—

By this opportunity I send down such of the Prisoners as could be conveniently assembled—I suppose it is not intended, that the familys (mostly Germans) who have taken the Oaths, and are settled on Farms, should be included, except such of them as are desirous of going down—There are also some women, who have their children still with the Indians, who request not to leave Detroit untill their children are brought in, also some orphans, and others who do not know their Parents—these I have fixed in Decent Houses, where they will be taken care of without being of the least expence to Government and where I shall let them remain 'till I hear further from you on the Subject.

I have the Honour to be Sir your most
obedient and most Huml Servt

AT. S. DE PEYSTER

Brigadier Genl Powell

Endorsed:—Major De Peyster Letter dated 27 August 1782 mentioning that He expected Captains Caldwell & Bradt would soon strike a Blow against the Enemy.

[B 123 p 300]

MAJOR DE PEYSTER TO SECRETARY MATTHEWS

DETROIT the 4th Sept 1782

DEAR SIR, The bearer of this letter Captain Isaac Ruddle was taken by Captain Bird who recommended him as a proper person to be fixed upon Hogg Island, where he has lived quietly ever since, but having conceived the Idea that an exchange of Prisoners will take place he is desirous of going down the country.

Give me leave to mention him to you as I did Capt. Orr.

I am Dr. Sir Your Huml & obedt Servt.

AT S. DE PEYSTER

Endorsed:—Captain Mathews Secretary to His Excy. Gen. Haldimand Quebec.

From Major De Peyster

4th Septr Recd. 10th Octr 1782

[B 123 p 309]

MAJOR DE PEYSTER TO GENERAL HALDIMAND

DETROIT the 4th Septr 1782

SIR, I have the honour to inform your Excellency that on the 21st Ultimo. Captain Caldwell with thirty picked Rangers and about two hundred Lake Indians were successful against a body of the Enemy at the Blue lick on the banks of the Ohio—the particulars of which I have forwarded to the Brigadier. But reflecting that your Excellency may be desirous to have Mr. Alexr. McKees original letter I herewith inclose it. I have reason to believe that Captain Caldwell conformable to my orders is at present encamped with the Rangers and local Indians at upper Sandusky, there to wait for a body of the Enemy which I am informed are to make another attempt upon that place.

By this opportunity I send down some Prisoners amongst which is the Commandant and superintendt of Indian Affairs at Post Vincent taken by the Scouts I sent to get intelligence.

Mr. Dalton was so well pleased with the treatment he received from the Indians on his way that he prevailed upon some of them to return from the Ouia to fetch his wife and family, which I have promised to take care of 'till your Excellency's pleasure with regard to him is known, he being desirous to settle in this country being tired of the rebel service.

We are quite out of Linnen and Strouds for shirts and Leggings. not having received the fourth part of what was returned wanting unless a supply should soon arrive I know not what to do.

I have the honour to be Sir

Your Excellency's Most Humbl & Most obedt Servt.

AT. S. DE PEYSTER

His Excely Genl. Haldimand

Endorsed:—Ent'd 1782 From Major De Peyster 4th Septr Recd 30th acknowledged C., Entered in Book marked B No. 3 Page 26

[B 123 p 310]

NUMBER OF INDIANS RESORTING TO MICHILLIMAKINAC*

		Persons
	Ottawas of L'Arbor Roche four hundred men with their families, amounting to	1000
	Dr. of the Grand River & Banks of Lake Michigan with their Families 500 men	1200
	Chipawas—Proprietors of this Island	100
For the most part Chiefs and Heads of Families who received presents from them.	Do. from St. Mary's	50
	Do. from Lake Huron Mississagi River La Cloche &c.	150
	Do. from Lake Superior	500
	Follevoines from La Bay and Lake Huron	250
	Indians of the Mississippi, Winipigoes	150
	Saies	250
	Renards (pxes or osogamis)	200
	Aswoés	50
	Scioeux Indians, Chiefly the Heads of Tribes who received Presents from their respective Villages	100
	Potewatamies	20
	Persons	4020

*See appendix

In all amounting to about four Thousand and Twenty Persons.

(signed) JOHN COATES,
Clerk to the Indian Dept.

Michilmakinac 10th Sept. 1782.
[B 98 p 136]

ACCOUNT

In the Indian Department at this Post were paid:

David Mitchell as Surgeon (formerly in receipt of pay at this post for his care of the sick of that Department—

1780. 15th Feb Alexander Kay
1st Mch. James Phillips.... } present with the Ottawas sent to Detroit

30th July Antoine Ignace.......
30th July Charles Langtan fils... } as Lieuts at 8s N. York Curry per day each. present with the Ottawas sent to Detroit.

1781. June. Blondeau to the Forces with them............
10th Octr. J. B. Cadot (at St. Marys).............
1st July. Roque (to the Scioux & formerly paid at the Post in the Scioux country....................
1st May. Thos. Stone as Ferry Keeper at old Michilimackinac @ 8s N. York Curry per day, for two Ferry Men @ 4s do. do. each............. } [illegible] Interpreters @ 8s N. Y. Curry per day each.

1st May John Waters as Storekeeper @ 8s do. present

1779. 8th Sept. Augustin Feltcan
1781. 1st April. Vasseur....... } as Blacksmiths @ 8s do. each present

1781. 1st May Louis Varin as Cooper @ 8s do. present

1780. 1st July John Coates as Commissary @ 8s per do. present
as Clerk @ 4s do. per do. present

(signed) JOHN COATES,
Clerk to Indian Dept.

Michilimackinac 16th September 1782
[B 98 p 129]

REASONS FOR THE PURCHASE OF CERTAIN PROVISIONS

MICHILLIMACKINAC 17th Septr. 1782.

In explanation of the causes of so large Quantities of Corn & other Articles of Provision having been purchased at this Post—

In order to have as large a Reserve of Provisions for the Garrison as circumstances would admit of, & a supply for the Indians and other uses of the Post, I held out the Prices of Corn & other Articles purchased for that purpose, at the same prices at which they were rated upon my arrival at the Post, being convinced of the necessity of having a large Quantity and that the Demand would raise the Price to the Merchant or Trader who furnished the Traders sold to each other, at the time above referred to, for the same prices charged to Government and without Force it would not have been procured at any other rate—

Endorsed:—Governor Sinclairs reasons for giving the Price he has for Corn, as well as for what purpose such quantities have been bought up.

[B 98 p 131]

ACCOUNT

Lieut George Clowes assistant Engineer @ 10s Half. Curry Per day, appointed 6th Septr 1782

Ensign Robert Pollard Chief overseer @ 5s do. same Time

Serjeant James Donaldson acting in the absence of James Phillips, Clerk of the Cheque 2s 6d do.

Corporals James Ellis 84th, Francis Huson 84th, Valentine 8th asst. overseers 2s 6d do.

Serjeant Hartman 84th Foreman to Caps 2s 6d do.

27 of the 84th 32 of the 8th Artificers, Labourers, Drivers &c 1s 3d to 2s.

Storekeeper, Alexander Kay @ 5s

In charge of Tools in use Corpt Davidson Rl. Arty. @ 2s

Michael Augé, overseer of Corveés @ 5s

48 Civilians, caps, & Masons, Axe men, Labourers &c 2s 6d to 5.

(signed) G. Clowes. Lt.
Assist. Engineer

Michilimackinac 18th Septr. 1782.

[B. 98 p. 132]

RETURN

Return of Carpenters employed in the Naval Department at the Post of Michilimackinac 19th Sept. 1782.

Names.	Quality.	Wages.
Angus McDonald	Master Builder	16s N. Y. Curry
Hugh Moore	Carpenter	8s
Joseph Laboise	Do.	8s

(signed) P. R. FRY
Ensign 8th Regmt.

Ensign Fry of the 8th Regmt appointed Naval Storekeeper 6th Sept 1782 @ 8s N. Y. Curry per day

Corporal Omar of said Regmt to act under him @ 1s Half'y per day

(signed) P. R. FRY.

[B 98 p 133]

LIEUT. COL. HOPE AND OTHERS TO CAPTAIN ROBERTSON

MICHILIMACKINAC Sept. 20th 1782

SIR, From the very heavy expences that have been incurred on account of Government at this Post, into which His Excellency the Commander in Chief has thought proper to direct us along with yourself to make Enquiry, and from the great abuses and neglect in different shapes that have appeared to us all upon this Inquiry—the following Regulations for your future conduct in the Command of the Post will in our opinion be absolutely necessary in order to reduce & correct in some measure these expenses, and abuses, and you are hereby directed therefore, agreeable to the power delegated to us by His Excellency's Instructions to that Purpose, to conform accordingly to the Regulations, as far as circumstances will possibly admit, until you receive orders to the contrary from Head Quarters—

First—That you should strictly observe the General orders of the 22nd of June 1781 not to make purchases and be particular in transmitting the Returns required therein, to neither of which does attention appear to have been paid, by your Predecessors, without any sufficient reasons to the contrary having been assigned or existing.

Secondly—That as well as to all other Instructions and orders that have been given, You should particularly attend to the Spirit of His Excellency's Letter to Lieut. Governor Sinclair of the 10th of May 1782 to answer one of the essential purposes in which it may be found upon Trial, a good Measure to post Trusty persons on some particular passes, leading to this Place, with a small quantity of Rum (when the state of that article in Store will enable you to furnish it) in order to give to the distant Indians who may be coming to the Post when not wanted, to engage them to return, to their Villages without advancing farther, the pass at St Mary's seems a very proper one to try this experiment at—

Thirdly—That you should be very particular in establishing some method and arrangement at the Post, both relative to the mode of issuing Provisions & to the quantity issued for a Ration in the Indian Department so as always to be able to calculate the supplies and consumption that will be necessary, as well as to have a check upon those persons who have charge of the Stores—in no part of which does there appear to have been any method—during the command of your Predecessor,—which has occasioned great abuses and been the cause of a considerable part of the expense incurred unnecessarily.

Fourthly—That as a sort of combination has evidently been framed by all the Traders at this Post to avail themselves of the necessity of Government, in keeping up the Price of Indian Corn, at a most exhorbitant rate, to defeat this in future, till a more reasonable & generous disposition appears among the Traders, as calculation has been made of the quantity at present wanted for the Public service, and the contractor for supplying this article should be immediately sent out to the neighbouring Villages of the Ottawa's at L'Arbe Croche to make his purchases at the first hands from the Indians themselves, as far as to the amount, of Two Thousand Bags before any other persons under the protection of this Post, be permitted to go out, to make theirs a measure which with any others of the same nature that may occur to yourself to adopt on a more extensive knowledge of these practices among the Traders, will we have no doubt meet with the approbation & support of the Commander in Chief & which therefore we strongly recommend to you—

Fifthly,—that as great stress is laid by His Excellency in his Instructions upon the great increase of appointments in the Indian Department here, which has been found by us all on this Inquiry, not only to have been considerably augmented since Governor Sinclairs command of the Post but also to be without any apparent necessity in so much as that except Blondeau, who is at present with the Ottigamies—Cadet at St Mary's. Rocque with the Scioux Indians & Langlade, le fils as an assistant to the established Interpreter, Gautier, no other in the line of officers or Interpretors seems to be at all requisite at this Post for the present—and these to be paid as heretofore, at Eight Shillings p. diem each, N. York Currency, and that only a storekeeper at twelve shillings p. diem and one Blacksmith at eight Shillings N. York Curry are necessary to be added to the above list, to which latter appointment your own nomination of the properest persons to be found upon the principles expressed in the Generals Instructions is thought right. You, are therefore hereby directed to strike off from this period all others of whatever denomination, that may be paid on the list of the Indian Department, until the Commander in Chief's further pleasure shall be signified to you upon this subject.

Sixthly,—that as an Engineer will be left to carry on the Works, You are hereby directed to discontinue all the appointments as they stand at present in that Line, and only to pay such in future, as he will point out, at the usual rates, and that you shall think absolutely necessary to carry on the service—that all those useless officers under the denomination of Naval Department, be likewise immediately abolished, and that a stop be put to working at the Vessel on the Rocks, & the people now employed on it be dismissed, as soon as the present materials collected are used, or that the Bulk of it is finished—

Seventhly,—that the small vessel which has been taken into the hire of Government by your Predecessor at such an Enormous rate, and contrary to the Generals regulation on this subject, should be & is, hereby directed to be paid off at the expiration of another month & be sent away to Detroit, the continuance of her in the Service for that period being allowed only on account of the assistance agree'd to be given to the Contractor for collecting his Corn to the Post on this occasion, and as she may also be of use in the exertion so necessary at present towards compleating the works, on the proposed temporary plan—

From an adherence to these Regulations, which we think highly necessary just now for the Service, and from the Zeal, with which we are convinced that you will carry them into execution, as well as every other measure that shall appear to you, condusive to that end, the most sanguine hopes may be entertained of a very material reduction so justly complained of at this Post.

We are Sir, with great regard your most obedient humble Servants

(signed)

Henry Hope Lt Colonel

(signed)

John Johnson

(signed)

James Stanley Goddard

(A true Copy)

Captain Robertson 84th Regiment Commander at Michilimackinac

[B 98 p 134]

SKETCH OF THE FORT ON MICHILIMACKINAC ISLAND.

Temporary Lines of Pickets.

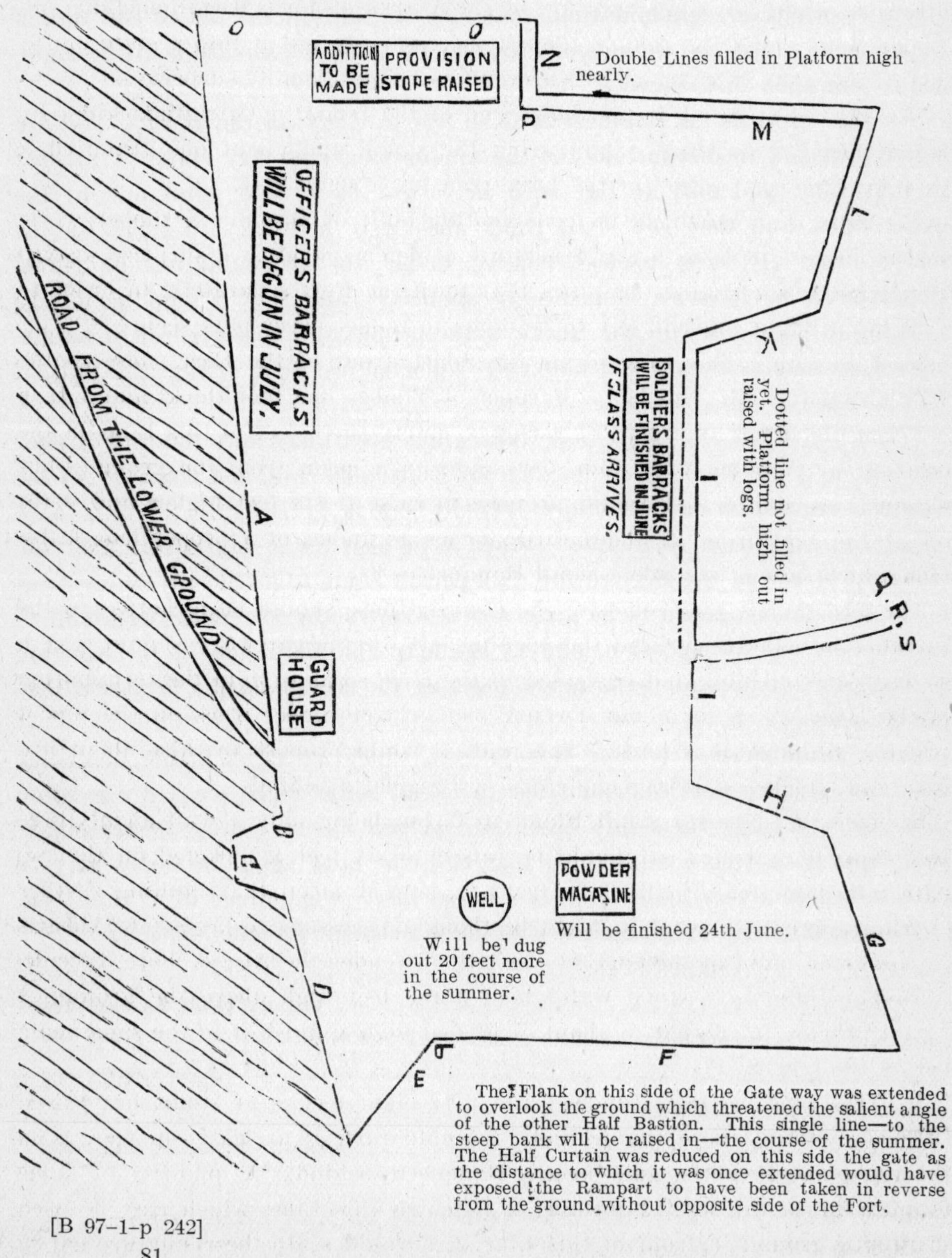
O
O
ADDITTION TO BE MADE
PROVISION STORE RAISED
N
Double Lines filled in Platform high nearly.
P
M
L
K
OFFICERS BARRACKS WILL BE BEGUN IN JULY.
SOLDIERS BARRACKS WILL BE FINISHED IN JUNE IF GLASS ARRIVES.
Dotted line not filled in yet. Platform high out raised with logs.
ROAD FROM THE LOWER GROUND
A
I
Q. R. S
GUARD HOUSE
I
H
B
C
WELL
POWDER MAGASINE
Will be finished 24th June.
Will be dug out 20 feet more in the course of the summer.
G
D
F
E
The Flank on this side of the Gate way was extended to overlook the ground which threatened the salient angle of the other Half Bastion. This single line—to the steep bank will be raised in—the course of the summer. The Half Curtain was reduced on this side the gate as the distance to which it was once extended would have exposed the Rampart to have been taken in reverse from the ground without opposite side of the Fort.

[B 97-1-p 242]

CONDITION OF FORT MICHILIMACKINAC.*

Report of the state & Condition of the Works of Fort Michilimackinac attended with a plan of what is thought necessary to put it into a state of Defence, before the Winter, as will prevent its being taken by surprize—

The Fort is situated at the South end of the Island of Michilimackinac on an eminence, about half a mile from the shore, and about one Hundred & Fifty feet above the level of the Lake fronting a small Bay.

The Fort is irregular in its construction built of masonry & timber work, but as no part of it is in a proper state of defence against a surprize, it will be necessary to examine the Lines that form the Fort separately, in order to shew what ought immediately to be done, to render every part secure

A—vide plan. This Line forms the South front of the Fort, close to the edge of a steep hill, and has a Parapet of Timber one foot thick, and 4 ft, 6 in high, supported by a wall of masonry Thirty three feet of this Line on the right is a dry stone wall, four feet high, on a mean from the ground—but without any Parapet—I would propose to raise it six feet higher and plant pickets on the top of it, about three inches as under, of a proper length, behind which should be made a small Banquette—

The left of this Line opposite the Guard House should be picketted to the entrance into the Fort—and the opening left for the gateway—should have a strong Barrier Gate—and traversed in the rear, so as to Join the termination of the Line, which for about Twenty feet is part timber work on the top of which a Stone wall is built. This wall I would propose to raise about five feet, plant picketts thereon and form a Banquette behind—

B—This line forms a small Flank to **C**, but being only a wall about three feet above the ground, it should be raised to six feet & picketed on the top with a Banquette. The Hill in front is so very steep that nothing further appears requisite—except it might be thought necessary to lay a few Abbatis in front and close to the edge of the Hill to render the Access more difficult.

C—This Line is a stone wall about three feet high above the ground, I would propose to raise it to about eight feet high & finish it in the same manner as the Line **B**.

D—This Line for one Hundred and fifty eight feet is of stone, but raised little or nothing above the ground. I would raise it at least ten feet, & on the top plant Picketts, and form a Banquette behind. A quantity of stone is quarried on the top, in forming a Ditch to this Line, which may be used in raising ground in front of this Line, & I would scalp the rising ground in front of this Line, of as much earth as possible to form a Banquette behind,

*[As the lettering A. B. C., &c, corresponding to that of the report was lacking in the diagram as received from the copyists, it has been supplied as seemed most obvious.—Ed.]

the picketing also lay an Abbâtis on this ground, so as to be flanked by the Line E, and indeed if Time permitted it would be proper to raise the Line D even fourteen feet, that the Provision Store may be properly covered, but also to prevent a part of the work being seen in reverse—About thirty two feet and nearly in the continuation of this Line, the Line is constructed of logs at A, but has no Parapet—If thought necessary a picketting may be fixed on it, and a Banquette formed behind.

E—This Line is constructed of Log work filled in with earth, within three feet of the level of the rampart, & its height from 12 to 14 feet above the bottom of the Ditch. I would propose to fill in the Timber-work with earth, even with the level, and plant a picketting on the top—Part of the Timber-work of the Parapet of this Line is formed at b, which I would also fill in, to the height of about four feet, above the rampart, so as to have as great command as possible on the rising ground before it. Two embrasures are formed on this Line. The wood in front of the Line should be felled to the distance of five Hundred yards, so as not to afford any cover to an enemy.

F—This Line is formed of Log-work filled with earth, level with the Rampart—one merlon is formed, but not filled. The Height of the work above the ground is from eight to twelve feet, the Breadth of the Ditch from ten to thirty feet wide. It will be necessary, the narrow part of the Ditch should be widened, & pickets placed on the Rampart, where the work is low, & particular attention will be requisite to secure the dead Angles, by widening & sinking the Ditch opposite to them—so as not to leave any footing for an enemy.

G—This Line is a Stone Wall, about five feet wide at top—The height of the wall is from 8 to 16 feet above the ground. The Ditch in Front is roughly excavated from 20 to 23 feet wide, and sunk below the Level ground from 6 to 10 feet. I would propose to slope the ground at the foot of the Wall, and throw the earth into the work to form a Banquette to the Picketting that is necessary to be placed where the wall is low, part of the Rampart to this Line is formed.

H—This Line is similar to G, its height above the ground is from 6 to 13 feet and the Ditch is sunk about four feet lower. The same alteration here will be necessary as to the Line G.

I—This Line is formed of Log-work and the Parapet nearly finished. There are two Embrasures on this Line. I would slope the Ground at the Foot of the scarf, and trim the ground taken out of the Ditch more in Glacis, to prevent an enemy lodging under cover of it, which at present may be easily done—The height of the work is from 9 to 11 feet above the ground. The Ditch is from 20 to 40 feet broad, and three feet below the level ground, but roughly traced. The ends of the Land-ties projecting from the work should be cut off, The entering angles formed by **H I** should be dug deeper, at least 5 feet, and the Stone wall raised about four feet, where it joined the Line **I** for the length of 30 feet on the Line **H** at the right and left extremity of this Line the Salient Angles are raised, on which are placed four wall pieces that have a tolerable command over the ground in front.

K—This Line is formed of Log-work and the parapet raised about four feet high above the Rampart, but not filled in, this should be done. The Height of the work is from 10 to 16 feet and the Ditch about 30 feet broad but roughly dug.

The Rubbish taken out of the Ditch should be trimmed more in glacis, from the work as observed before to prevent an enemy lodging in the hollow way in front. The parapet should be filled in and a Banquette made behind it.

L—This Line is a Stone wall, as high as the Level of the rampart, in height about 13 feet above the ground, on which a Log Parapet is partly framed, but not filled in, this should be done, and a picketting made behind it with a Banquette. The Ditch to the Line is dug about 16 feet broad. The would should be cut down to at least 500 yards back, that the rising ground opposite may be exposed as much as possible.

M—This Line is a Stone wall from 12 to 18 feet high. It is not material whether it is picketted, except about 20 feet from the re-entering Angle **d**, but, the Trees should be felled down, the Slopes of the Hill.

N—This Line is a Stone Wall and forms a Flank to **M**. It's height from 9 to 12 feet at the Salient Angle I would have the rocky Bluff lowered or have pickets planted on the Wall, and the planks laid to form a Banquette.

O—This Line is a Stone Wall, about 6 feet high, as it is the only Flank to the Road leading up to the Fort, & to the long Line **A**. I would raise the wall about 4 feet higher, to give it a greater command *a* fix a picketting with a Banquette behind. As the Slope of the Hill here is very steep and enemy would find it Difficult to break in at this Quarter.

Q. R. S—Two Flanks and a curtain of framed Log-work of unequal heights, which is now taking down, this Front in my opinion, is well constructed & forms a better Defence than any other part of the work. The Faces of the Demi-Bastions would have been properly defended if the work **G. H.** had not joined the shoulders, however, I think the Curtain and Flanks **Q. R. S.** should remain, and if time permitted would picket them, but as the Timber work of the Curtain has not been filled in with earth, I would lay Planks to serve as a Banquette. This will increase the Defence, by serving as an entrenchment to the work before it.

Gates ought to be made to the two Gate-ways which also should be traversed.

From the great Extent of the Lines of Defence, it appears the present Garrison is not sufficient for the defence of such a Fort, & from the great irregularity of the works, & being incompleat in so many places, it does not appear to me at this time possible to contract it, without exposing some parts to be surprised—It must therefore be secured on its Present Plan, and, would about one Hundred men be furnished as Labourers (exclusive of the different artificers) I am induced to think with a proper exertion that in about two months, the works might be put into such a state as to be secure against a surprize.

For this purpose every kind of Timber and Plank should be immediately collected & brought to the Fort, without loss of time, to strengthen the Place when requisite.

Reported by

(signed) R. Hockings
Engineer

Michilimackinac 20th Sept 1782.
[B 98 p 140]

FROM LIEUT. COL. HOPE. UNADDRESSED

Michilimackinac Sepr. 21st 1782.

Sir, As Lieut Governor Sinclair proposes going down to Quebec by the Grand River, I shall leave this Letter to be convey'd to Your Excellency by this opportunity, merely to inform you in general terms that your Commands have been executed by us at this post to the utmost in our power and to such purpose as will we hope in some degree have the desir'd effect and meet your Excellency's attentions & wishes, the particulars however of what has been done here I shall defer entering upon, till I have the honour of delivering to you our report in person which will I hope be very shortly after this can reach Your Excellency, & within the time prescribed to me, for we are upon the point of setting out for Detroit with a fair wind, and it may be two days yet before Lt. Governor Sinclair will be ready to proceed on his Route—tho' it is three days since at his own request, He gave up the command of the Post to Captain Robertson—

I have the honour to be, with great respect, Your Excellency's most obedient & faithfull—humble Servant

Henry Hope—

[B 98 p 148]

CAPTAIN MCKEE TO CAPTAIN CALDWELL

Block House Septr. 21st 1782 4 o'clock

Dear Sir, This moment a Runner is arrived from Wheeling who left it three days ago, his companions who were two Delawares give out upon the way, so that he says none are gone to your Quarter. they were sent to inform us that they took a Pris[r] near Beaver Creek who inform'd them that there was twelve hundred men assembled there to make an Expedition in the Indian country and that their design is upon the Huron Villages and were to set out in two or three days, so that this day or yesterday they are on their way. The Party who sent him consists of seventy men who he says will push to be in before the Enemy. they attacked a small Fort between Wheeling and Beaver Creek, but were unsuccessful and lost two men. Capt. Bradt is just arriv'd here likewise with the Rangers & a few Delawares.

I shall assemble all the Indians that can be found in this Quarter to oppose them. I wish the Hurons now to watch towards Koashawking & inform us of their discoveries from time to time perhaps upper Sandusky is their object. this only can be known by the way they take from Kooshoking or Tuskarawas. I wish you would forward this Intelligence to Detroit and Roche de Bout the Ottawas there may come at least in time to Sandusky.

I am Dear Sir, Your most obedt. Servant

(signed) Alexr. McKee.

To Capt Caldwell

Detroit I Ent'd. Copy of a Letter from Capt. McKee to Capt. Caldwell dated Block House Septr. 21st 1782 Entered in Book marked B no. 3 Page 32

[B 123 p 316]

CAPTAIN CALDWELL TO MAJOR DE PEYSTER

Sandoskie Sept 24th '82

Sir, This morning arrived here two Delawares who deserted from Ft. Pitt and informs us there were then twelve hundred Rebels gathered in that country to come against this place, part of them they says when he saw them were already crossed the Ohio, which makes me think they will be shortly with us, I send you a letter I this moment received from Capt. McKee.

I am sorry to be obliged to tell you that I will have but few Rangers to face them with as there is 38 of them sick. I could wish you to send all assistance you possibly can & be quick as possible—

I am Sir Yours &c

Signed— Wm Caldwell

To Major De Peyster.

Endorsed:—Detroit K Ent'd Copy of a Letter from Capt Caldwell to Major De Peyster dated Sandusky 24 Sepr 1782 Entered in Book marked B no 3 Page 32

[B 123 p 317]

MAJOR DE PEYSTER TO GENERAL HALDIMAND

DETROIT the 26th Sepr 1782.

SIR, I am honoured with your Excellency's Commands to send all the corn this Settlement can spare to the Post of Michilimackinac. When there is any to spare I shall not fail to do it, but I must beg leave to observe that, when we have an Expedition on foot in the Indian country, the Settlement barely produces what is necessary.

From the constant imployment we have had for our artificers and labourers, in order to put this place in a state of security, it has not been in my power to Erect a Mill, upon Hog Island, which no doubt Your Excellency has been informed of by Brigadier General Powell. The wheat raised this year, does not however, require much grinding owing to the Violent falls of rain, and, to the Indian Horses swimming around or breaking the Fences—The Quantity of Indian Corn raised amounts to about Eight Hundred Bushels which requires no grinding, and as the soil is better calculated for it, than for wheat, I shall humbly offer my opinion to give up the Cultivation of the latter, at least for the present, and stick to the raising of Indian Corn, and grazing of Cattle, for which the Islan is best calculated, the inconveniency of the Indian Horses excepted, which will ever be a plague, I shall therefore wait Your Excellency's further determination before I proceed to erect a Mill, which I now see will be more expensive than useful.

I have the honour to be Sir, Your Excellency's
most Huml & obedt Servt.

AT. S. DE PEYSTER

His Excellency the Comma. in Chief

A 1782 From Major De Peyster 26th Septr Rec'd 18th Octr.

[B 123 p 318]

LIEUT. GOV. HAY TO GEN. HALDIMAND

MONTREAL Sept 26th 1782.

SIR In consequence of your Excellencys intentions when I left Quebec of allowing me time enough to go to Detroit this Fall, I prepared myself on my arrival here, and even forwarded a part of the stores necessary for the use of my family, but have not yet been honoured with your Excellency's commands. Therefore beg leave to represent to your Excellency that the season is far advanced and that a little time will render my arrival there very precarious if not impossible this year, and that if I am detained here it will both hurt and injure me very much. That my remaining inactive may give rise to conjectures very much to my prejudice, & put me to great & unavoidable expenses which I am unable to bear. I actually now pay nine pounds per month for very indifferent lodgings, so that my whole salary will barely pay house rent, firing and lights, and consequently will render me incapable of supporting a numerous family. I hope your Excellency will take these things into your consideration, and favour me with orders and Instructions to proceed, & honor me with your confidence for the execution of them with zeal to the best of my ability, for the good of his Majesty's service.

I have the Honor to be

Your Excellency's most obedient and most humble servant.

JOHN HAY.

His Excellency Genl. Haldimand.

A 1782 From Mr. J. H. Hay Lieut. Gov. of Detroit of the 26th Septr. at Montreal Rec'd 29th.

[B 123 p 319]

MESSRS. MACOMB TO CAPTAIN MCKEE

DETROIT, 27th Sept. 1782.

DEAR SIR, We send you pr. the Wiandot I keg Contg 1 lb Hyson tea, 12lb. Coffee, 10lb. loaf Sugar & 1 keg brandy 7½ gall—

Sir John Johnson arrived here from Mich. yesterday & setts off this evening for Niagara; Lt. Governor Sinclair is ordered down You may equip, not for building churches—

We wish you may Injoy what we send you & Return safe and sound to this place

and b've Your most Hble. Servts.

MACOMB & MACOMB.

Alexr. McKee Esqr.

[Indian Affairs M. G. IV.]

MAJOR DE PEYSTER TO CAPTAIN MCKEE

DETROIT the 27th Sept 1782

SIR, I am just favoured with your letter and one from Capt. Caldwell, both reporting the Enemy advancing towards Sandusky, and requesting a reinforcement—in consequence of which I have assembled the Ottawas of the Miamis River and shall speak to them upon the subject.

I have also ordered a Detachment of fifty Soldiers, with Artillery properly officered to take Part at the Roche de bout, in order to support you in case you are obliged to put my former orders into execution, which are, should you find the Enemy too strong, to retreat and give time for the neighboring nations to assemble—Capt. Brant sets out with Capt. Potts, who will help to spirit up the Six Nations—

As matters are circumstanced, it is not in my power to allow Capt Potts to proceed further than the Miamie River, nor indeed would time allow him to join Capt. Caldwell before the enemy approach him. You will of course endeavor to form a junction with C. Caldwell, as soon as you are convinced that Sandusky is the object which the Enemy have in View. In every other matter I must leave you to act mutually as circumstances shall require for the good of the Service.

I am Sir, Your most Huml & most obedt Servt.

At. S. De Peyster

Alexr McKee Esqr Dy. Agent

P. S. It is thought best that the Detachment should take Post at the Block House, lately built at the mouth of the Miamie.

Indian Affairs M. G. III.

MAJOR DE PEYSTER TO GENERAL HALDIMAND

Detroit the 29th Sepr. 1782

Sir, I have the honour to inform your Excellency that I have given Lt. Coll. Hope and Sr Johnson every information they required—My list of Indian officers, and others imployed, may appear large, but then it is fluctuating, the Enemy take off some, and most of the others imploy'd by me, cease to be imploy'd at the end of a Campaign. Lt. Coll. Hope and Sir John, have been eye witnesses to the streight I have been put to with respect to the Indian presents not arriving in time, I have made every shift in my power and If we are not supplyed soon, I shall not know what to do; the Indians are really become troublesome a disagreeable prelude to what must soon happen. I have been advised to exchange Tobacco with Captain Robertson for the Article of Strouds. I am ready to do it, but circumstances has prevented my sending a vessel to Michilimackinac, and I hope to be supplyed from below, before I can exchange with Capt. Robertson, he shall nevertheless have the articles proposed from this place, as I understand he will want them. Lt. Colonel Hope took with him the Intelligence I received from the Indian country the day he left Detroit, and will before this reaches Quebec, have informed your Excellency of the steps I have taken in consequence thereof. Should the rangers be obliged to retreat, (which from the sickness among them may be very probable) or should Mr. Clarke from the other Quarter, push the Shawanesse, Captain Potts will be well situated to cover their retreat, till they can be reinforced from all Quarters. I have a very difficult Card to play at this post, and its dependencies, which differs widely from the situation of affairs at Michilimackinac, Niagara and others in the upper district of Canada. It is evident that the back settlers will continue to make war upon the Shawneese, Delawares & Wiandotts even after a truce shall be agreed to betwixt Great Britain and Her Revolted Colonies. In which case, whilst we continue to support the Indians, with troops (which they are calling aloud for) or only with arms, ammunition and necessarys, we shall incur the odium of encouraging incursions into the back Settlements—for, it is as evident, that, when the Indians are on foot occasioned by the constant alarms they receive from the Enemys entering their country, they will occasionally enter the settlements, and bring off Prisoners, and Scalps—so, that whilst in alliance with a people we are bound to support, a Defensive war, will in spite of human prudence, almost always terminate in an offensive one—

These matters considered I hope your Excellency will urge the necessity of the back Settlers holding out the olive branch, instead of setting on foot, one expedition after another—declaring on their setting out, that their intentions are to exterminate the whole Savage tribe. I wait with impatience to hear from your Excellency, and in the meantime I shall continue to discourage small partys as much as possible, and endeavour in every respect to act for the honor of the British nation.

I am with the greatest respect Sir,

Your Excellency's Most Huml. & Most obedt Servt.

AT. S. DE PEYSTER

His Excelly. The Commr. in Chief

Endorsed:—No. 19 Detroit 1782 From Major De Peyster 29th Septemr. Entered in Book Marked B No 3 Page 29—

[B 123 p 329]

GENERAL HALDIMAND TO LIEUT. GOV. HAY

QUEBEC 30th Sepr. '82

SIR, I have Received your Letter of the 26th Inst and am sorry that the present Situation of affairs in the upper country interferes with my Intention of permitting you to repair to your Government this Season, and obliges me to avoid making any change in the arrangement of affairs at Detroit in the present moment, as I should be responsible for the consequences—I hope this necessity can be attended with no other Inconvenience to you than the circumstance of House Rent mentioned in your Letter, in consideration of which, I shall take upon me to make you an allowance of one Hundred pounds to indemnify that Expence

I am &c——

(Signed) FRED: HALDIMAND

Lieut. Governor Hay

Endorsed:—(Copy) 1782 To Lieut. Governor Hay of the 30th Septr.

[123 p 223]

MAJOR DE PEYSTER TO CAPTAIN MCKEE

DETROIT the 1st Oct'r 1782.

DEAR SIR, I am favoured with your letter of the 22d and 26th Ultimo, by which the Enemy seem inclined to cut off the Huron and Shawanee Villages. By the accounts of their force in the present sickly state of the Rangers and the Indians being so much distressed I fear you will be obliged to retreat at least till you are joined by the Miamies. I have sent all the Indians I could muster particularly the Ottawas of the Miamie Riv'r. Egoushwa is also gone, and eight of the six Nations which arrived here in the last Vessels. You must be sensible that my soldiers are little acquainted with wood fighting and Ill equipped for it withall. I had therefore only ordered them to take post where they can secure the ammunition and provisions and support you in case you are obliged to retreat which I hope will still not be the case. If the Indians are as determined as they have hitherto shown themselves.

I am very unwell and have an ugly bruised thumb which will I hope apologize for the brevity of this Letter.

I am Dr. Sir Your hum'l obedt. Serv't

AT. S. DE PEYSTER

Alex'r McKee Esq.
Indian Affairs M. G. III.

FROM LIEUT. GOV. HAY. UNADDRESSED

MONTREAL October 8th 1782

SIR, I was honored with your Excellency's Letter of the 30th of Septr. a few days ago, and am extremely sorry, that your being responsible for the consequences of any change at Detroit, should oblige your Excellency not to permit me to proceed there this season.

The disappointment is the greater as your Excellency always gave me reason to believe I should repair to the post assigned me, from my first arrival at Quebec in the latter end of June, but since your Excellency has resolved to the contrary, my duty obliges me to comply with it, tho' not the less mortified. The article of House rent which your Excellency has made me an allowance for, and which you hope is the only inconvenience attending my being detained here, is the least of several.

Your Excellency I presume is not ignorant that I left a numerous family, and went voluntarily upon a disagreeable and unpromising service, fell into the hands of the Enemy, suffered a long confinement in prisons & Dungeon! received many indignitys, put to exhorbitant expences during an absence of four years, and finally laid down fifteen shillings pr. day on a presumption of entering into employ: instead of which I see another enjoy in quiet the Emoluments annexed to my appointment and seven shillings & six pence pr. day besides.

This will appear very strange to the person from whom I had the honor of receiving my commission: but as my reputation is at stake in several views, it will be incumbent on me to make it appear I suffer innocently after voluntarily: and that what was meant, given and received as a Reward, is (if I am to be thus suspended from my office) turn'd to a pecuniary and degrading punishment.

I have the honour to be your Excellency's most
obedient and most humble Servant
JOHN HAY.

Endorsed:—A 1782 From Lieut. Govr Hay 8th Octr Rec'd 12th.
[B 123 p 324]

SECRETARY MATTHEWS TO MAJOR DE PEYSTER

QUEBEC 15th October 1782.

SIR, His Excellency the Governor having received Instructions from the King's Minister to render an Exact account of all the Revenues in Canada, describing their nature and the amount of their produce respectively, for the last six years, has commanded me to signify to you His directions that you will, as soon as possible, transmit to him an Exact account of the Kings Rents Lots et Vents, and all Revenues whatsoever paid in the Settlement of Detroit

*See appendix

during your command at that place, in order that the same may be collected and paid into the Hands of the Depy Recr Genl.

I am &c.

(signed) R. M.

Major De Peyster.

Endorsed:—(Copy) 82 To Major De Peyster at Detroit 15th Octr.

[B 123 p 326]

MEMORIAL

To His Excellency Frederic Haldimand General and Commander in Chief of the Province of Quebec and dependant Territories &c. &c. &c.

The humble petition of Louis Chevallier formerly resident at the Post of St Joseph in the Upper Country.

And has the honor to show to your Excellency that under an order from Lieutenant Governor Hamilton of the 15th of October 1778, to raise and conduct to the Miamis the Pautawatamies nation, he has delivered to the Chiefs and their families goods to the amount of seven hundred and forty Livres old shillings of the Province according to the account annexed to the present request.

That having received a new order from Lieutenant Governor Hamilton of the 27th of February 1779, to cloathe thirteen Indians whom he sent from Post Vincennes to St Joseph, he had given to them in consequence goods to the amount of one thousand seven hundred and sixty eight Livres, which makes with the first sum a total of two thousand five hundred and twelve Livres old currency of this Province, out of which he has received nothing.

That the Petitioner takes the liberty of representing to your Excellency that he has always conducted himself with the most zeal when the interests of His Majesty are in question and on all occasions when he could be of any use; that he has himself taken the Indians to their Wintering Grounds, conducted them many times to the Post of Detroit and also to Michilimackinac, without having ever expected any reward, hoping only to have done his duty, but that he is obliged in the interest of his family to repeat what he has been able to expend for Government.

This considered, the Petitioner flatters himself that your Excellency will take his petition into consideration and will order payment of the amount of his account, and he will not cease to wish for his health and his prosperity.

Your Excellency's Most obedient & Most humble Servt.

LOUIS CHEVALLIER

Montreal 18th October 1782.

Endorsed:—Memorial of M. Louis Chevallier '82, of the 18th October with an account of the payments made for Lieutenant Governor Hamilton in 1778.

[B 98 p 156]

MEMORIAL

To His Excellency Frederic Haldimand General and Governor in Chief for His Majesty in the Province of Quebec and territories depending thereon in America Vice Admiral of the same General and Commander in Chief of His Majesty's Troops in the said Province and Frontiers &c. &c. &c.

THE PETITION OF LOUIS CHEVALLIER

Your Petitioner having for more than thirty years lived at St Joseph and being regarded as a well known man by the surrounding nations & attached to the service of His Majesty, Major De Peyster has honored him by sending a commission to watch over their conduct & has given him orders in many of his letters (which he can produce to your Excellency) to make the presents which he judges necessary to preserve their friendship; he has acted in all things in consequence of these orders and his accounts have always been approved of and payed by Major De Peyster with thanks for his good services, except the last which amounts to the sum of 6820″ making £284., 3., 4, and it would have been payed likewise if he had had the happiness to see Major De Peyster before his departure from Michilimackinac. Wherefore your Petitioner has already had the honor of representing to your Excellency that this sum was still due to him and he has every reason to believe that your Excellency is now informed of the justice of his demand having received advice from Detroit that Major De Peyster has notified Your Excellency that his accounts ought to be payed and that he was only surprised knowing the affairs in which he had been engaged that it did not amount to four times the sum; such an avowal from Major De Peyster who has also remarked that it would give him true pleasure and at the same time authorised Your Excellency to give your orders for payment to be made to him.

Your Petitioner has the honor to be very
respectfully Sir Your very obedient
and very huml Servt.

Louis Chevallier

Endorsed:—Memorial from M. Chevallier praying his account may be discharged.
[B 98 p 158]

* * * * * * * * * * * * *

ACCOUNT

Account of Merchandise furnished by Louis Chevallier at the Post of St Joseph for raising and bringing to the Miamis the Potawatamies by the order of Lieut. Governor Hamilton received the 15th of October, by an Indian named Windigo, & in consequence the following articles were delivered to the Chiefs and their families.

viz

4 Cloth Blankets	at 36"	144
4 White Blankets	at 24"	96
4 pr. Lavelle	at 12	48
4 Large Shirts	at 18	72
4 Pairs of Mitts	at 10	40
4 Gallons of Rum	at 36	144
4 Carots of Tobacco	at 32	128
6 lbs of Powder	at 8	48
12 lbs of Ball	at 2	24
		744

By orders received the 27th of February to cloathe thirteen Indians which he has sent from the Post where I have delivered, in consequence of the order, the following articles

viz

13 Cloth Blankets	at 36"	468
13 White Blankets	at 24	312
13 lbs Vermillion	at 24	312
13 Shirts	at 18	234
13 Pairs Mitts	at 10	130
13 Pairs Leggings	at 6	78
6½ Carots Tobacco	at 32	208
13 Large Knives	at 2	26
		1768
		744
Shillings old Currency of this Province		2512

The Presents given for the sum of two thousand five hundred and twelve Livres. One hundred and four Livres thirteen Shillings and four pence Halifax Currency £104 ,, 13 ,, 4.

Endorsed:—Account of Louis Chevallier

[B 98 p 149]

LIEUT. COL. HOPE TO GENERAL HALDIMAND

QUEBEC, Octr. 19th 1782.

SIR,—In obedience to your Excellency's Commands of the 15th of August last, I set out from Quebec on the following day, from Montreal on the 21st of the same month, & arrived at Michilimackinac by way of the Grand River on the 15th September, the twenty-fourth day from our leaving the Indian Village of Canesadago, having had the winds upon Lake Huron so strong as to oblige our canoe to lay by three entire days—on the subject of this very intricate navigation I shall not take up more of your Excellency's time at present than just to mention the several distances of the principal points on it with the number of carrying places only in each, where the Canoes with the Provisions and the Baggage of the Party were oblig'd to be transported by themselves, the particulars of which are as follows, viz. up the Grand River from Cansedago & Matonan (where we quitted it) 117 leagues with 16 Portages, up the little River to the entrance of Lake Nipipin 18 leagues with 15 Portages—Across that Lake 12 leagues—Down the French River 25 Leagues with 3 Carrying Places, & across Lake Huron to the Island of Michilimackinac 79 Leagues, the whole making 251 Leagues with 34 Carrying Places, after which when I observe to your Excellency that the shallowness of the water & rapidity of the current in these Rivers are such as to render it absolutely impossible to navigate them in any other craft but Bark Canoes, it is of course unnecessary almost to add that this communication can serve no other Military purpose than to forward expresses to the upper country, or perhaps to throw a very small reinforcement of men into either of the Posts of Michilimackinac or Detroit upon emergency, in case of any part of the other by the Lakes being intercepted for a time.

With respect to the business which Your Excellency gave me in charge along with Sir John Johnson and the other Gentlemen "of enquiring into the cause of the great expenses that had been incurred of late at Michilimackinac, and to apply such temporary remedies to the different abuses that might appear as were most expedient." I beg leave to refer your Excellency to our joint report upon that head which I have already had the honour to give in. As to the state in which I found the works at that Post, and the steps that appeared to me most proper to be taken with respect to them under present circumstances, the Engineer Dr. Hocking's report (whom Your Excelly. sent up with me for that purpose) will fully explain the former, as will the order I left with him & Captain Robertson shew the latter, much more might be said upon the subject of every branch of service, such as I found them at this Post, than can come within the compass of a General Report of this nature—

but having taken minutes upon every thing that struck me at the time—I can at any future period dwell upon such particular points as Your Excellency may think sufficiently interesting to engage your attention—so shall only further observe at present with respect to Michilimackinac, that as from the returns which I received there of what was actually arrived, and from the state of the transport that was going on, there will probably be in the stores by the time the navigation of the Lakes is closed this year an entire twelve months Provision of all species (& more of some) so from the resources of fish which they have at hand in great plenty, & of Indian Corn that might be collected from the Indian Villages in the neighborhood, that Garrison should be able to support itself in case of any impediment to farther supply next season till the navigation shall be open in the following Spring—

On the 21st Sept. as soon as the business at Michillimackinac was finished, I embark'd in one of the King's Sloops employed on that communication for Detroit, and arriv'd there late at night of the 24th, the Distance being 106 Leagues. But from the strength of the Current & a Bar, which there is in the narrows between the Lakes St. Claire & Huron, and which requires a strong leading wind to pass it, this voyage upwards is seldom made in less than ten or twelve days—Here I remained only till the Evening of the 26th of Sepr. having in that time inspected the state of the Garrison and of the Different Departments at this Post, agreeable to Your Excellency's Directions. But tho' I have furnished myself with every Information that was required, yet as Brigadier General Powell had so immediately preceeded me and is since come down from those Posts, who will have been able to make Reports to Your Excellency upon all these points in the fullest manner, it becomes unnecessary for me to trouble Your Excellency with an imperfect repitition, however on any particular branches you may do me the honor in future to demand my opinion, I shall ever be ready to give it with every information that I have gained to the best of my judgment—

Tho it was so early as the first of October that I reach'd Niagara, having traversed Lake Erie & Examined the condition, terms & mode of transport across that important carrying Place in the course of five days, yet no vessel being then on that side of Lake Ontario, or arriving till the 3rd Inst, and the weather being too boisterous to attempt the passage in a Boat, it was not till the 6th in the morning that I sailed from hence, with the full intention however of calling at Oswego, and according to Your Excellency's Instructions of visiting that Post, but after beating against contrary winds four entire days within sight of Niagara, and a Southerly wind then springing up, when we were upon the North Shore of the Lake, it was with much regret, that I was obliged to relinquish that object & to steer for Carleton Island, where we did not arrive till the 11th and as the time prescrib'd for my being here was then drawing on apace, I embark'd in a Bateau next morning and after visiting the post of Oswegatchie, & seeing those very ingenious & usefull cuts and Canals that have been made to facilitate the navigation up these amazing Rapids at Coteau du Lac and some other adjacent spots, the Current brought me down to Montreal, in something more than 48 Hours, tho' a Distance of near seventy Leagues—and which to ascend with loaded Bateaux even in the longest days of the summer season seldom takes less, I am given to understand, than fourteen days, and at this time of the year nearer twenty.

For the same reason assign'd already with regard to detroit, if Brigadier Powell's having so lately also left Niagara, and seen the State of the lower Posts, its is equally useless for me to take up your Excellency's time just now with particulars relative to them, as they must only be a repitition—

And as the Indian Department upon the very extensive communication when Your Excellency considers the magnitude of the object and the variety of matter for enquiry, it will occur that a much longer time than I could command at this advanced season, in the prosecution of a Tour of Two Thousand miles and upwards such as what I have made within two months—would have been requisite to gain that competent knowledge to report as fully to Your Excellency as it would appear that the subject requires, some notes however I have taken which I shall endeavor to digest into a sort of form which may aid a little in any future investigations, in the meantime from the pains which Sir John Johnson has taken, at the several Posts on this Tour that we have made together, to inform himself thoroughly of the various abuses that it is so apparent have crept into this Department, not only from the extraordinary number of appointments in it, but with respect to the vast expenses that the present mode of cloathing & feeding Indians leaves an infallible opening for, and indeed to make himself perfect master of the subject, I have no doubt but that Your Excellency will receive every satisfaction on this head that you could wish from him—

There is only one matter more then of the several subjects pointed out to me by Your Excellency's order to report upon, that I think necessary to intrude upon any more of your time will in this manner (being ready however as I have before observ'd to discuss the particulars of them all when your leisure will admit, as far as every Information that I have collected can go) but this subject it is highly proper that Your Excellency should be inform'd of, which is, that complaints are made at all the Posts from Carleton Island upwards that great quantities of the Pork & Pease arrive to them in so damag'd a state as even to be unfit for present use (one instance of which I was myself witness to in part of a Cargo that came to Michilimackinac during my stay there, owing it appeared to the badness of the Casks, that had left the Pork to corrupt in a Dry State—that the waste of these articles is not the only consideration, great as it is but the consequences of disappointment in the quantity of Provisions depended upon might as Your Excellency well knows be of a most serious nature—Now tho' from every enquiry into the subject, I am far from thinking that the whole damage accrues on the transportation, but that on the contrary there must have been some want of attention to the state in which these Provisions are set forward from La Chine, yet certainly a part may have been occasioned by some defects on certain parts of this communication that can I should conceive be easily guarded against before the ensuing season for the transport begins, and which, as this subject is so immediately connected with the Department in which Your Excellency has done me the honour to appoint me to act, I shall think it more indispensible a Duty hereafter to submit to your consideration.

If in these endeavors to execute Your Excellency's orders I may have the good fortune in the smallest degree to have succeeded to your approbation, permit me to add that every fatigue and pains will be amply repaid, having the honour, Sir, to subscribe myself with the greatest respect.

Your Excellency's most obedient
faithfull, humble Servant

HENRY HOPE
Lt. Colonel and Act'g Q'r Master General.

His Excellency General Haldimand

Endorsed:—From Lieut Col Hope 19th Oct'r containing proceedings in the upper country—after his return to Quebec—

[B 98 p 160]

GENERAL HALDIMAND TO MAJOR DE PEYSTER

QUEBEC, 21st Oct. 1782.

SIR, Altho' extreme Hurry prevents my writing fully at present, I wish to acknowledge the Receipt of your Letters by Lieut. Colonel Hope—The Defensive measures you have taken will I hope prevent the Enemy from prosecuting their Incursions into the Indian country, at least this season, or should they persist, render their attempt abortive—Your observations upon the consequences attending the unavoidable Hostilities between the Indians and the Americans upon the frontiers as long as the latter continue their present system of invasion, are very just, and I shall attend to them in their Place—In the mean time I have to recommend to your serious attention a steady adherence to the Instructions you have Received concerning a strict observance of Defensive Measures as far as the safety of your post will permit—Before any operations can be undertaken by the Enemy next Campaign, I hope to be able to send you such orders as will in all Events be decisive. for the present Your attention must be employed to restrain the Indians from every act of Hostility, except in their immediate deffence, and to that œconomy of the Public money I have so repeatedly and so earnestly recommended—Your List of Indian officers, and the amount of their Pay are enormous and greatly Increased in the course of your command, which ought not to have happened without my particular approbation & consent, and I now desire that you will make as great a Reduction in that Expense as the absolute indispensible necessities of the Service will admit of—for which the late adopted system of defence affords a very favorable opportunity, & I expect you will improve it to the greatest advantage, reporting to me thereon, and specifying the particular services those continued are Employed in—

Your reasons for Discontinuing the cultivation of Wheat and consequently the construction of a mill, are very proper & have my approbation—and as the soil and circumstances are more favorable to Indian Corn, I desire you will encourage by every means the cultivation of that article.

I am &c.,

(Signed) FRED: HALDIMAND.

Endorsed:—No 10 Ent'd 1782 Copy To Major De Peyster of the 21st Octr. Copy Entered in book marked B No 2 Page 27.

[B 123 p 327]

GENERAL HALDIMAND TO LIEUT. GOV. HAY

QUEBEC October 1782

SIR, I have Received Your Letter of the 8th Instn and having already communicated to you my Sentiments upon the material part of it, I have, on that, only to Repeat my concern that they should interfere with your wishes or convenience.——

As Grievences are often heightened by Imagination, and sometimes entirely Ideal, I wish to set you Right with Respect to those mentioned in your Letter of your having finally laid down 15 shillings pr day and the commanding officer at Detroit enjoying the Emoluments annexed to your appointment and seven Shillings and Six pence per Day besides——If you mean the 15s. per Day Which You received on Lieut. Govr Hamiltons Excursion as Major of

Militia, there not being any Precedent of the kind in the Province (altho' both French & English Militias are Established) I should never of course have taken upon me to continue it, & If the Emoluments aluded to, are the Rents and Lots & Vents of the Settlement at Detroit, I have Instructions Home to Render account of them for six years past, Which I shall certainly do, as well as for the time to come—The 7s 6d pr Day has always belonged to the officer commanding the Troops and Lieut Governor Sinclair now enjoys it only as a Military Man and having a Detachment of the Regiment he belongs to actually in Garrison with him.

I am &c

(Signed) F. H.

Lieut. Govr Hay——

Endorsed:—Copy 1782 To Lieut. Governor Hay of the Octr——

[B 123 p 331]

GENERAL HALDIMAND TO LIEUT. GOV. SINCLAIR

Quebec 21st October 1782

Sir, In answer to your Letter of this date I have to acquaint you, that you have not, in any Respect, personally incurred my Displeasure, that my Duty to the Public Engaged me to take the steps I have, with Concern, found necessary, & that as a full Investigation of the Expenditure of the Public Money at Michilimackinac under your direction will take place this winter, Your Attendance at Quebec will be indispensably necessary.

I am, Sir, &c

(signed)

Fred Haldimand

Lieut Governor Sinclair

[B 98 p 169]

GENERAL HALDIMAND TO HON. THOMAS TOWNSHEND

Quebec 22d October 1782.

The Right Honorable Thomas Townshend (No. 3:)

Sir, I do myself the Honor to transmit You the Triplicate of my Letter of the 16th July (No 1) to the Right Honble the Earl of Shelburn relative to complaints which had been Lodged in the Secretary of States office by Messrs Charles Hay, Calvert & Cuthbert. I do not send Triplicates of the enclosures as they are very voluminous, and that it is very improbable that the two former Dispatches should have miscarried—

Affairs on this Continent have not taken so favorable a Turn as will Justify any Relaxation on my part either of Vigilance or Severity with regard to the known abetters of France & America within this Province, on the contrary everything conspires to render it more necessary than ever for me to be upon my Guard, and to consider the Province as likely next summer, if not sooner, to become the Theatre of War. In these Circumstances, the necessity of supporting the authority of Government is obvious. I flatter myself with experiencing Your Protection and countenance as long as the good of the King's Service shall appear to be the motive which directs my conduct—

I have the Honor to be &c

(signed) F. H.

[B 55 p 228]

GENERAL HALDIMAND TO HON. THOMAS TOWNSHEND

QUEBEC 23rd October 1782.

The Right Honorable Thomas Townshend (No. 5.)

SIR, I have the Honor to transmit to you Copies of Letters I have lately received from the Commanding officer at Detroit, which will at once Shew You the Impossibility of entirely restraining the Indians from War while the Virginians continue their Incursions and obstinate attempts to dispossess the Indians of their Most Valuable Country—Our Southern operations have hitherto confined their abilities to partial attacks upon the Indian country and Menaces against the Post of Detroit—Our evacuation of that Country will now afford them the means of prosecuting that Plan upon a Larger Scale, and if the Overtures for Peace should not be more cordially Received than hitherto, it is probable an Early Campaign will be undertaken for the Destruction of the Indian Villages & the Reduction of Detroit; Which, tho' in a very good state of defence against any attempts that could hitherto have been made, is neither in point of strength or Garrison equal to oppose a great Force, particularly as the Affections of the Indians will decline in Proportion to the success of our Enemies, & the Evident Marks we have discovered of what they will (notwithstanding all that can be said to them) construe into a want of abilities to carry on the War. In conformity to the Instructions communicated to me by Lord Shelburn I have Regulated in the fullest manner in my Power to Brigadr General Maclean who commands in the upper Country, & to Major De Peyster, in the strongest Terms to discourage Hostile Measures on the part of the Indians, & to draw them as much as Possible from the Enemies Frontiers, but if they continue their Encroachments in the determined manner they have lately done it will be impossible to restrain the Indians.

From an apprehension, Sir, that the Disposition of the Indians, and the indispensible necessity of preserving their affections may not be Sufficiently understood at Home, I think it my duty to assure you that an unremitting attention to a very nice management of that People is inseparable from the safety of this Province, which has been indisputably preserved hitherto in a great measure by their Attachment. They must not be considered subject to Orders or easily influenced where their Interests or Resentments are concerned. Great Pains & Treasure were bestowed to bring them to act. They have suffered much in the cause of the War in their Lives & Possessions, in So much that, the Mohawks, who were settled in Ease & Affluence, have entirely lost their country—the rest of the Six nations (the Oneidas excepted) have been invaded, & driven off their Settlements. They have so perpetually harassed the Enemy that they Cannot look for Reconciliation upon any other terms than Abandoning the Royal Cause. They are Thunder Struck at the appearance of an accommodation So far short of their Expectation from the Language that has been held out to them, & Dread the Idea of being forsaken by us, & becoming a Sacrifice to a Vengeance which has already in many Instances been raked upon them. Foreseeing the Possibility of the Americans becoming an Independent Powerful People and retaliating Severely upon them, they reproach us with their Ruin, and while their Fears are thus alive, if the Americans are disposed to take the advantage of them, and are in a Situation to supply their wants liberally, The consequences may be very fatal. As long as the Six Nations are determined to act with us, Oswego, that great Key to this Province, is in security, but from the moment they become *even Neuter* (and they will not remain long so) we have everything to apprehend—I have been already to prolix, Sir, to enter upon the subject of the Western Indians & at Detroit, it is sufficient to inform You that on their Friendshp equally Depends the Safety of the Trade and Posts in that Quarter. The Expense attending our Indian Alliance is enormous it originated in the difficulty & necessity of bringing them to Act, and perhaps in some measure, in bad Management: but the present is not the time to Retrench, for they must be liberally supplied while we have occasion for their services—nor should they be forgotten afterwards—Interest, Humanity & Gratitude are concerned in granting them a yearly gratuity for their Services—That Establishment, when a Peace takes Place may be reduced to such Limits as to render a Bounty so well bestowed, of little moment to the Nation. The Promises we have been obliged to make to these People will be unviolated & their Confidence in us will secure them in future in our Interest

The Post of Oswego, tho' by no means finished is so far advanced as to resist, and to discourage any Attempts that can be made against it except in Force, which cannot be undertaken in the Winter Season.

It is necessary to acquaint You, Sir, that in the present Critical Situation of Affairs at Detroit, I could not hazard the removing an officer of Major DePeysters long residence in that Command, Experience & established Influence with the Indians, by sending Lt. Governor Hay to reside at that Post, which by the King's Order (giving the Lieut Govrs. Rank of all officers under a Brigadier General) must have been the Case. However mortifying & discouraging it must have been to an officer of Major Depeysters rank & long Service, to be commanded by a Half Pay Lieut, You may be assured Sir, that consideration should not have any weight with me, had not the good of the King's Service evidently forbid risking the consequences in the present moment.

I have the Honor to be &c

(signed) F. H.

[B 55 p 233]

FROM MAJOR DE PEYSTER UNADDRESSED

DETROIT the 23d Octr 1782

DEAR SIR, Capt. Potts this morning received your answer to his Letter from the Block House wherein you seem not to have had any late accounts of the Enemy. I have to inform you that Hazel arrived here last night in three days from Pipes Town where he had just spoken with two Deserters from Fort Pitt which place they must have left about the 12th Inst. As you are thoroughly informed of the accounts they bring before now, it is needless for me to say more than that you will see in the Inclosed Speech a copy of which I send by the Vessel to Sandusky—She takes Ammunition and Tobacco as pr inclosed which will be stored at Arundels to be delivered to your orders. About a week ago I sent four Barrels of Powder with a proportion of Ball and Tobacco to the Wyandotts & the like quantity to the Delawares of Sandusky, so that you will know how to distribute the present Cargo. I fear our Clothing Ship with the Indian presents to the Amount of Sixty thousand Pounds Sterlg. on Board, is either taken or lost, so that it will be late before I can supply the Nations with those necessary Articles. It is really unlucky the Enemy take it in their Head to come at this advanced Season when our Rangers are many of them like walking spectres, I shall however send them when they are able to move provided there is an absolute occasion for it. I hope something still may happen to prevent the Enemy from advancing, but should that not be the case the Indians must make the best of it. In fact they must strike in a body upon the first appearance of the Enemy, or they will run the risk of having their Hutts burnt, and what is of much more consequence their Spirits damped.

I am convinced you will direct all for the best and that matters may turn out better than we imagine is the sincere wish of

Dear Sir Your Huml & obedt. Servt.

AT. S. DE PEYSTER

P. S. If this Story does not blow over soon, you will I fear be late for a Voyage to Canada. I must observe one thing to you, which is that unless the Indians can assemble a body sufficient to make a stand, they had better disperse than to lead the Rangers into a scrape by sending for them, please to make them sensible of this.

Indian Affairs M. G. III.

GENERAL HALDIMAND TO HON: THOMAS TOWNSHEND

QUEBEC 24th Octr 1782.

The Right Honble Thos. Townshend

SIR, On the 29th of September I had the honor to receive your letter of the 31st of July (most secret) by His Majesty's Sloop "Drake" communicating the King's commands to fit out for the reception of Troops, and send with all possible expedition to New York, all the Transports & Victuallers at this place—In consequence of which I have the honor to acquaint you, Sir, that every possible effort was exerted in fitting out the said Transports, 23 of which sailed from hence the 10th Inst for the Island of Bic, when Captain Worth, senior Naval officer had ordered a proper convoy for their Protection—five more have since followed—this number I expected to send in the last Division, was unfortunately reduced by various accidents, out of Three Transports which I sent to Spanish River for coal, two were cast away in the River—The Transport "Maria" is so disabled as to make it necessary to discharge her from the service, & I am obliged to employ the "Amazon" to transport the officers of the 47th Regiment & Invalids of the Army to England—The loss of the coal ships & "Maria" in which I intended to send part of the Prisoners of War that do not go by Lake Champlain collected from the different Parts of this Province to New York, in order to be exchanged obliges me to send one remaining Transport, now refitting to Salem on that service.

I have the Honor to be &ca &ca

[B 57-2 p 476] (Signed) FRED: HALDIMAND

RETURN.

A Monthly Return of Indian Corn issued out of the King's Store at Michilimackinac from the 24th September to the 24th of October both Days Inclusive, 1782.

Corn 60 lbs per Bushel.	Canadians.		Indians.		Cattle.	
Date.	Bushels.	Pds.	Bushels.	Pds.	Bushels.	Pds.
September 24	33	30	......	......	1	16
25					1	30
26					1	20
27					1	30
28			2		2	36
29					2	.....
30					2	.....
October 1st					2	36
2nd				51	2	36
3					2	18
4			1	.....	2	18
5					2	18
6					2	36
7			2	.....	2	18
8					2	36
9					2	18
10					2	18
11					2	18
12					2	18
13					2	18
14					12	30
15					1	14
16					2	2
17					2	2
18					2	10
19			9	.....	1	30
20			2	.....	1	38
21			1	.....	1	38
22					1	54
23					11	58
24	46	46			1	46
Total	80	16	16	51	83	42

Total 180 Bush. 49 lbs.

JOHN WATERS
Engineer

[B 98 p 170]

GENERAL HALDIMAND TO HON. THOMAS TOWNSHEND

"Private."

QUEBEC 25th Octr 1782

The Right Honble Thomas Townshend

SIR, The present situation of Public affairs is such as necessarily employs the thoughts & attention of every person who has the honor to be employed by His Majesty, or who feels himself interested for the welfare of his Kingdom.

Equally sensible of your Friendship to myself, as persuaded of your attachment to the service of the King—I write this letter for your private Information, having an entire Confidence in the Indulgence with which you will receive any suggestions or Hints, which may be improved to the benefit of your Country—

The Evacuation of the Posts which has already taken, or which, may hereafter take place in the Provinces bordering upon the Atlantic, has engaged some Loyalists to seek an Asylum in this country— I have great reason to think that many more will follow their Example in hopes of getting Grants of Land here to compensate for those which they have forfeited in their own Country by their Loyalty to the King.

The unconceded Lands in this country are unfortunately of little value not improveable, not being fertile in themselves and at a great distance from the River St Lawrence.

I am assured by the Loyalists that in case New York is evacuated a very great number of Families who have taken refuge there at Different Periods of the War, will be obliged to seek an Asylum in Nova Scotia or Canada—The situation of these people Excites Compassion and requires every assistance which Government can afford them. In conversing with Major Holland who surveyed Cape Breton in the year 1776, it has occured to me that an Establishment might be procured for these unfortunate People on that Island, which in a few years would become comfortable to themselves, as well as beneficial to the Mother Country.

The Island contains a great Quantity of improveable Land, as well as many valuable Harbors & Stations for Fisheries. Its proximity to Newfoundland, the Island of St John's & Gulf of St. Lawrence is such that the Fleet or Cruizers necessary for its Defence, will be equally usefull for the Protection of the Trade carried on at these Places, but as Major Holland transmitted in a plan of Cape Breton to the Board of Trade, you will be able to form a better opinion from the Plan, of the advantages of situation, than from any Description which I can give. It may be presumed that these People having suffered so much Persecution for their attachment to the Crown of Great Britain, will transmit the same to their Posterity—In case Government should approve this idea, Cape Breton may be made an Asylum for the Refugees from the Sea Coasts of the Northern Provinces. There are already in this Province many Loyalists, and no doubt many more will soon arrive, from the Frontiers of New England & New York, perhaps an Establishment may be procured for them, at, or near Detroit. The Lands there are fertile & can be cultivated with ease. The climate is in every respect advantageous. A settlement of men at that place who by Principle and a sense of sufferings, are attached to Great Britain will be a great support to our Indian Allies, who have everything to fear from the encroachments of the Americans.

Besides such settlement would in a few years raise a quantity of Provisions sufficient for the Garrisons, which it will be necessary to keep in the Upper Countries & might prove an essential resource in case at any future period the communication between the Upper & the Lower Canada should be so far interrupted as the supplies of Provisions could not be sent from the latter.

The settlement ought to all intents and Purposes to be under Military Government, The officer appointed to that command should have at least the Rank of Lieut. Colonel in the Army. The Lieut Governor of Detroit is at present Mr. Hay, whose Rank in the Army is that of Lieutenant, his appointment of Major of Militia by Captain Hamilton at that time Lieut Governor of Detroit, giving him no Rank in the Army. Tho' I have no objection to Mr. Hay, yet that circumstance has put me under the necessity to detain him this winter at Montreal, as his taking the command from Major de Peyster at the time when the Enemy tho' repulsed in two actions, persist in their attempts against the Indian Country, might be attended with great inconvenience to the Service. Major de Peyster from having commanded there for some years is well acquainted with the nature & resources of the Service, & has acquired great Influence with the Indians. Tho' his zeal & Duty for the service might induce Major de Peyster to serve if ordered to remain at Detroit under the command of Lieut. Gov. Hay, yet that is a mortification which in the present state of things I think improper in me to impose upon so deserving an officer.

In case a Peace or Truce should take place during the winter, tho' I apprehend it is unnecessary, yet my anxiety for the good of the Empire makes me observe to you that in making the one or the other, great care should be taken that Niagara & Oswego should be annexed to Canada, or comprehended in the general words, that each of the contending Parties in North America should retain what they possessed at the time. The Possession of these two Forts is essentially necessary to the security as well as the Trade of the

Country. If any thing in this letter shall tend to assist you in the Department over which you preside I shall be happy.

I have the Honor to be &ca &ca

(Signed) Fred Haldimand.

P. S. Since writing the above Major Holland has favoured me with a copy of the Remark which accompanied the plan of the Island of Cape Breton in the year 1766. I have sent it for your Information. The plan is in the office of the Lords Commissioners for Trade & Plantations

(signed) F. H.

[B 57-2 p 489]

GENERAL HALDIMAND TO MR. BURKE

Quebec the 25th October 1782.

Richard Burke Esq. (No. 11).

Sir, In consequence of the directions from the Lords Commissioners of His Majesty's Treasury signified to me in Mr. Secretary Robinson's letter, (duplicate) of the 27th August 1781. I have required from the different officers of Government an exact account of all the Revenues in Canada for the last six years & have the honor to transmit the results to you for their Lordships Information.

No. 1 & 2 are the Accounts of the Duties received in consequence of the act of the 14th of His present Majesty. The duties collected and the monies paid by the collector into the hands of the Dr. Receiver General are stated in two different Columns, so that the Deficiency arising from the mode of payment as well as the expense of collection may the more readily appear. I beg leave to refer their Lordships to a variety of reports from the Committees of Council, which have been transmitted by Sir Guy Carleton and myself relative to the Province Duty. No. 3 contains an account of the Casual & Territorial Revenue from July 1775 to the 10th of October 1782—

I enclose copy of my letter to Lord North of the 25th October 1780—Wherein I proposed applying the money arising from this Revenue & which are now in the hands of the Receiver General & his Deputies to the particular purposes mentioned in that letter. I have to request that you will lay the same before their Lordships so that I may receive their Majesty's Commands on that subject.—No 4 is the account of the revenue collected at the Custom House in consequence of Acts 25 Car II 6 Geo & 4 Geo III & 7 Geo III In the last six years as it has been furnished to me by the collector & Comptroller.

Independent of these Revenues there are Quit Rents & other Territorial Rights due to the Crown for the Lands at or near Detroit.

I do not find that any account has been transmitted here of the Amount; I have applied to Lieut Governor Hamilton & to Major De Peyster the present commanding officer at Detroit for Information on that subject which I will take the earliest opportunity to transmit.

I have the honor to be &c.

(signed) F. H.

[B 55 p 218]

GENERAL HALDIMAND TO MR. BURKE

Quebec 25th October 1782.

Richard Burke Esq'r (No. 16)

Sir, I herewith inclose, for the information of the Rt. Hon'ble the Lords Commissioners of His Majesty's Treasury a List of the Bills, drawn by the Lieut Governor and Commanding officers of the Upper Posts between the 20th October 1781 & 24th October 1782 examined and compared, as usual amounting to £63,912, 13, 5 Stg. for which I shall grant a final warrant.

I have further to request you will communicate to their Lordships that Lt. Gov'r Sinclair has drawn Bills on me from Michilimackinac, exclusive of those already paid & included in the enclosed amount, to the amount of £65,-000 New York Currency, or thereabouts, which I have refused to accept, & shall in a few days (when the Bills would have fallen due if accepted) offer to pay to the holders such Articles of them as appear to be reasonable, leaving the remainder to a minute Investigation which I intend to order in the Winter, Particulars of all which shall be laid before their Lordships by the first opportunity.

I have the honor to be &c.

(signed) F. H.

[B 55 p 222]

GENERAL HALDIMAND TO MAJOR DE PEYSTER

Quebec 1st Novr 1782

Sir, Brigadier General McLean will, by this opportunity, forward to you Intelligence I have lately Received from New York, together with such Instructions as he shall think necessary in consequence thereof, and the circumstances of affairs with you shall Require.

Whatever may be the Intentions of the Enemy against the upper Country it is highly improbable that they will attempt any thing at this advanced season of the year, but if no change should take place in Public affairs in the course of the Winter, there is reason to Expect that whatever is intended will be undertaken Early in the Spring—And as the lateness of the Season will not admit of a Reinforcement being sent to you this fall, it will be the more necessary that you procure such Intelligence of the Enemy's Intentions, as will enable you to have Recourse to Brigadr General Maclean for early assistance—and if any communication with Michilimackinac should be necessary, you will not fail to send an Express to Captn Robertson, as well as to keep up an Intercourse with Niagara, as recommended in my last Letter—I have the Strongest Dependence on your Vigilance and attention to the Safety of your Post, and the Interest of Government in general committed to your care.

I am &c

(signed) F. H.

Major de Peyster

Endorsed:—No 17 1782 To Major De Peyster the 1st November—Copy Entered in book marked B no. 2 Page 28

[B 123 p 333]

MR. MCBEATH TO CAPT. ROBERTSON

MICHILIMACKINAC 1st Novr 1782.

SIR, As an opportunity now offers by the Grand River For Canada Thinks it my duty to inform you for the Benefit of the Plan, That its absolutely necessary to make application To His Excellency the Commander in Chieff, General Haldimand For a Particular Pass such as he was Pleased to grant for me, the latter End of this summer, For at Least sixteen Batteaus to be Loaded with necessarys for the use of this Post, so as you, Sir, your Garrison & what Things may be wanted for The use of Government at this place, might be had on Reasonable Terms, & not be obliged to pay as has Been the Case Heretofore Extravagant Prices. The Distance of this Place and the many causes of Goods Being Detained on the Communication during the Course of the Summer occasions my making so early an application & the Extravagant Cost of Bringing, Particularly Heavy Articles, up the Grand River, From the Justness of my Request and the necessity you see for it yourself will induce you To lay it before His Excellency as soon as possible and that if the Pass is granted to be given Messrs. Robert Ellis & James Grant, who will gett the Boats Fitted out and Forwarded as early as possible next Spring. Your complyance will much oblige Him who is with due Respect

Sir your most obt & most humble Servant.

GEORGE MCBEATH.

Dan'l Robertson, Capt. 84th Reg't Commandant &c. &c. &c.
[B 98 p 172]

CAPTAIN ROBERTSON TO SECRETARY MATTHEWS

MICHILIMACKINAC 1st Novr. 1782.

SIR, You will be pleased to lay the annexed Letter from Mr. McBeath to me before His Excellency the Commander in Chief, who, I hope will comply with the request as it may be the means of lowering the exhorbitant prices of Goods at this Post.

Mr. McBeath will set out early next Spring for the Mississippi, which I have already mentioned to Col. Hope, the Intention, and I have great hopes he will succeed in a great degree, of keeping those Indians from coming here, which must be a considerable saving to Government.

He wishes much to have Mr. James Grant here early, in order to do his Business while absent.

I am Sir your most obedient and most humble Servant

DAN'L ROBERTSON
Capt. 84th Reg't.

Capt. Mathews.
[B 98 p 171]

GENERAL HALDIMAND TO LIEUT. GOV. SINCLAIR

QUEBEC 2nd November 1782.

SIR, I have received your Letter of yesterday, requesting Permission to go to Britain which I am sorry it is not in my Power to comply with, having from necessity, determined that a full Enquiry shall be made this Winter into the Expenses incurred at Michilimackinac for the amount of which, my Duty has obliged me to protest your Bills, and in this Enquiry, your Personal Attendance will be indispensibly necessary.

I am &c.

(signed) F. H.

Addressed to Lieut Governor Sinclair 2nd Novr 1782
[B 98 p 173]

APPENDIX

VOLUME X—SECOND EDITION.

The pages to which the notes refer are indicated by the numbers in the margin.

54. The statements of this paragraph are incorrect; the writer seems to have had the Northwest Territory in mind, but his conception of its extent and location is also at fault. That part of the country, now known as Colorado and Nebraska, were never part of Michigan; the author, however, could have included without error, the eastern parts of North and South Dakota. The following is a very brief outline of Michigan's geographical history, condensed from Campbell's Political History of Michigan: Wayne county was established in 1796, by Winthrop Sargent, who was the acting governor of the Northwest Territory; it included all of what later became the Territory of Michigan as well as part of Ohio and Indiana. In 1800 Congress passed an act which threw into Indiana Territory all of what is now Michigan, except the eastern (about) half of the Lower Peninsula. In 1802 Congress authorized the people east of Indiana and south of a line drawn eastward from the south point of Lake Michigan, to adopt a constitution,—all north of this line to be annexed to Indiana. In 1805 Congress enacted—"All that part of Indiana Territory which lies north of a line drawn east from the southerly bend or extreme of Lake Michigan, until it shall intersect Lake Erie, and east of a line drawn from the said southerly bend through the middle of said lake to its northern extremity, and thence due north to the northern boundary of the United States, shall for the purpose of temporary government, constitute a separate Territory, and be called Michigan." In 1816 Congress authorized the establishment of the State of Indiana, fixing its north boundary ten miles north of the extreme south end of Lake Michigan. In 1818 Illinois was admitted to the Union with its north boundary at 42° 30′, and all the country to the north lying east of the Mississippi made a part of the Territory of Michigan. In 1834 all the territory west of the Mississippi river, north of the State of Missouri, and east of the Missouri river and White Earth river was added to Michigan. In June, 1836, congress passed an act providing for the admission of Michigan to the union with boundaries as they now are, that is, with the western part of the Upper Peninsula added, and the "Toledo strip" taken away from the original Michigan of 1805. A new chapter of the history of Michigan's boundaries must soon be written, as recent surveys show that Wisconsin is exercising jurisdiction over land that the Act of 1836 gave to the Upper Peninsula.

86. This reverend gentleman at that time claimed only a humble origin, but later became the hero of a romance which gave to him loyal lineage, in fact, made him the kidnapped Dauphin and heir to the Bourbon throne.

211. On July 27th, Andrew (André) entered the Fort at Detroit to assure Major Gladwin of his loyalty to the British,—see page 337, Vol. VIII.

216. Louis St. Ange de Bellerive was the first British governor of Illinois; he relieved Neyou de Villiers from the command of Fort Chartres in June, 1764. He was with Charlevoix in his exploring expedition and died in St. Louis in 1774. (Ill. and La., under French Rule, Wallace.)

225. Robert Rogers was born in New Hampshire in 1727 and died in London in 1800. He was a daring and successful leader of New Hampshire Militia in the campaigns about Lake George against the French. After the fall of Quebec in 1760, he received the surrender of the Northwestern French forts. After escaping on a technicality from the investigation here narrated, he went to England, where he appears as an author and a prisoner for debt.

If his published journal is to be relied on he fought two battles under the banner of the Dey of Algiers. When the War of Independence began he offered his services to Congress, but his sincerity was suspected and he was put under arrest, and then released upon parole, which he promptly broke by accepting a British colonel's commission and raising a regiment.

227. It may be safely assumed that there never was a place on the Mississippi called Louis Constant; it is undoubtedly an error of the copyist, either in London or Ottawa. The best way for the deserters to have gone to Louisiana would have been by the way of the Wisconsin river, and with a little change in spelling and capitalization we have *L'Ouisconsin.* In Vol. VII, of "Documents relating to the Colonial History of the State of New York, it is spelled "Lowis Constant."

228. Frederick Christopher Spiesmacher was appointed Lieutenant in the Sixtieth or Royal American Regiment in 1756, while a prisoner of war in France. In 1770 he was promoted to a Captaincy and received his majority in 1778. His command went to the West Indies in 1772, where it is supposed he died in 1782. (J. R. Broadhead, Ed. of Colonial Documents of N. Y.—Vol. VII.)

228. William Hay came to Canada with Gov. Guy Carleton in 1776 as Chief justice; he was succeeded by Peter Livius, a refugee from New Hampshire, in about 1779.

247. There was a Miami chief called Piedfroid, so we may safely conclude this should be Cold Feet. See "Maumee River Basin," (Slocum), from which most of the modern names here inserted were taken. Parkman quotes a letter from Raymond, who commanded at Miami under the French, to the effect that certain news brought in by "Cold Foot" might be relied upon as he was an honest man if any Indian could be said to possess such virtue.

248. It is difficult to determine the route here described. Several rivers have been called Huron, notably the Clinton and the Cass, besides the modern Huron. The Savoyard had also been called the Little Huron. The Clinton and the modern Huron are about equidistant, but not nearly so far as forty miles from Detroit. Perhaps it was the Raisin. The "Reccanamozo" is undoubtedly the Ke Kalamazoo. A. L. Williams is authority for the following Indian names of rivers: Raisin, *Nee-ma Sebee;* Huron, *Cos scut ee nong Sebee;* Clinton, *Not e way Sebee.*

285. Alexander McKee was a native of Pennsylvania, and in the British service became an Indian agent with the rank of colonel and was very active in setting the Indians on the Americans,—at least up to 1813. In April, 1778, John Proctor wrote to President Wharton: "Sir, I am able to inform you that Capt. Alexander McKee with sevin other Vilons is gon to the Indians, and since there is a serj't and twenty od men gon from Pittsburg of the Soldiers." (Penna. Archives.) Among the "sevin other vilons" were Simon Girty, Matthew Elliott, and Robert Surphlet.

368. The name of John Campbell appears among those who received land in Clark's grant, and as he received only 108 acres he must have been a private, as officers received more in accordance with their rank.

373. John Schank (born 1741, died 1823) had charge of the British vessels on the great lakes. It was he who built the Inflexible that defeated the American fleet on Lake Champlain, and made the bridges for Burgoyne's expedition. In 1822 he was appointed admiral.

448. Augustin Molin de la Balme claimed to have been a French Lieutenant Colonel and to have come to America with Lafayette. He enlisted about forty-five men at Kaskaskia and Cahokia and picked up a few more at Vincennes. It was at modern Ft. Wayne that his little band was nearly annihilated by the Miamis under Chief Little Turtle. (History of Maumee Basin, Slocum.)

450. Both Moore, in his "The Northwest under three Flags," and Parrish in his "Historic Illinois," as well as several historians, state that the expedition against St. Joseph, headed by Thomas Brady and Jean Baptiste Hamlin, took place in October, 1777. Both these authorities say that the Spanish expedition sent out by Gov. Cruvat left St. Louis in January, 1781, and returned in March of that year, and of this there can be no doubt, as there is ample documentary evidence at St. Louis and Madrid. Don Eugenio Pourre was the commander with Don Carlos Tayon for his lieutenant. Under their command were about sixty-five Spaniards and Frenchmen and as many Indians. The news of their return with the British flag from Fort St. Joseph was printed

in European papers in March, 1782 (note the perhaps intentional delay), and caused quite a stir in diplomatic circles, particularly attracting the attention of the American representatives at European courts, as it injured their claim to all the territory east of the Mississippi,—which probably was the ulterior object of the expedition. We must conclude therefore that the many histories which give 1777 as the date of the Brady-Hamlin attack are wrong, especially as Sinclair's letters, written from Mackinac, agree with De Peyster's. In Vol. XIX, page 600, De Peyster refers to both the Spanish Brady expeditions.

451. Thomas Brady ("M'sieu Tom") had been selected from among the inhabitants to command at Cahokias by Col. Clark; all accounts agree that there were only sixteen men in his party, whether, in accordance with the above named authors it occurred in 1777 or 1781. Now turn to the speech of the Indian on page 453 and note that he claims that there were one hundred whites and eighty Indians, a statement that De Peyster would not have passed unchallenged had it not been approximately correct; also note that De Peyster's letter is dated Jan. 8th, 1781, and that the capture was made on Dec. 5th, 1780.

467. Philippe Francois de Rastel de Rocheblave was a native of Dauphiny and had been an officer in the French service. Surprised in bed by Col. Clark and his Virginia militia, he surrendered Kaskaskia, which he had commanded under both French and British rule. He was sent prisoner in irons to Virginia, where he dishonored his parole and escaped to New York. See page 572.

475. This "point of rock" is seven miles above Grand Rapids and one mile above Waterville, Ohio, on the Maumee river.

478. This is the modern Coshocton, Ohio. "Doddridge's Notes" says that eighteen of the Indians having been identified by a friendly Delaware as warriors, were executed by order of Col. Broadhead, but that the rest of them were massacred by the militia without his knowledge or consent. The huts on the other side of the river were spared, not from oversight, but on account of the freshet.

482. Captain Linctot was one of Col. George Rogers Clark's militia officers, detailed as Indian agent. He was one of the Illinois Frenchmen who joined the victorious Virginia army.

512. The commander of this unfortunate expedition was Col. Archibald Loughry, who was County Lieutenant of Westmoreland, Penna. They were recruits on their way to join Clark at the Falls of the Ohio. (Winning of the West, Roosevelt.)

547. Both the Illinois and Kankakee have been called Theakiké, but at this date only the Kankakee was so called.

574. In the journal kept by Washington, which fell into the hands of the French after Braddock's defeat, there are many references to Half King, who seems to have been a staunch friend to the British and Colonists as against the French. Another diary of that time records that Half King had a very low opinion of Washington's military ability. (Montcalm and Wolfe, Parkman.)

635. The copyists seem to have been even more than usually unfortunate with this document. L'Arbor Roche should be L'Arbre Croche,—near the modern Cross Village in Emmet county, Michigan. The Indians designated "Dr." we can only guess may have been "Sr."—a not improbable abbreviation for Saulteur. "Follevaines" we may be quite certain were Folle Avoines or Menominees. "Saies" were undoubtedly Sacs. The two names in parentheses (pxes or osogamis) ought probably to be read (Foxes or Outagamies); for "Scioeux" read Sioux; Aswoes are probably Iowas,—which the French used to spell Aiouez and Ayoes.

652. These complaints refer to his capture at Vincennes in the spring of 1779 by Col. G. R. Clark, his journey to Virginia in irons and his imprisonment there.

GENERAL INDEX

TO

VOLUME X.

GENERAL INDEX.

A.

B.

D.

G.

H.

I.

K.

L.

M.

S.

T.

INDEX OF NAMES

INDEX OF NAMES.

*Error; should be J. B. Ide, of Climax.